INTERNATIONAL THEOLOGICAL LIBRARY

# THE
# ANCIENT CATHOLIC CHURCH

*FROM THE ACCESSION OF TRAJAN
TO THE FOURTH GENERAL COUNCIL*
[A.D. 98–451]

BY

ROBERT RAINY, D.D.
PRINCIPAL OF THE NEW COLLEGE, EDINBURGH

NEW YORK
CHARLES SCRIBNER'S SONS
1925

*The Rights of Translation and of Reproduction are Reserved*

Printed in the United States of America

# PREFACE

It was the duty of the writer to endeavour to combine in this volume the manifold detail which the student requires, with the points of view and the modes of treatment which make a book readable. How far he has succeeded, others must judge. He has thought it due to the subject and the reader to express frankly the impression on his own mind which the various topics have made. He hopes, notwithstanding, that he has not allowed personal bias to obscure the objective realities of the history.

In the Appendix, besides supplementary notes on literature a few details are added which had been accidentally omitted in the text.

# CONTENTS

|  | PAGES |
|---|---|
| INTRODUCTION | 1–2 |

## FIRST DIVISION: A.D. 98–180

### CHAPTER I
#### THE ENVIRONMENT

| | |
|---|---|
| Gentile life and religion | 5–9 |
| Popular feeling towards Christians | 9–11 |
| Attitude of the Government | 11–18 |
| The Jews | 18–23 |
| Extension of Christianity | 23–26 |

### CHAPTER II
#### THE EARLY CHURCHES

| | |
|---|---|
| Sense of unity—Public worship—Lucian's impressions | 27–32 |
| Leadership and organisation | 32–40 |
| Note.—Hatch and Harnack on the episcopate | 40–42 |
| Discipline | 42–44 |
| Martyrdom | 44–49 |

### CHAPTER III
#### THE CHURCH'S LIFE

| | |
|---|---|
| Apostolic Fathers | 52–60 |
| Apologists | 60–62 |
| Apocrypha | 62–65 |

### CHAPTER IV
#### BELIEFS AND SACRAMENTS

| | |
|---|---|
| Beliefs of the early Church | 66–73 |
| Early forms of creed—"Apostles'" Creed—Regula | 73–75 |
| Baptism—*Agape*—Eucharist | 75–79 |
| Forgiveness of sins | 79–81 |
| Easter controversy | 81–83 |

## CHAPTER V
### THE APOLOGISTS

| | PAGES |
|---|---|
| God and the world—The Logos—Man | 85–87 |
| The significance of Christ's coming | 88 |
| Relation to the thought of their time | 88–89 |
| Impoverished representation of Christianity | 90–92 |
| Harnack's view criticised | 92–93 |

## CHAPTER VI
### THE HERESIES

| | |
|---|---|
| A. Gnosticism | 94–119 |
| General description of the scheme | 94–111 |
| Leading Gnostic schools | 111–119 |
| B. Marcion | 119–127 |

## CHAPTER VII
### MONTANISM . . . 128–139

# SECOND DIVISION: A.D. 180–313

## CHAPTER VIII
### RELATION TO THE STATE

Action of the Government . . . . . . 141–145

## CHAPTER IX
### THE NEW PHILOSOPHY . . . 146–156

## CHAPTER X
### CHRISTIAN THOUGHT AND LITERATURE

| | |
|---|---|
| Leading names—What they hold in common | 157–160 |
| School of Alexandria | 161–179 |
| School of Asia Minor | 180–184 |
| School of Africa | 184–197 |

## CHAPTER XI
### CHRIST AND GOD

| | |
|---|---|
| How the question took shape | 198–202 |
| Justin Martyr | 203–205 |
| Irenæus—Tertullian—Origen | 206–209 |
| Monarchian theories | 209–211 |

|                                                      | PAGES     |
|------------------------------------------------------|-----------|
| Dynamical Monarchianism—Paul of Samosata             | 212–215   |
| Modalistic Monarchianism—Sabellius                   | 215–217   |
| Review                                               | 218–220   |

## CHAPTER XII

### CHRISTIAN LIFE

|                                                      |           |
|------------------------------------------------------|-----------|
| Teaching of Clement and Tertullian                   | 221–222   |
| Marriage—Asceticism—Family life                      | 223–226   |
| Charity—Public service—Doctrine of merit             | 226–228   |

## CHAPTER XIII

### WORSHIP

|                                                      |           |
|------------------------------------------------------|-----------|
| The Lord's day—The Lord's Supper                     | 229–232   |
| Public prayer—Baptism                                | 232–235   |
| Easter—Epiphany—The Christian dead                   | 236–239   |
| Church buildings                                     | 239–240   |

## CHAPTER XIV

### CLERGY

|                                                      |           |
|------------------------------------------------------|-----------|
| Growth of the bishop's power                         | 241–245   |
| *Chorepiscopoi*                                      | 245       |
| Election of bishops and presbyters                   | 245–247   |
| Minor Orders—Deaconesses                             | 247–248   |

## CHAPTER XV

### DISCIPLINE AND SCHISMS

|                                                      |           |
|------------------------------------------------------|-----------|
| Reception of penitents                               | 249–251   |
| The "lapsed"—Schism of Felicissimus                  | 251–253   |
| Schism of Novatian—of Heraclius—of Meletius          | 253–255   |
| Heretical baptism                                    | 255–261   |

## CHAPTER XVI

### MANICHEISM

|                                                      |           |
|------------------------------------------------------|-----------|
| Manicheism                                           | 262–267   |

# THIRD DIVISION: A.D. 313–451

## CHAPTER XVII

### THE CHURCH IN THE CHRISTIAN EMPIRE AND BEYOND

|                                                      |           |
|------------------------------------------------------|-----------|
| A. The Emperors                                      | 268–271   |
| B. The Church in transition                          | 271–276   |

## CONTENTS

|  | PAGES |
|---|---|
| C. Policy of the Christian empire in regard to religion | 276–279 |
| D. The Pagan Opposition | 279–285 |
| E. Christianity beyond the empire | 285–288 |
| F. Life in the Church | 288–290 |

### CHAPTER XVIII
#### MONASTICISM

| | |
|---|---|
| Eastern developments—Antony—Pachomius | 291–295 |
| Spreads to the West—Ambrose—Martin—Cassian | 295–298 |
| Jovinian and Vigilantius | 298–299 |
| Criticism of the movement | 299–304 |
| Divergences | 304–305 |

### CHAPTER XIX
#### THE CLERGY

| | |
|---|---|
| Minor Orders—Deacons—Presbyters—*Chorepiscopoi* | 306–308 |
| Election of bishops | 308–309 |
| Metropolitans—Patriarchates | 309–312 |
| Growing power of Rome | 313 |
| General conditions of clerical life | 314–322 |

### CHAPTER XX
#### NICENE COUNCIL

| | |
|---|---|
| The belief of the Church—Positions of Arius | 323–328 |
| Constantine calls a council | 328–330 |
| Proceedings of the council | 330–333 |
| Review | 333–338 |

### CHAPTER XXI
#### ARIAN CONTROVERSY—POST-NICENE

| | |
|---|---|
| State of Parties | 339–340 |
| To the death of Constantine (325–337) | 340–342 |
| To the reunion of the empire under Constantius (337–351) | 342–345 |
| To the death of Constantius (351–361) | 345–348 |
| To the council of Constantinople (361–381) | 348–352 |
| Gothic Arianism | 352–353 |
| Review | 353–355 |
| Note.—The Nicene Creed | 355–357 |

### CHAPTER XXII
#### MINOR CONTROVERSIES

| | |
|---|---|
| A. Apollinarius | 358–364 |
| B. Origenistic controversies | 364–369 |

|                                                      | PAGES   |
| ---------------------------------------------------- | ------- |
| Note.—Main points of the attack against Origen       | 370     |
| C. Professed Reformers                               | 370     |
| D. Priscillianists                                   | 371–373 |

## CHAPTER XXIII
### DISCUSSIONS REGARDING THE PERSON OF CHRIST

| | |
|---|---|
| A. Case of Nestorius | 376–392 |
| B. Case of Eutyches | 392–396 |
| C. Council of Chalcedon | 396–401 |
| Review | 401–404 |

## CHAPTER XXIV
### DONATISM

| | |
|---|---|
| How the schism arose | 405–407 |
| Character of African Christianity | 407–409 |
| The Donatist positions | 409–411 |
| Augustine's part in the debate | 412–421 |

## CHAPTER XXV
### ECCLESIASTICAL PERSONAGES OF FOURTH CENTURY

| | |
|---|---|
| Eusebius of Cæsarea | 422–423 |
| Athanasius | 423–426 |
| The Three Cappadocians | 426–430 |
| Hilary of Poictiers | 430–432 |
| Martin of Tours | 432–433 |
| Ambrose of Milan | 434–436 |

## CHAPTER XXVI
### FESTIVALS, CHURCH SERVICES, AND SACRAMENTS

| | |
|---|---|
| A. Festivals | 437–440 |
| B. Order of service | 440–444 |
| C. Doctrine of the eucharist | 444–445 |
| D. Baptism | 445–449 |
| E. Preaching | 449–451 |
| F. Objects of worship | 451–453 |
| G. Pictures and angels | 453–454 |

## CHAPTER XXVII
### DISCIPLINE . . . 455–459

## CHAPTER XXVIII
### AUGUSTINE . . . 460–467

## CHAPTER XXIX
### Pelagian Controversy

|   | PAGES |
|---|---|
| Life and teaching of Pelagius | 468–473 |
| Previous church teachers on human ability | 473–475 |
| Teaching of Augustine | 475–476 |
| The Pelagian positions | 477–479 |
| The positions of Augustine | 479–482 |
| The judgment of the African Church | 483 |
| The origin of Semi-Pelagianism | 483–484 |

## CHAPTER XXX
### Semi-Pelagianism

| | |
|---|---|
| The community at Lerins and their views | 486–488 |
| Cassian and Faustus | 488 |
| The Synod of Orange | 489–490 |
| Note.—Semi-Pelagian positions | 490–493 |

## CHAPTER XXXI
### Ecclesiastical Personages [who survived A.D. 400]

| | |
|---|---|
| Chrysostom | 494–496 |
| Cyril of Alexandria—Theodoret—Isidore | 496–498 |
| Jerome | 498–501 |
| Rufinus—Synesius—Cassian | 501–503 |
| Sulpicius Severus—Salvian | 503–505 |
| Leo I. | 505–507 |

## CHAPTER XXXII
### Processes of Change

| | |
|---|---|
| Canon of the N.T. | 509–510 |
| Creed and Regula—Stress on doctrine | 511 |
| Growth of the bishop's power | 512–513 |
| Conception of the Church | 514–516 |
| The sacraments | 516–517 |
| Formulation of orthodoxy—Councils | 518–519 |
| Multitudinism triumphant—Consequences | 520–521 |

# APPENDIX

| | |
|---|---|
| A. Literature of Church History | 523–525 |
| B. Supplementary Notes to Chapters | 525–531 |

# THE
# ANCIENT CATHOLIC CHURCH

# THE
# ANCIENT CATHOLIC CHURCH

## INTRODUCTION

AN earlier volume of the Series was devoted to the subject of Apostolic Christianity. The present narrative proposes to contemplate the life, growth, and influence of what, as distinguished from mediæval and later developments, is called the early Catholic Church. The period in view is nearly that which has been named the Patristic. It has also been denominated, but not perhaps very happily, the period of Christianity under its Antique and Classical form.[1]

The last survivor of the apostles, John, is said to have died at Ephesus near the end of the first century. Apostolic guidance had by that time become only a memory in most of the churches; but for years after, and deep into the following century, vivid impressions of Apostles and their sayings were preserved and rehearsed in various churches. Near the end, then, of the first century our task opens. The close might be placed as early as the pontificate of Gregory I., A.D. 590–604, or, on other accounts, as late as the reign of Charlemagne, say A.D. 800. The present volume carries the history down to A.D. 451. A subsequent volume will cover the rest, and also the transition period down to Gregory VII.

A great landmark in the history of the Early Church

[1] So Kurtz.

is furnished in the change by which, in the days of Constantine, the Roman Empire allied itself with Christianity. The year 313, when Constantine and Licinius published their edict of toleration, may here be most conveniently fixed upon.[1]

The period A.D. 98–313 finds a natural subdivision at the close of the reign of Marcus Aurelius, A.D. 180, or, which for some purposes is more convenient, at the close of his son's reign in 192. In the period succeeding A.D. 313, the year A.D. 451, with which this volume closes, corresponds pretty well with important changes in the affairs both of the Christian Church and of the Roman world, and may serve as a resting-place.

[1] So Müller.

# FIRST DIVISION
## A.D. 98–180

## CHAPTER I

### THE ENVIRONMENT

**Merivale**, *Romans under the Empire*, 7 vols. 12mo, 1868.
Friedländer, *Sittengeschichte Roms*, 3 vols. 8vo, 1881.
Mommsen, *The Provinces of the Roman Empire*, Eng. Tr., 2 vols. 8vo, 1886.
Hardy, *Christianity and the Roman Government*, London, 1894.
Neumann, *Römische Staat*, Leipz. 1890.

EARLY Christianity was born and grew in the Roman world. It reached, no doubt, into the regions beyond, but of its fortunes there we know little. The Church grew in a society always conscious of the Roman strength, gradually awakening to the peculiar genius of the Roman law, impressed with the sentiment of the Roman destiny. All these carried with them some impression of the religious tone which Rome itself cherished in connection with the State. The mental life was mainly Greek, taking colour in some regions from Italian influences, and in some from Oriental. The various social characteristics and influences, once associated with distinctive national types, were mingled now in the lively intercourse of the empire, which assuaged old barbarisms, but weakened old moralities; yet in the quieter regions the ancient ways of each people lived on, giving way gradually. No old religion was displaced; but each was losing something, most had lost much of their ancient significance and credibility. The educated people realised this most distinctly.

Politically, the history from A.D. 1 to 313 divides itself into three stages. First to A.D. 98, from the latter days of Tiberius to the end of Nerva's reign. It was a period during which the ruling persons on the whole evoked little attachment and created little confidence. In A.D. 98 Nerva performed his one great service to the State by calling Trajan to the succession. Trajan was the first of four great emperors whose reigns extended to A.D. 180. During their time the Roman order was well maintained, and the impression of care and justice in the highest quarters inspired confidence and tranquillity among their subjects. The twelve years of Commodus (to A.D. 192) introduced a third stage of prevailing disquiet and decay which lasted for a hundred years. During this long period some able and some public-spirited men rose to the throne; but, on the whole, it was a time of feeble and uncertain government, of civil wars, of incessant change of dynasty, of frequent pestilence and famine, and of severe pressure by the barbarians upon the weakened empire. Population, wealth, letters, all decayed: and though the strong fabric of the Roman administration and the Roman law held out through the evil time, the whole system was strained and shaken. Latterly a series of soldier emperors fought the empire out of its disorganisation and disgrace. Diocletian, a man of the same breed, who came to the throne in A.D. 284, completed the task; and he celebrated the last triumph Rome was destined to see. During this time of frequent calamity and distress, outcry against the Christians as the guilty cause stimulated governors to persecute; and about the middle of the third century some of the emperors, and those not the worst, judged it to be in the interest of the State to authorise new and special measures in order to put down Christianity. Persecutions then became very severe. But from the time of Gallienus, A.D. 260–268, these attempts ceased. When Diocletian set up his system by which the imperial power was distributed, and an emperor (Augustus or Cæsar) was posted on every dangerous frontier, the Christians, along with other citizens, enjoyed for a time the benefits of peace and order. But once more, in 303 (under the influence of his colleague Galerius), Diocletian authorised the persecution which is associated with his name. In A.D. 311 Galerius suspended these severities. Two years later Constantine and Licinius shared the empire between them, and by an edict, dated at Milan, they very expressly enacted liberty of faith and worship for all their subjects.

## Gentile Life and Religion

During the first century the popular paganism existed side by side with a great deal of disbelief on the part of thinking people. The character of the government and of the times inspired distrust and apprehension, rendered men cynical about truth and goodness, and disposed them to think, so far as they thought methodically, on Epicurean lines. Yet individuals could cherish ideals, and could sometimes live for them, generally clinging, in that case, to a Stoic creed.[1] But as we pass into the second century a change is felt. With better order in the State, and nobler examples in high quarters, serious thought took courage, and a reaction set in. It did not prevail universally; the wittiest monument of the cynical and mocking spirit exists in the second century in the writings of Lucian. But men possessed by moral aims could find an audience, and they were stirred by the consciousness of a mission. The effort to find theories by which moral and religious life could justify its aspirations, was resumed again; and religious systems like the mysteries, which professed to purify and to consecrate life, found sincere votaries. Unfortunately, the difficulties were great. Where could means be found for representing life as a career which has a real goal at the end of it? Besides, it was felt, almost universally, that for one reason or another the popular worships must in some degree be kept in credit. But they were not credible. Hence abundant insincerities

[1] Seneca, d. A.D. 65; Epictetus, from Nero to Hadrian.

accompanied really good intentions; and fine sentiments
of every degree of spuriousness circulated along with the
good coin of moral endeavour and seeking after God.

The medium through which these influences chiefly
worked was the fashion, widely diffused, of interest in
public discourse. Education under Greek methods was
largely literary; and it aimed at forming habits of effective
writing and speaking. It could hardly be said that books
were dear or scarce; but the prevailing taste preferred
lecturing and discussion. Large sections of the community had tastes of this kind, and rhetoricians abounded
who sought fame and livelihood by appealing to them. They
durst not meddle with politics; they found themes, however, in history, and in the great poetical traditions of
Greece; but obviously also the questions of human life,
of duty and destiny, which the philosophers had debated,
opened a wide field to eloquent persons in search of a subject. The views offered on such questions were not likely
to be profound. Still the field lay as naturally open to
them as social questions do to the eloquent persons of
to-day; and a professional rhetorician almost always was
prepared to pose as a philosopher also (Zeller, *Phil. d.
Griechen*, iv. 729). The section of society which cared to
hear him had its own habits of sentiment and of talk on
these subjects; and people of condition could even keep a
rhetorician (soi-disant philosopher) on their establishment.[1]
Men could combine these tastes with flippancy, scepticism,
and immorality; but they could be combined also with
serious thought upon the deeper questions of life. This
nobler side of things gains ground in the second century,
and it is represented and guided by notable men. Epictetus
carried over from the previous century his Stoic teaching,
enriched and deepened by a religious pathos. Plutarch of
Macedonia, the cultivated gentleman of literary eminence,
embodied in many works his outlook on life, and advocated
a tranquil and pious morality, drawing strength from the
better side of the popular religion, while dismissing what

---

[1] Hatch, *Hibbert Lect.* p. 35 fol., and Lucian, *de Mercede conductis*.

savoured of terror, distrust, and hatred. On a lower moral platform Apuleius may be named; on a lower intellectual one, Maximus Tyrius and Numenius. But perhaps no one more than Dio Chrysostom illustrates how men were drawn at this time to betake themselves with earnestness to the line of moral appeal. Dio, originally a rhetorician able to be eloquent on any theme, professes to have experienced, during his banishment from Rome, a kind of conversion to moral earnestness; and henceforth he makes it his aim to deal with topics which will heal and purify men's souls.[1]

The views on God, virtue, and (sometimes) immortality, cherished by these more serious minds, had a great interest for the Christians; they furnished the line on which the Christian appeal to the Gentile mind proceeded. It is natural to ask, further, how far Christianity itself had a share in producing and guiding this ethical revival. All the probabilities are in favour of its having had some share. Christianity was a contemporary stream of intensely powerful moral and religious life; that is an influence which always sets currents agoing, even in regions where it is repudiated. The religious seriousness, the tone of kindliness to men and of trust in Providence, which the wise Gentile of the second century cherished, must owe something, very likely not a little, to impressions received from Christian life and character. Men might decline to own any obligations to the religion of the crucified Jew. And yet the lives of His followers might awaken a great longing after a goodness and a moral strength comparable to that evinced by them.[2] At all events the growth of a serious and inquiring spirit opened a way for the Christian message in some quarters;[3] and the same cause made the gospel interesting to men who did not find it acceptable. Some of these were repelled by the claim of Christianity to

---

[1] Zeller, *Phil. d. Griechen*, iv. 729.

[2] Points of contact with Christianity in the writings of Seneca and of Marcus Aurelius have been suggested.

[3] *E.g.* Justin Martyr's account of his own conversion, *Dial.* ii. 2; also Clem. *Hom.* i. 1 f.

by the one true religion; that was claiming too much; and they pointed to aspects of the Christian story and the Christian teaching which struck them as incoherent or superstitious.[1] Others were evidently impressed by the sincerity and the goodness of the Christians; they mock them, but they do it with good-humour, and even with a certain contemptuous kindliness.[2] Generally it may be assumed that the cultivated Gentile world knew more about Christianity than it chose to say. It long remained a point of honour with most representatives of the old culture to make no references, or as few as possible, to this popular "superstition." It came from the barbarians, and it had no claims on the serious attention of a wise man. One might attack it, in the hope of destroying its power over some of its votaries; otherwise it was better ignored. But the influence which was not owned was felt.

As to the general world of Gentile life, those who wish to acquire impressions of it must consult works on that express subject.[3] On the whole, it was superstitious, and at the same time low in tone, coarse, and immoral. Still we must not forget the virtues which, even in a pagan society, the providence of God nurses and disciplines, the affections which soften and cheer life, and the religious longings which spring spontaneously in some hearts, and which anxiety and sorrow awaken at some times in almost all. Christian religion made way in this element by the assuredness of its belief, by the resonance of its strong morality, by the attractiveness of Christian character, and by the unsparing charities of the churches. Everywhere there were individuals, there were families, attracted, impressed; ultimately either carried over, or, if left outside, yet looking wistfully across the border. Such cases were incessantly occurring; but yet the sentiment of the masses towards Christianity was hostile. This swelled sometimes into rage, and it long continued to reveal itself energetically. Individuals could continue to be powerfully animated by this

---

[1] Celsus. [2] Lucian.
[3] Friedländer, *Sittengeschichte Roms*, 3 vols., Leipzig, 1881.

hostile sentiment even when, as the result showed, a complete revolution by conversion was on the point of befalling them.

### Popular Feeling towards Christians

The habits and industries, the courtesies and enjoyments, which made up Gentile life were all touched, more or less, with some reference to the gods and their worship; and earnest Christians had to purge this out, or stand aloof. Then there ran through all a strain of careless secularity, and very often of immorality, against which a Christian must protest. This element culminated in the theatres and in the various forms of spectacle so popular throughout the empire: hence the resolute opposition to these recreations which appeared among the Christians so early, and in which the Church was so much united. It does not follow that heathens could not be persons of high moral quality; but even those who could claim to be so regarded, tolerated, as inevitable, the low moral tone which existed around them: it was for them a spiritual ugliness which they disliked, but they hardly recoiled from it as earnest Christians felt that they must recoil. Beyond the idolatry, the immorality, and the frivolity, rose the question how far many current usages of Gentile life might be accepted by the Christians as simply human, or whether they ought not rather to be rejected as carrying with them temptations which a Christian should avoid. It was a question of degree, on which Christians of different tempers, and under different social conditions, were sure to differ among themselves. But a man could not be a Christian in any sense who did not make a stand somewhere.

Out of all this, then, arose in the Gentile world, speaking generally, an intense popular aversion to Christianity. For in regard to this whole region of human life the new religion seemed to threaten indefinite disturbance. It interfered with the established ways of society—with trade interests, with family life, with popular amusements, with accepted religious observances. There might be compliant

Christians, but the representative and influential Christians were not compliant. The Christians might be social among themselves, but for general purposes they were non-social in a degree that suggested *odium generis humani*.[1] For, indeed, if a Christian wished to escape friction and bitterness, it was natural for him to stand aside from the general life; and so he incurred the charge of *contemptissima inertia*, as well as of *lugubris cultus* and *malefica superstitio*.[2] The very expectation of the Lord's return, while it helped the Christian to bear persecution, might render him indifferent to current social interests. Then his purer morals and his more spiritual but exclusive religion seemed to mark him as one who claimed to be a superior person, and who disapproved of his neighbours. The Cynics had already made themselves unpopular by their censorious ways. They were meddlesome; they thrust their morality under the noses of people who did not want it; they were busybodies in other men's matters. But the Cynics were merely a disagreeable set of self-important philosophers. That kept them apart. Christianity, on the contrary, had a strange power of spreading, and found its way into the most unlikely quarters. How hateful it must have seemed when this mysterious influence got hold of a member of a family! He was estranged from his own circle, and entangled in a new society largely composed of slaves and low people; his money, too, if he had any, was drawn into the Christian communism. New questions rose about marriage. Nothing is commoner in the legends of female martyrs than the picture of a maiden of good social standing, who becomes a Christian, and refuses to carry out the marriage arranged for her by her family. Christians had scruples about festivals, about illuminating their doors at times of rejoicing, about undertaking public functions, about ordinary amusements,—about things in regard to which it seemed to the Gentile perfectly immaterial how they were disposed of. Then this religion of theirs — what was it? A very

---

[1] Hardy, *Christianity and the Roman Government*, p. 45.
[2] Tacitus, *Ann.* xv. 44; Suetonius, *Nero*, c. 16.

questionable business;—no temples, no shrines, no stately services; evening or nocturnal meetings in private houses. Stories went abroad of monstrous crimes perpetrated in these Christian meetings.[1] It was altogether a detestable infection from which no man's family was safe; and it was a satisfaction to believe the worst about it, that one might have the better excuse for hating it. This popular feeling had become strong long before the government, although it had decided to treat obstinate Christians as outside the laws, had yet acquired an impression that they were dangerous outlaws, or that the case required any very serious or systematic treatment. Add to all this that the regular worship of the gods was thought to guarantee the State against calamities, and that neglect of it might bring disaster upon the whole community. For, indeed, the public religion was the consecration of the State, and in a manner the basis of it. And the Christian, not contented with quietly disbelieving, must openly repudiate it. All this fermented together in the popular mind.[2]

#### Attitude of the Government

The popular aversion to Christianity was not without influence on the action of the government; for a Roman magistrate was ready enough to set himself against anything that disturbed the general tranquillity. But the case presented itself to him from points of view which must be separately described.[3]

Ancient laws existed, which forbade the practice of non-Roman rites, and these laws had not been repealed; yet the course of things tended to the discontinuance of

---

[1] Referred to in almost all the Apologies.     [2] Tert. *Apol.* 40.

[3] Increased precision has been introduced into statements on this subject as the result of recent investigations. Besides the works of Hardy and Neumann, an article by Mommsen—"Der Religionsfrevel nach römischem Recht," reproduced in *Expositor*, July 1893—is considered epoch-making. Discussions by Ramsay (*Church in the Roman Empire*) and by Harnack (*Texte u. Unters.* xiii. 4, on an edict ascribed to Antoninus Pius) have also thrown light on the subject—Ramsay especially.

prosecutions on this ground; and, practically, people who used non-Roman rites were not punished under the emperors unless some additional reason existed. These laws might have been revived and made operative against the Christians; or new laws, directed specifically against the alleged enormities of the Christian worship, might have been enacted. In either case a regular trial with well-known formalities would have been the method employed. Such a trial was called a *judicium*. But this course was not taken. It would not be easy to produce an instance of it. The laws against *sodalitates* or clubs were in full observance and application; but neither were these made the basis of action against the Christians.

The method adopted relied on general powers which the emperors claimed as preservers of the Roman peace, on guard against forces that might tend to disturbance.

These may be regarded as police powers; and they were wielded also by governors of provinces and the prefect of the city as the emperor's representatives. Discretionary chastisement could be inflicted, according to the necessities of the case, when these functionaries found what appeared to them to be movements or tendencies endangering the common well-being; and the penalty, especially for the obstinate and insubordinate, might be death. Still, especially when severe penalties were in question, it was no doubt felt to be important to keep within the line of approved practice. For it was the emperor's discretion that was exercised, and it had to be used in a manner likely to secure his approbation. The process by which a governor satisfied himself that a case had arisen for the exercise of this corrective power was not a *judicium*, but a *cognitio*—an investigation, in which, with less formality, the governor could take plain common-sense ways of satisfying his own mind. He might also use more discretion as to acting or not acting than a judge could, who must do right on a cause when once brought before him. It is to be remembered that whatever offence Christianity gave, the conclusive reason which justified a death sentence was the Christian obstinacy which persisted in the offence against authority and before the tribunal; and a governor could avoid giving the opportunity for exhibiting that final and fatal insubordination. Also a governor might exercise his discretion in both ways at once; some Christians being spared, while others were made examples. There was responsibility both ways. Very severe courses might appear to the emperor unwise and excessive; or, by great indulgence, a governor might let his province get out of hand, and accustom people to think that they might do as they pleased.

The emperors, all of them, were careful not to prohibit infliction of the extreme penalty in fitting cases; but some of them framed edicts which plainly enough suggested caution and forbearance.

The general heads under which this power was exercised in the case of Christians seem to have been chiefly *sacrilegium* and *majestas*, and it was easy to bring Christians under one of these categories.

The mere fact that Christians, as we have seen, awoke repugnance and irritation in many minds, was in itself enough to dispose a Roman magistrate to hostile action; the order and tranquillity of society were great public interests, and novelties that were troublesome, and that savoured of wilfulness, were never looked upon as entitled to much toleration. Besides, while Christianity as a body of religious beliefs might not be a matter of much importance, yet if a Roman magistrate began to consider it, first, as a perturbing social influence apt to spread, secondly, as interfering with the religious sanctions on which the system of the empire rested (and even with outward deference for them), and, thirdly, as creating an obstinacy of temper which refused to give way to admonition or to punishment, he was naturally led to think that, obscure and foolish as it might seem to him, it should be treated, when it had to be publicly noticed, as beyond the protection and permission of the law. Lastly, Christianity organised its votaries by a system of regulated administration. It formed societies in each place, and bound them all together,

Nothing could be more contrary to Roman imperial ideas than such organisation, when it took place without sanction or permission from the imperial authorities. Putting all this together, we have the case which to the eye of Roman authority seemed substantial enough to be noted as against the welfare of the empire, and proper to be visited with high penalties when it was obstinately maintained.

Still, the Roman authority was wielded generally by experienced men, who did not too readily arrive at conclusions. Christianity might be unpopular, and might involve its adherents in collision with the religious basis of the State. Yet these Christians were seen to be inoffensive people; they professed loyalty to the emperor, and prayed for him; and, as the organising tendencies of the Church came into operation gradually, they were not so noticeable at first. Hence a magistrate might see reasons for being temperate rather than sweeping in his application of the general rule. For the most part, governors aimed at getting Christians to submit, and not unfrequently they made this effort in a fairly humane spirit; but some of them evinced a savage determination to put down the new religion by ruthless severities, applying torture to compel submission.

The situation as now explained may render it intelligible that churches could exist, might continue and hold property for years together under the eyes of the authorities, if only the Christians abstained from forcing upon the authorities the character of their societies. One of the forms of association which even the jealous eye of Roman government regarded in a tolerant way was benefit societies, such, for instance, as burial clubs; and there is proof that Christians often held property in that character.[1] In the same way we are to understand the access of the Christians to the prisons to comfort and refresh their brethren who had been seized with a view to trial and punishment. No doubt, gaolers were paid by the Chris-

[1] It is understood that secret societies among the Chinese of Singapore avail themselves at this day of the same disguise.

tians for their complacency. But it was not inconsistent with a gaoler's duty to admit them, of course with proper precautions. The visitors were friends of the criminal; but the gaoler was not at all bound to know, or even to think, that they were criminals themselves.

Certificates could be procured to the effect that the bearer had given proof, by sacrificing, of his freedom from ground of challenge on the score of religion; in short, that he was a good pagan; and it must sometimes have been convenient to be provided with one. A specimen of such a certificate turned up lately in Egypt. Christians who had not sacrificed could procure such a certificate by favour or bribery, and so escape trouble. This was reckoned by the Church an act of virtual denial of the faith; and those guilty of it (*libellatici*) were put under discipline. They are not referred to, however, till the third century.

It may be convenient to describe here the detailed policy in regard to Christians pursued by successive emperors of the second century. It has been extensively maintained that Trajan first established the principle that the persistent profession of Christianity apart from other crimes was punishable with death. Mommsen has decided against this view,[1] which is, indeed, inconsistent with the documents on which it relies. He regards the practice as settled from the time of Nero. That seems to be established by the unanimous tradition of the Christians and the testimony of Tacitus and Suetonius.[2] It seems certain also that Christianity, as such, was punishable in the times of Vespasian and his sons (from A.D. 70). Domitian especially was remembered by the Christians in this connection. In his time occurred the famous cases of T. Flavius Clemens, condemned to death, and of Flavia Domitilla, relegated to an island. At the same date the

---

[1] See above, p. 11, n. 8.
[2] Tacitus, *Ann.* xv. 44; Suetonius, *Nero*, 16. Ramsay thinks that some proof of specific crime was required until the time of the emperors of the Flavian dynasty, who fixed the mere confession of the name as sufficient. *Church in Roman Empire*, p. 252 f.

Epistle of Clement to the Corinthians[1] makes reference to recent experiences, which had led the minds of Roman Christians to revert to the horrors of Nero's persecution. Trajan, therefore, must be regarded merely as maintaining and regulating established principles.

The correspondence of Pliny with Trajan on this subject belongs to about the year 112, Pliny's letters being written from Amisos in the eastern part of his province. Pliny, who had not previously filled the post of governor, or of prefect of the city, had no experience of Christian causes, and wished to be guided—apparently with a desire to be allowed some discretion on the side of mercy. Trajan's reply is temperate and brief. Christians should not be sought for, nor should they be cited on the ground of anonymous accusations. If they prove amenable to authority, and will sacrifice when required, they are to be dismissed; but persistent obstinacy in the face of warning is to incur punishment, *i.e.* death. These principles regulate the procedure under Trajan's two successors. Under Trajan are placed the martyrdoms at Jerusalem of Simeon, son of Klopas, a relation of the Lord (perhaps about A.D. 106), and of Ignatius, bishop of Antioch, who suffered at Rome (A.D. 115—unless Harnack's indication of a possible date some years later is accepted).

Hadrian was a man of intelligence and culture, and of restless curiosity. He noticed Christianity as an element in the religious ferment of the time, but with no particular attention or respect. To him, however, is ascribed a rescript to Minucius Fundanus, the true scope of which seems to be to repress tumultuary popular demands directed against the Christians, and to enforce regular and responsible procedure. It does not really alter the directions given by Trajan, though perhaps the language suggests to governors a mild use of their discretion.[2] Various

---

[1] 1 Clem. Rom. i. 1.

[2] "Si quis . . . probat *adversum leges* agere memoratos homines . . . supplicia statues." Justin Martyr is early and good authority for the edict. The Christians construed the rather vague language as relieving them from punishment unless specific moral crimes were proved.

martyrdoms are dated under Hadrian; among others, that of Telesphorus of Rome. Antoninus Pius also found it necessary to rebuke the riotous demands for Christian victims by edicts of a similar tenor.[1] To his reign seems to belong the first surviving plea for just treatment of Christians in the *Apology* of Aristides.

Marcus Aurelius of all the emperors was most anxious to fulfil the ideal of duty, and most willing to sacrifice himself in the process. Yet under him persecution of Christians became more common and more severe. Either he authorised, or he did not restrain these severities. He was not ignorant how the Christians suffered, for he speaks of their patience as something fanatical and debased; and perhaps we must say that, while he would have dealt gently with any wrong to himself, he could be hard and bitter against the representatives of a *malefica superstitio*, which he regarded as one of the influences that undermined the ancient Roman strength. In his time we meet with two points of practice not authorised by Trajan,—the Christians begin to be sought out by the authorities, and tortures are applied to overcome their fidelity. Still, all this was in the governor's discretion. Justin Martyr at Rome, and Polycarp at Smyrna,[2] are the most remarkable single sufferers. They simply suffered death, the one by the sword, the other by fire. But the narrative of the martyrs of Lyons and Vienne in Gaul (Eus. *Hist. Eccl.* v. 8) opens for us those scenes of incredible cruelty, vanquished by superhuman endurance, which meet us too often during the two succeeding centuries. Evidently a savage temper had been aroused which spread from the people to the

---

[1] With respect to the rescript, Πρὸς τὸ Κοινὸν τῆς 'Ασίας, see Harnack, *Texte u. Unters.* xiii. 4.

[2] Justin died perhaps A.D. 165. Polycarp's death used to be placed about 166. An interesting discussion of Waddington's set the date back to 155, a result accepted by great authorities (Lipsius, Gebhardt, Lightfoot, Zahn, etc.). Latterly it seems to have turned out that Waddington's argument fails in one of its main steps; yet the conclusion remains in all probability true that Polycarp suffered on 23rd February 155. See Harnack, *Chron. der altchristl. Lit.* i. 355.

magistrates, and which set itself to break the Christians down by all extremities of pain and shame.¹

In the reign of Commodus (180–192), who reproduced many of the characteristics of Nero, the general system continued unchanged. Apollonius, a man of culture, and, according to Jerome, a senator, suffered at Rome; and the first known African persecution, that of the Scillitan martyrs, fell perhaps in his first year. Yet an impression that the reign of Commodus was more favourable to the Christians than the preceding one is distinctly indicated in the Christian traditions. A ruler who was open to foreign superstition, and who neglected public interests, might very possibly press less hardly on the Christians than one who cared for those interests on the old Roman principles. But, besides, we learn from the *Refutation* of Hippolytus (ix. 12), that Marcia, the well-known mistress of Commodus, was in some sense a Christian ($\phi\iota\lambda\acute{o}\theta\epsilon o\varsigma$), and exerted her influence effectively, in one instance at least, to relieve and set free Christian sufferers.²

The main point favourable to the Christians in the action of Trajan and his two successors is, that they required the appearance of specific accusers. Influences which might deter men from appearing in this character are specified by Ramsay (*Church in Roman Empire*, p. 325). Still, it seems likely that the attempt to extract money from the Christians by threats of accusation would, in the circumstances, become a common form of extortion. We do not hear much of it in these three reigns, but it became common in the time of Marcus Aurelius, when informers against the Christians were encouraged.

## The Jews

The reconquest of Palestine and destruction of Jerusalem by the Roman armies (A.D. 70) had been accompanied

---

[1] Serious and prolonged calamities of war and pestilence are supposed to account for special exasperation of the popular antipathy to the Christians.

[2] Marcia's relations to Commodus might be contemplated by the Chris-

by frightful losses and humiliations to the conquered people; masses of them were slaughtered or sold into slavery; their whole territory was confiscated; and their religious prejudices (heretofore humoured by the Romans) were, in Palestine at least, trampled upon and outraged. Still, this did not generally or seriously affect the Jews of the Dispersion; and even those who remained in Palestine began, after a time, to experience more tolerant treatment.

But the spirit of the race was not yet broken. In the days of Trajan (A.D. 115) Jewish insurrections, almost incredibly destructive, took place in Egypt, Cyrenaica, and Cyprus. And when Hadrian, after some indications of favour, took steps which threatened to paganise yet more thoroughly Jerusalem and the holy places, one more great uprising under Bar Cochba (132–135), as Messiah, subverted the Roman authority in Palestine, and was suppressed only slowly and by great efforts. The suppression, however, was complete. Palestine was laid waste; Jerusalem, under the name of Ælia Capitolina, became a Gentile city, equipped with all the pomp of pagan worship. Circumcision, Sabbath keeping, and instruction in the law were prohibited everywhere; and no Jew might enter Jerusalem. This last rule continued long in force. The other prohibitions were soon withdrawn, or fell into desuetude.

A centre for the dispersed nationality arose in the Sanhedrim of Rabbis and teachers of the law which formed itself at Jamnia, and was afterwards transferred to Tiberias. Here at the end of the second century the traditional teaching began to fix itself in the Hebrew tongue as the Mishnah ("*repetition*"). Further discussions, distinctions, and inferences embodied themselves in the Palestinian Gemara ("*completion*"), about the middle of the fourth century, and the Babylonian about the middle of the sixth, both in Aramaic.

From the time of the destruction of Jerusalem by

tians as on her side the nearest approach to marriage of which the Roman ideas and laws admitted. While questionable, it might not appear to have the character of plain immorality. Lagarde, *Rel. Jur.* pp. 121–124.

Titus it must have been difficult for Jewish Christians, even for those who clung most to the law, to maintain friendly relations with official or devout Judaism; and after the war of Bar Cochba it became, as a rule, impossible. No Christian could support the movement of that warlike Messiah. Christians were henceforth denounced by Jews as apostates; and a formal curse directed against them became a tradition of Jewish worship. Authoritative Judaism, of the schools and of the synagogues, finally shut its doors against all kinds of Christians.

But a calmer Judaism existed which took various forms. The earlier history has shown how Jews in Egypt and the west were influenced by the Greek learning and speculation, and how those who lived eastward of the Jordan were attracted by Oriental forms of belief. Even when Judaism was strong and hopeful, it was not reckoned heretical for Jewish minds to be hospitable to a certain extent to such influences. But now the process was likely to go further. In the case of many, at least, confidence in Judaism, as it had been, was profoundly shaken, and a craving for new combinations was felt.

As regards the Christian Church, the effect of these events was to fuse the believers from the circumcision and those from among the Gentiles still more completely into one community. Almost everywhere this process had gone rapidly on. Already the second generation and the third had grown up under the general system of the Church and under the influence of its enthusiasm. Now, anything like aggressive Judaising could have little meaning and no future; and Judaism more emphatically than ever meant hatred and scorn towards every kind of Christianity.

Here and there, however, but chiefly in the neighbourhood of Palestine, communities of Christians still existed, of Hebrew descent, or formed under specially Hebrew influences, which could not yet resign themselves to be Christians merely. Two classes of them, not always very clearly distinguished, are indicated: one, which claimed for its members the right to keep the law, but did not seek to impose that yoke on Gentile Christians; another, which insisted that the law was binding on all believers. The former could be owned as brethren; the latter cut themselves off from fellowship, and became alienated from the Church in doctrine (*e.g.* as to our Lord's higher nature) as well as in practice. Both became separated from other Christians, ceased to exert influence, and sank into narrow and obscure sectarianism. But they lingered on till the fourth century at least, and eventually the name of Nazarenes was applied to the first class, and that of Ebionites ("the poor") to the second. It is not proved that these names were so distinguished during our first period. Both words no doubt had been applied to the early disciples of Jesus.[1]

Besides these, we must allow for churches in which the sentiment of the old Palestinian Christianity, its ways, predilections, and sympathies were partially maintained, and presented a type of Christianity which without intrenching itself in permanent points of conscience, lingered on, and only gradually merged itself in the common Christianity of the Church. Churches where the kinsmen of Jesus according to the flesh were held in honour, and traditions concerning James were cherished, would certainly have many interesting features which cannot be recovered now.

Distinct from these is a form of opinion the adherents of which were called Elkesaites, and they probably existed as a sect. Some suppose them to derive especially from the Essenian type of Judaism. They recognised Jesus as the Messias, rejected sacrifices, retained circumcision and the Sabbath, and made much of purifying washings. Jesus, according to them, is an incarnation of Adam, or of the ideal man; and so Christianity is a republication of the original religion, which has again and again been corrupted and again and again restored. Modern historians recognise the features of this teaching in the Clementine writings.[2]

---

[1] The Fathers derived the name Ebionite from a supposed leader called Ebion. Hilgenfeld has supported this view, *Ketzergeschichte*, p. 424.

[2] *Homilies* (Lagarde, 1865), *Recognitions* (Geisdorf, 1838), *Epitome* (Dressel, 1859). The *Homilies* appeared first in the *Patres Apostolici* of

In these a romance of the wanderings of a Roman, Clement, in search of lost friends, is made the framework of the doctrine. Peter appears in conflict with Simon Magus, and maintains against him that the religion of Adam and Moses, which had been corrupted, comes to light again in Christ, who is an incarnation of the same spirit. It is a Jewish or Ebionitic Gnosticism, set up against the Gentile Gnosticism which is imputed to Simon: at the same time, Simon is represented with traits which are intended to identify him with the Apostle Paul.

It continued to be felt needful to guard Christians against being perplexed by the arguments of Jews.[1] And efforts to propagate a Judaising Christianity occurred here and there in the early part of the second century. But the mass of the Church remained unaffected by any Judaising propaganda; and the mass of those whose fathers, belonging to the circumcision, had become Christians under apostolic teaching, remained in the fellowship of the general Christian Church, and shared in the common Christianity. Christianity, with whatever local variations, is seen everywhere receiving and prizing the Old Testament, yet everywhere marking itself off from Judaism; everywhere shaping its thought in ways that are not very congenial to the teaching of Paul, yet everywhere honouring and quoting him. A great influence from the Old Testament preparation is visible in the early Christianity, but it extends to the whole Gentile Christianity (excepting the Gnostics and Marcion), and not merely to a Jewish party in it. The view that a distinctively Jewish party carried on into the second century the flag of Judaism as against a Pauline or Gentile version of the faith, and powerfully affected the subsequent development, can be maintained only by signalising as distinctively Jewish,

Cotelerius, 1672. Attention was drawn to them by Neander, and Baur afterwards laid stress on the Clementines as supporting his conception of early Christianity. The *Homilies* preserve most distinctly the heretical element; see article (Clementine Literature) by Professor Salmon of Dublin in *Dictionary of Christian Biography*.

[1] So, first, Barnabas, c. 2 f.

features[1] which were common to the Christianity of the whole Church. The question certainly remains, however, whether the whole Church may not by degrees have Judaised in the way in which it construed its own religion; whether, beginning in the Spirit, it did not seek perfection in the flesh.

## Extension of Christianity

Christian writers of the second century and the beginning of the third speak in glowing terms of the rapid multiplication of Christians among all races of the empire, and also beyond it.[2] There is no reason to doubt the sincerity of their statements; but these are necessarily vague; and the most truthful men are apt to overrate and overstate the amount of adherence to their own cause, especially when they see in the progress of it something wonderful and divine. Historians therefore have felt it needful to check general statements by a close scrutiny of details, so far as these are accessible to our knowledge.

In Palestine and its neighbourhood Christians no doubt continued to be numerous. Here the conspicuous churches were in Cæsarea (Stratonis Turris), the capital of the province, and at Jerusalem or Ælia Capitolina, where the Church had now assumed essentially the type of Gentile Christianity. Palestine is flanked on either side by Egypt and by Syria. In both regions the influence of the new religion on many ardent minds is illustrated by the wealth of Gnostic speculation which flows out from both quarters during the second century. In Egypt, Alexandria, with its manifold population, Jewish and Gentile, its commerce and its schools of learning, became also a great centre of Christian thought

---

[1] Reference is here made to the Tübingen hypothesis. Evolved by a man of Baur's extraordinary powers, that hypothesis no doubt freshened the whole field of investigation. On its relation to the facts Ritschl's *Altkatholische Kirche*, 2nd ed. 1857, is still well worth reading.

[2] *Ad Diogn.* 7; Just. Mart. *Tryph.* c. 117; Tert. *Apol.* 37 *ad Scap.* 15.

and action. Tradition reckons the evangelist Mark as the father of its Church life. The beginning, no doubt, was among Jews and Greeks. But for the native Coptic population, also, it became necessary to prepare a translation of the New Testament, at least as early as the third century. Westwards of Egypt in Cyrenaica, eastwards in Arabia, Christianity must have existed in the second century. Tradition ascribes the origin of Arabian Christianity to apostolic labourers—Matthew and Bartholomew. Before the end of the second century Pantænus, the first conspicuous teacher in the Alexandrian catechetical school, is said to have gone as a missionary to India; but the word as then used might signify Yemen, or parts adjacent to Yemen, either in Asia or in Africa.

On the other side, in Syria, the wealthy and luxurious city of Antioch was also the seat of the leading Christian church. From hence the gospel spread far east and south, and before the end of the second century Christian martyrs are heard of on the Parthian borders. In this Syrian region Tatian laboured in the latter half of the second century, and left his mark durably on the literature of many Syrian churches. A romantic Christian interest attaches to Edessa, the capital of a kingdom created under Macedonian influences. Here a Christian king (Abgar Bar Manu) reigned from A.D. 176. The story ran that an earlier king, Abgarus, who was our Lord's contemporary, had written to our Lord, and had received a reply; and that, in accordance with a promise contained in it, Thaddeus was afterwards sent by the Apostle Thomas to carry on the work at Edessa.

In Asia Minor, Christianity had made very considerable progress even in the interior (notably in Phrygia), but was probably strongest in the western sections, where Ephesus and Smyrna were important churches. The most remarkable testimony on many accounts is that given in reference to Bithynia in Pliny's letter to Trajan (98–117). Christianity had spread over the province and among all conditions of people, so that the worship of the temples was greatly neglected. It may be true that of the state of things thus described Christians constituted the earnest side, while Gentile scepticism and indifference constituted the other. But the Christian element was strong and conspicuous. One thing should be noted. We are apt to assume that Christian societies formed themselves at this time only in larger and smaller towns, and hardly reached the country districts. But according to Pliny, in Bithynia country and town alike had become full of Christians.

In Macedonia and Greece, as might be expected, the Christianity planted by Paul had spread and formed new churches. For the West generally, the church of Rome was already beyond comparison the most eminent and influential. It numbered among its members representatives of distinguished Roman families, including the Flavian house itself. The Greek language as yet prevailed in the use of the Roman Christians; and in this way facilities existed for easy exchange of thought and feeling with Eastern Christianity, which became more limited at a later date. On the other hand, the same fact rather indicates a less successful propaganda, as yet, among the native Italian people.

The African province in all probability received its Christianity from Rome, and the African church from the first thought and spoke in Latin. Punic speech lived on among the common people, and use was made of it for Christian purposes, but little durable trace of this is left in history. The earliest African Christianity, probably, was among the Italian settlers, who were also the influential class. Very early in the third century African bishoprics had become numerous. It is likely on various accounts that Christian communities existed in Spain in the second century or even in the first, but there is a want of historical proof of it. In Gaul, on the other hand, we know that in the latter half of the second century Christian communities existed in Lyons and Vienne. This Christianity traced its origin not so much to Rome as to Asia Minor.

In regard to Britain and other outlying regions of the

empire, statements have come down which are either rhetorical and vague, or too late to be relied upon. In regard to those regions, therefore, nothing can be affirmed. Yet the probability is strong that a force so expansive as early Christianity proved itself to be, may have reached those regions in the second century.

In reference to the progress of Christianity, it is to be noted that our information is far from complete. Vigorous church life breaks on our view in the African province at the end of the second century: of its previous history we know little. Similar remarks apply to other regions — to Gaul, to Spain, even in a measure to Alexandria. Specially sensible is the lack of statistics. How many Christians were there in the empire at the end of the second century, how many in the middle of the third, how many in the beginning of the fourth? We have to content ourselves with guesses. Gibbon estimated the Christians of Rome in the middle of the third century at 50,000, perhaps a twentieth of the whole population of the city. Over the empire he conjectured that, say in 310, Christians might be five per cent. of the population. Strong reasons can be pleaded for reckoning this estimate too low.[1] Certainly the proportion might be, must have been, considerably higher in particular cities and regions. However this may be, in most places the Christians proper are to be thought of as surrounded by a large number of persons who were attracted, impressed, in some degree influenced, but not yet won. Outside of these stood the great mass of the indifferent and the hostile, capable of being stirred, at times, into wrath and hatred.

[1] Orr's *Neglected Factors in the Study of the Early Progress of Christianity,* Edinburgh, 1899.

# CHAPTER II

## THE EARLY CHURCHES

LITERATURE.—See Appendix.

IF we would represent to ourselves the physiognomy of the Christian Church in the second century, we must think of a number of societies, existing in towns and villages (but by no means as yet in every town) over a great part of the Roman Empire, and in some places beyond that limit. These communities varied much in size, sometimes perhaps not exceeding a dozen or two of people.[1] Wherever they existed they joined in common faith and worship, and they conceived themselves to be decisively set apart by a divine calling to a new life. They referred their own existence as churches to the interposition of Christ, and to the call proceeding from Him, administered by the apostles and by those who heard them. Amid the inevitable varieties of circumstance and attainment, all these communities have common features of organisation, of worship, and of Christian faith and practice. They exist independently,[2]— so far, therefore, little republics,—each regulating its own affairs. As yet no other plan would have been natural or practicable. Everywhere, indeed, ties were owned which bound all churches (as all Christians) together, as well as duties which each owed to each. Still, for most of the period no authoritative system existed by which those ties

[1] A provision for electing a bishop in places where twelve male voters could not be found, probably comes down from times comparatively early. (Διαταγαί 16 in Lagarde, *Rel. Jur.* p. 77.)
[2] This must be the general statement, even if we allow for little groups of worshippers who clung to the nearest large church, and identified themselves with it.

and duties should be expressed and regulated. Local councils of groups of churches do not appear till the period is closing.[1] It would be a mistake, however, to suppose that influences were not at work tending to intercourse, and to the maintenance of agreement. At this time the facilities for travel throughout the empire were great, and they were very freely used.[2] Christians, in virtue of the impulse given to their energies by the new faith, were likely to take a large share in the general stir. In particular, some Christians felt impelled to travel much through the churches, and must have promoted a constant circulation of ideas and of sentiments.[3]

Even apart from these influences, the recognition of the unity which comprehended all the churches was amply secured. All the churches felt that they had been called into existence by the same will and grace of God,—all were subject to the ordinances of Christ,—all claimed a position which was really supernatural, and was the same for all,—and all the churches owned the presence of the same Spirit of Christ. Hence not only the words of the Master, but all accredited teachings of the Spirit were to be everywhere received. So the thought of the one Church pervades all the churches. Sometimes this Church seems to be the empirical whole of Christians then in the world, of which each church claimed to be a part; sometimes it is the future company of the saved, by and by to emerge in its proper lustre, clear of mixture and defilement; sometimes it is an eternal divine ideal, realising itself so far in all true churches. The two latter thoughts unite in passages like 2 *Clem.* 14: "So, my brethren, doing the will of God our Father we shall be of the Church that is First, that is spiritual, that was created before the Sun and Moon. . . . Let us choose then to be of the Church of Life, that we may be saved." This ideal Church is sometimes conceived vividly as a spiritual personality or form,

---

[1] In connection with the Montanist movement.
[2] Zahn, *Skizzen*, c. v., Erl. and Leipz. 1894.
[3] See below on Prophets, Apostles, and Teachers.

existing somehow independently, but imparting its own identity to each separate church and to each Christian in it. There was therefore really no risk of the churches losing hold of the idea of the unity; but there were possibilities of practical divergence and misunderstanding, and specific safeguards with respect to these had hardly yet been devised. The dividing forces will be referred to in another place. It is enough to say, for the present, that by the end of the second century an onlooker could recognise various sects of Christians, who distinguished themselves from one another: "They divide and split, and everyone would have his own following"; and yet he could note that, in contrast to those sects, which were mostly small and local, a community of churches rose into view which was fairly distinguishable as the "great Church."[1]

The social aspect of a Christian church must have been in many cases very like that of a small dissenting congregation in an English town where dissent is feeble. Where the believing community was very small it ceased in a manner to be visible at all. Where, on the contrary, it was large, as in Antioch or Rome, the necessities of the time might lead to the congregation meeting, for many purposes, or for considerable periods, in dispersed groups.[2] Facilities for disunion might hence arise, if strong individual views and tendencies came to play upon the situation.

Our conception of the Christian meetings must be based chiefly on Pliny, the *Didache*, and Justin Martyr. Pliny gathered, as he tells the emperor, that the Christians had been in use to meet on a fixed day before sunrise, when they sang a hymn to Christ as to a God, and bound themselves by an oath (*sacramento*) to commit no wickedness. They met again at a later hour and took food together; but the later meeting had latterly been abandoned by some of his witnesses in deference to the imperial prohibition of clubs. Some of the persons examined by Pliny had renounced Christianity; but all alike testified to the moral

---

[1] Celsus in *Orig. contr. Cels.* iii. 9, 10; v. 59. Celsus wrote about A.D. 176–180.   [2] Justin Martyr, *Acts of Martyrdom* 3.

purity of Christian manners. Cross-examination and torture brought out nothing inconsistent with this—somewhat, apparently, to Pliny's surprise.

From the *Didache* we learn that in the churches whose practice it represents, in the Lord's day meeting they broke bread and gave thanks, but first they were enjoined to confess their transgressions, that their offering might be pure; and those at enmity were to seek reconciliation. Also those who were plainly doing wrong were to be denied fellowship until they repented. In the direction for the eucharist, brief forms of prayer are suggested, first with the cup, and then with the bread, and a longer prayer of thanksgiving follows; but a prophet may give thanks in what terms he pleases. It seems to be implied that the administration was connected with the social meal which had acquired the name of an Agape. Life, knowledge, the hope of immortality, the gift of spiritual food and drink, and life eternal through God's Son, are the blessings commemorated; and the deliverance of the Church, her perfecting, and her gathering from the four winds into God's kingdom, are earnestly sought. "Let grace come, and let this world pass away."[1] Fasting was to be observed on Wednesday and Friday, and the Lord's Prayer to be used three times daily.

Justin Martyr[2] says that on "Sunday" Christians hold meetings, and the memoirs of the apostles and writings of prophets are read, as time allows. "When the reader ceases, he who presides exhorts to follow what is so excellent. Then we rise together and offer up prayers. . . . And when prayer is ended bread is presented, and wine with water; and the president offers prayers and also thanksgivings, according to his ability; and the people assent, saying, 'Amen.' Then distribution and reception of that

---

[1] It must not be inferred that no other exercises of worship and teaching were contemplated as proper in the Lord's day service. The writer of the *Didache* felt it important to regulate the eucharistic part; most likely he conceived that what else was in use might be left to the discretion of the congregation and its guides.

[2] Justin Martyr, *Apol.* i. 61, 62, 65–67.

over which thanks were said take place, and it is sent to the absent by the deacons. Those who are well off and willing give as each sees fit, and what is collected is deposited with the president; and he aids children and widows, and those who are in want by reason of sickness or adversity, those who are in prison, or strangers who need hospitality; in short, he cares for all who are in want." In another place Justin mentions the mutual kiss after prayer and before the eucharist. In regard to baptism, he says that the candidates, previously admonished to prayer, fasting, and penitence, are taken to a place where water is, and baptized in name of Father, Son, and Holy Ghost.

It was a common experience in these churches that the nucleus of more earnest and thorough Christians was surrounded by a fringe of adherents of a less decided sort. This feature took shape in the post-apostolic age under some peculiar influences. It was not unusual for men who were interested in religious questions or experiences to get themselves initiated into one or other of the mysteries, and to practise its discipline assiduously for a time. It was an experiment. When they seemed to themselves to have got to the bottom of the secret discipline, and reaped the main advantages it offered, they then relaxed, and were ready for a new experiment. To such men Christianity might seem to be one more system, perhaps more pure and lofty, but which, without culpable irreverence, might be dealt with very much in the same way. Then among the poor who were drawn to the Christian community by the practical benevolence of the Christians, some, of course, might become earnest believers, but others might be no more than grateful dependants, professing the faith which brought alms and kindly ministries in its train. Add to these children of Christian parents, who adhered to their parents' religion with some reverence perhaps, but without profound conviction, and you have the unreliable element in the Christian societies, easily swayed by the temptations which, in different forms, assailed the Church.

In two of his essays Lucian sketches in his lively way some aspects of the Christian societies. His account of Alexander of Abonoteichus represents the Christians, along with the Epicureans, as the special foes of that ingenious impostor, and as the principal objects of his hate. Doubtless the Epicureans had too little, either of religion or superstition, to give in to a religious pretender; and the Christian faith was too deep-rooted and decided to dream of any communion with him. In Lucian's account of Peregrinus Proteus he tells us how that cynic passed himself off, somewhere in Syria, as a Christian, and imposed on the local church for a time. As a Christian who made himself conspicuous he was imprisoned, and would probably have been put to death, but the governor of Syria saw how his vanity was gratified by being the centre of a great sensation, and sent him about his business. Lucian's main point is the respect and deference the Christians paid to Peregrinus during his imprisonment, crowding to see him and listen to him, and ministering to all his wants. For Lucian they are sincere, silly, kind-hearted people, who are successfully gulled by a rogue. But it is quite possible that Peregrinus was one of those dramatic individuals who impose in some degree on themselves, as well as on others, in the various parts which they play.

### LEADERSHIP AND ORGANISATION[1]

From the *Didache*[2] we learn that apostles, prophets, and teachers appeared in the churches or in some of them, and were regarded with great respect. All three

---

[1] The immense mass of discussion on the earliest church order has been augmented and freshened of late years in consequence of the discovery of the *Didache*. Besides Lightfoot's Dissertation (*St. Paul's Epistle to the Philippians*), which must always be kept in view, there may be named—Hatch, *Organisation of Early Christian Churches*, 1882 (2nd ed.); also articles by him on Priest, Orders, Ordination, in *Dictionary of Christian Antiquities*; Heron, *Church of Sub-Apostolic Age*, 1888; Gore, *Ministry of Christian Church*, 1893.

[2] C. xi. f.

seem to be persons recognised as men of spiritual power and gifts, in whom the presence of the Spirit in an exceptional manner, fitting them for public service, could be discerned; and it does not appear that they were elected or ordained by any standing authority.[1] Of teachers as distinct from prophets no very clear idea is attainable. Perhaps their function aimed more at instruction, while that of the prophets added impression. But prophets and apostles seem to be adapted respectively to what might now be called the fields of Home and Foreign Mission. The prophet is not tied to any congregation, but may, if he sees fit, take up his abode in one, reside there continuously, and exercise his gifts; he takes a leading place in worship, and ought to be generously treated as to the supply of his wants. The apostle has been led to devote himself to a different kind of life. When an apostle appears in any settled church he is to be received as the Lord; but he is not expected to stay above a day or two; and it is a bad sign of him if he asks for money. His work is to push on—to preach the word and gather churches in places beyond. Apparently pretenders had been found who were willing to trade upon the feelings cherished by Christians towards such persons, and rules are laid down by which true men may be distinguished. Apostles and prophets alike must speak according to the received conception of Christianity, and their conduct must agree with it, especially in the point of being disinterested.

Prophets and men of prophetic gift come before us in several ways during the second century; Hermas of Rome probably considered himself to be a prophet, and he was considerably exercised about the state of the prophetic function in Rome in his own day, the claims made on its behalf, and the questions rising out of it.[2] As to apostles, the

[1] But this does not exclude acts of recognition, on the part of the churches, both at the beginning of such a career and afterwards. Cf. Acts xiii. 1, 2.

[2] The true prophet, according to him, is "gentle, quiet, humble, abstaining from all wickedness and from the vain desire of the world, making

New Testament applies the name to others besides the Twelve; but apart from the *Didache* we hear little of them afterwards. Yet a reminiscence of these early apostles, conceived perhaps in the manner of a later and a changed time, seems to be preserved by Eusebius (*Hist. Eccl.* iii. 3; also v. 10. 2). He describes a class of men content to be without possessions, and always pushing on in mission work; they were not standing officers of churches, nor, apparently, appointed either by the Twelve on the one hand, or by the churches on the other. They were greatly respected, they ordained office-bearers in the churches gathered by them, and "delivered to them the Scriptures of the divine Gospels." But Eusebius cannot name any of them except Pantænus, who is rather a late representative of the class.

Persons recognised in these characters must have filled a very important place in the life and worship of the churches which they visited or in which they abode. The fact, too, that such persons circulated from church to church would help to maintain a common consciousness, and common ways of thinking and acting; it would contribute also to make known everywhere the books recognised as canonical. On the other hand, the exploits of Peregrinus Proteus,[1] as reported by Lucian, receive some illustration, when we realise the existence and activity of apostles and prophets, and conceive how false prophets might work the situation.

The churches, however, also required and had standing office-bearers, through whom they were organised and represented, and who were charged with the functions that required to be constantly attended to. What they were has been the subject of a great deal of discussion, the rather because questions about the nature and transmission of Church power have been mixed up with it. The *primâ facie* impression which the materials suggest is that churches

himself the poorest of all men." The false prophet "exalts himself, is hasty and shameless, talkative, and takes hire for his prophecy" (*Mand.* xi.).

[1] *De Peregr. Proteo.* c. 13 f.

exist at first with two classes of recognised office-bearers, one known as presbyters or bishops, and the other as deacons. This is the concession with which Lightfoot sets out in his well-known essay.[1] By the time of Ignatius (A.D. 115 ?) the bishop is in some churches—Antioch and those of Asia—distinguished from the presbyters as holding a superior position, but not yet apparently in Philippi, or Rome, or Corinth. By the end of the second century the bishop seems to be very generally a distinct presiding person, although bishops are still often called presbyters, and although important writers still think of church officers as constituting two grades rather than three.[2] The advocates of an original threefold order argue back from the general and peaceful practice at the end of the century. They maintain that this result could not have come to pass by accident, nor grown without a real root in apostolic precept or example.[3]

The case might be discussed more amicably if it were kept in view that a church in the second century was practically what we call a congregation.[4] Now the experience and practice of almost all Christian communities may be held to prove that some strong motive or reason brings it to pass that a congregation is usually provided with one minister, whose whole and sole work it is to look after them, whatever other officers may coexist or may be appointed in addition. Since this prevails in all countries and ages, no one need wonder that things gravitate into this form as the second century advances.

It might be much the more wholesome way, and most accordant with the idea of the Christian Church, that a group of the most trusted and respected men should be charged with the official duty of guiding and watching over the society; and probably all churches lose something

---

[1] Lightfoot, *St. Paul's Epistle to the Philippians*, pp. 181-269.
[2] Clem. Alex. *Strom.* vi. 13.
[3] That even at the end of the century, however, the bishop was more than a presbyter with permanent presidency, is not proved.
[4] This ideal is still visible, *Ap. Const.* ii. 57.

where this system is not practically maintained. But yet in the early Church, as in all churches since, influences were at work which tended to complete the arrangement by the employment of one man as the centre of pastoral activities.[1]

If we suppose that the third order was developed from a state of things in which there had been only two, the following considerations are to be kept in view. In any body of presbyters someone must preside; and that arrangement becomes still more imperative in worship. The chair *may* be taken by all in turn; but age, services, character, and aptitude may lead to someone being preferred, particularly in worship. Teaching demands special aptitudes, which may require cultivation. The charities of the congregation, too, constituted a very great element of early Church life,[2] and even if generally watched over by all the presbyters, might best be systematised by putting one person in special charge, with control of the deacons who worked out the details. The worship of the congregation might require a good deal of arranging, especially if there was as yet no church building, and if the place of meeting was not always the same. A central person to serve the purpose of an inquiry office, and to exercise some care in providing for emergencies and regulating details, would be expedient. And the duty of carrying on communications with those outside, whether other churches or the civil authorities of the place, was a function by itself. Clement seems to have discharged it at Rome.[3]

So far no reason appears why these functions should not be distributed among three or four, and perhaps that was the method in some churches for a time. Each of the group in that case might be in the emphatic sense an *episcopos*[4] for his own department. But the persons are

[1] Here the case of very small churches is not dwelt on. In those, plainly, one active personality would absorb and satisfy all requirements; and it might not be easy always to find one.
[2] Hatch, *Organisation of Early Churches*, p. 40 f.
[3] Hermas, *Vis.* ii. 4.
[4] "Convener" would be the word in some modern churches.

not many who are willing to take on such duties, and are able to command confidence in the discharge of them, especially if large demands on their time are implied. A point would be reached when mere spare time redeemed from business would be found to be not enough to discharge duly the various functions required. This would be felt particularly in the department of pastoral care; for energetic action was needed to keep the church together, and to keep sight of individuals and details. Whatever distribution of duties continued to exist, the whole time of someone must be given to the work,—naturally the most energetic, able, and devout Christian attainable. Such a man must therefore give up secular business, and must be provided for. One such person might be enough at first; as churches grew the deacons would next require to be cared for in this way: the presbyters not till later. A presbyter placed in the position now indicated would inevitably acquire a character, an influence, and a stamp distinguishing him from others; and he would be felt to be in an emphatic sense " episcopos," the man whose *business* it was to look after things. He was the man also who must specially appeal to the loyalty of the congregation to stand by him in his special and incessant responsibilities. He became the centre of the system.

As character and services increased the influence of such a man, as the feelings associated with pastoral care gathered round him, and as converse with Christians and with Christian interests promoted his spiritual training, he might fall heir to much of the peculiar reverence given to prophets and apostles.

It is to be remembered that churches varied extremely in their size and circumstances. In some, one person to guide and lead in worship, with a deacon or two, might be as much as could be attained. It certainly continued for a long time to be the case that some bishops followed ordinary occupations for their support; but those must have been cases in which the church work was comparatively light. There might also be cases where churches grew so rapidly that it soon became necessary to relieve several presbyters from secular cares, and in such cases the development of the monarchical episcopate might be delayed. But that could not be usual. More commonly we can trace a period during which the bishop and deacons are the active persons, continually in contact with the church life, and presbyters though respected are not so much in front; but later they come into prominence again, probably because the growth of the churches now required and employed their whole time.

The writer does not lay great stress on the details thus sketched out. Very early, presbyters who were specially gifted may have been encouraged to charge themselves with exceptional responsibilities under influences too subtle to be satisfactorily represented. The points to be emphasised are that the episcopate, in the later sense, developed at a time when " a church " was still a congregation, and that an important step must have been made when a man was called upon to lay aside secular business and to devote himself mainly to the service of his brethren in church work.

It may be right to add that while presbyters and deacons, and from an uncertain date a presiding bishop, were men holding office, to which they were set apart and in which much respect was paid to them, they were not at this stage a professional class as we now understand the term. They were no more so than town councillors and justices of the peace are now. But their office was part of a divine system, and so it added to their character as Christians something which their brethren were not at all disposed to make light account of.

It does not appear that these officers were anywhere elected for a term, after which they should retire unless re-elected. They could be displaced for cause shown; and it is quite possible that in some cases early churches acted in this line pretty freely, in the way of giving effect to their impressions about merits or demerits. But as far as we know, men were called and ordained to office as something designed to be permanent; in short, *ad vitam aut culpam.*

Although the president-bishop during this period becomes visible enough as a distinct feature in the system, it would be difficult to name any function appropriated to him alone. Where he was present he no doubt presided; that lay in the nature of the case. As to public teaching, Justin Martyr mentions that after the reading of the Scriptures the "president" made an exhortation; but we hear also that in the same circumstances the presbyters exhorted in turn;[1] indeed the competency of a presbyter to preside in public worship was never questioned. So also as to the sacraments of Baptism and the Lord's Supper.[2] Probably much depended, as regards the ultimate settlement of the distinctive attributions of a bishop, on the fact that some administrations were felt to require, in a special manner, the presence of the complete church, and therefore of its official president. This applied to ordinations. Appointment of men to office, otherwise than as the act of the whole church, would tend directly to schism. The same principle applied also to the formal restoration of the fallen after discipline. The church had witnessed their penitence, and the church ought to receive them back in a solemn and complete assembly. The bishop could be and was present on all such occasions, and led the action; it would follow easily, after some time had passed, that such things were regarded as exclusively his. The same rule might perhaps have applied to the Lord's Supper. But as that was observed every Lord's day, as a bishop must be sometimes unwell or absent, and as separate gatherings for worship could not be avoided when congregations extended and affiliated groups had to be provided for, the practice of dispensing the ordinance through a presbyter never could be discontinued. Ignatius recognises, but does not like, celebrations of the eucharist without the bishop. At a later date, ordinations and authoritative

[1] 2 Clem. Rom. xvii. 3.
[2] See Tert. *de Coron.* 3, and *de Bapt.* 17. According to the latter passage *anyone* can baptize in case of need, but usually the administration ought to be respectfully left to the bishop.

release from discipline were recognised episcopal functions. We have no proof that as yet they were so regarded; but, in the way indicated, things might be in progress towards that result.

The value for a selected pastor as the centre of church administrations must have been greatly enhanced by the experiences connected with Gnosticism, and, in a less degree, with Montanism. All the heresies carried division with them: Gnosticism did so eminently: if it made progress, the churches must be demoralised, bewildered, and broken. The impulse must have made itself strongly felt in each church, in the case even of many who could not judge the merits of the dispute, to rally round the person who had been chosen as the church's strongest, wisest, and most representative man, and largely to trust his Christian instincts to carry them through.

Justin Martyr speaks of the "reader" (ἀναγνώστης), and the writer of what is called the *Second Epistle of Clement* seems to reckon that function as his own special work. Probably it was hardly as yet an office—rather a useful aptitude placed at the disposal of the Church. The reader of later times was certainly not expected to preach,[1] but there are indications that earlier he was presumed to have some spiritual gift. A certain distinct position in the congregation was probably allotted also to confessors, virgins (of both sexes), widows, and perhaps others as well.

NOTE

In regard to the Episcopate, Dr. Hatch, followed by Harnack, suggested a modified view, which has been supported very ably. It may be briefly stated thus—

1. The presbyters were not properly officers or functionaries, but an informal committee of the members—naturally composed of the older men (hence πρεσβύτεροι)—taking the management of the common affairs. Afterwards, in more numerous churches especially, they might come to be a select

[1] See some information on this obscure topic collected by Harnack, *Texte u. Unters.* ii. 5. *Lectoramt.*

body, chosen, and might thus approximate more to the type of office-bearers.

2. The bishops and deacons were from the first proper office-bearers, *i.e.* functionaries, servants or employees, of the congregation, and, therefore, of the presbyters.

3. The bishops, even in the earliest period, were not identical with presbyters, though bishops might be also presbyters, or members of the presbytery. The bishops were properly stewards, and two of their functions as such may be named: First, to superintend the revenue with its incoming and outgoing, therefore, specially, the charities of the congregation: here stress is laid on the importance of this in the early churches: second, to superintend arrangements for worship (including the Agape), and see that worship went on satisfactorily. Hatch dwelt more on the former function and Harnack on the latter.

4. The deacons were the younger aides-de-camp of the bishops, naturally required in connection with such functions.

5. From their function in reference to worship (Harnack), being at the same time generally energetic and capable men, bishops came to be expected to keep worship going, and to give it interest, freshness, and dignity, especially after prophets and apostles became more scanty or less trustworthy. Compare the *Didache*, "for they, too (bishops and deacons), minister to you the ministry of the Prophets and Teachers. Therefore despise them not, for they are men to be honoured with the Prophets and Teachers" (xv. 1, 2).

6. According to this view, there were at first no men in the Church having any proper authority, except the Apostles, Prophets, and Teachers. The bishops and deacons were servants, though honoured and trusted servants, and the presbyters were only a committee of the members. By the time of the *Didache* the bishops and deacons are becoming *authorities* (τετιμημένοι μετὰ τῶν προφητῶν καὶ διδασκάλων). And the bishop rose into the chief place because he did most work, while the presbyters somehow became his inferiors—partly perhaps because they had not been emphatically enough distinguished from the congregation to maintain superiority. Still the tradition of their presidency ensured them some place, and they settled into the second.

This theory has abundant suggestiveness. I cannot reckon it sufficient, for (1) I think that from the first pastoral care existed, with the amount of authority which that implies. (2) Presbyters, at the earliest mention of them, are more expressly chosen and settled in care of churches than this theory will allow. (3) I cannot doubt that the ἐπισκοπή, whoever was charged with it, was an oversight of spiritual health and Christian welfare primarily. (4) I see no reason on this theory why at first there should be plurality of bishops (Phil. i. 1), nor any explanation of how, eventually, the plurality was restrained to such emphatic singularity. (5) The implied revolution by which the presbyters, the original superiors, became subject to the bishop, the eventual superior, ought to have left deeper marks on the history.

The theory makes the presbyters have special charge of discipline, as the active representatives of the membership, in whom the power of discipline resides.

An accessible sketch of the theory by Harnack himself may be seen in the *Ency. Brit.*, article " Presbyters," vol. xix.

### DISCIPLINE

As regards the discipline of the congregation, we know that care of the conduct of believers was a recognised function of the Church, and that in the case of grave sins ordinary privileges were, to say the least, suspended. We must believe also that in proceedings concerned with this aspect of church life, the presbyters and, where he existed, the bishop in the distinctive sense, must have taken a leading part; for, in addition to all official attributes, they were the select men, more trusted and more representative than any of the rest. On the other hand, it cannot be doubted that in communities like those we are contemplating, the procedure taken in such cases must have been known to the community, and must have had their assent expressly or virtually. That seems implied in the conception of the Church which goes through the literature. The Christian concerns are the concerns of the whole body. The churches are exhorted to enforce discipline; the churches write letters of exhortation; the churches are supposed to be participant in proceedings. This does not exclude some special function of the office-bearers; but it includes some influence of the mind of the members. It does not appear, however, by what ecclesiastical order of things the function of the people was regulated or guaranteed. For a long time after our present period the common sentiment of the Christian congregations had great and recognised influence, but one sees very little trace of a precise or regulated method of exerting it. It endured longest, as a recognised element, in the election of office-bearers; this right continues to find some expression, and sometimes very vigorous expression, far down the history of the Church. But it seems to take effect in an ill-regulated, tumultuous way.[1] Perhaps it never was protected by very definite forms or rules. In a state of things in which bishop and presbyters were representatives of the congregation, and had the best reasons for maintaining a good understanding with them, fixed methods for ascertaining exactly the mind of the members were perhaps not felt to be very important. As affairs multiplied, therefore, they naturally fell more into the hands of the official persons; but in the common Christian mind a standard existed, which could be applied both to the personal behaviour of office-bearers and to the principles of their administration. Things could not be carried on unless that standard of opinion was respected. But it is not easy to say what the matters were in which it was thought the congregation must utter a distinct potential voice, excepting always the election of men to office.

As regards discipline, it is pretty clear that at the end of our period it was customary for the bishop, who was the official representative of the whole flock as well as their chief pastor, to officiate in restoring penitents to the communion of the Church. This was perfectly natural. Yet it had much to do with the growth of the episcopate as a distinct order with exceptional powers; for this, like the right of ordaining, came to be regarded as a function and a power divinely bestowed upon him. The Montanists objected to the exercise of this function by the bishops; but they do not seem to have set up against it a claim for

[1] Sidon. Apollinaris. *Epp.* iv. 25 ; vii. 9.

popular control, but rather that prophetic persons speaking in the Spirit should decide such matters. Sharp contentions were arising as to the severity or the tenderness which should prevail in dealing with penitents: and it becomes plain, at a later stage, that bishops had to reckon with very strong opinions on the subject among the members of their flocks.[1] But official power, aided no doubt by a wise regard to opinion in the exercise of it, was destined to prevail.

## MARTYRDOM

Part of the life of early Christianity was liability to persecution. The relation of the Christians to the laws has been described. We are not to suppose that martyrdom was an everyday business. In particular places, and at particular times, considerable periods might pass during which the Christians were little troubled. But the possibility was always present; and once called to an account, the Christian must reckon on high penalties, unless he was willing to save his life by apostasy.[2] There were friendly governors who suggested to the Christians expedients by which, without violating their conscience, they might avoid a direct conflict with authority.[3] But that was not usual. For the most part just, and even courteous, judges, who showed no delight in cruelty, still felt it their business to execute the law firmly. Others were cruel men; they applied torture to break down Christian constancy, and lent themselves to give judicial expression to the popular passions of scorn and hate.

Martyrdom might be solitary, but it was often social— those who had worshipped together dying together. Justin Martyr was accused at Rome along with Charito (a woman), Euelpistus, "a slave of Cæsar, but made a freeman by Christ," Hierax, Pæon, Liberianus. They appeared before Rusticus, the prefect of the city, who questioned them

[1] *Apost. Const.* ii. 14.
[2] Justin Mart. *Apol.* i. 11.
[3] *E.g.* Cincius Severus, Tert. *ad Scap.* 4.

rather haughtily as to their origin and their Christian profession, which they all acknowledged. From Justin he educed a short statement of his faith ("Are these the doctrines that please you, poor creatures?"), and in particular of his expectation of a blessed immortality ("You that are a learned man and knowing in doctrines, are you persuaded that if you are scourged and beheaded you will ascend into heaven and be rewarded? Do you imagine that?" "I do not imagine it, I know it, I am sure of it"). He also inquired as to where Justin lived and met his disciples, and was told he lived "above the house of Martin at the Timotinian bath." Finally, the prefect came to the point: "Come together and sacrifice to the gods." On receiving a refusal, he again warned them. Justin replied as before, referring to the great tribunal of the Lord and Saviour; and his humbler companions said, "Do what you please: for we are Christians, we do not sacrifice to idols." Then the prefect passed sentence: "Let these, who have refused to sacrifice to the gods and obey the commands of the emperor, be scourged and led away to suffer capital punishment, according to law." They were beheaded accordingly. Some believers secretly removed their bodies and buried them in a fitting place, "with the aid of the grace of our Lord Jesus Christ."

Eager Christians were for meeting the enemy half-way, and censured those who withdrew and hid themselves. The narrator of the martyrdom of Polycarp at Smyrna is evidently aware that some had censured the conduct of that venerable man in withdrawing for a time, and he is anxious to vindicate the consistency and the dignity of his behaviour. At the same time he points out that some, who rashly affronted persecution, did not prove steadfast in the end. Polycarp, an old man of 86, was arrested at a friend's house. He asked for time to pray, and poured forth supplications aloud and continuously for two hours. Then they brought him to the city and into the Stadium. The judge, as usual, tried to persuade Polycarp to save himself by compliance; then, irritated perhaps by the lofty tone and bearing of the old man, he threatened him with the wild beasts. It was in vain; the martyr's last word was, "Why do you delay? Do what you will." For certain reasons the wild beasts were not available, and Polycarp was appointed to die by fire. A multitude of Jews and Gentiles looked on; the process was slow, and the martyr's patience invincible; so the crowd wearied, and called for a finishing stroke, which was inflicted by the proper official; and a great gush of blood, remarkable for so old a man, ended the tragedy. This closed a persecution in which scourging, death by fire and by wild beasts, had proved the constancy of the Smyrnese church.

What seems to be the earliest form of the narrative of the Scillitan martyrs has recently turned up.[1] The date is probably about A.D. 180, and the account illustrates very well the grave and brief utterance of a Roman magistrate. Saturninus was the pro-consul, of whom Tertullian has said that he first in Africa actively persecuted the Christians. Three men and three women are named in the *Acts*, but there seem to have been others. The pro-consul offers them clemency if they will comply; if, for example, they will swear by the genius of the emperor. He refuses to hear them on the merits of the two religions, but brings them back to his offer four or five times. The Christians protest their innocence of crime, and would have explained their belief if allowed. On the main point, they steadily abide by their Christianity: Cæsar is to be honoured as Cæsar, but God is to be feared as God. Saturninus, "Will you take time to think of it?" Speratus, "In so good a cause there is no room for deliberation." Saturninus, "What have you got there in the wallet?" Speratus, "Books (Gospels very likely), and the Epistles of Paul, a righteous man." Saturninus, "Take a delay of thirty days and bethink yourselves." Speratus, "I am a Christian"; and all the rest agreed. Saturninus, the pro-consul, declared the sentence from the written form: "It is

[1] *Cambridge Texts and Studies*, i. 2.

ordered that Speratus, Nartzalus, Cittinus, Donata, Vestia, Secunda, and the rest, who have confessed to living according to the Christian rule, inasmuch as they have obstinately persisted, after opportunity given, to return to the Roman life, shall be punished with the sword." Speratus said, "Thank God." Nartzalus said, "To-day we are martyrs in heaven; thank God." Saturninus directed the herald to make proclamation in terms of the sentence. "And so all of them together were crowned with martyrdom, and they reign with the Father and the Son and the Holy Spirit for ever and ever."

The *Acts* of Justin and those last referred to are most likely based throughout on the official record; the *Acts* of Polycarp are a narrative by Christian onlookers, who testify what they saw and what they felt. But the gem of all *Acts* of martyrdom is the story of Perpetua and her companions.[1] She was a young Carthaginian lady, a wife, and mother of a young child, and she wrote the story herself down to the night before she was exposed to the beasts;—how she was imprisoned, how she was tried, how she was comforted, what visions or dreams she had, assuring her of victory. The narrative is completed by one who could report the closing scenes. The simplicity and the quietness of the whole give it a quite peculiar power. No one, probably, could read it aloud to the end with a steady voice. It is too long to insert, and would be wronged by summary.

Persecutions are mentioned of which we have no details, or only single features.[2] But the church of Lyons and Vienne drew up for the information of their friends in Asia and Phrygia an account of the bitter experience through which they passed about the year A.D. 177.[3] The proceedings look like a resolute attempt to terrify the church into submission; and suggest that perhaps Christianity was as yet feebly and scantily repre-

---
[1] Best in Camb. *Texts and Studies*, pt. i.
[2] *E.g.* Tert. *ad Scap.* 4.
[3] Eus. *Hist. Eccl.* v. 1-4.

sented in Gaul, and that the destruction of the church of Lyons might seem likely to be its deathblow in that country. The proceedings fell at the time of the great annual gathering in August. This Christianity had come from the East, and used the Greek language [1] (with Celtic also, as Irenæus (*Ref. Præf.*) intimates). The persecution was attended by furious outbursts of popular hatred. The prolonged and repeated tortures of ten or eleven persons are described; but a considerably large number were put to death, including some who had given way at first, but afterwards recovered their faith and confessed it. After the early stage of the persecution, in which severe and prolonged tortures were applied to the sufferers, the governor reported to the emperor (Marcus Aurelius). He replied, directing that those who confessed the faith should be put to death, and those who disclaimed it set free. The narrative of the martyrdom remarks that the most outstanding men of the two churches had been arrested —those who were most zealous, and who had done most to sustain the Christian cause in the places where they lived.

Naturally, scenes like these produced great excitement. Sometimes spectators, who had never before professed Christianity, became so impressed with what they saw at the scaffold, or with the spirit and bearing of Christian sufferers in prison, that they surrendered themselves to Christ and His religion, and accepted all the consequences. Sometimes Christian onlookers, who had not up to that time been themselves accused, could not resist the impulse of sympathy and indignation; they stood out, denounced the persecutor, and offered themselves to condemnation. Or Christians, carried out of themselves by the "passion" in which they felt it a privilege to share, could even join the sufferers, apparently without waiting to be either accused or condemned. Cases of the last kind could only be rare, and they could not be approved by the Church. But they

[1] It is noted that Sanctus replied to all questions *in the Roman tongue*, "Christianus sum."

could occur, and are recorded also with sympathy and admiration.[1]

[1] "Akten des Karpus," etc., *Texte u. Unters.* vol. iii.: "Now a certain Agathonike, standing and seeing the glory of the Lord which Carpus said he now beheld, and knowing that the call was heavenly, straightway lifted up her voice, 'This meal has been prepared for me: I must partake and eat of this glorious meal.' And the people cried out and said, 'Have pity on thy son.' But the blessed Agathonike said, 'He has God, who is able to show him pity, for He foresees all things; but as for me, wherefore am I come here?' and casting off her garment she threw herself triumphantly upon the pile. And those who saw it wept, saying, 'A terrible judgment: unrighteous ordinances!' And having been set in her place, and reached by the fire, she cried out thrice, 'Lord, Lord, Lord help me, for I have fled unto Thee'; and so she gave up the ghost and was perfected with the saints." The scene is at Pergamus, and the date assigned is the reign of Marcus Aurelius.

# CHAPTER III

## The Church's Life

**LITERATURE**

The **history of** Patristic Literature begins with Hieronymus, *De viris illustribus*. Among post-Reformation works on this subject may be named Dupin, *Nouvelle Bibliothèque*, Paris, 1688–1714; S. W. Cave, *Script. Eccl. Hist. Liter.*, Oxon. 1740; R. Ceillier, *Hist. Génér. des Auteurs*, etc., 14 vols., Paris, 1860. For the period covered by this volume, Smith and Wace, *Dict. of Christian Biogr.*, 4 vols., London, 1877; Donaldson, *Hist. of Chr. Lit. and Doctr.* (unfd.), 3 vols., Lond. 1866. For Latin writers, Schönemann, *Bibl. Hist. Lit. Patr. Lat.*, 2 vols., Lips. 1792, 1794, and Bähr, *Gesch. d. Röm. Lit.*, Suppl. I.–III., Karlsruhe, 1836–40, are convenient to consult. Harnack, *Altchristl. Liter.* (unfd.), Leipz. 1893 fol. Of older collections of works of Fathers, Gallandius, 14 vols., Venet. 1765 fol., is of most repute. Much more complete is the collection of Migne, *Patrologiæ Cursus*, etc., Paris, 1844 ff. (very inelegant), which reprints notes and dissertations from older editions. Texts only, edited with great care, of Latin authors, the series of Vienna Academy, 1866 ff.; and of Greek authors, first three centuries, series of Royal Prussian Academy, 1897 ff., both in course of publication.

In the second century we have hardly material for a continuous story. Various manifestations of a singularly strong and vivid life, individual and social, call for recognition and disappear. What united them all in one development we can divine, but we can hardly narrate. It remains to piece together the impressions we gather of the communities that at Smyrna, at Ephesus, at Philippi, at Corinth, at Rome, at Carthage, at Lyons, in Palestine, in Egypt, and "in every place," lived or died for Christ. The literature claims in this period more particular notice than will be needful at later stages; and we shall begin with it the rather, because some conception of the writings assists the mind in estimating the worth of conclusions drawn from them regarding the life and work of the post-apostolic Church. It has been usual to print a number of the earliest post-apostolic writings in a collected form, under the name of the *Apostolic Fathers*. The title implied that the writers, though belonging to the second or third generation, had been in contact with one or more of the apostles. In regard to most of these writings this assumption is misleading. But yet it is convenient to have them together, and the established title of the collection need not be disturbed. Speaking generally, the tracts included are of earlier date than the middle of the second century; some may even be ascribed with probability to the first. It is reasonable to include the recently discovered *Didache* (see below) in this collection; and Funck, in his edition, has set the example of doing so.[1]

The Apologists begin about the reign of Antoninus (A.D. 138–161), and constitute a class by themselves. This form of literary activity, however, continued long after the close of our present period.

Hardly less important for the student are the fragments of works no longer in existence, which have been preserved to us by Eusebius or other ancient writers.[2] Some of these are printed in recent editions of the *Apostolic Fathers*, and more might be included. Most of the Gnostic literature, and all its earlier portion, has perished; but important fragments are embedded in the works of later authors[3]; and the student has to realise the existence of this literature, and, as far as he can, to form an impression of its character. Lastly, Apocryphal Gospels, Acts, and Apocalypses were coming into existence for several hundred years; the origin of some of them may with probability be ascribed to the period now before us, although even these have generally been much altered and interpolated at later dates.

---

[1] Editions—*Cotelerius*, by Clericus, 2 vols. fol., 1724; Gebhardt and Harnack, 1876; Funck, Tüb. 1886; Lightfoot (unfinished), Lond. 1886.

[2] Collected, Routh, *Reliquiæ Sacræ*, 5 vols., Oxon. 1846.

[3] Hilgenfeld, *Ketzergeschichte d. Urchristenthums*, 1884.

### 1. *Apostolic Fathers* (*so-called*)

(*a*) Two "Epistles" pass under the name of Clemens Romanus, but examination has shown that they must be treated as distinct in character and authorship.

Somewhere about A.D. 96 a "$\sigma\tau\acute{\alpha}\sigma\iota\varsigma$" took place in the church of Corinth. The origin of it is not quite clear, but one effect was that the presbyters were no longer permitted to discharge their functions. The influence of the Roman church to heal the breach had been invited by the church at Corinth, or by some parties in it; and the letter from "the church that sojourns at Rome to the church that sojourns at Corinth" is the document known to us as the *First Epistle of Clement*. The writer is not named in the letter, though his name appears in the title as given in the MSS.; but unbroken tradition from the middle of the second century ascribes it to Clement, a notable presbyter or bishop of the Roman church. Still the letter is from the church, not from any individual. In it the Roman church interposes in favour of harmony, order, and respect for constituted authorities, at Corinth.

Thus the earliest extra-canonical Christian writing we possess is a letter from the church of Rome addressed to a sister church whose affairs were in confusion, and intended to restore order. The church of Rome, from its position, the character of its membership, and the habits of thought and action naturally acquired in a great centre of government, could interpose in such cases with advice which was likely to be wise, and felt to be entitled to deference. This letter is diffuse, and takes a pretty wide sweep of practical Christian exhortation and Bible citation, some of which strikes the reader as bearing only remotely on the practical questions that had to be decided. The Apostles Paul and Peter are referred to with equal reverence. The sayings of our Lord are frequently cited.[1] The Epistle to the Hebrews

---

[1] Very much in the line of our Gospels, yet with enough of variation of phrase to raise questions as to the sources on which the writer of the epistle relied.

has made a strong impression upon the mind of Clement, and its ideas and language have coloured his own in some passages. Also, in addition to echoes of Paul's teaching, his *Epistle to the Corinthians* is referred to by name. A little more explicitness as to the motives of the "movement" party at Corinth, and as to the arguments they adduced, would have been very welcome to modern students, even at the cost of displacing some of Clement's generalities. But, considering the value of what we have, it is hardly good manners to complain. The epistle is sent in charge of brethren, who from youth to age had walked blamelessly in the Roman church.

(*b*) What the MSS. and editions present as the *Second Epistle of Clement* cannot be certainly localised, though Rome or Corinth may be plausibly suggested as the place of origin. The recent recovery of the latter part has proved (what had previously been suggested) that this tract is not an epistle but a homily, prepared in order to be addressed to a Christian congregation. The writer's name is unknown, but he officiated as a "reader" among the people whom he addresses ("me who am reading among you," c. 19). An early date in the second century seems to be indicated by his use of the *Gospel according to the Egyptians* (afterwards rejected by orthodox churches), and by modes of expression which suggest that the collision between the general Christian sentiment and Gnosticism had not yet taken place. Probably some circumstance, to us unknown, gave this sermon special interest for the Corinthian church, and they preserved it along with the Roman epistle.

(*c*) While the birthplace of the treatise last described is uncertain, there is no doubt that the *Shepherd of Hermas* belongs to Rome. The book contains a series of visions and revelations which came to the author through the ministry first of a venerable lady, who proves to be the Church, and secondly of an angel of repentance who appears as a shepherd: hence the name. Hermas, the recipient of the visions, appears from his own indications to have been a Roman freedman, a married man with a family. He evinces a lively interest in the function of Christian prophecy, and dwells on the distinction between true and false prophets. It can hardly be doubted that he considered himself to be prophetically gifted. He also dwells on faults of the office-bearers of the church, which need to be repented.

The main subject of the book is the problem of post-baptismal sins,—how Christians are to think and feel about them, and what encouragement they have to seek forgiveness. Hermas is taught that *one* opportunity for repentance of (serious?) failures following on baptism is granted, in view of the near return of Christ to close the dispensation; and the importance of embracing this grace is pressed on himself, that he may in turn convey the offer to others. The discussion of the great subject of post-baptismal sin begins with Hermas. Incidentally, views on other points of theology, *e.g.* as to the Son of God and the Holy Spirit, are suggested, which have been differently explained.

All the lessons of the book are delivered by the supernatural instructors in connection with symbolical visions, which are afterwards interpreted. The book was certainly received with great respect, and even quoted as Scripture in the second and third centuries. Eusebius reckons it among the Antilegomena.

The author of the early catalogue of books (canonical and non-canonical), which goes by the name of the Canon of Muratori, says that the *Shepherd* was written by a brother of Pius (Pius I.) while the latter occupied the chair of the Roman church. According to the prevailing chronology, this would indicate for the publication a date prior to A.D. 150, and the actual writing might reasonably enough be carried back twenty or thirty years before that epoch. Hermas himself refers to " Clemens " as the proper party to circulate his revelations to other churches: and if this implies that the writer was really a contemporary of the notable Roman Clemens, the date of Hermas' work must be fixed still earlier—say, not later than 110. On the ground merely of the contents and style of the book the tendency among scholars at present is to place it early,—before A.D. 140 at latest.

(*d*) The epistle ascribed to Barnabas is also reckoned by Eusebius among the Antilegomena, and few nowadays will regard it as having been written by the Barnabas of the New Testament. The object of the tract is to impart what is described as valuable Gnosis, namely, the true view of the Old Testament, and specially of the Jewish law. The author writes with a considerable sense of his own importance; and his view is that the literal observance of the law was all along a mistake of the Jews, who ought from the first to have taken it allegorically. Of this allegorical sense various instances, many of them sufficiently grotesque, are explained. The last three chapters break away rather abruptly into a description of the two ways of life and death, *i.e.* the main articles of Christian morals. These three concluding chapters have an interesting relation to the opening chapters of the *Didache* (see below).

By general consent, this epistle should be dated high in the second century, perhaps in the earlier part of the reign of Hadrian (117–131). Some learned men would place it still earlier.

(*e*) An *Epistle to Diognetus* has usually been printed with the *Apostolic Fathers*. The only MS. ascribed it to Justin Martyr; but for various reasons this is discredited, and the author is unknown. It probably belongs to the second century, though some great authorities place it in the third; it would find its most appropriate place among the *Apologies*. The Christian author, writing to a friend, pleads for the truth and worth of Christianity with strong feeling, expressed often with striking ease and force. There was a Diognetus among the teachers of the Emperor Marcus Aurelius; the conjecture that he might be the recipient of the letter has nothing to support it, nor yet anything to render it impossible.[1]

---

[1] A curious suggestion as to the possible origin of this epistle may be seen in Donaldson's *Christian Literature*, i. p. 126, and in Cotterill's *Proteus Peregrinus*.

(*f*) Ignatius of Antioch, who suffered, it was said, under Trajan, was understood to have written epistles during his journey through Asia Minor to Rome, where he was to die. A rather intricate literary problem is connected with these letters.

Eusebius says that Ignatius was reported to have written seven letters to churches, which he names; and he makes a quotation from one, that to the Romans. This epistle, and also those to the Ephesians and to Polycarp, had already been quoted by writers earlier than Eusebius. After the revival of letters, and before the end of the seventeenth century, successive discoveries furnished the learned world with (setting aside obvious forgeries) a body of twelve or thirteen letters, in two recensions—seven of them addressed to the churches named by Eusebius. The recension which first turned up, distinguished as the longer, presented a good many features which critics regarded as difficulties. The other recension presented a shorter text, and one less objectionable, at least in the seven epistles named by Eusebius. It was natural to separate these seven, in their shorter form, and propose them as the genuine epistles of Ignatius; but even these had peculiarities which disposed a number of learned men to question whether the text even in this shorter form were reliable or pure. The authenticity was defended, however, by many Catholic and Anglican scholars.[1] Both these recensions existed in Greek, and also in old Latin translations. In 1849 Cureton published a Syriac *Ignatius*[2] containing three epistles (to the Romans, Ephesians, and Polycarp) in a still shorter text; and he gave his reasons for maintaining that these three—the only epistles cited by any early author down to Eusebius—were the only genuine letters of Ignatius. This theory implied that the process of interpolating and forging letters of Ignatius, which must in any view have begun in the fourth century, had begun before Eusebius wrote, and had gone to such an extent as to lead to his statement that

[1] Pearson, *Vindiciæ*, Camb. 1671.
[2] *Corpus Ignatianum*, London, 1849.

Ignatius (though really responsible only for three) was "reported" to have written seven letters.

Scholars are at present disposed to accept the short Greek recension of the seven letters named by Eusebius as genuine. The best statement of the reasons may be found in Lightfoot's *Apostolic Fathers*, ii. 1, 2.[1]

A prominent characteristic of the Ignatian epistles, and one that gave motive and energy to much of the controversy, is the earnest and reiterated exhortations contained in them to maintain unity in each church by adhering to the bishop and presbyters and deacons. In this connection the distinction between bishop and presbyter appears, as well as the importance attached to this gradation by the writer. The epistles, however, are remarkable also on other accounts. They embody an energetic expression of Christian religion, both doctrinal and practical, are often expressed in eccentric and startling phraseology, and reveal a strong and ardent character. In truth, the best proof of the genuineness lies in the very singularity of the writings. Interpolations or corruptions there may be; but the original stamp of the writings as a whole does not agree well with the suggestion of forgery.

If Ignatius suffered under Trajan, as tradition reports, the date of the epistles may be placed at A.D. 115. Lipsius and Harnack on different grounds argued that the date might be considerably later — say 130 or 140, — which would remove some historical difficulties. But the arguments adduced have not procured general acceptance for this position.[2]

(*g*) Polycarp stood at the head of the church at Smyrna; according to the testimony of his scholar Irenæus, he had listened to the teaching of the Apostle John. Irenæus also mentions that he wrote various epistles, including one to the Philippians. This alone has been preserved. It is written in reply to one from the Philippian Christians, and consists

---

[1] See also Zahn, *Ignatius*, 1876.

[2] Harnack, in *Altchristliche Literatur*, now says probably before A.D. 117, possibly a few years later.

mainly of practical exhortations. Various passages from gospels and epistles occur, generally without express citation. The genuineness is acknowledged by most; but as the death and the letters of Ignatius are referred to, those who continue to reject the Ignatian letters are led to reject that of Polycarp also in whole or in part. The date cannot be very long after the death of Ignatius—at a time, therefore, when Polycarp was comparatively a young man. His martyrdom is ascribed to the year 155. The interesting account of his death which is embodied in a letter from the church of Smyrna, must have followed soon after.

(*h*) The *Teaching of the Twelve Apostles* (Διδαχὴ τῶν δώδεκα Ἀποστόλων) became known in 1883, when it was published by Bryennius from a MS. found at Constantinople. It proved to be a writing once cited by Origen as "Scripture," ranked by Eusebius among the Antilegomena, and referred to by Athanasius as containing nothing heretical, and as fit to be read to those who are beginning to receive Christian instruction. Part of it had been worked up into another old book, generally known as the *Apostolic Church Ordinances*, and the whole of it was before the author of the seventh book of the *Apostolic Constitutions* (fourth cent.), who dealt in the spirit of a later age with the materials it supplied. The *Didache*, therefore, had a recognised position and considerable importance at an early period of the Church's history; but by the time of Eusebius and Athanasius it had become antiquated and was practically superseded, though treated with traditional respect.

The book (equal in size to one of the shorter Pauline Epistles) is a kind of "Institution of a Christian man"; only it embraces also simple instruction in church life and worship, such as might conceivably be very useful in smaller societies of Christians, whose ideas were in some respects rudimentary. It begins with plain Christian morals—the doctrine of the Two Ways. This is the same in substance with the closing chapters of the *Epistle of Barnabas*, only the items are differently, perhaps better, arranged. The influence of the Sermon on the Mount is distinctly visible;

but plain duties and gross sins are commended on the one hand and prohibited on the other with great particularity. A Jewish basis for this part of the book has been strongly maintained. The transition to the more ecclesiastical part is made by directing that, after the disciple has received the moral instruction of the first part, he is to be baptized. The manner of church services, administration of sacraments, and maintenance of discipline, are all touched, so as to give a vivid glimpse of the early Christian communities. One interesting feature is the recognition of apostles, prophets, and teachers as labourers in the churches. Of them much is said, while bishops and deacons are disposed of in a single sentence. The tract closes with solemn anticipation of the coming of Christ, and of the Judgment.

The date cannot well be later than A.D. 140. Some would carry it up to the very beginning of the second century, or even to the end of the first. The way in which the book bears on debated questions has some influence in leading different minds to lean in the one direction or in the other.

The title of the book is not meant to claim actual apostolic authorship for it, but only to indicate that the directions it contains represented faithfully the apostolic teaching as received in the churches. In later collections of church rules the apostles are introduced speaking, and are made individually responsible, each for his own contribution. A similar origin came at length to be ascribed to the twelve articles of the so-called Apostles' Creed.

We proceed to notice works of early writers of which no MSS. have survived, and which are represented by fragments, being citations of the lost authors by later writers. We owe most of them to Eusebius. Among the earlier may be specified Papias and Hegesippus.[1]

The remains of Papias are scanty. He was bishop of Hierapolis in Upper Phrygia; and Irenæus describes him as having heard apostles; which, however, Eusebius with reason doubts. He took a peculiar interest in collecting

[1] Collected in Routh's *Reliquiæ Sacræ*, vol. i., Oxon. 1846.

traditions of men who had seen and heard the apostles, and published a work in four books (λογίων κυριακῶν ἐξήγησις). The most important fragment is that referring to the origin of the Gospels according to Matthew and Mark, which has given rise to immense discussion in connection with the Synoptic problem. The other fragments give no high idea of the author's sense or discrimination. Papias is usually placed about A.D. 145-160.

Hegesippus lived till late in the second century; but about the middle of it he made an important journey of inquiry into the state and teaching of various churches. He is described as a man probably of Jewish extraction, at all events familiar with the *Gospel according to the Hebrews*, with Syriac and Hebrew writings, and with Jewish traditions. Hence Baur assumed, and argued from the assumption, that he was an Ebionite Christian; but this view is now generally rejected. He wrote five books of ὑπομνήματα (after A.D. 160 ?), from which Eusebius extracted historical notices. It is probable that he argued against rising heresies from the information he had gathered as to the history and teaching of various churches. If so, he inaugurated a line of argument which was to fill a large place in later discussions.

## 2. *Apologists*

More homogeneous than these tracts is the branch of early literature which takes the title of the "Apologists."[1] For our period the names included are those of Quadratus, Aristides, Justin Martyr, Tatian, Athenagoras, Minucius Felix (placed later by some authorities), Melito, and (perhaps) Hermias. The work of Quadratus is lost; that of Aristides has quite lately been recovered in a form which represents at least its main features.[2] Both are said by Eusebius to have addressed themselves to Hadrian; but the work of

---

[1] The characteristics of this Christian Apologetic are discussed in a subsequent chapter. The writings are collected by Otto, 5 vols., Jena, 1876.

[2] *Texts and Studies*, i. 1, Cambridge, 1893; *Texte u. Unters.* ix. 1, 1893.

Aristides, at least, appears to have been really addressed to Antoninus Pius (A.D. 138–161).

Of Justin Martyr we have two *Apologies* and an elaborate treatise (*Dial. c. Tryphone*) expounding the Christian argument to the Jews. They date about the middle of the century, and are of the highest value as historical documents.

Justin was a student of philosophy; sought satisfaction for his mind and heart in various schools; according to his own account was impressed and attracted to Christ by a venerable stranger whom he met on the seashore, perhaps in some part of Palestine. After his conversion he continued to profess himself a philosopher, for he believed that he had found the true wisdom. But he was at the same time a warm-hearted and courageous Christian man, and he was honoured eventually to give up his life for his faith. His pupil, Tatian, an Assyrian, has left an *Apology*, written with glowing scorn of the Greek wisdom, which Christianity, the religion of barbarians, puts to shame. Tatian is reproached as having lapsed into a heresy (Encratite), pushing asceticism to the extreme of condemning, as intrinsically evil, the created things from which, as an ascetic, he refrained. He imbibed also some Gnostic views. He returned to the East after the death of Justin, and put abroad a Harmony in Greek of the four Gospels, which long continued to be used for public reading in various Eastern churches. The substance of it has lately been recovered.[1]

Of the history of Athenagoras, "an Athenian and a philosopher," little is known; but he has left a pleading (πρεσβεία) addressed to Marcus Aurelius (prob. A.D. 176), in which the accusations commonly brought against the Christians are discussed and refuted. There is also a tract on the Resurrection, in which the difficulties suggested by that doctrine are carefully discussed. Theophilus was bishop of Antioch; among other works which are lost, he addressed to Autolycus, a man of education and culture, an

---

[1] Zahn, *Forschung. z. N.T. Kanon*, i., Erl. 1881; *Texte u. Unters.* i. 1883; Möller, art. "Tatian," in *Real-Encycl.*, 2nd ed.

argument in favour of Christianity. It is weak in logic and not particulary admirable in tone, comparing unfavourably with several of the early *Apologies*.[1]

All these wrote in Greek. The *Octavius* of Minucius Felix is in Latin. The author was a Roman lawyer; and those who wish to see how a Christian of that profession in the second century could occupy his holidays, ought to read at least the charming introduction to the argument.

Fragments only remain of the writings of Melito, bishop of Sardis. He, too, was an apologist; but he was much more, for he took an active part in all the questions of his time, and more than twenty of his writings are referred to by later authors. He recorded the result of inquiries about the canon of the Old Testament, debated against Montanism, advocated the Asiatic practice in regard to Easter, wrote on the incarnation, on baptism, and on various other topics. In him we see how, as the second century advanced, the importance of literary discussion becomes more sensible in connection with every Christian interest. A public existed who could be reached, and for whom it was worth while to write.

Other writers of the period whose works are lost, like Apollonius of Hierapolis (an apologist and controversialist), Miltiades, Dionysius of Corinth, and the like, it is unnecessary to dwell on. They remind us that Christian pens were active in the latter half of the second century.

### 3. *Apocrypha*

It is right, however, before leaving the literature to refer to the Apocryphal Gospels, Acts, and Apocalypses, which were already beginning to appear. Here a distinction must be made. Versions of the gospel narrative (resembling apparently our canonical Gospels) had come down from the previous century: they were in use in some circles, and are quoted by catholic writers, but were not eventually regarded as authoritative, and have perished. This descrip-

---

[1] Hermias may or may not belong to this century. His tract is a satirical attack on the Greek philosophy.

tion applies to the *Gospel of the Hebrews* and the *Gospel of the Egyptians*, of both of which we have fragments From them are to be distinguished a quantity of writings, due partly to the desire to satisfy a craving for romantic detail, and partly to the wish to find access, in this form, for new sectarian teaching. The dates of many of these writings are difficult to fix, all the more that many of them existed in several successive forms, the relations of which are not easily disentangled. The subject has a history of its own, which must be followed out in works specially devoted to the subject.[1]

The Gnostics were active in the production of this class of writings. They were no doubt read with avidity, and they could be made the means of insinuating opinions which were less likely to be acceptable if plainly propounded. To our period belongs the *Gospel of the Childhood* ascribed to James the less, afterwards worked up into the *Gospel of Nicodemus*. Recently a discovery in Egypt has made known to us considerable parts of the *Gospel of Peter*,[2] and also of the *Apocalypse of Peter*. The former was known, before the year 200, to Serapion, bishop of Antioch, as a gospel which betrayed docetic tendencies. The fragment recovered contains an account of our Lord's passion, of great interest, both for its agreement with, and its divergence from, the account in the canonical Gospels. The *Apocalypse* contains a representation supposed to be given by our Lord to Peter (after the resurrection ?) of the experiences both of the blessed and of the lost in the other world. It stands at the head of a great Christian literature, which has dealt with the hopes and fears of men through representations of this kind.

A work of considerable interest is the *Testament of the Twelve Patriarchs*, in which the twelve sons of Jacob are

[1] Thilo, *Cod. Apoc. N.T.*, Lips. 1832 f. Tischendorf, *Ev. Apocr.*, Leipz. 1876; *Acta Ap. apocr.*, Leipz. 1851; *Apocal. apocr.*, Leipz. 1866. And see, especially, articles by Lipsius on Acts, Apocalypses, Gospels, in Smith's *Dict. of Christian Biography*.

[2] Swete, *Gospel of Peter*, London, 1893. Text of both writings, *Texte u. Unters.* ix, 2, 1893.

introduced uttering, each upon his deathbed, prophetic intimations and warnings to his descendants. These lead up to the appearance and death of Christ, the supersession of the Jews, as the people of God, by the Christians, the destruction of Jerusalem, and so forth. The book may be earlier than A.D. 180—at all events earlier than Origen. It seems likely that the *Testament*, as we know it, rests upon an earlier Jewish work, of which ours is a Christian adaptation. At all events, the very conception of the book, and its execution, indicate a Jewish point of view, and the influence of earlier Jewish models.

In this connection it is to be noted that various Jewish works of an apocalyptic kind were received among Christians with great respect, and exerted considerable influence. The chief of these were—

(*a*) The *Book of Enoch*, preserved in an Æthiopic translation from a Greek original, which may itself have been preceded by a Hebrew one. Enoch, after some introductory visions, is carried through the whole universe, surveying the mysteries of earth, heaven, and hell, which he recounts to Methuselah; and visions follow, in which the history of the human race as related to righteousness, sin, and judgment is set forth. Some critics recognise several hands,—the work of one going back perhaps as far as the second century B.C.; and the book may have been revised in a Christian interest in the first century A.D. Christian authorship of cc. 37–71 has been strongly maintained.

In addition to the Æthiopic version of this book, which is familiar to scholars, a Slavonic *Enoch* has recently been discovered. It traces back to a Greek original distinct from that on which the Æthiopic is based, and it also is ascribed to the first century.

(*b*) The *Book of Jubilees* (also *Little Genesis*), with legendary explanations of the early biblical history. This also dates from the first century.

(*c*) The *Fourth Book of Ezra*, a kind of theodicy; also, perhaps, of the first century.

(*d*) The *Assumption of Moses*, which has survived in an

old Latin translation. The last editor, Mr. Charles, ascribes it to a date not later than A.D. 120.

An important Gnostic literature began to arise in the second century and continued into the third. The fragments which survive, especially of the earlier writings, are scanty.[1]

The accounts of martyrdoms have been referred to in another connection. They were very liable to be revised in the sense of a later time; hence the date and value of these narratives as we now have them is often very debatable. But the Acts cited on an earlier page are well established.

[1] Hilgenfeld has collected the fragments, *Ketzergeschichte des Urchristenthums*, 1884; *Pistis Sophia*, Berol. 1852.

## CHAPTER IV

### BELIEFS AND SACRAMENTS

Discussions for many years on the birth and growth of the Church have left an almost boundless literature on this subject. Besides all general histories, see F. C. Baur, *Vorles. ueber die Christliche Dogmengesch.* 1866, 4 vols.; Harnack, *History of Dogma*, transl. by Buchanan, vol. i., Lond. 1894; Loofs, *Dogmengeschichte*, Halle, 1893 On rites, Smith's *Dictionary of Antiquities*, London, 1875 (unequal).

VARIETIES of tendency and of attainment appear in any Christian society or set of societies. In the early Church, allowance must also be made for progress and change due to a time of rapid growth. Before the end of our period Gnosticism, and Montanism, and the special tendencies of the apologetic writers, all had time to make their impression. Some churches, too, were more sheltered from such influences, while on some they played incessantly. Hence old fashions could appear alongside of new ones. What is now to be said must be subject to the qualifications which this state of things suggests.

Perhaps the most needful preparation for appreciating the beliefs of the early Church, is to get rid of the assumption or impression that the post-apostolic Church started with the fulness of the apostolic teaching, as that is embodied, for instance, in the New Testament. That is a natural assumption, and it is often made without a thought; but it is entirely opposed to facts. What the apostles and some others of their generation taught is one thing; what the Church proved able to receive is quite another. The tradition of the apostolic ministry was vivid; the writings embodying its message, which we still possess, were circulating, and they were soon collected and set apart as a special deposit. But the Church, which had a glowing sense of the worth of Christianity, had as yet laid but feeble and partial hold on its treasures of wisdom and knowledge. Elementariness is the signature of all the early literature. It is not for that the less Christian; and anything else would be non-natural; but the fact must be emphasised. The Church had waded as yet but a little way into this wide sea. Great elements of apostolic teaching had hardly become at all audible. But, especially, much that did float round Christian minds, and that is rehearsed at times in the writings, has not revealed its significance. Its meaning is caught faintly; the thoughts it awakens are indefinite. The apostles speak with power and certainty of great spiritual facts and forces, whose being and whose laws are clear to them. But to their disciples the meaning is often dim and the impression dubious, so that the range of principles remains hidden. All this was inevitable; it would have been so with the wisest and the best of us in their place. Ages of study, of meditation, of controversies, of obedience, of devotion, of discipline were to work the meaning of the New Testament teaching into the mind of Christendom. It was enough for the early Church that some bright central certainties held them fast, filled and fixed their souls with full assurance. Under the influence of these, it was easy for them to believe that the great inheritance of truth and grace stretched much farther than their eyes could see.

Where doctrines have been crystallised by controversy it is easy to give an account of them. As that had not yet taken place, the state of the Christian mind must be indicated by description.

Perhaps nothing strikes one more than the singular moral heat — the enthusiasm about goodness — which we meet in the Christian writings.[1] To be good is no longer a doctrine of philosophy or a matter of taste; it is

[1] Donaldson, *Christian Lit.* i. p. 84.

a calling, a career; a summons, as imperative as it is wonderful, has awakened men to it. There broke into consciousness among the Christians a new relation to the moral standard. The standard itself is often set forth in terms not very different from those of the Stoic moralists, or in terms of the Jewish law idealised on Stoic lines. Often, no doubt, the inwardness of it, and the stress laid on love, forgiveness of wrongs, meekness, gentleness, humility, helpfulness, proclaim the new influences that are at work. Generally, however, it is not so much the definition of the standard that is important, but the new relation to it. It has become for Christians their inheritance to be realised, their proper destiny to be achieved, the field on which they are to make good the reality—the glory —of the religion which has taken them captive.

Already some approved asceticisms are beginning to be valued and to be accepted as rules of life. With some this expressed simply the wish to be like Christ, who was poor. Again, as all Christian goodness implies self-discipline and self-repression, as steady preference of the higher aim implies repression of the lower impulse, it becomes plausible to infer that increase of self-sacrifice will certainly be gain in goodness. Once more, the desire to make sure of one's own honesty and thoroughness, to make sure that no weakness is cherished and no hardness is declined, disposes some to reckon exceptional asceticism the safer and the worthier course. This does not go *much* beyond the legitimate liberty of choosing what seems best for a man's own Christian life; but it does go somewhat further.[1] Yet a benignant way of looking at natural ties, and a consciousness of God's presence in them all, are still able to avert extremes.[2]

This moral enthusiasm was supported and deepened by fear. For the difficulties were not disguised,—the strength of temptation, the weakness of the flesh, the sad possibility of falls. Yet, long as the race may be, and

[1] It figures as the *whole* yoke of the Lord, *Did.* vi. ; 2 Clem. Rom. vii. 3.
[2] In many passages—1 Clem. Rom. i. 1, 2 ; *Ad Diogn.* 5.

hard the battle, there is nothing for it but victory; nothing less than that will do. And what they seek is a victory of them all, as a company that would fain triumph together. "Let us turn with all our hearts, that no one of us may be lost. For if we have commandments (and keep them) to draw men from idols and to instruct them, how much more is it fit that no soul that has once known God should perish! So let us support one another, and stir up the weak in goodness, that we may be saved, all of us, converting and exhorting one another."[1] This morality was imperative for its own sake; but not only for its own sake. It was the only genuine form in which a man could respond to the divine compassion; it was the one approved career along which to reach the fulness of the life eternal.

In the closest connection with this is the vivid Christian consciousness of being face to face with the decisions of eternity. The whole weight of the contrast between good and evil was to embody itself in final weal and woe; and the day of this judgment was speeding on. It was near, though no man knew how near; at farthest death was not far off, and that sealed men up for judgment. The intensity of conviction as to this is one of the most striking things about the Christians. The uncertainty about a world to come in classic religion and philosophy is notorious. The Jews had speculations about it, which embodied the thought of retribution, but these lacked finality. According to their Apocalypse there is no last end of anything.[2] For the Christians, the hope of complete and unending well-being rose into view, in vivid contrast with the doom prepared for sin and apostasy. Almost no Christian exhortation omits these topics; and they came instinctively to the lips of the martyrs when tempted to deny their faith. These great alternatives were speeding on. And they were felt reaching into each day's business, and transforming the values of all things here.

The power which kept all this alive is to be found,

[1] 2 Clem. Rom. xvii. 1, 2.   [2] Harnack, *Dogmengesch.* i. p. 120.

beyond a doubt, in the Christian convictions about "the things surely believed among us." God had made Himself known.[1] Quite recently He had revealed Himself in the world through Jesus Christ; and this was His complete, His decisive revelation. Men had longed, had yearned, had looked and listened, had hoped and feared. Now God had spoken; He had emerged upon human souls. One, Spiritual, Supreme, Eternal, the fountain of all being and object of all worship; yet having a mind and care for each man, accessible to each man, intent on the character of each, calling each man to fellowship with Himself. He came, with perfect truth and effectual pity, recognising the problem of the world's sin and providing the remedy, by coming down into it in His Son. In this presence man's life assumed a new significance. The hour had struck for applying judgment. Former ages with their relaxed or depraved manners God had in some sense tolerated. Now He commanded all men to repent. Things became clear and sure.

In particular, Christ Himself was unique. In Him arrived the great illumination alike of duty and of destiny. By Him, God, and human life, the great choice, and the eternal issues, had been set in an intense blaze of light. Nor did He reveal only (which was easily expounded), He also saved. How He did so was not so well explained; but it was felt and believed. He washed us from our sins, broke the chain that bound us, brought life within our reach, made it an altogether hopeful thing for us to choose the better part. A great deal of New Testament teaching about this was apprehended not at all, or in the vaguest way; but the thing itself was sure. Also, Christ was coming again to judge quick and dead, and to fulfil all the promises. Along with all this the conviction that Christ was not merely human but divine went hand in hand, and is quite frankly expressed. With some it is more in the foreground of their thought, with others more in the background. We have already met

[1] *Ad Diogn.* 7; 2 Clem. Rom. i. 5-8, etc.

with Christians, generally of Jewish origin, who claimed for Christ only a pure and lofty manhood; and others, ascribing to Him a supramundane nature, thought of His manhood as something fleeting and unreal. But beyond all reasonable doubt the mass of Christians regarded Him as both divine and human. How many of them, if forced to explain themselves, would have explained in the line of later Councils, is debatable. But the two aspects of Christ were present, dimly or clearly. With the Father and the Son the Holy Spirit took His place in Christian minds; that was settled by the formula of baptism (Matt. xxviii.).[1]

As to the salvation of the individual under Christianity, two moods of mind strove with one another; on the one hand, the sense of divine goodwill and help—which must be all-sufficient; on the other hand, a sense of dangers which called for the utmost effort. When it comes to particulars, it often seems as if the Christian, after baptism, under the moral influences of Christianity, must get along as well as he can—must in that view save himself; yet, on the other side, the impression comes out with no less force that Christianity really brings life eternal within our reach, and expresses a benignity so near and real that no hopes can be too high.[2]

But, at all events, whatever perplexity might beset the question of the individual, something definite and bright rose to view in thinking of the Church. Certainly Christ meant to have a Church, and should not be disappointed; the Church is destined to victory and life everlasting. That did not imply the final well-being of all her children: as the Church fought her way onwards, many a member might be snatched from her by the powers of evil. But the Church must survive; through all assaults she is destined to victory; and meanwhile the loving presence of the Lord, of which the individual could not always assure himself, could be more confidently counted on in the Church. Hence association with the Church, cultivating

---

[1] This subject comes up again in the chapter on Christ and God.
[2] Implied, *e.g.*, in prayer, Hermas, *Mand.* ix.

its fellowship and observances, breathing the atmosphere of its common life, promoted present Christian comfort, and became the pledge of Christian hope. As the Christians held together in this line they could most fully feel the Lord's presence in the midst of them, and could be strong to overcome the world.

This was so much the more natural, because the power of evil, also, was conceived as a concrete system, a kingdom, with its Satanic head,[1] its inspiring and energising demons, and its concrete embodiments and agencies throughout the world. All that was unchristian or antichristian fell under this conception. The machinery of the great system was at work everywhere. How could a Christian feel safe, except as he felt himself participant of the common social life of the counter-kingdom, the despised but invincible kingdom of the Son of God?

Everything in Christianity was divine,—it came from divine revelation, and was animated by divine life. The Church therefore, which is the completest earthly embodiment of Christianity, must eminently be divine. It included much human weakness and inconsistency; but its institutions and its life were from on high. Hence a very visible tendency prevails to hold every institution and observance, which at any time found acceptance in the Church, as something divine, original, apostolic. Change went on, but the results of change were canonised. This is continuously exemplified all down the history.[2]

Christians lived in the expectation of the Lord's return in power and great glory, the resurrection of the dead, and the judgment, with the separate issues of the righteous and the wicked. These events, according to the general impression, were not to be long delayed; but no definite term was assigned. It has been said that two distinguishable styles of eschatology characterised two types of Christian thought—the one taking pleasure in concrete images of rest and delight, after the manner of Jewish Apocalypses, the

---

[1] *Barn.* c. 4, ὁ μέλας.
[2] Especially visible in the law codes—*Apost. Const.* etc.

other dwelling more on emancipation from material conditions, and contemplation of truth in God. But while the early writers may gravitate towards one or other of these two poles, the important thing to notice is that no Christian writer repudiates either. Those who are most philosophic, and most disposed to aspire after ἀφθαρσία, maintain also the resurrection of the body with all that it implies; and those who are attracted by the more millenarian expectations are far from meaning that earthly delights can satisfy God's children. The conception of the ζωὴ ἐπουράνιος could be approached on both lines.[1]

So much has been said, because very brief statements of belief hardly represent sufficiently the way in which Christian minds worked on matters of faith. But, of course, any religion existing in a cultured age—especially one that does not stand in ancestral customs pleasing to the Gods, but presents itself as a doctrine of light—must be able to say roundly what it means. When anyone came to be baptized, the question came clearly up, What does the neophyte accept? An understanding on the point would seem to be necessary just then; and there was every reason for its being expressed with care. Accordingly, some profession of faith in Christ—or of faith in the great name into which a man was baptized, Father, Son, and Holy Ghost—must naturally be supposed. So far we may feel sure. If a longer and more fixed creed existed, it must be inferred by reasoning back from later authorities.

At a later date various forms of creed existed in different churches—various yet very closely allied. They suggest an early form, in Greek probably, both in East and West, confessing faith in the Father and the Son and the Holy Spirit, and connecting with the third head brief clauses of Christian blessings and hopes. When the wording comes within our reach, we find it varying only slightly in the Western churches, and the Roman church claimed for its formula a direct apostolic origin, on which account it would allow no change upon the wording. In the East the original

[1] See Hermas, Papias, *Didache*, 2 Clem. Rom.

form, if we are to assume one, had been varied more freely in different churches to meet successive heresies; and in the East there existed no tradition for an apostolic origin of any creed.

The creed now known as the Apostles' is one form of the Western creed; it was used in Gaul as far back as the fifth century. But the old Roman form, which must have been in use A.D. 250, and for two centuries after, was a little shorter. It was in these words: "I believe in God the Father Almighty: and in Jesus Christ His Son, only begotten, our Lord; who was begotten of the Holy Ghost and Mary the Virgin, crucified under Pontius Pilate, and buried; the third day arose from the dead, ascended into heaven, sitteth at the right hand of the Father, from whence he cometh to judge quick and dead: and in the Holy Ghost, holy Church, forgiveness of sins, resurrection of the flesh." The phenomena of early creeds, in their likenesses and their differences, are conceived to point back to some form like that now quoted, existing in various Western churches in the second century. When a man asserted these articles he took Christian ground. The recognition implied or imposed upon him the state of mind called Faith. These things, being real, claimed his trust and allegiance, and he acknowledged so much in his creed.[1]

We find also in the churches, especially in churches where minds were active, a conception of the significance of the creed, or of the common belief, for Christian thinking. It was the common belief relating itself to the mental movement of the time, and taking ground in characteristic assertions. Christian revelation, so far as yet apprehended, left much unsettled. But it furnished thinkers and teachers with some fixed points in reference to the speculation of the time, which could be roundly expressed, though men did not use one unvarying form in which to embody them. This consent of Christians as to the meaning of their faith, or as to the common teaching received among them, was referred to as

---

[1] Greek σύμβολον, perhaps "watchword." Writers of the fourth century speak of the creed as never committed to writing, but handed down orally.

the κανών, or the *regula veritatis*. It assumes prominence in the beginning of the next period.[1]

Baptism was administered, in the name of the Father, the Son, and the Holy Spirit, usually, but not always, by immersion. A practice of baptizing in the name of Christ simply, comes into view from time to time; but it was always rather questionable. Baptism presupposed some Christian instruction, and was preceded by fasting.[2] It signified the forgiveness of past sins, and was the visible point of departure of the new life under Christian influences and with the inspiration of Christian purposes and aims. Hence it was the "seal" (σφραγίς) which it concerned a man to keep inviolate. When we come to Tertullian (*De Corona*, 3), we find various new circumstances attached to the administration. These, or some of them, may have begun in the present period, but there is no contemporary evidence.

The Agape or love-feast was a custom of apostolic times, and the celebration of the Lord's Supper had been connected with it. The Agape, in one form or other, continued to be observed for a long time; but in the second century[3] a change took place which disconnected the sacrament from the religious social meal, joined the former to the principal service of the Lord's day, and made it the crowning act of the worship of the congregation, when that was completely performed. Justin Martyr, writing near the middle

---

[1] Neither the *regula* nor the creed appear in the period now before us, but by the end of it there is much reason to think both were present. Whether the *regula* or the creed comes first historically has been made a question. The *regula* is plainly spoken of in Christian writings long before the creed is referred to in the same way. But that can be accounted for; and the order given above seems to the writer to be the more likely.

Statements of the *Regula*, Iren. I. x. i.; Tert. *de Præscr.* 13, *de Virg. vel.* 1, *adv. Prax.* 2; Clem. Alex. *Strom.* vi.; Orig. *de Princ. Proœm.* 4.

As to the Creed, among foreign writers, Hahn, *Bibliothek der Symbole*, Breslau, 1877; Caspari, *Quellen z. Geschichte des Taufsymbols*, 1869; V. Zezschwitz, *System d. Katechetik*, 1875; Harnack (*Apost. Symb.*) in Herzog, *Realencycl.*[3] vol. i. Among English writers, Heurtley, *Harmonia Symbolica*. Swainson, article in Smith's *Dict. of Antiquities*, and reff. there. Sanday in *Journal of Theolog. Studies*, vol. i. p. 3.

[2] *Didache*, vii.; Justin Mart. *Apol.* i. 61.

[3] Later than Ignatius, *Ep. ad Smyrn.*

of the second century, refers only to this form of rite; but the date must have varied in different churches, and the old connection with the Agape appears here and there later. We gather also from Ignatius that within one church the love-feast, with its sacramental commemoration of the Lord's death, might take place among smaller groups of worshippers, as well as in the set meeting of the Christian congregation as such.[1] Ignatius appears to dislike this practice. At all events, he is clear that no meeting of this kind should be held without the bishop's authority, and he presses the view that in one church there should be united observance, with all the constitutive elements of the organised church present.

Besides the observance on the Lord's day, the eucharist was celebrated after the baptism of a new convert, and no doubt at other times. The celebrant is referred to by Justin as the " presiding person," and there is nothing as yet to indicate that the validity of the ordinance was held to depend on " orders." At the same time, alike the celebration in separate groups, and by persons not specially authorised, could easily lend itself to schisms, and restriction in both respects was certain to be ultimately agreed upon. In churches whose practice is represented by the *Didache*, it was deemed desirable to have for the eucharist short fixed forms of prayer. The forms given are remarkable chiefly for the absence of clear reference to the suffering and death of Christ, to forgiveness or reconciliation. The leading thoughts are the unity of the Church, its eventual gathering to Christ, the spiritual food and drink imparted to believers, the light and immortality to which Christians are called, and the near coming of the Lord. The *Didache* recognises the right of the prophet to pray in such terms as he thinks fit, and Justin Martyr says the presiding person prays according to his ability. It is probable that the prayer in the earlier part of the Lord's day service took the form chiefly of supplication, and in the eucharistic part of thanks-

---

[1] Ignat. *Philad.* 4, *Eph.* 20.

giving. As early as Ignatius and the *Didache* the term εὐχαριστία occurs in application to the whole ministration of the sacrament, and even to the elements.

That in partaking of the consecrated elements the participation of the worshippers in the body and blood of Christ is solemnly affirmed, both on their part and on God's, may be said to be the common teaching; but what the nature of this participation is, according to Ignatius and Justin, and what the relation of the elements to that which they represent, is a question which will be differently answered, just as the statements on these subjects in the New Testament are differently understood in different schools.

This service has to be considered also from another point of view. From the earliest period probably it was customary for the people to bring gifts of various kinds of food, including especially bread and wine. These were needed for the Agape, and any surplus was available for Christians whose wants had to be provided for. From this supply the portions were taken which, after the eucharistic prayers, were employed in the celebration of the sacrament.

These contributions in kind were the δῶρα, which the office-bearers presented, as gifts brought for the service of God and of His Church. And it was not unnatural that the technical term for temple offerings (προσφέρειν [1]) should be applied to them, the rather that the term etymologically means simply to bring forward or present. This fell in also with the Christian feeling that the worshippers, as God's redeemed, had it for their duty and privilege to offer themselves to God—all they were, and all they had—and to do so then, especially, when admitted to the highest expression of fellowship with the Son and with the Father; so that the gift they brought with them was only a token of the surrender of all. In particular,

---

[1] 1 Clem. Rom. i. 44, προσενεγκόντας τὰ δῶρα. But it is not quite certain that these material contributions were as yet spoken of as δῶρα, and the phrase may refer to the prayers and thanks of the Christians, of which the presbyters were the mouthpiece. These also were eminently offerings. Heb. xiii. 15.

this feeling of grateful obligation necessarily animated the eucharistic prayer. Then, any sentiment of thankful offering to God which expressed itself in the δῶρα in general, must especially have followed that portion of them which, in the service, was as it were specially accepted by the Lord, and was honoured to become the expression of what Christ, on His part, gave and gives, in virtue of His sacrifice of Himself. In the portion so employed, what was brought by the Christian people to the Lord seemed to meet that which the Lord brought and communicated to them. Up to this point nothing hindered the thought of "offering" or presentation as embodying one aspect of the transaction. If that offering in itself was small, it was fashioned to great honour in the use for which the Lord accepted and employed it, and it was the token of the greater offering of loving hearts and lives. Such considerations make it intelligible that as early as Justin we find the whole service spoken of as the προσφορά. It was the Christian offering as contrasted with Gentile sacrifices. But this use of language rather obscured the main meaning of the sacrament; and it lent itself, eventually, to an impression that the thought of offering might be applicable indiscriminately to the whole religious transaction, and especially to the elements after consecration; so that Christ sacrificed for us is somehow the προσφορά which Christian men offer in the eucharist. Nothing in our period suggests that this conception (which supposes us to present to our Lord that which He, in fact, is presenting or representing to us) had taken being; but the form of language had already been provided out of which it was to grow. The eucharistic προσφορά appears as yet in Justin Martyr only.[1] In this connection it is to be observed that the thought of a special priesthood, alone qualified to make the offering, is also unknown. Justin, in connection with the eucharist, speaks of the whole Christian congregation as the high-

---

[1] Ignatius speaks thrice of the altar—*Philad.* 4, *Eph.* 5, *Trall.* 7. But this is an ideal altar, in allusion to the Levitical type. See Lightfoot.

priestly race (*Dial.* 116, 117) who offer true and pure sacrifices; and he goes on to identify these sacrifices as the Christian prayers and thanksgivings, and the Christian commemoration " in food dry and moist, in which the suffering of our Lord is remembered."

Generally, one sees the working of a set purpose to find a Christian sense for Old Testament sayings, and therefore to find aspects of Christian ordinances to which Levitical language can be applied. Such a tendency must be expected to exert itself, with special force, in connection with symbolical ordinances like the eucharist.

A lively sense of a wonderful union to Christ, specially brought home to us in the eucharist, dominates all the language used; and whatever benefits arise to men through union to Christ, might be suggested in this connection. Specifically, some writers suggest the idea that the sacrament received operates on our bodies as an influence disposing them to resurrection and immortal life.[1] But how far this is literally intended, it is hard to say; for, in any view, resurrection and eternal life are ours in union with Christ, and that living union is represented in the eucharist.

Sin and the forgiveness of sins were topics of which much had to be said; yet the doctrine of them was entangled in views and impressions arising from the Church's discipline. Baptism seals to men the forgiveness of sins.[2] No doubt actual forgiveness could not be assumed without reference to the state of mind of the candidate for baptism; for in him faith and repentance are required, and they might not be really present. Still forgiveness of all past sins is a blessing held out to faith in baptism. But how as to sins after baptism?

First, there are some sins which are also scandals.

[1] Ignat. *Eph.* 20.
[2] This is equivalent, according to Tertullian, to forgiveness at conversion, if baptism, though intended, does not immediately take place—if, for instance, it is reverentially delayed, "Fides integra secura est de salute" (Tert. *de Bapt.* 18); but baptism is the *sacramental* donation of forgiveness; therefore it is the visible epoch of forgiveness for Church purposes, and the sacramental seal of it to the believer himself.

When these become known they interrupt Christian fellowship, and the Church separates the sinner, until satisfied of his restoration to a better mind. Now the habit of early writers is to speak of the loss of the Church's peace and the loss of God's, also of the (legitimate) possession of the Church's peace and the possession of God's, as if the one interpreted the other. Hence, in regard to such sins (especially impurity, idolatry, and murder), the question about "forgiveness" is the question about the Church's right to restore. Many maintained that for these great sins there is no forgiveness after that which is sealed in baptism. Others (whose view prevailed more widely as time went on) allowed one more forgiveness upon penitence, but none after that. Lastly, there were those (but they are hardly visible till the third century,—yet the view may have been acted on before) who allowed more than one restoration. Those who restricted the Church's right to restore meant that, in such cases, the forgiveness of the sinner could not be presumed or assured. But they did not mean to shut out all hope. If the sinner continued penitent till he died, he might, or would, find forgiveness in the next world; but not in this one.

On the other hand, sins less aggravated were conceived to find forgiveness through current religious exercises with almsgiving; they required no more special provision for taking them away. But this was in its own nature an insufficient and unsatisfactory distinction. Which are the really great sins? Not necessarily those which bulk largest in human eyes. This difficulty was felt. For while sometimes the plenitude of grace was regarded as easily cleansing the occasional stains of a redeemed people,[1] at other times the Christian consciousness of sins became very pressing.[2] The special lessons of Hermas concerning his sins begin with the consciousness of a passing thought of evil;

---

[1] 1 Clem. Rom. ii. 3: "With godly confidence you stretched forth your hands to God Almighty, beseeching Him to be merciful to you, if ye had been guilty of any involuntary transgression."

[2] 2 Clem. Rom. xiii. 3, xviii. 2.

then his lack of good government in his family, and a habit of lying begin to come home to him. His whole life becomes so defective in his eyes, that the announcement of one more opportunity of repentance before the Lord comes, consoles him greatly. That is, he feels that the lesser sins in his case require as express relief as the greater might. This special grant of one repentance after baptism is not regarded by Hermas as a standing ordinance in the Church. It is allowed for once only, that men may be encouraged to prepare themselves for the Lord's return.[1]

Amid all that created exultation and called forth effort among Christians, the consciousness of sin, and a serious estimate of its ill-desert, could not but have a large place. On the other hand, the impression of the divine benignity and compassion towards the penitent was never lacking. But clear thoughts of the principles on which the Lord deals with men about sins, especially after baptism, never were attained. Out of this perplexity arose, after a long time, the Romish sacrament of penance.

In some churches there had been the practice, at an early period, of confessing openly whatever each member felt to have been a transgression on his part, with the view of clearing his conscience before common prayer and communion.[2] This would apply specially to any wrong done to a brother, but the rule may have applied to transgressions generally. No doubt this turned out to be inexpedient. But public penitence continued to be exacted in connection with grave or scandalous sins. We may believe the leading or ruling persons in congregations would be consulted, when a conscience-stricken believer was in doubt as to whether his own particular offence required to be dealt with in that way.

The yearly commemoration of the Lord's death and resurrection at Easter reveals itself, about the middle of the second century, by a debate which then arose. From a period which cannot be assigned, the custom had prevailed of distinguishing the Wednesday and Friday of

---

[1] Hermas, *Mand.* iii. and iv. 3, 4.  [2] *Didache*, iv. 14.

each week by some religious observances — of course, in addition to the first day of the week, on which the chief weight was laid. Annually, when the feast of the Passover came round, and when the observances connected with it became prominent in every Jewish community, the Christian churches could not but feel that the Christian worship of that week was coloured by the remembrance of the great events associated with our Lord's last Passover. This was the more certain because in the earliest days almost every church included members who were Jews, and strongly imbued with Jewish habits and associations. In the earliest period, indeed, many continued to observe the Jewish feasts. One way in which this situation worked was, that whatever the day of the week might be on which the Passover fell, the Friday (being the week-day of the Lord's death) took on the character of commemorating the crucifixion, and so, naturally, the next Sunday became the commemoration of the resurrection. This form of observance must have been very general; we find it prevailing in Syria, Egypt, and the West. But in Asia Minor they followed a practice according to which the Passover day in each year, whatever day of the week it might be, was devoted to commemorate the death, and probably in the evening the period of mourning ended, and the celebration of the eucharist introduced the period of rejoicing. This way was not less natural than the other, and might even claim, from one point of view, to be more exact. But as the Passover day was naturally accepted annually as fixed by the Jews, this had the effect of bringing the Christian celebration into constant coincidence with the Jewish one; while, on the former arrangement, such coincidence only happened occasionally. Charity might have regarded the Asiatic practice as embodying a constant protest against Judaism; but zeal suggested that it might be a form of Judaising.

At all events, after a time offence began to be taken at the Asiatic peculiarity in this respect. Hence, when

Anicetus (A.D. 154–166) was at the head of the church of Rome, Polycarp of Smyrna, then a very old man, made a journey to Rome, the chief object of which was to arrange the difference. The Asiatics were in a minority; but theirs was at that time a very vigorous ecclesiastical life; and besides, they traced their practice back to the Apostle John and other great authorities. They therefore did not feel they could give way; nor did the Romans on their side. At that time the two parties agreed to bear with one another, and Anicetus, in token of Christian friendship, made Polycarp celebrate the Lord's Supper in his church. Later, as we shall see, in the time of Victor (bishop of Rome, A.D. 189–198), the controversy revived with great bitterness.

# CHAPTER V

## APOLOGISTS

J. C. T. Otto, *Corpus Apologetarum Christianorum*, 2nd ed. 5 vols., Jenæ, 1876, is a useful collection.

THE Apologists fill, relatively, a large place in the Christian literature of the second century. They are by no means confined to that century; but it may be best to deal with them now. Aristides, Justin Martyr, Tatian, Athenagoras, Theophilus, Minucius Felix (probably), come within our period. Tertullian, Clement of Alexandria, Hermias, Origen, Arnobius, Lactantius, and others fall later.[1]

Their task was to represent Christianity, and defend it in relation to the alien and adverse forces which have been described. Their main concern, speaking generally, is with the Gentile world; but Justin Martyr has left an elaborate exposition of the case of Christianity *versus* Judaism; and Apologists often refer to Judaism as one of the alternatives naturally present to the minds of men at that time. As regards the Gentile world, the Apologists, speaking generally, have an eye to the action of the government; they plead for toleration. But at the same time they press the claims of Christianity on the classes that are capable of being influenced by writing. The *Octavius* of Minucius Felix is not on the face of it directed at all to the government or to the tribunals. It is rather a literary treatment of a current question. The same remark applies to the *Epistle to Diognetus*.

The Apologists put Christianity forward as the true and

[1] The date of the *Epistle to Diognetus* is contested.

the eternal religion. From first to last it has claimed the loyalty of men; but as announced by Christ, it is set forth, at last, adequately, so that in its purity and its certainty it may do its work among men. They assume the classes whom they address to possess the intellectual training of the age, referred to in a previous chapter, and to be furnished with the conceptions and schemes of thought which that training supplied. God,—Virtue,—a possible or probable survival of spiritual natures after death,—these were themes which the Platonic and the Stoic schools (often, by this time, fusing themselves together) had kept alive in the minds of men. Also the thought of a divine nature which mediates between the Highest God and the concrete world was extensively entertained.

What then is the Christianity which the Apologists propound to their contemporaries? Christianity, according to the Apologists, sets forth God as the only God, unapproached in nature and dominion, a pure spirit. He is represented much on the lines of those older schools which dwell on His essential remoteness from the material and the concrete. He is eternal and immutable, He is also righteous and good. He is sole Creator of the world, both physical and moral, and is the Lord of Providence. The world therefore is, essentially and in the main, beautiful and good (though graduated as to both qualities, and capable of evil), and it has been planned with a view to man, who unites the two elements of matter and spirit. It is therefore the same God with whom we have to do, alike in the moral region and in the physical; and He is the God who deals with us in salvation.

The ancient Church had a very lively sense of the importance of *certainty* as to all this. They held fast the double thought—on the one hand, that God is the principle and source of the world; on the other hand, that God, as immortal and eternal, stands in vivid contrast to the world as corruptible and transient. In the former it is involved that moral good presides, and in the end will be supreme. The same thought lent itself to the conception of creation as furnishing parables of redemption. On both grounds, commentaries on Gen. i. came to occupy a large place in Christian literature.

The revelation of this God, both in creation and to the creatures, is carried on by the Logos (also the Son) of God, the manifest and manifesting reason. He comes forth from the eternal Father; yet so that the Father loses nothing by the process.

Man, in particular, is so related to God that Truth is a common element for God and man. The highest truth, indeed, requires to be revealed, but man is apt for such revelation. There is, first of all, a revelation in the nature of man, a "seed of the Word" more or less present to all men. Hence it is, at least ideally, possible for men, even now and without further revelation, to attain sufficient knowledge of God; but it is difficult. There are, however, additional ministries of the Logos, which, in various degrees, have tended to the same end. All these are crowned and completed in Christianity.

The doctrine of the Logos could be connected, of course, with the νοῦς of Plato and the λόγοι of the Stoics, as well as with the λόγος of Philo, and it was connected on the Christian side with the person of Christ. In addition, the Apologists recognise as distinct the Holy Spirit (sometimes identified with σοφία); but this is an element suggested rather by their Christian faith than by their intellectual scheme.

Man has been endowed with reason and free-will; and he is destined to a life transcending earth and time. This blessed life is to be attained by a course of holy walking in the likeness of God. Virtue is conceived on the principle of surmounting desires and impulses pertaining to the body, and living spiritually. The natural morality is, to surpass nature and so find oneself related to God and man in a pure and lofty manner. By equanimity, indifference to want, purity, goodness, always under the influence of the Logos, man even here rises above the transient, and finds his way to the other world with its vision of God.

This, rather than the great **thought of love**, is the watchword of the Apologists: though with a consciousness that a gentle, helpful, unselfish temper is an element in it. Along with this spiritual hope the resurrection of the dead was firmly asserted; also the judgment and twofold retribution. Life lived under the influence of the Logos leads on to ἀφθαρσία—a state free from darkness and decay. As the peculiar manner of God's own existence is emphatically marked out by this same word, so the destiny for man which it indicates, suggests for him also a divine manner of existence. This thought is distinctly present as a matter of fact, and it continues to recur far down the Greek Christian literature. Man saved is in a manner deified. This connects again with the Incarnation as the fitting means towards such a result.

This view of the true good is so congenial to man, that the response to it was due on the part of men even from the beginning. Christian religion in this view has claimed men all along. But in our present condition the true knowledge and the right impressions have been hindered. Darkness and uncertainty beset men, and they are enslaved in lusts and in misleading beliefs. How has this come about? If there is in every man a seed of the eternal reason, if also the energy of the Logos has been, from time to time, put forth exceptionally in some men who have been examples and instructors to their fellows, why has truth so far failed to do its work? The main practical answer which the Apologists have to give is to refer to the influence of dæmons, who have in some way come into great power in this lower world, and whom men have allowed to establish a baneful influence among them.

Christian religion, then, is the truth concerning all these matters operating duly on men. In the case of an individual here and there, it might conceivably have been attained by the light of nature; but it has from the beginning been authoritatively revealed by the prophets, and now at last conclusively in the incarnation and life of Christ. Thoughtful men among the Greeks attained to a large measure of the truth; but for the most part their attainment was partial, and largely beset with uncertainty. Now, in the incarnation and in the ministry of the Word Himself, the teaching of the prophets and the sages has been confirmed and completed. Now, with decisive clearness and authority, it claims our obedience.

It may be asked in what way the Apologists make good their claim, that in connection with Christ's coming this religion has now received its conclusive certification. Often they are content merely to state the case, as if the mere statement spoke for itself. Sometimes (so Justin Martyr) they dwell on the thought that by the manifestation of the Logos in Christ a fuller participation of Him has become possible for men. But in general they rather remarkably abstain from maintaining that something new has been revealed by Christ. For their point rather is, that all essentials have been within our reach all along. On other terms they might have had to encounter a strong prejudice; for the thinkers of the day were not likely to admit that the eternal religion, the religion which is from the beginning true for man, should come to light *per saltum*, at a later epoch. The Apologists prefer to say that the whole prophetic dispensation was rich in predictions; and in the coming of Christ, and the results of it, those predictions have been verified. This directly proved divine insight and divine providence. When the Apologists survey the recorded history of Christ, their first thought about it, and their constant comment on it, is that in it prophecy has remarkably been fulfilled. Christ, therefore, appears in a radiance of fulfilled prediction which assures us who He is.

The Apologetic conception of the true religion fell in remarkably with the indications of the best Greek schools. The exceptions to this are the doctrine of the incarnation and the definite Christian eschatology, both of which the Apologists faithfully assert. But the unity of God,—His ineffable contrast to the material world,— the supreme worth of virtue,— even the general conception of what virtue is,—immortality as an assertion or as an aspiration, —and the general doctrine of a Logos,—were all reflected in the common thinking. Besides, many Gentile minds confessed, or did not disclaim, a craving for something like religious assurance,—for hope beyond the grave,—for conscious and personal relations to the immortal and the eternal. The Apologists were well aware of this approximation, and for some purposes they emphasised it. They took up a double attitude towards Greek thought. They accepted the evidence which Greek thought supplied, that the conception of religion presented in the Christian argument is indeed the true, the congenital religion for men; it can approve itself to man's better reason. The "seed of the Word" in every man (aided sometimes by hints from Jewish prophecy and by special influences) can bring men so far. On the other hand, they feel entitled to treat Gentile philosophy with disdain, because—(1) it deferred to the national idolatries and entered into compromises with them; (2) it proved to be fluctuating and divided; (3) it lacked certainty; it could not inspire confidence or sustain hope. This double attitude in different degrees characterises all the Christian representatives except, perhaps, Arnobius, whose attitude is that of contempt only. Tertullian, too, professes to disdain the schools; and he lays stress only on the views which common sense suggests to the ordinary unsophisticated man.[1] But what he so accepts is materially the same thing which other Apologists commend as the reasoned conclusions of the better philosophers.

The Apologists, then, hardly ask the Gentile mind to change much in its better thoughts about God and virtue; but they offer to it the new certainty and the new encouragement which Christianity imparts. For the sake of these, Greece might well accept the articles which embody direct divine interposition in the incarnation and the eschatology. Christianity is a religion in which the life of well-doing becomes an assured career. That which has heretofore been an ideal no doubt remarkably put in

[1] *Testimonium Animæ naturaliter Christianæ.*

practice by some select souls, was now to come home, convincingly and fruitfully, to men in general, to common men and maidens, not less than to the wise. The goal seems to be much the same as before; nay, the force which is to carry men to the goal is substantially the same—the influence of Truth upon the mind. But now, Truth is cleared of doubt; now it can operate in a victorious manner; and it is reinforced by Hope.

It has been felt and said that in taking this ground the Apologists reveal a scanty appreciation of their own religion, and are silent as to some of its greatest promises and prerogatives. They do not dwell on the significance of forgiveness; they do not insist on the need, or the fact, of a new beginning by a new birth. They do not seem to feel (here, however, Justin Martyr and the writer to Diognetus must be excepted) that the incarnation and the experience of our Lord embody a redemptive energy, unless we reckon to this the assumption that those who now believe are enabled by the Holy Spirit to throw off the power of the dæmons. Our Lord's appearance (this seems to be their leading thought) became the great fulfilment of prophecy, and at the same time it possessed men's minds with a quite new sense of the reality of that Logos influence which was more secretly dispensed before. Harnack, therefore, has remarked that the Apologists made a very bold stroke in asserting identity of contents as between Christianity and the better forms of pre-existing theory, for thus they claimed for their cause the suffrage of the world itself; but they did so at the cost of neutralising the significance of all the specific features of the religion they defended.

In order to do justice to the Apologists, it must be considered that their business was to address the cultured mind of their time. In doing so they were bound to put forward aspects of the case to which they could hope that mind would respond. Their business was, or seemed to be, to insist on the affinities between Christianity and Greek thought, to suggest the help which the Greek mind might receive from Christian teaching, but not to insist on what might seem alien or opposed. Their personal Christianity, therefore, might be of a richer strain than their *Apologies* reveal.

Another thing must be said. The significance of Christ in connection with the scheme of truth and duty may be conceived barely by these writers. It may be often little more than this, that in His person the immediate *imprimatur* of the Logos Himself was stamped on the moral contents of His religion. But the feeling of the writing means more. The writers are filled with the sense of a new beginning set for men, and for each man, in Christ's religion. Just as in the final judgment, so resolutely asserted by them all, the justice is signalised which upholds moral distinctions, and gives to the world a moral constitution; so, in the incarnation, the grace which cares for men, and knows no limits to its condescension for their sake, the Love which was set on saving, was felt, though hardly at all explained. It was something *there* which made all new, and rendered it so hopeful, obligatory, and inspiring, to forsake all and follow Christ.

And this, too, it is which, as it were unconsciously, baptizes their moral code. They do not themselves know why or how their morality differs from the pagan codes,— at least they most imperfectly tell us; but when morality comes into a world of love, and takes relation to the grace of Him who took flesh and died for us, it is unawares transformed, inspired, and glorified. Still, the impression gathered from the writings is that the early Apologists disclose, substantially, all that had attained, in their minds, to the condition of a reasoned case. What further impressions they had of something rich and strong in Christianity were largely inarticulate. Their minds were on the whole filled and held by the conception, already explained, of Christianity as related to current thought. With various proportionings of things they agree with one another in the main. One must say, therefore, that in these representative men the Christian mind took up a conception of Christianity which impoverished the representation of it. The effect was that the ways of thinking and speaking on the subject, the utterance, in short, of the early Church, was powerfully influenced in the arid direction by these writings.

This may be the place to notice an interesting reflection of Harnack's.[1] He says, "Here lies the difference between Christian philosophers of the type of Justin, and Christian philosophers of the type of Valentinus (the Gnostic). The latter were seeking for a religion; the former, without being clearly aware of it, being already in possession of an ethical view of the world, were seeking for a certification of that view. The attitude of both towards the complex Christian tradition—in which, no doubt, many elements could not but attract them—was that of strangers; but the second class sought to make this complex intelligible to themselves, while the first class were content to take it that here was revelation,—that this revelation, whatever else was in it, testified of one spiritual God, of virtue, and of immortality; and that it had power to lay hold of men and guide them to a virtuous life. These last, then, externally considered, were no doubt the Conservatives; but they were such because almost at no point did they reckon seriously with the content of the Christian tradition: the Gnostics, on the contrary, sought to understand what they had read, and to get to the bottom of the message which had reached them. . . . In short, the Gnostics tried to ascertain what Christianity is *as a religion*, and under the conviction that it is the absolute religion, they offered to it as a gift . . . all that they reckoned lofty and sacred, while they removed from it what appeared to them to be only subordinate. The Apologists devoted their efforts to place religious illuminism, along with morality, on a stable foundation; to render impregnable a view of the world in which, if it were impregnable, they could feel certain of eternal life. It was this they found in traditional Christianity."[2]

This is so far true, that the Gnostics insisted on think-

[1] *Dogmengesch.* i. p. 375.  [2] Compare also p. 171.

ing out a complete theory of the world, including Christianity, in which both the prevalence of evil and the victory of redemption were vividly embodied, and relations to supernatural beings and forces were powerfully asserted. But in doing this the Gnostics transformed Christianity as it had been delivered to the world; and, indeed, they may be said to have transformed morality too; for both are subjected to a thoroughly fantastic rationalism. The Apologists, as far as their writings inform us, conceived Christianity in a scanty manner; but at least they respected its great outlines and remained within them; and it was a tribute to the power with which traditional Christianity held these men, that they did not venture to traverse its positive teachings. It was safer, and more accordant with a believer's attitude, to begin the work of knowledge with one aspect of things, although that might be provisional and inadequate, than to try to complete it at one huge and reckless stride. In particular, to insist that Christian religion fulfils itself always on moral lines was true, and the assertion of it by the Apologists was a signal service to the cause of a sound theology. Finally, the decisive point is that the Gnostics, notwithstanding their vivid sense of the significance of Christ's appearance, really destroyed the faith of the incarnation. The Apologists barely develop the significance of that great event, but at least they remain under the influence of it. Some, as Justin Martyr and the writer to Diognetus, should have much more ascribed to them. This is the dividing line, which proved to be decisive. "Suo igitur sanguine redimente nos Domino, et dante animam suam pro nostra anima, et carnem suam pro nostris carnibus, et effundente Spiritum Patris in adunitionem et communionem Dei et hominis— ad homines quidem deponente Deum per Spiritum, ad Deum autem rursus imponente hominem per suam incarnationem, et firme et vere in adventu suo donante nobis incorruptelam, per communionem quæ est ad eum—*perierunt omnes hæreticorum doctrinæ*" (Iren. v. 1. 1).

## CHAPTER VI

### THE HERESIES—GNOSTICISM

The chief early writers on heresies, now extant, are Irenæus, *Contra omnes hæreticos* (Stieren, 2 vols., Lips. 1853, and W. W. Harvey, 2 vols., Camb. 1857); Hippolytus, *Refutatio* (Duncker u. Schneidewin, Gött. 1856), both in Clark's Anti-Nicene Fathers; Epiphanius, *Panarion* (Oehler, 4 vols., Berol. 1857), to which are to be added various works of Tertullian, Clemens Alexandrinus, and Origen, which discuss the Gnostics or refer to them. In modern discussion the *Essays* of Massuet, ed. of Irenæus, and of Petavius, ed. of Epiphanius, are reproduced in the editions mentioned above; Neander, *Entwickelung d. Gnostischen Systeme*, Berlin, 1818; Matter, *Histoire Critique*, 3 vols., Paris, 1844; Baur, *Die christliche Gnosis*, Tüb. 1835 (also in his *Kirchengeschichte*, Tüb. 1860, and *Dogmengeschichte*, Leipz. 1866); Möller, *Geschichte der Kosmologie*, Halle, 1860; Mansel, *Gnostic Heresies*, London, 1875; Harnack, *Hist. of Dogma*, transl. by Buchanan, London, 1894; Lipsius, *der Gnosticismus sein Wesen*, u.s.w., Leipz. 1860, with series of articles by Lipsius in Smith's *Dict. of Christian Biography*, London, 1877–1887; Loofs, *Leitfaden*, Halle, 1893. These are selections from an immense literature.

THE churches were liable to disturbance, not merely from the government and the populace, but from questions raised among the Christians themselves; and some churches, in virtue of their composition and their situation, were more in danger of it than others. When these questions concerned permanent principles of Christian truth and Christian duty, the risk of persistent divisions made itself felt. No doubt a very wide field of matters lay open, on which the churches did not profess to have attained a common judgment,[1] and

---

[1] One sees from Justin Martyr that differences of view about the Person of our Lord were already felt in his time, and were apparently tolerated, at least in some churches. These preluded the Monarchian disputes. It seems

did not try to impose any. Variety of individual thinking could be tolerated in many points. On the other hand, however, the Christianity which lived in the churches was felt by all earnest Christians to have a definite character which must be maintained; it was a mode of spiritual life, conscious of the difference between food and poison. So when eccentric teachers inculcated views which threatened to transform Christianity, to alter, as it were, its centre of gravity, or to pivot it on some new axis, resistance was instinctive. How to distinguish the various cases, and how to have the requisite agreement about them, was, no doubt, the difficulty. In the earlier years of our period, the disturbing influences felt seem to have been mainly, first, a tendency to Judaise; and, secondly, a tendency to Docetic notions, *i.e.* to treat our Lord's human nature as unreal and apparent only.[1] Neither tendency seems to have operated widely or given much trouble. The second claimed to give a purer and more spiritual conception of Christ, and was indeed an early stage of the Gnosticism of which we are presently to speak. The first was a belated effort of a dying party; but it could base itself on the authority of the Old Testament, universally received in the Christian churches as Holy Scripture. From that source it was always possible to press the literalities of Judaism, or some selected forms of it; and Christians could be bewildered, and needed to be put upon their guard.[2] Still the general mind of the Church recoiled from everything distinctively Jewish with decision, and even with antipathy.[3]

These were not formidable dangers. But from about the year 130 [4] a flood of speculative theories poured out upon the churches, which pretended to give the deeper

more convenient to survey these in one connected view, and to reserve them for that purpose to a later chapter (Chap. XI.) under next period. The Elkesaites have been noticed, in connection with Judaising, in Chap. I.

[1] Ignat. *Epp. to Trallians, Smyrnæans.*
[2] *Barn.* 2, and see Eus. *Hist. Eccl.* vi. 12. 1.
[3] *Didache*, c. viii. : "Do not fast along with the hypocrites (the Jews), for they fast on Monday and Thursday; but do ye fast on Wednesday and Friday."
[4] Manifestations of the same tendency appear a good deal earlier, but did not then operate powerfully or extensively.

and the truer view of Christianity. Varying in detail they had much in common, and together they embodied a mental tendency of the age. In some of their prominent features they are so fantastic that the modern mind finds it difficult to treat them seriously; but on closer consideration they are found to embody ideas and impressions that cannot be so lightly set aside. Moreover, the representative Gnostics, in point of freshness and force of mind, were probably on a level with any Christians of the second century. Valentinus, Basilides, Heracleon, Ptolemæus, Marcion, Bardesanes, — a selection from a much longer list — were thinkers; some of them, in their way, poets. The conceptions which held such minds could not but appeal with force to a good many Christians, particularly to men of education, conscious of the intellectual ferment of the age. That the various Gnostic teachers agreed so far, bears witness to common impressions and common cravings which they all expressed; that they differed as they did, indicates the wilfulness of their method. These men were not expounding a revelation; they were arranging their impressions and their conjectures. Yet all of them had felt the vitalising force of Christianity.

The elements out of which the Gnostics build their theories are, in general, these—first, the grand distinction is that between matter and spirit,—the one the element of grossness, darkness, deception, therefore of evil and vice; the other of light, truth, reality, therefore also of goodness. Second, the world we know, with its hierarchy of beings from man downwards (including human religions, politics, in short the whole scenery of the world), is a mixture in various degrees of the two elements, the rational and the irrational. How is it to be understood? It is the case of a better nature imprisoned in a worse. A kind of "wisdom" goes through all the world, rising here and there to clearer manifestation; but it is a captive wisdom, gone astray, entangled in a foreign element. It has become carnal. Thirdly, belief in God, goodness, and salvation, means belief in a higher world, where the better element exists in purity and power; it exists in hierarchies of beings (the æons),[1] graduated perhaps, yet all divine, and all manifesting the central source whom we call God. That world is the Pleroma.[2] Fourthly, returning to this world, we note that not merely is matter pervaded by a certain "wisdom,"—it is amenable so far to order and can palpitate into life,—but the world has something architectonic about it; its vault of heaven, its plain of earth, its tribes of animals, its kingdoms of men with traditions and laws. Someone[3] has been here ordering, disposing; but if so, it is someone who from his birth has never conceived any higher work, otherwise he would not have busied himself with this. This is the Demiurge, the Maker, the great carnal Worker. Fifthly, as to the religions of the world, they are classed as evil— the pagan; medium — the Jewish; good — the Christian, gnostically understood. The Demiurge is the God of the Jews, and of the Old Testament. He is doing what he can to make the world perfect, with no great success; and the Jews are his special people, with whom he has taken particular pains. He has promised them a Messiah, and an earthly triumph under his guidance. When the supreme God, or the joint wisdom of the Pleroma, interposes at last, in Christianity, the administrations of the Demiurge are taken possession of by this higher power and are made vehicles of higher influences. Sixthly, Christ is a wonderful concentration of the light and virtue of the Pleroma. He comes forth in fitting time to deliver what can be delivered of the captive element. There are men, there have always been, in whom the divine spark comes out more clearly and victoriously, or in whom it can be roused into decisive manifestation. These are souls susceptible of the true salvation. The coming of Christ is the signal for their emancipation. Deliverance comes home to them as they catch sight of the significance of His coming, and

---

[1] The numbering and naming of these æons is the **most fantastic element** in Gnosticism.
[2] The fulness.
[3] It might be a company—angels, star spirits, etc.

become possessed with the true view of things; and this effect is promoted by various rites. About Christ Himself (*e.g.* in His relation to the man Jesus), and about the influence He exerts on different classes of men, a variety of views existed. Some systems provided a kind of inferior well-being for Christians of the letter who are not capable of Gnostic insight, nor therefore of Gnostic salvation. Seventhly, the hope of the Gnostics was to rise clear of all material entanglement into the realm of light, knowledge, incorruption. What this would prove to be remained very vague; no details could be given.

Some particulars of the various systems will appear below. Meanwhile let us observe what the points were on which Gnosticism challenged Christian thought, and so accelerated its development.[1]

Only let this be emphasised in the first place, that the Gnostics with whom we have to do were Christians. Justin Martyr says that the followers of Simon, of Menander, of Marcus, were all called Christians. Apart from general repute their own teaching proves it. Wild as their speculations were, still for all of them Christianity was not only a true religion; it was the absolute and final religion. The coming of Christ was the great interposition, the decisive crisis of the world. On it the destiny of all spiritual natures depended. Neander[2] has remarked how striking the testimony is which is thus rendered to the impression produced by Christ and the gospel; for, indeed, this conviction about Christ became the starting-point of some of the strangest Gnostic theories. They paid this tribute to a sect despised by Celsus, scoffed at by Lucian, everywhere spoken against. In connection with no form of teaching of that century but the Christian, do we find such an eager host of cultivated and speculative men, inspired with the conviction that in the gospel they have found the centre of truth and life; yet resolute to con-

---

[1] This outline would have to be modified in various details to fit to particular Gnostic systems. This is specially true of the system of Basilides.
[2] Neander, *History* (Clark's transl.), ii. p. 5.

strue it into harmony with intellectual prejudices which they feel to be imperative.[1]

First, then, Christianity is a remedial scheme. The problem it proposes to deal with is sin. Deliverance from other evils will follow sooner or later if this be healed. The Gnostics accepted this Christian thought. They confessed an evil which needed for its cure an interposition from on high; and they recognised this interposition in the person, history, and teaching of Christ.

But they judged that the problem to be solved by redemption reached farther than the ordinary Christian supposed. The Gnostic did not begin with a world which is good, or is neutral, and then conceive sin coming into it, or arising in it, to mar it. For him human sin is only one feature of a larger evil — the pervading evil of the world itself, rooted in its very constitution.

That there is a difficulty about the world, and about the course of providence, was not concealed in the Old Testament or the New. Anyone who looks closely into life is apt to have suggested to him some deep disease in the nature and course of things. Yet neither Scripture nor the faith of the Church could be moved from the conviction that the moral problem — the problem created by human wills—is the essential one for man, and is that with which redemption must deal.

Still the problem of the world is a perplexing one; and in some moods it presses on the mind with dangerous force. More seems to be wrong than only the sin of erring wills. Pain, death, decay are everywhere; the world suggests a good which it does not impart. The theory that man's fall brought evil after it for other creatures, seems inadequate to explain the mystery. The very constitution of things by which man is partaker of animal life, and is pressed by all kinds of physical necessities, seems of itself to bring in and begin the irreconcilable conflict. In this very constitution are not the sources of evil already present, the influences which lower life and baffle its aspirations?

[1] See Harnack, *Dogmengesch.* i. p. 171.

The Gnostic thought so; and he asserted his conviction in the most emphatic way. Evil in man's life is only a particular case of evil present everywhere in a world that is essentially base, disappointing, perverse. This system of things has about it just so much of a suggestion of something better, just so much of a *nisus* towards that, as to stamp it with the character of defeat and disgrace. It is radically mistaken and evil. So evil in man and world alike has a deep root. It is in the nature of things.[1]

On this system one clearly could not speak of the creature, man, as having fallen, nor yet of the whole creation as fallen. Rather, the creation is itself the fall. That is, the mere constitution of this world, or of any world that has a material fabric, is its disgrace, its fault. If some wisdom, and therefore some goodness, can be traced in the world, it is a fallen wisdom, and it is a goodness fettered and imprisoned under forces too strong for it. Sin in man is but the concreated defect—the same in principle throughout the whole creation.

Probably the Gnostic was not so consistent in all this as to leave no room for responsibility—for men being possibly better or worse within certain limits. Still the tendency of the scheme was towards fatalism, which is always strongly charged upon the Gnostics by their opponents. That came out not only in the doctrine of sin, but in the classes of men (pneumatic, psychic, hylic), who are determined to be such by their natures and cannot be other. This brought out the thinkers and teachers of the Church on the subject of responsibility, which they

---

[1] Possibly the Gnostics felt themselves all the more entitled to lean in this direction, because they perceived among their fellow-Christians a mode of thought on the subject which was superficial. Those who put to the front the freedom of the will as the clue to man's condition were apt to think of sins merely as isolated acts of transgression, or at worst, as habits formed by such acts. Thinkers of this class certainly existed at the end of the second century (*e.g.* Clement), and might well do so at the beginning of it. The Gnostic might feel himself entitled to correct this in the interest of a profounder view. Sin in men is not merely acts of sin; it is a state which is the fruitful mother of acts.

grounded on an extremely resolute, and not very discriminating, assertion of the freedom of the will. Gnosticism, in this view, may be taken as the earliest advocacy on Christian ground of a kind of necessarianism by natural law. It began a great debate which was to take many turns and to assume many forms.

The Gnostic view of the world represents an impression of it which exists in all periods. Not many years ago it was vividly expressed by Mr. J. S. Mill, when he declared that if we assume a Maker of the world, he must be regarded as either not able, or not willing, to make it very good. Accordingly the Gnostic doctrine of the world reacted on their doctrine of God. So imperfect a world must have a very inferior author, far below the Supreme Truth and Goodness. Hence, although creation is still regarded as containing an element or an influence which holds remotely from the Supreme God, yet creation ceases, properly speaking, to reveal Him. The purpose and plan and work of creation are no longer His; and the same has to be said of ordinary providence. At the same time, we lose hold of everything that helps us to think of God as personal. He retires to an unapproachable distance. True, the spiritual element in the world is referred to Him by emanation; but it is rather material to work with than any determinate presence of God with creatures. The world, therefore, when it comes into existence, has a certain connection with God; there is an element in it which has fallen or has been stolen from Him; but the world is not the creature of His hand, nor the object of His care. As to redemption, on the other hand, some of these systems seem to make it to originate at a point lower than true and and original Godhead,—in which case redemption also would only remotely reveal God. Yet all of them regard redemption as originating in the Pleroma, and as aiming at restoring men, or some of them, to the region of divine light and influence. And some systems trace redemption clearly enough to the purpose and love of the Highest God. This was emphatically the case with Marcion. In such systems the true God is at last revealed in Christ, and, more or less explicitly, with a character of loving-kindness.

Against these views the Church set the Old Testament doctrine of God as the maker of all things. His creatures, though far below Him, do yet so far manifest His power and glory, and are the objects of His government. Also, He who became incarnate as Redeemer was the especial agent in creation. Very likely there might be among the members of the churches, even apart from full-blown Gnosticism, many who were disposed to account for the defects of creatures by postulating a ministry of angels as the immediate authors of them. But if so, these thoughts were speedily suppressed in the Catholic affirmation of God the Maker. Ever since those days the question, in what sense the world testifies of God and reveals Him, has been in hand, and it is active yet.

Besides the assertion of God the Maker, the Church had two other specific articles to set against Gnosticism at this point. One was the goodness of the creatures. As creatures they are all good, each in its place. Henceforth asceticism, however zealous and exaggerated, had to combine its self-denials and its repudiations of creature comfort with the acknowledgment that the creatures thus renounced after all are good. To have failed at this point was the chief heresy imputed to Tatian.

The other article was man's creation in the image of God. Man, therefore, as man, is capable of fellowship with God. Not only is he a creature good in his degree, but it is a very high degree. He ought to aspire to be man, nothing less and nothing else. In those days it often happened that the experience of inward defeat, division, and disgrace bred a sad conviction that human goodness was impossible. The only hope left was that of being transferred into some state of being that denied human conditions. The Gnostic theorised that feeling. The Church, confessing human weakness and danger, yet maintained that " in the image of God made He man."

The Gnostic, while he took no high view of man as man,

yet held that certain men are constituted so as to be capable of knowing God, and are destined to the upper world as their proper home. These are men in whom the divine spark asserts itself above and against the seducing and depressing flesh; they have this eminence by nature, as others by nature have it not.

Not merely the Gnostic teaching about the world, but the Gnostic mood or attitude of mind upon the subject, received its most picturesque expression in the doctrine of the Demiurge.[1] Not only is there a Sophia or an Achamoth who has diffused herself, or has diffused her influence, throughout the masses of matter of which the world is composed, making all in some degree amenable to form and law, but, below her and after her, there has been Somebody at work trying what he can make out of the material so prepared. In this Demiurge was summed up for the Gnostic the utmost and highest that the ordered fabric of the world suggests. He is the king of carnal natures; the chief instance of a wisdom caught somehow from on high, which has become permanently fettered in a material environment. He is ever looking downward, ever labouring about material things and conditions, or about men considered as beings with conditions and aims like his own. He strives constantly and vainly to perfect what cannot be perfected; he spends on such work care and pains which the Gnostic counted irrational, and which is doomed finally to disgrace; in short, he is the great busybody—περίεργος—who goes out incessantly into the divided, the external, the manifold. In his dealings with men he strives to order them by laws and penalties, and with very partial success. The Jews are his favourite people, and show the utmost reach of his plans. He has promised them a Messiah to endow them with terrestrial weal. This kingdom of the Demiurge was what the Gnostic, looking round the great world, seemed to see; and he renounced and defied the kingdom and the king. It suggests strange thoughts of the temper and the experience of

[1] Δημιουργός = creator.

those days, that such an attitude towards nature should be possible. Perhaps we may add that, in a form lamentable enough certainly, we see here the intensity of the Christian feeling as to good and evil imparting itself to the Gnostic mind. There is a sombre intensity about it, which could hardly proceed from the Greek schools, nor even from the Oriental dualists.[1]

As regards the Redeemer's person, the Gnostic view of matter excluded a real incarnation. To be incarnate would imply so far a captivity to evil. Therefore the Saviour from the Pleroma, who is purely spiritual, descends upon the Messiah prepared by the Demiurge, and makes him the organ of the higher plan—the supreme purpose of salvation. On this scheme he who dies on Calvary is the Messiah of the Demiurge, and the Saviour is conceived to have previously departed from him. It is another version of the same general theory when the human nature of Christ is treated as illusive—a mere deceptive show.

Heretofore apparently the Church had not encountered much doubt as to our Lord's true manhood. A vague docetic tendency had indeed appeared before the days of formal and express Gnosticism,[2] but it does not seem to have been very definite. Manhood was the aspect of our Lord that pressed upon the senses of men during His life on earth; and the first error was to assert that He was no more than man, or was only a man elevated by divine influence at His baptism to a higher capacity. Against this was set the assertion of our Lord's pre-existence in the higher nature. But in Gnosticism, while pre-existent divinity (in the shadowy sense in which degrees of it are admitted by

---

[1] There is a pervading difference between the mood of the Gnostic and that of his Greek models. With them the sense of evil was weak, though the sense of deformity might be strong. The effect of the material element was therefore more calmly and mildly conceived; matter was the element of defect; it can never be brought up to the ideal. In the Gnostic there is a certain bitterness and disdain. His Christianity operated here; or else some old Oriental conceptions revealed their peculiar way of working.

[2] Ignat. *ad Trall.* and *ad Smyrn.*; *Gospel of St. Peter*, as read by Serapion of Antioch.

Gnosticism) is ascribed to Christ, the human nature is denied or explained away. Here then the Church had to assert the human nature, the true birth and the true human experience of the Son of God; and men were led to dwell on the benefit achieved for us in that way.[1] In regard to His higher nature also stress was laid on His being the Only-Begotten; not one of many, holding more or less remotely of the divine nature, but the Father's only and perfect Son—whose incarnation therefore carries to us a quite unique expression of divine care and love.

It cannot be said that the Gnostics undervalued the thought of redemption. Rather it may be true that the Gnostics had a livelier sense of a great deliverance than was cherished by a good many of the so-called orthodox among their contemporaries. Christ's coming was for them the epoch of a great extrication. The sparks of divine nature in all susceptible souls were to be gathered to Christ as their true centre, and to the upper world as their true home. In a sense this came to pass by faith, if faith be understood as a form of thinking. The Gnostic Christian became aware of his relation to this Saviour and this destiny, and, becoming conscious of it, he possessed it and reaped its fruits. Some of them might lay stress on the necessity of its being *such* a consciousness as could animate and inspire the life. At any rate, Christ's appearance *is* the redemption. It would be congruous to this to hold that Christ's interposition operates only as it is illuminative, as it vividly illustrates the true relations of the universe, and lays the foundations of a teaching able to come home to those who are to be gathered in. That would seem to be, theoretically, all. Yet it is true, perhaps, that many Gnostics conceived the coming of Christ to have a mystical influence (not capable of further explanation) which somehow emancipates the æonic natures, and breaks the spell which held them captive. With this side of things might be connected observances, ascetic and ritual, on

[1] Irenæus, iii. 18. 6, 7, and elsewhere often. Ignatius had previously led this way with great decision. *Eph.* xix. etc.

which we know that **various** Gnostic sects **laid stress**; but these we are not in circumstances to conceive with clearness.

The Church, of course, had no objection to the stress laid on the illuminative function of Christ. But her teachers maintained against the Gnostics the reality and also the importance of His death, though no remarkable success attended their efforts to explain the grounds of it as part of the divine plan. On the other hand, against the Gnostic method of salvation by illumination, operating in souls of a certain susceptible class, the Church laid stress on the surrender of the will, and asserted it to be, by grace, open to all kinds of men everywhere.

The Gnostics divided men into classes, two classes according to some, according to the more popular teaching three, pneumatic or spiritual, psychic or carnal, and hylic or material, *i.e.* gross and low. On this classification a place was provided (among the psychic) for the ordinary Christians—the men of mere *pistis* as opposed to *gnosis*—who take Christianity in the letter, and who regulate their conduct by the rules of civil righteousness. These have a relative acceptance, and, eventually, a kind of lower blessedness which suits them. But the true ideal Church consists only of the Gnostics, who, being by their nature akin to the upper world, respond to the revelation of Christ, discern its true significance, and experience its power. Many Gnostics were disposed to veil the effect of this part of their scheme, to keep their connection with the churches, and to assume the character of a select class of Christians, but yet in fellowship with the larger membership. In proportion, however, as the Church realised the true position of the Gnostics on this point, it was felt to be intolerable. The distinction between faith and knowledge was recognised by the defenders of the Catholic belief; but the sufficiency of faith to procure an interest in the peculiar blessings of Christianity was always maintained; often, however, it must be confessed, on principles that were unsatisfactory and confused.

The distinctions just referred to were, of course, carried

out by the Gnostics in reference to the final destiny of individuals. Speaking generally, the men of each class are assigned by their nature to the destiny appropriate to them; and since, even in the case of the most select men, only the pneumatic element in them could go so high as the Pleroma, some systems were led by considerations of consistency to assert a final disintegration of human beings, one element, for example, of the spiritual man going to one destiny and another to another. In this connection the Gnostic way of thinking dropped the whole eschatological expectation of the Church, and did not even try to replace it by any substitute that might appeal to the imagination. Emancipation from the flesh and from the forces of the lower world were for them everything. The Church asserted, on the other side, the old eschatology—the return of Christ, His glorious kingdom, and the resurrection of the body. In this last article the Church at the end, as at the beginning, maintained the essential goodness of human nature.

The attitude of the Gnostics to the Old Testament and to Judaism must be understood in the light of the corresponding attitude of the Church. The Church repudiated Judaism, with all that was national and ceremonial in Jewish religion. At the same time it claimed the Old Testament as a Christian book—Christian in its true sense. The Christians, of course, had no difficulty in taking possession of that in the Old Testament which was obviously moral and spiritual. For the rest, they thought it proper to maintain that the Jews greatly misconceived the character and end of the law imposed on them, or, at all events, had always missed the main sense, *i.e.* the evangelical sense, the reference to New Testament events and truths; for these must be understood to be all along the main purpose of revelation. The Christians therefore resorted extensively to allegorical interpretation, in order to make out a sense in harmony with their assumption.

Now the Gnostics, or most of them, could allegorise, and they did. But to allegorise to the extent necessary to adapt the whole Old Testament to their theories would have been absurd. The Old Testament and Judaism spoke too plainly of a God who created the world and cared for it; who set apart a land for His people, provided for them, punished them, ruled them by laws. That was the character which the Gnostic ascribed to the Demiurge; he is therefore at once Maker of the world and God of the Jews. The Old Testament, therefore, is mainly the revelation of the Demiurge; and the view taken of it fluctuated according as Gnostic schools either regarded the Demiurge as mainly hostile to the higher world, or judged his influence more mildly as leading to order and justice, though on a low plane and within narrow limits. On either view, however, the Gnostics could confess that the Old Testament contains passages of a higher strain. These are utterances of spiritual men who arose in Judaism from time to time. They appeared in the kingdom of the Demiurge, but really belonged to the higher kingdom. They were generally misunderstood, and could not at that time make head against the system in which they were involved. The Old Testament, therefore, was a very miscellaneous book, and a process of very free thought could be applied to it.[1] On the whole, it might be a book not unprofitable to simple Christians on condition of their always translating it into a Christian sense; but the larger part of it could be accounted for only by ascribing it to an author distinct from the Spirit of Christ. Very likely this did not seem to the Gnostics the most formidable part of their system to maintain; yet nothing operated more conclusively against them than just the fact that they ascribed the Old Testament to another and a lower being than the true God. Many of their speculations could have been forgiven to them, but not this.

Against the Gnostics the Church maintained the apostolic position: it clung to the Old Testament. But in doing so it showed little aptitude to understand or appre-

---

[1] See especially the remarkable letter from Ptolemæus (Valentinian Gnostic) to Flora, Epiph. *Panar. Hær.* 33.

ciate either the Pauline explanations or those advanced in the Epistle to the Hebrews. Men simply laid stress on the right to allegorise, as furnishing the means of bringing out the required evangelical sense. In fact, the view was that large parts of the Old Testament must be taken in a non-natural or not obvious sense, if its position as Christian Scripture was to be maintained. Hence Origen lays it down (*de Princ., Præf.*) as universally agreed that the Scriptures have not only the plain sense but a concealed one, and that it is the judgment of the whole Church that the Law is to be spiritualised. Also (iv. 8) he says that it is because the heretics take many Old Testament Scriptures in the plain sense, that they do not ascribe them to the highest God.[1]

In regard to the Canon of the New Testament, it is likely, on every account, that such a challenge as Gnosticism addressed to Christians with respect to what was to be believed, should set men on to settle definitely the sources that could be appealed to as reliable and authoritative in regard to the main tenets of the religion. In the beginning of the second century ideas on this point were probably vague among all parties. The Gnostics, like other Christian schools, claimed the possession of traditions which connected them with the authoritative times of the Christian faith; and we read of gospels, some of which might be Gnostic versions of the Christian tradition, but they seem rather to have been treatises on the Gnostic theory of the universe—"Philosophies of the Plan of Salvation." Marcion, of whom something will be said presently, proposed a canon of New Testament books, and that step, of course, was a fresh motive to the orthodox Church to set

---

[1] Harnack has remarked that as long as the strain of the Gnostic controversy lasted this principle was not applied to the New Testament by the orthodox: it was the Gnostics who held that the allegorical key might be applied to the events of Christ's life and to His sayings as well as to those of His authorised followers, by the same right by which the Church, from their point of view, applied it to the Old Testament Scripture. Origen's rules of interpretation include the application of allegory to the New Testament; but this rather shows that the Gnostic crisis had passed.

forth and lay stress on a canon of her own. But while the Gnostics had a literature, partly apocryphal, as the orthodox also had, it does not appear, except in Marcion's case, that there was any prolonged conflict over the canon. Probably it soon became evident to Gnostics as to Catholics that there was, after all, a limited and tolerably definite set of books which could claim respect as undoubted monuments of the apostolic teaching. In the fragments of Gnostic literature still surviving, what strikes one is the habitual appeal on their part, as well as on that of their opponents, to our well-known books. In fact the Gnostics seem to have produced the first regular commentaries on writings of the Apostles Paul and John, as well as the first regular discussions of theological themes.[1] That is, the writings of Paul and John seemed to men of this type to have significance, in the way of thoughtful setting out of principles, which was little appreciated in the churches; and what they said of flesh and spirit, of the true God and the God of this world, of the Pleroma, and many other topics, could be shown to imply the principles of an esoteric scheme differing widely from the common Christianity of the churches. Hence, while they criticised the Old Testament, the Gnostics set themselves to discuss the monuments of the Christian tradition, and thus to base themselves not merely on speculation, but upon authority too.

The Church joined issue with the Gnostic teachers as to the real meaning of these books. But this was not judged to be a sufficient defence. Hence the belief of the great apostolic churches was put forward, in the form of the *regula*,[2] as the decisive test of the essentials of Christianity. Scripture was to be used on that foundation and within those limits. Some Gnostics also appear to have had a *regula*, and not so very unlike that of the orthodox Church as one would have expected.

The Gnostics based their ethical teaching upon the antagonism between the spiritual and the sensuous element in man. It has often been remarked that any system

[1] Basilides, Valentinus, Heracleon.  [2] See Chap. IV.

which does this is capable of development in two opposite directions. It was so with the Gnostics. Some of them in all good faith strove to suppress the sensuous element, and with that view inculcated a strict asceticism. Others regarded the sensuous element as indifferent,—it did not affect the real man, the spiritual being; and on this line of thought they became libertine, or at least secular and careless. In general, the orthodox could not but approve of the asceticism of the strict Gnostics, as far as it went. But the dualistic basis on which they placed it was peremptorily challenged and condemned.[1]

The leading Gnostic schools must now be described. Cerinthus has already been mentioned. The main article of his teaching, so far as known to us, was the assertion that the creation of the world was due to certain inferior angels. Speculations as to the agency of angels in creation had been current among the Jews. But the Gnostic type of the thinking of Cerinthus is fixed by this, that with him these angels are ignorant of the supreme God, and suppose themselves to be the highest existences.

Carpocrates and Epiphanes had no great influence. Their interest lies in the circumstance that a more Greek and a less Oriental character attaches to their scheme. It is energetically Antinomian. The "law of ordinances," the narrow and negative rule of the lower powers, was rejected by Christ in the strength of His knowledge of a higher world; and in rejecting it, he found His own emancipation and became the Saviour of others. In taking this attitude, however, towards the Jewish law, Carpocrates and his son took the same attitude, apparently, towards all restrictions upon human life and freedom. If they tried to restrain their own principle and to reconcile it with some view of regulated life, we do not know how this was attempted.

The name Ophites may be taken as designating a con-

[1] There was a ceremonial and ritual side of Gnosticism, which is believed by some writers to have powerfully influenced the eventual development of the same element in the great Church. But it is difficult to produce conclusive proof. See Loofs, *Leitfaden*, p. 73.

siderable body of Gnostics, whose thinking seems never to have found an authoritative expositor; consequently, it varied a good deal. But they so far had a common character and deserved a common name, because they drew into their scheme a widespread fancy of the ancient world, according to which the serpent form embodies or represents both the Agathodæmon and the Kakodæmon; with this they combined speculations suggested by the serpent of the temptation (Gen. iii.) and the brazen serpent of Moses. As the opponent of the Old Testament God, the serpent could be regarded as a good principle that bestows wisdom; yet in some theories a serpent form appears also as embodying a lower and evil principle which has to be overcome. Among the Ophites may be reckoned the Naassenes, the Peratics, the Sethians, and the followers of Justus.

A Gnostic scheme described by Irenæus (*Ref.* i. 30. 1 f.) is often ranked as Ophite in its affinities. This scheme affirms the existence of an original Light—the Father of all —also called the First Man; an Emanation, who is the second man; a third, the Holy Spirit, conceived as feminine, who is the first woman; and a fourth, son of the first woman, who is Christ. These four form the true Ecclesia—the Eternal Church. But another child of the first woman descends into the depths, becomes entangled in matter, and sets agoing the history of the lower world. Here a presiding Hebdomad of planetary spirits is developed, with Jaldabaoth,[1] the God of the Law, at the head of it, and a counter Hebdomad of lower quality presided over by Naas in snake form. The Demiurge himself, too, is not reconcilable to the supreme God, and he and his kingdom eventually fade away.

Types of Gnosticism which appear to be more distinct in themselves, and to bear clearer tokens of originating in single minds of some force, are those of **Saturninus**, **Basilides**, and **Valentinus**.

Saturninus holds a pretty early place in the Gnostic chronology—perhaps as early as the age of Trajan. His system is more simple, perhaps we should rather say more

---
[1] Child of Chaos.

crude, in some of its aspects, and the Oriental elements are more prominent than in the schemes of Basilides and Valentinus.

According to Saturninus,[1] the supreme God has created various angels and powers. Seven of these (planetary spirits ?), of whom the God of Judaism is one, have made this lower world. Man is their creature—created after an "image" which gleamed out upon the angels from the supreme God, but which they could not retain. Man as made by them is a failure; but God pities him as one made in His image, and sends out a spark of life, by means of which man accomplishes his earthly existence; but he returns to God at death. Satan is opposed to the world-creating angels, and under the influence of the Dæmons an evil race of men arise, over against the good who possess the divine spark from on high. Marriage and, according to some, the use of animal food are due to the influence of Dæmons. God has sent Christ, who is incorporeal and invisible, to free those who believe in Him (those who possess the divine spark) from the Dæmons.

Under the name of Basilides [2] two distinguishable systems are described—one by Irenæus (i. 23), one by Hippolytus (*Ref.* vii. 14 f.) supported by Clement of Alexandria. The latter is generally considered to be the more authentic. The former resembles closely the scheme of Saturninus: only, Basilides is said to have postulated a development of five æons from the supreme God, and to have increased the number of the spirits from the seven of Saturninus to 365. To the last seven of these the creation of the visible world is ascribed. The first of the æons is sent as Christ, to vanquish the powers of the lower world. His appearance is docetic, and Simon of Cyrene is crucified in his room.

But the Basilides of Hippolytus and Clement has ascribed to him a more remarkable speculation. It is not a system

---

[1] Or Saturnilus.
[2] Perhaps in the reign of Hadrian (A.D. 117–138). He claimed to have been instructed by Glaucias, a companion of the Apostle Peter.

of development downwards, but after the first stage one of evolution and ascent.

He begins with an antithesis which may be denoted as that of the Potential and the Actual. God is the non-existent.[1] In some way for which we can find no analogy, He creates a world, in the form of a world-seed ($\pi\alpha\nu\sigma\pi\epsilon\rho\mu\acute{\iota}\alpha$). All that is or can be is in it, undefined and mixed. From this point a process of evolution sets in,—each element is attracted upwards, and has an inherent *nisus* that way; so the elements sort themselves out, till each thing is found at last in its own distinct and appropriate place.

In the world-seed are three Sonships, all of one essence with the non-existent God, and all of which strive upwards towards His transcendent beauty and goodness. The first Sonship[2] is the most subtle element; it severs itself from the world mixture and rises with the speed of thought to the non-existent God. The second Sonship—less subtle—needs the aid of the Holy Spirit, and, each helping each, they reach only to the border of the non-existent God and the first Sonship; this, therefore, is a state still short of the supreme ineffable blessedness, but near it — a state in which an "odour" of Sonship abides. The Spirit now becomes the limitary spirit between the mundane and the supramundane. The third Sonship remains as yet below, needing purification, receiving benefit and imparting it. Now comes the development of the world. First the great Archon, the world prince, rises to the firmament and forms the visible world. He does not know that there exists one greater than himself. Out of the world-seed he begets himself a son greater and wiser than himself, admires his beauty, and sets him at his right hand. His seat is conceived to be above the seven planetary spheres,—therefore it is the Ogdoad. A second archon then arises, and finds his place in the Hebdomad, the last of the planetary spheres; and he also

---

[1] The strongest expression of God's remoteness from all we can conceive as existence—beyond even the Ideal.

[2] The pure Ideal?

begets a son greater than himself. How far Basilides and his followers imagined further developments analogous to these to have taken place in the constitution of the world, is not clear. But supposing the world to have taken shape, the main interest attaches to the redemption of the third Sonship, which still remains in the πανσπερμία or in the lower world. This third Sonship remains there, "in order to do good and to receive good";—to do good, apparently by exerting influence on creatures of lower element, and to receive good in ways not made very clear, but probably connected with effort and discipline. But it, too, must rise at last to its proper place. This takes place by the gospel—which passes through all the higher spheres, not by a real descent of any Saviour, but as an energy—compared to a flash of fire which even from a distance produces its effect. This travels through the worlds and reaches the great Archon, whose son (here beginning to be spoken of as Christ), sitting by Him, first apprehends its meaning and opens it to the Archon— who is awed and converted. The same process repeats itself in the Hebdomad: and, finally, the influence reaches Jesus the Son of Mary. Through its illumination, the purification and elevation of the third Sonship sets in. Jesus Himself yields up the various elements of His personality to their proper spheres,—some remaining in the corporeal world, some mounting to the Hebdomad and Ogdoad, but the highest—the proper Sonship—rises up above all these. This last Sonship, indeed, proves to be the purest and most powerful, and stimulated by the light from on high rises of itself to the region of supreme good. So He inaugurates the general purification and distribution by which everything comes to its proper place.

Finally, the world from which the three Sonships have departed is not abolished, as in other schemes, but remains in peace. Everything has come to its own place; and, to maintain the adjustment, a great ignorance is poured out upon all stages of the Kosmos, so that no element may be tempted to aspire beyond its proper limits.

On this system the third Sonship represents the pneumatic element as it exists in man, or possibly also in higher beings next of kin to man.

Valentinus formed the most popular and attractive of Gnostic systems. He was at Rome about 140—and his peculiar teaching cannot be of later date. His system begins with thirty Æons which successively emanate from the supreme God, in pairs male and female. One of these Æons, Sophia, falls from the Pleroma—and brings forth Christ, who frees Himself from all taint of mortality and hastens back to the Pleroma. Further, the fallen Æon brings forth the Demiurge, and also a being, the left or sinister one, who presides over the sheer material, as the Demiurge does over the psychic element. These two influence this lower world. Also, one Horos separates the first Æon, Bythos, from the other Æons, and another separates the Sophia from the Pleroma. In the development given to Valentinianism by Ptolemæus, a higher and a lower Sophia find their place, the latter being only a thought or dream of the former; and Christ and Jesus (who are distinguished from one another) are conceived as eminently derived from the strength and glory of the Pleroma. The scheme of Valentinus is brightened by touches of poetry and romance. While it embodies, like the other versions of Gnosticism, a theory of the world and its forces, it seems, more than any of them, to reflect in a measure the sentiment and the pathos of human experience.[1]

[1] Tatian, disciple of Justin and Apologist, afterwards an Encratite, is said to have cherished Gnostic notions about the material world and about Æons (latter half of second century); and Bardesanes of Edessa (A.D. 154-230) believed in Syzygies of Æons, which were alluded to in his hymns. Both of these continued to hold relation to the life of the Church. There were forms of Gnosticism which made large use of magical formulæ, and embodied ideas in connection with them which it is usual to refer to the old religion of Babylon. Elements of that kind invaded the West with great force during the second century. Some Gnostics provided sets of formulæ, which, being learned by the disciple during life, would prove available after death to guarantee him against hostile powers, in making his perilous way through different regions of existence up to the Pleroma. See Anz, *Texte u. Unters.* xv. 4, and Schmidt, *Texte u. Unters.* viii. 1, 2.

We have still to speak of Marcion. But before we leave the theories that have been before us, the question may be put by readers, "Where did the temptation to Gnosticism lie? How should speculations so conjectural, theories of the universe so fantastic, be seriously meant and seriously entertained? Why should one theory be preferred to another; and why lay stress on any of them, whether you call them Gnosis, knowledge, conjecture, or any other name?"

It is difficult, no doubt, to sympathise so far as to understand. But we may remember that for ages salvation by knowledge was the only kind of salvation which thoughtful men had been able to plan, or had found it hopeful to attempt. "Know yourself," and know your world: then, under the influence of that knowledge, you may be expected to act wisely, which is as much as to say, act rightly. That way of thinking was carried out in Christianity by many besides the Gnostics. Now Christianity seemed to reveal forces and relations for which none of the systems of Greek wisdom could make room. And to the Gnostics it seemed to carry suggestions which must be reduced to an intelligible scheme of the world, if men were to have an order of conceptions in their minds, under the influence of which a new outlook and a new wisdom should arise. The bare statements of the creed might be enough for merely practical people; but true children of light must live by theory.

Gnosticism was, after all, only an extreme case of a general tendency. It was a very general thought that the divine excellency of Christianity must then be ours when we find it rising upon the soul as a deep, pure, comprehensive, wonderful knowledge. Before Gnosticism, around it, after it, we must conceive this mood existing as a general diffused tendency, operating in very many influential minds, and very strong among Christians. The author of the Epistle ascribed to Barnabas, Justin Martyr, Clement, Origen, are all conspicuous instances.

For most people the greatest difficulty in taking

Gnosticism seriously is the introduction of the lists of Æons, those shadowy personages, higher and lower, interposed between the supreme God and the world with which men are acquainted. There is nothing like this mob of metaphysical identities in Greek philosophy: and even admitting that the conception in general of such intermediate existences might be entertained, what could possibly set men on to number them and name them, when the very attempt might seem to be a declaration to all the world, that those who did so were indifferent to the distinction between fact and fiction?

One can only say, that in accounting for a mixed world, it might seem an ease to thought to postulate a variety of principles, inferior to God, but above and before the world, to which the various phases of being, and the various grades of good and evil, could be referred. In Plato's time it had been felt sufficient to think of a world of ideas in the divine mind which impress themselves more or less successfully on the Hyle—the matter which is the basis of the world we know. For the Gnostic that was not sufficient; for, first, he had a darker sense than the early Greek thinkers of the energy of evil in the world, as an adverse force to the divine ideals; and, secondly, Christianity had taught him to conceive the world as embodying a history, a conflict, and a redemptive crisis. That seemed to import ideas which are also forces—are, indeed, persons. At this point what he believed of the interposition of Christ had also much to do with fixing the character of the Gnostic thought. Christ was a person. On the same type the world might be conceived as energised by a background of dim personalities. From among these Christ interposes; only He is (at least in the more thoughtful Gnostic systems) the most divine, illustrious, and victorious of them all.

The second century was a time in which all over the Gentile world, and among its best thinkers, the tendency to explain the world by the assumption of manifold beings, less than God and more than man, was extremely prevalent.[1] The Gnostics were too Christian to allow the heathen gods—the "dæmons"—to occupy this place, and they filled it with Æons. We need not suppose, however, that they ascribed any rigorous certainty to the detailed naming and numbering of Æons. In the case of each system those details represented the number and character of distinct principles which the Gnostic's survey of the world had led him to assume; but even in the same school, the disciples did not hesitate to vary such details.

Lastly, we must take it that we know Gnosticism mainly through unsympathetic reporters. One or two Gnostic tracts survive, indeed, to show that Gnosticism could be as dreary and as absurd as any page of Irenæus or of Epiphanius represents it. But there were forms of Gnosticism round which the common Christian interests continued to cling, and which had perhaps some inspiration not altogether estranged from Christian faith and love.[2] In these more Christian forms the error could be more insidious; perhaps the wilder forms were more fascinating to weak people.

### Marcion

Marcion is commonly associated with the Gnostics; he had, in fact, adopted some of their most characteristic positions. He rejected the Old Testament, and he distinguished the God of the Old Testament, who is the Creator of our world, from the God and Father of our Lord Jesus Christ. But the Gnostic elements of his teaching have no special importance: they are not very original, and are not consistently worked out. The moving forces which determined his position came from another quarter. He furnishes, therefore, a distinct illustration of the times, and of the influences then at work in the world.

Marcion came from Sinope in Pontus, where his father,

---

[1] Friedländer, iii. 485.
[2] As expounded, for example, by Ptolemæus (*ante*, p. 108, note), Heracleon (Fragments in Clement and Origen), Apelles (the follower of Marcion), and Bardesanes.

according to some authorities, was a bishop. He is said to have been himself connected in some way with shipping, and appears to have possessed means. It is also said that before he left the East he spent some time in ascetic retirement. Later writers say that he departed from Sinope under scandal on account of some immorality; but neither Irenæus nor Tertullian, though they both dislike the man extremely, allege anything of this kind. Marcion's rule of life was severe, and neither of these writers suggests that his own conduct had been inconsistent with it. It is of Marcion the story is told that meeting Polycarp of Smyrna in Rome, whom perhaps he may have seen previously in the East, he asked Polycarp, "Dost thou know me?" and received the reply, "I recognise thee for the firstborn of Satan."

Probably it was not far from the year 140 that Marcion first appeared in Rome. By 150, about which time Justin Martyr's first *Apology* was written, many had joined him; for Justin says, "There is Marcion, a man of Pontus, who is even at this day alive, and teaches his disciples to believe in some god greater than the creator; and he, by the aid of devils, has caused many of every nation to speak blasphemously, and to deny the God of this universe, and to assert that some other being, greater than He, has done greater works." Again, he says, "As we have said, the dæmons put forward Marcion of Pontus, who is even now teaching men to deny that God is maker of all things in Heaven and Earth, and that the Christ predicted by the Prophets, is His Son. And this man many have believed, as if he alone knew the truth. And they laugh at us, though they can produce no proof, but are carried away irrationally, as lambs by a wolf." Marcion's system spread rapidly, not as a mere opinion, but as embodied in a regular church, organised over against the Catholic; and this church proved durable, for Marcionites were still numerous in the fifth and sixth centuries. After the emperors became Christian, these dissidents had to endure Christian persecution, as before they had endured pagan. Nor did Marcion purchase adherents by concessions; he enforced a stern discipline, and exacted strenuous self-denial.

It is no wonder that Christian writers speak bitterly of a man who held Marcion's views, and taught them so successfully. And yet there is much reason to believe that Marcion's impressions were fundamentally Christian. He seems to have been one of those intense natures in whose case one aspect of things takes such vehement possession as to exclude all complementary or compensating considerations. Certain aspects of Christianity seemed to reveal themselves to him as evidently divine, worthy to be for ever asserted and enforced; and the religious value of these impressions regulated everything else. He found it difficult to believe that others could resist the views which came home so forcibly to himself. When he came to Rome, he held conferences with the presbyters: and to the end there are indications that he had not ceased to think it possible the great Church might be reconciled to his view.

Marcion believed that he had discovered the secret of Paul:—an open secret, for to him Paul's meaning was plain; yet a secret, for Paul seemed to be universally misunderstood. This discovery was not merely a discovery of the Pauline way of thinking, but at the same time, as Marcion felt, an unveiling of the divine genius of the gospel. According to Paul, the gospel was first and essentially a revelation of grace—of an amazing divine goodwill—which delights in saving and enriching those who have no claim upon it. This breaks out in the gospel as something hidden from ages and generations, but now made manifest. Therefore, the inspiring principle at the bottom of all is faith, conceived as trust in the benignity of grace. In one view this does not make practical Christianity an easier business; it does not open to us a smooth road. The love that saves inculcates the rejection of much that the flesh desires, and sets us on to seek our portion in regions which the flesh dreads to enter. If this involved hardships, these were nothing in the light of what was believed concerning the divine benefits present and future. The hardships in the case of the Marcionites were certainly not small. They shared the persecutions of the Catholic Christians, often enduring martyrdom with equal fidelity; they accepted a rule of life which involved many privations; and they experienced, at the same time, enmity and repudiation at the hands of other Christians. Marcion addresses his followers as "companions in distress and in reproach."

Marcion regarded Christ as the revealer of this divine grace and goodwill, and perhaps (owning no personal distinction) he identified Christ with the good God Himself. Following the Apostle Paul, he owns a special virtue in the crucifixion, as the ransom by means of which the divine goodwill becomes conclusively effectual; and apparently emphasis continued to be laid on this, as the central thing, among his followers. It is a doctrine not easily reconciled with some other parts of Marcion's teaching. But, as we have said, views which have vividly come home to him are strongly affirmed, without much care to smooth out inconsistencies.

So far, one does not see why a collision should arise between Marcion and the Church. The Church received all the Pauline forms of statement upon which Marcion laid so much stress. He might feel, indeed, that while his mind thrilled to the wonderfulness and the newness of all this, the Church in general apprehended it languidly, and failed to give it due effect. Yet, if that were all, it would hardly explain the breach which followed.

But Marcion's vivid appreciation of the teaching of Paul expressed itself in a vivid realisation of the contrast it presented to the current Christianity. Christ and Christianity, as described by the apostle, seemed to Marcion to stand in the sharpest opposition to the Old Testament and to Judaism. The one was grace, the other was law. The one wrought by inward attraction and by trust, the other by external authority and constraint. The one aimed at inward freedom and an inward goodness finally made perfect, the other was shut up in earthly conditions and earthly prospects. Had not Paul himself marked this contrast? Had he not shown what the religion of the law is, and what it comes to, and what a weary yoke it imposes? Had he not brought out over against it the spirituality and liberty of the Spirit of Christ?

The Church held that all these things were, after all, consistent. You could take a view that reconciled them as terms in one series: nay, the Old Testament could be interpreted so as to teach what the New taught, and the New could be taken as only a plainer utterance of the Old. But this way of huddling things up seemed to Marcion to amount simply to evacuating the glory of Christianity. At all events, it was incredible that the God of grace, the author of the gospel, should have gone on for hundreds and thousands of years, in the track of Jewish history, commanding, threatening, punishing, inculcating the yoke of ordinances, administering elements of this world, making nothing perfect. To associate this with the gospel was to shut one's eyes to that in the second which was incompatible with the first. And then, as Marcion said to the orthodox, "If your system is the true one, what that is new has Christ brought? Has he come only to enforce what, according to you, was in the world long before?"

No doubt, as the authoritative documents stood, even as the Pauline epistles stood, it might seem that this harmonising of old and new had been sanctioned and accepted from the beginning. But to Marcion that seemed impossible; and remarkable passages in the Pauline epistles plainly enough brought out the weakness and earthliness of Judaism, the poverty and fruitlessness of the law. Did not these passages give the clue to the apostle's real and central view?

The reform Christianity needed was to force home on men's minds this great contrast. But Marcion could not conceal from himself that the Church's error, if it was an error, did not date from yesterday. It was rooted in her tradition; it ran through all that passed for apostolic literature; it seemed to be as old as the apostles. Yes, but did not some Pauline sayings prove that this was exactly what Paul himself had found to be the case? He, too, could not agree with the elder apostles. The explanation, after all, was just this, that the apostles themselves had mistaken Christ; they had succumbed to the influence of those tendencies which are apt to prevail over Jews. Their Lord's teaching was in their minds biassed and misrepresented. This was what made it needful that a new revelation should be made to Saul of Tarsus, in order that the true scope of Christ's mission and work might be made clear. And yet even after Paul had done his work, the inveterate prejudice had prevailed; it had corrupted the record even of his teaching. The Gospels had been polluted with the evil leaven; and the very epistles of Paul had here and there been tampered with. A real reform must go deep; it must deal with the Christian teaching from the beginning.

Now, if the Old Testament was to be thus resolutely contrasted with the religion of Christ, what view was to be taken of it? Either it was a sheer self-deception from first to last,—a view which for many reasons was not likely to seem either probable or acceptable to Marcion,— or it was the manifestation, the revelation, of a different God. This God is severely strict—just in that sense; of abundant law, regulation, prohibition; always employing force and penalty. That need not hinder many of his rules being good as far as they go. This Being proclaims himself to be the God of creation, and therefore no doubt he is so.[1] Here Marcion is seen, like the other Gnostics, giving up this world without reluctance to the "just" God, whom he distinguishes from the good one. It was the common sentiment of meditative men in that time to regard the material world as something mainly to be surmounted and got rid of. But in this he differs remarkably from the Gnostics, that, taking the Old Testament account as he found it, he supposed human souls as well as bodies to originate in the creative act of the just God. The Gnostics usually maintained that something in men, a

---

[1] Various things suggest that Marcion took the apostolic references to the Old Testament as establishing the truth of its historical statements.

distinct and distinguishable something in the more select men, was derived, not from the Demiurge, but from a higher source. Marcion does not appear to have followed in this track. As men we are wholly the creatures of the God of the Old Testament; and under his government we find ourselves subjected to hard conditions which we cannot meet, and are always on the verge of disappointment and of punishment.

Marcion, as has been said, recognised the Old Testament as a truthful book. For the same reason he believed its promises; and therefore he expected the coming of the promised Messiah of the Old Testament, who should set up an earthly kingdom, and establish it by force.

Having made up his mind to fix the contrast between Christianity and Judaism in this startling form, Marcion carries out the scheme with a certain wilfulness and animosity. The good God, unknown before, resolves at length to interpose and rescue the unhappy subjects of the "just" God from his sway. Suddenly, therefore, in the fifteenth year of Tiberius, Christ appears at Capernaum (Luke iv. 31). His preaching is rejected by those who have succeeded in some degree in commending themselves to the just God; they hope that they have reached his standard of righteousness, or, at anyrate, they are filled with deference for his law. But those who are sinners and transgressors lie far more open to the new message, and become partakers of the new kingdom. So also when Christ, after His crucifixion, appears in the place of departed souls to offer them His benefits, those who were counted pious under the Old Testament do *not* respond. They do not want to throw away their position with the God whose favour they have gained, and they fear that Christ's mission may be a device of his to try, and even to ensnare them. They therefore reject the benefit intended for them; while the rebels of the Old Testament, such as Cain, embrace the offer, and enter Christ's kingdom. It was not necessary to Marcion's scheme to imagine all this; and it must pass mainly as a brusque and audacious way of underscoring the points in his scheme which were most adapted to affront both Jewish and Catholic piety. In the end, the unbelievers are left to the consequences of unbelief: the goodness of the good God is not construed to the effect of disposing Him to save all. The inconsistency between His character, as Marcion himself represents it, and the ruin which falls on unbelievers, is got over (apparently as an afterthought) by various versions of the explanation that unbelievers are *left*, merely, to the consequences which arise to them from the nature of their own God, or from causes not well defined.

The creatures on whom the good God has compassion, and whom He delivers, belong, as to their origin, wholly, body and soul alike, to the kingdom of the just God. But Marcion follows the common Gnostic conception, by making the Christian salvation apply to the souls only, not to the bodies. The souls are seats of mind and of deliberate action, and so far worth saving; the bodies are not.

Marcion represented Christ as divine, and His incarnation as apparent only, not real. Christ announced a new kingdom, and promised to save His people from the world, and from the God under whose yoke they groaned. All that He did was right contrary to what that God would have done; and at last the friends and servants of the "just" God crucified Him. But in doing so they blindly served Christ's purpose, for the crucifixion is the ransom which freed His people from the dominion of the Old Testament God. As Christ's incarnation is docetic only, on Marcion's showing, the stress laid on the crucifixion is an unexplained inconsistency in the scheme.

Marcion faced the whole question of the documents to which Christianity can appeal: and the way in which he dealt with this question is not the least important nor the least fruitful aspect of his activity. As we have seen, he rejected the authority of the Old Testament: that was in no way the revelation of the God and Father of our Lord Jesus Christ. Some of the Gnostics had attempted to analyse the Old Testament, with a view to discriminate in it diverse planes of principle and of moral view, due some to a lower and some to a higher source. Marcion took it as one whole: and the chief book he wrote, so far at least as argument goes, was the *Antitheses*, in which he exerted himself to bring out contradictions and inconsistencies between the Old Testament and the teaching of Christ.

As regards Christianity, Marcion had to maintain that, from a date very near the beginning, preverting influences had misled the apostles, and had polluted the documents that might otherwise have passed as authoritative. He undertook, therefore, to criticise the sources, and to bring out a version of them which might serve as a standard for his followers. He produced for this purpose a Gospel and ten Epistles of Paul. The Gospel was a retrenched and altered version of our Luke, beginning with iii. 1[1] and then passing on to iv. 31. The selected Epistles of Paul also were purged of passages which struck Marcion as inconsistent with his view.

Marcion's rule of life, it has been said, was strict and ascetic. In particular, he required married persons to separate, and unmarried persons to consent to remain so, as a condition of baptism. Those who could not make up their minds to this, had to remain in the stage of catechumens; and as considerable numbers occupied this position and continued in it, the catechumenate seems to have acquired a greater importance, or a higher rank, in Marcion's Church, than in the Catholic.

Marcion and his followers were frank and outspoken. Many of the Gnostics adopted an insincere attitude, both towards the Christians and towards the heathens. The Marcionites, on the whole, seem to have been prepared to speak out, and take the consequences.[2]

---

[1] Among the Marcionites this was known probably, not as the Gospel according to Luke, but rather as the "Gospel of the Lord," or the like· and the later Marcionites believed it to have been written by Christ Himself.

[2] This sketch of Marcion is in general agreement with the views of Harnack, *Dogmengesch.* i. 197 f.; and Loofs, *Leitfaden*, p. 73. The chief early source is Tertullian, *Adv. Marcionem*; also Hippolytus, *Ref.* vii. 17; *Dial. Adamantii de orthodoxa fide*, among Origen's works.

# CHAPTER VII

## Montanism

In connection with discussions of Tübingen theories, Schwegler directed particular attention to Montanism, *Nachapostol. Zeitalter*, Tüb. 1846. On the other side, A. Ritschl, *Altkatholische Kirche*, 2nd ed., Bonn, 1857. Prophetic utterances in Hilgenfeld, *Ketzergesch.* p. 591; Bonwetsch, *Gesch. d. Mont.*, Erl. 1881.

MONTANISM appeared first at the town of Pepuza, in Phrygia, about the year 156. A Christian called Montanus (who is said to have been a heathen priest before his conversion) claimed to be a prophet, and, indeed, to be the representative of a new prophetic gift; for in him appeared the Paraclete whom Jesus had promised to His disciples; and this was to be the closing revelation preparing the Church for the coming of Christ and the last things. Two women, Prisca and Maximilla, were associated with him as prophetesses; and utterances were given forth with great enthusiasm about the Lord's expected return, and about the preparation the Church must make with a view to it. For the standard of Christian life was to be strained to a higher pitch; more fasting was required, and more careful separation from the manners and enjoyments of the world; celibacy and martyrdom had great value set upon them, and second marriages were prohibited. A stricter discipline was announced, in virtue of which Christians who fell into offences of the graver class must not hope for restoration to communion; God could forgive them, on their penitence, but did not authorise the Church to do so. It was not denied that this system of Christian administration, taken altogether, involved elements that went beyond the practice of apostolic times. But the Spirit of God was free to prescribe new rules in new circumstances; and the time had come for calling the Church to assume the responsibilities of riper age. In general, Montanism aimed at regaining what it conceived to be the genuine and original spirit of Christian life, only in an intenser form and with additional guarantees. In this connection various things which had heretofore been discretionary were now to become imperative and universal.

The Montanists did not teach any doctrines opposed to the general views of the Church[1]; for though they were accused of identifying Montanus with the Holy Spirit, that seems to rest only on their owning him as the Paraclete—whom they understood to be an inspired personage that should arise in the Church under the influence of the Holy Spirit. But the whole movement seemed so dangerous and unsettling that many churches in the East, under the influence of their pastors, broke off communion with the followers of Montanus, and expelled them from their fellowship. On the other hand, whole congregations in some places, indeed the whole Christianity of considerable districts, especially in Phrygia, would seem to have adhered to Montanus. Besides this, a large number of Christian people throughout the Church showed a disposition to think favourably, or at least gently, of Montanism. This suggests that Montanism is not to be accounted for from mere local circumstances. The churches of Lyons and Vienne, not far from the time of the terrible persecutions which they endured under Marcus Aurelius, sent letters both to the East and to Rome (the latter carried by Irenæus, then a presbyter), deprecating extreme action against the Montanists. According to Tertullian, a bishop of Rome, perhaps Eleutherus, perhaps Victor, was on the point of interposing on their behalf, when he was withheld by the influence of Praxeas, who brought unfavourable

---

[1] Some Montanists at a later stage are represented as accepting Patripassian views.

accounts of them. Afterwards the same bishop became their resolute opponent.

Montanism established a footing elsewhere than in Asia Minor, especially in the African province, no doubt because some of the tendencies out of which Montanism had sprung were strong there. At first we find it as a form of view and feeling within the Church. The *Acts* of Perpetua and Felicitas reveal those sufferers as probably Montanists, or tinged with Montanism, although they were within the Church, and have always ranked as Catholic martyrs. Here too, however, perhaps as a consequence of the prevalence of adversaries at Rome, it ceased to be possible, or men could not count it possible, to live together in one church; and the Montanists became a separate community. It is not easy to decide how far claims to inspired utterance existed among these Montanists of the West. At all events, they believed in the revelations given to Montanus and his associates; and they possessed written records of the utterances of these Phrygian prophets. They regarded these as revelations, supplementary to those of the Old and New Testaments. The African Montanists found a spokesman in one of the most remarkable Christians of the time, Tertullian. In addition to his works, a certain amount of Montanistic literature appeared, which perished early.

The method or form in which this movement displayed itself was in some respects new, and yet in others not so. The exercise of prophetic gifts in congregations was not new. In all probability the general sense of the churches at that time was in favour of the existence, or certainly of the possibility, of genuine Christian prophecy, although some began to maintain that, if genuine, it must be calm and conscious, not—like the Montanistic prophesying—ecstatic; and others still, carried away by the spirit of controversy, appear to have rejected the idea of prophecy altogether, and along with it the writings of the Apostle John, which seemed to them to foster it. Prophecy was not new. But it was new that a man claiming to be a Christian prophet should assert for himself such a presence of the Holy Spirit as to constitute him the Paraclete promised by Christ, and should claim to bring in a new dispensation, in advance of the apostolic one. So also the points announced as characteristic of the new dispensation and imperative on those who lived under it, were new only in so far as rules, formerly reckoned discretionary, were now to be peremptory. Chiliastic expectations of Christ's return were no novelty. The importance of great strictness of life and abstinence from various pleasures and indulgences was a familiar thought. The principle that certain sins should not receive the Church's testimony of forgiveness was probably no novelty at all, but had been applied in various churches; perhaps, however, with no strict consistency.

To complete this sketch it is necessary to keep in view what the Montanists felt it needful to oppose. They were in conscious opposition to Gnosticism and everything connected with it. They were opposed to the authority which office-bearers, especially bishops, were attaining in the churches, or, at least, to the manner in which that authority was exercised. They were opposed to the adjustment of Christian life to worldly ease and convenience, which they believed was prevalent in the Church; and they set themselves against the tendencies to relaxation of discipline. Finally, they were, of course, opposed to every mode of view and feeling that was content to postpone indefinitely the prospect of the Lord's return.

Such, in general, was Montanism. The phenomenon is best understood as a reaction against a condition of the Church, and of the Christian life, which seemed to the Montanists to be pitched too low, and also to have decayed from an earlier and purer standard. It is likely, in fact, that in the Christian congregations features appeared that suggested a falling off from an earlier and intenser time. Probably, in spite of the persecutions which Christians had to bear, there were symptoms of worldliness of life, and of accommodation to Gentile notions. There might be coming into the modes of worship and into the method of Church management something of a mechanical order of things, contrasting sensibly enough with the freedom, the vivacity, the spiritual impulse of an earlier day. Probably enough, also, the Montanists were predisposed to exaggerate what might truthfully be set down under these heads.

Suggestions have been offered from various points of view as to the state of the churches at this time and as to the Montanist impression of it; and, indeed, various influences might conspire to produce the situation. One may be noticed which, perhaps, has been too much overlooked. The mere natural progress of human affairs tends to bring about a situation such as Montanism presupposes. In any great religious movement a stage is by and by reached at which a natural cause begins to operate as a source of change. And this has repeatedly received conspicuous illustration in the history of Christian churches.

The advent of a new religion, making serious and impressive claims to embody a new revelation from on high, is not a frequent occurrence. But frequently enough great religious awakenings have attended the advent into a country or district of a new sect, which breaks in on a conventional or slumbering Christianity, and claims to republish authentically and effectually the original Christian message. The awakened become partisans of the new sect; the new sincerity and devotedness of many of them enhance the general impression and give a fresh impetus to the progress of the movement. At the same time, such persons are found to lay stress on the ecclesiastical peculiarities, or, still more, on the points of Christian practice, self-denial, and the like, which happen to characterise the movement. Perhaps certain forms of emotion, or of expressing emotion, come to have particular value attached to them. Perhaps, also, stress is laid on the principle that Church fellowship should be pure, that is, that it should be confined to persons who afford individual and substantial evidence of adherence to Christ and of separation from the world. So there arises and grows a new embodiment of Christianity.

But Time has his office to discharge, testing, moulding adjusting, in many ways which need not be dwelt on here The thing to be especially noted is that a point is reached at which the composition of the body begins to change. Time was when the accessions to it were almost entirely in the form of persons, who, as the result of inward conflict and crisis, broke with their old ways, with the associations and habits of previous life, and gave in that way a sufficiently impressive pledge of the earnestness of their profession. But by and by it comes to pass that the bulk of the accessions, or a very large portion of them, are from the children of the members. Of these, some, after consciously standing out alike against the Christian influences and the sectarian peculiarities of the body, come distinctly, by a great change, to new views of things, and give themselves up consciously and freely to the fellowship of the saints as their fathers did. Some—far more—are cases of another kind. They have been nurtured in Christian homes; they have been sheltered as much as may be from undesirable influences; they have manifested on occasion tokens of seriousness and upright purpose; and they are willing, as their friends are willing, that they should take their place as believers. Nor has anyone a right to form an adverse judgment of the reality and sincerity of their profession; theirs may often be the more consistent and reliable type of religion; and yet certainly very many of them will differ in their development from the old type. Instead of the question being how far they ought to go in the way of defying and renouncing fellowship with a world they have known too well and are now forsaking, the question will often rather be, why restrictions should be accepted, and whether this or that indulgence, which the society conventionally reckons worldly and unbecoming, might not be adopted without any real harm or danger.

When this new element begins to form a large proportion of the whole, and when the new tendencies begin to operate strongly, a crisis is apt to take place. For there will be many who cling not only to the old faith, but to the old ways of embodying it. Those on the other side will be for moderating the ancient rigour, for broadening the platform, and for freer accommodation to what they reckon simply human in the world and its ways.[1]

Turning back now from modern sects to the undivided Church, one sees that the same thing must have occurred there. In the various countries in which it was settled there came a time, earlier here, later there, when the recruits from among the children of Christians, trained up to be Christians, came to bear a very sensible proportion to the accessions from the outside and to the general mass of the membership. It is impossible to fix an exact date for this; but probably in the countries where Christianity made its beginnings under the influence of apostles, some time about the middle of the second century may be as near an era as it is possible to assign. Of course the case of the Christian Church planted among the nations must differ, in various ways, from that of any sect forming in connection with religious awakening in a territory of professing Christianity. But the one case illustrates the other. There might well be a perceptible difference of tone and tendency between the time when the churches were chiefly composed of, and were generally led by, men who had themselves passed over from heathenism by a memorable act of personal decision, and the time when Christianity was largely represented by persons who were in the Church because they had been brought up to it, who had always looked forward to life as to be lived in a Christian profession, who had from the first foreseen all life's experiences as necessarily taking shape under that influence.[2] Many of these might indeed be intensely,

---

[1] This process has been exemplified a hundred times. There are congregations scattered over our country, arising out of the religious awakenings of the end of last century and the beginning of the present, in which the process has visibly been accomplished. On a larger scale one may refer to the Mennonites of Holland, to the Society of Friends, in some degree also to the Wesleyan Methodists, and various other bodies.

[2] A very good instance is supplied by the Christian expectation of the Lord's return, with the great events it was to bring with it. To many early

irrationally, loyal to all the old traditions. But many also would be of another type. A tendency could not but arise to reconcile with Christian profession a good many modes of life, enjoyments, occupations, social actions and customs, from which the first Christians had recoiled. In their minds these were associated with secularity and idolatry, while their successors might come to regard them as not necessarily evil, but simply neutral and human. And in times and places where there was not much persecution, people could become and continue Christians who neither were nor professed to be very devoted persons.

When these tendencies became operative, tension would set in. Many would be vexed. Was this Christ's promise of the Spirit? Was this the power and presence of the Church's head? With these good people might join many who were not so really under the spiritual power of Christianity, but with whom religion stood very much in the observance of the accepted peculiarities. These, too, would bewail the change, and vote for holding on to the old ways.

Presently this feeling would express itself in another direction: it would lay hold of the discipline of the Church. Has not Christ qualified the Church to keep herself pure? Can she not frame such rules, and so apply them, as to keep out and put out this lazy, self-indulgent, worldly-minded style of Christianity? Here would set in, by a fatal necessity, a collision between this party and the majority, the great majority of the rulers of the Church. It would prove so, for this reason among others, that those who have permanent responsibilities in connection with discipline acquire an experimental knowledge as to what discipline can do and what it cannot; in particular, they learn that discipline must proceed not upon wishes and impressions, but upon definite rules and conclusive proofs.

Christians, who brought with them from heathenism sad memories, and materials of much inward conflict, and whose conversion broke many ties of friendship and kindred, the conviction that Christ would soon come might be animating and cheering. But young persons, born in the Church, and looking forward to life and its experiences, might regard the prospect in a different way.

Further, such persons could not overlook, nor afford to overlook, the elements of conscience and of Christian character among those who took the milder view. Hence would come mutual suspicions:—on the one hand, a tendency to regard church rulers as not alive to the necessities of the Church, as perceived by spiritual men; and, on the other hand, the tendency on the side of church officers to regard those we speak of as insubordinate and disorderly.[1]

The same tendencies might come into collision in another field, that of the public teaching and the public worship. The earlier practice of the Church had been more or less to employ in worship under the presidency of the pastor or pastors, the gifts of the congregation. This feature was now retiring. Things were falling into a set order, and public utterance was being restricted to those who were regarded as having special aptitudes to edify the people, and who were called to office on that ground. If so, we may well believe that some would impute to the methods so coming in, the lack of vitality and the failure of power which they were disposed to recognise as prevailing evils.

On lines like these one can understand the spread, here and there, in the Christian churches,—especially perhaps among the humbler members, so far as these were earnest and clung to memories of earlier days,—of a feeling of dissatisfaction and distrust. It would aim at having room made and effect given to impulses and convictions which the Spirit of God inspires in Christian hearts, as against secularity and worldly conformity, as against set methods that turn Christianity into a mechanical system going on of itself, as against worldly wisdom and philosophy; finally, as against the hierarchy and the centralised ecclesiastical authority which seemed to leave no room for the

---

[1] One point of difference was the way of dealing with those who, by common consent, *ought* to be subjected to discipline. In this point, also, extreme rigour was more apt to commend itself to those who theorised from a distance, than to those who had to deal with the actual sinners.

free upburst of the Christian heart to assert its desires and make good the result it longed for.

There might be a great deal of prejudice and short-sightedness at the bottom of all this; probably there was also a great deal that was worthy and sincere. Dangers did lie before the Church against which it would have been well to guard. But the dissatisfied section were too apt to assert as the true marks of real Christianity—of the Spirit's presence and power — certain approved forms of self-denial and methods of work righteousness; and they were apt to drive at these by what seemed to them the readiest means; as if when they got these things to be required and to be complied with, they would then have real and satisfactory Christianity. Thus, they too went astray with their own forms of externalism. And they deprived themselves by so doing of all durable influence; for it could with perfect truth and fairness be maintained against them, that no such yoke as they would impose had been laid by the Lord upon His Church.

Such feelings existed and operated, most likely, in all parts of the Church, and very many of those who shared them never became Montanists; but the mood of mind described, furnished the materials to which Montanism appealed. In its special form Montanism was a Phrygian phenomenon, due, no doubt, to tendencies to religious exaltation and excitement, which had characterised the Phrygian people for ages; and it availed itself of the elements of awe and wonder suggested by the expectation of the coming of the Lord. Hence feelings and convictions, which existed in many quarters, there found expression in persons who had been looked on as prophets before, or who appeared in that character now, but who claimed at all events to have received a quite new mission. They spoke in a remarkably ecstatic manner. No doubt the epidemic nervous excitement was present, which has often manifested itself in connection with religious enthusiasm.[1]

[1] See Hecker's *Epidemics of the Middle Ages*,—Publications of Sydenham Society.

The conclusion was drawn at once that a special visitation of spiritual power had been vouchsafed to authorise and to emphasise the new teaching. When this stream of ecstasy and prophecy began to run, to certain minds it seemed conclusive. Here, men said, is a new era and a new power. Now we see the secret of our vexations and our disappointments. The era of the Paraclete had not come, and so things could not be set right. But now he has come. Now at last, not through bishops or synods, but by the Spirit Himself, the Church will become a society worthy of its calling; and Christians, shaking themselves clear of entanglement and compromise, will be raised to the posture that becomes them, as disciples awaiting the coming of the Lord.

This seems thoroughly to explain the various phenomena of Montanism. It explains how Montanism kept clear of new doctrine, excepting the modification of the idea of the Paraclete; and how its whole energy was directed to disciplinary preparation for the coming of the Lord. It explains also how ecclesiastical authorities in the neighbourhood of its first appearance, saw in it a dangerously subversive movement that required to be instantly checked; and also how it came to pass that large-minded bishops in regions farther off, seeing in it what it had in common with the feelings of many good Christians everywhere,—feelings which they respected, and perhaps partly shared,—were slow to commit themselves to a collision with it, and were anxious to treat it in a tolerant spirit as long as they could. That plainly implies that they saw mixed up with it Christian aspirations which deserved to be regarded.

From the human point of view, it must be regarded as a calamity that the assertion of the Church's dependence on the Spirit, in those ministrations of His which are not limited to clerical character or standing arrangements, but belong to all believers, was made in a form so indefensible and fanatical. That soon blew over, as all fanaticisms do; Montanism as a concrete thing fades away early in the third century, although its influence lasted longer. Meanwhile the Church more and more provided for the doctrine of the Holy Spirit, by practically chaining His influence to the hierarchy and the sacraments.

The mood of mind above referred to as diffused through the churches, and as existing in places where it refused to accept the form of Montanism, reappears from time to time, especially in the disputes regarding discipline, of which Novatianism and Donatism are conspicuous instances. With respect to the local Phrygian conditions which gave to Montanism its sensational features, it will be useful to read Professor Ramsay's account of Glycerius the deacon.[1] The incident falls two hundred years later, and belongs to Cappadocia; but it is not the less illustrative and suggestive.

[1] *Church in Roman Empire*, p. 443.

# SECOND DIVISION
## A.D. 180–313

## CHAPTER VIII

### RELATION TO THE STATE

Aubé, *Les Chrétiens dans l'empire Romain*, Par. 1881, and *L'église et l'état*, 1886. Neumann, *Römische Staat*, Leipz. 1890. Hardy, *Christianity and the Roman Government*, London, 1894. Mason, *Persecution of Diocletian*, Cambr. 1876. Ramsay, *Church in Roman Empire*, deals professedly with the earlier period, but throws much light also on this.

THIS period was on the whole a dark one for the empire. Famines, pestilences, earthquakes, disastrous inroads of the Northern tribes, and arduous wars upon the frontier tried the State, while weakness from political causes gained ground within. But Christianity grew. It reveals its existence in distant regions, in Arabia, India, and Persia; and in every province of the empire, where its earlier existence had been questionable or feeble, it becomes conspicuous during the third century—in Africa, Spain, Gaul, Britain, in all the Romanised provinces on the German frontier and along the Danube. The growth in numbers continued throughout the century, and an uneasy anger on account of it haunted the pagan mind. To Origen the progress in this respect is so remarkable, that he argues an early supersession of other religions by the mere continuance of the process which he sees going on.[1]

[1] *Contra Celsum*, 3.

ACTION OF THE GOVERNMENT

During the reign of Commodus (180–193), the Christians (*ante*, Chap. I.) suffered continually; but the central government, so far as we know, did not stimulate the local severities, and the influence of Marcia, the imperial concubine, could be exerted to release Christian captives.[1] Septimius Severus (193–211) was in friendly relations with individual Christians, but he specifically prohibited conversion to Christianity and to Judaism. As his reign proceeded, he became more actively hostile, and sharp persecution set in at Alexandria and in the African province about A.D. 202. In this persecution, Leonidas, the father of Origen, was among the sufferers. Caracalla (211–217) and Heliogabalus (217–225) inherited from Julia Domna, the wife of Severus, a tendency to Eastern worships, and a disposition to fuse together the more popular elements of various faiths. The same spirit appeared in a worthier form in Alexander Severus (225–235). It was a mood which detached men from the old Roman maxims, and it disposed them to examine Christianity with interest and respect. The Christians reaped the benefit in the form of comparative tranquillity; but the legal position had not changed.[2] Maximinus, the first babarian emperor (235–238), was unfriendly, and directed the presidents of the churches to be especially aimed at,—perhaps because the significance and the growing power of the hierarchy were now attracting the notice of the government. Pontianus, the bishop of Rome, and Hippolytus were sent to the mines of Sardinia, and in Cappadocia a sharp persecution took place under the proconsul Serenianus. Under the two Gordians (238–244) and Philip the Arabian (244–249) public troubles occupied the government, and the Christians were let alone. A tradition existed that Philip was or became a Christian; if so, this unedifying convert is the first Christian emperor.

---

[1] Hipp. *Ref.* ix. 12, see p. 18, *ante*.
[2] Ulpian at this time collected the laws bearing on Christians. His work has not survived.

Babylas, bishop of Antioch, is said to have refused him entrance to the Church until he confessed and made satisfaction for his fault.[1] Alexander Severus also was believed by some Christians to have become a convert. He venerated Christ, at least, and valued some elements of His teaching. He left no trace, however, on the laws or on the life of the empire.

A new state of things set in with the reign of Decius (249–251), and lasted till the end of the reign of Valerian (253–260). Decius belonged to a class of emperors vigorously represented in the third century. While the empire was losing faith in itself, in its gods, in its old beliefs and maxims, and was bewildered by its troubles, and while imperial families of Eastern origin and Eastern sympathies amused themselves in devising new religions, bold soldiers, who had to confront the barbarians, fought their way up to power. They were apt to think it their business to recall together the old Roman maxims and the old Roman triumphs. Such a man was Decius. The growth of Christianity seemed to him ominous; he saw that persecution as hitherto practised had not greatly hindered it. Under his authority special legislation was undertaken with a view to suppress the objectionable religion. The edict of A.D. 250 decreed that all Christians should be cited to perform the ceremonies of State religion; those who fled were to have their goods confiscated, and to be put to death if they returned. Those arrested were subjected to successive severities intended to break them down; priests were to be promptly put to death; torture and death soon became the portion of all Christians who stood out. Decius died in battle next year, but his laws remained; and a fresh impulse was given to the action of the authorities by Valerian (253–260). He was a good though not a fortunate emperor, and no doubt acted conscientiously. Beginning with a system of pressure, which did not prove sufficiently effective, he went on to decree the execution of clergymen, degradation and confiscation of goods for men of rank, followed by death for

---

[1] Aubé, *Chrétiens dans l'Empire*, p. 461.

the obstinate, banishment for women, working in chains for members of the imperial service. Fabianus of Rome, Alexander of Jerusalem, Babylas of Antioch, and other bishops are named as martyrs under Decius; Sixtus of Rome, Cyprian of Carthage, and others under Valerian. Direct instructions from Rome to the provincial governors are mentioned in some of these cases.[1]

This hard onset broke down the fidelity of very many Christians. Some hastened to abjure; others gave way when pressed; others still signed declarations that they had sacrificed, or procured certificates to that effect. The fallen were so many that all the old discussions as to the Church's duty in relation to such persons were resumed with eagerness, and led to fresh divisions of opinion.[2] Some of the letters of Cyprian convey a vivid impression of the situation thus created.

But Valerian fell into the hands of his Persian adversaries, and his son Gallienus (260–268), a less resolute ruler though a more cultivated man, ere long terminated the persecution. It does not appear that he reversed the old presumption of the Roman law in regard to Christians, but he must have withdrawn the special measures of Decius and Valerian,—and this manifestation of his goodwill must have been a warning to governors to use their discretion gently. Aurelian (270–275) is said to have had thoughts of taking measures against Christianity, but his life ended without any steps of that kind. Days of great confusion had overtaken the empire; and the series of soldier emperors who followed had hardly time, in their short and stormy reigns, to do more than meet the most urgent necessities of government. They fought the empire out of its most serious difficulties; and Diocletian, a man of the same type (284–305), completed their work and

---

[1] Cyprian, *Ep.* 18, and see *Acta* 1.
[2] Name for those who sacrificed, *sacrificati*; those who offered incense, *thurificati*; those who emitted declarations of conformity to paganism, *acta facientes* (χειρογραφήσαντες when personally signed); those who procured certificates to the same effect, *libellatici*.

inherited the fruits of it. From the accession of Gallienus, therefore, to the year 303, the Christians for the most part were free from serious trouble.

During the whole period, Christianity, as far as the law was concerned, existed on sufferance: but yet the religion and its leaders were very well known to the authorities, and the sect continued not merely to exist but to own property, and to deal with the authorities from time to time about its temporal interests. The Christians availed themselves of laws which sanctioned *collegia tenuiorum*—societies for charitable and co-operative purposes, which could hold property, acquire burial-grounds, and so forth; and the authorities might not choose to *see* that under these forms they were dealing with Christians. But even apart from that artifice, it is to be remembered that a Christian was reckoned a bad subject because he refused to sacrifice; and as long as a magistrate chose to assume that the Christians known to him might be good subjects, who *would* sacrifice if called upon, he might not incur much responsibility by raising no questions. That would not apply to times when laws were in force like those of Decius and Valerian, but in ordinary times it was possible. Christianity, in fact, was steadily becoming more and more conspicuous, and its place in the community was notorious. Hence from time to time it is frankly taken notice of. Alexander Severus adjudged to the Christians a site beyond the Tiber, the title to which was disputed; Gallienus wrote to the Egyptian bishops that their cemeteries and meeting-places should be restored to them, and that they should not be disturbed. Aurelian was actually asked to interpose in the question between the orthodox and Paul of Samosata, and he professed to decide it according to the opinion of the Roman bishop.[1] Church buildings certainly existed *eo nomine* in the time of Diocletian, and probably a good deal earlier.

In such circumstances, and after forty years' immunity from serious disturbance, the Christians must have imagined

[1] There were obvious political motives for his action.

that they had virtually established their "right to be" ("Christianos esse passus est"); but in the year 303 Diocletian, persuaded by his colleague Galerius, began to set in motion the last great persecution. For some years previously steps had been taken which indicated a determination to discourage Christianity. The actual persecution continued for eight years. It did not affect the whole empire with equal severity. Probably Asia Minor, Palestine, and Egypt suffered most,—Italy and the central provinces not quite so continuously,—Spain, Gaul, and Britain under Constantius Chlorus were comparatively spared. This Cæsar demolished churches, *verum autem templum quod est in hominibus incolume servavit* (Lact. *de Morte*, 15). Constantine succeeded his father in the West in 306. In 311 Galerius, in his last illness, issued an edict owning the failure of his efforts, and announcing the termination of the persecution. After a little it was renewed in the Asiatic provinces by Maximinus. But in 313, Constantine and Licinius divided the whole empire between them; and in the same year they published at Milan a joint edict of universal toleration.

# CHAPTER IX

### THE NEW PHILOSOPHY

Harnack, article "Neo-Platonism," *Encycl. Brit.*, 9th ed. Plotinus, *Opera Omnia*, Oxf. 1835, Lips. 1856 (*Enn.* ii. 9 contains the attack on Gnosticism ; on this see Neander in *Wissenschaftl. Abhandlungen*, Berl. 1851). Porphyry. Fabricius, *Bibl. Græca*, v. Zeller, *Philosophie der Griechen*, Leipz. 1865, 3rd ed. vol. iii. 2. Relations to Christianity, *Church Histories* of Neander and Baur, and *Dogmengeschichte* of latter. Augustine, *Conf. B.* ii. Tzschirner, *Fall des Heidenthums*, 1849. Hüber, *Philosophie d. Kirchenväter*, 1859. Vogt, *Neuplatonismus u. Christenthum*, 1836. Jahn, *Basilius Platonizans.*

EARLY in the third century a new speculative effort made an epoch in the history of philosophy.

Before the Christian era the efforts of the older Greek schools to supply a positive basis for thought and life had begun to give way to a sceptical tendency, represented by various schools of doubt. Yet alongside of this and after it, the desire to believe gained ground again; and it proved vigorous enough to make head against strong sceptical tendencies. After the time of discouragement, men began again, in the first and second centuries, to postulate a divine derivation both for reason and for religion, on the assumption that the better mind of the race had all along been, in a manner, inspired. Thus reason and religion were to combine their strength, and men hoped to find, not only light, but warmth, which seemed unattainable on other terms. A tendency this way works variously in men like Philo, Plutarch, Apollonius, Numenius, and indeed also in Seneca and Epictetus. It took shape finally and deliberately in the school of the New Platonists, as they were called. Alexandria, where a great school of learning had long existed, was the cradle of this latest effort of Greek thought; there, at anyrate, early in the third century, the New Platonism came into evidence.

It was, once more, a philosophy; but it did not profess to be a new philosophic sect. Rather, it claimed to combine the strength of past speculation, emphasising what might be held to be the best wisdom of it all. More than any of the noted older schools, it aimed, also, at religion,—confessed the need of it, and professed to supply it. But here, too, it was not to be a new religion, but was to disclose the true secret, the reasonable significance of all religions. The new school hoped thus to supply a devout enthusiasm, and a reason for it. It was therefore a philosophy striving towards religion. The older forms of Greek thought did, no doubt, recognise God or gods. But the conception of life according to reason, which ruled those systems on their practical side, drew little inspiration from the gods. Things would have been much the same if the gods had been left out. The new scheme professed to get beyond reason, into a region of religious experience, of fellowship with the unseen and eternal; and yet this was to be grounded on a reasoned conception of existence and of the world. It is possible that some such effort would have been made, even if Christianity had not been a growing force. But it would be foolish to doubt that the pressure of Christianity intensified the craving for religious help and hope, and did something to give shape to the system.

The founder of the school was Ammonius Saccas,—said to have been once a Christian. For us he is a name, and little more. The most remarkable personage, and the first of the school to leave writings, was Plotinus (d. 269); Porphyry (233–305) comes next, and then Jamblichus (d. 330?) Proclus (412–485) was perhaps the last conspicuous teacher; but the school continued to have representatives down to the time of the Emperor Justinian (d. 565) and later. In its effort to combine what was strongest, both in the various philosophies and in the traditional religions, New Platonism met a prevailing tendency, and it might hope in this way to create something like conviction. Nothing tended more to engender doubt than the conflicts of the schools and the variety of the religions. But this was a scheme for which its supporters claimed a common consent of men; they put it forward as the system which combines all the philosophies and explains all the religions; this was the truth which had lived in them all. Perhaps on these terms a sense of rest and of assurance could be gained for men. At the same time, the sufficiency of the old Greek foundations was virtually maintained, and the peremptory claims of Christianity as a positive revelation were rejected. The New Platonists made a last rally for the old world; they drew into their line of battle all its resources, and strove to marshal them as one consistent whole.

Plato's thinking contemplated the world as the realisation of supersensible ideas which exist in, or constitute, an ideal world. The divine Being therefore was the Supreme mind,—the home and fountain of ideas,—those eternal forms of order, goodness, and beauty which in this world are imperfectly and transiently realised. The New Platonism followed the same track; but it tried to carry speculative analysis a step farther. Plotinus said,[1] "When we come to feel the worth of our own soul, we cannot but ask what is that universal soul which breathes life into ourselves and into all nature? Next we cannot but ask, what is that mind by which the universal soul receives and preserves its own life-giving power? Lastly, we ask, what is that first cause, that supreme unity and goodness from which even mind itself has birth?" This Unity (τὸ ἕν), therefore, is something more abstract and inscrutable than mind; something higher than reason. It is characterised also as the good,—but good in a sense that transcends all types of goodness known to us. From this first energy cannot but arise all that is; the One flows forth into division and manifoldness; but for the first two stages, in the reason (νοῦς) and the soul (ψυχή) of the universe, a certain unity and a certain supreme divinity remain. These three therefore (τὸ ἕν, ὁ νοῦς, ἡ ψυχή) con-

[1] See a good article on Neo-Platonism by Mozley in *Dict. of Christian Biography*.

stitute the Neo-Platonic trinity. From this point multiplicity comes in, and we have passed from the region of supreme divinity. But we are still in a region of very pure and elevated beings,—spirits next to God,—some invisible, some identified with the stars; after which follow dæmons, who are superhuman beings, but participant, in some degree, of sensuous conditions. Places were found in these ranks of intermediate beings for the gods of paganism. Then came men, then animals, finally mere matter. Spirit alone has true existence; matter is rather $\mu\grave{\eta}$ $\check{o}\nu$, a kind of negation of existence, which is supposed to arise when the stream of influence has proceeded far enough from its source.

So far Neo-Platonism kept hold of ancient modes of thought—it presented what claimed to be a credible theory of existence. At the same time, it provided a basis for the accepted forms of religion. These were all good in their way; for the dæmons who occupied the stage above humanity had been allotted to preside over various departments, and had been worshipped from of old in the manner suited to them. Such worship was a proper tribute; only, the wise man should remember that not much was to be expected from the worship of these gods, except some temporal advantages, along with a certain exercise of devout feeling; and he must guard always against excessive superstition. True fellowship with the divine nature was to be sought on another line. Christianity itself could have a place conceded to it, in so far as Jesus, according to the New Platonists, was a wise man who had anticipated New Platonism in some of its practical aspects. But Christian religion, as it affirmed the peculiar glory and grace of Christ, and set itself against idolatry, was a corruption of Christ's original doctrine—a vulgar dogmatism of unintelligent disciples.

Reference has been made to goodness, $\tau\grave{o}$ $\dot{a}\gamma a\theta\acute{o}\nu$, as an equivalent of supreme Godhead. The intensely real existence of this One implies goodness, for what truly exists is truly good. Evil is not a positive or substantial thing; it is privation, lack of reality. Spirits, however inferior to

God in their manner of being, still *are*,—are participants of νοῦς and ψυχή, and so are good, and can own relation to the One. Matter, as already said, is a kind of negation of existence, and here therefore evil is found; but this does not directly apply to material substances as we know them, but rather to that ultimate something which gives to all such substances their common nature as material. The material world as we know it arises by the agency of the true existence flowing out on this limiting factor—or, to change the figure, by the light of existence reflecting itself in this region of negation.

This conception of evil is not very intense; and the material world was not for the New Platonists an object of scorn and hate, as it was for the Gnostics. The world had to be, and it was all right in its place; it was as good as it could be. Men, pre-existing as spirits, good in their degree, had a legitimate relation to this world, as something beneath them. But they prove liable to be unduly interested, to be too much attracted, and so they become entangled in an earthly existence, and are so far participant of evil.

The proper destiny, however, of human spirits is to be set free from matter, and brought finally into due fellowship with God. The discipline of earthly life, of successive or multiplied lives (hence transmigration), tends this way; it varies according to men's characters and deservings. Meanwhile the truly wise man can attain the desirable end by a shorter road. He may so use this life as to accelerate the result, or even secure at his death an immediate and permanent elevation above material conditions; and he may attain during this life to anticipations of the mystic fellowship with God.

At this point the system prepared itself to supply a career and a discipline, involving a religious experience, and leading up to final well-being.[1] Heretofore in Greek philosophy what had been set down for the conduct of life—what was reckoned good for man—was mainly to live rationally; morals were reduced to that consideration. The insub-

---
[1] Only, however, for select men, not for the herd.

ordinate and irrational elements were to be subjugated, and life conformed to an ideal type. Among the later Stoics this moral thinking became suffused with a faint pathetic glow of trust in a divine presence and providence; but it was dim and distant. Something implying a more decisive elevation and a securer goal was now felt to be needed.

According to all its principles and its reminiscences, New Platonism had to seek what at this point it wanted in the region of contemplation. Contemplation of the divine, which is as much as to say contemplation of the ideal, must be both means and end. But into this contemplation the New Platonists threw a mystic element. It was to be no longer merely the thought of the individual thinker brooding on truth. It was to be a process in which man's consciousness should meet the divine consciousness,—or the divine Something which is above all consciousness,—the one entering into the other. So fellowship with the divine Being is attained and realised.

Here was set the type of a kind of religious exercise (proceeding on a religious theory) which was taken up from the New Platonists by successive Christian schools; and in some ages it has played a great part. Meditation is to be directed along certain lines, while outward impressions and, as much as may be, our own individuality are to be suppressed. Thus we may reach a state in which we find the divine energy bearing us on into union with God. The eye of the body must be closed, and the eye of the soul opened. From the presence of the manifold world we must draw inward, fixing the mental eye on forms of supersensible truth and beauty and goodness, to which our minds by their origin are akin. The human soul has fallen into a kind of captivity to mortal and material conditions; but the forms of truth are, after all, congenital to us; and they rise in their own purity to the vision that steadily purges itself from the influence of the material world.

So far, however, we might still imagine ourselves to be near the regions of the old philosophy. But now three distinctive elements enter into the scheme:—

1. In order that the mental eye may be disposed to fasten on its proper objects, and may be clear of hindrances which affect it in its present state, a discipline is required. This was, in general, ascetic. It is distinguishable from the rational life recommended by the older schools. That was simple and sometimes severe, and among other benefits, it was conceived to aid in strengthening and clearing the mind; but it was conceived to do so mainly in the way in which sincerity, and fidelity to accepted principles, necessarily give health to the inward man. The ascetic discipline of the New Platonists was meant to fit the mind for a peculiar process, which gives access to an upper world.

2. The ideas or forms of truth and goodness are conceived in a mystic manner, as entrancing the soul with a contemplative amorousness, tending to enthusiasm, yearning, ecstasy. As the ideal forms come into view a Presence makes itself felt behind them; they are heralding an influence, a life beyond themselves. The system is here preparing to take wing from the merely rational or speculative region, and to rise into devout experience and satisfaction.

3. The object that is all along in view determines these efforts. That object is, to rise into the region of divine existence that we may share its pure life, the human consciousness merging itself in something higher, and touching at last the Highest. This goal of all, which in this life for the most part is only apprehended and aspired after, very rarely attained, determines the character and direction of the lower steps and stages; the disciple fits himself to rise into final union with the inscrutable Unity—the eternal and absolute One. He, indeed, is above all thought; so contemplation can never reach Him. But a mystic experience or intuition is possible, in which, from the last heights of contemplation, we rise into the ineffable fellowship, and lose ourselves in the One. This ecstatic state is the crown of all attainment; it anticipates the experience which awaits the wise and good when the bonds of sense shall be broken. Plotinus, it was said, reached this experience four times in the course of his life, and Porphyry once.

The preliminary discipline prescribed for the preparatory stage was, according to the proper theory of the system, purely negative; it was to remove from the soul what might hinder the positive progress which was desired. But it could easily be stretched so as to include any practical elements likely to contribute to the dignity or the promise of the system. As a matter of fact, the scheme in this department borrowed largely from Christianity, and appropriated to its own purposes phrases and ideas which it could not have excogitated.[1] At the same time, it is perhaps true that moral culture was not the strong point of New Platonism. These teachers certainly desired pure and noble life, and some of them exemplified it. But enthusiasm for morals gave way to enthusiasm for the mystic process, which was to rise alike above the moralities and the intellectualities.

The second element of those specified above—contemplation of the ideal as a world of entrancing divine beauty—could inspire enthusiasm, rising in devout natures into a kind of worship; but, in practice, this mood could not easily be sustained in so thin an air. The third element, the mystic self-identification with supreme Godhead in a region above reason, opened the door to nervous trances. Here the weakness of the scheme is revealed. While human nature was longing for some substantial communication from above, New Platonism, like the other philosophies, could only provide for the mind's exercising itself upon its own ideas. Attempting something more, it sank, and crowned its superb idealism with an ecstasy which depended very often on morbid physical conditions. On this, too, there followed a wider range of misleading superstition. Admit the process of attaining to God to be never so authentic, yet success in it was rare; and for most natures this inscrutable Unity, possessed of no determinate attribute to distinguish it, or Him, from mere void, could give little satisfaction. Therefore, though He (or it) is highest of all, might not men, even the wisest men, advantageously seek communion with some

[1] See Porphyry's *Ep. ad Marcellam* (his wife), ed. H. Mai, 1810, which was taken at first to be a Christian document.

of those intermediate dæmons, and find them to be in a sense mediators, steps towards what is highest? And would not this afford more real satisfaction, a sense of warm and real presence, of living ones bending from above, not so far removed from men themselves? From the first, or nearly from the first, it had been admitted among the New Platonists that certain magic rites—theurgic ceremonies and processes—could lend aid to the disciple; if they did not positively raise the spirit Godwards, yet they could purge and dispose the material conditions of human nature, and so remove hindrances to the spirit's upward flight. But might not such processes do more? Might they not avail to bring nigh to us some of those intermediate yet lofty spirits, helping us to discern them and hold communion with them? The place which New Platonism gave to the popular worships favoured such suggestions. Entering by this door, mere superstition and magic made good their footing.

The New Platonism is considered and represented here mainly in relation to the claims and the competition of Christianity.[1] It was a great and memorable effort. For it, God transcends all thought inconceivably; He is that intense reality and goodness in which existence culminates. All that really is derives goodness from Him; and in some wonderful way a consciousness of God is attainable which is victory, emancipation, and blessedness. The progress towards this goal and the attainment of it give life a consecration, and tinge it or bathe it in a religious experience; and yet all is based professedly on reason,—on a just perception and estimate of spiritual possibilites on the one hand, and of the sensible world on the other. Along with this idealism the sensible world retains, for the New Platonists, all the goodness a sensible world can have. Its basis, indeed, is an element which is the negation of true existence, and so the negation of good; yet into this is thrown from the higher

---

[1] Plotinus seems to avoid direct attack on Christianity, though he criticises Gnosticism. Porphyry's attack, in fifteen books, was able. κατὰ χριστιανῶν λόγοι πεντεκαίδεκα. *Opusc.*, ed. Nauck, 1866.

region as much of light as can be reflected from it. That which is lowest and worst has an aspect towards something higher, towards the highest. The true view of man and man's surroundings calls him to a career than which none could be better or higher.

This vision was presented so as to supersede the unwelcome "vulgarities" of positive revelation; it dismissed the thought of God interposing to save the world at a certain recent date, and by an individual man, and rejected the idea of adhering to the cause of a crucified Jew. Instead of these "foolishnesses," Plotinus retained the ancient grand and calm foundation; he rested his teaching on the nature of the universe studied and considered by the reason of man. And he represented God's relation to the world and to human souls as for ever equal to itself; yet on this foundation he teaches that God can be *found*.

Meanwhile also the old worships were retained: they were to have a place, though not the highest.[1] Even the magic and the marvels of legend could be welcomed; they were eddies in that wondrous stream of sympathetic influence which binds together all being from the highest to the lowest. It was contrary to the whole genius of the system to admit the idea of an individual Saviour. Yet against the influence exerted by the life of Christ, it was felt needful to present religious individualities like Apollonius of Tyana as carrying an exceptional influence from the unseen world, and attracting and justifying human trust.[2]

This way of thinking supplied, during several generations, the intellectual basis for those who, rejecting Christianity, clinging to the spirit of the classic literature, and making the best of the world as it was, still wished to have life ennobled and idealised. It was accepted by several of the Roman emperors of the earlier part of the third century,

---

[1] Though Plotinus teaches a Supreme Unity his system is Pantheistic, and his sympathies are with Polytheism. "To think worthily of God is not to shut him up into a unity, but to display divinity as manifold."

[2] Apollonius was one of the philosophico-religious adventurers of the time. His life was idealised and put in literary form by Philostratus.

disposing them on the whole to be hospitable to all religions, as, all alike, variations on one fundamental theme. From this it sometimes followed that Christianity should be gently treated; but sometimes also, chiefly with those who saw deeper, that Christianity, as the most dangerous foe of this philosophy, should be rebuked and punished for its obstinate and peremptory claims. For Neo-Platonism, though willing to provide an honourable place for Christ, dreaded and detested the conquering might of Christ's religion. Julian, in the next century, was the complete embodiment in a Roman ruler of the spirit of the New Platonism. In a word, this system became the storehouse from which cultivated men, who would not be Christians, drew plausible and attractive thoughts in the degree in which they felt it helpful to do so, either to vindicate or to dignify their lives.

But the power of Neo-Platonism to hold and stir the minds of men, appears most strikingly in the influence it exerted on Christians. Its doctrines could be appropriated on the side on which they approached the Christian positions. It conceived all existence to be related to the supreme existence, and pointed to that relation as in some way the source and pledge of well-being. To many this seemed the true point of departure in efforts to harmonise faith and reason. The conception of evil, as in itself nothing,—rather the negation or privation of true being,—fascinated Christian thinkers who were striving with the question of the whence and the whither of evil. And the method of retreat inwards from the world of sense upon the great ideals, in the faith that in and behind them we shall feel the pulse of the eternal life of Godhead, was embraced by one Christian school after another. In all these points men seemed to meet with something true, so set forth that it seized and held them. The idealism could be appropriated and the methodism could be baptized. Origen, Basil of Cæsarea, Synesius, Augustine, are early instances of various forms of this influence. And though Neo-Platonism as a school disappeared, the influence of it as an element in the history of the Church has been recognisable at all periods.

## CHAPTER X

### CHRISTIAN THOUGHT AND LITERATURE

See works on Patristic Literature, p. 50. On special schools, literature is noted below.

CHRISTIAN apologetic continued to be more or less active on the old lines: that is, we have works that attack the popular idolatry, and defend Christianity against current objections. Hermias, Arnobius, Lactantius may be named. Some place Minucius Felix in this period. The $Ἀληθής$ $Λόγος$ of Celsus elicited a notable reply from Origen.[1] The attack of Porphyry (d. 304) was met by Christian controversialists of the next period (Methodius, Eusebius, Apollinarius, Philostorgius); that of Hierocles by Eusebius, and, perhaps, Macarius Magnes.

But with the opening of our period a great literature begins, embodying the thoughts of leading Christian minds upon their own religion. Irenæus, Clement of Alexandria, Origen, Tertullian, Hippolytus, Cyprian are the most important names; Gaius, Dionysius of Alexandria, Gregory Thaumaturgus, Julius Africanus, Commodian, Novatian, Victorinus, Pamphilus, Methodius, Lucian of Antioch are also remembered. The central impulse was the stimulus which Christianity applied to moral and intellectual life; but this in turn was powerfully affected by the Gnostic and other theories which had been suggested within the Church, and also by the attitude and movement of the non-Christian minds with which Christians had to reckon. All that is greatest in this literature had been produced before A.D. 230; the remaining years of the period are marked by smaller

[1] Patrick, *The Apology of Origen in Reply to Celsus*, Edin. and London, 1892.

names, and have left us comparatively little. The wave of effort rose and died away, to be succeeded in the fourth century by another, which spread wider and endured longer.

This literature is conveniently divided into three schools. In examining the special bent which distinguishes each of them, we must not fail to appreciate the remarkable agreement which unites them all. They all (against the Gnostics) received the Old Testament, the ancient Scriptures, as sanctioned by the Lord and His apostles. They all agree in a free use of allegorical interpretation of it, though (at least till Origen) they had no determinate principles to guide them in the matter. Allegory did not imply a disposition to question the truth of the literal history; but as Christianity has at length revealed the true mind of God, who is unchangeable, His Spirit must have been intent of old on the same things which are now believed among us. The inference was that the Old Testament must be pervaded throughout by Christian meanings, and that it is now the privilege of Christians to discern and expound them.

The life and teaching of our Lord were, of course, central for His followers. A wealth of information on this subject existed in various forms, not all equally reliable—traditions, narratives, collections of sayings. During the second century the four Gospels had been everywhere received as the authoritative sources, and a divine wisdom was recognised in furnishing the Church with these and no more.[1] The Epistles also of the apostles had now been sedulously gathered, discriminated, and formed into a collection.[2]

---

[1] Irenæus, *Ref.* iii. 12. 8.

[2] The limits of the New Testament Canon were not drawn quite in the same way in every Church nor by every writer, but the general position was common to all. It will not be denied that Irenæus holds the Gospels and Epistles as settled Christian authorities. So also Clement clearly recognised the principle of the New Testament Canon (*Strom.* vii. 16). It may still be questioned whether the authoritative writings of the New Covenant had come to be regarded exactly in the same way as those of the Old were. As to this, it is to be observed that the mere antiquity of the Old Testament, and also the way in which it was held to speak from that antiquity to a far later age, suggested something peculiarly miraculous. The authority of the New Testament writings was not less, but they impressed the mind differently. They

Something shorter and simpler, however, was available to indicate the outline and basis of Christian religion, and this, too, was matter of substantial agreement among the writers before us. The Gnostic speculations claimed to be Christian, and proposed to set forth a profounder interpretation of the Christian writings. They claimed, too, the possession of secret traditions by which the deeper teaching of the apostles had been transmitted to the Gnostic leaders of the second century, and they named the persons through whom those traditions came. It was perfectly reasonable to set against these claims the public and notorious tradition of the churches, especially of the greater and older churches. This tradition was a fact of first-rate value in the middle of the second century. If the whole literature of Wesleyanism were suddenly annihilated, the consent of the greater and older Methodist congregations would to-day be excellent proof of the fundamental principles of the body. Just so if, in the middle of the second century, a man came to Rome with a system which, in its essentials, was a novelty among Roman Christians, that system might be never so admirable, but it could not be Christianity. For people knew in Rome what had been taught for Christianity to their fathers and grandfathers.

The churches are believed on good grounds to have had forms of baptismal confession, agreeing pretty nearly though with verbal differences. But the early writers of our period appeal especially to what they call the *regula* or standard of belief. As already explained,[1] this is a statement of Christian fundamentals, but with no fixed form of words, so that a given writer may sometimes amplify the statement and sometimes condense it. Either way one feels that

spoke mostly straightforward religion and morality, while those of the Old Testament spoke also mysteries, symbols, oracles. Let anyone observe, for example, how the Old Testament relates itself to such a mind as Origen's (*De Principiis*, iv. 23 *al.*). Now, on the Old Testament, Origen did not occupy a position substantially different from that of other Christians, only he was more inquisitive, suggestive, and intense. He extended the allegorical principle to the New Testament also; but that was not the earlier view.

[1] *Ante*, p. 74.

the writer is not merely conscious of phrases in a creed, but of a way of thinking and feeling regarding those great articles to which he may confidently appeal. Origen calls this rule also κήρυγμα, the Church's proclamation. Whether shorter or longer, the *regula* is understood to apply only to fundamentals like those in what is called the Apostles' Creed. On points more specific no uncontradicted common consent was available. They had to be determined from apostolic teaching and from the analogy of the faith.[1]

Therefore a common attitude towards the faith and a common sentiment about it belong to all the writers now before us. For all of them Christ is pre-existent in the divine nature; is identified with the Logos, who has given being and laws to the universe; has become man, being born of the Virgin; has ascribed to Him at once the divine glory and the human lowliness; also, was and is at once Word and Son. With the Father and Son is associated the Spirit, who dwells in Christ and dwells in the Church as the Spirit of Christ, who was concerned specially in the preparation of Christ's human nature, and who is the immediate source of all hallowing influences. The prophets, who prepared the way for the coming of Christ, spoke by the same Spirit. Christ by His incarnation and sacrifice, has brought in the forgiveness of sins, has opened to us a way and a hope of salvation through repentance, has called us to holiness in the fellowship and under the influences and ordinances of His Church. The hope which awaits the faithful is that of perfect purity and great blessedness. For evil-doers is appointed a condemnation which the common teaching, echoing the language of the New Testament, represented as hopeless. Only the esoteric teaching of leading Alexandrians spoke of it as a purifying pain which could not but at last achieve its end.

[1] Irenæus, i. 1, and i. 10. 1; Clem. Alex. *Strom.* vi. p. 803; Tert. *de Præscr.* c. 13; Origen, *de Princ.* i., *Præf.* 4-9.

## 1. School of Alexandria

Clemens (Titus Flavius) Alexandrinus, *Opera*, Potter, Oxf. 1715; Dindorf, Oxf. 1868; Migne, Paris, 2 vols. 1857, transl. in *Ante-Nicene Fathers*, Edin. The chief writings are the *Protrepticus*, the *Pædagogus*, and the *Stromata*. Origen, *Opera*, De la Rue, Paris, 4 vols. fol. 1733–59; reprinted by Lommatzsch, 25 vols. 12mo, Berol. 1831–48. Thomasius, *Origenes*, Nürnberg, 1837. Redepenning, *Origenes*, 2 vols., Bonn, 1841–46. We owe also to Redepenning a very useful edition of the Περι Αρχων, Lips. 1836. Bigg, *Christian Platonists of Alexandria*, Oxf. 1886. De Pressensé, *Histoire des trois premières Siècles de l'Eglise*, Paris, 1861, 2me serie, vol. ii.

We begin with the Alexandrians. In their hands the work of the Apologists was followed up in a profoundly sympathetic spirit. In illustrating the place and worth of Christianity, they aim at doing justice to the better thought and life of the pagan world. Pantænus is reported as the earliest representative of the School; but he left no writings. For our purpose he is merged in his disciple, Clement.

Clement's birth can hardly have fallen earlier than A.D. 150 or later than 160. While still ignorant of Christ, he had devoted himself to philosophy; and Neander has aptly suggested that the sketch of such a career, put into the mouth of Clemens Romanus in the *Recognitions*,[1] might well enough describe the actual career of his Alexandrian namesake. After he came under Christian influences, he continued to be a seeker, wandering to and fro in search of the wisest and most helpful teachers. He commemorates some with special gratitude,—one from Syria whom he met in Greece,[2] one from Egypt whom he met in Magna Græcia.[3] Others he encountered in the East. Lastly, in Alexandria he comes upon Pantænus, "the true Sicilian bee, gathering spoil from the flowers of the prophetic and apostolic meadow"; and now he found rest.

Pantænus, who came to Christianity through a Stoic training, held an interesting position. Alexandria was at

---
[1] See *ante*, Chap. I. p. 21.  [2] Tatian has been suggested.
[3] Perhaps Theodotus.

once an important provincial capital, a great commercial centre, and the seat of a remarkable school of learning. Many streams flowed together in its population; and all that was plausible in speculation found disciples and expositors. The need had been felt of setting apart someone who knew how minds were working, and who was qualified to deal with them, in order to train those who at Alexandria were entertaining the question of Christian discipleship. So the catechetical School had special significance there, and Pantænus was at the head of it. His philosophy apparently did not chill his Christianity; for, by and by, he left the libraries, the society, and the disputations of the city, to go on missionary work among uncultivated people. This may have taken place about A.D. 189. Then probably Clement succeeded him. In A.D. 202 the persecution under Alexander Severus drove Clement from Alexandria. Perhaps he returned before his death, which is usually dated about A.D. 220.

Clement brought to the service of Christianity a full and ready mind. No one of his time has quoted so largely from the store of Greek literature. He loved beauty and goodness, and he found their traces everywhere: accordingly, he counted on a response from human hearts, when appealed to in the name of beauty, and goodness, and God. The position in which he was placed, and the work he had to do, called upon him to present Christianity to his hearers as the crown of all worthy human thoughts: it was a creed in harmony with all that men had found to be valid, supplying what men had felt to be lacking. Clement believed all this; he devoted his resources to make it good; and in so doing he set the type of the earlier Alexandrian Christian teaching.

He took up afresh thoughts we have already met with in Justin Martyr; but he presented his case with more wealth of suggestion and more warmth of appeal. He had little value for continuous exposition; on the contrary, his convictions gush up in a kind of fortuitous disorder. His great successor, Origen, was to state the case with more argumentative power, more continuity of thought, more patient working out of detail; also with astonishing subtlety of speculation. But Clement retains a charm of his own—the charm of the impressionist. And the aim of Clement, not less than of Origen, is to present a clear intellectual conception of Christianity. That was dictated by the situation in which both teachers found themselves. They had to commend Christianity to men sharing the culture of the time, and interested in the questions which it raised. To influence such men, to grasp them permanently, intellectual method must come clearly into play, and ideals must be presented and pressed. Again, Christianity had to be exhibited as tenable against the philosophies which claimed to embody all that was discoverable of the good, the true, the fair. Christianity must either own a certain helplessness as compared with them, or must transcend them and beat them on their own ground. Again, Christianity at that time had to be stated as distinguished and as vindicated from Gnosticism. Now Gnosticism presented a conception, and so far a solution, of the great problem—the being, the history, the catastrophe of the world. There were various Gnostic schemes, but all worked with the same materials, and on similar lines. The best way of ousting all these was to present the true Gnosis, embodying elements which, if once accepted, must explode all the Gnosticisms. It may be added, that the Gnostic theories were recognised already as only one large and rank species under the general head of heresies. These were forms of thought which claimed the Christian name, had affinities on some sides with Christian faith and feeling, and yet proved irreconcilable with great and permanent convictions on which Christian faith and life rested. These schemes could be encountered in detail. But to the whole class, Christians were beginning to ascribe a common character, for they associated them all with ideas of wanton fancifulness and insubordinate self-will. It was natural to think, then, that, in contrast to all these, the genuine Christianity could be set forth on grand lines of thought,—few, sufficient, self-evidencing,—and so might take possession of the minds of men, convincing and steadying. Perhaps this remark applies more to Clement: Origen's theorising, which aims at the same object, is not quite so simple; he is more prone to theoretic detail.

For Clement, Christianity is first and chiefly the coming of the Logos into the world, in the person of Christ. He had been in the world before; for as He made all, and is the sustaining reason of the universe, so He has never failed to solicit human minds with truth. The whole history of the race bears token of His presence. Yet this ministration, though it had many eminent fruits, was not sufficient for the highest ends,—it was not sufficient to bring about complete agreement with God, nor to open the gates of the true blessedness. It is the ministration of the Word as actually come among us in His incarnation, revealing and attracting, which proves able to flood the soul with light; it is this that persuades us to make the decisions in which we become completely His disciples and His friends.

But that result does not come to pass with all, even of those whom the message of Jesus reaches. The reason is that men cannot be absolutely swayed by any power, not even by Truth itself in its clearest dispensation. Men can shut the door against it, or can detain it in unrighteousness. For Will is an essential feature in human nature, and the essence of Will is to be free,—it is always free. Being so, it can reject reason and prefer unreason. Still, the human heart feels that Truth has a claim to be heard and welcomed, and even perverse wills must in some measure own this. Hence the importance of that divine ministry of truth and discipline combined, which not only carries on the culture of those who have believed, but also besets the unbelieving with successive lessons and with fresh motives, so that they may yet surrender to that which they have resisted.

Hence, then, comes the division between those who have received the light and those who resist it. What the final issue of this division shall be is not so clear in Clement. Probably he, like Origen, looked for a final victory of light over all natures capable of light, however long continued the processes of discipline might have to be, by which that victory should be attained. At all events, over against this array of human wills, with their responsibilities and their persistent freedom, stands the divine equity, always aiming at men's welfare, but steadily aiming at it by dealing with men according to their desert. Hence all conditions and all distinctions among men are finally accounted for by this, that their merits have so determined for them. Will is continually confronted by justice with its discipline; it always encounters the lessons which ought to be prescribed to it; yet it retains always its inherent freedom to make its own decisions. This $\delta\iota\kappa\alpha\iota\sigma\sigma\dot{\nu}\nu\eta$ $\sigma\omega\tau\dot{\eta}\rho\iota\sigma$ of God, taking relation to the $\alpha\dot{\upsilon}\tau\sigma\epsilon\xi\sigma\upsilon\sigma\dot{\iota}\alpha$ of man, is the abiding key to the moral history of the world and of all individual souls.

If it be asked how those are justly dealt with who died before the Saviour came, or who have never heard of Him,—some of whom searched for truth so earnestly,—the answer is that for the purposes of salvation the truth they attained was insufficient; but nothing hinders the divine equity to prolong their training after death, and to vouchsafe to them revelations, and guide them to decisions, in which they may reach the level of believing and baptized Christians.

It is admitted, however, that Truth and Goodness not only have existed before Christ came, but they have swelled into great proportions. They have done so chiefly on two lines, the Jewish and the Greek. These were the historical preparations for the great advent. Greek thought, as well as the Jewish law, was a schoolmaster to bring us to Christ.

On this scheme the view to be taken of the material world is not the Gnostic view,—that it originates in a fall,—but mainly this, that it is subservient to the trial and the discipline of spiritual beings. For this purpose it is fitting and good. The natural result of this explanation would be to regard everything material as transient. Clement does not say so; but perhaps he betrays the pressure of a tendency in this direction. He held the incarnation and the resurrection; but touches of docetic tendency occur here and there in his references to Christ's human nature; and one does not see that the resurrection holds any important place in his thinking.

Clement's teaching placed Christianity in a setting which had various advantages. It presented a tenable way of thinking about the world, as framed on a plan into which Christianity enters as the proper complement. It recognised the attainments of the Gentile mind, without sacrificing the necessity and supremacy of Christianity. It emphasised the benignity of the Logos in pre-Christian as well as in Christian dispensations, and asserted the interest and the claims of Christ in connection with every aspect and every stage of human progress. While it sympathised with the emphasis with which most ancient thinkers exalted the spiritual as contrasted with the material, it still was able to claim importance for the material world as the intended and the fitting scene for discipline and trial; and so it could retain the Hebrew and the Christian doctrine of God the Creator, and of the intrinsic goodness of the creatures. It took possession of all the hereditary enthusiasm of the schools for truth and knowledge, because it conceived Christianity as the complete Truth, which did its work as a light, victoriously correcting and persuading. At the same time it shut out the fatalistic tendencies of Gnosticism and Pantheism by the energetic assertion of creature independence as involved in the freedom of the will; while yet the element of irregularity and disorder, that seemed necessarily to break in at this point, was held in check by the conception of a divine righteousness, strong, watchful, and benevolent, which perpetually relates itself to every movement of every will, and administers incessantly the discipline which the action of each calls for. So the history of the world and the processes of Christian salvation evolve themselves on lines which are simple, attractive, intelligible, which may charm away speculative doubt, and secure room for the moral and spiritual teaching to do its work unimpeded. This doctrine, propounding a philosophy and a theology hand in hand, appealed strongly to the age. And it was really much more than merely a doctrine of the second or third century. A way of thinking in substance the same has revived again and again down to our own time; it has been represented by very beautiful and attractive minds. It embodies one of the ways of conceiving Christianity,—one of the great alternatives for thinkers who strive to combine Christian convictions with a free outlook into the experience and the thinking of men.

The defects of it have at all times been obvious. Claiming to exhibit the relation between God and men, it has no feasible account to give of the moral and spiritual condition in which the race finds itself. Its exponents have often been distinguished by moral enthusiasm and sincerity; but their theory in its own nature tends to attenuate sin, and reduce it to mere error. The need and the fact of the Atonement and the Christian doctrine of grace are foreign to the scheme, and therefore must be somewhat slightly dealt with; and redemption turns wholly on the soul being flooded with light, combined with the lessons of experience. Yet while these defects must be pointed out, it is right to acknowledge that what is not adequately presented by thinkers of this class is not necessarily or always denied. Christianity is full of compensations for human defects in the appropriation of it. Those who think mainly on Alexandrian lines have often approximated in various ways to the positions which they felt unable to assert.

The scheme recalls features of Gnosticism in the stress which it lays on enlightenment, and in its conception of the function of the Logos as the great appeal of mind to mind. Clement loves to think of the ripe Christian as the true Gnostic; and he did share in some respects the point of view of the earlier Gnostics, and their intellectual tendencies. But the contrast between him and them is marked. He had no sympathy with the fantastic romance of Gnostic speculation; he abhorred its fatalism, its way of conceiving the relations of God and creatures, its conception of fundamentally diverse classes of human beings. He threw himself on the Christian doctrine of creation, and of the responsibilities of the creature, and (in his own way doubtless) he carried these through. One effect of the intellectualism may be noted. On his scheme a consistent divine benevolence is asserted, which is also one with justice. This benevolence aims at highest well-being, and therefore may be said to be equivalent to love. Yet the *thought* is not so much of love, but rather of light, with its essentially beneficent influences.

The chief features ascribed to Clement apply also to the teaching of Origen. But Origen was far more conscious of the obligation to think out his theories. He left a remarkable illustration both of Alexandrian tendencies and also of Christianity itself, as including peculiarities which he recognises, and for which he endeavours to provide.

### ORIGEN

Origen was born at Alexandria about A.D. 185. His father, Leonidas, was a Christian of some position and means. Origen received a liberal education, and was trained also in the Scriptures, learning many portions by heart. His strange, deep questions led the father to augur a remarkable career for his child. In A.D. 202 the persecution of Alexander Severus broke out, and Leonidas was apprehended. Origen burned to share his fate; and when prevented by his mother and other friends from giving himself up, he sent a message to his father imploring him to be staunch to the end. Leonidas was put to death, and Origen found himself at seventeen years of age without means. He resolved to make his way by teaching. Soon the mental energy and the unflinching Christian devotedness of the youth led the bishop to intrust to him the care of the catechetical School; for Clement had found it expedient to leave Alexandria when the persecution began. Origen's courage and devotedness, joined to his remarkable gifts, ensured for him the affection and admiration of his scholars. Some time during this period of his life, desiring to make any sacrifice that might conduce to the purity and success of his work, he was led to the rash act of self-mutilation, which he afterwards condemned.[1] Till past middle life Origen continued at Alexandria. But during occasional visits which he paid to Palestine he preached in the church at Cæsarea, in presence of the bishop and, later, received ordination as a presbyter. These steps, taken without the leave of the Alexandrian bishop, were fitted to give umbrage; most likely also parts of his teaching were disapproved. Proceedings were taken, and he left Alexandria, in so far as the Alexandrian church was concerned, a deposed and excommunicated man. But the churches in Palestine and in some other regions refused to recognise the sentence, and Origen found refuge at Cæsarea (in Palestine), where the bishop, Alexander, was an old friend. His life was diversified by various journeys,—in one of them he came to Rome; but Cæsarea continued to be his headquarters, until in A.D. 251, escaping to Tyre to avoid the Decian persecution, he was taken prisoner. He survived the persecution; but, broken by suffering, he died in A.D. 254.

His labours as a scholar and writer were enormous; hence probably the name Adamantius often given to him. The greater part of his work was expended directly on the Scriptures. Of the rest the most important are his sketch of a system in four books ($\pi\epsilon\rho\grave{\iota}$ $\dot{a}\rho\chi\hat{\omega}\nu$, *De Principiis*), and his reply to Celsus,[2] who had written against Christianity in the previous century. The *Hexapla* was a gigantic effort to establish a good text of the Septuagint version of the Old Testament, accompanied by the Hebrew, and by other Greek versions besides the LXX.[3] These materials were exhibited, at least in a large part of the work, in six columns. Nothing

---

[1] His later judgment on it will be found in *Comm. on Matth.* xix. 12; Lomm. iii. 327, 331.
[2] Patrick, *The Apology of Origen in Reply to Celsus*, Edin. and London, 1892.
[3] *Hexapl. quæ Supersunt*, F. Field, Oxon. 1867-74, 2 vols. 4to.

so elaborate was attempted with respect to the New Testament; but it appears that a corrected copy, which Origen used, became a source of subsequent copies. For the rest, he commented on books of the Old and New Testaments in three different forms (Scholia, Homilies, and Commentaries, τόμοι), and these expositions form the bulk of his surviving work; but much has perished.

It should be mentioned that in more than one case Origen was sent or was invited to churches where alleged heresies had been broached, and composed the differences by leading the innovators to withdraw what had given offence.[1]

As an interpreter Origen is famous for having theorised the principle of allegorical interpretation, already generally applied to the Old Testament. That, as Origen himself points out, was one of the commonplaces of orthodoxy in his day, only it required to be systematised. But the method, as he maintained, was applicable also to the New Testament, *i.e.* to all inspired Scripture. There are three senses—the literal, the moral, the spiritual, which he compares to body, soul, and spirit; but not all passages have all the three senses. Origen's own interpretations are no doubt often fantastic; yet he has the merit of inculcating strict grammatical exegesis as the foundation of all else; and he did a great deal of useful scholarly commentating by which all his successors have benefited.[2] Sometimes his literal interpretation is *too* literal; it overlooks the *essential* figurativeness which gives life to all language. It is usually said that Clement and Origen hold a more liberal theory of inspiration than other early writers do; but it would be difficult to prove it. It is true that the allegorical method gives a comfortable latitude in dealing with difficult passages; but Origen himself enforces the importance of every syllable in the text from which your allegory starts. It is true also that Origen asserts that, *e.g.*, in historical books, you may meet with statements impossible in the letter, which are

---

[1] Cases of Beron and Beryllus of Bostra,—obscure speculations on the Godhead. Dorner, *Lehre v. d. Person Christi*, i. 536-61.

[2] Lightfoot, *Comm. on Galatians*, p. 227.

meant to force you to look out for a deeper sense. But that, in his view, is the triumph of inspiration, not the defect of it.

It remains to say something of Origen's scheme of theological thought. It might be more lightly passed over if its importance were estimated by the number of its adherents; for few probably, even in his own day, adopted it throughout. But its interest lies in the revelation of the way in which the most remarkable Christian of the third century could think. Moreover, it is the first Christian system, the first scheme of ordered Christian thought which aims at method and completeness. In sketching it, it will be most convenient to begin at the beginning—with God and creation; only the reader will do well to remember that, in such schemes, what were really the decisive and organising thoughts for the system-maker are found in the middle of the system, rather than at the beginning.

Origen opens with an enumeration of the points which ought to be regarded as settled and agreed upon among Christians. It is a statement of the *regula*, as he conceived it, and it coincides in substance with statements of the same kind by other writers (see *ante*, p. 159); only Origen goes into more detail, and betrays more distinctly the common tendency to claim the benefit of the *regula* for inferences whose value was becoming apparent, as well as for positions which had been longer recognised. Beyond this common ground he recognises a region open to reverent discussion, on the grounds of Scripture and of reason. Here he finds topics and questions of which the Church has nothing final to say; but to search for treasures in this field is the duty and the privilege of Christians who are competent for doing so. Origen, looking out from the central certainties into these regions beyond, forms his own conception of the Unity of Truth, and the eternal order of the ways of God.

God is pure spirit or intelligence, immaterial, exalted far above all creatures. His attributes are, properly speaking, unnameable. Yet Origen was to maintain that He is essentially self-revealing. Accordingly, he ascribes to Him proper personality and immutable truth and goodness. He is absolutely without beginning and without end. Otherwise He is not absolutely without measure. If He were, He could not comprehend Himself. On this Origen speaks with some emphasis.

Here comes in the doctrine of the Logos. At this time men's thoughts vacillated between the ascription to the Logos of full divinity, but so as, at the same time, to merge Him indistinguishably in the Father, and the ascription to Him of distinct or distinguishable being, but in expressions which seem to imply a later and lower nature. Origen leant to the latter alternative, because he was anxious to assert strongly the distinct personality. The Logos was an eternal existence like the Father, eternally begotten. Origen, like others, conceives the Logos as one in whom the divine nature becomes the divine manifestation,—seed and ground of all creatures. But He is distinguished from Philo's Logos, and from Plato's world of ideas, by this, that He is unambiguously personal—possessing life, thought, and power. The Christian doctrine of the Incarnation dictated this difference.

Through the Logos, who is thus the eternal radiation or reflection of the Father, the Holy Ghost takes being, receives wisdom, and becomes the channel of both to the creatures. Origen has spoken of the kingdom of the Father as including all things, of that of the Son as including the rational and the hallowed, and of the Spirit as including the hallowed. This disparity, however, is ultimately adjusted; for, as we shall see, on the scheme of Origen all that is irrational vanishes at last, and all that is rational becomes ultimately holy.

This scheme turned really on the doctrine of the Second Person; and two interests were to be provided for. *First*, the conception of the universe as related to God, having its reason and ground in Him; *second*, the conception of the Saviour as realised in Jesus Christ. The latter determined the conception of the full personality of the Logos. Looking at Christ, Origen felt that though He is in the Father, and with the Father, and from the Father, and though He lives by the Father, yet He is *not the Father*. The distinct personality is therefore emphasised, and that in a form of subordinationism. But another interest, the first noted above, acted on the other side. If the Christian view of creation was to be maintained, the universe must be traced up to God, as an expression and revelation of Him. Therefore the Logos, who is specially the Creator, must be conceived so as to sustain that view. In the Logos there must be no arbitrary wilfulness of a creature, polluting and confusing the work. The Logos must be a pure echo, if we may phrase it so, of the Father. Origen meant to give effect to this thought.

The picturesque peculiarities of Origen's thinking become more apparent when we go on to the doctrine of Creation.

Existing tendencies have to be remembered at this point. It was common to assume that mind alone has any value, and to set down what is material in the universe as the element of disadvantage or deformity. Evil of all kinds was accounted for as arising from material conditions. The scheme was then completed by assuming that all minds are portions of God, or emanations from God (so the Gnostics, —the Neo-Platonic doctrine tries to refine on this); and that matter is the lowering and darkening element which seduces us from our proper good, as it hides from us our true nature. It was congruous to this mode of view to think that the emancipation of men and their final well-being depended mainly on an intellectual triumph over the delusions of sense. Origen shared the common tendency so far, that he, too, could not think any form of being worthy to be called into existence by God, save mind—intelligence. But, as a Christian, he could not regard matter as *not* God's creature, nor as necessarily evil; nor could he regard created spirits as parts or modes of God's own being. Also, he had learned as a Christian to give a more decisive place, both for good and evil, to the decisions of the will, than to the exercises or the accomplishments of the understanding. It may be added further, that the Gnostics, as we saw, traced up not merely the present state of the mixed world, but its origin, to a primeval fall from the Pleroma. Origen, too, was not disposed to think of the material world as other than the result of a fall; and yet, as just stated, he was not to condemn it as evil. How was he to wind his way through these various conditions?

God, as Origen considered, did not begin to create, as at an era before which creation was not. He has never been without a world of creatures. And His work has consisted in causing to exist a great, but not an infinite number of intelligences. From the inconceivable "beginning" these spirits have existed. They must be conceived as equal to one another in position and gifts so far as God is concerned,—anything else were inconsistent with divine equity. They are, then, at first blessed, all of them equally, with a full view of truth and full delight in goodness, for they are all in unimpeded fellowship with the Logos. Though they are akin to God, they differ from the Holy Spirit (and, of course, from the Logos and the Father) in this, that He has goodness essentially by nature, but they are capable of partaking of it, and also of losing it, by will. Being in possession of goodness they may become saturated with it, may relax in their intentness, and become subject to some degree of evil. They can cool from the glow of primeval goodness.

This, in fact, is what Origen conceives all of these creatures to have done, more or less, through the play of their own freedom (all, unless there be *one* exception); a descending process thus sets in which proceeds in various cases to various lengths. The devil is he who has gone farthest, and Origen conceives that it was he who began the process of defection.

Here now comes in the actual experimental world. A spirit, $\pi\nu\epsilon\hat{\upsilon}\mu\alpha$, sufficiently refrigerated [1] in the progress of its decline from the glow of primeval goodness, becomes a human soul, $\psi\upsilon\chi\acute{\eta}$, and acquires a material vesture adapted to its precise conditions; also, the material universe takes shape by divine appointment precisely in the form

[1] Origen connected $\psi\upsilon\chi\acute{\eta}$ with $\psi\upsilon\chi\rho\acute{o}\varsigma$.

adapted to be the scene in which spirits so situated shall pursue the course of further experiences. As compared with the prior and happier conditions of spirits, the world we know is thus a kind of prison and place of correction, while in relation to abodes of yet lower quality it may be a place of relief. This is the explanation of how men are born; an intelligence, so far fallen, has become incorporate in each little child. Other spirits which have not fallen so far, have their own conditions, more ethereal than ours, but material still. The sun, moon, and stars are all, for Origen, instances of spirits less fallen than we, yet in a disciplinary captivity in those lucent forms of theirs, from which they shall one day be delivered.[1]

The spirit of each man at death is supposed to ascend or descend, as his previous course deserves. There is not, however, for the present, at the death of each man, an exact adjustment of externals to his internal state; only an approximation. But when the Æon, or world age, ends, then a full rearrangement takes place. The Logos becomes intensely present to each soul; each fully realises his own character and his past doings; and then a full readjustment takes place, a new world arises, and a new start is made.

A succession of such world ages is to be supposed, how many and how long enduring none can say. The whole process is meant to reclaim the fallen; and at last, after many successive æons, the great result will be attained,— the whole universe of intelligences will return to their primeval good state. This is the greater world close, which concludes, not an æon merely, but the "ages of ages." That such a close is relatively near, Origen inferred from Christ's incarnation, for that must be supposed to indicate that all was to be made new. Yet, end when it may, this immense process cannot, apparently, be supposed to occur only once for all. Change will set in again through free will, and the problem will rise and be resolved again,—in

---

[1] There are passages, however, in which the alternative is suggested, that all spiritual beings (except the Trinity) possess an extremely refined material vesture.

general on the same principles, but with interminable variety in detail. This last point lies in the connection of the system, and it is indicated by Origen as at least possible; but he does not dwell upon it.

The Logos, meanwhile, has been ever soliciting the minds of His creatures with truth. Philosophy, Law, Promise are all effects of His activity. But these prove to be not enough; and so, in one æon, after much evil, the Logos Himself comes,—who does not come in many æons,—He comes incarnate. Our Lord's appearance is the most striking instance of one principle enunciated by Origen, namely, that while in general all intelligences are placed in stations corresponding to their merits, yet sometimes the good and pure are found in stations far below what would otherwise be their lot. This takes place by way of condescension and sympathy. These benefactors descend to minister to the good of others.

Origen attached great weight to the presence of the human soul of Christ in the incarnation. Probably many Christians were confused or unsettled on this point. In his view it was unsuitable for the Logos to unite Himself directly with a material body; He is in union with a human soul, and with the body through that. But this human soul, this ψυχή, had to be explained, as far as possible, in conformity with Origen's general doctrine of souls. He taught, therefore, that this spirit, like all others, has preexisted through indefinite ages. This one, however, unlike all others, has constantly adhered to the Logos in unfailing and inextinguishable love, has grown continually into nearness and ardour of attachment, has become, as it were, one spirit with Him. So it could appropriately have the distinction, and could accept the trials of the human soul of Christ.[1] Thus the principle of remunerative righteousness is carried

---

[1] It has often been remarked that this explanation leaves out of account one element in Origen's theory of souls in general; for, according to that, a πνεῦμα becomes a ψυχή, and acquires a material vesture only through a process of moral refrigeration. But Origen's resources are not easily exhausted, and perhaps he had a reply ready for this difficulty.

out even here. The human soul of Christ has earned the place it occupies. And while the actual incarnation takes place only once in the consummation of the ages, the union of the Logos with the spirit, who is the human soul of Christ, became a durable fact quite apart from the incarnation, and apparently in no connection of time with that event. Apparently, also, in the final state of things, the material part of Christ will vanish, but the union with this spirit will remain.

As to the redeeming energy of Christ, the main thought is that He operates as an enlightening influence. Yet Origen felt a meaning in the death of Christ which this thought did not adequately bring out. Three ways of looking at this matter have been pointed out in various parts of his writings. First, he gives some weight to the idea, current in his day and long after, that in subjecting Himself to the malice of Satan, our Lord ousted that enemy from the dominion which he had over us as sinners,—a dominion usurped as it relates to God, but having a certain right to be, in so far as our sin brought us under that dark yoke. Secondly, in a sense Christ's death was substitutionary, and as such relieves us from punishment. Punishment, according to Origen, is not vindicative, it is always and only disciplinary; but sacrifice on the part of another may, even in this view, so far fulfil the ends of punishment as to replace it. Lastly, Origen seems to have thought that the death of the holy sufferer has a mystical or magical power to defeat the onset of evil. It breaks the spell, and sets man free.

The pathway by which the individual soul reaches the great result through repentance, faith, baptism, and perseverance, is conceived by Origen as an ascent to God, in a manner that recalls the teaching of the New Platonists, and also of the later mystics.

At death the soul, separated from the body, but still retaining a finer material vesture, has special experiences to go through. Even the good, who proceed, in the first place, to paradise (somewhere in the earth), pass to it through a lively apprehension of their own sin, and an inward judgment of it, which is their punishment. The same experience awaits others also; but these cannot pass through, and they sink to those regions that are suited to their state. From paradise the good ascend, not usually to consummate blessedness, but to some higher region adapted to a character which is not yet perfected. All this was a contribution to the doctrine of purgatory. The punishment of the wicked is perhaps chiefly to be conceived as an intense manifestation of the Logos, which confronts the soul with its sins, and forces in upon it the sense of their intolerable evil. Each man really lights his own fire, rather than sinks into fire prepared for him. " Walk in the light of your fire, and in the flames which ye have kindled." And the fuel is our sin, which Paul (1 Cor. iii. 12) calls wood, hay, stubble. "So the soul, when it has collected into itself a multitude of evil works and an abundance of sins, at a fitting time glows into punishment, and bursts into penal fire." Very striking representations are made of the way in which past sins may take hold of the sinner. The process, with its unknown progressions—for who can tell what purging pain the great Healer will apply?—is always in the long-run designed to heal and to restore. God is at last to bring all to the result described as subjection to Christ (1 Cor. xv. 28). "What is that subjection? I believe it is that subjection which we long for, that which apostles and saints experience. It is such subjection as includes the safety of those subjected. For David says, 'Shall not my soul be subject to the Lord; from Him comes my salvation.'"[1]

Origen's theology is a theme on which much might be written, if this were the place. Let it suffice to say, meanwhile, that in a great degree he saw and settled what the questions are which dogmatic theology raises, and in a great degree also, the relation in which they stand to one another. He also raised into prominence the question of the boundary

[1] Origen, at the same time, had given the consentient teaching of the Church in these words: "The soul departing out of this world will be dealt with according to its merits, either partaking the inheritance of eternal life and blessedness, if its own works allot this to it, or committed to eternal fire and punishment, if the guilt of its evil deeds binds it over to this" (*De Princ.* Præf. 5).

between that which is of faith and that which should be open among Christians. Where should that line be drawn? And ought it at all times to be the same? It is a question that has been variously dealt with since, and it is not yet closed. Origen's answer to it is in the earlier chapters of the *De Principiis*.[1]

In passing from this system, we may remind ourselves that a man does not always live by the speculations which he thinks. Apparently the older Origen grew the more he lived in the Scriptures, and the less he cared for anything outside of them. It is not wonderful, however, that umbrage was early taken at the freedom of Origen's speculation. At first, this applied mainly to his speculations about the origin and history of souls, including his theory of matter.[2] As regards his way of speaking on the higher nature in Christ, the charge of heresy on that ground was a later development.

For some time all Eastern theology was influenced by Origen, but in various degrees. Dionysius, after presiding in the catechetical school, became bishop of Alexandria, and was distinguished as "the Great." He opposed Chiliasm, and criticised unfavourably the claims to canonicity of the Book of Revelation. His utterances on Logos doctrine are referred to below (Fragments in Routh). Gregory Thaumaturgus, a scholar of Origen at Cæsarea, afterwards a very successful bishop of Neo-Cæsarea in Pontus, wrote a Panegyricus on Origen (among Origen's works, Lommatzsch, vol. xxv.). Methodius, bishop of Olympus in Lycia (died a martyr, 311), attacked Origen's Anthropology, and his doctrine of Eternal Creation (*Opera*, Jahn, Heid. 1865, transl. in Clark's *Ante-Nicene Fathers*). His conception of salvation as emancipation from sense makes him a glowing advocate of celibacy. Against various attacks Pamphilus (died 309 by martyrdom), aided by Eusebius, wrote an Apology for Origen, of which the first book remains (in Routh, and among Origen's works, Lomm. vol. xxiv.). Separately must be named a learned layman, Julius Africanus, older than Origen, and one of his correspondents. He wrote five books of Chronography, long influential, and a medical book, Κεστος; fragments in Routh, ii. 219, 509.

---

[1] For the rest, the reader may consult the remarks of Harnack, *History of Doctrine*, noting especially what he says as to the art with which, in Origen's scheme, each element slides into the next, and sharp contrasts are avoided See also Thomasius and Redepenning, *ante*, p. 161.

[2] Methodius, in his works on the *Resurrection* and on *Things Created*.

## 2. School of Asia Minor

There existed in Asia Minor during the second century a vigorous church life, and a lively tradition of Christian teaching.[1] There Irenæus was impressed in his youth by the character and reminiscences of "Presbyteri Apostolorum discipuli." Characteristic thoughts of Ignatius, of Polycarp, and of Melito receive emphasis and illustration in Irenæus. This is less conspicuously true of Hippolytus; yet he is commonly referred to the same school. Irenæus and Hippolytus both found their field of work in the West; but they continued to think and write in Greek—and their peculiarities are Asian rather than Western.[2]

Irenæus is important, because he represents the central forces of the Christianity of his time. Alike his training and his character disposed him to avoid eccentricities, and

---

[1] Melito of Sardis, Apollinarius of Hierapolis, Miltiades, Apollonius. The rise of Montanism, and the conflict with it, imply vivacity and susceptibility.

[2] Irenæus, born in the East—perhaps A.D. 130 (Zahn says, 115), not later than 140, in his early days saw and heard Polycarp at Smyrna, said to have spent some time at Rome after 155, became bishop of Lyons on death of Pothinus, 177—and is known to have been alive in 190. That he was martyred under Septimius Severus (202) has been asserted, but on no sure grounds. Besides his work against *Heresies* (chiefly the Gnostic), which has survived in a very old Latin translation (considerable fragments also in Greek), Irenæus also wrote letters and tracts on current questions, which were quoted by later writers. (Edd. Stieren. 2 v. Lips. 1853; Harvey, Cambridge, 1857, contains additional fragments from the Syriac.)

Hippolytus was by far the most learned man in the Roman Church of his day, yet his position there has been matter of great debate. He was influential from about the beginning of the third century, but disapproved of the action of Pope Zephyrinus, came into serious collision with Callistus (217-222), and is believed by Döllinger and others to have been an opposition bishop of a sect in Rome (but see Prof. Salmon in Smith and Wace's *Dict. of Biogr.*). About 235, in a time of persecution, he was banished to the mines of Sardinia along with Pontianus the Roman bishop, and probably died there. He was afterwards venerated at Rome as a martyr, which suggests that the quarrel had been composed before he died. His most important work, perhaps, was his *Refutation of all Heresies*, recovered in 1851. But about forty others are ascribed to him, of which the smaller part has been preserved. The forty titles may not represent in all cases as many distinct works. *Remains*, Lagarde, Lips. and Lond. 1858; Migne, *Patr. Gr.* x.; *Refutatio*, Duncker and Schneidewin, Gött. 1859.

to recognise the main interests to which Christian teaching ministers. Some of his contemporaries were trying to interpret Christianity in terms of philosophy; and the whole mass of Gnostic theories ran out into the wildest speculations. Irenæus distrusted this so-called science, but there is nothing irrational in the position he takes up about it. "If a man cannot find out the reason of everything that is asked after, let him consider that man is infinitely less than God; man is not yet equal to his Maker. Now, just in so far, in point of knowledge and searching out of reasons is he less than Him who made him. For, O man, thou art not uncreated, nor always coexistent with God as His Word is; but from His goodness thou hast received a beginning of being, and gradually dost thou learn from the Word, the arrangements of God who made thee. It is no wonder that we find ourselves so situated in regard to things heavenly which are matters of revelation, since even of the things that are before our feet, I mean the visible parts of creation, many escape our understanding; and these, too, we must commit to God" (ii. 25. 3; 28. 2).

On a former page, reference was made to a scheme of thought which frequently suggests itself as underlying early Christian utterances, especially in the case of the Apologists and their successors (*ante*, p. 89). It is a rather scanty and starved conception of Christianity. Irenæus also speaks, not unfrequently, according to the same scheme. But he inherited from his predecessors in Asia Minor an impression of something richer and deeper. His mind is often occupied with thoughts of salvation as standing in wonderful benefits or gifts which Christ has achieved for us, and which are ours in union to Him. The great comparison between Adam and Christ, suggested by the Apostle Paul (Rom. v.), is his point of departure. We ought to own, he says, a twofold *recapitulatio*. Adam was our head, holding on our behalf excellent gifts. What we lost in him we receive again—that and more—in Christ. So He became what we are, that we might become what He is. This thought runs into many illustrations. It constantly appears how important it was for Irenæus (as for Ignatius before him) to maintain the full reality of our Lord's human nature. And we see him brooding on the question *how* the interposition of Christ shall be conceived to avail to restore so victoriously the state of man. He is full of suggestions in which picturesque contrasts between Adam and Christ indicate how the latter undoes and repairs the fault of the former. Yet he hardly succeeds in giving connection to his thoughts, or bringing out a tangible theodicy of Redemption. Generally every circumstance, and every act of the life of Christ, has for him a redeeming force with reference to some aspect of the sin and shortcoming which it counterworks.[1] Naturally, the Incarnation and the Cross chiefly hold his mind. His doctrine of the incarnation will occupy us later. Irenæus felt sympathetically the place which the death of Christ occupies in the New Testament. "He gave His flesh for our flesh, and His soul for our souls." Since Christ is our Head, His death is in some sense our death: and it blotted out our debt. But how? More than one later theory as to this floats before us in the language of Irenæus. How far any of them can be fairly imputed to him as corresponding to his deliberate judgment, is a question which cannot be fairly answered without discussion, which is not possible here.

One theory, already referred to in connection with Origen, and which will meet us later, proceeded on the ground that men, by complying with Satan's temptation, became subject to his dominion. If from this dominion they had been rescued by sheer force, Satan could have maintained that the deliverance was unjust. The death of Christ then operated as a ransom, especially in so far as Satan, working his will on Christ by his instruments, put himself finally in the wrong, and was ousted from all claims. Baur ascribed this theory to Irenæus.[2] And Harnack has followed him

---

[1] *E.g.* the disobedience of Adam was disobedience *in the tree*, and the obedience of Christ was obedience *on the tree.*

[2] *Gesch. d. Versöhnung*, p. 31.

(relying on the same passages), so far as that Irenæus, according to him, at least recognises something in this direction which rests his mind. It is certain that Irenæus believed the human race, as one of the consequences of its transgression, to have fallen under Satan's dominion in some sense; and in saving men Christ delivers them from the power of the adversary. Also Christ does this, not βίᾳ, by violence, but in a way more worthy of God. All these are ideas suggested in Scripture, and generally received in antiquity. But, according to Irenæus, the power to produce this effect belongs to the whole incarnate actings of Christ, not merely to His death; and as far as appears, the redemption from the "apostasy," or from the kingdom of evil, proceeds by Christ's reversing all that is wrong in human history,—embodying for us and imparting to us a perfect status and a new life. So Satan's power falls of itself.

Irenæus speaks of the Lord's Supper as involving an offering on our part; but this offering consists in the elements which we bring and it is sanctified by the purity of the heart that offers. These elements, being blessed, cease to be common bread or common wine—they become eucharist, and the communicant partaking of them receives the body and blood of Christ. He does so in such a sense that his own body and blood are enriched thereby, and are elevated with a view to the resurrection life.[1]

In regard to the Old Testament, Irenæus represents the line of treatment which prevailed ever after. Barnabas seemed to hold that the Christian meanings drawn from the Old Testament allegorically, had been all along the one divinely intended sense. Irenæus distinguishes the Decalogue, as the natural and essential moral law, from the ceremonial; the latter is to be allegorically interpreted in the way usual in the Church; but yet the literal sense also was valid and obligatory before Christ came. It

---

[1] εὐχαριστία ἐκ δύο πραγμάτων συνεστηκυῖα, ἐπιγείου τε καὶ οὐρανίου, οὕτως καὶ τὰ σώματα ἡμῶν μεταλαμβάνοντα τῆς εὐχαριστίας, μηκέτι εἶναι φθαρτὰ τὴν ἐλπίδα τῆς εἰς αἰῶνας ἀναστάσεως ἔχοντα, iv. 18. 5, see also 3. 4.

served a necessary pædagogic purpose, placing men in a kind of bondage for a time; but now under the gospel we are set free. Thus both the unity of the Old Testament with the New, and also the difference, are emphasised.

Irenæus held decidedly to the literal fulfilment of the promises. He believed, therefore, in a state of things in which the risen saints should enjoy an earth of peace and gladness. In that state of things the ideal relation of the material world to man's nature should be realised, and so the order of creation should be justified. Beyond this he appears to admit the prospect of something ineffable. Eye hath not seen it.

To the same school as Irenæus, Hippolytus is reckoned. He, too, wrote in Greek, though his ministry was in or near Rome itself. Probably the Roman Church was passing, in his time, from the Greek stage of its existence to the Latin one; but in that case Hippolytus must have served the Greek section. He was probably more extensively learned than Irenæus, but hardly on a level with him in point of Christian sagacity and insight. His book against Heresies, which has acquired the rather misleading name of *Philosophoumena*, is on the whole the most important work we owe to him; and it reveals passages in his own career which have led to much curious discussion. Features of his theology will be referred to in connection with the discussions on the divine nature and the person of Christ. He represented in the West the learned inquisitiveness and the literary activity which Origen, his younger contemporary, exhibited in the East; but Hippolytus possessed neither the imaginative resource nor the systematising genius of Origen.

### 3. School of Africa

A third type is recognised in the writers who inaugurate the Latin Christian literature. This comes to light first on African soil, and its earliest representative is Tertullian. He was born probably before A.D. 160, became a Christian about A.D. 192, and was attracted to Montanism somewhere about the close of the century. He had become a presbyter, probably at Carthage, and he no doubt led the Montanist party in that city. He had received an excellent education, had studied law, and had read extensively in history, which he valued, and in philosophy, which as a Christian he distrusted. As a pagan he had shared in the ordinary life of Carthage; as a Christian he entered keenly into all Christian interests, resisting and resenting compromise and evasion. He may have died before 240. Some of his surviving writings were composed while he was still a member of the Catholic Church; others represent his later Montanistic position.[1]

Tertullian possessed the gift of vivid, pithy, often scornful phrase, and he set the example of a Christian style in the Latin tongue with triumphant energy, but with striking peculiarities.[2] No man of his age is so much alive; and no man so much as he carries the reader into the Christian life of the time;—often combative, often extreme, but always vigorous and suggestive. He combined in himself the Puritan and High Churchman, with even a touch of the Fifth Monarchy man thrown in. He was a married man, and one supposes might not be quite "easy to live with"; yet he might well be greatly esteemed and greatly loved. Besides those which are lost, more than thirty of his writings have come down to us. He knew Greek, and composed some tracts in that tongue; but to us he is known only through his Latin writing, which doubtless reveals him at his best.

Tertullian was acquainted with the work of Irenæus; and we sometimes find in him the same ideas, as it were advanced a stage. It was an orthodox commonplace to

---

[1] *Opera*, ed. F. Oehler, 3 vols., Lips. 1854, is the most useful edition: improved text (without notes) by Reifferscheid and Wissowa, in *Corpus Scriptor. Eccl. Latin.*, Vindol. 1890; Kaye, *Eccl. History, illustrated from the Works of Tertullian*, Cambr. 1829; Neander, *Antignosticus or Spirit of Tert.*, transl. by Ryland, Bohn, Lond. 1851.

[2] Contrast the style of Minucius Felix, not far from Tertullian's period, and, like him, a lawyer.

plead, as an argument against the wilder heretics, the consent as to the essential verities of Christianity expressed in the teaching of the greater and older Churches. We have met with this in Irenæus. But in the hands of Tertullian [1] it turns into a method of controversy with heretics by which you could deprive them of all right to be heard on the merits—could, in fact, shut the door in their face, and refuse to be troubled with them. For, as Tertullian virtually points out, it was all well to draw truth from the Scriptures, and especially to seek in the Scriptures, as a man had opportunity, fresh light and fresh impulse. But when a heretic came impugning any of the notorious verities, was a Catholic Christian to go to sea with him, as it were, in a fresh examination of Scripture on the point? Tertullian says, No. The Catholic might have limited acquaintance with Scripture, imperfect access to it, no right conception of methods of interpretation, might be liable to be bewildered with allegories and non-natural interpretations, and might be led into the most lamentable mistakes. His duty was to say,—" We, who live in the well-known faith, which has been continuous in the churches since the apostles' days, are the owners of the Bible; it belongs to us: you who are outsiders have no business with it; it is sacrilege for you to meddle with it. Therefore, we will simply pay not the least attention to a single word you say." There was much to be said for this attitude with reference to heretics who, like Valentinus, or Basilides, or Marcion, propounded as Christianity things unheard of till they came, unheard of especially in the old and large churches whose teaching was public and notorious. And Tertullian only means his principle to apply to the great articles, whose conspicuous place in Christian creeds was undeniable. In a wider application the grounds on which he argues will not hold; and, indeed, the debates which were to occupy the third century could not fairly be excluded by any arguments he adduces, as those might be which the Gnostics had raised in the second. But the principle was

[1] *De Præscriptione adversus hæreticos.*

immensely convenient; it could be made the bulwark of traditions, even when these had become far less clear and authoritative than those were in whose favour it was first pleaded. Every writer who appeals to the test advocated by Tertullian betrays the influence of the temptation to stretch it beyond the point which his own grounds will warrant. This is one of the lines on which the Catholic doctrine of the authority of the Church was destined to develop until it covered the whole heavens.

Tertullian, like Irenæus, distrusted philosophy, and, as we see, he urged the authority of tradition. Yet he was quite prepared to argue for Christianity as the religion which is intrinsically related to the reason of man. It is adapted to human nature and demanded by it. Hence the title of one of his treatises, *Testimonium Animæ Naturaliter Christianæ*. Tertullian therefore is a thinker. He had been trained in the Stoic philosophy, and his Christian thinking bears strong marks at various points of the bent his mind had received in that school. He refers with predilection to Seneca,—"Seneca, pæne noster."

Still Tertullian is the last man to idealise away his Christian beliefs. Rather he affirms them roundly, and is ready to materialise the objects of faith that he may conceive them energetically, and hold them firmly. Reality is for him associated with some sort of corporeity; at least he cannot speak of the real, so as to satisfy himself, without using language which implies as much.

Tertullian received and reproduced the ideas already before us (in connection with Irenæus) regarding the "recapitulation" of men, first in Adam and afterwards in Christ. But the second of these did not, apparently, greatly occupy his mind. The first did: he vigorously developed the conception of an inherited sinfulness—a *vitium originis* —which taints us all. In this connection he threw important thoughts and pithy suggestive phrases into the theology of the Western Church, and prepared the way for Augustine. His concrete way of conceiving things, and also his traducian views of the origin of human souls, contributed to deepen his impressions. It cannot be said that Tertullian put the doctrine of original sin into any very precise or final form. But he had a strong impression of the presence of it as a force operating ever since the Fall, and he contemplated all ordinary human *descent* as receiving into itself more or less of this influence, which is therefore a constant fact in human nature. Still a seed of goodness remains in men; infancy can be spoken of as innocent;[1] and the freedom of the will continues. On the other hand, as already stated, the influence of Christ's headship of men hardly occupied the mind of Tertullian as it did that of Irenæus. Yet one general result of Christ's coming and of our faith in Him is strongly affirmed. This is grace: a force which Tertullian does not define, but it is stronger than nature. It is emancipating; it gives play to man's free-will, too much put to disadvantage before, and reinforces it in its efforts towards attaining eternal life. Grace is, for Tertullian, a kind of inspiration; and he often speaks as if he conceived it under physical or material forms.

It has been remarked, and truly, that with Tertullian grace is opposed to nature, but not to merits. Indeed, he conceives life and salvation to be the result of merit with truly mercantile strictness; grace operates by potentiating the free-will of men, so that it becomes able to merit, if it chooses. Hence, too, the energy with which he inculcates those forms of Christian life and work that tell, as he believes, with greatest force in this line. Just so he regards the sins of believers after baptism (those that are remediable) as put away by voluntary endurances and sacrifices. In this connection he develops a doctrine of satisfaction, and is the first to use that word in Christian theology. With him it is a process of paying for our sins by our self-denial and humiliation.

Doubtless the controversy with the Gnostics had some effect in disposing Tertullian, as it did Irenæus, to assert solicitously the freedom of the will, as an actual practical

---

[1] *De Baptismo*, c. 18. But the innocence here intended is not necessarily absolute.

fact in all states of men. But the tendency of Christianity itself to deepen the sense of moral responsibility also acted here. Neither of them means to assert grace in any sense that would interfere with this freedom. At the same time, neither of them can be said to have thought deeply on the conditions of freedom, or on the sense in which bondage arises under the influence of sin.

Tertullian, as we have seen, could appreciate the congruity of Christianity to the essential nature of man; he could also appreciate the importance of Christlike dispositions. But, in general, the habit of his mind disposed him to think of Christianity in statutory forms. "Do this and live" was the law which came naturally to his lips. A faith and a life are inculcated, and our business (under Christian aids) is obedience, which, if rendered, becomes merit. Perhaps he felt personally safest when he presented to himself this aspect of things, and bowed his rugged self to this yoke. Certainly, though he owned a place for grace, the Pauline wealth and tenderness associated with that theme are strange to his thinking. Yet he cherishes a sense of the greatness of Christianity which goes beyond his schemes of thought; and he is intent on making earnest work of Christian religion, on realising it as something great and decisive.

Tertullian, finally, is the most human of the Fathers, keen, witty, sarcastic, argumentative, morally intense, intellectually extreme, capable of love and wrath and scorn, and, in the midst of his strong assertions and high moral imperatives, a lowly man, conscious of his own sin and ashamed.[1] His must have been a notable mass of Christian manhood; and the vitality of his writings is extraordinary.[2]

In the same African province Cyprian[3] arose a genera-

[1] *De Patientia*, i.; *De Penitentia*, 12; etc.
[2] Some expressions are constantly quoted—such as *adv. Praxean*, 1: "Prophetiam expulit et hæresim intulit: paracletum fugavit et patrem crucifixit." But a large anthology could be collected, *e.g.* "faciunt et vespæ favos, faciunt ecclesias et Marcionistæ."
[3] *Opera*, Is. Fell, Oxon. 1682, with Pearson's *Annales*, S. Baluzius, Paris, 1726, both fol.; D. J. H. Goldhorn, Lips. 1838–39, 8vo; best text, Härtel,

tion later. He, too, came over to Christianity after he had reached manhood. He found inspiration and resource in the writings of Tertullian, but presented in his own person a very distinct type. The rather turbid fervour of Tertullian is replaced in him by dignity, sagacity, and leadership. We are told that before his conversion he had practised oratory and had taught literature. Possibly his aim had been to make way on those lines to promotion in the official hierarchy of the empire. At all events he was a man of cultivation and of independent means, intellectually and morally distinguished, sure of himself and prompt to guide others. He combined marked gentleness of manner with firmness in essentials. Such a man, called to be bishop of the church of Carthage, and fully alive to the obligations and the possibilities of his office, could not but be a great churchman.

First of all, however, he was a Christian; and he carried into his Christianity a fine thoroughness and singleness of heart. Before his conversion his mind had been exercised about the lofty standard of purity and well-doing which Christianity proposes; and at that stage he judged the moral change it called for so difficult as to be impossible. But when, persuaded at last,[1] he came to baptism, accepting and claiming the life of the new kingdom, then doubts vanished, light broke in, what had been impossible became practical, that in him which had served sin became subject to God; and he could appeal to those who knew him as to the decisive character of the change. This was God's doing, as he tells us, "it is of God, of God I repeat, all our life, all our strength, the vigour of the present, the hope for the future." Believing that thorough Christianity implied self-denial as to wealth and ease, he resolved to remain unmarried; and he sold his property that he might distribute the proceeds among the poor.[2]

---

3 vols., Vindob. 1867. Life by Pontius the deacon in 3rd vol. of Härtel; Archbishop Benson, *Life and Times*, Lond. 1898.

[1] The presbyter Cæcilianus was the chief agent in his conversion. As to what follows, *vid. ad Don.* 5.

[2] Considering the period and the literary training of Cyprian, he might

He early attracted the notice and confidence of the Carthaginian church, almost immediately became a presbyter, discharged his duties with fervour and efficiency, and in A.D. 248, while his baptism was still comparatively recent, was elected bishop. Older presbyters might naturally resent so rapid promotion of a neophyte, but the church would have it so. This personal element had its share in creating some of the troubles he afterwards encountered.

The chief debates in which he was involved were those regarding the proper treatment of the lapsed, and the re-baptism of heretics. In the second year of Cyprian's episcopate the Decian persecution began. The Church had enjoyed comparative tranquillity for thirty years, and the suddenness as well as the severity of the blow told heavily. Cyprian speaks of his church as devastated by the rush of defection which set in. It involved even a number of his presbyters. But very many of those who stretched their consciences to comply with pagan rites, in order to avert persecution, had no wish to be finally separated from Christianity. What was to be done about these "lapsed"?

It was not reckoned unfaithful in Christians to avoid persecution by withdrawing from their usual dwelling-places to live where they were less known.[1] Rather, such persons, especially if the withdrawal involved serious loss and discomfort, were regarded as, in their degree, confessors. The lapsed were those who, in some way, denied their faith, generally by some act of conformity to paganism.[2] All these—*sacrificati, thurificati, acta facientes, libellatici*—were held to have denied their Lord, and by that sin they had

have been in danger of cultivating the far-fetched and tawdry style affected by the later rhetoricians. There is one passage (*Ad Don.* 1) in which one seems to see a trace of that kind of fine writing. But if so, Christianity, fixing his mind on great interests, came to the rescue. His style, in general, is notably clear, manly, and effective.

[1] An extreme party condemned this course, but not Cyprian, nor the Church generally.

[2] See *ante*, p. 143, note 2.

fallen from their position as members of His Church. These people were numerous, some of them no doubt were influential, not a few were near relations of persons who still held their position in the church, and they pressed to be restored.

The ground taken by the bishop contemplated eventual restoration as the rule; but not hurriedly, nor as a matter of course, nor in the heat and disorder of the persecution. Cyprian succeeded in procuring the approbation of neighbouring bishops for this policy. Moreover, the same question having arisen at Rome, Cyprian succeeded in securing the adherence of the authorities of that church also for the policy which he approved.

Both at Carthage and at Rome the contention on this subject led to schism, a lax party separating at Carthage, an ultra-rigorous one at Rome. Both organised as independent churches; but the schism at Carthage was shortlived. The Roman separatists, headed by Novatian, became a sect known in the West for the most part as Novatianists, in the East more commonly as καθαροί, puritans, and it continued to exist for centuries. Some details of these disputes will meet us elsewhere. Certain effects of them may be adverted to now.

The assertion of the right to separate, and to carry on church life on separate lines, raised questions that were new in some respects. Gnosticism had been got rid of by an appeal to the consent of the churches as to the known fundamentals of their faith. Montanists had been more kindly regarded by many catholic Christians; but their assertion of a new revelation led to consequences so unmanageable, that in the end of the day they were practically treated, by general consent, as having placed themselves outside of the true Church. Now, however, societies were starting in which the common faith was retained, and which based any peculiarities of practice upon traditions that had a plausible claim to authenticity. They claimed that under constraint of conscience they were exercising a right, or performing a duty, pertaining to orthodox Christians; and they carried with them, as they held, the life and powers, the character and the functions, of churches of Christ. If this claim was valid, cases of the kind would multiply, and the influence of the great Church, as representing or embodying Christianity, was likely to be impaired. Cyprian was exactly the man to see the danger; and he met it by asserting that such societies were no part of the Church, and calling on catholic Christians to treat all claims, proceedings, and administrations on the part of separatists as simply null and void. Men who separated were as truly outside of Christianity as the heretic or the apostate.

This is the theme of the tract, *De Catholicæ Ecclesiæ Unitate*, which was written in 251. It is the next great step in succession to Tertullian's *De Præscriptione* in the way of building up the fabric of church power. It is short (about twenty pages), trenchant, and peremptory. God is one,—Christ is one,—He appointed His Church to be one. That unity is first embodied in the apostles, then in the bishops, who are in communion with one another all over the world. To break loose from the authentic bishops (assuming them to be orthodox and recognised), is to cut oneself off from Christianity and from salvation, for it is to cut oneself off from the Church. We lose salvation by schism as well as by heresy. He has not God for his father who has not the Church for his mother. All the topics are here—the ark, the dove, the spouse who is the only one of her mother, "Thou art Peter," the ray, the fountain, the unity of the Trinity, Korah and his company—which have found their place in confirmation sermons century after century. Hence those who claim to be bishops and priests in the separated societies can do "nothing": their administrations are vain, and their sacrifices are no sacrifices; their martyrdom when they suffer is no martyrdom. They may be able to prophesy and cast out evil spirits, but Christ answers that in Matt. vii. 22. Nothing can be more clear, thorough, and relentless. The unity of God, of Christ, of truth, of love, is to be manifest in the Church. But the Church must chiefly hold together through its bishops, who are, besides, the most representative men in all the churches. Therefore the unity is the unity of the faithful with the (united) episcopate.[1] It so happens that Cyprian was right in the main both in principle and in spirit against the dissidents at Carthage. But whether the unity he postulates is the kind of unity which Christ chiefly desires to see in His Church, and whether variation from it entails necessarily the consequences which Cyprian denounces, is quite another question. The point on which there can be no question is the ecclesiastical efficiency of the principle laid down. Also it is simple, and saves a world of discussion. Possess men's minds with the conviction that separation from the official framework of the Church is equivalent to renunciation of Christ and of His benefits, and you erect the strongest possible defence against schism. Unfortunately, while Cyprian and his followers are eloquent about the lack of love on the part of the separatists, they have not seen that the passions of scorn and hate are the effective forces in the system by which they themselves propose to fortify the unity.

The episcopate occupies a decisive place as the criterion of unity on Cyprian's principle. Yet Cyprian does not suppose that the bishop can claim despotic power. In regard to discipline, for example, he contemplates the faithful members of the flock, as well as the inferior clergy, joining in examining the cases, and the decisions are to be such as satisfy them. But he evidently contemplates the general principles on which discipline is to proceed as proper to be episcopally fixed. Therefore he strengthened his position by assembling councils of the bishops, as far as they could be got together. When they approved the method which Cyprian proposed, that method could then be insisted on,

---

[1] The unity of the Church is reflected and guaranteed in the unity of the episcopate; but Cyprian does not lay stress on orders strictly so called. He does lay stress on a bishop being duly elected and settled in his church with the proper consents of people, clergy, and neighbouring bishops, but he does not test apostolic succession more precisely. And the fact of a schismatic congregation having procured the presence of authentic bishops to ordain ministers for them would not better their case in his eyes.

at Carthage or anywhere else, as having the sanction of the Church. This is one of the ways in which the episcopate acquired the exceptional strength needed, if they were to occupy the decisive place ascribed to them by Cyprian's theory. Bishops meet in council and agree about general rules; then the flock may have a considerable voice in the application of them, under the presidency of their own bishop.

Very soon another question arose which threatened the episcopal unity on which, according to Cyprian, so much depended. It was that concerning the rebaptizing of heretics. This dispute brought Cyprian into collision with Stephen of Rome; but it was not pushed to an issue at this time.[1]

Cyprian shared the feeling that the world was in its decaying age, that the Lord's return to judgment was not far off, and that meanwhile persecutions were the natural indications that Antichrist might soon be revealed. Yet, remarkably enough, for practical purposes he counts upon the existing persecution ending, and the Church having peace to put her affairs again in order. This seems to indicate that Christianity was so rooting itself in the life of society, and had become so visibly a part of the existing world, that persecution was felt to be anomalous and unreasonable; it was a line of action which would have to be given up by practical statesmen.

Meanwhile, under Valerian, persecution continued on an extensive scale. In the Decian persecution Cyprian had withdrawn into concealment, judging it his duty, as far as he could, to prolong his services to his church at a critical time. His opponents in Carthage at that time could represent his conduct in this respect as pusillanimous; but Cyprian was not misunderstood by the mass of his flock, and he was able from his retirement to give the requisite guidance. Under Valerian he seems to have decided that reasons no longer existed for avoiding arrest, although probably he could have done so with success. It would have been convenient for the procurator of the province, at that

[1] See below, Chap. XV.

time an invalid, to try him at Utica; but Cyprian chose to be tried at Carthage, and he brought that to pass. The last letter in the collection of his epistles runs thus,—

"Cyprian to the presbyters, deacons, and the whole people,—

"Having received information, brethren most beloved, that warrants had been issued for my removal to Utica, I was advised by my friends to retire for a time from my gardens;[1] and I agreed to do so for a reason which I judged sufficient:—it is fitting, namely, for a bishop to confess his Lord in the city in which he presides over the Lord's Church, that so His whole people may be glorified by the bishop's confession in their presence. For a bishop, who is called to confess his faith, speaks in that moment under a divine afflatus, and as the mouthpiece of all. Now then the honour of our church, our glorious church of Carthage, will suffer loss, if at Utica I should make my confession and receive sentence, and thence depart as a martyr to my Lord;—therefore it is my part, on your behalf and my own, to pray continually, making all possible supplications, that among you I may make my confession, suffer and depart. I am waiting therefore in this retired hiding-place for the return of the proconsul to Carthage, and then I shall hear from him what the emperors have ordered with respect to Christian laymen and bishops, and will say what the Lord in that hour will give me to speak.

"Ye meanwhile, beloved, according to the rule which at all times I have delivered to you from the Lord's words, and according to what you have often heard me preach, keep peace and quietness; do not let any of you create disturbance for the brethren, nor offer yourselves ultroneously to the Gentiles. For, when a man is apprehended and delivered up, then he ought to speak, inasmuch as God dwelling in us speaks in that hour; and He desires us rather to confess than to profess. What else it is suitable

[1] A pleasant residence, inherited apparently. Cyprian had sold it at the time of his conversion, but friends repurchased it for his use.

for us to attend to, before the proconsul passes sentence on me as a confessor of the name of God, we shall arrange in personal conference, with the Lord's guidance. My beloved brethren, may the Lord Jesus deign to preserve you steadfast in His Church."

No opportunity occurred for any such remarkable testimony as Cyprian had thought it might be given to him to utter. He was perfectly firm and dignified, answering the judge's questions with Roman brevity. The proconsul apparently thought it his duty to the emperor to speak severely to Cyprian as the ringleader of a wicked sect, whose death might be a warning to the rest. But, on the whole, the martyr seems to have been treated with the consideration due to a remarkable personality. He received sentence with the response, "Thanks be to God," and died by the sword A.D. 261. The proconsul, it was remarked, pronounced sentence with difficulty, and he died a few days after.

## CHAPTER XI

### Christ and God

EARLY Christian thinking included various elements in which Jews and Gentiles could claim their part. But always, whether in the foreground or the background, is the conviction about Christ, "We know that the Son of God has come, and hath given us an understanding that we might know Him that is true; and we are in Him that is true, even in His Son Jesus Christ: this is the true God and everlasting life." This great belief transformed and lifted everything; it gave new significance to every old thought which it happened to appropriate.

Hence the subject destined most profoundly to exercise the Christian mind was the question about Christ. What is, essentially and adequately, the Christian way of thinking in regard to Christ? In regard to the various lines of investigation that might be pursued under this head, a modern student may ask whether the Church adequately pursued them all, or, if one had to be selected, chose wisely that which she preferred. That, however, is a question which must not be hastily answered. In the early Church much that concerned Christ certainly was left to the inartificial treatment of devout sentiment and homiletical meditation. The line of inquiry on which Christian minds gradually settled was that which concerned the nature of Christ as related to His Father, and also as related to man or to human conditions. For the questions here arising were those on which it was felt needful to be prepared with "Yes" or "No," if clear conceptions were to be formed of the meaning of Christ's appearance, the kind of benefit He brought, and the attitude which the Christian mind should take towards Him. It was not unnatural that in thinking out the world of personalities and facts and forces to which a Christian belongs, a leading question should seem to be *where*, in that world, Christ should find His place.

It is to be observed, however, that specific influences outside of the Church conspired to detain men's minds upon the same question. Reference has been made to the activity of non-Christian thought. But that thought laboured much upon the problem of the unity of the world,—in particular, how the world we know, the world of decay and change, should be conceived to derive from an immutable and immaterial source; and how the ideal elements, the goodness and beauty which mind discerns, ally themselves to that which is not mental but material. Theories had been struck out, and phraseology had been elaborated, of which use could be made in explaining Christian thoughts about Christ. This experiment, no doubt, had its dangers. The explanation offered in the light of these materials might expound the faith or might betray it. Yet the effort could not be escaped. Certain ideas were in the minds of men; and ideas must be compared if men wish to come to an understanding with one another.

Meanwhile among the Christians themselves different ideas were found, and it had not yet become clear how far these could coexist permanently in the same Christian fellowship. Many Jews had expected the Messiah in the character of a remarkable or highly favoured man. There were Jewish Christians who had accepted Jesus as such a Messiah;[1] and from time to time afterwards, as we shall

---

[1] Justin Martyr, *Dial. c. Tryph.* 47. These received the name of Ebionites, the poor—perhaps originally a name of humility, which became a name of contempt. Whether the Nazarenes or Christians of the circumcision, who maintained a church fellowship apart from that of Gentile Christians, were also Ebionites in the sense of rejecting the divinity of Christ and repudiating the Apostle Paul, is a question which has been much discussed. The result seems to be that while some of the Judaising Christians held higher views of our Lord's person and of the authority of Paul, and others held lower, the

find, teachers appear, not apparently Jewish, who put forward a view radically the same, but varied in detail. On the other hand, there were Docetists who regarded human nature, at least in its material elements, as impure, and unfit to be assumed by the Saviour; they held, therefore, that our Lord's body was apparent only. This was a phase of Gnosticism, or, at least, Gnosticism absorbed it. Docetism soon died out. Various theories owned the reality of the Lord's body, but conceived it to be animated not by a human soul but by some spiritual being from a higher sphere. Besides, those who asserted with great emphasis the divine nature of Christ, sometimes attenuated the significance of the human nature, while recognising it in terms.

These varieties existed, and some of them may have existed more widely than can now be established by proof. Yet, after all, the broad impression, to start with, is that for the general Christian mind Christ was both divine and human. Everything about Him suggested it. On the one hand, He was born of a woman, grew to manhood in a human family, companied with men, suffered and died. On the other hand, He revealed the Father, He achieved redemption, He was the object of Christian trust and worship, He presided over the destiny of men, He was to be their judge. He stood before the Christian mind, unique, the meeting-place of God and man. In such a personage it was not difficult to own both a human presence and the divine. But when men came to explanations they had to deal with the problems set for them, first, by the great faith of the divine unity, and, second, by the unity of Christ Himself; and the solutions were apt to be biassed by the element which took the lead. One may believe that Christ is divine and also at the same time human, or that He is human and also at the same time divine. The positions

---

proportion of adherents of the two views varied at different times; and that the application of the term Nazarene to denote peculiarly a more orthodox and, as regards the Gentiles, a more friendly section, distinct from the Ebionites, cannot be proved for the second and third century, though we meet with it in the fourth. Epiph. *Hær.* 30.

are equivalent, and are both true from the point of view of Church orthodoxy. But different tendencies can attach themselves to the one and to the other. The first suggests that thought should begin with our Lord's pre-existence in the higher or highest nature, and proceed to the assumption of the human. The other does not exclude this view; but to some minds it has rather suggested ideas of human fidelity in goodness, attaining at last a certain deification. The first was decidedly the line of thought which prevailed in the Church, and those who took it believed themselves to be followers of the Apostles Paul and John, and the writer to the Hebrews. The second took shape in theories which contemplated human nature in the man Jesus as responding to happy influences from above, until exceptional attainment is rewarded and crowned by divine dignity and dominion.

The thread of which the Christian thinking chiefly availed itself for guidance amid competing alternatives was that indicated by λόγος, the Word or Reason. The νοῦς and the Ideas of Plato, and still more the λόγος or λόγοι of the Stoics, had fixed attention on a divine element, a presence in the world, which makes the creation rational, and which makes man, at least, a reasoning creature. More lately, Philo had concentrated attention on this thought, because he made the Logos the centre of the explanations and combinations by means of which he philosophised the Hebrew Scriptures. The fact itself (the unity, persistency, and energy of the rational principle which pervades the world) was certain, whatever name men called it by; but the name, and the thinking which had gathered about it, had concentrated attention on the thing. On the one hand, this is true of God, that He yields a rational energy which gives being and meaning to the world; on the other hand, it is true of the world, that amid all its variety and its instability, it is pervaded by this constant element or influence, purer and higher than itself. The world embodies the ideal. It was felt then by Christians to be a vivid and helpful thing to say to the educated thought of the time,

"Christ is the Logos, manifesting His personality, and coming among us in the flesh, that He may effectually heal and save us." But the expression was not only vivid, it was authorised; it had been sanctioned in this sense by the Apostle John in the prologue of his Gospel.[1]

But while the discussions of the higher nature of our Lord were destined to follow by preference the trains of thought which this word suggests, it must not be imagined that the main articles of the Church's faith concerning Christ hang solely on this phrase. The divinity of Christ, and His special concern in originating and sustaining creation, are involved in utterances of His own, and are taught by Paul and the writer to the Hebrews, as well as by John. And so the writers who precede Justin, such as Clement and Ignatius, perhaps also Hermas (whose teaching, however, is peculiar), have no difficulty in expressing their faith without the use of the Logos line of speech. The round assertions of Ignatius in particular are very striking.[2]

The train of ideas which the Logos suggested had an obvious interest and value for the Apologists. It enabled

---

[1] No doubt it is possible to suggest a different account of the matter. It can be said that a Christian school early in the second century, thinking out the problems about Christ, found courage to make this bold advance on Philo, and to assert Christ to have been the Logos personal and incarnate. Then we may suppose Justin Martyr to have taken up the theory either under the influence or apart from the influence of the Johannine Gospel. That Gospel itself, originating, on this view of things, about the same time, may be thought to grow, as far as this element is concerned, out of the same sources. But apart from detailed critical arguments, all this is improbable. It is incongruous to suppose that Justin Martyr could affirm the Logos doctrine so unhesitatingly as he does, unless he felt that he had behind him conclusive Christian authority. And the only authority, but then an adequate one, was the wonderfully impressive assertion of the same thing in the Gospel which bore the name of the beloved disciple. Justin and the rest speculate with courage about the Logos, because Logos is for them an authentic and accredited truth of Christianity, which demands to be explained and understood.

[2] *Eph.* 7. "One only physician of flesh and of spirit, generate and regenerate, God in man, true life in death, Son of Mary and Son of God, first passible and then impassible." On the last clause, see note in Lightfoot.

*Pol.* 3. "Await Him who is above every reason, the Eternal, the Invisible, who became visible for our sake, the impalpable, the impassible, who suffered for our sake, who endured in all ways for our sake."

them at once to define the Christian conception of Christ in relation to an immense mass of pre-Christian thought, just because the word Logos belonged to that region of thought, and had been borrowed from it. And as Christian faith must understand itself not only by brooding on itself, but by comparison and contrast with the thinking of the world in which Christianity lives, this aspect of it may well be of permanent value. Yet for the domestic interests of the faith, the use of this word is not indispensable. The Church has framed all her great creeds without employing it.[1]

The Logos doctrine brings out the point in which Christ exceeds all philosophies, and all philosophies stop short of Christ. Philosophy aims at the immanent timeless Ideal, ever equal to itself. But Christianity asserts an essential historical crisis, making all new—the Word was made flesh.

Difficulties which beset this line of thought become plain enough in the case of its earliest representative, Justin Martyr, as well as in most of his successors. In the most important respects Justin affirms what the prevailing faith of the Church has affirmed ever since. The Logos belongs to the sphere of the creating nature, not of the created. He is identified with the divine reason or wisdom, and that in such a sense that to Him is ascribed not merely a seed of it, or a likeness of it, but the whole, the fulness of it. Yet this is not to be taken so that the Logos is merely a power or attribute of the Father; He is, on the contrary, "something numerically distinct";[2] in some sense or other there is plurality. The physical image which Justin prefers to use in order to illustrate the relation of this second to the first, is that of a flame which lights up another flame; the second is of the first, it has the nature of the first inscrutably communicated to it, but it subsists as something distinct.

[1] It is introduced in the Creed of Chalcedon, 451, but even there holds no important or decisive place.
[2] Ἀριθμῷ ἕτερον τι.

Now, as Justin contemplates the Logos as the divine wisdom, so far as that can be recognised in creation or providence or revelation, he accepts ideas which may be roughly represented by saying that God in His prime perfection is above all thought and all contact with the creatures, best conceived by contrasting Him with all that we see or know in nature and history; and this is the Father; while the Logos is God as He condescends to plan and care for a world of creatures, and at last appears on earth for their salvation. In this way the contrast between the Father and the Logos becomes emphatic. While the Father recedes into regions which transcend thought, the Logos seems to be the first step down towards creatures, and exists, as it were, for the sake of creatures and with a view to them. And this impression is deepened by another element in Justin's scheme. He identifies the Word with the unbeginning wisdom of the Father. But he appears to teach that the Word was not with the Father always, as $ἀριθμῷ$ $ἕτερόν τι$. Primarily existing only as the wisdom of the Father, that is, as an attribute, He was evoked into personal subsistence with a view to the creation of the world,— and in this sense *He* had a beginning, though the divine wisdom as such had none; and He owes His beginning to the $δύναμις$ and $βουλή$, might and counsel, of the Father. These were modes of view offering points of attachment with which, as thought developed, lower views of the Logos might connect themselves. But it is to be remembered always that Justin himself unequivocally affirmed the complete divinity of the higher nature of Christ, and in particular that the Father begat Him $ἐξ ἑαυτοῦ$, out of Himself, not, as the creatures, out of nothing, $ἐξ οὐκ ὄντων$. He adjusts his scheme by accepting the incongruous thought that a personality in Godhead emerges; it is an event which takes place with a view to the other event of creation. But this incongruity (which lay near at hand, since the Word is "of God") must not lead us to suppose that Justin hesitated in his main thought. For him the Logos belongs to the sphere of the Creator, not to that of the creature.[1]  So much has been said of Justin, because the scheme which he exhibits is upon the whole that of a school of early writers.  Something distinctive can be ascribed to each of them,—to Athenagoras, Theophilus of Antioch, Clement of Alexandria, even Hippolytus.  But these are shades of thought and language which belong to the special history.  These writers all are busy with the problem which occupied Justin.  They all, like him, avail themselves of creation as the function by which the Logos is identified; this aspect of things controls their thinking; and hence the eternity which they ascribe to the divine wisdom does not for them attach to the Logos as a divine personality.  Some of them attenuate the personality of the Logos.  Some emphasise His subordination to the Father; but the general outlook is the same.  They all tend more or less to seclude the Father as such from contact with creation or creatures, and they sometimes go far to identify the Logos with the κόσμος νοητός of Greek philosophy.

The extreme to which language can go, in this direction, is already indicated by Justin when he speaks of Christ, as once or twice he does, as a second God.[2]

[1] The scheme of Philo is modified in Justin's thought by two forces.  One is the personality of Christ; therefore, the Logos must be personal, and as person distinct from the Father; the other is the Old Testament view of creation as beginning; therefore the Logos finds His function beginning, and *as a person* then Himself begins.

[2] The effort of Bishop Bull to efface the variations from Nicene orthodoxy on the part of those earlier Fathers fails, because he interprets their language by distinctions which cannot be shown to have been present to their minds.

To conceive a Divine Person originating as an event with a view to something else; and, again, to assert His Divinity and yet regard Him as a preparatory approach to creation; were ideas which might hover in the Church's mind for a time, but which were sure eventually to create a crisis for a number of persons.  When that crisis came men might emerge from it in one of two ways.  On one side they might say, "We cannot accept such internal changes in Godhead,—yet we abide by the faith that Christ is God,—only, not as a distinct person.  He embodies not a distinct person, but a distinct mode of the Divine activity *ad extra.*"  And we can imagine such a person to say to Justin Martyr: "You yourself identify Him who appeared as Jesus Christ with the eternal reason and wisdom of the Father.  But the eternal reason is not another *person* with the Father; it is the Father Himself contemplated in one aspect.  And why speak of this reason or wisdom being evolved at some

Irenæus on this, as on other subjects, keeps free from extremes, and represents the main current of the Church's thinking. He freely employs the conception of the Logos (rendered both as *verbum* and *mens*) in explaining the Christian view of Christ. He therefore recognises the relation of Christ to creation. But he intimates that this does not exhaust the significance of the Logos;[1] also, the question as to the beginning of the personal Logos is averted by declining to ascribe a beginning to the process of His forthcoming.[2] In these points Irenæus anticipates the positions permanently occupied by the orthodox Church, a remark which holds also of his way of conceiving the incarnation. Naturally he has much in common with other

crisis into personality? Is it not enough to say that both in the creation of the world, and also in the person of the Redeemer, God in a certain mode of divine manifestation is set before us to contemplate? So we hold the one God and the Divine Incarnation." This was the view represented in various forms by Patripassians, Sabellians, and, perhaps, by some forms of dynamical Monarchianism. On the other side men might say: "We also can admit no such intrinsic changes in God; but we cannot shut our eyes to the fact that Christ is not the Father; He is one who is of and from the Father. The only reasonable course, therefore, is to admit that He is not truly within the sphere of Godhead. However great, since He is of the Father and sent by the Father, He is not the Father, and therefore He is not that one God. He can only be a wonderful effect of God's power." And such a person might say to Justin: "Do not you yourself speak of Him as begotten with a view to creation? Surely that assigns to Him a beginning, and a position limited to time and to created things. Surely He was not before He was begotten. You say He pre-existed as the Father's eternal wisdom. But surely the wisdom was not a distinct person; for then there had been no need of begetting: but if there was a begetting, *He* was not before He was begotten; and when He was, He could not be of the Father's essence, but ἐξ οὐκ ὄντων. You cannot reasonably mean more than this,—that with a view to creation there was summoned into existence one so stamped with the likeness and filled with the wisdom of God, that He is eminently His Son, and in relation to all the works committed to Him He is the manifested Wisdom of God." This was Arianism. The one way of it sacrificed the personality, the other the Divinity. Each might attach itself to one side of Justin's thinking. He meanwhile was neither a Sabellian nor an Arian, but was trying to hold the divine personality of the Word considered as of and from the Father.

[1] iv. 14. 1. Before Adam, before the creation, He glorified the Father, and was by the Father glorified.

[2] He has no beginning of being brought forth. Cited by Dorner, i. 474; see also Iren. ii. 13. 8.

writers of his age; but his distinction is that in discoursing on these arduous topics he never really sacrifices either the personality on the one hand, or the essential Deity of the Son on the other.

Tertullian, a richer but a less tranquil thinker, does not follow Irenæus here. He takes his place in the line of thinkers who followed Justin, but with peculiarities of his own. It should be remarked, however, that at the time that his writings appeared in the West, and those of Origen in the East, a powerful reaction against the prevailing teaching had begun to show itself, and the vigorous logic of Tertullian is animated by the sense of conflict. This reaction will be described presently, but it is more convenient to postpone notice of it till the teaching of Tertullian and of Origen has been reported.

Tertullian, like others, explains the relation of the Word to the Father by postulating an emergence—a coming forth into subsistence—of a divine Personality. This takes place with a view to the creation of the world, and also with a view to its redemption. But according to Tertullian three stages are to be distinguished in the development of the Logos. There is, first, an eternal quality or capacity in God, which is, as it were, the preparation for a second Person. Second, there is a forthcoming to create, to constitute the universe. This is the generation of the Son; but the personality is not yet so distinct or full as it might be. Thirdly, there is the incarnation. In this the full personal manifestation takes being: the hypostasis, if we may say so, is completely extricated. In this connection Tertullian could, to use Bull's phrase, "Dare to say that there was a time when the Son of God was not." For he applies the word "son" to denote the Logos, as completely distinguished and hypostatised. This took place when Godhead came forth into manifestation. Then was the generation *of the Son*; but before then the Word or Wisdom was; which in a sense is identical with the Son, but was not yet the Son, because not yet subsisting as a personality. For Tertullian, therefore, the Logos is no creature; He is truly and wholly divine: and the eventual distinctness of His personality is carefully secured, which for Tertullian was an important matter.[1]

Tertullian unquestionably maintained the true divinity of the Logos. Yet as He takes subsistence by a change in Godhead, and as His personality at least is essentially implicated in creation, the question was sure to be pressed whether some Monarchian theory were not more reasonable.

Tertullian's theories are crude, drawn in strong lines, and modelled on material analogies. Origen draws out the Logos doctrine into a speculation in which the transitions are gentle, provisional, and fleeting, and every element slides into the next without a jar. The scope of Origen's theological system is sketched, so far, in an earlier chapter,[2] and we shall avoid repetition. But his theory of the Logos occupies a specially important place in the history on several accounts. In reference to its orthodoxy as compared with the Nicene standard, it has been bitterly attacked and keenly defended. And it certainly exerted great influence for a time. It disposed men to affirm the distinct personality of the Logos, in connection with a certain subordination; but what that subordination really meant or really implied might be doubted. In some ways faith in the divine and uncreated nature of the Son of God was strengthened; for the Word of God, who was also the Son of God, appeared in Origen's teaching as eternally begotten of the Father, as the coeternal progeny of that eternal mind. This conviction was retained by many who dropped as an eccentricity Origen's

---

[1] The theological grounds on which Tertullian argued are not for this place; but it is worth observing that his three stages represent a natural order of impressions. It was accepted teaching that in thinking of the Logos we begin with the eternal divine wisdom; but antecedent to the existence of creatures there may seem to be nothing to suggest that this wisdom is personal. It is a phase of the divine existence. When an ordered universe comes in sight with its tokens of pervading mind, something seems to have separated itself for our contemplation, but it seems hardly yet to have concentrated itself into personality: it is not quite a person,—rather a presence and a potency. Still, as it originates creature existence and sustains it, it must be personal so far. But when Jesus Christ comes before us, in whom all treasures of wisdom are hid, now personality is rounded and complete.

[2] *Ante*, Chap. X.

speculation as to creation also having no beginning. On the other hand, the Logos, while sometimes spoken of as possessing the fulness of Godhead, so that all divine attributes are His, seems at other times to be contrasted with the Father, in Origen's thinking, in ways that suggest a lower nature with lower qualities and significant limitations. For us, indeed, looking upwards, Origen seems to say, Christ comes no way short of the Father's glory; but in His own knowledge and in the Father's that is far from being simply so. At the same time, one remembers that for Origen, limitation, in this direction or that, is not inconsistent with true Deity; indeed, the Father Himself, in Origen's view, has His limitations. On the whole, Origen was felt to affirm the divine peculiarity of the Logos; and yet not without some qualification. For in some minds the idea of the Logos fluctuated between distinct personality and impersonal influence or agency; in others it fluctuated between true divinity and a sublime form of creaturehood; and Origen, with his skill in suggesting connections, might seem now to reach out a hand in the one direction and now in the other. But on the whole he was understood to assert the true divinity, if you make room for the possibility of forms of divine existence that exist with limitations. One line drawn by Origen is, perhaps, decisive as to his intention at least. He holds the divine nature to be immutably good, while the creatures are essentially mutable. Now this immutable goodness which, though free, is inaccessible to any taint of evil, is ascribed by Origen to the Son and to the Spirit, as well as to the Father.

Tertullian and Origen, writing each in the third century, both refer to uneasiness existing in Christian minds with reference to the line of explanation which in various forms has been before us; and this uneasiness showed itself in persons whom they did not regard as heretically disposed.[1] This mood must have existed, more

---

[1] Origen tells us of some who "when they heard the divinity of Christ dwelt upon were troubled, though they desired to be religious, fearing that it was the introduction of two gods." And Tertullian reports, "Those who are

or less, much earlier than these writers. The remark of Justin Martyr as to some in his time who held lower views of Christ has been quoted.[1] Already in the second century distinct forms of Monarchian opinion had begun to be put forward; and this line of discussion constituted the main theological interest of the third century.

Two classes of Monarchian theories have been distinguished. Some represented our Lord as primarily and properly a human person, but elevated to exceptional place and power, even to an attributive Godhead, by divine influences which descended on him. It was natural to fix on our Lord's baptism as the epoch at which the decisive elevation took place. Inasmuch as these Monarchians regarded Christ as a man *potentiated* by divine influence, modern writers often style them dynamical Monarchians. Others regarded Christ as truly divine, but in order to avert personal distinctions in the Divine Nature, they identified Christ with the Father. In Christ they recognised a mode of the Father's subsistence graciously assumed, and in this special *mode* of subsistence, uniting Himself to our flesh, He is the Son. These, therefore, are called modalistic Monarchians. Perhaps it may be said that the latter opinion represented the impression naturally enough formed in Christian minds, not concerned in speculations about creation, but mainly occupied with the two thoughts of (1) the one God, and (2) the Divine Saviour. Down to the incarnation they thought of the one God of the Old Testament. At the incarnation something new certainly appears upon the scene; but this something new is the manhood which makes a quasi-personal impression on our minds, yet is not truly a distinct person.

In the case of both forms of Monarchianism the desire to safeguard the doctrine of the Divine Unity, and simple, not to say those who are thoughtless and unenlightened, who are always the greater portion of believers, knowing that the very confession of their faith implies that they have passed from the many gods of the Gentiles to the only and true God, tremble at the οἰκονομία (manifestations of divine persons). We hold, say they, the Monarchy."

[1] *Ante*, p. 199.

to avert difficulties in regard to it, acted as a disposing force.

Another motive is also to be kept in view, connected with the manner of thought of dynamical Monarchianism especially. There have always been in the Church tendencies to make much of the superhuman, the divine in Christ, even at the risk of sacrificing or suppressing the human aspect. But there have been always also tendencies to make much of the human, at the cost of losing sight of the divine, or of denying it. A *tendency* this way has its own rights. It is connected with the sentiment of attraction to Christ as our model, our example, our leader, the man in sympathy with men, the Captain of salvation. It can also own Christ as our representative. It is occupied with the ethical aspects of salvation; with the thought of the aim, the effort, and the achievements of moral life; and it dwells on Christ as the centre of all this. This side of things was too genuinely Christian to be absorbed by a sect. But as the Church theology, in its anxiety to understand and guard the higher nature in Christ, undoubtedly leant in the opposite direction, *i.e.* to overshadowing and limiting the human, the tendency we speak of threw its force into various forms of protest, often extreme. It proved apt to be not only Monarchian, but Nestorian, Pelagian, Adoptianist,—and probably its influence is recognised in Paulicians, Bogomiles, Cathari among the mediæval sects, not to speak of more modern exemplifications. Some considerations seem to point to the Syrian church as the region in which Christian theology was most liable to be swayed in this direction.

While we might on these accounts be prepared to meet, without surprise, considerable symptoms of the influence of the lower or dynamistic Monarchianism, it must be owned that the actual symptoms are scanty. Three persons are named; and nothing indicates much influence as exerted by any of them.

Certain Alogi appeared in Asia Minor as opponents of Montanism, and are said to have rejected the writings ascribed to the Apostle John,—perhaps also the whole

Logos doctrine. But we do not know their opinions exactly. Dynamical Monarchianism appears as intelligible theory in connection with the two Theodoti ($\sigma\kappa\upsilon\tau\epsilon\grave{\upsilon}\varsigma$, $\mathring{\alpha}\rho\gamma\upsilon\rho o\mu o\iota\beta\acute{o}\varsigma$) and Artemon. According to them, Jesus is, physically, a man only. But his birth was supernatural (apparently this was acknowledged), and he became the bearer or vehicle of divine power in an extraordinary degree. He lived a life of steadfast righteousness, and was enabled to reflect the divine likeness, and convey the divine message, with consummate fidelity and completeness. Thus Jesus attained to a divine Sonship; and our adoption takes place on the model of his. Accepting the received New Testament Canon, they had to explain what is said of the Logos by the Apostle John. Apparently they denied any Logos $\dot{\epsilon}\nu\upsilon\pi\acute{o}\sigma\tau\alpha\tau o\varsigma$, *i.e.* as a true personality. The Logos is the revelation of the Father, *i.e.* He is the Father in the aspects in which He sees fit at any time to reveal Himself. Christ, then, more eminently than any other of the elect, but substantially in the same way, bears the image of the Father. The Logos may be said to have become man from age to age, less perfectly in the prophets, more perfectly in Christ; in both cases by representation, not by personal incarnation. Harnack has proposed to call this tendency Adoptianism, because its characteristic is to assume an individual man, Jesus, who is *taken* into Sonship, and is in a manner deified.[1] The details of this teaching may have varied in different circles; but probably most of them made much of our Lord's baptism. The descent of the Holy Spirit upon him was, for them, the decisive event, the era of that connection with divine power which rendered the man Christ unique. In this way the Spirit's presence with Christ would be considered as an impersonal divine influence. But there were some whose theory appears to have differed from this in an interesting way. They regarded the Holy Spirit as having a personal character, and as being

---

[1] See below as to Paul of Samosata. Adoptianism has long been the accepted designation of a theory which emerged in Spain in the time of Charlemagne.

the Son of the Father in the true and highest sense. Then, at the baptism, this Person descends in a special manner on the man Jesus. The precise nature and effects ascribed to this union are obscure. But Jesus became qualified, in consequence of it, to be our Master, and his manhood experienced at the same time a kind of divine elevation or deification. It was a question among some of them whether Jesus as yet had become God at his baptism, or not till after the resurrection; and they are thus led to contrast the Holy Spirit as true Son of God, with the man Jesus as adopted Son.[1] With these views were connected some strange speculations about Melchisedek.

To this type of Monarchianism also belongs the more elaborate scheme of Paul of Samosata, who was bishop of Antioch after the middle of the third century. We know a little more of his theory than of those just referred to, and can see the way and the degree in which, beginning with the manhood, he tried to fill out the conception of Christ as in some sense a divine Saviour. Paul became bishop of Antioch about 260 or earlier. At that time Antioch was part of the shortlived kingdom of Palmyra, under Zenobia, and by her favour Paul maintained his position until 272. But before this three successive synods had assembled in reference to his opinions. Two were baffled by his explanations and arguments; the third, perhaps in 268, excommunicated him. His style of life and government are unfavourably characterised by orthodox writers, possibly under the influence of prejudice. He had evidently shaped his doctrine so as to avail himself in defending it of all the sources of strength which contemporary opinion seemed to offer to him. He held it resolutely, and it bears the stamp of a clear and strong mind.

Paul thought it necessary to bring a Logos doctrine into

---

[1] Some such view is often ascribed to Hermas, especially in *Sim.* 5, and it is natural enough so to interpret that passage. Yet allegory, with which one has here to do, lends itself readily to mistake; and the counter argument from the general drift of Hermas, as presented by Bull and Dorner, should not be lightly set aside. See also Zahn, *Hirt des Hermas*, p. 245 f.

his form of statement. At the same time he was a Monarchian,—he owned no personal distinctions in the Godhead. On the one hand, then, he owned a Logos not only abiding in God as His Reason or Wisdom, but in a certain sense set forth, begotten, so that the term Son of God may be applied to it. But this Logos or Sophia, though in a certain sense an existence, a persistent influence or power, is, after all, no more than a power. It is an impersonal Logos, ἀνυπόστατος. It never does nor can come into individual manifestation, but is known only as a power influencing one or other of God's creatures. This Logos worked in the prophets, but more eminently in Christ, who was supernaturally conceived of the Virgin. Jesus then is from below (ἐντεῦθεν or κάτωθεν); the divine Logos works in him from above (ἄνωθεν). It is an inspiration which Christ receives. The Logos does not take substantial or personal being in Christ, —it is with him, not personally, but as a potency (οὐκ οὐσιωδῶς ἀλλὰ κατὰ ποιότητα). The position of Christ is thus remarkable in various ways, but the decisive element is found in his moral attitude and career. The only unity that can exist between two distinct beings is unity of disposition and will, and such unity comes to pass through love. This is more valuable than any unity that might be constituted by nature. Jesus, by the strength of his love and the invariableness of his consent to God, has become one with Him. As Jesus maintained this unity through all trial and conflict, he was endowed with power, and has become the Saviour. At the same time this union to God becomes indissoluble, so that he is now one with Him in will and operation. Therefore he has a name that is above every name, has received divine honour, and power to judge. "He is God from the Virgin." He pre-existed in the determination of God—not otherwise.[1]

---

[1] In Christ, therefore, manhood grows to Godhead. The following are some of the expressions used to describe this doctrine: ἐξ ἀνθρώπου γεγονέναι τὸν Χριστὸν Θεόν—κάτωθεν ἀποτεθεῶσθαι τὸν Κύριον—ὕστερον αὐτὸν ἐκ προκοπῆς τεθεοποιῆσθαι. The affinities to Origen's scheme and the differences are interesting.

In connection with this case of Paul, the Synod of Antioch condemned the word ὁμοούσιος, which was afterwards the watchword of orthodoxy. It is still a question on what ground they rejected it. Had Paul taunted his opponents with using it in a Sabellian sense? or did Paul himself use it in application to his non-personal Logos, and was it regarded by the bishops as virtually denying the distinct personality?

We have still to refer to the modalistic Monarchians. They held that the Father Himself had taken flesh and become incarnate. Such was Noetus of Smyrna, before the end of the second century. He taught that Christ is Himself the almighty God and Father, and that the Father Himself, therefore, has been born and died in the flesh. Such also was Praxeas, who appeared in Rome in the time of the bishop Victor. He came from the East, where he had been in collision with Montanism.[1] Victor of Rome is said to have leant for a time to the opinions of Praxeas about the person of Christ, as he undoubtedly was influenced by him against Montanism; and, if Hippolytus may be believed,[2] the bishops Zephyrinus and Callistus, who succeeded, also betrayed Monarchian leanings. But it must be remembered that the Logos doctrine was held by Hippolytus in a form which might dispose him to be a somewhat prejudiced judge of their phraseology.

On this scheme the pre-existence of the Son of God is denied, because its advocates confined the term Son to God as incarnate, as appearing in the flesh. As incarnate He is or becomes the Son; in His primeval glory and Godhead He could not suffer, but He suffered in or with the Son; hence the name Patripassian. This theory proposed to start from a high view of the simplicity and peculiarity of the Divine Nature. But it lay open to an obvious difficulty. There is no denying that, according to the Gospels, Christ deals with and speaks to His Father, as person with person,

---

[1] Hence Tertullian, to whom his Antimontanism and his Monarchianism were alike distasteful, said of him that he drove away the Paraclete and crucified the Father.

[2] *Refut.* ix.

as one with another. How is this to be accounted for in harmony with the theory? Either the Gospels use a deceptive way of representing things, depicting earnest dealings between two, when really it is one, in the most absolute personal simplicity, who acts both the parts. Or, there has really emerged, at the incarnation, a new personality—another with the Father. If so, how? Either there has at last emerged in the Divine Nature a duality, a new personal centre, so that in Godhead one is set over against another,—but this is inconsistent with the original motive of the scheme; or, the new personality must turn on the humanity; it is the man who is the new or distinct person; the human nature must bear the weight of that. In this case it cannot but seem simpler to say, with the dynamical Monarchians, that the man is personally distinct from the Father—that is to say, from God; and that the divine influence which he may have experienced, whatever it was, must not be conceived as an incarnation of the Father's own person. One sees, therefore, that a road existed by which modalistic Monarchianism might pass over to the dynamical type.

The form of modalistic Monarchianism which may be said to have endured in the minds of men, as the most worthy of consideration among such theories, was Sabellianism. According to Hippolytus,[1] Sabellius appeared at Rome early in the third century, was for a time in close relations and in theological concert with Callistus, but was afterwards excommunicated by that bishop. From other sources[2] we only hear of Sabellius at a later period working in the Ptolemais (Egypt). His doctrine was marked by considerable originality in several respects.

Other Monarchians had occupied themselves chiefly or exclusively with the question of the Father and the Son. Sabellius provided in his scheme a place also for the Holy Spirit. He asserted a trinity, not of personal distinction, but of successive manifestation,—God acts three parts, or reveals Himself in three modes. The same who is the

[1] *Refut.* ix. 11.      [2] Basil, *Ep.* 207.

Father, the same is also the Son (in this connection Sabellius used the term υἱοπάτωρ), and the same is also the Holy Ghost. Either Sabellius or some of those who shared his views seem to have had a speculation according to which God is, first of all, a Unity unrevealed, Θεὸς σιωπῶν, and then, secondly, reveals Himself, and so becomes Θεὸς λαλῶν or λόγος; so that Logos would not denote the second person, but would comprehend all the three phases—Father, Son, Spirit.[1]

Sabellius, or some of his followers, spread his doctrine abroad with great success in the Libyan Pentapolis after the middle of the third century, so that Athanasius says it had nearly come to pass that in this church the Son of God should not be proclaimed at all. Hereupon Dionysius, bishop of Alexandria, interposed with great energy; and in asserting the personal distinction and place of the Son, he went so far as to declare the Son to be a creature and work of the Father. But on the interposition of the Roman bishop of the same name, who dwelt upon the unity of nature between the Son and the Father, the eternity of the Son, and the importance of distinguishing generation from creation, the Alexandrian bishop modified his language, and, in particular, recognised the *Homo-ousia* of the Son. But as he had at first gone so far, the Arians at a later period appealed to his authority to shelter their teaching.[2]

Obscure theories were put forward by Beron, whose name is associated with that of Noetus, and by Beryllus of Bostra. Origen is said to have convinced them of their error. These appear to have been elaborate attempts to get over the difficulties which apply to every form of modalism.

Of the two forms of Monarchianism, that which is now

---

[1] This was proposed by Baur as the true view of Sabellius' own speculation; and his representation was for a time generally accepted. But Zahn, in his *Marcellus*, followed by Harnack, declines to ascribe to Sabellius any Logos speculation whatever, or any distinction of the *Monas* as resting behind the *Trias*. Harnack, *Dogmengesch.* p. 632. Some such Logos speculation seems to have floated before Callistus. Hipp. *Refut.* ix. 12.

[2] Athan. *de Sent. Dionysii, Op.* i. p. 477.

called dynamical might seem more agreeable to common sense, and less beset with obvious internal difficulties. It may also have been earlier present in the Church, and it may have continued longer. But as it failed to assert roundly the divinity of the Lord, it could not make itself extensively acceptable to Christians. The modalistic Monarchianism spread wider, and gave far more trouble. To many minds, most likely, modalism came as a way of expressing old convictions and modes of feeling, which seemed to be in danger. A simple Christian persuasion obtained, that one God must be owned in room of the many, and yet that Christ was both divine and human, therefore a wonderful Saviour. Men knew Him as the Son of God, and rested there; they wished to say no more. They accepted what the Apostle John said of the Logos, but were not led by that into more specific determinations.[1] But during the second century, and as it passed into the third, the Logos doctrine was more extensively canvassed. A distinction of persons, Father and Son, antecedent to the world of creatures, was forcibly presented to the mind. We have seen from the testimony of Origen and Tertullian[2] that recoil and apprehension were thus created in Christian minds; and Epiphanius[3] tells us that the Sabellians used to say to plain, pious people: "Well, my good friends, what are we to say?—Have we one God or three?" with the effect in many cases of gaining them over. As the supporters of the Logos doctrine were thus charged with Ditheism or Tritheism, so they, with a view to bring out a unity of authority and origination between Father and Son, and yet to mark a distinction, were prone, as we have seen, to emphasise the subordination of the second person; and they had not surmounted the view that the emergence of the second person is an event, just preceding the creation of the world. These explanations did not avail to quiet the minds that were troubled on the subject of the divine unity; and they might well seem unsatisfactory in their bearing on the

---

[1] The modalists dealt with this as somehow figurative or allegorical.
[2] *Ante*, p. 209, note. [3] *Hær*. 62.

glory of Christ; since even as to His higher nature, qualifications and distinctions were multiplying.

To some, also, it might appear that modalism was the more evangelical view, on this further account, that it started not so much from the thought of the Creator, but rather from the thought of the Saviour. God was manifest in the flesh, that we might be saved. Now the representatives of the Logos doctrine seem first to settle the rank of the Logos in view of a scheme of creation, or a theory of the origin of being; and then the soteriological part is adjusted to that as an additional chapter, or an appendix merely. It must be added that the same writers, in developing their subordinationism, are tempted to speak of the second person in a way that might grate on pious ears. Dionysius of Alexandria has been alluded to already. Take also Hippolytus. He undoubtedly meant to assert the true divinity of the Logos. Christ, he says, is God over all. Yet elsewhere he gets into a strain which allows a remark like this: "God did not mean to make you (*i.e.* his reader) a God, but a man. *If He had wished to make you God, He could have done it,—you have the example of the Logos*; but wishing to make you man, a man He made you. But if you wish also to become God, be obedient to Him who made you," etc. It was not unnatural that some should ask, " But what sort of divine nature is this after all, that can be spoken of so?"[1]

With all these advantages, however, modalistic Monarchianism could not maintain itself as a system. It revealed its weakness when put in form. If the see of

[1] Hipp. *Refut.* x. The Logos theology at this time was associated with forms of thought, and in some degree with speculations, borrowed from the rising Neo-Platonism. The class of people from which modalistic Monarchians took their rise may best be conceived perhaps as rather repelling philosophy. Yet when they came to elaborate a theory and defend it, they give tokens of affecting specially the ideas and the logic of the Stoics. And it is curious to note that their opponents suspect a Stoic notion of God as at the bottom of their theory, and charge it upon them. They were thought to *go no higher* than the Logos God of the Stoics, who pervades creation, without rising to the *Farther God.* The dynamical Monarchians found Aristotelianism suit them best, and drew their weapons from that armoury. See Harnack, *Dogmengesch.* i. 604–5.

Rome temporised, or hesitated on the subject during two or three episcopates, that could only be a temporary hesitation, and it caused no serious division; for ere long we find a resolute assertion of the Trinity in Unity as the doctrine of the West.[1]

As the third century closed and the fourth began, the Church was still conscious of being in presence of a problem which had proved arduous. The Logos doctrine—that is, the doctrine that our Lord pre-existed with the Father, as His Word and Son—held the field; but regarding this, also, different forms of statement were possible. The great influence of Origen recommended the doctrine of the eternal generation, but in other respects favoured a pretty decided subordinationism. The tendencies of thought existing in the Church were to be finally revealed in the Arian controversy.

[1] Dionysius of Rome in the case of Dionysius of Alexandria. Routh, *Rel. Sac.* iii. 373.

## CHAPTER XII

### CHRISTIAN LIFE

THE question how to follow Christ in earthly life has always been in hand; to some Christians in every age it has been a matter of supreme interest. The great prohibitions of the moral law in regard to outward conduct have always been asserted. But as Christians are called to spiritual obedience and to a life of spiritual aspiration, a "how much more" comes into view; and the precise meaning of it for each Christian is debatable, though for genuine Christians it is always great. It is difficult, therefore, to report truly and usefully on the Christian life of our own age,—much more on that of an age far removed from ours in time and manners, and represented by imperfect records.

In the period before us the standard of Christian manners becomes a subject of deliberate discussion. It occupied the thoughts of Clement of Alexandria in the East and of Tertullian in the West, and both have written largely about it,—Clement more systematically. The two men were very different in many respects: moreover, Clement was not influenced by Montanism as Tertullian was, and Tertullian attempts no methodical exposition like that in Clement's *Pædagogus.* Yet in their way of approaching the subject, and inculcating its lessons, there is less difference than might be expected.

Both of them are influenced by what the New Testament urges in reference to self-denial and in reference to the supremacy of spiritual affections, and both wish to show how these principles are to be carried out. In making the attempt they are guided by the conception they have formed of the contrast which Christian life should offer to that which is worldly. For Clement the Christian is the true Gnostic,—he rises above the material and the sensuous, and that recoil determines his Christian conduct. Tertullian's principles, too, operate largely by recoil; in his case it is recoil from the concrete life of his time, which was self-indulgent paganism, and his moral thinking has a Stoic turn. Neither of them, in the main, attains to a steady grasp of the positive moral forces which make life Christian, because they make it participant in the life of Christ; and neither of them attains a clear view of the essential evil or defect of worldly life. Hence a too negative conception of Christian excellence, and too great a disposition to multiply prohibitions and rules, and to urge them in a legal way. Yet both of them were honest Christian men, striving to be loyal to a Master whom they loved.

What we learn from the catacombs and from other sources make it clear that Christians were by no means so sparing in matter of ornament, for example, as the writers named exhorted them to be; and art, which in pagan hands was always ready to overstep the limits of morality, took service with the Christians, but learned among them to sit at the feet of goodness as well as of beauty.

Christians could not but set themselves against the delight in immoral action and immoral suggestion which was common in paganism, and so they turned from the theatres and spectacles, as well as from whole classes of pictures and statues. Actors, and craftsmen who ministered to idolatry had to forsake their callings in order to be received. Generally, Christians refused to sympathise with distinctively pagan art, and with all that savoured of pagan beliefs and worships. Yet here there was a borderland which must have been debatable. Phrases, symbols, usages, which carried some touch of pagan meaning, might be repudiated or rejected by some Christians, while for others they passed as mere conventions which had lost all distinctive religious significance. Persons in active business relations to the life of the day would admit a large latitude. Again, elements of the current mythology could even be Christianised. In the paintings in the catacombs, while scenes appear from the Old Testament, scenes also suggested by our Lord's parables, and (within this period) perhaps one or two instances of direct representation of scenes from our Lord's life, myths like that of Orpheus are made to yield a sense which Christian artists, or Christians who employed non-Christian artists, had no scruple in appropriating.

The practice of self-denial for its own sake was regarded and commended as eminent Christian virtue. As embraced by the Christians it applied to food and raiment; but it had a very special application to marriage. The abuse of the sexual relation had gone so far in the Gentile world—it was such a fertile source of evil, and men's minds were so habituated to accept that evil as inevitable—that the Christians felt it to be their part to recoil from it vehemently. Marriage itself had been debased by the low tone of feeling in regard to it. The Christians, on the whole, maintained the legitimacy of marriage as a divine institution, and an appointed part of the order of the world; but it was habitual for those who led sentiment on the point to think and speak of it as a concession to the weakness of human nature, and as fixing life on a level lower than the highest. Hence, though marriage was always guarded against the imputation of being in itself evil, yet entrance into married life could hardly be dissociated, as it seemed, from a certain sense of inferiority, and abstinence implied a superior virtue. Early in the second century Christians who have renounced marriage and have been faithful to this purpose during their lives, are spoken of and pointed to with satisfaction.[1] Second marriages were opposed by some as wholly unlawful for Christians; and at all events persons who, after being once married, and having lost their partners, embraced henceforth the widowed life, were regarded as worthy of special commendations. So also the dislike grew to bishops or presbyters marrying after ordination. Many of them were

[1] Justin Martyr, *Ap.* i. 15; Athenagoras, *Presb.* 6-33.

married when ordained; and a disposition appeared to require those who were married to live separate from their wives. But the right of married clergy to live with their wives was on the whole upheld throughout our present period.

The ascetics did not withdraw from society: they lived in their own homes, and mingled with other people; but, of course, it was regarded as fitting that they should avoid temptations which might shake their purpose. In some churches, as already noticed (p. 40), ascetics had a distinct place in the meeting for worship.[1]

Perhaps before the end of our period there were cases of ascetics binding themselves by an express permanent vow. At anyrate, eventual marriage, in the case of those who had once become ascetics, could only be regarded as a descent from a higher level to a lower; but the marriage was not regarded as invalid. The strange moods of mind which might arise in connection with ascetic life continued to be illustrated by the scandal of the συνείσακτοι, or sub-introductæ,[2] against which Church rulers like Cyprian had sedulously to watch.

The prevalent sentiment of the ancient Christians on this subject it is not easy to appreciate with perfect justice. Strong recoil from actual evils was, in the circumstances, healthy and right, and the determination to give effect to the hate of evil at all costs was magnanimous. There might be, as there still are, excellent reasons for many Christians remaining unmarried, if they perceive that in this way they are likely to serve God and man more faithfully; and the ancient Christians who so decided were within their right, and used their own liberty. There may be times, and there may be classes of persons, in respect to which such practical decisions may become exceptionally important. But the mistake involved in holding that the

---

[1] Hierakas, near the end of the period, gathers ascetics round him, whom he leads and instructs,—thus verging towards distinctively monastic life. But according to Epiphanius he was a heretic, and his followers a sect. He is said to have absolutely condemned marriage.

[2] Celibate clergy had in their houses women, often consecrated virgins, their relations with whom, professedly innocent, were open to great suspicion.

unmarried state is in itself better or purer than the married (which emphatically it is not), became a source of almost boundless evils. It perverted the principles on which Christian conduct is to be appreciated by men, and is measured by God; it ascribed an unreal merit to ascetic life; it fixed a note of moral inferiority upon the state of marriage, and so disgraced the sanctities of family life; it became the occasion of leading many persons into a snare which ruined them. But nothing of this was foreseen by almost any. The ascetic life was regarded as an unmixed good, and received not only commendation but adulation. The young Church made here an experiment which young Christians often repeat: the experiment of seeking the victory over evil in rules and in severities of their own devising. Very few, perhaps, could conceive it to be practicable to dissociate the commendation of the "virgin life" from the assertion of its superior merit. Finally, those who have read the exhortations addressed by Church teachers to virgins are aware of one inevitable element in the situation: the minds of those addressed were detained on topics and questions which could only be unhealthy.

Marriage with pagans or Jews, also with heretics, was discountenanced, and eventually prohibited by councils.[1] But it could not be regarded as invalid; and while such marriages might be avoided by earnest Christians, it is certain that they were not uncommon.[2] Besides, there was the large class of persons who, though having some connection with the Church, were not yet baptized; and their conduct in this and other matters could not easily be controlled. A well-known passage in Tertullian describes the discomfort and the risks of such marriages.[3] It was expected that Christians should marry with the approbation of the Church, and with a rite in which the parties received the Church's benediction. But this also was not essential to the validity of the marriage.

The exaggerated importance attached to the virgin life

[1] Illib. Can. 15; Arel. Can. 11; Laod. Can. 10, 31.
[2] Cypr. *de Lapsis*, 6.     [3] Tert. *ad Uxor.* ii. 4.

tended, as we have seen, to depress the conception of the Christian value of married life. On the other hand, however, Christianity pervaded the home with influences and with a Presence which gave new sacredness and sweetness to all its relations.[1] Hence, domestic life became a new thing; all the more because the strong faith of life to come gave worth and dignity to every member of the Christian family. The family became the school in which the Christian order of life was enjoined and practised; and a habit of moral self-command was formed which, if it existed at all among the pagans, did not reach so far, and in most cases was much more feeble. Even the family life of less careful Christians was reached and influenced by the consciousness of what the common sentiment demanded, and by the discipline of the congregation.

Brotherly kindness and liberality to the poor were conspicuous features of Christian life. As far as we know, every Christian church cared for its poorer members;[2] and in times of persecution, ministration to sufferers was zealously pursued. Captives were ransomed. Kindness to the poor generally (not merely to those who were Christians) was also commended and cherished, and came out sometimes remarkably in times of pestilence, such as those which darkened the third century. This virtue also had its theological support in the doctrine of the efficacy of almsgiving to take away sins. Texts in the apocryphal books of the Old Testament supported that doctrine; and in this way those Christians might be persuaded to give who were conscious of a good deal of sin that required to be put away. The difficulty of bestowing charity so as really to benefit the receivers had not been apprehended, and all seemed to be gained if purse-strings could be opened. The result on the whole must have been to promote the sense of brotherhood, and to establish in the general mind the claims of the weak and

---

[1] Tert. *ad Uxor.* ii. 8.

[2] In the middle of the third century the church of Rome had 1500 widows and poor persons on its lists, and it contributed liberally to aid churches in distress.

helpless classes. In addition, the process of spending money unselfishly reacted beneficially on the rich. Unquestionably the Christian Church brought home to the richer classes the feeling of stewardship, and of accountability for the use of property, in a manner previously unexampled. And the poverty of our Lord, as also His compassion for the poor, were incessantly appealed to as irresistible arguments.

The relation of Christianity to a heathen state, whose functionaries were in direct contact with popular licence as well as popular worship, naturally led Christians to avoid public office. This was part of the foundation for charging them with at least passive disloyalty; and the same charge had also a further ground in the Christian hope that the whole existing order of things would soon be superseded. Christians, however, conscientiously obeyed existing authorities when they could do so without sin: otherwise, they suffered submissively; and they prayed regularly for their rulers and for the public peace. They did avoid public employment, especially posts in which they came into official contact with idolatry, or might have to pass sentence of death. But here, as in other matters, no absolute rule could be carried through; and as the third century advanced, the number of Christians increased who found reason for accepting public responsibilities, sometimes to the detriment of their religion. It could not be easy to be a Christian in the army, and the Christian feeling deprecated entering a calling in which a man's business was to fight and kill. Yet it is quite evident that there were Christian soldiers, some of them prepared to suffer for their faith;[1] and when Diocletian began to take measures against the Christians, the discharge of Christian soldiers from the ranks of the legions was one of the earliest steps.

The exercise of good works was supported by the widespread doctrine of merit, and the grosser sins were discouraged by the Church's system of discipline. As regards the former, asceticism and almsgiving were the popular form of virtue to which the doctrine of merit was most

[1] Tertullian's treatise, *de Corona*, itself implies it.

emphatically applied. The virtue to efface sin and to secure heaven was ascribed to good works in a strict legal way, so as to suggest that once a man was baptized, and had cleared old scores, he had to work out the balance of his merits and demerits as best he could. Cyprian perhaps goes furthest in this direction.[1] Sins before baptism are purged by Christ's blood; but as the laver of baptism quenches hell fire, so by alms and good works the flame of their faults is abated for justified men. Prayers and fasts cannot purge away sins, but alms can: God is satisfied by righteous works, and by the merit of mercifulness sins are purged. This is, in fact, the method by which post-baptismal sins, that do not require formal discipline, are remitted. Only it must not be thought that other motives for good works did not exert their influence along with these.

In the language of Christian oratory, those who live meritoriously in peaceful times will receive from the Lord a white crown, those who suffer for Him will have the higher honour of a purple one.[2] Or, using another illustration, ordinary Christians who live well are those who bring forth thirtyfold, ascetics answer to those who bring forth sixtyfold, martyrs to those who bring forth a hundredfold.

It will be seen that a somewhat external way of appreciating character and weighing merits prevailed.

The Christians were aware that the disposition and the motive are the decisive elements in true service of God; yet the external distinctions drew the eye, and were treated as decisive. When this is the case a double morality inevitably arises. A low and rather negative Christianity, along with church standing, can prove a pathway to heaven. A more heroic and self-forgetting style of service and endurance is owned to be, after all, the true ideal; but it is not imperative. Only, those who select and adopt it will earn an exceptional reward.

[1] Cyp. *de Op. et El.* 1-5.      [2] Cyp. *ibid.* 26.

# CHAPTER XIII

## WORSHIP

VERY interesting changes and developments took place before the end of the present period. They were certainly not due to previous consultation, and must therefore have suggested themselves locally. Yet while differences on some points continued to exist, a very considerable agreement in practice over the Church obtained in the end. With respect to the differences, two moods of mind are visible. Some defended the right of churches to differ on minor points; while some, without precisely denying that, were impatient of differences, and aimed at uniformity. In all such matters the practice of a few of the greater churches must have exerted much influence.

In Justin Martyr's account of Christian worship, one recognises reading of the Scriptures, preaching more or less formal, prayer, and the Lord's Supper. This already indicates one considerable change. He says nothing of the Agape, nor of the connection of the Lord's Supper with it. The Agape continued to be held as a pious and cheerful Christian meal (Tert. *Apol.* 39); it assumed various forms, and was often held in churches, but at a later period the use of the churches for the Agape was prohibited. The Lord's Supper, however, had been transferred to form part of the chief service of worship on the Lord's day. There is not a trace of the manner in which the change came to pass, nor of any discussion about it. Wherever and by whomsoever the practice began, it recommended itself and took place throughout the Christian communities. When transferred to the close of the Lord's day services, and made the culminating point of the whole, the solemnity and impressiveness of the Lord's Supper were probably enhanced, and the impression deepened of a wonderful and sacred meaning, bearing on Christians only, which was embodied in the ordinance. Already in the second century Christians like Justin, and still more Clem. Alex., show a consciousness of some analogy between the contemporary mysteries and this Christian transaction; and they may have felt that the impressiveness and awe aimed at in the mysteries by the restriction of admission to the initiated, might advantageously be secured for this Christian service; the rather that in any view the eucharist embodies a confidential meeting between the Christians and their Lord. This feeling grew in intensity and in the range of matters affected by it, so that a fashion of secrecy about the specialities of Christian faith and worship grew up which was not very rational nor very edifying. This is commonly referred to as the *disciplina arcani*.[1]

On the other hand, a total exclusion of catechumens from public worship could not be thought of; and the unbaptized generally could be shut out only at the cost of losing many likely converts. Accordingly, the service was divided into two parts: the first part included the reading of Scripture and the explanation or exhortation which was based upon it, with various prayers, mostly short, and singing; all this was open. Then the various classes of persons who constituted the uninitiated or the lapsed part of the audience were dismissed, sometimes with a short prayer for each; and the special service for the baptized alone began with a long prayer, and the communion elements were brought in, the kiss of peace exchanged by the worshippers preceding or following. The first part of the service eventually came to be known as *Missa catechumenorum*,

---

[1] Applied to the eucharist with its forms, baptism, the creed, Lord's Prayer, and the like. All these were to be adverted to with precaution, so as not to reveal details in the presence of the unbaptized, nor in works published to the world. Romanists have exaggerated the extent to which it operated.

the second as the *Missa fidelium*. At the latter, certainly in many parts of the Church,[1] baptized children were present and participated (*Const. Ap.* viii. 13. 4). The confession of sins mentioned in the *Didache* was dropped, though a warning against enmity and insincerity was retained. The bread was usually leavened, and the cup contained wine and water. Clement of Alexandria and Cyprian mention some who took upon them to celebrate with water only.

In the minds of Christians the ordinance retained the significance explained in speaking of the earlier period.[2] Christians brought their gifts (δῶρα) of created things, as the appointed and acceptable token of their self-devotion. In this connection the prayer enlarged on the power and goodness of God in creation. But the celebrant also rehearsed the words of institution, and followed these (but not at Rome apparently) with prayer that the Holy Ghost might be sent upon the offering, that He might manifest the bread and wine to be the body and blood of Christ, and that the participants might receive the various benefits of redemption. Those who expound the ordinance sometimes explain the sacrament allegorically,—it is a wonderful figure through which the realities are presented and brought home to Christians; sometimes dynamically,—a special virtue to carry the blessings is imparted to the elements by the Holy Ghost; sometimes the thought is that Christ or the Logos appropriates the elements so that they are related to Him as His body is, and carry His presence and virtue in a special manner with them.

Reference was made under the former period to the way in which the thought of offering or sacrifice, originally arising in connection with the gifts, was extended in the current use of language to the whole eucharistic service That is still more plainly the case during this period; the sacrament is spoken of as the offering or sacrifice;[3] yet it is not common to find the idea presented that the congregation offer Christ to God. Rather the thought is that they

---

[1] Africa and the East.  
[2] *Ante*, p. 77.  
[3] προσφορά, θυσία.

are allowed to make an offering, in which, as it proceeds, Christ makes Himself present, so that the access and the privilege of the worshipper become singularly great. But already one meets with language which literally means more, as when Cyprian says that the passion of the Lord *is* the sacrifice which we offer (*Ep.* lxiii. 17).

In connection with these conceptions, the idea of the priesthood of the higher clergy took root. In Justin the whole body of believers are the high-priestly race who are able to offer acceptable sacrifices. But when the Lord's Supper became the great and mysterious sacrifice which crowned the service, then, as none but the bishop and presbyters were thought entitled to transact it, nothing was more natural than to go back to the Levitical dispensation, and find in the bishop and presbyters the high priest and priests of a better dispensation. (The bishop has the complete priesthood, especially for Cyprian; the presbyters have it in a more subordinate and dependent way.) The bishops having apostolic authority on the one hand, and (with their presbyters) exclusive sacerdotal aptitude on the other, the whole dispensation is in their hands, and a mysterious sacredness and ritual power is supposed to be lodged in them. The ascription of the name of priest to the Christian minister begins with Tertullian (about A.D. 200), though he himself maintains vigorously the priestly character of all Christians as such. The language of Cyprian is strongly sacerdotal.

No one can wish to minimise the degree in which the grace of Christ came home to these early believers, as in other ways so in the Lord's Supper. It must be said, however, that, in the rite which crowned Christian worship, the impression of an inexplicable wonder tended to occupy the mind to the injury of the spiritual impressions at which the ordinance aims. This made it easier to cherish notions of an efficacy, mechanical and meritorious, by which the participants benefited.

The specimens we have of common prayers, suggest a style of prayer formed originally by the practice of free supplications; but a tendency to fix the forms used, especially in the administration of the eucharist, was natural. Administrations regarded as having mysterious sacredness and virtue, might seem to require specially consecrated and adapted words to secure their authenticity; and forms believed to embody the petitions used by venerated predecessors in the more solemn parts of the rite, would acquire authority and sacredness. But though many phrases, which afterwards became liturgical, had doubtless already fixed themselves in the usage of public prayer, and forms had established themselves more or less, yet historical evidence for liturgies falls later.

The case of baptism reveals the disposition to make much of Christian ordinances by enriching them with imaginative allegorical ceremonies. It was usually performed by immersion, or by pouring water on the head while the candidate stood in what served for a font, or by both together.[1] But before the end of the third century a group of ritual circumstances preceded and followed. The catechumen experienced a preparatory imposition of hands, and in some parts of the Church a preparatory anointing. When his Christian instruction was closing, the form of the creed and of the Lord's Prayer was delivered to him. A form of exorcism, or of renunciation, one or both, was gone through; for to the early Christian mind the world was in captivity to the wicked one; his emissaries pervaded it; adjuration and prayer in the name of Christ could drive them away; and the man who passed from that kingdom at his baptism, ought himself to renounce it. In the renunciation the candidate faced the west, and with a thrusting motion of his arms he renounced Satan thrice; turning to the east, with outstretched hands, he invoked and acknowledged Christ or the Trinity.

After baptism there was the kiss by the bishop and representatives of the faithful, the baptized tasted milk and honey, they were anointed, and received imposition of hands,

[1] Sprinkling came to be considered appropriate only in baptism of sick persons.

with prayer for the Holy Spirit. Other ceremonies and usages appear immediately after the close of this period, and may have obtained before it closed.[1]

The rule was that baptism should be administered by the bishop and his clergy, as a great function which interested the whole church. At the same time, in case of need, presbyters and clergy of the lower ranks might baptize, and in special circumstances laymen also; this latitude was hardly, and very grudgingly, extended to women. The anointing and laying on of hands was considered to be especially appropriate to the bishop. Hence, in baptism administered by clergy of lower rank, the reservation of these parts of the ceremony to a time when the bishop could perform it. But this separation obtained chiefly in the West. Ascribing to each part of the ceremony a distinctive meaning, baptism was considered to be connected with washing away sins, and the unction with imposition of hands intimated the gift of the Holy Spirit. The solemn and ceremonial baptisms were usually carried through on the eve of Easter or of Pentecost,—especially the former. The catechetical preparation had occupied the previous season, and the neophytes communicated for the first time at the great Easter celebration. Later, the right to have these solemn ceremonial baptisms was a privilege of the bishop's church. But this restriction had to yield eventually to necessities arising from the number of the candidates, and the growing custom of infant baptism.

All through the present period, and for a good while after, the conspicuous and prevailing type of baptism is baptism of adults. That was so, of course, at the outset, when the Church was busy gathering in her converts; and it still continues to be so. Nevertheless, infant baptism was recognised already in the second century, though it is not certain that the statement applies equally to all parts of the Church. The passage of Irenæus, quoted on this subject, seems conclusive in the light of his customary use of

---

[1] The lively ceremonial of the renunciation, as given above, is from authorities in the fourth century.

language.¹ Tertullian recognises the practice, though he disapproves of it; and he would almost certainly have stigmatised it as a novelty if he had known it to be recent. Apparently, therefore, two practices existed side by side, both of which had considerable authority. There seems to be no trace of infant baptism in Clement of Alexandria; passages which imply it occur in Origen, in works written after he left Alexandria; and it has been inferred that infant baptism was not yet practised in the Egyptian church at the beginning of the third century, though it was then received as an apostolic tradition in Palestine. Some recent historians have suggested that there may have been a time when children of Christian parents were not supposed to require baptism at all; but that seems most unlikely, and there is no valid support for the notion. Tertullian argues that the benefit of baptism will be greater when it is received by the adult, who desires remission of sins committed in his wayward youth. And parents probably experienced a collision of opposite interests in the matter,—sometimes yielding to the reasons alleged by Tertullian, sometimes, on the other hand, to the dread that delay might lead to their children dying unbaptized.² In connection with infant baptism, sponsors, who vowed on behalf of the children, appear as early as Tertullian (*susceptores —fidei jussores*). Against some who advocated baptism on the eighth day after birth, according to the rule of circumcision, Cyprian recommends baptism on the second or third day.

The practice of standing at prayer on the Lord's day instead of kneeling as at other times, is one instance out of many how a distinction, which must have originated in some locality, commended itself generally to Christian hearts and imaginations, and became a rule. On the Lord's day they stood, because it was associated with the joy and victory of the resurrection. A similar prevalence of a practice, of whose origin there is no trace, is the practice of turning to the east in public prayer.³ No doubt the motive was a reference to the rising of the Sun of Righteousness. Another

---
¹ Il. ??.  ² *de Bapt.* 1?.
³ Tert. *Apol.* 16, *ad Nat.* i. 13.

case is the observance of Wednesday and Friday for weekday meetings. There were cases, however, in which this unanimity was not attained; for example, in regard to the celebration of Easter.

The earlier history of this matter has been referred to in Chap. IV. Some observed the 14th Nisan on whatever day of the week it fell, while the greater part of the Church observed Friday and Sunday in a week fixed so that Easter Sunday followed 14th Nisan.[1]

Those who observed on 14th Nisan were called Quartodecimans (τεσσαρεσκαιδεκατίται): they were themselves not quite at one, apparently, as to the meaning of their own observance. Those again who, with the majority of churches, kept Good Friday and Easter Sunday, had their own difficulty in attaining the harmony they desired. For the basis of all Easter calculations, at least from the third century, was the day of the spring equinox: now that was not reckoned alike in all places; and so in different churches Easter might fall in different weeks, and in some even before the true equinox.[2]

The diversity of practice, as already mentioned,[3] came into discussion about A.D. 155, when Polycarp of Smyrna visited Anicetus of Rome. Each maintained the right of his own church, but they parted in peace. In or after A.D. 192 Victor of Rome took steps to elicit the mass of opinion favourable to the practice of his church, and to concuss the Asiatics into conformity. He proposed to cut them off from communion in case of contumacy. Polycrates of Ephesus defended the Asiatic tradition, and as Irenæus with other influential bishops deprecated the violent

[1] All accounts of the origin of this difference are conjectural; but even the exact nature of it has created lively dispute. The historical questions have been biassed by considerations connected with the controversies about the Fourth Gospel. See article by Steiz, *Realencycl.* xi. 140, and revised by Wagemann, *Realencycl.*[2] xi. 270.

[2] The Jews at this time neglected the equinox, and carried on their computation on principles which gave very irregular results. Till the third century the Christians followed them: and even later a party stood out for this observance.

[3] *Ante*, p. 83.

measures of Victor, his plans failed, though communion between Rome and Ephesus probably was suspended.

The πάσχα was originally conceived as the commemoration of our Lord's suffering and death, which had its centre in the Friday. The fast might begin earlier (one day, two days, four days,—the extension to forty days came later), but it ended on the Sunday morning, on which the eucharist was celebrated and the gladness of the resurrection commenced, which extended to Pentecost. It became usual for the assembled congregation to watch during the night preceding Easter Sunday, and baptism was then administered to the candidates who had been in preparation. On the fortieth day after Easter the Ascension was commemorated, on the fiftieth the descent of the Holy Spirit at Pentecost. During the whole time of Pentecost no fasting took place, the eucharist was celebrated daily, and the congregation prayed standing, not kneeling.

The only other festival, unknown as yet in the West, but observed in the East, was Epiphany, on 6th January. It commemorated the manifestation of Christ—especially in His baptism. There seems to have been a Gnostic celebration of Christ's baptism on this day, and that, no doubt, was grounded in the idea that at his baptism the man Jesus received a higher potency and became the Redeemer. In the orthodox celebration some reference to the birth of Christ, as the preliminary to all the rest, was natural; but it was subordinate; and the day was not supposed to be the true anniversary of that event.[1]

The way of feeling and acting about the Christian dead [2]

[1] The extended reference of this feast to Christ's manifestation to the wise men (as representing the world) and in His miracles (at Cana), seems to be connected with the adoption of the feast during the fourth century in the West: where also the idea suggested itself that these events, as well as the baptism, all took place on 6th January.

[2] Baptized persons dying in the fellowship of the Church were so regarded. Martyrdom, or death for the confession of the Name, was equivalent to baptism in the case of persons not yet baptized, and to restoration in the case of the fallen not yet restored. The idea that the purpose to be baptized may stand for baptism in the case of persons unexpectedly overtaken by death, is also expressed, but not so authoritatively (Tert. *de Bapt.* 18).

was significant. They "slept in Jesus": therefore the burial-ground became the cemetery or sleeping-place; and Christian burials, whatever natural sadness attended them, were characterised by thankfulness and hope. Of the two ways of burial practised in the empire, cremation and inhumation, the latter was adopted by the Christians because it fell in better with the hope of resurrection, and with reverence for the body which had been consecrated to the obedience of Christ. Otherwise minor national customs, which were not idolatrous, could be continued. No impurity was conceived to attach to the remains; and they were accompanied to their resting-place with singing. Christians showed the common feeling of reverence for graves, and of anxiety that they should be preserved inviolate. Objects of ornament or use which had an interest for the departed while they lived, were often deposited in the tombs. It was also felt to be natural that the Christian dead should be associated together; hence Christians early provided common burial-places; or Christians of position, who had family cemeteries, admitted the interment in them of Christian brethren of all degrees. But the bodies of unbelievers were not admitted, though it was reckoned a seemly thing for Christians, in case of need, to render the last offices to the heathen also; and in times of pestilence the courage and kindness of Christians in this department became conspicuous.[1] In the neighbourhood of large cities excavations in beds of soft rock were resorted to; hence the catacombs at Rome, Naples, and other places.[2] It does not appear that the Christian catacombs could have served as places of worship in times of persecution; but no doubt they were resorted to by members of families under the impulse of pious affection, and later they became places of pilgrimage. They have preserved to us the early efforts of Christian art.

The Christian dead were in fellowship with Christ and

[1] Cyprian, *Vita*, 9, 10.
[2] De Rossi, *Roma Sotterranea Christiana*, 3 vols. 1864–77; Northcote and Brownlow, *Rom. Sott.* 1879.

with the one Church in earth and heaven, and the desire to express this conviction found expression in various ways. The most impressive related to martyrs. All instances of martyrdom were hailed with triumph, and the martyrs themselves were regarded as specially honoured of God. It was felt to be a privilege to continue to associate them with the Church's service; they came therefore to be named in the eucharistic prayers, and those who were joined in the prayer were conceived to experience some benefit by it. This usage was extended to the Christian dead generally. Besides, it was usual to visit the graves of the departed on the anniversary of death, and to engage in exercises which came to include offerings and supplications for their repose. Tertullian is the earliest authority: he adduces the practice as one of those which has no warrant in Scripture, but rests on custom only (*de Cor.* 3). All this appears to have been grounded on the Christian feeling, that for Christians death does not break the fellowship of life in Christ. It led, however, into the practice of prayer for the dead, which is without New Testament example; and that led in turn to a craving for definite conceptions as to the benefit which might accrue to the dead in this line, and as to the elements in their state which made them capable of such benefits. Hence came by and by the doctrines of purgatory, of the twofold punishment of sin, and of the distinct conditions under which each is remitted. In the next period prayers for those departed in the faith are found in almost every form of eucharistic rite.

Not much is known directly of the form and arrangement of the places in which Christians met for worship. As the number of Christians grew, these arrangements must have varied. Before the end of the period buildings set apart for Christian worship [1] existed in various places. At an earlier period Christians met where they could,—in large rooms, in halls erected for public purposes but hired by the Christians, or in private houses. The central court of a large Roman mansion might often serve for this purpose.

[1] κυριακόν, οἶκος ἐκκλησίας, ἐκκλησία.

The description of Christian worship in the second book of the *Apostolic Constitutions* is supposed to date from the third century. It recommends for the building an oblong form looking to the east, entering presumably from the west. It contained the table for Communion[1] (called also altar from the time of Tertullian and Cyprian), and an elevated place for the reader and probably for preaching. At the east end was to be the chair[2] for the bishop, with a bench on each side for the presbyters. The Christian people were in the middle or nave, the sexes separate. Farther down were the catechumens, the penitents, the energumens, and unbelievers: these classes were called upon to withdraw before the administration of the eucharist. At a later period the classes just referred to were expected to stand in a vestibule divided off at the west end (*narthex*); and the eastern end of the church, containing the holy table and the clergy, was also more decidedly separated from the rest. The churches which had been erected towards the end of the third century, and which were destroyed or confiscated in Diocletian's persecution, may generally have approached this type. But there was another plan, circular or hexagonal, which probably existed then, as it did later. The former type had its precedent in the Basilica—the hall of justice or of business in imperial cities. The latter may have been suggested by the mortuary chapels, if one may call them so, in which families met to commemorate departed friends. These had been in use among Christians as well as among the heathen. And in times of persecution they were protected by the laws regarding burial, and by the Roman sentiment on that subject.[3]

[1] Mensa, τράπεζα; Ara, θυσιαστήριον.
[2] καθέδρα.
[3] Baldwin Brown, *From Schola to Cathedral*, 1886.

## CHAPTER XIV

### CLERGY

FROM the beginning of this period we find in churches a presiding person, distinguished as the bishop. At the outset, indeed, tokens of the earlier relations still survive: Irenæus often speaks of bishops as presbyters; and while the three grades are present to the mind of Clement of Alexandria, as a matter of fact which he knows and accepts, yet in principle and for ideal purposes he sees only two functions, those of elders and of deacons.[1] But these symptoms soon disappear, and the episcopate gains continually in influence and distinction.

It is true that episcopal authority was not despotic; and if modern writers call it "monarchical," it was at first a very constitutional monarchy. The presbyters, as the standing council of the church, had to be consulted and carried along: in important matters Cyprian frankly takes for granted that the church as well as the presbyters must have its voice. Even in matters that were left in the bishop's hands, the conscience of the church demanded that he should act by rule, and carry out principles: and all good bishops desired to fortify that conviction. Moreover, as the church existed by the consent, the support, the love and prayers of its members, no sane bishop could propose to himself to defy their disapprobation or to disregard their opinions. During this whole period the evidence is ample that the membership of the church felt keenly interested in the church affairs, and had no hesitation in forming and expressing opinion. The bishop therefore lived in an atmosphere which he could

[1] Clem. Alex. *Strom.* vi. 13; vii. 1.

not disregard. He might feel it his duty to resist popular tendencies: Cyprian would not yield to the cry for lax discipline; but in order to hold his ground he had to rally opinion, and to consider well where he should make his stand. But episcopal influence and authority kept increasing. In every church the bishop was the most representative man. Also while other office-bearers might have departments allotted to them, the bishop had general oversight. In every function of the assembled church he presided: in those rites, the administration of which came to be reserved to him,—nay, even in those which fell to him usually, though not always,—the sacredness of the rite accrued to the dignity of the man. The public teaching of the Church fell largely into his hands; but where other office-bearers taught, they were conceived to do so under his sanction.[1] Round him the general sacredness and supernaturalness of the Church tended to concentrate itself, because he stood alone: what was supernatural in the Church was most adequately represented by the bishop. This was the tendency of the system, realised more fully in the case of remarkable and energetic bishops. It did not prevent bishops being roughly handled when human infirmities on either side gave occasion; but it was a force in reserve which came into play eventually, and generally prevailed.

The tendency thus existing developed itself in theoretical forms which made it more effective. Everything that existed rightfully in the Church, being regarded as part of a divine plan, must express a divine intention. The bishop existed rightfully, therefore this principle eminently applied to him. The distinctive divine intentions in regard to the episcopate were conceived inferentially. The tradition of the churches had been appealed to, quite reasonably, as fixing the main articles of Christianity against the Gnostics. But the obvious way of making that argument tell, was to name the men [2] who were believed to have stood successively at

[1] With the same sanction instructed laymen also taught the congregation, *Const. Ap.* viii. 32, and *Conc. Carth.* iv. 98.
[2] Polycarpus a Joanne, Clemens a Petro ordinatur, etc. Tert. *de Præscr.* 32.

the head of those churches, each reproducing and guarding in his own day what he had previously imbibed as Christian teaching. This, therefore, was one thing divinely intended in the case of bishops, namely, to afford a special guarantee for doctrinal continuity and purity. It was to be presumed that somehow divine care enabled them to be sufficient for this function. Hence Irenæus speaks of their *charisma veritatis*, though this is not much dwelt on, and is nowhere defined.[1]

Again, Montanism had striven to assert the prophetic element in the churches, so as to embody a dispensation of the Spirit among the members that should outweigh the office-bearers. Montanism had failed: the Church in the continuity and order of its organisation had repelled Montanism. The Church, however, continued to have the Holy Spirit: the functions by which His operations were expressed were administered by the office-bearers, and the chief of these functions usually or exclusively by the bishops. Ritually, the office-bearers, but eminently the bishop, gave the Holy Spirit. Therefore, according to the logic then current, he *had* the Holy Spirit in such a sense that he *could* give Him.

It was only by degrees that such impressions produced their effect on the general Christian mind. The full realisation of them depended on the improvement of opportunities by eminent bishops. But it is easy to see how such impressions as they grew strengthened the bishop's position, especially as regards the effect of his negative voice. Relations in a society may be confidential, friendly, and frank. But if there is one man in it whose "*non-possumus*" is likely to stop everything, he *must* be treated with exceptional deference. Cyprian never says that a bishop is infallible, or that his power is absolute, or that he is entitled to govern his flock at his own sole will. But he does convey the impression that his dignity and authority are unique, that his decisions are to be treated with great deference, and that opposition to him involves exceptional responsibility. And he does tell a contumacious deacon in another church that, as the Lord

[1] *Contr. Hær.* iv. 26. 2.

appointed bishops, whereas deacons were instituted merely by apostolic authority, a deacon should as little take liberties with his bishop as a bishop should take liberties with God.[1]

Synods met to discuss important questions, and in the third century they met regularly in various provinces once or twice a year. Though presbyters also attended, the episcopal vote soon became the decisive one. The bishops were the men who were best entitled to speak in their own name, and best entitled to speak in the name also of their churches which had elected them. Provincial Synods, as a rule, were summoned by the bishop of the metropolis of the province, met in his city, and under his presidency. Hence such bishops acquired a recognised authority and precedence ($Mητροπολῖται$), perhaps carried out with greater regularity in the East. In the two African provinces, Mauretania and Numidia, the bishop who happened to be oldest presided; in proconsular Africa, always the bishop of Carthage. Early in next period other distinctions were developed: but already the bishops of Rome, Antioch, and Alexandria were exceptionally important, and influenced many neighbouring churches. In the West, Rome had the further distinction of being the only apostolic see.

Much was decided when the relation of bishops to the multiplying flocks in each city or each neighbourhood was fixed. Originally (*ante*, p. 35 fol.) the bishop was chief minister of one flock.[2] As Christians multiplied in great cities, to assemble the whole church became more difficult. It could only be attempted on very special occasions. Local sectional gatherings acquired more and more importance. Gradually they assumed the character of distinct communities—*quasi* churches. At each stage, in a gradual process, adaptation sets in. The one bishop remained, the staff of lower clergy was increased. This arrangement naturally extended itself to the suburbs and nearer country districts. Hence, where Christianity was growing, the same bishop became president of different companies

---

[1] *Ep.* iii. 3.
[2] This is still the ideal in the sketch of a church in *Const. Apost.* ii. 57.

of Christians, and these were regarded as members of one church, which formed his παροικία. This is the decisive step towards the hierarchy. One does not see, from the point of view of early episcopacy, any objection in principle to the constitution of each distinct congregation (to use our modern phrase) into a bishopric. But feeling, and also, in some respects, the natural development of affairs, were against it. These influences decided the course of affairs in the populous centres where Christianity grew most quickly; and so the type was set for the organisation elsewhere. The bishop was thus released from his strict connection with one flock, emancipated in some measure from the influences which surrounded him there, and put in the way of becoming a more conspicuous and influential person. In each of the separate Christian communities which begin to multiply under him, he is by and by replaced by a permanent parish presbyter, who for most purposes performs the acts which the bishop performed in the earlier single congregation. In Rome about the middle of the third century there were forty-six presbyters; about the end of the century there were forty churches. Probably the principle of connecting a presbyter permanently with each special flock and building had been accepted.

Yet villages in the country had in many cases been provided with bishops who came to be called country-bishops (χωρεπίσκοποι). They were really bishops who had but the one local flock to attend to. Probably, too, they often had few or even no presbyters. They continued for a considerable time, but came more and more to be regarded as anomalous in the general system of the Church. They were ultimately superseded, and their flocks grouped under bishops on what, in later phrase, we may call the diocesan plan.

Bishops were appointed by public election conducted in the face of the congregation, the voice of the clergy, at least the presbyters, and that of the people being required. It is not till a good deal later that we have any detailed accounts of procedure in actual cases; but the impression one forms is that, while certain principles were kept in view, the methods were loose, and therefore worked uncertainly. Filling of civil offices by election continued to exist in the Roman Empire, and probably the methods of the Church were conformed to those of civil society. In both cases presiding persons had considerable authority in regulating the proceedings. The election was not complete until the presiding officer formally pronounced the result (in respect of which he was often said to appoint or "create"); he was entitled to be satisfied as to the legal qualifications of the candidate, as well as with respect to the sufficiency of the vote; and in certain circumstances he could take the initiative by himself proposing a candidate.[1] All these features are found in one case or another of ecclesiastical elections. In the third century, the consent of the church members as well as that of the clergy was certainly held necessary to an election. But how cases were worked out when a serious division existed or threatened, we do not clearly see.

It is likely that for some time, at least in some churches, the elevation of one person to preside as bishop was accomplished within the church concerned, without aid from the outside. Apparently such an arrangement survived at Alexandria long enough to attract attention.[2] But in the course of the third century the rule is found operating, that the neighbouring bishops, not less than three, at the very least two,[3] ought to be present, and, of course, preside at the formal election and instalment of a bishop. Many reasons recommended some such arrangement. But the feeling or doctrine that bishops only could make a bishop became accepted as the conclusive and all-sufficing reason, it is difficult to say when. The same difficulty applies to the conception of a distinct ecclesiastical character attaching to the bishop as distinguished from the

[1] See Hatch, article on Ordination, *Dictionary of Christian Antiquities*, ii. p. 1503.
[2] Hier. *Ep. ad Evang.*
[3] The presence of one only was regarded as indicating something unfair or factious, unless special circumstances established a necessity, and absent bishops gave written consent. See Hefele, *Conciliengeschichte*, i. p. 378.

presbyter. The formula in the eighth book of the *Apostolic Constitutions* (generally referred to the early part of the fourth century) directs the deacons to hold the gospel over the head of the new bishop during the prayer: imposition of hands is not suggested. As the relative might of the bishop grew, his distinct order or grade would be assumed as self-evident.

The priesthood ascribed to bishops and presbyters has been referred to in connection with the eucharist (p. 232).

Probably election by the church had been the original way of appointing all office-bearers, subject perhaps, as before indicated, to considerable initiative and control on the part of the presiding person or persons. Under the episcopal constitution we now find the bishop practically nominating to the presbyterate and other offices; but in the case of the presbyterate, at least, in the presence of the congregation, and inviting their consent. That consent was seldom likely to be withheld from proposed additions to a large existing staff, the names proposed being in most cases previously concerted with the existing clergy. Naturally, therefore, such nominations assumed eventually the character of authoritative appointments.

New offices were added during our period to meet wants which before had been supplied by spontaneous zeal of members, or which were arising out of the growth of churches. The work of the deacons was supplemented by subdeacons, the rather that there was an indisposition to extend the number of the deacons in a church beyond the seven of Acts vi. Acolytes (attendants) took up other ministerial duties. Exorcists dealt with persons afflicted by evil spirits. Readers (*lectores*, ἀναγνῶσται) read the appointed portions of Scripture. Doorkeepers (*ostiarii*, πυλωροί) took charge of the place of meeting. These are the recognised orders in the West. In the East the exorcist was not regarded as holding an office, but as the subject of a gift; and that was so also in the West as late as Tertullian. On the other hand, singers (*cantores*, ψάλται) seem to have a clerical character in the East but not in the West, and *fossores* (gravediggers) come into view as functionaries, but not as clergy. Subdeacons, acolytes, exorcists, readers, doorkeepers came to be accepted as the Western arrangement, and these are commonly referred to as minor orders.[1] The appointment to minor orders was settled generally in the bishop's hands. Cyprian's practice was to consult his clergy and people as to all clerical elections. When, during his absence in time of persecution, he appoints readers and a presbyter, he specifies his reasons (*Ep.* 38 and fol.).

The place given to women as regards Church service is not quite clear. There were deaconesses or female servants of the Church in the apostolic age, and apparently also in the age of Trajan (Pliny's *Epistle*). But widows also are referred to in the Pastoral Epistles, and we hear only of widows, as a recognised class in the Church, during greater part of our period. As widows were supported by the Church, those of them who were qualified were employed, *e.g.*, in instructing female catechumens, and probably in charitable care of the sick; and they appear to have had some charge of the female members. This arrangement continued in the West for a time. But in the East, towards the end of this period, the deaconesses appear as an order (*Apost. Const.* iii. and viii.), and receive regular ordination. The first General Council recognises the function, but seems to forbid ordination; which, however, was recognised at Chalcedon [2] (A.D. 451).

---

[1] According to the later and the modern Church of Rome, subdeacons are reckoned to the sacred orders, and only the other four to the non-sacred. "Clerus minor" occurs first in *De Rebaptismo*, c. 10 (among Cyprian's works—before A.D. 260), but not so as to make its meaning quite definite. In the civic arrangements of the empire, the name "ordo" was commonly applied to the body of persons holding recognised rank in a community; but sometimes it signifies "rank" simply, lower as well as higher. The same holds in substance of the Greek word κλῆρος. These words were applied in Christian speech, sometimes to express any rank or class, but more usually to denote those who had place in the ecclesiastical hierarchy, and were distinguished in that way from the Christian plebs. (Compare "classes and masses.") All such belonged to the ordo (or ordines), Gr. κλῆρος, as distinguished from the plebs or λαός.

[2] *Conc. Nic.* Can. 19; *Conc. Chalc.* Can. 15.

# CHAPTER XV

## DISCIPLINE AND SCHISMS

In the early Christian writings of the West, *disciplina* denotes the conception of ordered life which the Church strove to impress on her members. In modern use, the word suggests the principles and processes in conformity with which Church power was exerted to uphold order and to repress transgression. This is the sense in which we use the word here.

Some reference has already been made to it in speaking of the early churches (p. 42). The Church had from the first asserted the right to guard its character by excluding scandalous and unruly persons (1 Cor. v.). Sins and imperfections attached to Christians, which were to be borne with, as common infirmities; and they could be the more easily borne with because, at least virtually and in general, they were confessed and regretted from week to week. But there were scandalous sins which implied a deliberate revolt from Christ's rules, or a conspicuous fall, under prevailing temptation, from the standard which Christians were bound to maintain. In such cases, both for the sake of the sinner himself, and also for the sake of maintaining in the society the cherished conception of their common calling, it was needful that the sinner should be taught, and that he should own, how he had separated himself from his Master and his brethren; and it was needful that the Church should have some ground to believe in the seriousness and sincerity of repentance before proceeding to restoration.

Early in the second century a strong disposition existed

to refuse restoration in the case of scandalous sins committed by Christians. Murder, sins of impurity, and apostasy, or lapse into idolatry, were chiefly in view. The practice thus advocated was based upon the theory that "one repentance" was expressly sanctioned with a view to forgiveness and Christian standing—that, namely, which is sealed in baptism; no second repentance is provided for, nor is the Church authorised to accept it. It was admitted (usually or always) that persons so situated, if they continued penitent to their life's end, should be encouraged to hope for eventual forgiveness at the hand of God; but they had lost their standing in the earthly fellowship. A high moral enthusiasm and a resolute purpose to defend the purity of the Church inspired this practice. At the same time, many cases must have occurred, leading men to question the fitness of so stern a rule; and most likely the practice of different churches always varied in some degree, but with a leaning on the whole to severity. Hermas (*Vis.* ii. 2) announces a second repentance—*i.e.* one after the baptismal one—as open; but he connects it apparently with the special circumstances,—the dispensation was about to close, and this exceptional door was opened by the Lord on that account. In this, as in other matters, the Montanists appeared on behalf of the stricter view of the Church's traditions and practice. But at the end of the second century the advocacy of that view was certainly not confined to them. On the other hand, Dionysius of Corinth (Routh, *Rel. Sac.* i.), writing to the Amastrian church, exhorts them to receive penitents returning from falls of any kind.

The reception of such penitents, however, even where it was in use, was regarded as something remarkable and difficult. It had to be sought by confession before the church, enforced by humiliation and supplication, which continued for some time, and was regarded as a satisfaction to the congregation and also to God. The restoration was, or came to be, by stages, which towards the end of the period appear as four: the penitents take their place, first, as προσκλαίοντες, *flentes*, or χειμάζοντες, in the court before the door of the church, beseeching those who enter to pity them and support their application; second, as ἀκροώμενοι, *audientes*, allowed to be present in a remote part of the church at the earlier part of the service to hear Scripture and sermon; third, as ὑποπίπτοντες, *substrati*, who took part in the whole service to which catechumens were admitted, kneeling at the prayers; fourth, as συνιστάμενοι, *consistentes*, who witnessed, standing, the administration of the eucharist, though not themselves participating. After this came formal restoration by imposition of the bishop's hands, the kiss of peace, and participation of the eucharist with the brethren. From various notices (*e.g.* canons of Ancyra, A.D. 314, and Nice, A.D. 325) it appears that several years, as a rule, might be spent in the three latter stages. But some discretion was left to the bishops. And while these prolonged exercises of penitence might be held up as the ideal, one acquires the impression that in various special circumstances the process was very greatly abridged. In particular, the intercession of confessors (Christians undergoing suffering for their faith) was allowed to operate on the side of leniency.

Early in the third century Callistus of Rome (A.D. 218–223) sanctioned principles which many reckoned lax, both in regard to some moral questions and also in regard to receiving to penitence persons guilty of sins of impurity. Hippolytus opposed him (*Ref.* ix. 12)[1] on this as well as on doctrinal points, and a schism appears to have arisen in the Roman church. That passed away, however, and the milder practice remained in force at Rome.

Some years after this the Decian persecution gave occasion to lively discussion of the Church's duty to the fallen. The circumstances have been referred to in the notice of Cyprian (p. 191). The immense number of the lapsed rendered the question very important: it also created a great pressure in favour of laxity, since not only the fallen, but

[1] Origen also apparently (*de Orat.* viii. 10). Tertullian, as a Montanist, energetically denounced the laxity.

doubtless also many of their friends, desired easy terms of restoration. But there was another complication. Cyprian's elevation to the bishopric of Carthage (A.D. 248) had been opposed by five presbyters, who thereafter ordained a deacon by their own authority, and set themselves to embarrass the action of the bishop: this led to their being excluded by Cyprian from church fellowship. Elements of controversy were therefore already present: and when the persecution was running its course, fresh matter of dispute was furnished by the confessors, who were moved to issue *libelli pacis*, certificates of restoration, sometimes in very wholesale terms;[1] and Cyprian speaks of thousands of such certificates issuing daily (*Ep.* 20). The African Christianity was very responsive to influences of this kind. According to Cyprian, there was something like a popular uprising throughout the province to constrain the guides of the churches to give way (*Ep.* 27. 3). Cyprian seems to have leant originally to the severer principle in cases of this kind. But first of all he insisted on delay until the churches with their bishops and clergy could deliberately examine the cases and make the requisite discriminations;[2] later, he conceded that in case of apparent approach of death, the confessions of persons recommended by confessors might be received by presbyters or deacons, who should administer the eucharist to the penitents. Next, penitent *libellatici* (see p. 143, n. 2), as the less flagrant offenders, were readmitted. And, finally, the general restoration of the fallen, who were penitent, was authorised by a Synod (A.D. 252, Cyp. *Ep.* 57), partly on the ground that fresh persecution seemed impending, and it was desirable to give every encouragement to those who by fidelity in a new trial might still be enabled to retrieve their former fall. Cyprian's principle on the whole, therefore, was eventual restoration, but not without serious discipline, and prolonged evidence of penitence. In all these steps Cyprian was able to carry with him the bishops of the African

---

[1] *Communicet ille cum suis*, Cyprian, *Ep.* 14. A universal form, *Ep.* 23.

[2] This he contemplates as taking place at a meeting of the church, expressly including the laity.

province, and also the clergy and confessors of the church of Rome.[1]

Out of this controversy a shortlived schism arose at Carthage under a counter-bishop, the dissidents being on the side of more lenient treatment of the fallen.[2] A more durable division took place at Rome in the opposite interest.

After the martyrdom of Fabian, bishop of Rome, A.D. 249, the chair had remained vacant for a year and a half, and the presbyters had dealt with the necessary business of the church. Among these presbyters, a distinguished place was held by Novatian, a man in high repute, some of whose writings are still extant. Official letters from Rome to Cyprian had been penned by him, and he was a party to the approbation accorded by Rome to Cyprian's measures. Novatian was put in nomination for the bishopric, but his party proved to be in a minority, and in A.D. 251 Cornelius was elected. Novatian's supporters were of the more rigid party, and they brought accusations of laxity against Cornelius: he had held fellowship, they said, with fallen bishops, and had received the unworthy to communion from interested motives. This party had influential confessors on their side, and they set up Novatian as counter-bishop against Cornelius. Cornelius excommunicated them, and laid down the principle that all sorts of fallen persons should be received to penitence, of course with proper precautions. Novatian and his followers, on their side, fell back on the principle that none of those who after baptism fell into the great acts of sin, regarded as deadly, ought to be restored to communion; to do so was to usurp God's prerogative and imperil the glory of the Church. Such persons are to be commended to the divine mercy, which they may still receive, but the Church is not authorised to readmit them. Among those who joined Novatian was Novatus, a leading person among the presbyters who had opposed Cyprian at Carthage. In joining Novatian, he went from

---

[1] The see of Rome was vacant for part of the time, but the presbyters signified their approbation of Cyprian's line of action.

[2] The leader was Felicissimus, a deacon, and Fortunatus was the bishop.

one extreme to the other. But Novatian soon lost the support of the more influential Roman confessors. Cyprian also promptly acknowledged Cornelius, and supported him energetically. Some bishops countenanced Novatian; Fabius of Antioch and Marcion of Arles were the most important; and Novatian congregations sprang up in many parts of the Church. They had the reputation during subsequent discussions of being generally on the side of orthodoxy, and they continued to exist for some centuries.[1]

The same principles, or principles nearly as severe, continued to be cherished by many who did not feel it necessary to join the Novatians, and in some branches of the Church sins were specified which were too grievous to admit of restoration even on deathbed. In the church of Rome itself fresh troubles broke out during the bishoprics of Marcellus and Eusebius (A.D. 307 fol.), the leader of opposition being one Heraclius; but this time the Roman authorities seem to have been opposed by a party which desired to reduce discipline to a nullity.[2] During the Diocletian persecution, Peter, the bishop of Alexandria, laid down rules which contemplated restoration of the fallen under careful conditions as to due manifestation of penitence.[3]

In more than one of these debates personal antagonism, or jealousy, was the motive of division. But sensitiveness on the question of discipline, involving the purity of the Church on the one hand and compassion to penitents on the other, furnished the pretext on which popular parties were formed. On this subject men really felt strongly, and so could be induced to take decided action.

It is also to be observed that while the party which condemned the admission of post-baptismal repentance seems at first sight stern and pitiless, they are the party which

[1] In the East called καθαροί, which was the name they preferred.
[2] This is the usual interpretation of the inscription in the catacombs; but a quite opposite interpretation is possible.
[3] The schism of Meletius, bishop of Lycopolis, who took upon him to usurp the power of the Alexandrian bishop (A.D. 306), seems to have found a pretext in these matters of discipline; but no clear contrast of principles was evolved.

more fully recognises the distinction between the Church's function and the Lord's. According to them the Church either had no power to restore, or was restrained by the Spirit of God from exerting it, in the cases which were in question; but the hope of salvation to the penitent, even in this painful exclusion, was proclaimed. On the other side, the admission of the penitent to Church privileges was associated with the belief that in this way they were brought again into the position, and under the influences (not, indeed, which would secure salvation), but without which salvation is not ordinarily possible.

The schism of Donatus in Africa will be noticed under next period.

### Heretical Baptism

Cyprian, *de Unitate* and *Epp.* 70–75; on the other side, *de Rebaptismo*, among the works of Cyprian. Benson, *Life of Cyprian*, Lond. 1898, and article in *Dict. of Christian Biography*, vol. i.

Closely connected with the discussions just referred to is that which arose regarding the baptism of heretics, and therefore it may be referred to here.

It has been matter of general agreement, that baptism is an ordinance which ought to be administered only once in the history of a disciple. Cases, indeed, may be suggested in which it can be plausibly urged that a second or supplementary baptism might be reasonable. But these plausibilities have not been allowed to disturb the rule that the impressive uniqueness of baptism, as standing, once for all, at the outset of proposed discipleship, must be maintained. The one baptism, however, must be real baptism. And so the question what should be taken for real baptism has to be dealt with.

With the deepening impression of the unity of the Church, and of her function as alone possessing the ministrations and alone constituting the fellowship through which we have life, it was easy to infer that no Christian ordinance could be authentic or valid unless it was administered by her authority, and reached the individual through her ministers. The tendency, in fact, was all this way; yet in regard to baptism the application of this principle became debatable.

When sects, heretical and schismatical, formed themselves, as they did in the second century, all or most of them administered baptism, though some varied the form of the rite. Sooner or later some persons so baptized joined the greater Church, doing so, no doubt, as Christians who saw reason to exchange what they now regarded as a less satisfactory form of Christianity for one more perfect or more authentic. Some of these sects differed less from catholic Christianity and some more; and it does not seem likely that any one rule could have at once obtained as to the recognition which Christianity so initiated was to receive. It seems most likely that persons who came over in such circumstances were welcomed as Christians who needed to be taught the way of the Lord more perfectly, and that no question was raised about their baptism, unless some known peculiarity in the ceremony, or in the words used, rendered it specifically questionable. But a stronger view of the nullity of heretical baptism had developed itself by the end of the second century, and had formed the practice in some churches, while others opposed it.

In these circumstances Cyprian's whole influence was directed to secure uniformity, at least in Africa. He had developed energetically the doctrine of the unity of the Church. He maintained that as the Church, which is catholic, distinguished from all dissidents, is alone the authentic fellowship of salvation, and in it alone Christian benefits are enjoyed; therefore any Christianity professed outside of it is spurious and null, and any Christian rites professedly administered outside of it are also null. This was applied even to orthodox sects like the Novatians. The administrations of such separatists are an offensive mimicry. Baptism in their case is no baptism, the eucharist is no eucharist, martyrdom is no martyrdom. It followed that persons coming from such sects [1] to the Catholic Church were really for all Christian purposes unbaptized, and must now be baptized again. The question of baptism was the important one. There was no need to discuss the value of the eucharist, as received in a heretical or schismatic sect, because henceforth the convert would receive it in the catholic way. But if baptism was not readministered, the Church would acknowledge the convert to be baptized already, *i.e.* would concede that the heretical baptism was baptism. Cyprian of Carthage and Stephen of Rome took sides against one another on this point.

Cyprian appealed to the tradition of his church, for it was important to maintain that the practice had been so from the beginning. He refers to a council held by Agrippinus,[2] a predecessor at Carthage, which sanctioned his view,—although this seems to imply diversity of practice as even then existing.[3] Apparently Callistus of Rome (218–223) had sanctioned rebaptism; but contrary to the tradition of his church, as Hippolytus maintains (*Ref.* ix. 12). It seems certain, however, that rebaptizing obtained in Cappadocia and neighbouring regions, and it was sanctioned as ancient practice by synods at Synnada and Iconium (perhaps before A.D. 236). Meanwhile an opposite practice was in use, certainly at Rome, and, no doubt, in many other churches. Cyprian himself seems conscious that his argument from tradition and history is not conclusive; his main strength is in his church theory.

Those who took the other side regarded baptism, though administered by heretical hands, as substantially valid, requiring only to be completed by accession to the authentic Church. Such accession took place by the con-

---

[1] *I.e.* baptized in them. Perverts baptized in the Catholic Church, carried away by heresy, and afterwards returning, had been truly baptized, and so needed only to be received as penitents.

[2] Date uncertain, A.D. 180? 215?

[3] Augustine suggests that Agrippinus **and his council** *introduced* the practice of rebaptizing those who had been baptized in heresy. But that view is probably an inference from what Augustine believed, rather than a fact resting on evidence.

fession and submission of the convert, and the imposition of the bishop's hands.[1] Cyprian did not believe that the difference afforded a ground for breaking off communion between bishops. But it seemed to him so important in connection with church principles, that he felt justified in doing his utmost to maintain it.

Cyprian's case is summed up in the treatise *de Unitate*, composed before this dispute broke out (c. 11): "They suppose that they baptize, although there can be no baptism but the one; when they have forsaken the fountain of life, they offer the grace of the living and saving water. In their hands men are not cleansed but rather defiled; their sins are not purged, but rather heaped up. That kind of nativity generates children not to God but to the devil. Those who are brought forth from unbelief lose the grace of faith; those cannot come to the rewards of peace who have broken the peace of God by the fury of discord." Besides arguing in general from the doctrine of the unity, he maintained (*Ep.* 72. 1, 73. 7) that baptism, as it includes forgiveness of sins, was granted by our Lord to Peter on behalf of the episcopate and those in union with them, was therefore valid only as administered with their sanction. Reasoning *ad hominem*, he pointed to the admission of his opponents, that in the cases debated, the imposition of the bishop's hands was needful; but that meant the communication of the Holy Spirit. If the Holy Spirit had been lacking from the heretical baptism, how could it be baptism at all? It might be a kind of external judaical ceremony; but that was all. It was argued on the other side, that the faith professed at such baptisms might be that of the Church. But this was not sufficient; besides, as a matter of fact, it was doubtful. In cases where the baptism was merely in the name of Jesus Christ, who could be sure what the faith was? Finally, the argument from history or usage, and from the consistencies of church practice in dealing with

---

[1] This was a rite applied in many ways; in all its applications it signified the Church's recognition of the candidate's purpose, and her benediction in connection with it.

the array of conceivable cases, was handled by Cyprian with great energy, strength, and effect.

Stephen, who succeeded Cornelius at Rome, upheld the practice of his church, and strove to impose it on others. He sent letters to the East threatening to break communion with those who should persist in rebaptizing, and he necessarily came into collision with Cyprian on the subject. Possibly Stephen was willing to find a pretext for doing so. The influence of Cyprian was becoming extraordinarily great, and in his letters to Rome his tone of friendly independence and of plain-spoken counsel, verging on injunction, could hardly be welcome. Cornelius had owed too much to Cyprian for vigorous support against Novatian, to be willing to break with him; but Stephen may have thought the time was come to make a stand, and to reduce the African bishop to his proper place. Stephen maintained that he had on his side ancient custom—especially the tradition of Peter's see, which ought certainly to prevail. He referred also to Paul's rejoicing in the preaching of the gospel, even if preached through envy. The main position was that the efficacy of the one baptism depends not on the administrators, but on the institution of Christ. Those who are baptized in the name of Christ, even by heretics, have been validly baptized, and ought not to be baptized again.

On the principles then received it can hardly be doubted that Cyprian had the better argument. For both sides admitted the theory of church unity which Cyprian expounded. And if the principle is to be admitted in regard to church institutions that the institution is Christ's whoever may administer it, then it cannot be confined to baptism; it must be extended to all those institutions, those sacraments as Rome reckons them,—confirmation and orders, as well as eucharist,—to which Romanism declines to apply it.[1] Archbishop Benson points out that, according to Cyprian, the visible

---

[1] The arguments by which a distinction between baptism and other sacraments is supported may be seen, *inter alia*, in Hefele, *Conciliengeschichte*, i. 105.

Church includes the worst moral sinner, in expectation of his penitency, but excludes the most virtuous and orthodox baptized Christian who had not been baptized by a catholic minister.[1] This is not quite accurate. But apart from that, Cyprian had a right to ask, *Was the* virtuous person baptized? just as the archbishop claimed the right to ask in regard to the most virtuous dissenting minister, *Was he* ordained?

But it was a happy inconsistency which the Roman tradition in this case carried down into the principles and practice of the later Church; and it proved to be possible to theorise it, without sacrificing the exclusive attitude towards heretics and schismatics on which both sides laid so much stress.

The dispute was hot while it lasted. Stephen denounced Cyprian as a false Christ, a false apostle, and a deceitful worker; while Cyprian referred to his opponents as aiding Antichrists; and Firmilian of Cæsarea, making common cause with Cyprian, told Stephen that in trying to cut off others from the Church's unity, he had cut off himself. Dionysius of Alexandria meanwhile exerted himself to bring about mutual toleration (Euseb. *Hist. Eccl.* vii. 5).

At this stage the opposing theories were boldly and roundly asserted; Cyprian was for rebaptizing the disciple even of the most orthodox schismatic sect; and Stephen, apparently, was against rebaptizing the disciple even of the most heterodox, and was prepared to accept baptism in the name of Christ, without reference to the Trinity. After the death of Stephen the conflict died out, each church maintaining its own custom. But probably the weight of authoritative practice was already against rebaptizing. Moreover, cases differed, and in many cases the maintenance of the principle that the man proposing to come over to orthodoxy was still unbaptized, offended against common sense. The Roman view gained the day, but with slight modifications. The synod of Arles (A.D. 314) decided that baptism in heresy should be recognised, if it appeared that Father, Son, and Holy Ghost were owned in the administra-

[1] Smith, *Dict. of Christian Biography*, i. 752.

tion. The great council of Nicea, however,[1] seemed to sanction a construction of this decision which questioned the validity of baptism in the case of sects regarded as unsound with respect to the Trinity, even though the formula prescribed in Matt. xxviii. had been used in the administration. With this qualification, the exact amount of which is debatable, the practice advocated by Stephen was ultimately acquiesced in by the Church.

[1] Canon 19.

# CHAPTER XVI

### MANICHEISM

I. de Beausobre, *Hist. crit. de Manichée et du Manichéisme*, Amst. 1734.
Flügel, *Mani*, Leipz. 1862.

WHILE the Christian religion was settling itself on fixed lines, the problem of the world and of human life was suggesting new efforts of religion-building. Manicheism took origin in the third century. This form of dualism did not seriously affect the Christianity of the empire until the fourth century; from that time it appears and reappears, though carefully suppressed by Church and State whenever it became visible. Properly speaking, it was not a Christian heresy, but an extra-Christian religion. Yet some appropriation of the name and the institutions of Jesus entered into the scheme of Mani himself; and this element may have been expanded in the hands of his disciples, as Manicheism moved westwards, and made its appeal to the Christians of the Roman world.

Mani (or Manes) was a Persian, born about A.D. 216. He found Parsism in power, as the popular and the State religion. Mani appears also to have inherited from his father some ideas which traced up to materialistic and magical elements of Babylonian idolatry; and elements of Buddhism have been recognised in his system, connected, doubtless, with the journeys in far eastern regions which he is said to have undertaken. He felt in himself the impulse to take ground as a religious innovator. Like Mahomed afterwards, he claimed to be the last and greatest prophet, and he sent forth emissaries to preach in his name.

Eventually he returned to Persia and aimed at great things there; but religious antipathies and political suspicions became too strong for him, and sometime after 272 he was cruelly put to death. His disciples also were bitterly persecuted. But the man had impressed his followers, and his ways of thinking could appeal with force to many minds. Manicheism was nowhere adopted as a national faith, or as the characteristic religion of a race. But as a sect, it maintained a prolonged existence in the East, having its centre at Babylon and afterwards at Samarcand, and stretching out to India and China.

Manicheism appeared in the Roman Empire before the close of the third century, and created active discussion during the fourth. It made itself known as an ascetic religion resting on divine revelation, claiming to embody the true view of the universe, and the true securities for human welfare in a future life. Further, it professed to embody a corrected Christianity, which it naturally claimed to complete as well as to purify. Hence it appealed to passages in the Gospels and Epistles; but it regarded all these as more or less corrupted. The canonical books of the sect were certain writings of Mani. The recognised officials were (1) teachers (twelve, apparently, to correspond with the apostles—one of whom might specially represent Mani); (2) bishops (seventy-two according to Augustine); and (3) presbyters. The adherents of the sect fell into two classes, *electi* and *auditores*. The elect abstained from animal food and wine, from material occupations and labours, and from marriage; they might not injure even plant life, and therefore their vegetable food must not be gathered by their own hands, but be supplied to them by the *auditores*, and they were bound to frequent and rigorous fasting. The *auditores*, who were imperfect members, might engage in the ordinary relations and occupations of society; but in addition to the observance of moral rules, were expected to put no animal to death, to prefer a simple and retired life, and to provide for the wants of the elect, and pay them great respect. The intercession of the elect was supposed to avail vicariously for the welfare of the comparatively imperfect *auditores*. Augustine was led to suspect that a good deal of hypocrisy and make-believe existed among the Manichean elect, and he mentions circumstances which had produced that impression. But inconsistency might exist in some degree, and still more it might be imputed by opponents, without supplying any good ground for doubting the sincerity and earnestness of the sect in general.

There could be no great show of external evidence for Mani's claims to be a medium of revelation. The sect must have made way, therefore, on the strength either of its theory of the universe, which might be reckoned credible and impressive, or of its system of life and worship, which might be accepted as worthy and helpful.

The force with which the conception of the world, as the scene of conflict between two originally opposed and irreconcilable principles, is able at some times to lay hold of the minds of men, has here one more illustration. The life enjoined on his followers by Mani was based on a system of dualism, fanciful in its details, but possessing some important distinctive features. It differed from the system of Zoroaster in a more intense conception of the entanglement in evil in which human spirits are involved, and also in the stress it laid upon a redemptive process, and a life conformed to that process. From Christianity it differed, not merely in its dualism, but especially in the demand it made, that the elements of evil in the world should be fixed as concrete material things, and should be precisely named and numbered. Then the true life must shape itself in opposition to these things, and by deliverance from them. Anything less concrete and less material than this would have seemed to Mani unreal, missing the substantials and going astray among shadows. Yet along with this he enjoined the usual moralities, mostly in the negative form.

Good and evil, in this system, are identified with light and darkness, also with purer and more impure substance.

The kingdom of light and the kingdom of darkness, each

with its personal king, stand over against one another. A time arrives when the kingdom of darkness makes its effort against the kingdom of light. The first man, who is God's firstborn, leads the five pure elements into war against the powers of evil; he is overthrown, but eventually delivered; yet a part of his light has been carried off captive by the darkness. With a view to extricate this captive nature, the God of light causes the universe we know to be organised. The object of its living processes, at least of its plant life, is to afford channels by which the captive element may physically make its escape from the elements of darkness which detain it. Along the zodiac the particles of light, as they escape, reach the sun and moon, where they are purified and passed on to their proper home. The sun is the dwelling of the first man (Jesus *impatibilis*); the moon, of the mother of life, through whom he came into existence. And those two luminaries are ships which, moving in the sky, carry on the processes of redemption. Against all this the Prince of darkness creates man, in whom the captive element of light, so far as available, is concentrated, but fatally entangled with sensuality, covetousness, and sin; so that every man may be regarded as having a soul that is akin to goodness, but also an evil one. Generation expresses the line along which the Prince of darkness would have evil triumph in human history. But the powers of light join battle on this arena of human history and character, so that here the moral element comes in. In addition to mere physical processes by which light is either held captive or is emancipated, human thought and choice now come into play; the unconscious world-process has added to it the element of conscious effort; but largely in the way of calling men to recognise the proper physical distinctions, and to give effect to them. Prophets also have appeared in the world, to do the work of the kingdom of light; but not Moses and the Jewish prophets; for Judaism, like heathenism, is on the side of darkness, and Manes rejected the Old Testament, no doubt because it frankly owns the good of material life Jesus appeared, docetically, in the form of a human body;

but his teaching has been corrupted and misrepresented by his followers. Still, in all these ways men have been invited and attracted to a way of life in which their better soul may escape from the power of darkness and of matter. Finally, Mani, the last and greatest prophet, appears as the Paraclete of Jesus and the true guide of men.

Men are to experience this redemption under the guidance of Mani, by due separation from the sensual and the material, and by appropriating—eating, in fact—the creatures which yield elements of light. Full members of the Manichean church (*electi*) accepted a threefold seal,—*signaculum oris*, which implied renunciation of animal food and wine, as well as of impure speech; *signaculum manus*, which implied all possible abstinence from activity about the material things and interests of the world; and *signaculum sinus*, which implied complete chastity. Severe fastings and regulated prayers, with sacred washings, were also enjoined; the prayers were addressed, so far as is known, to God, to the kingdom of light, to angels, and to Mani himself. The *auditores*, or catechumens, as already stated, were much less stringently treated; and many adherents of the sect were content to remain in this stage, and were allowed to believe that they might in this way attain Manichean salvation. The worship in which the *auditores* joined seems to have been unimpressive and bare. In March a festival was held (replacing the Easter of the Christians), in which an empty pulpit or desk (*Bema*), representing the authority of Mani as teacher, was devoutly venerated. For the elect a baptism with oil, and an observance modelled on the Lord's Supper, are said to have been in use.

This system may have been welcome to some, because it reduced the mysteries of good and evil to concrete and tangible forms; also because, in its own way, it turned the world into a parable of the great struggle, and a source of endless allegories to set it forth. Besides this, it could be so propounded as to awaken expectation of a progressive enlightenment, in the course of which the neophyte's difficulties would gradually melt away, and a deeper secret meaning would appear. This was one, perhaps the main, motive which drew Augustine to listen to the teaching. In due time he saw it to be pretentious and baseless.

An edict of Diocletian, dated at Alexandria (perhaps of the year 287), authorises the suppression of Manicheism. During the following century it grew in various provinces of the empire, particularly in Africa. From the time of Valentinian I. edicts were issued against it by Christian emperors, and it was sedulously suppressed. The tendency to distort Christianity in the Manichean direction continued, however, to exist, and showed itself in new forms in various later sects.

In the intention of its founder, and according to the main drift of its teaching, Manicheism was not a version of Christianity; it was a new religion, claiming to be universal, which had appropriated some Christian elements, and especially had found a place for Jesus in its account of the divine plan. But the name of Jesus comes with power wherever it does come; and in the case of many of its adherents, especially in the West, Manicheism may have been practically a Christian heresy. It embodied from the first the aspiration, so remarkable and so pathetic, after a life above the sensual. In that form its founder proposed to find and to embrace a better part. And as glimpses of a redeeming care and power in connection with Jesus crossed its teaching, it is possible that Christ found His own sometimes even among the Manicheans.

# THIRD DIVISION
### A.D. 313–451

## CHAPTER XVII

### The Church in the Christian Empire and beyond

Broglie, *L'Église et l'Empire Romain au IV<sup>me</sup> Siecle*, Paris, 1866. W. Bright, *History of the Church 313–451*, London, 1869. Sohms, *Kirchengeschichte in Abriss*, 1888. Gibbon, *Decline and Fall*. Tillemont, *Hist. des Empereurs*, folio, Venice, 1732, vols. iv.–vi.

#### A. THE EMPERORS

In A.D. 313 Constantine and Licinius divided the empire between them. Both of them at that time announced a policy of toleration, though Licinius some years later became a declared enemy to the Church. In 323 Licinius was overthrown, and from that time Constantine reigned alone. His victory decided also the religious question. The ruler of the world became the patron of the Christian Church.

During the rest of the period three families successively supplied rulers for the empire, viz. that of Constantine, that of Valentinian, and that of Theodosius.

Constantine I. died in A.D. 337. He was succeeded by his three sons, Constantine, Constantius, and Constans; but at the death of Constantine (A.D. 340), Constans assumed the government of his provinces also; and when, in A.D. 351, Constans fell in battle, Constantius became sole ruler. In A.D. 361 he was on the verge of war against his cousin

Julian; for the legions of Gaul, where Julian commanded, had saluted him as Augustus, and Constantius would neither share the empire nor resign it. At the critical moment, however, Constantius died, and Julian succeeded without a struggle. He declared himself a worshipper of the old gods, and made his famous effort to rehabilitate paganism. In less than two years he died in battle against the Persians, and his projects fell with him.

After the short reign of Jovian (A.D. 363–364), Valentinian inaugurated a second dynasty. He was a good soldier, was orthodox according to the standard of those days, and at the same time was fairly tolerant in religious matters. Leaving the East to his brother Valens, he ruled the West till his death, A.D. 375. His sons—Gratian by his first wife, and Valentinian by his second; the first a youth, the second a child—became joint emperors of the West. In connection with the insurrection of Maximus in A.D. 383, Gratian was put to death; but Maximus accepted Valentinian II. as his colleague, and ruled for five years. At the end of that time he was overthrown and put to death by Theodosius. Valentinian II., supported by Theodosius, continued to be nominal sovereign of the West until another insurrection in A.D. 392 led to his death also.

Meanwhile, in the East, Valens reigned from A.D. 364 to 378. In church affairs he was an active Arian; in those of the State the weakness of his government was revealed when the pressure of the Goths upon the frontier had to be dealt with. Valens fell in the great battle of Adrianople; and he left the Eastern empire in extreme danger. Gratian, who was still a youth, and whose hands were full with Western troubles, could do little to retrieve the disasters in the East. Happily for the State he called in Theodosius, who became emperor in the East, A.D. 379.

Theodosius I. founded a third dynasty. He belonged to a notable Spanish family; and perhaps his occasional bursts of furious passion, his resolute orthodoxy, and his disposition to repress heresy by persecution, were all connected with his Spanish blood. However that may be, his courage and success earned for him the title of the Great. He brought the Gothic wars to an end, restored the order of the State, and vigorously discouraged Arianism. In A.D. 388 he went to the aid of Valentinian II., who was then assailed by Maximus. In A.D. 394 he once more invaded the West to overthrow Eugenius, who had usurped the throne on the death of Valentinian. After achieving a complete victory Theodosius died in the West, A.D. 395.

The empire, East and West, had been for a moment reunited in his person; at his death it was again divided. Arcadius (A.D. 395–408), Theodosius II. (A.D. 408–450), and Pulcheria (to A.D. 453) represented the line of Theodosius I. in the East; in the West, Honorius (A.D. 395–423) and Valentinian III. (A.D. 425–455).

So far therefore the form of the Roman Empire had been maintained, and up to the death of Theodosius I. its dignity and strength might seem to have not yet failed. But decay was going on; feeble rulers paralysed the State more than strong rulers could invigorate it; and the impulses which propelled the barbarians into the empire never ceased to operate. In the West, especially, revolts and invasions followed one another. In Africa the revolt of Firmus (A.D. 372–374) and that of Gildo (A.D. 386–398) preluded the conquests of the Vandals (from A.D. 428). Italy was invaded by Alaric, by Radagaisus, by Attila.[1] Gaul and Spain, after being overrun by various tribes, were restored to nominal connection with the empire, at least in part, by the Visigoths, who had left Italy, and who posed in Gaul as the allies of Rome. But in these provinces civilisation had been shaken to its base, and their inhabitants had learned that Rome could no longer protect loyalty or reward it. Britain, which had sent various usurpers to the Continent, finally resolved to provide for its own safety; and so did Armorica. Honorius sanctioned the arrangement: but as regards Britain, the Saxons were soon to come and take possession. The sack

[1] The last in A.D. 451 or 452. But he had vexed the Eastern empire for years before, and had invaded Gaul in A.D. 449.

of Rome by Alaric in A.D. 410,[1] and the devastating conquests of Attila (453), resounded through the world as the knell of Roman glory. Not only the whole West, but the European provinces of the Eastern empire were repeatedly wasted by these calamitous invasions. For the present the Asiatic and the Egyptian provinces were more fortunate.

The period ends, therefore, in political confusion and social misery. But at the beginning it promised well. To Christians, in particular, the accession of Constantine must have seemed most propitious. God had raised up for them a great deliverer; the ruler of the world was now a servant of Christ; his arm had proved strong to conquer peace and to maintain it. In those days it seemed as if, under Christian auspices, the empire might essay a new career, more benignant and not less prosperous than of old. A hundred years later Christian pens were busy in explaining that the Roman State was too bad to be saved, too thoroughly pervaded by principles of earth and sin to escape from overthrow.[2]

### B. THE CHURCH IN TRANSITION

Christians must have multiplied rapidly during the third century, particularly after the accession of Gallienus;[3] doubtless at the end of the century they were still very much in the minority;[4] but they were a very compact, resolute, and growing minority; they alone, indeed, were sure of their ground, and confident of their future. Their progress, whatever the rate of it may have been, was undoubtedly impressing the minds of many who were not Christians. It roused the advisers of Diocletian to try

---

[1] That by Genseric the Vandal followed, A.D. 455.
[2] Orosius, Augustine, Salvian.
[3] Gregory Thaumaturgus was said to have found seventeen Christians only at Neo-Cæsarea, when he became bishop there, and to have left only seventeen of the inhabitants still heathen at the date of his death (perhaps A.D. 238-270). This, like much else told of him, is at least exceptional.
[4] Gibbon's estimate, however, is too low.

one more persecution; but it must have impressed others in a quite different way. It forced men to recognise that the forms of traditional religion were played out, and that, whether Christianity were divine or not, the future lay with it. As each generation passed, this impression spread wider. Enthusiastic Neoplatonists might persuade themselves that the old worship could be rationalised; Roman sentiment might cling to old Roman rites, especially among the noble families of Rome itself; and the population of rural districts, where Christianity made less progress, could resist the influences that made for change. But the educated people, and indeed all who felt the stir of the world, must have had an uneasy sense of the feebleness of their own religion, and also of the energy with which Christianity pressed forward to supplant it. In fact every Christian congregation was a focus of thought. It lived by energetic convictions which set people a thinking. Paganism, on the other hand, was little more than a set of customs, having only the faintest connection with intelligence, and its priests were mere performers of rites. Of those who wrote against Christianity not one was a priest of the old religion. In reference to the movement and questioning of the age, that religion was deaf and dumb.

In the current confidential talk of the town populations and of educated people, during several generations, the moral of all this must have been drawn. They might not care about Christianity; they might not even regret the persecution of Diocletian, though probably they regarded it as foolish, perhaps as annoying. But when that ended in confessed failure, it must have been silently owned by masses of men that this faith, which had once more outworn the strength of the empire, was like to grow into a great mountain and fill the earth. The extent to which these impressions existed is proved by the action of Constantine. When he decided that it was safe and wise to stand forth as the protector, and afterwards as the patron, of the Christian faith, he must have known very well that the Christians were a minority. But it might well be that a majority agreed with him in thinking the acceptance of Christianity as the coming religion to be no bad policy. Nothing vital existed that could be set against it. And from that day onwards no real popular rally for the old faiths was possible. Those, and they were very many indeed, who did not love Christianity, yet felt no call to interpose on behalf of paganism. When it became evident, then, that Christianity was to be the favoured, and the only favoured religion, many became willing to adopt it, and many more to let their children adopt it. It was the faith which had a future; and now the adoption of it was no longer to hinder a man's worldly prospects, but rather to help them.

Of course this indifference was not universal. Not a few continued to cherish regard for the old deities and the old rites. The preference might be aristocratic at Rome, philosophic at Athens, a popular passion in some towns and in many rural districts. For this paganism, here and there, a man might be found willing even to die. There is always some tragic fidelity to lost causes. The great sea of paganism did not empty itself into the Christian Church at once; but a great stream of converts flowed in incessantly and for a long time. Gradually it came to be taken for granted, all but universally, that those who cared to have some religion should have this one.

Long before Diocletian it was plain enough that the churches numbered many members whose sincerity was very doubtful. Influences were already at work that attracted a good many to Christianity without subjecting them to Christ.[1] But after Constantine's adhesion, the world began, inevitably, to pour into the Church. Thus a new stage of her history sets in; for forces, which had indeed more or less been operating all along, began to operate with new energy and greatly increased effect.

The Church's relation to the State is one department of

---

[1] So common an experience hardly needs proof. But see the character of many converts of Gregory Thaumaturgus, *Epist. Canonica*, and the canons of councils in the beginning of the fourth century, as Elvira. Hefele, i. 122.

this subject; but it is better to think first of the Church's relation to the world.

Various causes now rendered it creditable, expedient, customary for men to become Christians. The advantages of doing so were increased, certainly, by a variety of influences governmental and other. But the radical fact was that the ruler of the empire had adopted Christianity, did not conceal his preference for it,[1] and (at best) left paganism to reveal all its weakness, without countenance or succour. After that, there could be no lack of reasons to induce careless, worldly, or unprincipled people to associate themselves with the winning side. Relations between Church and State (whether right or wrong) might be superinduced on this situation, but this remains fundamental.

When the Christian Church finds herself in such circumstances, there must, no doubt, be duties which, then specially, it falls to her to discharge, with a view to maintain her character as the witness to truth and righteousness, and her fitness for the functions committed to her. How far such duties were rightly conceived, or rightly discharged, by the Church in the fourth century, this is not the place to discuss. The point to attend to is that, at all events, the Church was subjected to new experiences, and that the strain was applied to her whole system in a new direction. Fidelity to Christ might still bring its penalties; but as far as the Christian name and association with the Church were concerned, discouragement had passed away and the approbation of society had begun.

With such a flood of questionable disciples the standard of Christian feeling and of Christian life could not but tend downwards, and new difficulties were prepared for those who tried to raise it. Secularising influence asserted itself everywhere.[2]

---

[1] Whatever may be thought of Constantine's personal Christianity, it soon became clear that the emperor took a keen interest in the religion he professed, and the same was true of most of his successors.

[2] No better proof need be offered than some of Augustine's statements in the Donatist controversy, all the more because Augustine's sympathies with spiritual life are so pronounced, *e.g. Contr. Ep. Parm.* iii. 13, 14, 15.

On the other hand, Christian teaching could now command the ear of the Roman world. The message of salvation could be made common news, and men in general could be confronted with the Christian ideas. These were the compensations. How the loss and the gain balanced one another in that great revolution will be differently judged by different minds. Even those who take dark views of the proximate effects, will not forget how strong Christianity proves to be, even at its weakest, and what power of recovery and reform it can command. For the present, at anyrate, it became matter of course to profess Christianity, both on the part of those who cared much for it, and on the part of many who cared little or nothing. A great mass of unfixed opinion, of worldly and loose life, made itself at home in the Church. And the maintenance of a conflict at the risk of all things, for the name and faith of Christ, such as had so often recurred during the first three centuries, had ended. For the enemy was disarmed; outwardly in the empire Christianity was to be oppressed no more. In that sense there were to be no more confessors or martyrs.

These forms of influence, it has been pointed out, must have revealed themselves forcibly, even if the conversion of the emperor had not been accompanied by the formation of ties between the Christian Church and the State. But no one thought of that as natural or possible. Immunities, privileges, revenues, were conferred on the Church. The clergy became important public functionaries; ere long it was thought appropriate to apply discouragement, in various degrees, to the enemies or opponents of the true faith. Then, moreover, the State had to form a judgment as to the Christianity it should and the Christianity it should not favour. It could apply influences to the clergy whose influence it owned, and it had to decide which types of error called for discouragement, and what degree of discouragement they deserved. In all these departments the mind of the Christian community, asserting itself through all the successive confusions, did, no doubt, powerfully control the eventual decisions of the State. But, on the other hand, the

State and its representatives, mingling as a domestic force in the Church's affairs, exerted a continuous influence, both paralysing and secularising, on her agents and her action. The secular life of a corrupt time infused so much the more easily its method and its spirit into the great organisation known as the Catholic Church. This cannot be overlooked by any student. The reaction of the genuinely Christian spirit against the perplexities and temptations hence arising is not less deserving of attention.

### C. POLICY OF THE CHRISTIAN EMPIRE IN REGARD TO RELIGION

Constantine's public favour for Christianity had opened with a strong disclaimer of intolerance, and recognition of the principle that each man should regulate his own religious affairs. Nor did he afterwards violate flagrantly the principles then announced. He set forth laws against divination and magic, but these followed precedents already set by heathen emperors; and in forbidding rites connected with immorality or fraud, he might be looked on as protecting public order. Towards the end of his reign he despoiled or closed various temples, either to weaken idolatry, or to adorn his new capital, or to turn the buildings and revenues to Christian uses. But in many places these temples had begun to be forsaken by their worshippers, and that might afford a pretext for finding a new use for them. There seems to be doubt as to an alleged law against sacrifices, issued late in his reign.[1] In any case, the measure does not seem to have been carried out in practice.

The sons of Constantine acted more decidedly. Constantius ordered the temples to be closed, and forbade sacrifices on pain of death. The law was certainly not universally enforced. However, from this time, under Christian emperors, the public worship of paganism was liable to challenge. After Julian, however, a short period

---

[1] *Nocturnal* sacrifices had often been objects of special prohibition, and the alleged law might apply to them.

of partial toleration obtained (*bloody* sacrifices were forbidden, but not incense). Theodosius himself did not go much beyond this till about 391, when he forbade the frequenting of the temples altogether. The temples themselves were to be maintained as public monuments; but the zeal of Christian mobs outran the laws, and in various places temples were pulled down. Paganism, in fact, was growing weaker, and emperors and people alike felt free to treat it with less ceremony. In 392 Theodosius forbade all kinds of idolatry. Under his successors in the East the actual suppression of pagan worship was carried out—often by swarms of ascetics, who attacked the temples and put down the idolatrous practices by force. In the West paganism was more vigorous; and amid the confusions in that part of the world, the struggle between the two religions had various fortunes in different districts, so that people suffered both for Christianity and for paganism. The suppression of the altar of Victory in the Roman senate, decreed by Gratian and followed up by Theodosius, was one landmark in the process. In the remoter districts zealous bishops led on their flocks to demolish temples,[1] but reactionary pagans were sometimes equally violent. In the end many local ceremonies, associated with paganism, were carried over, with the necessary changes, to the Christian worship. The whole situation in the West was powerfully modified by the fact that the Goths, though heretics, were by profession Christians: other invading German races, that had not accepted Christianity, took little interest in the religious question within the empire.

Since the policy of the emperors, in adhering to Christianity and recommending it, was bringing to the Church many new adherents, buildings and ministers were wanted to meet the situation thus created; and the resources of the Church could hardly be equal to the strain. This might be a special reason for the State contributing to her necessities. But probably Constantine did not think any argument to be required in order to justify his showing favour, out of

[1] Sulp. Sev. *Vita Martini*, c. 13

the public revenue, to the religion which he preferred. He contributed in various forms to the supply of churches and the support of ministers; but many of these arrangements were local and temporary. The nearest approach to a permanent establishment was an edict appointing an alimentary allowance of corn to be made for the support of the clergy (σιτηρέσιον, σύνταξις τοῦ σίτου) from the treasuries of the various towns. It is not clear whether this extended to the whole empire. The provision was withdrawn by Julian; and, after his death, it was restored only to the extent of one-third, because the local revenues could not bear a larger contribution. The clergy, however, still depended mainly on the offerings of the people; and the growth of the ecclesiastical wealth came much more from gifts and legacies (which the Church was now legally authorised to receive) than from the State. Chrysostom, indeed, expresses a doubt whether the Church was not the poorer for such help as the State did give, inasmuch as the public aid had chilled the private generosity of the Christian people.[1] Constantine exempted the clergy from public offices, such offices being of the nature of burdens imposed on persons possessed of property; but he soon found it necessary to modify this regulation, because rich men joined the ranks of the clergy in order to escape their public responsibilities. Constantine sanctioned the observance of the Lord's Day— *Venerabilis dies solis*—by the intermission of many kinds of employment. Constantius relieved the clergy from the poll tax, and from some other occasional exactions. In addition, the custom of resorting to the bishop for arbitration was recognised in cases where both parties consented; and his award was made valid in law. Intercessions of bishops in behalf of those who were in danger of severe punishments were allowed considerable influence; and a right of sanctuary in churches for accused persons came to be legally recognised, at least in certain cases and for a limited time.

In the legal system of the empire improvements had

[1] *Hom. Matth.* xxvi. 67.

been in progress from a period much anterior to Constantine. A livelier sense of the equality of races, of the common rights and interests of human beings, of the claims of equity and piety, had gained ground in the empire during the second and following centuries. These reforms were guided by great lawyers. Amid the caprices of despotic government, and the vicissitudes of stormy times, they still cherished high legal ideals, and gave effect to them when they could; and their thoughts were widened by the variety of legal traditions which the empire included. Improvements therefore were not solely due to Christian influence,—but that influence, too, was telling. A sterner tone was taken towards immorality; gladiatorial contests were by degrees suppressed.[1] The interests of oppressed classes—of slaves, children, women, especially widows and orphans—were better guarded. On subjects like marriage, legislation began to conform to Christian ideas, *e.g.* as to forbidden degrees, and even to Christian prejudices like that which disapproved of second marriages; and the laws against celibacy were repealed. But this approximation could only be gradual; for example, large liberty of divorce continued; and it is remarked that punishments became more severe and savage.

### D. THE PAGAN OPPOSITION

Neander, *Julian*, 1813. Merivale, *Boyle Lectures*, 1864–5.

Those who still worshipped the old gods persisted for the most part silently; but sometimes they defended themselves by force against Christian assailants, and sometimes they revenged themselves on individual Christians for the wrongs they suffered. The Christians whom the Alexandrian bishop Theophilus urged on to assail the temple of Serapis (A.D. 391) were resolutely met, and only prevailed after a bloody struggle. Collisions of this kind were, however, most apt

---

[1] They lingered longest at Rome, where they were abolished in the time of Honorius. See story of the monk Telemachus, whose self-sacrifice brought the butchery to an end, in Theod. *Hist. Eccl.* v. 26.

to happen in remote places, where a population, predominantly heathen, clung to its old rites.¹ In most places observances survived—spectacles, popular usages, and festivals—which retained a heathen character; and nominal Christians shared largely in them. Yet this really indicated that in the opinion and feeling of the people heathenism as a serious business was passing away.

It is well to note, however, the character of representative men who maintained the dying cause. Among the Roman nobles the most interesting upholder of paganism was Q. Aurelius Symmachus, who was prefect of the city in A.D. 384. He led the remonstrants on the question of the altar of Victory—which might almost be said to symbolise the right of Roman senators to worship as their fathers did. In A.D. 382, 384, 392, and perhaps again in 403 or 404, he exerted himself to move the Christian emperors to make this concession, and once incurred banishment for his pertinacity. A member of the college of pontiffs, and strict in the performance of his office, he was also well descended, and a man of great wealth; but he was especially valued for his high personal qualities. Symmachus was on friendly terms with eminent Christians, and Christian writers speak of him with unvarying respect.² Such was the man, and such his surroundings, who pleaded for toleration of the altar of Victory, and could not prevail.³

Another form of eminence which furnished some advantage in withstanding Christianity, was distinction in

---

¹ All the more because it was believed that on these rites being duly performed, health, crops, and other forms of prosperity depended.

² It is interesting to know that the influence of Symmachus (then prefect at Rome, — previously he had been proconsul of Africa) was successfully exerted in favour of Augustine, when the latter, weary of the ways of Roman students, sought a post at Milan. Augustine was not yet a Christian; but his transference to Milan, where he was to come under the influence of Ambrose, was a step in that direction.

³ Of the religion of his son, who also held high office, we are uncertain. His great-grandson, who was eminent before A.D. 525, was a Catholic Christian. Members (probably) of the same family were friends and correspondents of Gregory the Great at the end of the sixth century. See Smith Dict. of Christian Biography, art. "Symmachus."

literary studies. Assiduous study in the ancient writers tended naturally to create spiritual loyalty to the ancient world, to its culture and its literature. Now the whole way of thinking which pervaded that literature was attuned to a conception of the world which Christianity overthrew. To men of this class, therefore, the faith of Christ came as a disturbing influence; they disliked and resented it; if any of them professed Christianity, it was usually Christianity of the lukewarm and dubious type. These men of letters could still maintain the impression that something barbarian and illiterate clung to the new religion; and this was a note of inferiority which, in their eyes, discredited its claims.

No better specimen of this class can be named than Libanius the rhetorician. His works have the fatal emptiness and artificiality inevitable to a man of letters who, living in the past, cuts himself off from the interests and the forces which are vital in his own time. But the man himself appears to have been a person of good sense and good feeling, very capable of friendship, and deserving of respect. He obtained regard or consideration from Christians like Athanasius, Chrysostom, Basil, and the Gregories.

Men of this type might be men of no religion at all,— the old mythology merely clinging to their minds as a world of gracious forms which they would not discard. But most of them accepted the Neoplatonic principles; they believed, therefore, that something true and good, in its degree, really pervaded the pagan worships, and that the supreme goodness might fitly be approached through the avenues thus furnished. A kind of belief—a certain real religiosity on pagan lines—must be recognised. But it had a twilight character. Ardour or passion of conviction cannot be ascribed to such men as a class; and, when they plead their cause, the toleration they ask for seems tolerance for their tastes rather than for anything higher. Here and there, doubtless, the flame burnt more intensely.[1]

Certainly an intenser mood must be ascribed to the

[1] And with a denser smoke of superstition: Jamblichus may be named.

remarkable Emperor Julian. His recoil from Christianity has, naturally enough, been accounted for from his peculiar history; it has been traced to the wrongs inflicted on his family by Constantius, the precarious tenure by which for years he held his life, and the self-suppression with which he had to guard his thoughts and feelings from the Christian tutors, who were also spies, in whose charge he was. Constantius himself, the author of Julian's adversities, was an ardent Christian in his way; and so when, as an alternative, a plausible non-Christian conception of life offered itself, it found Julian predisposed to embrace it. All this must certainly count for something. Yet in the case of Julian's brother, Gallus, the same causes failed to produce a similar result.

Julian, like other members of the house of Constantine, was religiously disposed. Religion interested and attracted him. Had he been a Christian he would have been, most likely, a keen and restless one. Without being a Christian, he was sincere and devout in his regard to the supernatural, and he combined his piety with a high moral standard, and a resolute effort to be true to it. Now for such a man the age offered an alternative. In an earlier chapter[1] we have sketched the way in which Neoplatonism appealed to some minds in the third and fourth centuries. Julian doubtless felt the force of that appeal; and something in Christianity repelled him. It was too positive, too peremptory, too sure of itself; it assigned to its disciple a place too lowly, and it had too much to say of sin. Also it scorned all other religion as futile and null; but that might stir Julian to resolve to confute it on that very point. There was plenty of religiosity in the world,—there were portents, faith healings, apparitions, apprehensions of the supernatural, worships, mysteries;[2] and these, it seemed, were all to be trampled down or waived aside at the bidding of Christianity. But why? Why should all that had flowered out from the classic

---

[1] *Supra*, p. 146.
[2] How all these held their place in the common mind, see Lucian "Philopseudes," and also "Alexander of Abonoteichus."

mind and heart wither and die? It needed to be rallied: it needed to be moralised, dignified, made practical and venerable. With a view to that, men must be in earnest with the New Platonism; paganism must be made to take itself seriously. The popular rites must be filled with the awe of worship, and made to ally themselves with moral purpose and spiritual aspiration. For Julian had certainly learned to appreciate some of the forces of Christianity: its resolute faith, its great ideas inculcated by preaching, its moral intensity. Let the old worship, then, be quickened by the doctrines of a congenial and friendly philosophy; let it be as believing as Christianity, as assiduous in preaching, as conscious of the dignity of moral life. Julian was serious in all this. He was himself religious without Christ, and religious in a sense that gave glow and expectancy to his existence; and he was so little opposed to the supernatural, or distrustful of it, that he was ready to meet it everywhere. If he could live this life, then the world, too, could do so. It was *not* needful to sacrifice the culture, the thought, and the worships of Greece to a barbarian creed.

Philostratus (A.D. 182–245) had made an effort to show that what was admirable and desirable in Christ could be had on pagan terms. He had exhibited Apollonius (living in the end of the first century) as a reformer and renovator of heathen religion, who exhaled goodness, and who carried the supernatural with him wherever he went. That was in a book. But could it not be done in the face of the world? Could not one inspire and energise the heathen religion to make the best of itself, and to embody in actual life the Neoplatonic dream? Perhaps only an emperor could attempt it; but when Julian, after anxious vicissitudes, attained the empire—was not this providential? Was not the time come, and the man?

One sees that Julian, with his sincere religious intensities, had no great religious depth, or he would not have undertaken to reproduce in paganism the features that made Christianity remarkable, and the forces which made it successful. He did not really know what these were, or he knew them only on the surface. But this, after all, makes it easier for us to realise Julian's sincerity. He combined with really great qualities a certain egotistic simplicity and mental *gaucherie*, which reminds one of James VI. of Scotland; only James was far less truthful than Julian was. Julian was a brave and essentially sincere man, with much ability, with intellectual and moral aspiration, and with benevolent impulses. But something that was perverse and even laughable adhered to his best qualities.

Besides descending in person into the literary arena (his κατὰ Χριστιανῶν λόγοι were answered by Cyril of Alexandria),[1] Julian annulled the privileges that had been conferred on the Church by his predecessors, and he restored to the temples the property of which they had been deprived. He probably meditated promoting in the service of the empire only those who were not Christians; and he ordained, in reference to schools, that the ancient literature should be taught only by those who believed in the ancient gods. He showed a certain animosity in dealing with conduct on the part of Christians which he reckoned violent and contumacious: but this is not wonderful: and, on the whole, we must ascribe to him a praiseworthy spirit of tolerance and self-control. It is rather surprising that his enterprise against Christianity had not more success. A certain number of unstable Christians went over to him; but he himself could not reckon them numerous. He stood practically alone. His enthusiasm for pagan rites and magical divinations outran the sympathy even of pagans, while it awakened Christian contempt. Besides, his reign was too short to give play to his projects; and his early death impressed the world with the feeling that the Fates themselves were adverse. All things resumed their former course as soon as he left the scene.

Christianity could be controverted: philosophy could be made plausible to speculative minds: and a materialised system of symbolic worship might be put forward as better

---

[1] *Contra Julianum*. From this source Julian's arguments have been restored by Neumann, Leipsic, 1880.

fitted for the mass of men than the worship that is in spirit and in truth. But Christianity was irresistible. Something might be done by philosophising Christianity, and something by paganising it, but no direct attack in front could be successful.[1] Yet long after public paganism had ceased, intelligent men existed who continued to cling to some form of the pagan traditions.

In the foregoing sketch, those who openly adhered to Christianity and those who made some stand for paganism have been chiefly in view. But in closing, a third class must be kept in view. A mass of people, probably a great mass, who obeyed the emperors, who made no resistance to the abolition of paganism, and who made no objection to the elevation of Christianity to be the State religion, still remained neutral. They had no religion, or rather, they retained enough of superstition to supply the place of one. This superstition might gradually receive Christian elements. But probably a considerable time passed before this great section came to regard Christianity as their own religion, and the offices of the Church as their own inheritance.

### E. CHRISTIANITY BEYOND THE EMPIRE

The most important extension of Christianity at this time was among the Goths. In their case it took the form of Arianism; and in this form it was propagated in turn to other German races. Christian influence seems to have

[1] The New Platonists believed the ancient worship, while it had an element of truth and worth, needed to be purified by being idealised. This reform, which they reckoned practicable, was interfered with by Christianity; and they regarded Christianity (whatever truth it might contain) as mainly a new superstition of barbarian origin. The acceptance of it they regarded as a great mistake, perplexing the proper movement of the world. The attitude of Erasmus and some other Humanists to Lutheranism may be compared. The later New Platonists, including Julian, were led or constrained to throw themselves, much more than the earlier, on the supernatural element in their system, and they did so with conviction. Proclus (412-485) had *seen* Apollo, who cured him of an illness; he had various other experiences of the same kind, and was minute and devout in worship of the ancient gods. On Julian, see Neander, *Kaiser Julian*, Leipsic, 1812; G. H. Rendall, *Emperor Julian* 1879, and a careful article by J. Wordsworth in *Dict. Christ. Biogr.*

reached the Goths first through Christian captives from Cappadocia and other Asian provinces. Later, Gothic tribes settled in the countries on the north bank of the Danube and came into contact with the Christianity of the Eastern empire. Constantinopolitan Christianity was then Arian: and it is to be remembered that even the earlier Christian agents, from Cappadocia or elsewhere, cannot be assumed to have taught a doctrine which was definitely Nicene. Far the most influential person in diffusing and organising Christianity among the Goths was Ulfilas, who was under Constantinopolitan influence, and who was consecrated bishop for the Goths in A.D. 348. He appears to have been an Arian of the Eusebian type. To him the Goths owed their translations of the Scriptures. When the overthrow of Arianism took place under Theodosius, Ulfilas made efforts to avert the catastrophe, and he died at Constantinople, which he had visited in that interest. But his people (specially, the Visigoths) adhered to his teaching, and it spread remarkably among kindred tribes, first among the Ostrogoths and the Vandals. Near the end of our period the Suevi in Spain, and the greater part of the Burgundians in Gaul, adopted Arianism, after having for a time professed Catholicism. The invasion of these races carried a fresh Arian influence into the empire, where that doctrine was dying out. But, on the other hand, the race antagonism between Roman and Goth became religious antagonism between Catholic and Arian. There is little trace of any high culture, any originality, or any great amount of influence among the Gothic clergy. On the whole, the Goths seem to have been fairly tolerant to their Catholic subjects in the territories which they conquered. The Vandals, after their conquest of Africa, form the great exception to this statement. The barbarous persecutions of the African Catholics (under Genseric and Hunerich) fall chiefly later than our period.[1]

[1] C. Anderson Scott, B.A., *Ulfilas, the Apostle of the Goths*, Camb. 1885; K. G. Krafft, *Gesch. der Germ. Völker*, i. Berl. 1854; Gothic transl. of Bible, E. Bernhardt, Halle, 1875.

The Christians in Persia[1] had to endure very severe persecutions, partly because the Persian monarchs regarded Christianity, from the days of Constantine, as a Roman, i.e. a hostile, faith, but partly also because they became fanatical supporters of the Zend religion. Two notable persecutions took place, one in the latter half of the fourth century, the other in the beginning of the fifth. The Persian Christianity was naturally in close alliance with the Syrian, and when Nestorianism was banished from the empire its disciples found shelter among the Persian Christians. Nestorian Christianity, denounced and persecuted by the Romans, was so much the less objectionable in Persia; and from that time the Persian Christianity, in its Nestorian form, maintained its existence with little or no relation to that of the Roman Empire.

The fortunes of Christianity in Armenia[2] also were affected by the repeated wars between the Persians and the Armenians, or between non-Christian Armenians supported by Persia, and Christian Armenians supported by Rome. The struggle on the part of the Armenian Christians was very gallant and resolute. The Persian Government, after years of persecution, found it necessary to adopt a policy of toleration. This Church owed its translation of the Scriptures, and, indeed, the foundation of a native literature, to Mesrob (d. 441). Monophysite influences early prevailed in Armenia, and that doctrine is still professed by the official Armenian Church.

The Christianity of Britain was destined to be crushed over a great part of the old Roman province by the invasion of the heathen Saxons, which began about the end of our period (A.D. 449). But meanwhile Patrick[3] (said to have

---

[1] Rawlinson, *Seventh great Oriental Monarchy*, Lond. 1876; Nöldeke, *Aufsätze zur persischen Geschichte*, Leipz. 1887.

[2] J. St. Martin, *Mémoires Hist. de l'Armenie*, 2 vols., Paris, 1819; Elisæus, *Hist. of Vartan*, translated by C. F. Neumann, Lond. 1830; Neumann, *Gesch. der Armen. Liter.*, Leipz. 1836.

[3] *Life*, etc., by J. H. Todd, D.D., Dublin, 1864. Two writings ascribed to Patrick are believed to be genuine, the *Confessio* and *The Epistle to Coroticus*, in Gallandius, *Biblioth.*, tom. x.

been a native of Kilpatrick on the Clyde, and to have been carried into slavery for a time by sea rovers) became the Apostle of Ireland. His teaching seems to have encountered little serious opposition, and Christianity spread rapidly through the island (from about A.D. 430).

A kingdom called Axum [1] existed to the south of Egypt, coinciding generally with what we now know as Abyssinia. Early in the fourth century a ship, freighted by merchant adventurers, was wrecked on the coast. Two youths, Frumentius and Aedesius, escaped drowning, were brought as slaves to the capital, passed into the service of the king, and gained his favour. By and by they were allowed to return northwards, and at Alexandria Frumentius was consecrated by Athanasius to return as missionary bishop to Axum. The work of Christianity was afterwards pushed on by monks from Egypt, and naturally became subject to the Alexandrian Patriarch. When the discussions regarding the person of Christ were developed, this church took the Monophysite side. It seems soon to have fallen into an inactive and unprogressive state, and it is characterised by some features of a curiously Jewish kind, which are not easily accounted for. It has preserved a literature of its own, which includes Æthiopic translations of early Apocrypha not preserved in any other form. In connection with it a Christianity existed for a time in Southern Arabia; but this was eventually overwhelmed by the onset of Mohammedanism.

#### F. LIFE IN THE CHURCH

Gradually the populations of the empire assumed a Christian tinge. We have no statistics; but even those who did not form any regular tie to the Church acquired some acquaintance with churches, festivals, popular preachers, —also in some degree even with the objects of Christian

---

[1] H. Ludolph, *Hist. Æthiopica*, ed. 4, Frankf. 1681, and *Commentaries*, 1691, App. 1694; Dillmann, *Anfänge des axumitischen Reichs*, Abh. Berl. Ak., 1878, 1880.

faith: they could sometimes mingle in the discussions of Christian parties, and they could appreciate the popular and picturesque side of Christian worship, so far as that was revealed to unbelieving eyes. It was now possible in some places to have Christian *mobs*, ready to fight where Christian interests were supposed to be concerned.

As to the special life of the Church proper, we may remember, in the first place, that the change which Constantine achieved was attended with a great exhilaration for Christian minds. Since the empire had bowed to Christ, no hopes could be too high. For a time this imparted to the Church, and especially to its earnest ministers, new courage and a certain grand style of thought and action. This was never wholly lost, even when times of perplexity and discouragement returned. Then, whatever may be truly said of the progress of a secular and worldly spirit among the Christians and their clergy, it is clear that in the case of individuals and families a powerful religious life, simple, sincere, and resolute, reacted against these influences. The fourth century is an age of great churchmen, and in the case of very many of them they are seen rising out of families in which piety made its home: that is the influence which, in the end, brings about their decision to serve Christ.

The questionable converts, whose presence lowered the average state of the Christian society, were therefore confronted by devoted Christians. Still, the canons of councils reveal the difficulties with which Church discipline had to contend. The indulgences, diversions, and frivolities of a society reared in paganism acclimatised themselves in Christianity, and the coarser sins, though they continued to be resisted and condemned, became commoner incidents, and so more familiar. On the other side, no doubt in many sections of the population marriages, funeral usages, superstitions (as to dangers and deliverances) conformed increasingly to a Christian type, and great Christian festivals became gradually observances which pervaded the community.[1]

[1] A good many local features, arising from old popular feelings and habits, attached to the Christian celebrations and observances in many places. The

In dealing with all this the representatives of the Church too often took a line that was essentially weak. It was very convenient to assume that in baptism a foundation had been laid on which it was necessary only to build some items; and it became a prevalent fashion to insist (as indispensable) on, first, the avoidance of gross sins (the Church's discipline being accepted in case they were incurred); and, second, the cultivation of ecclesiastical virtues, prayer, almsgiving, fasting, which were often recommended expressly on the ground that they take away minor sins. This seemed perhaps the only way to make something of the disciples whom one had in hand, the only formula likely to be intelligible and operative. It tended to give a sanctioned position to a great deal of Christianity that was only a compromise between religious forms and pagan dispositions.

But that the Christian message, represented by the great preachers of the fourth and fifth centuries, could at least stir consciences and awaken lively solicitude, we have a strong proof in the phenomenon of the monastic life which now claims our attention.

effort of the churchmen of the fourth century was to suppress these, and to produce conformity to the methods of the great churches. Ramsay, *Church in Roman Empire*, chap. xvii.

## CHAPTER XVIII

### MONASTICISM

Bingham, *Orig.*, vol. iii. Helyot, *Histoire des Ordres Monastiques*, Paris, 1714. Möhler, *Geschichte d. Mönchthums: Schrift. u. Aufsätzen*, ii A. Harnack, *Das Mönchthum*, 1886. Athan., *De Vita Antonii*, Opp. i. Sozomen, *H. E.* i. c. 12-14. Theodoret, *Hist. Relig.*, Opp. iii. (ed. Hal.) 1886. Jno. Cassian., *Coll. Patrum* in *Corpus Scriptorum Latin.*, Vindob. 1888.

WE have seen that forms of self-denial as to food, marriage, etc., had been adopted by some Christians from a very early period.[1] They aimed, on this line, at Christian thoroughness, and they were known as ascetics. If it was good to begin this kind of life, it must also, of course, be good to persevere; hence declension from a declared ascetic purpose was looked upon as, more or less, a fall. The declared purpose therefore became virtually a vow.[2] Still, those who, after beginning an ascetic course, chose to discontinue it, though thought to be in peril, were not at first regarded as having made total shipwreck. They were, in a sense, within their right, though they were making a questionable use of it.

Such asceticism came to be regarded as the appropriate expression of Christian devotedness, at least for those to whom it was practically open. It was the "whole yoke of the Lord," according to the writer of Clem. Rom. *Ep.* ii. It is the angelic life, according to Methodius (*Conviv.* vii.). In the case of virgins, especially, it acquired a significance that was romantic as well as sacred; for in the light of the Song of Solomon, and of other passages spiritually inter-

---

[1] *Ante*, pp. 68, 223, 224.
[2] Not expressly, apparently, till far on in the third century.

preted, the consecrated women were contemplated as brides of Christ.[1] This view became the source of many inferences.

The earlier ascetic life did not imply separation from the family, nor from ordinary associations. Now it assumed the intenser form of a retreat to the wilderness, so as to part from all of common life that could be parted from. In the desert, distractions could be avoided, temptations to common forms of indulgence must presumably be absent, time could be devoted completely to devout exercises, and the flesh could be chastised. It is not quite clear when this Christian ἀναχώρησις began to be important. There might be stray instances at any time. It has been said that some who fled to the desert to escape the Decian persecution, in the middle of the third century, became enamoured of the lonely and simple life, and continued it after the persecution had passed away.[2] But the historical indications suggest that the stream of Christian hermits began to flow early in the fourth century during Diocletian's persecution.

In taking this course, Christians were only following the example of men of other religions. All religions which preached either the evil of material existence, or its unreality and vanity, were apt, when intensely apprehended, to throw Eastern men on ascetic life. This was the way in which to trample on material ease, and to assert, through solitude and meditation, the supreme worth of spiritual existence. This was the way in which to break through the deceitful shows which entangle us, and find entrance into the region of reality. Egypt, by its soil and climate, lent itself to such a life, or rather, suggested it to meditative men. Accordingly in Egypt there had already existed the Therapeutæ of Philo; and there also the New Platonists, following older schools, had developed their theory of asceticism. In conforming to such examples the Christians found Christian reasons for the course they took, but they could hardly fail

---

[1] Methodius, *Convivium*, iv. 5.
[2] This is implied in the life of Paul of Thebes (by Jerome, *Opp.* ii.); but that authority is not trustworthy.

to imbibe also something of the mode of view of their predecessors. Hence among the Christians themselves the ascetic life was denominated "the philosophy," *i.e.* the practical wisdom. The Christian anchoret was carrying out, in the Christian way, suggestions which had visited even Gentile thinkers.

At first solitude was a chief condition aimed at by the ἀναχωρητής, who thus became μονάζων or μοναχός. The model of the life was Antony, whose story had been written by Athanasius.[1] Antony is said to have been born about A.D. 250. He inherited wealth; but about A.D. 270 the text in the Gospel concerning the rich young man led him to distribute his goods among the poor, and to retreat from the world in order to devote his life to God. He found refuge first in a tomb, then in an old castle, then in a desert place where he could live on dates. Friends brought him some supplies half-yearly; and by and by many sought him for miraculous help or for counsel, and other ascetics gathered round him for guidance. His influence became great after the year 311, when he appeared in Alexandria, during Maximin's persecution, to minister to the martyrs and to denounce the persecutors. Forty years later he once more came to Alexandria, to support the cause of Athanasius during the Arian troubles. He died A.D. 356, it is said at the age of 105. The story of his life contains much that is extravagant and even ludicrous; but an attentive reader will find interesting traits of Christian feeling, and of Christian wisdom also, gleaming through. He seems to have remained a humble man, and he withdrew himself as far as he could from the adulation of his admirers.

The tide of Christian devotees began to flow apparently from the time when Antony became famous. Egypt long continued to be the country most noted for hermits; but early in the century waste places in Palestine and Syria began also to be resorted to. The impulse reached

---

[1] The authorship has been questioned on account of the extraordinary nature of a good deal of the contents; but the evidence for it seems to be conclusive.

Pontus, Cappadocia, and Armenia somewhat later. Far in the East towards the Euphrates the same condition of things is proved by the writings of Aphraates before 346.

Solitude was the ideal of this life; but yet it was a natural tendency for the hermits to draw together and form groups, especially around some exceptional personality. Indeed it is wonderful that the theory of a social being, like man, finding his perfection in solitude, should have been entertained at all. It was soon found, as a matter of fact, that the life of solitude exposed the hermits to dangers and mistakes, both from lack of sympathy and lack of control. It was a gain, therefore, when monastic villages or settlements (λαῦραι) were formed, the ascetics living each in his own hut, but all able to assemble for common worship; and still more when a company of hermits was formed into a society with a regulated common life, the dwellings being arranged with a view to this. The inauguration of this system is ascribed to Pachomius. This ascetic, before A.D. 340, formed a monastery on the island of Tabennæ in the Nile (μοναστήριον, κοινώβιον, place of common life; μάνδρα, fold). Besides the gain to the credit and profit of the ascetic life which seemed likely to arise from the method of Pachomius, it gave to the multitude of hermits an organisation through which they could be connected in an orderly way with the general system of the Church. This was of great importance in an age in which the Church's sanction and benediction were so much prized. It is true, no doubt, as we shall see, that some who revolted from the Church's authority became ascetics, and asserted liberty or eccentricity in that guise. But the opposite tendency was stronger. All the great churchmen of the fourth century were friendly to asceticism, and all of them advocated the regulated common life as the safest form of it. At the same time a good deal of spontaneity and variety must at this period be supposed. People planned and carried out their own ways of it, and these approximated in various degrees to the settled type which eventually prevailed. A period of probation soon came to be imposed on those who desired to be monks or nuns. The features of the life on which they entered [1] were chiefly celibacy, laying down of possessions, obedience to a presiding person (Abbas, ἀρχιμανδρίτης), fixed times for worship (three daily at first, afterwards six, finally seven), for meals, for occupations; adoption of some simple and homely dress which became common and distinctive, and submission to discipline for offences. A common place of abode—house or cluster of houses—was necessary. Manual labour to provide the necessaries of life was enjoined, at least in the East. In the West, for a time, this does not seem to have been the practice. Food was always simple; the quantity was not at first prescribed, though comparative abstinence came nearer to the ideal that was in view. Those who ate more were expected to work more. Many leading bishops of the later half of the century had passed through discipline of this kind; for instance, Epiphanius, Basil of Cæsarea, Gregory Nazianzen, Chrysostom; but in their case the earlier and freer attitude of men who adopt the rule so long and so far as themselves judge it to be helpful, is still perceptible. Apparently it was under Basil's influence, first, that monastic societies—existing before in retired country districts—were introduced into towns.

The impressive features of monastic rule, its sudden popularity, and its power to lay hold of individuals, were reported in the West as a rumour, and it was soon to be realised among themselves. Augustine, before his conversion (about 385), heard at Milan of the life of Antony, and records the impression which the report made on him.[2] Also his friend Pontitianus told him how he had been one of a group of four officers of the Imperial court at Treves who one day walked by two and two in the public gardens there. One

---

[1] None of the "Rules" ascribed to names of the fourth century (they are collected by Holstenius, *Codex Regularum*, i. par. 1663) are in their original form. They are believed to have been modified under the influence of later experience. Two bear the name of Pachomius and two that of Basil of Cæsarea. The shorter of the latter, ὅρος κατ' ἐπιτομήν, is regarded as nearly representing Basil's own work. *Opera*, Garnier's ed., p. 199.

[2] *Conf.* viii. 6.

pair stumbling on a hut where some religious persons had begun to live a recluse life, found there the life of Antony. And after looking into it, one of them, deeply moved, said to the other, "What is the utmost we are aiming at? Imperial favour? and how precarious it is! and how long shall we be of attaining it? And to think that I could become the friend of God this very moment!" So after a little agitated meditation he continued, "I have broken with my former purposes, and am determined to serve God. I begin here and now. If you do not choose to imitate me, do not oppose me." Whereupon the other declared himself to be his associate in that warfare and reward. Then Pontitianus, with the fourth of the company, coming in search of the first two, was told of their decision; and though they were not minded to share it, yet they lamented their own case, and begged the prayers of the others. So two remained in the hut, and two returned to their quarters. The first two were both of them betrothed; the ladies, when they heard what had happened, dedicated their virginity to God.

But, though Augustine did not yet know it, Ambrose had already founded a religious house in Milan; and the West already had its famous hermit in Martin of Tours, whose sacrifices and conflicts, joined to his resolute and commanding character, were thought to place him on terms of equality with the greatest ascetics of the East. He had passed from a soldier's life to that of a religious recluse, and lived as such in various places before he was called to the bishopric of Tours.[1]

From this time the monastic life spread rapidly in the West, beginning with Italy, Africa, Northern and Southern Gaul. Ambrose in Italy, Martin in Northern Gaul, and Cassianus in Southern, impelled the movement. The authority of Athanasius had already recommended it in Rome, and there the zeal of Jerome called forth warm support and also bitter opposition. In Africa the system had the support of Augustine and of the more devout

[1] Sulp. Severus, *Vita*.

clergy; but there also a popular sentiment of irritation and contempt was strongly manifested.[1]

In reference to this sentiment, it is to be remembered that the asceticism which withdrew from ordinary life, renounced possessions, and affected visible privation, was native to the East; but in the West it was an importation. When the new tendency began to operate extensively, many in the West regarded it with dislike and resentment. Some might be irritated by the disturbance to families and breaking of social ties; some might be unwilling to think of their religion as demanding such sacrifices; some might recoil from the sordid aspects of the business, and from what struck them as its extravagance. But there were those also who discerned the principles involved in the enthusiasm, and disapproved of them. The resistance, therefore, while it included much that was worldly, found also some very respectable representatives. But it was borne down by the general sentiment of religious people. Most of these took it as settled, not only that the monastic life embodied a high effort of Christian virtue, and that it offered the best method of seeking salvation, but that it was, in fact, the appropriate form of thorough decision,—of forsaking sin, renouncing self, and following Christ. Hence the more ordinary Christianity, that which was contented to be the more ordinary, was relatively imperfect: nevertheless, it might suffice as a Christianity of the lower grade. The inferences which these positions were to yield were not yet all clearly drawn. They were destined to affect profoundly the moral life of Christendom.

The best way, probably, of learning what the early monastic *mood* was, how it felt itself related to both worlds, is to read the life of Martin of Tours by Sulpicius Severus,[2] along with the Dialogues in which he compares the glories of Eastern and Western monks. The order of a monastic house may be gathered from any of the rules already referred to (p. 295). The details of dress, of admission and

[1] Salvian, *De Gubern. Dei*, viii. 4.
[2] In *Corpus Scriptorum Latin.* i., Vienna, 1866.

subsequent life, of nightly and daily worship, may be found, with a great deal of curious material, in the first four books of John Cassianus, *de Institutis Cœnobiorum*.[1] The remaining eight books are occupied with the eight principal vices against which monks have to contend; which are tendencies to gluttony, impurity, covetousness, anger, sadness (mental depression), *akedia* (indifference, often in the form of a restlessness which can settle to nothing), vainglory, and pride. A fuller survey of Christian duty and attainment, according to the views cherished in early monasteries, may be found in another work of Cassianus, *Collationes Patrum*, in which he professes to report discourses addressed to their monks by eminent Egyptian abbots. The controversial defence of the system against opponents is contained in works by Jerome against Jovinian and Vigilantius.[2] His positions were reviewed and moderated by Augustine.[3]

Jovinian (about A.D. 390, d. before 409) did not argue against the celibate life; he was a celibate himself; but he denied the superior merit ascribed to it, as well as to fasting and martyrdom, and thus would have cut the roots of the current enthusiasm. He appears first at Rome, afterwards at Milan. Vigilantius of Calagurræ in Aquitania (after 394), worked as a priest in Spain and Gaul. He, too, objected to the honours paid to martyrs and their relics, and, like Jovinian, he challenged the exaggerated estimate of monastic holiness. Also he opposed the tendency to celibacy of the clergy, partly on the ground that the moral effects were often bad.

Vigilantius, after his death, was regarded as a heretic. The teaching of Jovinian was condemned at Rome during his lifetime. Jovinian, perhaps, went deeper of the two into theological theory. He was charged with holding that those baptized with the Spirit cannot sin; that all sins are equal; that in the next world there is but one degree of punishment on the one hand, and of reward on the other.

---

[1] In *Corpus Scriptorum Latin.*, vols. xiii. and xvii., Vindob. 1886–88.
[2] Hieron. *Adv. Jovinianum* and *Contra Vigilantium*, Opp. iv. 2, p. 214.
[3] *De bono conjugali* and *Retract.* ii. 22.

These charges seem to indicate, on Jovinian's part, speculations based on the Pauline writings, and probably misunderstood by those who reported them. Both the men evinced strong convictions and steadfast character in encountering, as they did, the stream of sentiment which ran in their day; and it might well be that the strain of so difficult a position betrayed them into some exaggerations. They reveal to us religious earnestness opposed to the growing superstitions, which has left little trace otherwise.[1]

The ascetic life, as placed under rule in the monastery, was accepted and accredited by the Church; and both as a fact and as a force it became an element of first rate importance in practical Christianity. It agreed with the asceticism of the $\dot{a}\nu a\chi\omega\rho\eta\tau o\iota$ (that of Antony and his followers) in prescribing the sacrifice of all possessions, though, in practice, life in the monastery was less rude and precarious than life in the desert, It added to mere asceticism the advantage of rules, and especially it restored something of the social tie. The ascetic, pure and simple, broke loose from all human ties, as if they were all nets to ensnare him, and as if sheer individualism made a man ready for God. The system of the monastery still sacrificed the same ties, but so far replaced them, in that a company of men or women living together must own relations and obligations. Still further, a great element in the monastery was the obligation to obey the ruler. At first, probably, this obtained only in the degree necessary for good order in a religious house. But it was early recognised as furnishing the opportunity for mortifying self-will. The habit of complete submission to men or women clothed with authority found here a special consecration. It became one of the recognised points of Christian perfection.

The significance and the power of the movement lay after all in this,—it embodied an effort to give effect to one

---

[1] Besides references in last page, Siricii *Epist.* 7; Ambrosii *Rescript. ad. Sir. Epist.* 42; Aug. *Ep.* 35; *De Hær.* c. 82; G. B. Lindner, *de Joviniano et Vigil.*, 8vo, Lips. 1839; Haller, *Jovinianus* in *Texte u. Unters. N. F.* ii. 2 Lips. 1897.

of the most fundamental truths of Christianity. Genuine Christianity includes the surrender to a new principle, the recognition of a new master, the response to a new motive, and the acceptance of all sacrifices which so great a change implies. Life is to move to a new goal, and concentrate on one great attainment. "Except a man forsake all that he hath, he cannot be My disciple." "Take up the cross, and follow Me." Up and down the churches we may be sure there were not a few Christians in whom this had begun, in whom it was going on. But the general aspect of things seemed rather to imply a consent of Christians that nothing so serious should be pressed. The old heroisms of the persecutions had ceased. The tide of easy-going converts swelled the churches. A man's Christianity passed unchallenged if, having once been baptized, perhaps in infancy, he maintained a negative goodness, joined with some attention to ordinances. The worst of it was, that the way of conceiving Christian principles which, it may be said, was universal, weakened in an extraordinary degree the power of challenging this nominal Christianity, even on the part of those who felt it to be dangerously defective. The decisive something had taken place at baptism, and after that it seemed the only question that could be raised was the question of a little more or a little less of Christian observance. Meanwhile this "Christianity," which was less and less distinguishable from indifference, lived on easy terms with the manners and the spirit of the decadent empire. Against it the spirit of Christianity itself revolted. Men who were awakened, even if they did not judge others, still refused to be content for themselves with so dubious a religion. And, in the spirit of their time, they demanded that the genuine Christianity should have a definite outward form, so that one could make sure of it. Asceticism was the answer to that demand. It has a deep meaning that the monastic life came to be spoken of as "religion," and the entrance on it as "conversion," and that Jerome could say that to become a monk was to have, as it were, a second baptism. The monastery was not to question the validity of the common Christianity which the Church sanctioned; but the monk was resolved not to be content with it for himself.

The external form which was consecrated to hold this place was, after all, a human contrivance. And we may regard it as dangerously misleading. We may agree with Luther that the common callings of human life supply the proper opportunities and the proper discipline for a Christian. We may be persuaded that both by what it claimed for itself, and by what it implied as to the outside Christianity, this system wrought indefinite confusion in men's thoughts regarding Christian duty and attainment. But, whatever we may think to be the dangers or the errors of monasticism, we must not belittle the enthusiasm which flowed into the monasteries.

The general state of the Church was depressing, and undoubtedly the monasteries themselves very often shared in the untoward tendencies of the time. But an effort in favour of more thorough and strenuous Christianity was the spring of the movement. When we can follow the steps of individuals—of Basil, of the Gregories, of Chrysostom—we often find that a gracious religious life, pervading a whole family circle, has nursed the thoughts and purposes which led the individual to the ascetic life; and, in other cases, the purpose was born in the experience of a great change in which men felt themselves turning from sin to God. Hence Augustine has no difficulty in appealing to the movement as a proof of the divinity of Christian religion. It was seen exerting a power which no other religion could rival.

Certainly from this point of view one must own the energy revealed by the Christianity of the fourth century. Environed as the Church is with relaxing and lowering influences, moving away from the old heroisms of the persecutions, torn by heresies, swamped with worldliness and with worldlings, we see a great uprising of men who claim to be Christian in another style. A few begin, but they begin enthusiastically and unreservedly, and in all directions kindred souls catch fire, and resolve not to be left behind.

As to the method from which so much was hoped, its concentration and its reiteration could, no doubt, produce habits of religious thought and feeling which were remarkable. They were not always healthy. However the plan might answer in some cases, yet when presented, as it was, as the true form of sincere Christianity, it was doomed to prove a sad mistake. It was essentially artificial, external, one-sided; an experiment made by the young Church, as it is often made still, at the same stage, by the young Christian. It must be remembered that this life did not then contemplate systematic service of others;—everything was concentrated on the man's own perfecting. It was not wonderful that morbid symptoms were frequent. The *Tristitia* and the *Acedia* of Cassian's book were only instances of a large class of effects due to an unhealthy discipline. Sometimes mere intellectual and moral torpor resulted.

The stimulus which was applied to the fancy and to nervous tendencies, is revealed also by the extraordinary harvest of visions, demoniacal assaults, and miracles which followed in its wake. The occurrence of some marvels had been associated all along with Christian history, in times of persecution especially, and in other cases of great trial. But both in type and in number these had hitherto occupied a comparatively modest place; and the Christian feeling had been that miracles comparable to the gospel miracles had for good reasons passed away. But from Antony onwards the miraculous element increases, and by the end of the fourth century it had overflowed the world. Asceticism was one cause; another, which operated in the same way, was the mood of mind now prevailing in regard to the relics of the saints. Illustrations of the first may be found abundantly in Sulpicius Severus.[1] For the effect of relics, note how Augustine, who, in earlier days, recognised the comparative absence of the miraculous from Christian

[1] Especially the *Dialogi*.

experience, in later life qualifies and virtually retracts the statement.[1] For in the meantime not only had asceticism begun to bear fruit, but the relics of St. Stephen had come into Africa, and miracles everywhere followed in their train; and such miracles![2]

Various motives led men to the monasteries. Even the religious impulse included different elements, which might be mingled in different degrees. First, there was the feeling that a life which aims at friendship with God ought to include an element of self-punishment. The ascetic pain was to operate as expiating sin. Secondly, as already suggested, it was a way of trampling on the material element and on its claims, a way of achieving emancipation from the world of sense and deception. This associated itself with ideas of the essential baseness of matter; also, with aspiration after the aristocratic intellectualism of the philosophers. Thirdly, Christianity demands and promises a supremacy of spiritual affections, a subjugation of all else to the main aim. The ascetic life offered itself as the way of being true to this faith. And this was the motive most akin to the spirit of the gospel, —however legal and external the method was which it embraced. Fourthly, it was in general a way of testing one's own sincerity; religion that goes too easy may be suspected; sacrifice accepted tests devotion. Fifthly, in all these ways and in others it was a methodism,—a ruled-off way of being good,—so plain and distinctive that one might rest in it, dismissing questions and doubts. How dear this is to human hearts a thousand instances have proved!

It is to be remembered, finally, that persons could become monks and nuns without experiencing very deeply the peculiar influences of the system. Almost from the beginning there were low types of monastic life, and low motives leading men to embrace it. On the other hand, the monasteries sometimes became simply places of shelter

---

[1] *Retract.* i. 13. 7. See also a case in *De Mir. S. Stephani ad Evodium*, ii. 3, in Aug. Opp. vii. App.

[2] See *de Civitate*, xxii. 8, for specimens. Four are cases of raising the dead.

for people who could have found shelter nowhere else, and who were glad of a quiet and regulated life.

### DIVERGENCES

The monks were laymen, and they must often have felt themselves to be more pious than many of the clergy; they practised what was held to be a more complete Christianity. It was obvious, therefore, that the anarchical and revolutionary spirit might develop among them. But very powerful and influential men had exerted themselves to secure for the monastic life on the one hand the approbation, on the other hand the control of the official Church. The monasteries took their place as subject to the bishop, and as participant, through a resident presbyter or otherwise, in the regulated worship of the Church. Still, ascetic life was apt to break out into vehement excitement, or into extravagant and demonstrative self-torture. And sometimes these forces carried the monks into excesses which had to be condemned as schismatic or heretical. Some lived a wandering gipsy life sustained by herbs ($\beta o\sigma\kappa o\acute{\iota}$). Some grouped themselves in towns in small companies and earned a common livelihood without much rule, and so often with no good repute (Remoboth, also Sarabaites). Some refused to hold Christian fellowship with any who lived in marriage, or who retained private property (Apostolici). The followers of Audius declared separation from the official Church in Syria, apparently on account of its laxity (Audiarii). The Euchites lived in constant prayer, begging for their support, denouncing even the earning of wages by labour; and they undervalued the sacraments. Some of the monasteries in the East, previously in good repute, became infected with this spirit. The Eustachians, whose tendencies were imputed to Eustathius of Sebaste, practically set up a Christianity and a church of their own. They denied the possible salvation of all married people, and of all rich people, would have nothing to do with martyr feasts and Agapæ, and rejected the ministrations of married priests. They were condemned at the synod of Gangra in Paphlagonia (after 360). "Stylites" was the name given to ascetics who, like Symeon (near Antioch), spent years on the top of a pillar. These anomalies gave way, sooner or later, to the powerful influences exerted to bring the monastic institute into harmony with the system of the Church.

On the other hand, the morbid symptoms are not less apparent. Almost from the beginning we encounter complaints of low types of monastic life, and low motives leading men to embrace it. Thus early did it appear that the acceptance of an external law, however holy it seemed to be, might be very far indeed from fellowship with Christ.

# CHAPTER XIX

## THE CLERGY

Bingham, *Christ. Antiq.* i. and ii. Tomassini, *Vetus et Nova Disciplina*, Paris, 1691.

THE rapid increase in the number of Christian worshippers naturally required great additions to the clerical staff. Besides the grades already mentioned, attendants on the sick (Parabolani) and gravediggers (κοπιάται—fossores) now appear; they became very numerous in the great churches, and took the form of guilds under the bishops. The civil law sought to limit their number;[1] for turbulent bishops could employ them as agents in disturbing the peace; and those who wished to escape public burdens could get themselves enrolled for nominal service in these orders. A similar increase, though not so great, took place in all the *ordines minores* (p. 248).

In the Diaconate, however, the increase was not so great; indeed some churches, at least the church of Rome, held to the number seven. The necessities of the time were met rather by multiplying the sub-deacons. The deacons proper, therefore, rose in importance as the special agents of the bishop, his eyes and hands in worship, finance, charities, and discipline. Signs appear that, conscious of their own importance, the deacons were disposed in some cases to take precedence of the presbyters.[2] An official who is found in great churches from the very beginning of this

---

[1] Five hundred and six hundred Parabolani at different times in Alexandria, nine hundred and fifty and eleven hundred in Constantinople.
[2] *Conc. Arelat.*, Can. 15.

period, is the leading deacon or archdeacon; he acts as chief of the staff to the bishop. That was the position of Athanasius at Alexandria before he was elevated to the episcopate. The deacon who held this post was a natural candidate for the bishop's place in case of a vacancy; and ordination to the higher rank of presbyter might seem to him unwelcome as tending to spoil his prospects (Hier. *in Ez.* 48).

Presbyters necessarily became much more numerous, for ministration of ordinances required more ministers. As the number of Christians increased in each locality, the expedient adopted was to increase the staff of presbyters; and these at first, speaking generally, were equally related to the whole flock, and ministered to particular sections of it as might from time to time be arranged. The alternative plan of multiplying bishoprics could not but seem likely to lower the dignity and influence of bishops, and it might also seem to infer more frequent and serious rearrangement. New bishoprics were therefore discouraged, except in the case of mission fields, and in the case of towns which rose into new importance sufficient to justify the presence of a bishop (Can. Sardica, 6).

Already, however, from an older time had come down the institution of country bishops (χωρεπίσκοποι), who ministered to village communities, but sometimes to a cluster of villages each with its own presbyter (Bas. *Ep.* 142, 188, 290). Such villages, on the system now preferred, would be regarded as sufficiently provided for by a presbyter under the city bishop. The older system therefore began to be discouraged over the larger part of the Church (Ancyra, (314), Can. 13; Antioch (341), Can. 19; Neocæs. Can. 14, and Nic. Can. 8), the powers of the chorepiscopoi were limited, and they were placed under the superintendence of the city bishop; but they continued to exist for a considerable time. Of the numerous bishops in Africa some must have been practically chorepiscopoi; but they do not seem to have ranked lower than the city bishops of those provinces.

Presbyters put in charge of country places might acquire a durable relation to the portion of the flock intrusted to them sooner than city presbyters did; for the latter might more easily take duties in rotation and circulate from one congregation to another; and distance helped to give greater independence to the country parts of a bishop's "parish." But alike in the town and in the district attached to it, the Christians were regarded as members of one episcopal flock. And in the cities themselves it was ere long found expedient to attach particular presbyters more or less permanently to particular churches. This can be proved for Alexandria in the fourth century, and for Rome and Constantinople in the fifth. It was the germ of the later parochial system. Such a presbyter gradually became to his congregation what the bishop had been to the early Christian community of the whole place; he was their pastor and they his flock; only he was not competent to ordain office-bearers, and they could not receive a complete separate organisation. At Rome, a presbyter so situated did not himself consecrate the sacramental elements, but dispensed what the bishop had consecrated previously (Innoc. I. *Ep. ad Decentium*). The city presbyters took precedence of the country ones.

An arch-presbyter, corresponding among the presbyters to the archdeacon among deacons, existed; but the office never attained great importance.

The right of the bishop to nominate to vacant positions among the inferior clergy was now well established. Such nominations, especially the more important, were no doubt usually made with the advice of his clergy. In regard to presbyters the *view* persisted, and was expressed in the ordination service, that they took office by the consent of the congregation; but practically this was tending to become a form.

In regard to the bishops themselves, the ancient right of a church to elect its own bishop was more vividly remembered; for the bishop was that one person with whom every Christian must hold relations, so that his appointment created a definite and a pervading interest in the whole Christian community. But while in theory the clergy and the people must assent to the election, the neighbouring bishops, or more precisely, the bishops of the province, who were to consecrate, and who must receive the new bishop into their fellowship, had also a right to be satisfied, both as to the regularity of the proceedings and as to the competency of the man. And their power in the election preponderated. The wishes of the local clergy and the people were not without influence, especially if they were united in their choice; and they were occasionally exerted with such decision as to be irresistible. But we cannot trace adequate securities for those wishes being definitely ascertained, or regularly made effectual. Moreover, the growing numbers of Catholics in each bishopric would increase the difficulty of collecting and interpreting the popular voice. Very often, therefore, the person preferred by the bishops of the province and approved by the Metropolitan could be appointed. Still the "election" proceeded in face of the clergy and people, and with some forms of inviting their suffrage; and the theory was never allowed altogether to drop, that the choice of the clergy and assent of the people were required. In most cases, one may believe, friction was avoided by circumspection and good sense on the part of the provincial bishops who presided. The presence of three bishops was necessary to a canonically regular consecration; and that rite seems to have very often taken place upon the spot, as soon as the election was over. While the ordinary course of things followed these lines, great divergences might take place. A surge of popular feeling might lead to the disregard of ordinary rules, as in the case of Ambrose of Milan and others. On the other hand, imperial favour often determined the appointment to great bishoprics, especially in the East.

The grounds of necessity and expediency which had led to the institution of synods, had led further to these synods being provincial, *i.e.* composed of the bishops of each (political) province of the empire. The same reasons had led to one bishop being fixed on as the convener and president of these meetings, as the depositary of any powers which might be usefully exerted between the meetings, and as the authorised organ of communication with other regions of the Church. He had a right of visitation in his province, and to see that rules were not broken. The ordinary bishops required his permission to make distant journeys.

This order was well established at the beginning of the period now before us. The president was usually bishop of the city, recognised as the political metropolis of the province (hence "metropolitan"), but not always. In Africa proper, the bishop of Carthage was the metropolitan by right, while in Numidia and Mauretania the leading bishops (Senes) were not occupants of one fixed see. In Pontus the oldest bishop of the province was the presiding person. Generally, however, the civil precedency of the metropolis determined also the ecclesiastical primacy of its bishop. Hence an increase of metropolitans is said to have taken place when Diocletian increased the number of the provinces by subdivision. But in Italy there had not been quite the same division into provinces which obtained elsewhere in the empire; and there the metropolitan development was hindered still further by the impressive influence of Rome. Diocletian at length instituted eighteen provinces in Italy; but that made no great alteration ecclesiastically in regard to the ten provinces of lower Italy. In Northern Italy, Milan, Ravenna, and Aquileia acquired metropolitan rights during the fourth and fifth centuries. The two former were for a time imperial residences. The council of Nicea directed two synods (Can. 5) to be held in each province yearly; but circumstances might, and often did, prevent compliance with the rules. The synods could frame rules which were imperative on Christians within the province; they were the court of appeal in complaints of lack of justice at the hands of bishops, and, generally, in disputes regarding ecclesiastical rights; and they superintended all Christian interests within the province which did not properly fall to particular bishops. In these provincial synods the conceptions of ecclesiastical order and administration were worked out which were proceeded upon in the œcumenical synods. The members having voice and vote were bishops;

these might be attended by some of their presbyters and deacons, who might also occasionally be allowed to address the synod, but could not vote. A bishop necessarily absent might commission a presbyter to represent him, who could vote in his name.

It was felt, however, that districts greater than the provinces constituted units of church life and work, within which ecclesiastical authority might and should be brought to bear, and throughout which the common mind of ecclesiastical authorities might be applied to provide for the order and welfare of the Church. Under the influence of this feeling the Patriarchates established themselves, and were recognised. Here again the political divisions of the empire—themselves dictated, of course, by natural and social cleavage—suggested a basis. Under Constantine and his successors the empire was divided into four great præfectures, namely, the East,[1] Eastern Illyricum, Italy, and the Gauls. These præfectures, again, included fourteen " dioceses " of various sizes, each of which might in turn include many provinces; as, for example, the diocese of the East included fifteen provinces and that of Rome ten. The idea of forming each diocese into an ecclesiastical province with a great bishop at its head was entertained; and accordingly, along with Alexandria for Egypt, and Antioch for the East (in the more limited sense), Ephesus was named for Asia, Cæsarea for Pontus, and Heraklea for Thrace (Const. Can. 2), all as equal ecclesiastical magnitudes.

But this proved to be a somewhat *doctrinaire* attempt. In truth, there were three bishoprics which by the splendour and antiquity of the see outshone all others. These were Rome, Alexandria, and Antioch. To these came to be added Constantinople,—the new Rome,—the centre of power

[1] The word Oriens in this period is ambiguous,—it might denote the Præfectura Orientis, or it might denote only the Diœcesis Oriens, one of the five into which that præfecture was divided. It is the latter and more limited sense which corresponds most nearly to the ecclesiastical Patriarchate of which Antioch was the mother see.

and law for the Eastern empire. These sees really held an exceptional place. Rome had oversight, without question, of the ten suburbicarian provinces of Italy; besides, she stood first in dignity among all Christian sees; and she had an influence through all the West, the extent of which was not yet ascertained. Alexandria easily held her place as the presiding see of the diocese of Egypt, and Antioch in the diocese of the East. And the political strength of Constantinople enabled her not only to claim the obedience of Thrace, but also that of Asia, Cappadocia, and Pontus. Sees like Ephesus, Cæsarea, and Carthage, though undoubtedly above the rank of common Metropolitans, and allowed to claim distinctive privileges, still proved unable to contest the superior rank of those great sees. The latter accordingly are known as Patriarchates. At the close of our period, Jerusalem, on the ground of its historical associations, was allowed to dissociate itself from Antioch, and its bishop received Palestine as his Patriarchate. The name Patriarch begins to be restricted to these great bishops in the fifth century. Previously it had been more widely and uncertainly applied. Bishops who, though not Patriarchs, occupied sees which were regarded as conferring presidency over dioceses (in the civil sense of that word), or at all events as entitled to the obedience of several metropolitans, were often called exarchs,—a name derived from the civil hierarchy.[1]

Patriarchal sees held their position in virtue of the age, historic importance, and greatness of those churches. The ecclesiastical force, however, which formed the *ultima ratio* of their authority in case of need, was the exclusion from their communion of the bishop who seemed to give sufficient cause for that step. If the case was wisely selected, the example was sure to be followed by other churches of the

---

[1] The name ἀρχιεπίσκοπος also had at this time no very settled range of attributes. Πάπας was the common name at Alexandria for their bishop, and was superseded there by the title of Patriarch in the seventh century. The Greeks called the bishop of Rome Patriarch, but that title was not usually given to him in the West.

Patriarchate. This created what was always a difficult and perplexing position for the bishop in question, and was extremely likely to raise trouble for him at home. If, however, the public opinion of the churches generally regarded the step of excluding from communion as unjustifiable, the bishop assailed might find support enough to enable him to hold out. But the situation was at best trying; and even in the days when the fundamental equality of all bishops was most strongly asserted, a provincial bishop had many motives for avoiding unfriendly relations with the occupant of the "apostolic" see. Rome earliest realised all that could be made of this state of things. In the second century Victor was on the point of breaking off communion with Eastern bishops who followed the Quartodeciman celebration of Easter, and in the third Stephen took a similar attitude about heretical baptism. These were cases in which Rome was in danger of prematurely straining her power; but they reveal her disposition to assert it. Innocent I., who was Pope at the end of the fourth century, signalised his pontificate by the boldness with which he asserted the powers of his see; and many of these assertions were successfully translated into fact by the great Pope Leo I. A.D. 440–461. By these successive representatives, Rome, which was acknowledged to be the primatial see, virtually claimed the whole Church as her Patriarchate. The process by which the unique authority was made good over all the West (and often asserted in the East), is a subject by itself. It is enough here to say, that the alleged episcopate, at Rome, of the Apostle Peter was all along the main ground relied on by the Roman church. But at first they were content to say that the Church, in honour of Peter, had agreed to accord a special authority to the church and bishop of Rome.[1] Later, the assertion came to be that to Peter the Lord had made promises, which secured to the church in which he presided, and to his successors in its chair, perpetual stability in the true faith and authority to rule the whole Church.[2]

[1] Innoc. I. *Ep.* 29 ; Zosim. *Ep.* 2.   [2] Leo I. *Ep.* 10.

### General Conditions of Clerical Life

Two ways of arranging service in the Christian ministry have been distinguished (p. 37); it could be undertaken as an addition, an honourable and responsible addition, to some ordinary calling—a farmer's, a merchant's, and so forth; or it might become the sole calling of a class of men who must be provided with a professional income for their proper support. The first way of it prevailed in the earliest practice of the churches. Yet from the first it was recognised that approved Christian service demanded grateful acknowledgment; and that when it absorbed much of a man's strength and time, it was incumbent on the Christian brethren to provide for his temporal wants (1 Cor. ix. 14; *Didache*, 13, 15). This obligation must naturally be more stringent when a laborious ministry was undertaken at the call of the local church. The change from the first method to the second was still proceeding in the present period, but had not been completed. Accordingly regulations appear which contemplate Christian ministers engaged in secular callings, but forbid occupations that were reckoned improper or unbecoming, as well as offices properly secular (*Can. Illib.* 19, 20; *Can. Ap.* 7). The two methods evidently coexisted: each prevailing more or less, according to the circumstances of different churches.

It is quite plain that, by the time we have now reached, bishops in larger towns had to devote their whole time to their work, and they had also to maintain a representative position and show hospitality; similar considerations applied in a less degree to most of the presbyters in such churches, and perhaps to all the deacons. At the other end of the series some of the minor orders, now come into existence, would equally require a regular provision. On the other hand, in smaller and more rural churches other conditions could prevail; the gratitude of the flock, or a modest honorarium added to the gains of a secular calling, might still be counted recompense enough; it is possible that some of the clergy in the greater churches also were similarly situated. With this state of things we may connect the fact that Christian laymen, especially men of some position, made efforts to be ordained and numbered with the clergy in order to escape public burdens.

The Christian ministry, however, was becoming more completely a profession, or distinct calling, in which men could expect to be provided for as to their temporal wants, whatever higher aims might influence them in addition. On this footing, in later times, young persons could begin to prepare for the ministry as their chosen career. But as yet, in general, a state of things continued which we may represent to ourselves in this way—that, on the one hand, the congregation and its guides picked out Christian men, likely to be useful, and asked them to take the ministry upon them;[1] that, on the other hand, an aspiration after work of this kind led individuals sometimes to offer themselves for service.

A line of approach to the more important posts had been created by the development of the minor orders. In those orders lads and men could begin official service with less of responsibility on their own part, and less of risk to the Church's well-being. They became familiar with ecclesiastical duties, were in contact with the older clergy, received influence, formed habits, acquired insight, and meanwhile revealed in some degree their own character and aptitude; thus they could be promoted step by step. It was, therefore, a system not of formal study or methodical training, but of apprenticeship. Apprenticeship long continued to be the method of preparation in other professions besides the clerical, and it has its own advantages and disadvantages. Among the latter may be reckoned this, that in churches where the bishop and presbyters did not include men of exceptional religious power and depth, the tendency among the "apprentices" might be to cultivate aptitude for the external duties of the ministry, without much perception of its proper spirit. Men like Basil, Chrysostom, and Augustine exerted themselves to remedy

[1] A strong feeling existed that men so called were bound to respond.

this evil by inculcating right conceptions of the nature and the responsibilities of the spiritual office. At all events, this line of approach to the pastoral care offered itself so naturally that one sees a tendency to make a rule of it. But it never became universal. The Church could summarily call to its service in important posts any Christian it judged proper. Augustine, happening to make a journey from Tagaste to Hippo, and entering the church in the latter place, was promptly pounced upon by the bishop and his people to fill a vacant post of presbyter; and he had to submit, at that time much against his own judgment. Ambrose, not yet baptized, nor even a catechumen, was suddenly elected bishop of Milan. Such cases, however, more and more became exceptional. To rise through the established grades was held to be the safer practice. Hence, even when men were to be introduced at once to the work of deacons or presbyters, it came afterwards to be reckoned fitting to pass them rapidly, *pro formâ*, through the minor orders.[1]

Men could begin their career on these lines with very little of mental cultivation or acquired knowledge, and no system of special education was inculcated or pursued over the Church generally. In particular places there existed facilities for mental training on Christian lines,—at Alexandria, at the Palestinian Cæsarea, at Antioch, and at Constantinople; and we cannot doubt that use was made of these facilities. But they could be available only to an inconsiderable minority; and it is to be remembered that the system of apprenticeship confined men to their own church and gave little scope for seeking advantages elsewhere. We have every reason to believe that the attainments of many Christian ministers were extremely elementary. Augustine and others sought to meet these wants by persuading their clergy to live together under superintendence, after the model of the monastic life; and in the regulation of the society so formed, place was

[1] A monk was presumably an earnest Christian; his life had given him opportunity for meditation; and his asceticism recommended him. Hence a disposition to seek in the monasteries recruits for the clerical life.

found both for mental and for religious discipline. As regards the numerous clergy of the various grades who were not favoured in some of these ways, one can only say further, that reading must in all cases have been regarded as an appropriate occupation for men who served the Church. The Scriptures, and more or less of the Greek Christian literature in the East, of the Latin in the West, must have been usually accessible, opening a way for a certain amount of self-education.

But we must equally make room in our minds for a considerable number of men who had profited by the school education of the period. Relatively good schools existed at all events in most large towns, and were able to bestow a literary training, preparing men of religious minds to pursue what further studies they chose. So that we must think of the attainments of the clergy rather as exceedingly uneven than as uniformly low. Who can doubt that in all the great cities where a certain culture was affected by people of condition, the clergy—animated by a strong *esprit de corps* and stimulated by Christian thought and Christian controversy—would create among themselves a certain standard of knowledge; and this, in the case of those who reached the higher grades, could not be contemptible.

It is to be remembered, finally, that the ranks of the clergy were recruited by some who had been in touch with all the culture both of the schools and of the administrative hierarchy of the empire. From the time of Constantine the Christian ministry began to attract remarkable men, at least on a level with the highest education of the time, and some of them of great force of character. Men felt they could be more free, vigorous, and dignified in the Church's service than in the hierarchy of the State; but often that impression was itself subordinate to the more personal sense of indebtedness to Christ and desire to serve Him. They came from a long career in the schools, in which they had exhausted all that was reckoned to the heads of literary refinement or speculative thought,—and now the call to be scholars and teachers in a higher school came home to them; or they came from the service of the empire, expert in business and in statesmanship, to administer a more spiritual kingdom; or, after years of ease as wealthy Greek and Roman gentlemen, they tired of a life aimless and self-indulgent, apt to be frivolous even when it was far from wholly selfish; and they felt a call to place their means and themselves at the disposal of the cause which comprehended the best they knew or could conceive. The change might follow on some great conscious crisis in the inner man, or might be marked by a meditative period of retirement, after the manner of the monastic life, or might be gradually reached in advancing life, an attraction that had been felt for years becoming at last irresistible. In any case it brought to the service of the Church men who had freely dealt with the culture of the time in its heathen as well as in its Christian form, men who brought whatever the age possessed of reading, or of eloquence, or of passionate and questioning thought, or of poetry, or of refined and gentle life. No doubt it was their pious fashion to utter warnings against many of the paths by which themselves had passed; for instance, against the study of the heathen classics.[1] But such men as Basil, Gregory of Nazianzus, Ambrose, Chrysostom, Jerome, Augustine, Paulinus of Nola, and many more set a type the influence of which was no doubt widely felt. Recruits from the service of the State, in particular, continued from generation to generation to pass over to the service of the Church.

It was felt necessary to guard the clerical function against the entrance of those whose previous mode of life created offence, as performers in the theatres, and even as soldiers, if the candidate had followed that career after his baptism. Also slaves, and even freedmen were inadmissible unless completely set free from the obligations to an earthly superior, usually attaching to those two classes. Certain immoralities, also, in the previous life of baptized persons, even if repented, excluded permanently from clerical office, and so did some kinds of previous marriage which were

[1] Basil, πρὸς τοὺς νέους.

held less reputable. Similar exclusion applied to persons baptized on sick-bed, because they were liable to be regarded as having accepted the ordinance under fear of death rather than by choice. But in this case, and indeed in some of the others, the prudential reasons on which the exclusion was founded could be overcome by prolonged evidence of confirmed Christian character. Neophytes, *i.e.* persons recently baptized, had been from the beginning specified as not eligible for office; but here, too, eminent exceptions occurred, as Ambrose and Synesius. As a rule, a candidate for the deaconship was to be not less than twenty-five, and a presbyter thirty years of age.

Bishops, presbyters, and deacons were not forbidden to engage in traffic, handicrafts, and husbandry for their support. But they must not personally travel about to push their business, nor burden themselves with trusteeships and business not their own. Gain by lending money at interest was reckoned usury, and was specially forbidden to the clergy (Conc. Illib. Can. 19, 20; Arelat (A.D. 314), Can. 12; Nic. Can. 17; Chalc. Can. 3).

The clergy had some encouragement to engage in business, from the fact that they were set free from duties charged on certain industries. But this immunity was afterwards very much restricted.

Early regulations had warned clerical persons against undertaking any civil functions; but apparent violations of this rule occur pretty frequently, often, perhaps, in cases where plausible special reasons could be pleaded.

More special restrictions on clerical life were implied in the efforts of Eusebius of Vercelli, and of Augustine, to arrange a *quasi*-conventual mode of life for their clergy; but these experiments had no extensive or permanent effect. On the other hand, a mode of view and feeling was rising in the Church which favoured clerical celibacy. Asceticism had long been regarded as a proper expression of pronounced religious earnestness, and the development of monasticism had intensified these feelings: that the clergy should exhibit this token of sincerity and devotedness was the inference;

and one must suppose that many of the clergy, in point of fact, had accepted the principle for themselves. On the other side was the fact that from the very beginning married men had been chosen to office, and chosen by preference; and that such unions, existing by divine authority, could not be dissolved. Yet the council of Elvira, in Spain, A.D. 305, laid it down that married bishops, priests, and deacons must live apart from their wives. The council of Nicæa declined to adopt this principle; but the rule seems to have been generally accepted and enforced, that clergy in those orders must not marry a second time on the death of the wife, and that those who were single men when ordained must not marry afterwards. In the West, moreover, Pope Siricius, before the end of the fourth century, is found demanding cessation of conjugal intercourse after the husband's ordination. The Eastern Church, on the contrary, continued to abide by the rule just stated as regards priests; in some cases working it with a disposition to require all candidates for priesthood to be married before ordination. As regards bishops, however, the feeling in favour of celibacy gained ground, and finally prevailed. Various eminent bishops of the fourth century appear to have been married men.[1] When Synesius was suddenly called upon to accept the bishopric of Ptolemais (about A.D. 400) he made it a condition that the acceptance should make no change in his conjugal relations. He thought, therefore, that the other course might be expected; but was assured that the maintenance of his condition as a married man was within his rights.[2]

The luminaries of the time—from Athanasius down to Leo—show what Christian ministers of the fourth and fifth centuries might be,—what power, zeal, and fidelity, mixed, no doubt, with other qualities, they could bring

[1] The father of Greg. Naz., Gregory of Nyssa, and Hilary of Poictiers are usually cited.

[2] In judging of the effect of regulations like these, it must be kept in view that a very large proportion of those called to be presbyters or bishops were persons more or less advanced in life, selected from the membership of the congregation.

to the discharge of their duties. On the other hand, indications are not wanting that pronounced selfishness and secularity were also very visible, that men sought the ministry and pursued it under the most earthly motives, and did not care to disguise those motives. One acquires the impression that gross immorality could, in particular cases, exist and be winked at, without awakening great concern; but the proportion of such cases cannot be fixed. *Charges* of gross sin were far from uncommon; they constituted a weapon which theological opponents used pretty freely. But a certain discrimination appears in the use of them. Such charges were employed to destroy Eustathius of Antioch. But nothing of the kind was seriously alleged in the case of Athanasius. The new charges brought against the young bishop of Alexandria were such as might seem plausible against a man of high, resolved, imperious character. A similar remark applies (with some modification) to the charges advanced by the enemies of Chrysostom.

One of the influences affecting the personal character of the clergy was the conventional deference accorded to them. This was most remarkable, naturally, in the case of bishops, but by no means applied to them exclusively.[1]

[1] There were substantial powers, partly noticed already: bishops were recognised arbiters in causes brought before them by consent, and in such cases their decisions were accepted by the Courts as valid; accusations against clergymen were, under considerable limitations, relegated, in the first instance, to their ecclesiastical superiors; and bishops had a vague but effective right of interposing to procure mitigation of severe—especially of capital—sentences in the criminal courts. But the main point is that they were regarded as centres of legitimate influence, the source of which was sacred; and the motives under which it was exerted were to be presumed to be worthy. Influence of this kind could be made much of by strong men and by men of venerable character, while in other hands it was less potent.

The social and ceremonial position receives its chief illustration from the etiquette according to which the emperor bowed his head to a bishop, to receive his blessing, and kissed his hand. Philostorgius has reported an amazing instance of sacerdotal impudence in this department, which was probably unique (Gies. § 91, No. 24); yet see Sulp. Sev. *Martini Vita*, 20. The polite conventions of the clergy are exemplified in their correspondence. In the third century Cyprian, addressing a bishop of Rome, was content to say

The clergy had become highly important persons in the Christian communities before Constantine; the Christian emperors accorded to them the full amount of respect which they enjoyed among their flock,—the imperial religion was to be glorified by the dignity of its representatives,—and so a social convention on the subject took place throughout the empire. The clergy benefited by it, and adopted among themselves the extravagant formulæ of courtesy characteristic of the Eastern Court.

"Cyprianus Cornelio fratri"; but in the fourth Jerome writes to Augustine, "Domino vere sancto et beatissimo papæ Augustino"; and in the fifth the bishops of Dardania write to the Pope Gelasius, "Domino sancto Apostolico et beatissimo patri patrum Gelasio papæ Urbis Romæ humiles Episcopi Dardaniæ (*Epistolæ, Arillana Collectio*, No. 80). This, of course, was mainly form; but it was significant, and also influential. An official dignity and sanctity were suggested which fitted in too well with the growing disposition to make much of externals.

## CHAPTER XX

### NICENE COUNCIL

Newman, *Arians of Fourth Century*, Lond. 1871. Gwatkin, *Arian Controversy*, Lond. 1889; *Studies of Arianism*, Lond. 1882. Stanley, *Lectures on the History of the Eastern Church*, Lond. 1862.

THE shadows of the long Arian controversy were darkening over the Church in the very hour of her emerging into the region of imperial favour and protection.

The Monarchian theories had been practically rejected. The existence of the Divine Word or Son, personally distinct from the Father, incarnate in Jesus Christ, maintained itself as the belief which the Church was to assert. It was a belief not free from difficulties. It had been associated with ideas of a certain derivation from the Father, and a certain subordination to the Father, by which, it was conceived, the unity of Godhead was guarded, while yet the distinction between the First and Second in the Godhead was made tangible. From Justin downwards expounders of this doctrine had been led by various motives, intellectual or religious, to ascribe to the Son characteristics that seemed to draw Him somewhat nearer to the creatures, —a limited sphere, a definite origination, a particular destiny;—but then they balanced these ideas against others which imported essential connection with the Father, and derivation from within the Father's being. How far these explanations could be carried, and how far they could be deemed successful or safe was not yet clear. Dionysius of Alexandria, opposing Sabellius, had found himself on the point of collision with Dionysius of Rome. Going back a little further, no writer had exerted more influence than Origen, and he had familiarised many minds with the thought of the Son's generation as eternal. Yet the true construction of the modes of speech on this subject, which he brought together, has been matter of debate ever since. All this holds true of the East especially. In the West, Rome was the place most accessible to waves of influence of this kind; but in the West, generally, a simpler and steadier mood prevailed, and that counter influence prevailed at Rome on the whole.

Arius proposed to clear the way through this region of thought by making thorough work, as he conceived, with the great distinction between uncreated God and created beings. With the Church in general, he owned that He who became incarnate pre-existed as the Logos, personally subsisting, presiding over creation, the source of existence to all beings lower than Himself. But this Logos, though thus exalted, is not, according to Arius, within the sphere of Godhead; is not, therefore, divine in the proper and primary sense, but is only the first and greatest of creatures. Terms which suggest divinity are indeed applicable to Him, because He is the creature who stands nearest to the Father, and most fully represents Him. How far lofty terms of this kind may be carried in the case of the Logos, was a subject on which Arius probably fluctuated. But the assertion of the Logos as the central and personal element in Christ, and, at the same time, the denial of His proper and essential divinity and the assertion of His essential creaturehood, was Arianism. The Arians maintained this to be the only logical way of escaping Sabellianism.

Arianism commended itself to men who wished for a scheme of thought running clear, apparently, from end to end, and not, on the surface, offering difficulty or incoherence. This seeming advantage was secured at the cost of sacrificing all the main interests for the sake of which the Church's mind had laboured. The Church had spoken of Christ as divine and human;—some, supposing themselves driven to make a choice, had asserted one aspect so as to wrong the other.  According to Arius, Christ, who was not divine, was not truly human either. He had the body of a man, but the Logos (a creature of a higher order) supplied the place of the soul.

The opinions of Arius have sometimes been considered to be a development of those of Origen. Others have traced them to influences which had their home at Antioch.[1]

A remarkable presbyter, named Lucian, had lived and worked at Antioch during the latter part of the third century. Like his namesake, the author of the *Dialogues*, he was said to have been born at Samosata. He was trained at Edessa, and early in his life he settled at Antioch. It is said that during the episcopates of the three bishops who followed Paul—Domnus, Timæus, and Cyrillus (A.D. 275–305), Lucian was not in the communion of the Catholic Church at Antioch. But all this time he was growing into celebrity as a teacher, especially as an interpreter of Scriptures. He must have been reconciled to the Church eventually: his reputation continued to be high, and many who became distinguished in their generation had formed their theology under him. In 312 he was arrested by the civil authorities and removed to Nicomedia; he died there as a martyr, enduring suffering with fortitude.

As he had so long continued separate from the party at Antioch recognised as orthodox and opposed to Paul, it was a natural suggestion that Lucian shared Paul's errors. Again, as Arius was among his pupils (as were various churchmen who afterwards sympathised with Arius), it is equally natural to infer that Lucian might be the real author of Arianism. Both views have been maintained, though they are not obviously compatible; a dynamical Monarchian (which is Paul's theological label) being very different from an Arian.[2] It would certainly

---

[1] Newman, whose theological antipathies were energetic, traces the course of Christian thought at Antioch in lurid colours. *Arians*, 3rd ed. 1871, pp. 1–25.

[2] Harnack has ingeniously tried to show how the combination might be accomplished, and ascribes to Lucian, on the strength of this speculation, an articulately Arian position. *Dogmengesch.* II. vii. 1.

seem, however, that Lucian's teaching, whatever it was, influenced in an Arianising direction the minds of many who had been under him. Arius, writing to Eusebius of Nicomedia, appeals to him as Sylloukianistes—Fellow Lucianist.[1]

Arius is described to us as a Libyan by birth, who had visited different centres of church life. Latterly he is found as an influential presbyter at Alexandria. A parochial system had developed there, and Arius was in permanent charge of the church called Baucalis. He valued himself much on his reasoning powers. Indeed, Alexander, the bishop, imputed to him and his followers a spirit of boundless arrogance; they spoke, he said, as if they, and they only, were the enlightened portion of the Church.[2] However, Arius was not merely logical, but enthusiastic also; and he lived an ascetic life, using the scanty dress at that time becoming usual with ascetics. When the dispute attracted the attention of the Church, Arius was already sixty years of age—a tall, thin, eager, excitable man, with something strange in his appearance, and yet with great gentleness of voice and manner in his calmer moods. He had a considerable following among Christian ladies in Alexandria.

It is said that the bishop Alexander, expounding in the church the Christian doctrine of God, asserted a unity in the Trinity—$\dot{\epsilon}\nu$ τριάδι μονάδα εἶναι.[3] Arius controverted this, and charged the bishop with Sabellianism. In the earliest letters bearing on the controversy,[4] Arius objects to the co-eternity of the Logos, and asserts in more than one form the precedency of the Father. Therefore, "there was when the Son was not";[5] and he already argues that the Son was called into existence "out of nothing."[6] He was willing

[1] Theodor. *Eccl. Hist.* i. 4.
[2] Theodor. *Eccl. Hist.* i. 3.
[3] Socrat. *Hist. Eccl.* i. 5.
[4] One of Alexander of Alexandria to his namesake of Constantinople; one of Arius to Eusebius of Nicomedia; and one of the Arians to Alexander of Alexandria. Theod. *Eccl. Hist.* i. 3, 4; Athan. *de Synodis*, 16.
[5] ἦν ποτε ὅτε οὐκ ἦν.  [6] ἐξ οὐκ ὄντων.

to emphasise the unique position of the Son. Though He is neither the unbegotten, nor part of the unbegotten, yet " by the divine counsel and will He took subsistence before the ages ";[1] and he is willing to confess Him to be " fully God, only begotten and immutable."[2] Afterwards he developed more resolutely, both the distinction from the true God and the participation in creature qualities,—positions which were certainly implied in his radical assertion that the Son is one of the creatures, though the first and most glorious. Thus his later teaching asserted that the Son is by nature capable of going wrong as well as right; and he argued that the Father must be to the Son also, as well as to others, incomprehensible and " invisible," known by the Son only, as it were, along the same lines on which some knowledge of Him opens to others.[3] These and similar developments appeared in the *Thalia*, a versification of his principles with a view to popular impression.[4]

[1] πρὸ χρόνων καὶ αἰώνων.
[2] πληρὴς Θεός, μονογενής, ἄτρεπτος καὶ ἀναλλοίωτος.
[3] Arius originally spoke of the Logos as ἄτρεπτος ; but that perhaps concealed an ambiguity, for the idea of the Logos, both in the superhuman sphere and in the human, by trial and fidelity turning a position that was precarious into one that was assured, seems to have been an original element in his thought. Take the scheme of Paul of Antioch, and you have Christ as mere man, but, under an impersonal Logos influence, making good His standing by virtue. He might have fallen, but He stood. Make the Logos personal, but created, substitute this Logos for the Soul of Christ, and suppose Him to be peccable, but at all stages, before and after His human birth, to overcome all influence and surmount all risks that might shake a creature, and you have Arianism. In both schemes God foresees the moral victory, and so appoints the office of Saviour to the victor. Lucian of Antioch *may* have suggested this modification of Paul's view. If this was the original scheme of Arius, his earlier ascription to the Logos of the attribute ἄτρεπτος must have referred only to the divine foreknowledge.

[4] Athanasius has preserved for us some of these strange verses (*de Syn.* 15), *e.g.*—
" God as He is in Himself, exists by none comprehended,
He alone has no equal, no like, no sharer of glory;
Unbegotten we call Him, comparing Him with the begotten,
And praise Him as unbeginning in contrast with him who began.
Thus He, the beginningless, gave to the Son beginning of being;
He brought Him forth as a child, and Him to be Son He adopted.
In His own substance the Son has nought that to Godhead pertaineth,
Nor consubstantial is He, nor equal in ought to the Father," etc. etc.

Still, while the Second Person, in the judgment of Arius, is a creature, called into existence out of nothing by the will of the Father, He has divine perfections so communicated to Him that no creature can surpass Him;[1] all other creatures are called into existence by His ministry, and He stands completely between the Universe and the Father. There are therefore two Gods, the unbegotten (who corresponds to the abstract and unknowable God of the philosophers) and the only-begotten God—inferior, even infinitely, to the first, yet the object also of faith and worship.

Sabellius had explained away the Three as transient phases of One. In the course of efforts made, against Sabellius, to emphasise the reality and the distinction of those blessed personalities, a tendency had appeared to carry subordination of the Second to the First so far as to turn distinction into separation. Arius gave decisive expression to this tendency; he did so with all the more animosity, because men were beginning to guard against it; while, in his view, it ought rather to be more roundly and logically carried out. He seems to have been possessed, too, by a real enthusiasm for the Divine Unity, which seemed to him to be subverted by the Athanasian doctrine.

A local council,[2] numerously attended, met at Alexandria and deposed Arius, with Theonas and Secundus, bishops who favoured him, and several deacons. Arius sought support among his friends, who occupied important positions in various churches.

Indeed it soon appeared that the breach could not continue merely local. Churchmen were taking sides upon it in different places. When the debate began Egypt was under the government of the Emperor Licinius. Constantine won his victory in 323; and Egypt, with the East, passed under his sway. All the more that Constantine

---

[1] "One that is even as the Son is, God can beget at His pleasure. But one that excels Him, or better, or greater, not even He can." *Thalia*; Athan. *de Syn.* 15. Beget is for Arius equivalent to create. It mainly suggests to him beginning of being.

[2] Date uncertain; A.D. 320 or 321 has been assigned; see Hefele, *Conciliengeschichte*, i. p. 235.

had committed himself to Christianity, a violent conflict about the Christian faith was unwelcome to him. Already (A.D. 314) he had experienced, in connection with Donatus, the obstinacy of ecclesiastical parties; and he was anxious to suppress this new strife. The debate seemed to him a needless one which might be dropped, and he interposed his good offices through Hosius, bishop of Corduba, to reconcile the parties. This proved to be impracticable; and we may reckon it likely that the report of Hosius would dispose the emperor to take the anti-Arian side. The bent of the Christian West had long been to affirm plainly both the Godhead and the manhood of Christ, and to abstain from minute speculation. Hosius no doubt shared this tendency; and Constantine, so long resident in the West, might be familiar to some extent with the manner of thought and speech which this disposition suggested. If so, the elaborate effort of Arius to break down the divinity of Christ, while he continued to call Him a God, could hardly fail to repel Hosius, and might well seem to Constantine a provoking and needless sophistication. For the present, however, he does not seem to have indicated any bias. With the advice, doubtless, of ecclesiastical persons, he resolved to call a council, œcumenical enough to represent the whole Church. Only under a Christian emperor could such a convention have taken place; and it is very possible that the imagination of Constantine was fired by the idea of occupying a position in which he could seem to elicit, and in some degree to control, oracular decrees in connection with the religion which he had adopted.

The importance of the step thus taken ought to be well considered by the student of Church history. Local councils had been in use for a considerable time, and had exerted authority. In dogmatic questions such councils were understood to formulate the actual tradition of the Church, their authority in that respect depending mainly on the feeling that their agreement afforded a reasonable guarantee for a correct account of that tradition, and carried with it a share of that general presumption as to divine guidance and care which it was pious to associate with ecclesiastical actings. But the first council that could claim to be œcumenical must have been contemplated as something new and great. It would have the character of the collective Church speaking by its authentic voice. And whatever of the sacred and the supernatural, whatever presumption of divine guidance and care was associated with the Church as a whole, might easily be imputed to such an assembly. Hence its decisions might have something more in them than record of tradition; they might have a more oracular character. The significance of it might not be realised in anticipation. Yet it must have been felt to be excitingly new. It came to pass afterwards that a council was a recognised ecclesiastical expedient, became so far a part of the machinery of church life, and presented plainly enough to observers the tokens of "human nature" in its procedure. As yet this was something new,—part of the new world into which the Church had come.

Nicæa lies east of Constantinople, across the Bosphorus, at a distance of some forty-four miles. The council assembled there in May or June 325. Practically it represented Eastern Christendom,—there were not ten bishops from the West: the distance and the growing disuse of Greek in the West were obstacles. Sylvester, bishop of Rome, being old and feeble, was represented by two presbyters. The number of bishops present has been reckoned variously from 218 to 318, the latter is the figure which is generally accepted. Hosius of Corduba, Eusebius of Cæsarea, Eustathius of Antioch. Alexander of Alexandria, are the personages most prominent, at the outset at least, and among them the presidents of the meeting must be sought. Athanasius was in attendance on his bishop, and took part, perhaps, as his spokesman in some of the discussions.

No continuous and consecutive account of the proceedings has been handed down. Arius was present, and about eighteen bishops, headed by Eusebius of Nicomedia, were in general agreement with him. It would appear that at a pretty early stage, explicit statements of the views of Arius were elicited, including passages of his *Thalia*, and these drew forth energetic disapprobation. A creed was put forward drawn up by the eighteen, the terms of which have not been preserved; but it was rejected, and torn in pieces. Perhaps it was at this point that Eusebius of Cæsarea rehearsed the creed of his church, which he conceived might be accepted as a sound and adequate statement of the Church's doctrine.[1]

This creed is given by Eusebius himself in his account of the proceedings at Nicæa, contained in a letter to his flock (Theodoret, *Eccl. Hist.* i. 12). The last sentence, and perhaps the one before, do not read like clauses in a creed, and may embody rather assurances with which Eusebius accompanied it, when he submitted it to the council.

The Arians by this time, we are told, had become aware of the position in which they stood; they saw that they must, if possible, shelter themselves under the terms of some decision which, without sanctioning their views, might be interpreted as not excluding them. They showed themselves ready to accept the Cæsarean formula, but this suggested to their opponents that they meant to interpret it in an Arian sense. On this the Alexandrian party (who had the powerful support of Eustathius of Antioch, Macarius

[1] "I believe in one God the Father Almighty, Maker of all things both visible and invisible: and in one Lord Jesus Christ, the Word of God, God of God, Light of Light, Life of Life, the only-begotten Son, the firstborn of every creature, begotten of the Father before all worlds, by whom all things were made; who for our salvation was incarnate, and lived among men, and suffered, and rose again on the third day, and ascended to the Father, and shall come in glory to judge the quick and dead. And we believe in one Holy Ghost. We believe that each of these Three is and subsists, the Father truly as Father, the Son truly as Son, the Holy Ghost truly as Holy Ghost: as also our Lord, sending forth His own disciples to preach, said, 'Go, and teach all nations, baptizing them into the name of the Father and of the Son and of the Holy Ghost.' Concerning which things we affirm that this is so, that we so think, and that it has long so been held, and that we remain steadfast to death for this faith, anathematising every godless heresy. That we have taught these things from our heart and soul from the time we have known ourselves, and that we now think and say this in truth, we testify in the name of Almighty God, and of our Lord Jesus Christ, being able to prove even by demonstration and to persuade you that in past times also thus we believed and preached."

of Jerusalem, and also Marcellus of Ancyra), without objecting to anything in the Cæsarean formula, set themselves to strengthen and make it more effective in excluding Arianism, by the insertion of appropriate words and clauses. It would be interesting to know in detail the process of discussion by which this took place. But only scattered glimpses are afforded us. The creed ultimately took shape as follows:[1]—
"We believe in one God the Father Almighty, Maker of all things visible and invisible: and in one Lord Jesus Christ, the Son of God, begotten of the Father, only begotten, that is, of the substance of the Father, God of God, Light of Light, Very God of Very God, begotten, not made, consubstantial with the Father, by whom all things were made that are in heaven or in earth; who for us men, and for our salvation descended and took flesh, and became man; He suffered and rose again the third day, ascended into heaven, and cometh to judge the quick and dead: and in the Holy Spirit. But those that say there was when He was not, and before He was begotten He was not, and that He was made out of nothing or of some other substance or essence, or that say the Son of God was liable to perversion or mutation, them the Catholic and Apostolic Church anathematises."

The word consubstantial—$\dot{o}\mu oo\acute{u}\sigma\iota o\varsigma$—henceforth became the banner of the orthodox, although "of the substance" —$\dot{\epsilon}\kappa\ \tau\hat{\eta}\varsigma\ o\dot{u}\sigma\acute{\iota}a\varsigma$—was perhaps the phrase which Athanasius valued most. The Arian teaching was effectually shut out by these phrases, and by the condemnatory clauses at the close.

[1] Πιστεύομεν εἰς ἕνα Θεὸν, Πατέρα παντοκράτορα, πάντων ὁρατῶν τε καὶ ἀοράτων ποιητήν· καὶ εἰς ἕνα Κύριον Ἰησοῦν Χριστόν, τὸν Υἱὸν τοῦ Θεοῦ, γεννηθέντα ἐκ τοῦ Πατρὸς μονογενῆ, τουτ' ἔστιν ἐκ τῆς οὐσίας τοῦ Πατρὸς, Θεὸν ἐκ Θεοῦ, Φῶς ἐκ Φωτός, Θεὸν ἀληθινὸν ἐκ Θεοῦ ἀληθινοῦ, γεννηθέντα, οὐ ποιηθέντα, ὁμοούσιον τῷ Πατρί· δι' οὗ τὰ πάντα ἐγένετο, τά τε ἐν τῷ οὐρανῷ καὶ τὰ ἐν τῇ γῇ· τὸν δι' ἡμᾶς τοὺς ἀνθρώπους, καὶ διὰ τὴν ἡμετέραν σωτηρίαν κατελθόντα, καὶ σαρκωθέντα, καὶ ἐνανθρωπήσαντα, παθόντα καὶ ἀναστάντα τῇ τρίτῃ ἡμέρᾳ, ἀνελθόντα εἰς τοὺς οὐρανούς, ἐρχόμενον κρῖναι ζῶντας καὶ νεκρούς· καὶ εἰς τὸ Ἅγιον Πνεῦμα. τοὺς δὲ λέγοντας, ἦν ποτε ὅτε οὐκ ἦν, καὶ πρὶν γεννηθῆναι οὐκ ἦν, καὶ ὅτι ἐξ οὐκ ὄντων ἐγένετο, ἢ ἐξ ἑτέρας ὑποστάσεως ἢ οὐσίας φάσκοντας εἶναι, ἢ κτιστὸν ἢ τρεπτὸν ἢ ἀλλοιωτὸν τὸν Υἱὸν τοῦ Θεοῦ, τούτους ἀναθεματίζει ἡ ἁγία καθολικὴ καὶ ἀποστολικὴ ἐκκλησία.

The question was whether the formula thus built up could secure acceptance in a measure sufficient to constitute it an utterance of the Church. The emperor's influence was freely employed to promote this object, and in the end almost everyone signified acquiescence. A letter of Eusebius of Cæsarea[1] to his church exists, in which he explains his signature of the creed,—evidently conscious that he might be charged with having acted against his convictions. Most of the eighteen bishops who had supported Arius signed; but Eusebius of Nicomedia with Theognis of Nicæa, demurring to the condemnatory clauses, were deprived of their sees and banished. It is alleged, however, that before the end of the council or soon after it, they were induced to submit and were restored.[2] Arius also was banished, and some of his more obscure followers also shared this fate.

The Nicene Council might not at once disclose all its significance to its contemporaries and to those who took part in it. That is common in the case of great events; the actors are occupied with the details and the temporary forces. But the first general council crystallised and embodied in a new form the idea of the Church: it exhibited the form in which, as regards faith and duty, the Church could appear, and speak, and act in time and space. A presence heretofore believed, shall we say worshipped, found means of gathering itself into a tangible shape, in a Bithynian town, during some weeks of the autumn of 325.

Heretofore the Church spoke as from the past. Men and companies of men professed to receive and reproduce her genuine tradition, cherished by the constant faith of her members. To the great subject of the nature of our Lord men had striven to do justice by selecting and combining Biblical phrases. In doing this the inevitable expository function, in the exercise of which we declare *our* understanding of that which has come to us, was not idle.

[1] Theod. *Eccl. Hist.* i. 11.
[2] It is more likely that their return to position and influence fell somewhat later.

But men had striven always to keep the attitude of reproducing what was undeniably ancient. The Nicene Council felt itself competent to go further, and to give a more independent expression to its utterance of the distinctive faith. The decisive words οὐσία, ὁμοούσιος (ὑπόστασις), had been employed, or had been allowed to pass, by some eminent teachers.[1] But they had not been regarded with uniform satisfaction, and they were understood to be welcomed by Sabellius and his followers. No very authoritative tradition applied to them. But the council chose them to define what it judged to be the true sense of the received faith concerning Christ.

This liberty, which is indispensable to the theologian, is also surely not forbidden to councils. And councils may be—it is to be hoped are—inwardly persuaded that their exposition is absolutely just. But much depends on whether, once made, it is held to be final, irreformable, infallible.

Consciously or unconsciously the Nicene decision really meant that ways of thinking and speaking which hitherto had been open must cease. Esteemed teachers had admitted speculation which either leant in the direction of merging the Son in the Father—in that case with risk of construing the distinct personality of Christ as human merely—or, for the sake of escaping that danger, they emphasised the distinct personality before the human birth, and tried to make that conceivable by ascribing to this personality a later origin and a restricted class of attributes, as of one hovering between God and the creatures. But in the presence of Arianism, with its created God and its creature God, this had to end. The contrast between the Creator and the creature must be emphasised,—and the personal distinction between the Son and the Father must be associated with the resolute assertion of Christ's true and essential Godhead.

Theologically, the writer believes that the turn of thinking on this high subject sanctioned at Nicæa, was the just outcome of the whole discussion. Whether the terms em-

---

[1] Origen sometimes, Hippolytus (*Ref.* x. 33), Dion. Alex. in Athan. *de Sententia*, xviii.

ployed to express it are the best or the only ones, has been questioned. Those who do so, object to metaphysical and non-Biblical terms; and they point to the history of varying meanings attachable to οὐσία, ὁμοούσιος, ὑπόστασις. But it is not needful to track all these windings in order to understand the Nicene Creed. The subject in hand determines the range of meaning. Οὐσία is etymologically = Being or Essence; and it suggests that whatever that manner of existence is which differences God from all creatures, that is to be ascribed to the Son as well as to the Father.

It can be maintained, indeed, that this term οὐσία and others do not apply to God with certainty or clearness. These terms are derived from our thoughts of existences nearer to ourselves. Amid the changing appearances and relations to which they are subject we ascribe to each object something abiding, its οὐσία, which makes it what it is, and is the source and secret of its properties. It may be said we do not know that οὐσία in any of the shades of sense of which it is capable is at all applicable to God. But the answer seems to be that if we think of God at all we do, in our thoughts, ascribe to Him Being, and a manner of Being, which is peculiarly His. We cannot most likely clear these words of implications which originate in our dealing with objects presented to our senses. But terms which have been found indispensable must be presumed to have a right. It is a saying which carries its sense clearly, that if and when we ascribe to God οὐσία, as we shall inevitably do, we are to ascribe the same also to the Son of God because He is divine.

This conviction had substantially prevailed in the Church before, but not so consistently and clearly, nor expressed so inevitably, as now it was to be.

But while this may be maintained theologically, ecclesiastically it is a question whether the Church was prepared for the Nicene decision. Was the council itself so united on it as it seemed to be? Face to face with Arianism, from which they recoiled, impelled by the clearness and consistency of those who led on the Alexandrian side, influenced eventually by the emperor's concurrence with the proposers of the creed, those members who might have preferred something short of it found no standing ground. They were embarrassed perhaps by the circumstance that the course of procedure which their views suggested had been early put forward by the bishop of Cæsarea, and had been discredited as fitted to shelter the Arians. But it is very possible that many of them, in adopting the phrases of the creed, went further than their own convictions warranted, and would have preferred to rest in expressions of earlier creeds less peremptory and precise. When they departed to their churches, and found themselves again in contact with brethren who had not experienced the influences of the council, a change came for many in the direction of relaxation or recoil. In no other way can we explain the course of subsequent events.

Of those who, refusing to accede to Arianism, yet proved to be dissatisfied with the Nicene Creed, there might be various shades; but on the whole they may be referred to two classes. One was composed of men who simply wished to abide by the language already familiar to them, and felt uneasy as to the amount of change and also of exclusion which the Nicene phrases might turn out to carry with them. The other class were Semi-Arians proper. They had adopted subtle theories about the Logos, which really were attempts to find a middle category between the creating nature and the created. They did not sympathise with the resolute clearness of Arius in ranking the Logos among the creatures, called into existence "out of nothing"; but neither did they sympathise with the corresponding clearness of the Nicene Creed on the other side. They believed in a middle ground. These two classes shaded into one another, and it was the interest of both to find common phrases and to act together.

Such persons could unite in objecting to the phrase of the creed, as leaning to Sabellianism. For some of them this might be merely a good popular cry; but in the case of others it was a genuine apprehension. The assertion of the ὁμούσια, as they felt, so identified the Father with the Son that the distinction between them could not afterwards be maintained. The word itself also had had a questionable history. In using it the council were consecrating a suspected phrase.

Some justification for such suspicions was furnished by the case of Marcellus of Ancyra. He had been prominent at the council as an opponent of Arius, and afterwards continued to support the Nicene Creed. But he held a peculiar doctrine, which was eventually disclosed in a book written by Marcellus, against Asterius an advocate of Arianism. Marcellus, as we shall see, did not own a real distinction between the Father and the Logos. He was felt to deny both the pre-existence of Christ and His continued existence after the consummation of the Church. He had no motive therefore, and hardly a feasible ground, for any doctrine of the Holy Spirit.

The energy and success with which the Athanasian view was carried through at the council against every hostile or temporising tendency, seems to be reflected in the attitude of Constantine. There is reason to suppose that before the council began he had been made acquainted with the creed of Cæsarea (proposed by Eusebius), and had thought it might suffice. If this be so, his change of attitude, and his resolute advocacy, at last, of the creed eventually adopted, indicates that the way in which the Homoousian doctrine was pressed and carried had impressed him deeply, and led him to think it his true policy to rally the Church on that line, and break down opposition or hesitation. This memorable decision of Church and State —uttered by a new organ, in the very dawn of the new day, must have fallen with weight on the minds of men. Yet the elements of reaction existed, as we have seen, in many minds, and the Arians, as well as the more advanced and dogmatic Semi-Arians, resolved to take advantage of this to shake the authority of the Nicene formula. Constantine was by and by won to their views.

What proved to be at first the policy of the party

was not to repudiate Nicene doctrine, but to administer the Church with liberal toleration for Arianising views; to smother the Nicene Creed in numerous formulas less precise; and to contrive pretexts for discrediting and destroying leading advocates of the Nicene decision.

# CHAPTER XXI

### ARIAN CONTROVERSY—POST-NICENE

Gwatkin, *Studies of Arianism*, Lond. 1882. "Arianism," in *Real-Encycl.*

THE chief sections into which the Church divided during subsequent discussions may be distinguished thus:—

1. Those who defended Nicene theology in Nicene terms, led, of course, by Athanasius. Their distinctive words were ὁμοούσιος, ἐκ τῆς οὐσίας.

2. The Arians. For them the Son was a unique and wonderful creature, called into existence before the ages to be the Father's representative to all other creatures. For many years the most of them were willing to be confounded with the next party (No. 3); for their great object was to defeat Nicene theology. Eventually ὅμοιος became their watchword; but a more resolved party took up separate ground (see 4).

3. Between 1 and 2 the ground was occupied by a large party, very strong in the East, whom the orthodox designated Semi-Arians; but it included (*a*) a section that repudiated all sympathy with Arianism, and proposed to maintain the divinity of the Son in language more safe and more approved than that of Nicæa; for they thought the latter to be capable of a Sabellian sense, and in any case to be too new. These were led, for some years, by Basil of Ancyra, and were accustomed to appeal to certain creeds of Antioch. Eventually their distinctive word came to be ὁμοιούσιος. (*b*) A body of men who either verged towards Arianism, but did not like to go the whole length and tried to find a middle ground between Creator and

creature, or who did not know their own minds and were at the mercy of circumstances. This party could often use the phrases of dogmatic Semi-Arianism; but they were more attracted by the convenient vagueness of the Arian ὅμοιος.

4. An extreme left wing of Arianism became apparent in the later stages. The natural utterance of Arius was to say that the Logos was like the Father. Yet in respect of the contrast between Creator and creature, He must be also unlike; and Arius had virtually said this too. A section of his followers conceived it to be proper to lay the emphasis on the unlikeness, and they did so in coarse and offensive terms. They said plainly ἀνόμοιος.

The debate went on for fifty-six years.

We fix four stages, and give account of them in succession. The first extends from the Nicene Council to the death of Constantine (325–337); the second, to the reunion of the empire (previously shared among the brothers) under Constantius (351); the third, to the death of Constantius (361); and the fourth, to the Council of Constantinople (381), which was preceded by the accession of Theodosius (379).

I. Constantine had approved the Nicene formula, and promoted the adoption of it in the Council. That was in A.D. 325. But a change in his policy appears by 328. Various influences have been suggested as explaining this, among others that of his sister, the widow of Licinius, who was herself influenced by Eusebius of Nicomedia. Something was due, perhaps, to mere change of residence. Constantine had come from the West, where the divine and the human aspects of Christ were roundly stated, and where there was no propensity to speculation; in particular, no anxiety to relate the definition of church theology to philosophical theories. It is likely enough that Constantine by degrees became more aware of the intellectual world in which the Greek mind worked, and of the various lines of thought and argument by which it was held; and he might begin to think it wiser and more conducive to eventual peace to pursue a policy of comprehension. This, at all events, was the nature of the change which took place. Constantine resolved to administer things so as to comprehend men of different shades, instead of exacting full and precise acceptance of the Nicene definitions. There was, however, no repudiation of the Nicene Creed. That for a man like Constantine would have been a questionable step; it would have amounted to the admission of a mistake. But there might be different ways of regarding the creed, and of administering affairs under it.

The men who chiefly influenced Constantine in this direction, or who naturally became his chief advisers when once his face was set this way, were Eusebius of Nicomedia and Eusebius of Cæsarea. Both men must have agreed in desiring a less stringent enforcement of Nicene doctrine; but the former was an Arian or something very near it, while the bishop of Cæsarea belonged to one of the shades of what would have been called Semi-Arianism at a later period. Eusebius of Nicomedia was nearer to the ear of the emperor, and he was the more astute manager of men. He had been banished at the close of the Nicene Council, but reappears in his see about A.D. 328 or 329. Arius also was recalled, or was allowed to return from banishment. Meanwhile Alexander of Alexandria had died, and Athanasius, in spite of bitter opposition, was elected to the vacant see, A.D. 328.

It must always be kept in view that Arianism proper, in its own name and for its own sake, could have done little to disturb the Nicene decision. The Arians for the present maintained their position by supporting the great middle party, which in a general way goes under the name of Semi-Arianism in the pages of Church history.

The Eusebians began the attack; the Nicene leaders were assailed, but not on the ground of their Nicene faith. Eustathius of Antioch was deposed about 330 on charges, mainly, of immorality. Several more were got rid of in the following year; and charges of false doctrine were directed against Marcellus of Ancyra,[1] while against Athanasius

[1] Marcellus really held a peculiar doctrine, though his friends were unwilling to see this, and he himself seems for a time to have concealed it.

various impossible charges were brought, not theological, but personal and political.

Athanasius was made to appear at a great council at Tyre (335), which deposed him; and the emperor soon after banished him to Treves in the West, but did not at this time allow his see to be filled up. In 336 Arius, who had made a confession satisfactory to the authorities now in power, was ordered to be received into the fellowship of the Church at Constantinople; but on the evening before the day fixed for that purpose he died suddenly. In A.D. 337 Constantine himself died, having been baptized on his deathbed by Eusebius of Nicomedia. All this time the Nicene form of creed had not been openly rejected, scarcely even controverted. Athanasius, Marcellus, Eustathius of Antioch, Macarius of Jerusalem, were prominent at this stage on the Nicene side. Hosius had retired to his remote bishopric in Spain. Eusebius of Nicomedia led the anti-Nicene party, which had not yet disclosed its internal differences.

II. In the next period (extending to A.D. 350) we start with three emperors, of whom Constantius ruled the East (including Egypt), Constans had Italy and Illyricum, and Constantine II. Spain, Gaul, and Britain. Constantine's

---

He had energetically opposed the Arians at Nicæa, and lent useful help in connection with the creed. But in a book which he put forth he was understood to maintain that the Logos, which is the essential Reason of the divine nature, is not, as such, personally distinct. In the Incarnation, however, it assumes a distinct character and becomes the Son; but this is not durable; for when, at last, the Son, having accomplished all the ends of His work, gives up the kingdom to the Father, He is again merged indistinguishably in the Father's essence. This was Sabellian, because the personal distinction in the Godhead was explained away; it was also denounced as savouring of the error of Paul of Samosata.

Marcellus, like some others, returned to his see after Constantine's death, but had soon to leave it again. He was in Rome as a refugee during the pontificate of Julius, and met the accusation against him by reciting the Roman creed. This sufficed for the time, but eventually his friends had to acknowledge his defection from sound doctrine. The phrase "of whose kingdom there shall be no end," in the later form which passes under the name of Nicene, was levelled against Marcellus. Zahn, *Marcell. v. Ancyra*, 1867.

life soon ended, and his inheritance was taken over by Constans.

The new emperors allowed the deposed bishops, Athanasius, Marcellus, and the rest, to return to their sees. Constantine II. and Constans were at least not unfavourable to Athanasius, and Constantius probably deferred to their wishes. But next year (338) Athanasius was again expelled from his see and fled to Rome; so did various other ecclesiastics, including Marcellus. Julius, bishop of Rome, proposed to hold a council on these troubles, and invited the attendance of the Eastern bishops; but they procrastinated and finally declined. In 340 Julius held his council. About fifty Western bishops met at Rome, acquitted Athanasius, as well as Marcellus, and reported their decision to the Eastern bishops. The irregularity of a Western council disregarding the decision of an Eastern one in the case of Eastern bishops, and their shielding the errors of Marcellus, were henceforth added to the doctrinal causes of division and distrust. The case of Marcellus was regarded in the East as an illustration of the Sabellian teaching of Nicene men.

In 341, on the occasion of the dedication of a great church, a council was held at Antioch[1] which illustrates very well the situation in the East. This council put forth successively four creeds, all differing in terms from the Nicene, and it confirmed the sentence on Athanasius. It was regarded in later times as an Arian or Eusebian assembly; resolute criticism has been applied to its utterances, and the key to its proceedings has been found in insincerity and heresy combined. But that was hardly so. The council was a meeting of Eastern bishops, exhibiting the usual varieties which at that stage might be expected at such gatherings. Some were Eusebians; but none of these professed to hold the Arianism condemned at Nicæa. Others no doubt represented, in different shades and degrees, the

[1] Antioch was not only the seat of a Patriarchate, but at this time it was the court residence of the Emperor Constantius.

sentiment which distrusted the Nicene way of asserting our Lord's divinity; Dianius of Cæsarea (in Cappadocia), for instance, certainly believed in our Lord's true divinity, but held the question still to be open how it might best be expressed. In these circumstances the aim of the Eusebians was to bias the proceedings in a manner favourable to their own policy, but they could only do so by adopting a very cautious line of action. There is nothing heretical in the four creeds: three of them condemn Arianism, and all are efforts to come near to the Nicene faith, while abstaining from Nicene expressions, especially from the ὁμοούσιος. They level condemnation also at Marcellus, who was still supported by the Nicene champions; but this condemnation was just. Finally, they confirmed the deposition of Athanasius on charges of oppression, etc., a step which must have given satisfaction to the Eusebians. But they did so as upholding the sentence of the synod of Tyre, against the contrary judgment of a Roman synod, which they no doubt considered to be intrusive and irregular.

Meanwhile Constans in the West was pressing for a general council of the whole Church, and the political circumstances were such that Constantius did not think it prudent obstinately to resist the proposal. The place fixed was Sardica, within the frontier of the Western empire. This council was held A.D. 343. The Eastern bishops refused to enter the council unless the deposition of Athanasius and Marcellus, as confirmed at Antioch, was held to be valid. The Western bishops refused, proceeded with the examination of the cases of both the accused, and acquitted them. They declared adherence to the Nicene Creed, and framed some canons to regulate existing disorders. The Eastern bishops meanwhile had adjourned to Philippopolis. There they denounced the bishops at Sardica as patrons of the errors of Marcellus, and set forth a creed nearly in the same terms as the fourth creed of Antioch. Another council at Antioch (343) once more affirmed the same creed with long explanations (hence called μακρόστιχος). Also they afresh condemned Marcellus, and now also his disciple

Photinus of Sirmium.[1] But, on the other hand, they condemned certain Arian phrases, and strongly affirmed the unity of the Son with the Father. All these utterances, in fact, embody the same effort—to come as near as possible to the West in doctrine, while they still try to win a victory on the personal questions. Arianising Semi-Arians, and also some who were Arians simply, might choose to take shelter under these formulæ; but the plain sense of the creeds adopted was unfavourable to both these forms of doctrine. Hence a certain measure of forbearance appeared. The West still continued to uphold Marcellus, but they gave up the defence of Photinus. Meanwhile the Arian occupant of the see of Alexandria died, and Constantius, pressed by Constans, ordered Athanasius to return to Alexandria (346). During these years the influence of Julius of Rome was powerfully exerted in favour of Athanasius. Eusebius of Nicomedia died in 342. He had practised throughout the policy of holding together, as far as possible, all who were on any ground dissatisfied with Nicene phraseology.

III. Constans died in A.D. 350, and Constantius became sole ruler; but troubles in his empire hampered him until 353. Then it turned out that while some progress had been made towards mutual understanding as between the mass of the East and the mass of the West, Constantius and his chosen clerical advisers were bent on courses which perplexed everything, and which won for Arianism a temporary triumph throughout the empire. In these ecclesiastical matters Constantius was resolute to rule. But his conception of the form of doctrine which he should cause to prevail was not always the same.

In the East Marcellus and Photinus were again deposed as early as 351, a step which could not reasonably be complained of. But in 353 the emperor began to act with vigour. He succeeded in inducing the members of a

---

[1] Photinus advanced a doctrine very nearly the same as that of Paul of Samosata. The divine Logos did not become personal in Jesus, as Marcellus seemed to teach · but the unique humanity of Jesus was a subject of special divine influence.

Western council at Arles, with one exception, to condemn Athanasius for the crimes alleged against him. In 355 the same sentence was affirmed again at Milan. Hilary of Poictiers here comes into view; he was sent into exile for standing out against the emperor's will. Only in this indirect way as yet was the Nicene faith attacked in the West. Soon after, Athanasius was again driven from his church by an armed force (356).

Still, therefore, affairs continued to present the same general aspect as they had done ever since the reign of Constantine. That is to say, Arianism, so far as it existed, was content to shelter itself behind Semi-Arianism or conservatism. Some of the phrases in which the Nicene faith was expressed were questioned, and it was maintained that all legitimate interests connected with the doctrine of our Lord's higher nature could be sufficiently provided for by other definitions, and these were put forth in various creeds. Further, Marcellus and Photinus were attacked, but for false teaching peculiar to themselves, and Athanasius, but for alleged personal crimes.

At the same time the prolonged discussions had done something to produce dispositions in East and West tending towards peace. But at this point influences were thrown into the situation which produced a scene of great confusion.

In the first place a set of Arians began to make themselves heard, who were much more unmanageable than the politic men about the court; in fact, were more extreme than Arius himself. They were hard, shallow, and conceited men, but they had the courage of their opinions. They saw no mystery in God's being, or in any kind of being; and they proclaimed broadly and coarsely that the Son, being merely a creature, is simply *not* like the Father, $\dot{\alpha}\nu\delta\mu o\iota o\varsigma$; whence they were called Anomœans (also Exoukontians, Heterousiastians, and the like). Such men were Aetius, Eunomius, Eudoxius.[1] Probably by plain, strong state-

---

[1] Against them the famous *Orations* of Gregory Nazianzen are chiefly directed, at least in the portions which have regard to the divinity of the Son. Eudoxius was sometimes separated from the Anomœans as an Arian simply.

ments they made an impression on that class of persons which is indisposed to recognise mystery. But those Semi-Arians [1] who had mostly at heart the maintenance of our Lord's divinity, were now driven by recoil to realise more fully the amount of their agreement with the Nicene theology.

About this time, however, certain court bishops who were practically Arians, though less coarse and more politic in the expression of their Arianism, gained the confidence of Constantius; and they began to devise plans for giving to the utterances which were to define the Church's faith a more Arian character. Conspicuous among these men were Valens, bishop of Mursa (in Pannonia), and Ursacius of Singidunum (Belgrade). With them Acacius of Constantinople acted for a time. The emperor exerted his authority in this direction, but sometimes for a more Arian and sometimes for a less Arian formula.

Under these influences certain creeds of Sirmium came into play,[2]—the second, third, and fourth,—associated with successive meetings in that city. The second (357) asserts the primeval generation of the Son, disclaims all theories about the οὐσία, and emphasises the superior majesty of the Father. It was recognised as framed in the interest of Arianism, but Hosius was induced to sign it, and so purchased his release from exile. The third (358) verged towards the conservative Semi-Arians; for the emperor had, for a little, come under their influence: it went on the lines of one of the creeds of Antioch (341). Liberius of Rome signed this, and obtained leave to go home. The fourth was planned at a small meeting (359). Like the second, it repudiates all terms that suggest οὐσία, but confesses the Son to be like the Father in all things (κατὰ πάντα), as the Scriptures declare. This repelled the Semi-Arians, for they were aware

---

[1] Semi-Arians began now to be more habitually distinguished by this name.

[2] Sirmium was frequently the residence of the Court. The first creed of Sirmium was adopted at a council which met there 349 or 350. This creed was identical with the fourth of Antioch (341-2).

by this time that the term "like" as used by Arians applied merely to imitative attributes in a creature; hence they claimed that the likeness must apply to the nature underlying the attributes, and this they henceforth expressed by ὁμοιούσια. In the summer and autumn of the same year (359) the great double Council of Ariminum (for the West) and Seleucia (for the East) was held. More than five hundred and sixty bishops attended at the one place or the other. It is said that the majority at Ariminum was Nicene, at Seleucia conservative Semi-Arian; but the fourth creed of Sirmium, or rather a modification of it in a rather more Arian direction, was pressed upon both;[1] and by force and persuasion a general signature by both parties was at last attained. Of all the bishops who attended, only Hilary of Poictiers seems to have finally refused to sign.

The emperor had thus secured a general submission of East and West alike, and had committed the Church to a formula planned and welcomed by Arians. The Nicene Creed seemed to be supplanted, and therefore virtually cancelled. Opinions, however, had not really changed; and one effect of the proceeding was to draw together conscientious men from the two parties of the Homoiousians and Homoousians. But yet for some years the Church, bewildered and baffled, seemed content to remain under the general formula of Homoiism,—the doctrine of indefinite likeness. The term was vague enough to cover different alternatives; and there seemed to be no end of trouble if anything more precise were aimed at. Hilary of Poictiers is conspicuous during this period on the Nicene side. The more orthodox Semi-Arians were led by Basil of Ancyra. The Arianising Semi-Arians were represented by Acacius of Cæsarea, and the Anomœans by Eunomius and Eudoxius along with Aetius, a "sophist," evidently of very considerable ability, but constitutionally irreverent and self-confident.

IV. In 361 Constantius died, and Julian his cousin succeeded to the throne. Julian professed toleration; and

[1] It omitted κατὰ πάντα.

he allowed all banished bishops to return to their sees, not without the hope that Christian dissensions might in this way be intensified. On the whole he was disappointed. The more grave and thoughtful Christianity was not Arian, and it gained ground in most places by its moral weight.

About this time or before it, fresh movements came to light. Those of the Semi-Arians who were now known as Homoiousians, began to discuss in a fresh and careful way some of the terms employed in the controversy, such as φύσις, οὐσία, ὑπόστασις, πρόσωπον. These discussions tended in the direction of an understanding with Athanasius and his friends. Stress was still laid on the reasons which led them to judge ὁμοιούσιος the more fitting word. They grant that the Father and the Son are ταὐτόν in so far that they are both πνεῦμα; but in so far as they are distinct hypostases, they can also be said to be *like*.

Athanasius had already come some way to meet these views in his treatise *De Synodis*, which dates from 359. It was an important effort at conciliation. He granted that he who says that the Son is of like nature with the Father —and also says that the Son's οὐσία is " of the Father's" —is not far from saying ὁμοούσιος. For this is equivalent to saying ὁμοιούσιος ἐκ τῆς οὐσίας. He still exerts himself to show that ὁμοούσιος is, however, the right word. Further, in a synod held at Alexandria in 362 he procured a declaration that men who were willing to accept the Nicene Creed should be owned as in communion, without regard to past misunderstandings. It was of even more importance that he recognised the ambiguity of the word hypostasis, and granted that one might say, in one sense (like the Nicene Creed) one hypostasis, but in another sense three hypostases.

Julian fell in battle in 363. Jovian, his successor, died in 364. Valentinian came to the throne, and allotted to himself the government of the West. He ruled on the whole in a wise and tolerant spirit. In these circumstances the native bent of the West asserted itself, in the election of bishops and otherwise, against Homoiism and in favour of the higher teaching. In 369 a synod at Rome again declared for the Nicene faith.

The government of the East had been left by Valentinian to his brother Valens. Here were to be found Anomœans on the one hand, Nicene Christians on the other; between them both stood Homoiians who represented the creed dominant in the later days of Constantius, and also those conservative Semi-Arians who stiffly maintained their own formulas (those of Antioch) against the other three parties: they were now generally affirming the *homoiousia*. Valens supported the Homoiians. They were still probably the strongest party, and therefore even on grounds of policy might seem best deserving of the support of the emperor.

Disturbances in the Eastern empire, which for a time absorbed the attention of Valens, encouraged the Homoiousian party (as distinguished from the Homoiians) to assert themselves. They re-enacted some of their old creeds, and deposed, or affected to depose, Homoiian bishops. When the political troubles passed away, Valens showed his resentment, and vigorously supported Homoiism throughout the East. His action caused some trouble to Nicene men; but apparently it bore still more hardly on the Homoiousians. As the result, this party, already realising the possibility of friendly relations with the Nicene theologians, began to move still more decidedly in that direction. This was the main importance of the reign of Valens.

Athanasius was now becoming old; he died in 373. The three "Cappadocians," Basil and the two Gregories, became the leading Nicene theologians. They had started (Basil certainly) from the thought of "likeness," or from the Homoiousia.[1] But from the beginning their face was set towards the Nicene theology, and now they were labouring to bring about a full understanding. They exerted important influence in reuniting those who were accessible to the lessons of the time. Reunion was delayed by natural difficulties regarding terms, by the influence of old alliances, by suspicions, by the movements of reactionary sections.

[1] Basil, *Ep.* 361.

Still, from 370 to 380, the intermediate parties tended to break up; and the new currents set, not towards the Arians, but towards the Nicenians.

It was important that the policy of Valens should have driven the conservative Semi-Arians to seek this alliance, leaving the Homoiians in the enjoyment of imperial favour. The Homoiian formula had really no definite meaning: that was its recommendation: and when outward influences ceased to hold its adherents together, they proved to have, as a party, no strong ties, no pervading enthusiasms. Those, on the other hand, who adhered to the creed of Antioch evinced a certain constancy in keeping their ground against Arianism. Indignation and resentment at the treatment they experienced reinforced other influences which were drawing them towards the Nicene party; and by the end of the reign of Valens they were in a large measure ready to make common cause with them. If, on the contrary, this party had been favoured by Valens and had been in possession of a strong position at the end of his reign, they might have proved more stubborn and more difficult to deal with than the Homoiians proved to be in the same circumstances.

An illustration of the tenacity of conservative Semi-Arianism occurred in connection with the doctrine of the Holy Ghost. Bishops who could have given up their controversy with Nicene modes of statement regarding the deity of Christ, continued to make difficulty about the corresponding doctrine in reference to the Third Person. And when the question, which had been left open for a time, was pressed to a decision, they maintained their ground and suffered for it. These received the name of Macedonians—from Macedonius, then bishop of Constantinople.

All over the East there was great confusion of parties, of creeds, one may fear also of Christian manners. But in 378 Valens fell at Adrianople in the great battle with the Goths. Presently Theodosius was summoned from Spain to assume the empire of the East, and to avert the ruin of the Roman State. As soon as he had restored the framework of the empire, and secured a respite from its most pressing dangers, he called a council at Constantinople, which met in 381. The council was a meeting of Eastern bishops, and mustered about one hundred and fifty members. The new emperor was resolute for the Nicene faith. Those who could not be conciliated were the Anomœans, who were deprived of their churches without ceremony, and that portion of the Semi-Arians who stood out on the doctrine of the Holy Spirit. Their case was contemplated with some regret, and efforts were made to bring them in. But they too withdrew from the council and gave up their churches. The council reaffirmed the Nicene faith, and condemned certain heresies, among which was that of the Πνευματομάχοι, opponents of the divinity of the Holy Spirit.

The contest was at an end. Within the empire the Church was to be Nicene. There must have been many surviving Arians, and Arian congregations here and there still struggled with the difficulties of a lost cause: especially among the cultivated classes individuals might take leave to doubt what was so confidently asserted as the faith. It continued to be the part of orthodox teachers to state and argue the case against Arianism. But for the Church of the Græco-Roman world the question was closed.

Arianism continued, however, to be the national religion of the Goths. Sporadic Christianity had existed among the Goths for more than a century, but energetic and organised missions among them dated from a time when opposition to the Nicene formula was very prevalent in the East. The Christian leaven thrown into the Gothic nationality through this channel retained its Anti-Nicene character. One cannot doubt that this Arianism was represented by some devoted ministers, and it diffused a powerful Christian influence among a vigorous barbarian stock. But in addition to all the disadvantage implied in Arian teaching, it was a great loss alike to clergy and to laity among the Goths, that they were in this way cut off, in the East and the West, from religious fellowship with the thought, the worship, and the life of the great Church. This Gothic Arianism failed to make any deep mark on history as a religious force. No doubt the imperfect civilisation of the Goths was reflected in their church life. As the result of conquest, or by the policy of Gothic rulers who, sooner or later, concluded that the time had come to give up their peculiarity, the races which had received an Arian Christianity eventually passed over into the Catholic fold. Ostrogoths, Visigoths, Burgundians, Vandals, Lombards— all are alike in that respect. One would like to know more of the type and working of this Christianity; but if there was ever much to tell, the tale has fallen silent. One may guess that it assumed the character of a distinctive race religion, and surrendered itself too willingly to the influence and impulses of the Gothic nationality. The only personality that stands out impressively is the venerable form of Ulfilas, whose memory was cherished as the great evangelist of the Goths, and who gave them the Scriptures in their own tongue. He died in 381. The Gothic version of the Scriptures is still accessible in the beautiful MS. which is preserved at Upsala.[1]

In the long struggle, the course of which has been surveyed, two parties held positions that were clear,—Arians on the one side, supporters of Nicæa on the other. Between them were various forms of expression, upon which men of different shades of view could take their stand; and of these men often availed themselves, who desired rather plausibly to conceal their views than plainly to express them. The Arians and some of those who passed for Semi-Arians often acted disingenuously, and their history affords little evidence of religious depth or of moral tone. On the other hand, of the Nicene bishops too many were apt to give way under pressure; but the party was nobly led, and it certainly comprised far more worth and conscience than the Arian. But another party, who were charged with Semi-Arianism, while they themselves claimed

---

[1] Waitz, *Ueber das Leben u. die Lehre des Ulfila*, 1840; Bessell, *Das Leben d. Ulfilas u. die Bekehrung der Gothen*, 1860; Krafft, *De Fontibus Ulfilæ Arianismi*, 1860; Gwatkin, *Studies of Arianism*, 1882; C. Anderson Scott, *Ulfilas*, etc., Cambridge, 1885.

to be the heirs of the ancient teaching, must be looked upon as serious and self-respecting men. They conceived that they expressed the divine nature of Christ in safe and approved terms; but they were apt to argue themselves into questionable positions, and to slide into alliances not favourable to their best qualities. Still they were genuinely opposed to Arianism, and many of them were not far, in their views, from their Nicene brethren.

The Nicene Creed proved to be the line of statement on which, at the stage of human thought then reached, the doctrine of the Godhead and the manhood of Christ could be upheld as a church doctrine against Arianism. But for the interposition of the civil power the result would have been earlier reached: even with that interposition, and in spite of all efforts to avert the consummation, Nicene Christianity wore its opponents out by intellectual and moral strength and constancy. This fact ought to impress us. Even those who may think that terms like ἐκ τῆς οὐσίας, ὑπόστασις, and so on, cannot claim permanent dominion over our thoughts,—who may wish to dismiss them for more Biblical expressions,—may still reasonably feel, that having (at the critical stage which we have traversed) been found practically indispensable, these terms have won a permanent significance. They have become associated with meanings and references with which the Church cannot part, and for the sake of which the terms themselves must have permanent importance.

A question has been raised, whether the Nicene faith, as explained and defended by Basil and the two Gregories, is quite the same with that faith as explained by Athanasius.[1] It can be maintained, for instance, that some new phraseology and some new illustrations are put in play by the Cappadocians. In particular, the distinction between οὐσία and ὑπόστασις is permanently fixed in the Church (see, however, *ante*, p. 349, as to Athanasius' decision on this point), so that now, while one *ousia* continues to be owned, three hypostases are emphasised. It can be said, therefore, that the

[1] Harnack, *Dogmengesch.* II. chap. vii. 8.

distinction of the Persons is now more marked, and the unity not so much; or again, that Athanasius held the Unity with the Trinity as the mystery, while the Cappadocians held the Trinity with the Unity as the mystery. It is pointed out also that in the Cappadocians we find a tendency to resume speculation, after the example of Origen, on the significance of the relations in the Trinity, to dwell on the relations of the λόγος to the κόσμος, and, in general, to make extensive use of Platonic doctrines. All this, if it be so, seems to amount to no more than the shade of difference necessarily arising when new minds are embarking in a great discussion.[1]

The real result was that the true and full divinity of Christ came to recognition throughout the Church, through an agreement between Egypt and the West on the one hand, and the party which now formed the mass of the East upon the other.

### NOTE.—*The Nicene Creed.*

The authentic decree of Constantinople (381) is contained in the first canon. It is in these terms:—
"The creed of the three hundred and eighteen fathers who met at Nicæa in Bithynia shall not be annulled, but shall remain in force; and all heresy shall be anathematised, and, in particular, that of the Eunomians or Anomœans, and that of the Arians or Eudoxians, and that of the Semi-Arians or Pneumatomachoi, and that of the Sabellians, the Marcellians, and that of the Photinians and the Apollinarists."

An opinion, or impression, early gained currency that the Constantinopolitan fathers had sanctioned a new version of the Nicene Creed, or had issued the Nicene Creed with certain changes of phrase, and additional clauses. The later form, therefore, came to be regarded by many as the finally

---

[1] I should admit that Athanasius is best understood as holding the identity of the οὐσία in the strict sense, sometimes spoken of as "numerical identity," which is also the habitual mode of Augustine's thinking; while Basil has no difficulty in saying that ὁμοούσιος denotes only specific identity,—sameness of nature,—as when we say that two men are the same in nature or essence. I am not able to answer for Athanasius, but I should be surprised to find him saying so.

sanctioned form of the creed, and in that character it appears (with a further change,—the clause of twofold Procession) in the service of the Church of England, and in the Roman Missal. But there is no real evidence that the Constantinopolitan fathers changed the terms of the Nicene Creed, or authorised the later form in its room.

The well-known words of the creed in its later form are:—
"We believe in one God the Father Almighty, Maker of Heaven and Earth, of all things visible and invisible: and one Lord Jesus Christ, the only-begotten Son of God, begotten of the Father before all ages, Light of Light, true God of true God, begotten, not made, consubstantial with the Father: who for the sake of us men, and for our salvation came down from heaven, and was incarnate of the Holy Ghost, and of Mary the Virgin, and became man: He was crucified for our sake under Pontius Pilate, and suffered and was buried, and rose on the third day according to the Scriptures, and ascended into Heaven, and sitteth on the right hand of the Father, and cometh with glory to judge quick and dead; of whose kingdom there shall be no end: and in the Holy Ghost, the Lord the Life Giver, who proceedeth from the Father,[1] who with the Father and the Son is together worshipped and glorified, who spake by the prophets: and in one Holy Catholic Apostolic Church. We confess one baptism for the remission of sins; we look for the resurrection of the dead, and the life of the world to come."

There is no reliable, no contemporary report that the council of Constantinople revised the Nicene Creed, or set it forth revised. It is very unlikely that they should have done so. Up to that time all the Nicene men had refused to alter the Nicene Creed in any particular. Moreover, the alterations are unaccountable, particularly the omission of the clause ἐκ τῆς οὐσίας τοῦ πατρός—on which Athanasius set so much value. Still further, the creed is older than the council. Its characteristic features appear in the *Ancoratus* of Epiphanius, a work which appeared in 374. It has been suggested, therefore, that this was not a revision of the Nicene Creed, but a revised form of an older creed of Jerusalem (a creed used in baptism in that church) which may have been readjusted and enriched with some Nicene phrases by Cyril of Jerusalem when he returned to his church (after deposition) in 362. This is the view which best accounts for its special features.

[1] "And from the Son," in later Western form.

The ascription of it to the Constantinopolitan council can only be accounted for conjecturally. Cyril of Jerusalem had been associated with Semi-Arian men and counsels, and at Constantinople he might quite possibly meet with suspicions as to his soundness in the faith. To remove these he might recite the creed of his church, and procure an attestation of it as orthodox. Some tradition of this might exist, and there might be a disposition in some quarters to recur to it on account of the clauses regarding the Holy Ghost, which are fuller than the Nicene. No mention of it occurs at the council of Ephesus (431). At Chalcedon (451) reference seems to have been made to this form of creed as having been authorised at Constantinople, and though the statement seems to have created some surprise, it appears to have been acquiesced in.

The fact that Epiphanius appealed to this creed, or something like it, in the *Ancoratus* is explained by his original connection with the Palestinian church; the creed in use there had special associations for him.

See Gwatkin, *The Arian Controversy*, p. 159 ff., and Hort, *Two Dissertations*, Camb. 1876, p. 73 ff. Hefele, *Conciliengeschichte*, ii. pp. 9 and 422, 451, maintains the older view, that this creed was sanctioned at Constantinople.

# CHAPTER XXII

## Minor Controversies

### A. APOLLINARIUS[1]

Works and fragments are collected by J. Dräseke, *Apollinarius von Laodicea, Leben,* u.s.w., Leipsic, 1892. Athanasius, *De Incarnatione contra Apollinarium.* Basil Cæs. *Epp.* 265. Greg. Naz. *Epp.* ci., cii., ciii. Greg. Nyss. *Antirhet.,* in Zacagni, *Collectanea,* tom. i., Rom. 1698; Migne, vol. xlvi. Leontius, *Adv. fraudes Apollinarist.,* in Mai, *Spicileg. Romanum,* xii. Dorner, *Person Christi,* i. p. 957 fol.

During the debates concerning the higher nature of our Lord, questions about His manhood must occur, and some men were already taking positions[2] upon the subject. Arius, for instance, ascribed to our Lord a human body, but not a human soul. But variations on the point, where they existed, had not as yet attracted much attention. Apollinarius first proposed and urged a doctrine which, by its theoretical coherence, the energy of thought applied in its support, and the range of consequences connected with it, was felt to challenge a decision.

Apollinarius is on all accounts an interesting personage. In mental force he, perhaps, equalled any of those who signalised themselves in later controversies on the same field. Yet he did not command the attention of men in general, nor did he succeed in concentrating on his opinions the amount of interest which, in the form of hate or friendship, waited afterwards on Nestorius or on Eutyches. Arianism was

---

[1] By the Latins especially the name is written Apollinaris; but the other spelling is better authorised.

[2] See survey of previous impressions in Dorner, *Person Christi,* 3te Epoch, 2te Abth. capp. 1 and 2.

still in the field, contending for its life, and the minds of men were preoccupied. Hence, although leading theologians felt the edge of the argument of Apollinarius, and were constrained to weigh carefully the reasons on which he relied, and though the council of Constantinople rejected his peculiar opinions as heresy,—yet none of the sensations were awakened that attend a great process. Apollinarius was dislodged, and dropped with little noise. Yet he had already realised the significance of questions which were to be hotly agitated in the fifth century.

Two persons of the same name—father and son—have to be distinguished, of whom the younger concerns us now; the father was born probably about the beginning of the fourth century, and the son died about 392. Both were men of literary enthusiasm; and when the Emperor Julian prohibited the admission of Christians to the schools of classic literature, the two undertook to produce new classics on the basis of the Biblical writings. Among other efforts in this line were a tragedy called " Christus Patiens," and a Homeric version of the Psalms. Whatever the unwisdom might be of making this attempt, there is no doubt as to the Christian zeal which prompted it. Afterwards the son became bishop of Laodicea. He signalised himself by taking part, ably and usefully, in the discussions then going on. He wrote in defence of Christianity against Julian and Porphyry; he controverted the Manicheans and the Arians; he appeared against Marcellus. He was on friendly terms with the great defenders of the Nicene orthodoxy, such as Athanasius and Basil of Cæsarea. A synod at Alexandria (362) is conceived to have condemned the Apollinarian error without naming the teacher.[1] It was about 375, however, that Apollinarius began to separate, or to be separated, from the Church. The council of Constantinople (381) named his followers along with other sects whose tenets were rejected.[2]

[1] See on this Dorner, i. p. 984. It can be argued that Apollinarius, who was not named, was not aimed at.
[2] Can. 1. In philosophy, Apollinarius is said to have been a follower of Aristotle mainly.

Arius, as already noticed, held that our Lord took *flesh* only, *i.e.* a human body,—the created Logos taking the place of the soul.[1] He taught also that Christ was mutable, in the sense of liability to fall. However, for Arius that mutability applied not only to the incarnate Christ, but to the higher pre-existent nature as well. That, being no more than a creature, might possibly go astray. Apollinarius, on the other hand, attached great importance to our Lord's sinlessness; and he valued highly the Nicene assertion of the Son's essential divinity on this account as well as on others, that Christ as the Eternal Son abides immutably in the Father and in the truth. But this might lead him to scrutinise with peculiar keenness the doctrine of the Incarnation, in order to make sure that the interest he cared for was secure on the human side also.

It appeared to him that the union of complete God to complete man was an incongruous thought. It could never make a real unity. You may call it a unity; really it is and can be only a collocation of two. On that footing, then, there are two Sons, the divine and the human: and these may be related to one another, but two they continue to be. The mind of Apollinarius was strongly held by these impressions. There is, for example, a confession of faith in the Incarnation, which is printed among the works of Athanasius (Migne, iv. 26), but which is now ascribed to Apollinarius. All through, what he protests against is the idea of *two* in Christ—two Sons, one who is worshipped and one who is not. This is so strongly emphasised that older editors argued that the tract must be later than Athanasius; it must be the work of someone who wrote in the fifth century, when Nestorianism was under discussion, and who wished to refute that error. But the protest embodied in the tract is apparently not against Nestorius, but against the consequences which Apollinarius believed to be involved in the common doctrine of the Incarnation, and which he was determined to fasten upon it.

---

[1] The Nicene Fathers probably had this in view when they not only used the common phrase of *taking flesh*, but said also that our Lord *became man*.

On the common representation, then,—so Apollinarius argued,—there are two in Christ; and if there are two, God is not incarnate; the man is another than He. Further, each of the two will have his own history. What kind of history will it be? Here we come upon the main motive of Apollinarius,—the danger which he seemed to see, and which he was resolute to avert.

If there is here a complete man, with all the elements of human nature, then there must be free will. Now free will in a creature means liability to sin, in such a sense that there almost must be sin sometime. But supposing sin to be avoided, it is avoided by the same free will; and our redemption turns on the precarious effort of a man. If Christ is to avail for us, what He does must not be ascribed to a human subject;—neither His sinlessness nor His death. It must be a divine act. Redemption must proceed in a way that is perfect and divine. But if you ascribe it to one who is really possessed of a complete personal life apart from God, then you have only an inspired man, subject to the inevitable human infirmities.

To escape all this Apollinarius reverted to the threefold division of human nature; body, soul, and spirit. Christ, he said, assumed the human body, $\sigma\acute{\alpha}\rho\xi$, and the soul or principle of animal life, $\psi\upsilon\chi\acute{\eta}$; but the Logos is the rational and spiritual centre, the $\nu o\hat{\upsilon}\varsigma$, the seat of self-consciousness and self-determination. The Logos, therefore, in this case is, or takes the place of, $\pi\nu\varepsilon\hat{\upsilon}\mu\alpha$. The usage of language favoured this speculation. It was usual to speak of God as $\pi\nu\varepsilon\hat{\upsilon}\mu\alpha$. The Logos therefore was so. But we ascribe to man also $\pi\nu\varepsilon\hat{\upsilon}\mu\alpha$, as the highest element in him. If in the case of Christ the Logos is present, why suppose a second (human) $\pi\nu\varepsilon\hat{\upsilon}\mu\alpha$ to occupy a place which is filled already? Holding this, Apollinarius conceived himself able to assert without embarrassment the unity of Christ; *e.g.* the material body is His, His very own Just as in my own case my body is part of me—it belongs to that intellectual nature which is myself, so in the Incarnation the body was the body of the Logos, was part of Him, and with Him is worshipped.

The Logos Himself becomes νοῦς in Christ: so He concurs in constituting that supernatural man, and so the Unity is secure. The Logos, then, did not " assume a man," as was sometimes said (very often in the West— *assumpsit hominem*), but was *found in fashion as a man*, and *in the likeness* of sinful flesh. The union is perfect. God in Himself has no passions, but through the flesh which is His, He has them. On the other hand, the flesh is wholly taken into the nature of the Second Person; —one subject possesses, as inseparably His, all the elements, capacities, and experiences. In this way we have the moral and spiritual immutability really guaranteed. *This* πνεῦμα cannot fail. To the advocates of the ordinary scheme, Apollinarius would have said, According to your theory, you have in Christ two natures, which must be two persons, whether you own it or not. But now, on my showing, there is but one nature, just as, in man, body, soul, and spirit are one human nature. The σάρξ and the ψυχή are now aspects of the one nature of the Incarnate Word, μία φύσις τοῦ Θεοῦ λόγου σεσαρκωμένη, οὐδεμία διαίρεσις τοῦ λόγου καὶ τῆς σαρκὸς αὐτοῦ ἐν ταῖς θείαις προφέρεται γραφαῖς, ἀλλ' ἐστὶ μία φύσις, μία ὑπόστασις, μία ἐνέργεια.

Apollinarius connected all this with a remarkable and interesting speculation. There is a sense, according to him, in which, before the Incarnation, the divine nature of the λόγος is eminently and ideally human. Man was made in the image of God. But if the Word of God is God's true essential image, then He is not foreign to the spirit of man, is rather man's perfect archetype. When He fills this place in the Incarnation, in some eminent sense it is His own place. The Logos even before the Incarnation is the heavenly man (the second, spiritual Adam, the Lord from heaven); Godhead in Him was destined to Incarnation. It is in some ways His nature to come among us as He has done. We are weak and unfinished without

Him: we are not, indeed, true men until we are joined to this truest man. The striking thing about Apollinarius is, at how many points he anticipates later developments and speculations.

Those who opposed Apollinarius were not prepared to meet all his instances with conclusive answers. The point about free will was not very satisfactorily dealt with; and the question, how it should be thought, assuming the presence of perfect and complete human nature, that the personality is one only and not two, was not very distinctly answered. What men mainly held by was the conviction that the Incarnation meant the assumption of *all* that pertains to manhood, in order to the redemption of it all.

Apollinarius embodied fully in his thought a tendency of the time to think of Christ as one in whom the divine presence practically supersedes human experiences. That tendency, indeed, was to prevail for ages. But even the men who in some degree exemplified it still felt, when it was thus put into theoretical shape, that it contradicted the genuine teaching of the Gospels. They appealed to the recorded life and thoughts and words to bear them out in asserting the true manhood as well as the true Godhead. It was felt, therefore, that according to the manhood Christ is ὁμοούσιος with us. And that was eventually declared at Chalcedon.

Apollinarius did not leave a very large number of followers, but they were attached, confident, and some of them not very scrupulous. Knowing that their master's teaching was not to be received under his own name, they were dexterous and diligent in fathering works of his on approved orthodox names, in order that his thoughts, at least, might find approbation. This was observed and complained of in antiquity; but for a long time one could not be sure how far the complaint was well grounded. Recent writers, however, have established a number of instances; for example, the κατὰ μέρος πίστις,[1] among the works of Gregory Thaumaturgus, the ἔκθεσις πίστεως among

[1] See Dräseke, *op. cit.*

those of Justin Martyr, and others among the works of Felix and Julius of Rome. One among those of Athanasius has been quoted above. Hence some of his expressions acquired for a time the credit of having been authorised by Athanasius.[1]

### B. ORIGENISTIC CONTROVERSIES

The questions raised by Apollinarius did not, at that time, awaken much attention. Fully forty years (from A.D. 381) were to pass ere the subject became pressing. Meanwhile discussions regarding the teaching of Origen created some disturbance.

In that great teacher's own time, and in the generation which followed, some of his tenets had been questioned.[2] The discussion turned up again at the close of the fourth century, and it was destined to revive at a still later date.

Origen's teaching, as it lay in his own writings, included very free speculation, but it was pervaded by Christian enthusiasm; and the wish, at least, to render the great articles of the faith credible and acceptable could be seen even in his eccentricities. Besides, his writings were a storehouse of learning and suggestion, and his character had left an ineffaceable impression. Gratitude and admiration were the sentiments cherished towards him by the leading minds of the century following his death. The champions of orthodoxy during the Arian controversy treated his name with great respect. Athanasius cites him against the Arians, maintaining that his main express teaching, positive and negative, was good, and that stress should not be laid on what he had said hypothetically, or had hazarded in controversy. The three Cappadocians, also Didymus of Alexandria, Hilary of Poictiers, and Ambrose take the same tone.

But at the end of the fourth century prolonged dogmatic

---

[1] Even as early as Cyril of Alexandria.
[2] Orig. *Ep. ad Amicos*, Lomm. xvii. p. 6; *Homil. in Lu.* xxv., Lomm. v. p. 182; Pamph. *Apol.*, Lomm. xxv.; see *ante*, p. 179.

controversy had produced its usual results; the feeling that error was the truly fatal evil was growing, and the craving was strong for a coherent order of Christian statement, in which security and rest might be found. Not every one could fairly estimate Origen as a whole. And men whose attention was arrested mainly by his brilliant singularities, could be startled and repelled.

It is true that Origen sincerely professed to hold all the great articles recognised as binding in his day. But, wishing to make them comprehensible in their relation to the world of experience, he had projected an imaginative history of Creation and Redemption. It was a kind of evangelical Gnosticism. He undertook to find a place for all the articles of the creed in this new setting; but it could hardly be doubted that some of those articles were severely pressed, and even intrinsically modified, by their new environment. And the men of A.D. 390 did not know how different the conditions for a Christian thinker had been in A.D. 220. They judged him by the light of their own day.

Epiphanius (born in Palestine perhaps *circ.* 315) spent some years of his early life in Egypt among the religious recluses. Already he found there two distinct tendencies, exhibited in a friendly or in a hostile attitude to the works of Origen; and he was himself associated with the latter party. He devoted himself to ascetic life, and returning to Palestine built a monastery at his native place. In 367 he became bishop of Salamis; about the year 374 he wrote his *Ancoratus*, and before 377 his *Panarion*. The latter is a review and confutation of heresies so far as known to Epiphanius, and exhibits him as a man of sincere and narrow orthodoxy, of extensive reading, of little judgment or discrimination, and of great zeal. In both works he takes ground earnestly against Origen, although his conception of the faults in Origen's teaching is confused and superficial.[1] These literary per-

[1] *Panarion*, lib. ii. t. i. 18. This article extends to nearly a hundred and fifty pages in Oehler's edition.

formances had procured consideration for Epiphanius; and a reputation for saintship, which gave him much influence, had been earned by his zealous and self-denying life. By and by alarming reports reached him of the respect for Origen cherished among the recluses in Palestine.

In Palestine, devout persons from various quarters had formed communities for the purposes of retired religious life. Some of them were men of scholarly instincts and habits; many were disposed to seek edification in mastering the full range of Christian knowledge. The two impulses wrought together in promoting the study of Christian literature. Far the most distinguished man among them was Jerome (Hieronymus), who had settled at Bethlehem about A.D. 386. Rufinus (commonly called of Aquileia) had settled at the Mount of Olives in 378. They were old friends, and for a number of years continued to cherish great regard for one another. Jerome had felt the attraction of the genius, the learning, and the Christian enthusiasm of Origen: though he had not imbibed his peculiar doctrines, he had already translated some of his writings, and during his stay at Rome had written with great scorn against those who decried Origen. In the year 386 Cyril of Jerusalem was succeeded in that bishopric by John. He, too, was a man of scholarly sympathies, and resented the tendency to sacrifice the reputation of Origen to what he regarded as ignorance and bigotry. This was the situation the report of which awoke the anxieties of the bishop of Salamis.

In 394 Epiphanius found or made pretexts for visiting the scene in person. In Jerusalem he spoke and preached against the tenets of Origen, came into sharp collision with John the bishop, and exerted all possible pressure upon Rufinus and Jerome. Rufinus, with John, disregarded his remonstrances, and treated him as a well-meaning but an unreasonable person. Jerome, on the other hand, gave way: he resolved to repudiate his early enthusiasm for Origen as inconsiderate, and he became henceforth an opponent. It is not easy to believe that his motives were worthy. Apprehension regarding his own reputation for orthodoxy and his influence in the Church may naturally be supposed to have swayed him. Yet allowance should perhaps be made for a growing difficulty in the situation. It was becoming more difficult to disguise the extent of Origen's divergences from ordinary teaching, and more difficult, also, to offer a successful defence or palliation of it to the minds of ordinary people. This irruption of Epiphanius into the bishopric of John had the effect both of creating serious trouble for that prelate, and of alienating Rufinus from Jerome. They were reconciled to one another afterwards (in A.D. 397), partly through the good offices of Theophilus, bishop of Alexandria; but the misunderstanding broke out again more fatally than before. For Rufinus, returning to Italy with his friend and patroness Melania, continued to translate and recommend Origen, and in doing so, appealed to the good opinion of him which Jerome had in earlier days expressed. This at once produced a strained situation, and bitter controversy followed.[1]

The scene now changes to Egypt. The bishop of Alexandria was Theophilus (since A.D. 385). This prelate was disposed, at first, to protect the reputation of Alexandria's greatest Christian scholar; his most intimate friends were among the Nitrian monks who studied Origen with predilection; and when the trouble arose in Jerusalem he sympathised with John, and exerted himself to restore good feeling between Jerome and his bishop, and also between Jerome and Rufinus. Moreover, he dealt sharply

[1] Rufinus translated the *Apology* for Origen by Pamphilus, and issued a tract on the corruption of Origen's writings by heretics; this being the plea by means of which he accounted for many of Origen's more startling expressions. Origen himself had made the same complaint. Then Rufinus translated the Περὶ Ἀρχῶν with a preface, in which he referred to Jerome's translations, and to the praise which Jerome had bestowed on Origen in earlier days. This led Jerome to remonstrate, and also to prepare a new translation of two books of the Περὶ Ἀρχῶν, in order to reveal the heterodoxies which the translation of Rufinus had concealed. An "apology" by Rufinus and a sharp letter (now lost) to Jerome began the acrid stage of the dispute. Jerome's *Apology*, especially in the third book, written after becoming fully aware of what Rufinus had published, gives vent to the tone of contempt and anger which Jerome maintained towards his former friend to the end of his life. All this, of course, fastened attention on the less orthodox side of Origen's thinking.

with monks of the less cultured party who ascribed to God a material form, and he seemed resolute to suppress that foolishness. Yet he gradually became aware that too ardent an advocacy of Origen might involve him in trouble. Ere long something like a monastic insurrection against Theophilus was evoked by the question about God's nature, and vehement monks could easily stir up the suspicion and wrath of the Christian populace of Alexandria. Theophilus evaded his difficulty by a sudden zeal against the errors of Origen.[1] He condemned these, and he insisted that the Nitrian monks, including his old friends and agents, should concur. It was in vain they pleaded that they did not adopt Origen's questionable tenets, but were entitled, under Origen's banner, to oppose anthropomorphism. Theophilus proceeded in person to the Nitrian mountain and carried his purpose out amid great tumult and violence. The vehemence, arrogance, and self-will of the man, and his unscrupulousness when thoroughly roused, were first clearly revealed in these proceedings. Yet he was a person of ability, not without theological attainments, and not without insight into the Christian ethic, which he violated so conspicuously in some passages of his life. It seems likely that resentment on account of opposition to some of his arbitrary proceedings was mingled with other motives in the mind of Theophilus.

Many of the Nitrian monks refused to comply with the commands of Theophilus; they were driven into exile, and appeared as fugitives in Palestine and beyond. Four of them, known in Church history as the four "long brethren," had occupied a leading place in the society. They had been known and trusted by Theophilus, and one of them (Isidore) had been his confidential agent. After some stay in Palestine these monks took refuge at Constantinople, hoping to find countenance there. The Constantinopolitan Patriarch was John Chrysostom, and he gave them shelter provisionally,

[1] More than once, in the course of Christian history, Origen, or his posthumous reputation, is turned out like a bagged fox, to be hunted, when it becomes expedient to divert the chase from some other object.

writing meanwhile to Theophilus in their behalf. As Theophilus had excommunicated them, John did not meanwhile receive them to communion. Soon after, however, the imperial government was induced (but not by Chrysostom) to summon Theophilus to Constantinople to explain his conduct. The indignant bishop of Alexandria obeyed the summons; but he did so with a resolution to destroy Chrysostom, and he succeeded in that effort. Chrysostom was deposed and banished, though not on charges connected with Origen's tenets. At the same time, the question between Theophilus and the Egyptian monks seems to have been compromised.

It appeared, therefore, that the most important tangible result of the whole controversy was the downfall of Chrysostom, who really had nothing to do with it. But undoubtedly a deeper note of disapprobation had been fastened on the writings and on the name of Origen. Progress had been made in bringing it to pass that men must be ready to denounce Origen if they were to have credit for orthodoxy. This marks the development of that peculiar but well-known mood of mind, which in the interest of orthodoxy demands that questions shall be settled by a cry. He who will not join in the cry is an unsound man.

In this case, however, it must be owned that the censure of Origen was not wholly undeserved, though on all accounts it should have been more justly and more gently measured. Origen's defenders were accustomed to speak much of misrepresentation, and of heretical interpolation, as accounting for the charges against their hero. But the main articles of charge permanently pressed against him are really sustained by his authentic writings. The facts are not doubtful. Only, if Origen's time and circumstances, especially if his manner of thinking and his undoubted services had been duly weighed, the facts might have been found largely pardonable. To make reasonable allowances on such grounds was becoming a difficult business at the end of the fourth century.

### Note

The main points dwelt upon by those who attacked Origen were: first, his tendency to spiritualise the material and the concrete; second, his ideas about creation, about the constitution of human nature, about the eventual restoration of all spiritual existences, and about the resurrection. These are the points chiefly called in question by Methodius in the third century. Besides, the results of his scheme as regards the person of Christ were questioned, especially as to the human soul of our Lord and its peculiar history, and as to the duration of His mediatorial kingdom. Lastly, there was the kind of inequality between the Father and the Son which some passages of his works certainly seemed to assert. But on this point more than others, some, at least, of his early assailants seem to be conscious that another side of his thinking qualifies this one. They do not know very well what to make of it, and pass from it with brief notice. And certainly modest men might feel that it was not incumbent on them to frame a charge against Origen on this article, when Athanasius had refrained from doing so.

### C. PROFESSED REFORMERS

Jovinian and Vigilantius have already been referred to in the chapter on Monasticism. Aerius[1] is said to have been a friend of Eustathius of Sebasteia (in Pontus), and was still alive about A.D. 375. After Eustathius was promoted to the bishopric, Aerius is said to have founded a sect which renounced worldly possessions. They were severely treated, and excluded from social as well as ecclesiastical fellowship. The doctrines ascribed to him are—(1) assertion of equality of presbyters and bishops; (2) rejection of festival of Easter as Jewish; (3) prayers for the dead were useless and injurious; (4) fasting should be regulated by the soul's inward condition, not by set times. As the attitude of Eustathius in the Arian controversy was extremely variable, it is very possible that his early friend might share the uncertainty on that great controversy which characterised many portions of the Eastern Church.

---

[1] Epiphanius, *Panarium Hær.* 75, is the only authority.

### D. PRISCILLIANISTS

Syn. Cæsar-August., Hefele, *Concilien*, ii. Sulp. Severus, *Chronicon*, ii. 46–51 ; *Dial.* iii. 11. Prisc. *Quæ supersunt*, Schepps, Vindob. 1889 (with Orosii Commonitorium de errore, etc.). Schepps, *Priscillianus*, Wurzburg, 1886. Loofs, *T. L. Z.*, 1886.

Priscillian was an earnest Spanish layman, whose real views it is not easy to make out, and the recent discovery of a lost treatise of his does not illuminate the situation very much. It is obvious that he found the church around him to be in a relaxed condition, and some of the bishops corrupt men. On the other side, his own piety, which was uncompromising, seems to have connected itself with fanciful speculations. He ascribed a measure of inspiration to various writings outside of the Canon which attracted or impressed him. And as his earnestness applied itself especially to the ascetic side of Christianity, so it found support, apparently, in gnostic or semi-gnostic conceptions of the origin of souls, and of the evil powers with which they have to contend : the souls of men originate with God, and have strange conflicts to go through before they reach the earth.

Priscillian was a man of good family and of culture, and evidently could powerfully impress others. He drew people about him as a religious leader, and the circle included some bishops. The trouble began with the imputation of sectarian courses, the members of the party withdrawing more or less from ordinary church meetings, setting up conventicles, and practising asceticism to unusual degrees. The synod of Saragossa (A.D. 380) emitted canons believed to have been directed against Priscillian (though he is not named), and the features just mentioned are those against which the canons are levelled. It is also said that this synod excommunicated Priscillian and his friends without giving them a hearing.

We know from orthodox sources that some of the bishops opposed to Priscillian were believed to be very bad men. It was natural, therefore, that those who believed his influence to be good should rally to him. He continued to find support, and is said to have been himself consecrated to the bishopric of Avila.

He was now accused of magic and Manicheism, and an edict, decreeing his banishment from Spain along with his chief supporters, was procured from the civil authorities. Priscillian, with some adherents, made a journey into Italy to plead his own cause at headquarters. Ecclesiastical men like Damasus of Rome and Ambrose of Milan declined to show him favour, but the Emperor Gratian reversed the decree of banishment. Priscillian could now return to Spain, and his chief enemy, Ithacius, bishop of Emerita, was obliged to leave, convicted of unworthy conduct. Just at this time, however, the usurper Maximus established himself in Gaul, and Ithacius was able to persuade him and his advisers to bring Priscillian and his friends to trial at Bordeaux. Priscillian, after torture, was put to death. This hitherto unheard-of procedure was at once and strongly denounced. Siricius of Rome, Ambrose of Milan, Martin of Tours, all took the same view. The two latter refused to hold communion with the bishops concerned in it,—Martin at last making some concessions in order to obtain, in return, a cessation of persecution for the Spanish Priscillianists. The two bishops chiefly responsible for the enormity had to leave their sees.

Priscillian professed adherence to the common creed (Apostles'); but his ardent celebration of "the one God, Christ," is capable of a modalistic interpretation. And, as has been said, a gnostic tinge characterised his thinking He is to be regarded as in sympathy with the piety of his time, and earnest in it, but disposed to speculations which were felt to be questionable.

The whole case reveals to us the existence (not universal but general) of a worldly-minded clergy in his part of Spain, and also ascetic earnestness asserting itself against this. It reminds us also that as the Manicheans held their ground mainly by the fame of their self-denial, any asceticism that seemed exclusive or eccentric could be brought under suspicion of Manicheism. Finally, it reveals the Christian recoil from death-punishments on alleged heretics, which still happily prevailed in the Church.

The Priscillianists lingered on in Spain as a sect for a couple of centuries.

# CHAPTER XXIII

### DISCUSSIONS REGARDING THE PERSON OF CHRIST

THE theology of the Church was now to proceed on the fixed assumption that our Lord, in His higher nature, is consubstantial with the Father.[1] This was the common ground. Yet in working out this assumption through the processes of thought, speech, and worship, divergences could arise. Here, in Christ, are two—God and Man; and these two in Him are One; but how two, and how One? The differences at this point slowly came to light; and so the Christological controversies set in, which were to absorb theologians during many generations.

The tendency which at first preponderated, proceeded naturally from the great victory over Arianism. Christ being owned as first, and from eternity, true God, then, whatever He became as man, the vitality of Godhead is thought of as penetrating everything. This tendency culminated in the Monophysite heresy. Along with this, however, enough came over from the theological past, and enough was present in the Gospels, to maintain a consciousness of the reality of the human nature of the Lord. And a school arose which was to claim special attention for the distinctive life of the humanity of Christ. In doing so it was to incur the charge of ascribing to the humanity a separate self, and was denounced as Nestorianism. This tendency found its home at Antioch; the opposition to it

---

[1] The Arianism of the Gothic and Teutonic races continued: it enveloped the empire and penetrated it; but it ceased to operate on the Church of the empire as a domestic influence.

centred at Alexandria; and the ecclesiastical rivalry of the great sees mingled with the theological interests which were felt to be at stake.

Antioch, the capital of Syria, had long been a seat of intellectual life. Its Christian history was associated, through Paul (*ante*, p. 213), and also through Lucian (*ante*, p. 325), with debates, which at least implied active thought, and also stimulated it. Here, as elsewhere, the Nicene teaching had finally triumphed; and no ground exists for impeaching the sincerity with which the school of Antioch adhered to it. During the later stages of the Arian debate Diodorus stood at the head of the school; and Theodorus of Mopsuestia, Chrysostom of Constantinople, Theodoret of Cyrus, were among its distinguished representatives.

Theodorus was the most famous theologian of the East; and he preserved to the end of his life the respect and admiration of his brethren. After his death his memory was assailed, and he was denounced as the true father of Nestorianism. At all events he, chiefly, developed ideas with which Nestorianism has a natural affinity.

If Theodorus is truly represented, his teaching ran on these lines: Man has been appointed to be the centre of the created universe and the turning-point of its destinies. When man fell, the creation fell with him: but in Christ, the second Adam, it is restored. Throughout this history, the part which man plays must be the result of his own free decision. By such a decision man fell: by a decision as truly free, human, independent, the restoration must be effected. In Jesus this takes place: and it must come to pass (apparently) in a way more independent and more simply human than it could be, if Jesus were from the first identically and simply the Eternal Son of God. That would supersede the human choice. Rather we should think that the great decision comes to pass by Jesus, as man, affirming his own adherence, and his union, to the Son of God. Through such a decision he passes into that complete union in which a final and indestructible harmony is attained. Here ideas and connections of thought were presented which remind one, in different ways, of Origen and of Paul of Samosata. It would seem that Theodorus conceived himself able to assert a certain union of the two natures from the first; but not, from the first, the consummate and final union. It does not appear that this way of construing the person of Christ is to be imputed to any other member of the school of Antioch: but it could hardly have been developed without contradiction, except in a school to which it was congenial to emphasise the significance of our Lord's human nature, and the worth for our redemption of his human conflict and victory.[1]

Besides what has now been said of the school of Antioch, we may add that it was ethical rather than mystical. Also it was capable of developing a rigorously rationalistic tendency; but as regards the representative men, this possibility was powerfully restrained by their sincere participation in the faith of the great articles of the creed.

It will be seen, then, that special interest was felt by the theologians of Antioch in our Lord's human nature, and in the conflict and victory achieved in it. Here they found thoughts of our Lord as our Example, our Leader, our Representative, the Captain of our Salvation, the Second Adam, which they valued as authentic and instructive. In the interest of this mode of contemplation they were naturally disposed to claim as much room as possible for the human development, the human exercise, and the human decision of the Lord Jesus. This was a perfectly valid tendency, and necessary to the completeness of Christian theology. Effect could be given to it in an extreme and one-sided way. The counter tendency, characteristic of Alexandria, will be described later.

### A. CASE OF NESTORIUS

It had not yet appeared that these tendencies, Antiochian and Alexandrian, existed in a form that would

[1] There is a careful article on Theodorus by Dr. Swete in the *Dictionary of Christian Biography*, and one in *Real-Encycl.* by W. Möller.

endanger the peace of the Church, when, in 428, the see of Constantinople became vacant by the death of Sisinius. At his election, two years before, factions had harassed that church: at his death these were immediately renewed; and as no local candidate could be elected harmoniously, the emperor decided to summon Nestorius from Antioch. He had lived an ascetic life, had become a presbyter, and had established a great reputation as an eloquent preacher. He was, if possible, a little too conscious of the sincerity of his motives; and his whole procedure shows that he had not dreamed of his orthodoxy being questioned. He came to Constantinople to set people right in doctrine and practice, so far as that might prove to be required. He therefore immediately attacked various heresies — Arian, Novatian, Macedonian, Quartodeciman—with great vehemence. His ambition was to " purge the earth of heretics."

At Constantinople the phrase $\theta\epsilon o\tau \acute{o}\kappa o\varsigma$, mother of God, as applied to the Virgin, attracted the attention of Nestorius. At Antioch probably it had not been so current; or if it had, Nestorius had noted it with disapprobation and made up his mind to discourage it. For him it was an erroneous phrase, suggesting that the divine nature could have a human mother. A presbyter, Anastasius, who came with Nestorius from Antioch, preached against the use of the word, ascribing to it, seemingly, an Apollinarian sense; and when this created sensation and debate, Nestorius himself preached to the same effect. There was, no doubt, enough of factious and disappointed party spirit at Constantinople to lay eager hold of the occasion thus afforded for assailing the bishop. But in any case he could hardly have escaped a storm; for the phrase which he attacked had become one of the forms of speech in which men held fast the wonder of the Incarnation;—He who was from everlasting God of God, became in time the Son of a human mother.[1] The

---

[1] The *familiar* use of the phrase as a designation of the Virgin must have been recent. It is certainly rare in Athanasius, and one cannot, I think, be very confident of the text in all the cases in which it does occur. But all Nicene men held, of course, that He who was born of the Virgin was the

term has no Biblical authority, and is one of those expressions of which the startling effect depends on imputing to the Person, denominated only from His divine nature, things that are true of Him in respect of His human nature, while yet all mention of the latter nature is suppressed. It is fitted, therefore, to suggest more than any serious supporter of the phrase intends it to mean. And when used, not in connection with explanations of the Incarnation, but as the brief denomination of the blessed Virgin, it lends itself to ideas about her to which the New Testament gives no countenance. It stood connected, however, with the enthusiastic assertion of the wonder of the Incarnation, and it embodied in itself the tendency, already setting in, to magnify and extol the Virgin. On these grounds it required to be handled with far more care and discrimination than appeared in the action of Nestorius.

Anastasius and Nestorius had attacked the phrase mainly as expressing the objectionable idea, that the divine Nature could be brought forth by a woman. They did not apprehend danger in standing strongly on this ground, because they felt that the only accurate statement of the Virgin's position was to say that she was honoured, in the order of providence, to contribute as a mother the human element by which the Incarnation came to pass. Still He who through the human nature became her son, was the Son of God. The "$\theta\epsilon o\tau\acute{o}\kappa o\varsigma$" was valued as bringing out vividly that thought. Nestorius and his friend could be accused of trying to explain away the thought, and so, *in that interest*, trying to suppress the word.

We do not possess the sermons in which Nestorius embodied his position, but great debate arose at Constantinople, and news of the debate were forwarded to other ecclesiastical centres, especially to Alexandria. Here a

Eternal Word and Son. I have not found the word in Basil. It occurs once or twice in Gregory Nazianzus,—and not so as to suggest that the usage is novel. It had been occasionally used by theologians of various schools, during a considerable time.

lively sensation was awakened, and Cyril, the archbishop, thought it his duty to preach a course of sermons, addressed chiefly to the clergy and monks, in which he vigorously defended the use of the phrase θεοτόκος and the mode of view it was intended to express. In order further to strengthen his position, Cyril communicated with the great Patriarch of the West, Cœlestinus of Rome, forwarding also copies of his sermons. Cœlestinus played a waiting game: he kept silence for months, pleading that the documents must be translated into Latin before a satisfactory judgment on them could be given.

Alexandria had already earned the character of an aspiring and enterprising see. Distinguished men had occupied it,—recently Athanasius. Something in the constitution and circumstances of the Egyptian church seems to have easily suggested strong measures to the great prince-bishop at its head. Perhaps more than any other Patriarch, the Alexandrian bishop had behind him a great mass of religious life at high pressure; and that was force, or could be converted into force. At all events Alexandria was older and as yet more famous than Constantinople, and saw with jealous eyes the precedency which almost inevitably accrued to the bishop of the imperial city. Theophilus, the predecessor and uncle of Cyril, had gained a memorable victory for Alexandria over Constantinople when he drove Chrysostom into exile. To humiliate and trample on Nestorius might seem a not undesirable sequel.

At the same time the part which Alexandria and its bishop took in the contest cannot be ascribed merely to ecclesiastical motives: the Alexandrian school of religious thought differed really from that of Antioch. Here we must find the reason and motive of Cyril's antagonism to Nestorius, which the Church approved as orthodox; and also of the whole monophysite development, which, a little later, the Church condemned.

This tendency could appeal to the usage of speech with orthodox writers before the controversies of the fifth century began. Those writers, affirming the true Godhead and the true manhood of Christ, loved to present Him as a marvellous unity: of Him might be predicated what belongs to Godhead and what belongs to manhood; both being referred to the same identical subject, however incompatible they might seem—*e.g.*, that He was begotten from Eternity and begotten in time, that He was invisible, yet seen and handled, that He was the Lord of Life, yet dead and buried. Their wish was to express forcibly the perfect and abiding union in Christ of all that makes Him capable of being thus spoken of. So it should be felt that He, He himself, really became man. The strength of feeling on this subject led the monophysites, who represent the extreme of the Alexandrian tendency, to assert, finally, that after the Incarnation we are to own only one nature, the μία φύσις of the Incarnate One.

With these habitual modes of view a mystic devoutness was associated. It might partake largely of the nature of Christian piety: largely, also, it might be due to the way in which the imagination was stimulated by paradoxical combinations of ideas in regard to the Person of Christ.

These tendencies prevailed in the Alexandrian Christianity at the beginning of the fifth century. They found their extreme development, as we have said, in the utterance and action of the declared monophysites. Effect was given to them meanwhile, in a more considerate way, by the great bishop Cyril. He had already occupied the see for sixteen years. He was a man of exceptional force of character, and prone to resolute, even passionate, self-assertion. At the same time he was a theological thinker of great power, and undoubtedly he felt the religious value as well as the intellectual or systematic importance of the doctrines which he maintained.

It has been mentioned that Cyril preached at Alexandria upon the questions raised at Constantinople, and that he spoke plainly on the theology which seemed to him to underlie the withholding from the Virgin of the title θεοτόκος. Letters passed between him and Nestorius, and Cyril wrote besides to the bishop of Rome, desiring his support in the debate which was arising, but professing to leave very much in his hands the question of further steps. The Pope approved of Cyril's view, and entrusted him with letters in that sense directed to various parties in the East. One of these was addressed, in very harsh terms, to Nestorius himself. It required him, on pain of exclusion from church-fellowship, to recant within ten days of receiving the letter. These letters of Cœlestinus are very discreditable to him on this account, that they contain no statement of the grounds on which he proceeds. Nestorius is denounced as a heretic; Cyril is commended as orthodox; Nestorius is called upon to recant; but all is couched in vague generalities which leave undefined the doctrine (as yet defined by no council) which the Roman bishop professes to be so anxious to support.

About the same time John, bishop of Antioch, comes upon the scene. His promotion at Antioch had been nearly contemporary with that of Nestorius at Constantinople. Letters which he received from the bishop of Rome convinced him that a serious storm was gathering, and he could have little doubt that Egypt, Macedonia, and large districts in Asia would repudiate the position Nestorius had taken up. He wrote, therefore, a very friendly remonstrance to Nestorius, advising him to give up the question about the word $\theta\epsilon o\tau \acute{o}\kappa o\varsigma$, since it was capable of reasonable explanation, and was endeared to men by usage. In this way the cause of offence would be removed. John shared the point of view common to the Antiochian school, and therefore might hope to have the more influence with Nestorius. But the latter declined to comply; he owned that $\theta\epsilon o\tau \acute{o}\kappa o\varsigma$ was not quite incapable of being taken in an inoffensive sense, but he reckoned it dangerous and misleading. He was inclined, as a compromise, to offer the word $X\rho\iota\sigma\tau o\tau \acute{o}\kappa o\varsigma$.

In the meantime Cyril, who could act not only for himself, but was now also empowered to represent the bishop of Rome, and to transmit to Nestorius the epistle of the latter, thought fit to prepare the way by convoking a synod of his own clergy at Alexandria. This synod sanctioned a severe letter to Nestorius, in which they call upon him to concur in the doctrine they set forth. In this statement they reject various phrases used by Nestorius or imputed to him, partly as insufficient to express the unity of the person of Christ, partly as tending actually to suggest the idea of two persons, a human and a divine one, closely conjoined but still remaining separate. To this synodical letter were attached twelve *anathematismi*—so many propositions, each branded with anathema. Cyril had prepared these, and they became famous. Nestorius was called upon himself to anathematise the same propositions. These *anathematismi* were met by Nestorius with twelve counter *anathematismi*, in which he strove to turn the imputation of heresy against Cyril. The Alexandrian declarations were sent also to John of Antioch. He evidently regarded them as involving some positions that were erroneous, and as embodying an attack not only upon Nestorius, but upon the theology of the school of Antioch; accordingly, he engaged Theodoret to furnish a reply.[1] In Cyril's *anathematismi* some statements occur which his admirers have had to explain away.[2] Hence, though the defenders of the Church's doctrine have always been exceedingly chary of taking exception in any case to Cyril's teaching, this (third) letter to Nestorius, with the appended *anathematismi*, has never been clothed with the same authority, as a standard of orthodoxy, as has been

---

[1] Cyril had accompanied each *anathematismus* with an exposition (ἐπίλυσις). Theodoret responded to each in an ἀνατροπή, and Cyril finally replied in an ἀπολογία. The three manifestoes—the *anathematismi*, the criticism of Theodoret, and the apology of Cyril—are printed together in vol. v. of the Halle edition of Theodoret's works, and they present a good view of the controversy as then stated,—the interests which each side wished to guard, and the liabilities to suspicion and misunderstanding which operated. Andreas of Samosata also wrote a book against Cyril, to which the latter replied in an *Apologeticus adversus Orientales*.

Besides Mansi, iv. and v., Fuchs, *Bibliothek d. Kirchenversammlungen*, iii. p. 477 fol., see good statement in Hefele, *Conciliengeschichte*, ii. p. 127 fol.; Bright in *Dict. Christ. Biogr.*, art. "Cyril," p. 766; Tillemont, *Mémoires*, xiv. pp. 358, 360.

[2] Particularly in the third, where he asserts a ἕνωσις φυσική.

ascribed to some of his other writings. Theodoret, on the other hand, in his criticism of Cyril, has been accused of leaning unduly in the Nestorian direction, especially in his treatment of the fourth *anathematismus*. But he obliged Cyril, in reply, to explain himself more carefully on some points. More particularly, Cyril explained that he used certain language only against the pronounced Nestorianism which he alleged to be his opponent's real doctrine.

As to the real position of Nestorius, it is obvious that if he was to vary from what has proved to be the Church's teaching about the person of Christ, he was in danger of doing so rather in the way of dividing the Person, than of confusing the natures. But how far he did vary is obscure. It is plain that Nestorius [1] maintained the doctrine of two natures and the integrity of each; that he sincerely rejected Arianism and Apollinarianism; that he refused to admit that Deity in itself could be born or could suffer; that the phrase θεοτόκος was rejected by him on this, as the main expressed ground, that according to its proper meaning it implied Deity in itself to have been born of Mary and to have taken origin from her (which would be not so much heretical as monstrous); also he admitted that in a certain sense, and with explanations, he could allow the term θεοτόκος itself. All these were orthodox positions. On the other side, it is true that he shrank from the language which, on the ground of the unity of the Person, who is both God and man, applies to the person identified by the one nature descriptions which are literally and immediately true only by reason of the other nature.[2] He shrank from this, because he thought it a practice which led to misapprehension; probably also, though on this he was less explicit, because he thought it tended to attenuate the significance, and the peculiar discipline, of the human nature in Christ. And yet it is not obvious that he would have shrunk so much from the language if applied only to the Saviour Himself (*e.g.* Before

---

[1] See Hefele, *Conciliengesch.* ii. p. 140, who is here followed.

[2] This usage is called the *communicatio idiomatum* by Catholics, and by the Reformed: the Lutheran *c. i.* is differently explained.

Abraham was Jesus is); but he felt it to be going beyond bounds when a mere human being, the Virgin Mary, began to be characterised habitually as related to God (without further discrimination) *as*, in virtue of His humanity, she was related to Jesus Christ.

In comparing the early statements of Cyril on the one hand and of Nestorius and Theodoret[1] on the other, one sees that on the latter side there is more anxiety to preserve the manhood distinctly before the mind, and to hold apart, in thought and speech, what belonged to the manhood and what belonged to the Godhead. The Virgin, *e.g.*, was directly and immediately related to the manhood, she was the mother of the manhood or of the man; only *then*, because the man is one with the Son of God, one owns that this comes to mean that she is the mother of the Lord. Cyril, on the other hand, owns that it is through the manhood the Son of God holds special relation to the Virgin; and he says that if there were the smallest danger of anyone supposing that the divine nature derived origin or being from the Virgin, it might be right rather to say ἀνθρωποτόκος. But Cyril's mind is held, not by the nature which takes relation to the Virgin, but by the Person who in that nature does so. Cyril brings out the unity of Christ by the assertion of one φύσις, and Theodoret brings out the twofoldness of the Godhead and the manhood by the assertion of two ὑποστάσεις. Both phrases are objectionable from the point of view of the phraseology ultimately settled; both are pardonable at the stage then reached; and they indicate, when compared, a divergent tendency;—but not necessarily so divergent, on a fair construction, as to exclude the doctrine, ultimately accepted, that the divine Person assumed the human nature,—the Person continuing to be one, in the two natures.

This is the orthodox phrase, and it is easy to waive difficulties by means of it; but anyone who thinks, becomes aware that personality is an idea full of mystery, and there-

[1] But Theodoret differed from Nestorius in admitting from the first the disputed phrase θεοτόκος.

fore of difficulty.¹ And perhaps we may best represent to ourselves the relation of minds at that time by saying that Nestorius and Theodoret thought of each nature, the human for instance, as continuing to have attached to it, if it is to continue to exist in its integrity, a certain *shadow* of personality, a spiritual identity of its own; but Cyril shrank from the thought, because to his mind it threatened to bring in two persons, and so to annul the wonder and the grace of the Incarnation. There is no evidence, however, that Nestorius held a doctrine of two persons after the Incarnation; though in dealing with the difficulties of the subject he is more anxious than Cyril to emphasise the sphere of relation proper to each nature. The question of his precise view is by no means so important as in the case of Cyril, for Nestorius, as a theologian, is not nearly of equal rank. Nestorius is best understood as guarding against Apollinarianism; for that doctrine abridged the human nature in order more completely to make out the union of it with the divine. His misfortune was to have incurred boundless suspicion and dislike, by attacking a phrase which had acquired so many theological and devotional associations.²

Nestorius himself had suggested to the emperor that a general council might assuage the trouble which had arisen; and in replying to John of Antioch's remonstrance he had expressed his expectation that if a council met, the difficulties would disappear. Similar suggestions had reached the emperor from some of Nestorius' opponents. Accordingly, on 19th November 430, Theodosius II., in his own name and in that of his Western colleague Valentinian, issued a summons for a council,

---

[1] "Person" explains itself to us by the personal pronouns; but it is not capable of dialectical limitation so as to afford means for defining the real manner of existence of that which the term denotes.

[2] The counter anathemas of Nestorius may be seen in Hefele, vol. ii., Fuchs, vol. iii. All that Hefele has to say of them is that they tilt at windmills, in so far as Nestorius imputes to Cyril opinions which were not his, and that the heretical views of Nestorius himself here and there "durchschimmern."

to meet at Ephesus on Pentecost of the following year.[1]

The story of the general council of Ephesus (A.D. 431) is interesting in its way, but it must be briefly touched here. The council had been indicted for the 7th of June. On that day Nestorius had arrived, and Cyril and various parties of bishops presented themselves during the following days; but the representatives of the see of Rome on the one hand, and, on the other, John of Antioch, with a large body of Eastern bishops, had not arrived (though they were understood to be not far off), when on the 22nd the council, at the instance of Cyril and those who agreed with him, resolved to open its proceedings. This step was taken against the remonstrances of Nestorius, of a considerable number of Eastern bishops, and of Candidianus, who represented the emperor. Nestorius, in reply to repeated messages, refused to attend until those who were on the way to the council should have arrived. The council proceeded in his absence; and on the same day, 22nd June, they caused to be read the Nicene Creed, the second letter of Cyril to Nestorius, which was approved, the reply of Nestorius, also the letter of Cœlestinus of Rome, and the third letter of Cyril with the *anathematismi*.[2]

Two bishops who had been sent to summon Nestorius were examined as to what passed at their interview. Passages from the works of twelve older teachers of the Church were read (many to the effect that the Son or Logos was born and suffered in the flesh). Lastly, about twenty passages from the writings of Nestorius were produced, which were alleged to establish the peculiarity of his point and mode of view.

Then the decree of the council was formulated as follows:—

"As the ungodly Nestorius, in addition to all else, has refused to obey our citation, and to receive the bishops sent

---

[1] It is interesting to know that a very special invitation was sent to Augustine, but he had already died on 22nd August.

[2] Apparently approbation of this letter was not asked.

to him, we have found it necessary to proceed to the examination of his impious utterances. And discovering from his letters and treatises, and also from his utterances in the metropolitan city, which have been borne witness to, that he cherishes and proclaims impious doctrines, we are constrained by the canons, according to the letter of our most holy father and fellow-servant Cœlestinus, bishop of the Roman church, to come with many tears to this sentence: Our dear Jesus Christ, who has been blasphemed by him, has determined through this most holy Synod, that Nestorius is excluded from the episcopal dignity, and from all priestly fellowship."

All this was done on the one day, the 22nd of June. Four or five days later John of Antioch with his bishops arrived, expressed his grave displeasure at the course taken, and formed a protesting counter-council. These proceedings were reported to the emperor, who at first decided that Nestorius on the one hand, Cyril and Memnon of Ephesus on the other, should all alike be regarded as deposed. But eventually, under whatever influences, he altered his attitude. The deposition of Nestorius was maintained, and he was sent into exile, but Cyril and Memnon were sent back to their sees.

Plainly the decree of Ephesus was inequitable, because Nestorius had no fair trial on the merits, and the merits, as regards his real position, are obscure to this day. Besides, the doctrine condemned was not stated, nor the counter doctrine defined.

Whatever view we may take of the position of Nestorius, his judges no doubt apprehended that in the line of his statements Nestorianism in the technical sense (the Nestorianism of the Church histories) was approaching; and the council resolved to shut it out.

The course they took, however, left it uncertain what they condemned and what they sanctioned, for no theological light is emitted by the decree.[1] Perhaps the result may be summed up in this, that the term $\theta\epsilon o\tau \acute{o}\kappa o\varsigma$ was sanctioned. The sense intended in that term has ever since been generally accepted by believers in the Incarnation, inasmuch, namely,

---

[1] The second epistle of Cyril, however, had previously been approved.

as He who was born of the Virgin was the Son of God,—just as the same Son bore our sins in His body upon the tree. Most Protestants, however, have disapproved and avoided the phrase itself, as lacking Scripture authority, and as tending to produce mental confusion. The Virgin became the mother of the Lord, which is the safe and satisfying Christian phrase. In addition to this, the word "theotokos" became, as it was likely from the first to become, not so much the means of uttering faith about the Lord, but rather of associating the Virgin with God, and taking an attitude towards her which is idolatrous.

John of Antioch and many of his followers, while they did not believe that Nestorius had fallen into any serious error, yet regarded his conduct of the case as unwise, and felt that he had made it difficult to defend him. They regretted his attack on a phrase which had high authority in usage, and which was associated with strong religious feelings. After the council, it becomes pretty plain that the party are more disposed to charge questionable expressions upon Cyril than to accept the odium of vindicating Nestorius.

The two parties, however, were not really much removed from one another, and steps were taken to avert schism. Probably John early made up his mind to let Nestorius fall, a course which Theodoret could not persuade himself to adopt. But John was resolved that if he gave satisfaction to the Alexandrians in this form, he must receive a *quid pro quo*. He demanded that Cyril should accept a statement on the debated points satisfactory to the Antiochians. We possess this statement, and it is very nearly the same with one which the Antiochians had drawn up as a manifesto of their position, and had forwarded to the emperor for his information, probably in August 431. Most likely it was originally drawn up by Theodoret. Cyril agreed to accept it. His action in doing this enhances the impression of his power as a theologian and his ability as a leader. A weaker man would have hesitated. John, on his part, agreed to accept the decree of Ephesus and to anathematise the teaching of Nestorius. The formula in which he did so gave prominence to the motive of restoring the peace of the Church as leading him to this course.

The statement accepted and adopted by Cyril begins with an introduction :—

"We wish now, since this has become necessary, briefly to declare, according to the Scriptures and the traditions of the Church, what we believe and teach concerning the Virgin, theotokos, and concerning the Incarnation; not in order to add anything new, only for the satisfaction of others, but not to adjoin anything to the faith expounded at Nicæa. As we have said, that creed is fully sufficient for the knowledge of religion and for the repelling of heretical error. And we do not give this explanation as if we would grapple with the incomprehensible, but in order that by the confession of our own weakness we may repel those who impute that we expound what is to men incomprehensible."

Then follows the belief :—

"We confess that our Lord Jesus Christ, the only begotten Son of God, is true God, and true man of a reasonable soul and a body consisting, before all time begotten of the Father according to the Godhead, but in the end of the days for us and for our salvation born of the Virgin according to the manhood; of like essence with the Father in respect of the Godhead, and of like essence with us according to the manhood; for of two natures a union has come to pass. Therefore we confess one Christ, one Lord, one Son. On account of this union, which is without mixture or confusion, we confess also that the Holy Virgin is the Theotokos, because the Logos became flesh and man, and even from the beginning united Himself with the temple which He assumed from her."

What follows was added on the occasion of the compromise between Cyril and John :—

"As to what concerns the Evangelical and Apostolical utterances concerning Christ, we know that theologians apply some, as bearing on the One Person, to both natures in common, but separate others as relating to the two natures."

Cyril's acceptance of this formula was responded to by a letter from John embodying in frank language the conditions agreed to upon his part. So a *modus vivendi* was established, and it was announced that peace was restored.

The settlement thus reached was disapproved and resisted by some on both sides. Among the bishops of John's patriarchate, the majority followed their patriarch; but two distinct parties formed and took action in the opposite direction. The more extreme declared against the views of Cyril as plainly heretical; they regarded John's compromise as treacherous; and they, of course, refused to concur in the condemnation of Nestorius. A more moderate party, headed by Theodoret, were willing to acknowledge that Cyril's signature of the new formula might be held to be a proof of his orthodoxy (though some of them maintained that he ought, in addition, to disclaim some of his previous statements); but they regarded the whole transaction as having too much the aspect, on the Antiochian side, of acknowledging defeat,—especially as four Antiochian bishops besides Nestorius had been deposed, and were not to be restored. They also, like the first party, protested against recognising the justice of the condemnation of Nestorius. Not receiving satisfaction on these points, a considerable number of bishops, on the one set of grounds or on the other, declined to hold communion either with John or with Cyril. But John took resolute action, and the emperor came to his aid. Eventually most of the malcontents gave in,—Theodoret himself returning to fellowship on the footing that he should not be required to say anything about Nestorius. Fifteen bishops who held out were driven from their sees. These bishops and their adherents were, in time, driven out of the empire; they took refuge under the Persian monarchy; and a Nestorian Christianity was inaugurated which long continued to operate, and to operate beneficially, in the remote East.

On the other side some of the followers of Cyril were gravely dissatisfied. They blamed Cyril for accepting the statement proposed to him by John, and they regarded the renewed fellowship with the mass of the Eastern bishops as equivalent to the reception of impenitent heretics. Some of the dissatisfied, perhaps, misunderstood the true nature of Cyril's action; but it cannot be doubted that many of them were already monophysites, and maintained that doctrine as the true orthodoxy. The tendencies that way were strong in Egypt, as we have seen. The exceptions taken against his action were energetically met by Cyril in various writings, in which he offered elaborate explanations; and in the course of these he takes up afresh and defends phrases, which afterwards were strongly appealed to by the monophysites, especially a sentence ascribed to Athanasius which spoke of the μία φύσις τοῦ λόγου σεσαρκωμένη—" the one incarnate nature of the Word." [1]

Cyril succeeded in averting ostensible schism among his followers, the rather because in procuring the general acceptance of the decision of Ephesus he had inflicted a substantial defeat on the tendencies of the Antiochian school; but there remained in Egypt and elsewhere a strong monophysite party, which ere long was to reveal itself clearly.

After all this Cyril opened an attack upon the writings of Theodore of Mopsuestia. He did so at the instance of Rabulas of Edessa, who was one of his adherents in the East. Theodore had died (A.D. 428) before the Nestorian controversy broke out. Now that Nestorius and his writings were condemned, men of Nestorian principles, it was said, were circulating writings of Theodorus, and also of Diodorus of Tarsus, and some of these were being translated into the Syrian, Armenian, and Persian languages. The name of Theodorus was venerated in the East, and his writings found ready reception.

The bishops of Armenia, apprehending danger, sent to Proclus, now bishop of Constantinople, to ask for guidance in regard to these writings. Proclus drew up a treatise adverse to the teaching of Theodorus, and Cyril published others in the same line. Men now began to speak of anathematising Theodorus; and Armenian monks, in their

[1] Athan. *De Incarn.*, Migne, vol. iv. p. 25. This, therefore, was already ascribed to Athanasius in Cyril's day. See *ante*, pp. 360, 363.

enthusiasm, went so far as to denounce utterances of his which were plainly orthodox. It was clearly undesirable to push the matter further, and the emperor published an edict exhorting to peace, and deprecating the condemnation of men who had died in the fellowship of the Church. About this time Rabulas died. He was succeeded by Ibas, who belonged to the opposite school, and who venerated the memory of Theodorus. The controversy then dropped for a time. The bias, however, which these proceedings gave to the Armenian church may prepare us for the adhesion to monophysite principles which finally fixed its dogmatic position.

Nestorianism had no future within the empire. The school of Edessa, from the days of Ibas onwards, did lean somewhat in that direction, and distrusted the theology of Cyril; but that school was destroyed by the Emperor Zeno in 489. Under the Persian monarchy, on the other hand, the Nestorian Christianity developed an active life. For a long time their patriarch resided at Ctesiphon or at Bagdad; and in the thirteenth century twenty-five metropolitans, it was said, owned his authority. The invasion of Tamerlane fell on these Christians with peculiar severity. A very small remnant now survives.

The Nestorians never called themselves by that name. They professed to abide by the Nicene Creed; in the interpretation of Scripture they chiefly followed Theodorus.

### B. CASE OF EUTYCHES

The reconciliation between John of Antioch and Cyril took place A.D. 433. During the years which followed, although the dispute had ostensibly ended, suspicion and jealousy continued to exist. In particular, the more extreme men of Cyril's school identified the Church's orthodoxy with their own party, and in their opinion a strong presumption of concealed Nestorianism attached to all followers of the Antiochian school. They felt entitled, therefore, to take active steps on any promising opportunity, and they relied, not without reason, on the sympathy of the imperial court. Shortly before the middle of the century signs of returning strife multiplied. Ibas (see last page), who had succeeded Rabulas at Edessa, was subjected to severe trouble by accusations of various kinds; his position became finally untenable about 448. In the same year Irenæus, a friend of Nestorius, who (about 446) had become metropolitan of Tyre, was driven from his see. Theodoret also was placed under some restrictions. At this time the see of Constantinople, after being filled successively by Maximian and Proclus, was held (from 447) by Flavian. He was certainly opposed to Nestorius, and in particular had showed himself to be in sympathy with the hostile action against Ibas. He was, however, not in favour with Chrysaphius, who guided the counsels of Theodosius II.

There was at Constantinople an aged archimandrite (head, in fact, of the famous monastery called Studium) whose name was Eutyches. A devoted follower of Cyril's teaching, he conceived orthodoxy very much as opposition to Nestorius, and felt that safety lay solely in that direction. His contemporaries did not think highly of his abilities, though his character and his position were venerable. As happens to such men, he conceived himself to be an authority on the questions in dispute. Like many of his party, he would not hear of the continued existence of two natures after the Incarnation; and this had shaped itself in his mind to an impression and assertion that Christ's nature is not consubstantial with ours. What he meant is not, perhaps, clear; it was imputed to him by some that he held our Lord to have brought His human nature from heaven; but this he repudiated. He must have contrived to create in various quarters some uneasiness by the form he gave to his Antinestorianism, if it is true that Domnus of Antioch, and others also, had contemplated a formal challenge of his theology. But the assault came from another quarter.

In the course of the year 448 Flavian had assembled

a "synodos endemousa"[1] to dispose of some business which required attention. When that was concluded, Eusebius, bishop of Dorylæum, rose to make a formal charge of heterodoxy against Eutyches, and to claim that he should be summoned to answer for himself.

This Eusebius had shown some animosity against Nestorius, and, therefore, so far belonged to the same party as Eutyches; but, according to Eutyches, Eusebius was a personal enemy, whose accusations proceeded from malice. However this may be, all we read of Eusebius suggests a personage who loved to be loud and prominent in theological disputes, and who, once embarked in them, was mainly concerned about securing his own reputation by winning the battle. On the other hand, Flavian and the council seem to have treated Eutyches, on the whole, in a considerate manner. Eutyches, astonished probably to find accusations of heresy levelled against himself, was very unwilling to appear at all, and, when he did, he made statements that were not very clear. He repudiated the imputation of teaching that our Lord brought His human nature with Him from heaven; on the other hand, he declined to speak of two natures after the Incarnation; also, to admit that our Lord's humanity is consubstantial with ours. The synod finally came to this conclusion:—"Eutyches, heretofore priest and archimandrite, has by his earlier statements and by his present confessions proved himself to be entangled in the perversions of Valentinus and of Apollinarius, and has not been persuaded by our instruction and admonition to receive the pure doctrine. Therefore we, bewailing his complete perversion, do, in the name of Christ whom he has wronged, declare him deposed from office as a priest, excluded from our communion, and deprived of the presidency of his convent. All who henceforth hold communication with him are to know that they also receive the pain of excommunication." This sentence was concurred in by Florentius, a lay official of the emperor, reputed to be a skilful theologian, who had been sent by the emperor to

---

[1] *I.e.* composed of bishops who happened to be at Constantinople.

take part in the proceedings, no doubt with a view to protect Eutyches as far as possible.

Eutyches had still the powerful friendship of the emperor's favourite, Chrysapius, who was his godson. He was therefore by no means disposed to submit without a struggle, and both sides exerted themselves to procure support. Dioscurus of Alexandria was ready enough to take part in the strife on the side of Eutyches. He had come to the bishopric at the death of Cyril in 444. He appears to have been a resolute monophysite; and he embraced cordially, and followed out unscrupulously, the Alexandrian policy of improving doctrinal uneasiness with a view to advance the power of that see. Apart from him the most important men to gain were the bishop Leo of Rome and the emperor. Leo took time for consideration until all the papers were before him; he then decided that Eutyches was justly condemned, and that Flavian had acted rightly. The emperor, on the other hand, was from the first prepossessed in favour of Eutyches, and ere long he resolved to call a council to reconsider the case. Leo saw no need for this, and would have had the emperor act under the guidance of Flavian and himself; but as the emperor proceeded to summon the council, Leo sent representatives to it. He also sent to Flavian a long theological statement upon the matter in dispute, which became very celebrated.[1]

The council was summoned to meet at Ephesus, 1st August 449. The emperor appointed that Dioscurus should preside. He also forbade Theodoret to be present.

About one hundred and thirty bishops assembled; and, apparently at the very first sitting, after reading the papers in the case, but without reading the letter of the bishop of Rome, or giving any proper hearing to Flavian, or to Eusebius of Dorylæum, Eutyches was restored, and Flavian and Eusebius were deposed. All this took place at the instance of Dioscurus, and seemingly amid much confusion and violence, and amid threats, which acted as compulsion

· Leo, *Ep.* xxviii., "The Dogmatical Epistle of Leo."

on the bishops who might have stood by Flavian. Only one of the legates from Rome seems to have ventured on an attempt to discharge his duties; and he was glad to escape and to find his way back to Rome incognito. Flavian died shortly after, owing, it is said, to the rough handling he received. Writers near the date of the council report (though this does not appear in the extant acts) that Domnus of Antioch also was deposed, along with Theodoret and some other bishops. In room of Flavian, Anatolius was appointed to the see of Constantinople, and Maximus to that of Antioch in room of Domnus. Such were some of the features of what Leo stigmatised as the Latrocinium Ephesinum.

On receiving information of these proceedings, Leo exerted himself, successfully, to rally the West to the doctrine condemned in the person of Flavian. He also wrote earnestly and repeatedly to the emperor, and to others in high position in the East. The question as to the see of Constantinople had also to be dealt with. Leo declined to recognise the new bishop, until he received satisfaction regarding his orthodoxy. His efforts to reverse the decision of Ephesus might, however, have fallen short of success, had not Theodosius II. died, 28th July 450. His sister, Pulcheria, came to the throne, assuming Marcian, an able statesman and soldier, as her husband and co-regnant. Pulcheria had already satisfied herself that Flavian and Leo were in the right. In order to restore the Church's peace, another council was summoned, to meet at Chalcedon 451. On this occasion, also, Leo deprecated the project of a council: he had received satisfactory letters from Anatolius, and he thought sound doctrine could be vindicated by dealing firmly with cases in detail. But as the imperial authorities persisted, Leo acquiesced, and sent deputies. The meeting-place, Chalcedon, was near Constantinople, on the other side of the Bosphorus. This council was far more numerously attended than any that preceded. The numbers given vary from 520 to 630; but none were from the West except the Pope's legates, and two bishops from Africa—

wanderers, perhaps, whom the Vandal persecution had set adrift.

### C. COUNCIL OF CHALCEDON

At the council of Chalcedon it was well understood that the violent proceedings at Ephesus could not be supported, and no great difficulty was found in constraining Dioscurus, the ringleader in those proceedings, to sit apart from the rest of the council, as one whose conduct required to be investigated. But after the preliminaries had been arranged and the necessary documents read, it was a delicate question what step should next be taken. A considerable section of the council had monophysite prepossessions, and large districts of the empire sympathised with these feelings. On the other hand, the "Orientals" could not be willing to lose the opportunity of retrieving the defeat they had experienced twenty years before; and the West, which, through the bishop of Rome, had taken its ground so explicitly, was not likely to be contented with an ambiguous result. A considerable number of those in the East who had heartily opposed Nestorius, were now willing to think that Eutyches had gone astray in the opposite direction, and they resented the maltreatment of Flavian and the arrogant conduct of Dioscurus; but they were anxious and sensitive as to the theological position which, in connection with Dioscurus' overthrow, they might be called upon to accept.

The council, however, began with a question of less difficulty. The conduct of Dioscurus had been indefensible, and he was now deposed. That step had no precise theological significance, but it meant much; practically, it operated as a warning to all waverers. Those who had been conspicuous as supporters of Dioscurus at once felt themselves in danger; appeals to the majority of the council to act mercifully began to be heard.

The next step was to express adherence to received doctrinal determinations, including certain explanations of Cyril, but including also the dogmatical epistle of Leo. This received general assent; but it appeared that many

Egyptian bishops demurred, not, however, ostensibly on the ground of dissenting from the teaching, but on the ground that until they received a new patriarch, under whose guidance they could act, it was utterly unsafe for them to become responsible for the declaration proposed. This could hardly be regarded as other than a pretext, but it was met by an order not to depart from Chalcedon until they should have given satisfaction. Then the council proceeded to deal with the question of Faith, as raised by the teaching of Eutyches, and by the proceedings, in his case, of Flavian's council. There had long been great unwillingness to add anything doctrinal to the creed of Nicæa,—the council of Ephesus of 431 had avoided doing so in the case of Nestorius. But it was becoming evident that no official security against error could be provided by merely deposing particular men without saying what their error was, or what the form of teaching against which they had offended. This became very plain in dealing with the case of the monophysites. In regard to Nestorius, it could plausibly be said that he diverged from the declaration of the Nicene Creed, which taught that the only begotten Son of God was born of the Virgin Mary. Eutyches granted the assumption by our Lord of the human nature: the effect of that assumption was the point he brought into question; and if any doctrine on that point was to be maintained, it required to be articulated. Some time had to be spent on maturing a statement; and some hesitation over Leo's phrases was manifested, especially on the part of some Illyrian bishops. At length a form was settled. A long introduction set forth the relation of the council to previous discussions regarding the Incarnation of the Lord, and various errors were condemned, last of all the error of those who say that before the union there are two natures, after it only one. And so,—

"Following the holy fathers, we teach unanimously the confession of one and the same Son, our Lord Jesus Christ, perfect, the same, in the Godhead, and perfect, the same, in the manhood; being, He the same, truly God and truly man, of reasonable soul and body; consubstantial with the

Father according to the Godhead, and consubstantial, He the same, with us according to the manhood; in all things like unto us, sin excepted; before the ages begotten of the Father according to the Godhead, but in the latter days, He the same, for our sake and for our salvation, begotten of Mary the virgin mother of God according to the manhood; and the same Christ, Son, Lord; owned in two natures, without confusion, without conversion, without division, without separation; the difference of the natures not being taken away by the union, but rather each nature being preserved in its propriety, and concurring to one person (πρόσωπον) and to one hypostasis; not parted or divided into two persons, but one and the same Son, only begotten, God the Word, Lord Jesus Christ, as the prophets of old, and the Lord Jesus Christ Himself, have taught us, and the confession of the fathers has delivered to us." This was followed by denunciation of deposition or excommunication on those who teach otherwise.[1]

[1] A curious question exists about a critical clause in this decree concerning the Faith. As given above it reads, "owned in two natures (ἐν δύο φύσεσι), without confusion, etc." In the Greek copies, however, it stands as ἐκ δύο φύσεων, "of two natures"; the Latin copies support the other reading. Two things may be noticed. One is that the introductory part of the decree condemns those who say that before the union there are two natures, but after it only one. Now, "of two natures" was the phrase affected by this very party. The other is that when the question of the decree was under consideration, the committee charged with forming it brought up a report in the fifth sitting of the council, which was strongly recommended for adoption by Anatolius of Constantinople. It was objected to as not sufficiently decisive, as capable of being interpreted in the sense of Dioscurus. The document has not been preserved, but one criticism upon it has survived. Flavian of Constantinople had been condemned by Dioscurus and his followers for having said that in Christ there *are* two natures: the committee's formula said that Christ was *of* two natures. That was in itself sound enough, but it could be interpreted as meaning "*of*, but not *in*; Christ is of two natures, but in one nature after the union." The imperial commissioners therefore remarked that the doctrine of Leo on this subject must be embodied in the decree. It looks as if at this fifth sitting a disposition had existed to settle the matter in the terms proposed by Anatolius, —perhaps because it was so desirable to end the disputes,—perhaps because the fathers dreaded the division likely to ensue if the matter were pressed further. They might for such reasons be willing to think it enough to mention two natures, but not so as to ensure a collision with the mass of monophysite sensitiveness. But when it was put to them, "Dioscurus says

The creed as thus adjusted was received with acclamations.

The sittings of the council were still prolonged in order to dispose of some matters of ecclesiastical interest. Men like Theodoret and Ibas, who had been deposed by the robber-synod for alleged Nestorianism, claimed to be vindicated and restored; and canons had been planned to which the council's assent was invited.

The main charge against Ibas was that he had impugned the orthodoxy of passages in Cyril's *anathematismi*. He had not, however, resisted the understanding between John and Cyril, and he had no difficulty in condemning Nestorianism. He was therefore restored.

Theodoret of Cyrus had not objected to the term Theotokos, but he had vigorously controverted Cyril in the early days of the controversy, and had charged him with erroneous teaching. However, after Cyril's acceptance of the formula sent to him by John of Antioch, Theodoret approved of the quarrel being dropped. But Cyril made it a condition that John and his bishops, each for himself, should anathematise Nestorius. Theodoret, who believed that Nestorius had been misrepresented, refused. He agreed with the Church in condemning what now went by the name of Nestorianism, but he declined to anathematise Nestorius himself.

Meanwhile, however, it had been accepted as a settled token of orthodoxy that Nestorius should be anathematised. All the procedure against Eutyches, all the efforts to restore the balance between conflicting tendencies, went on the basis of anathematising Nestorius, and then going on to anathematise Eutyches as well. When Theodoret was introduced [1] into the council of Chalcedon in order to his being

*of* two natures, Leo says *in* two natures, which will you follow?" they could only give one answer, and the formula was recommitted for amendment. In these circumstances the amended form, which was brought up later in the same day, could hardly fail to read ἐν δύο φύσεσι. Baur and Dorner, however, have judged that the Greek copies ought to be followed; against them may be named Tillemont, Walch, Gieseler, Neander, Hahn, Hefele, Harnack, and Loofs.

[1] At the eighth sitting. He had appeared at the first, but the personal matter had not then been disposed of.

restored, he was prepared to give ample proof of his personal orthodoxy by referring to well-known definitions which he *ex animo* embraced; and he tried once and again to get the council to accept satisfaction in this form. It was quite in vain. He was met with shouts of "anathematise Nestorius." And now at last Theodoret gave way. "Anathema," he said, "to Nestorius and to every one who does not call the blessed Virgin Theotokos, or who divides the only begotten Son into two Sons. Also I have signed the decree of the council, and the letter of Leo." That gave satisfaction, and Theodoret was vindicated.

Probably Nestorius by this time was dead; and Theodoret had this excuse, that the condemnation of Nestorius had come to be a theological flag, which had to be hoisted if he was to gain credit for the faith which he really held. Theodoret had long been true to the memory of his old friend. It was with a pang, perhaps, that he consented to sacrifice it at last.[1]

Monophysite teaching was condemned at Chalcedon, but it was destined to appear and work energetically for generations after. It may be fitting to say something here of a tendency which proved to be so strong and so durable.

It has been pointed out already that early writers who desired to hold fast the truth of the Incarnation, and to impress men with the wonder of it, were led to dwell on the Unity of Christ—one Christ, God and Man. In doing so they certainly followed in the line of memorable New Testament declarations. They had therefore to think of Christ as that identical subject of predication, to whom there might be ascribed what belongs to the Godhead and what belongs to the manhood, both at once, both with equal truth. He was begotten from eternity and begotten in time, impassible yet crucified, the Lord of life yet dead and buried.

---

[1] The canons of Chalcedon were twenty-eight or thirty in number. The only one which created much discussion was the twenty-eighth, asserting that the civic dignity of Constantinople, as New Rome, carried with it corresponding ecclesiastical rank and privilege, so that Constantinople must take the second place in precedency—and, apparently, a not inferior place to the first in substantial authority. This canon was indignantly rejected by Leo.

Now those who, in their zeal against Nestorianism, took up monophysite ground, thought that these views and impressions could be secured only by monophysite forms of speech. They loved to think of our Lord's person as a sublime effect of divine wisdom and goodness, a mystery too glorious to be fathomed. They therefore resented explanations that proposed to bring things in this department to the level of human experience. They clung to the thought of the oneness between the divine nature and the human, realised in the person of Christ, the Son of God Incarnate. This was the bond between God and men in which Christians rejoiced. To introduce at this point anything like division was to mar the very centre of Christianity: it was to break the keystone of the arch. The wonder of all the wonders was that the divine and the human attributes and experiences are ascribed not to two, but to one, simply and singularly one. And when they met with distinctions of the two natures in Christ, their impulse was to say, "We will have here no two natures. It is *the* nature of Christ to have all these things true of Him at once. This is *the nature* of the incarnate Word." With these views was often associated a certain type of mystic devoutness which in its extreme forms passed into Pantheism.

There might be much in this tendency to which sympathy could be yielded, and the language of its representatives may deserve to be benevolently interpreted. Their assertion of the one φύσις has been apologised for on the ground that the sense of terms was still very unsettled, and that to many minds φύσις might carry the sense of person, rather than that of nature. There is something in this, but hardly enough. It is reasonable, perhaps, to go further and admit that when the monophysites brought out the unity of Christ—the complete harmony of all that belongs to Him—by asserting the one nature, that, by itself, might be capable of being explained. In that case it would have to be understood as a way of expressing the χάρις ἑνώσεως, the grace of the union; and, in particular, as meant to bring out the permanent and perfect character of that union,—that we may rest in it as a permanent reality, just as we do rest when we have fixed or assigned to anything its permanent *nature*. So taken, the assertion would not exclude the continuance of the divine nature and of the human nature in the union of them both, each retaining the essential features or attributes appropriate to each. And this I take to be the real position of Cyril, who acceded to the form of teaching indicated by John of Antioch, and yet continued occasionally to use the phrase of the μία φύσις σεσαρκωμένη. But the monophysites asserted the one nature, so as to declare resolutely against the acknowledgment, in any sense, of two natures. Christ is *of* two natures, but not *in* two natures. So they involved themselves in inferences which led them far. For what was this "nature" which was neither divine nature simply nor human nature simply? Practically the effect, in general, was to lead them to explain away the true human nature of our Lord. He is not now consubstantial with us. If they had been content to assert simply that in *some* sense we may speak of one nature in Christ, that might involve an inaccurate and confusing use of a word, but might be allowed to pass; but when the phrase was expounded into the formal denial of the continuance, without confusion, of essential human nature with the divine nature, it was impossible then to avoid the tendency to merge the manhood in the Godhead, and to explain away that which is human in the Lord Jesus. In doing so they took from Him what is needful that He may be our head, representative, and surety; and in the same proportion they drifted towards a style of religious feeling to which these views of Christ are not essential or even important. These tendencies among the Monophysites were illustrated in a lively sectarianism, the movements of which will claim attention in a subsequent volume.

To sum up. In the unity a twofoldness was acknowledged. Christ is διπλοῦς, as the three great Cappadocians often say. Presupposing the Nicene assertion of our Lord's true divinity, Nestorius emphasised this διπλοῦς; his opponents wished to give it the gentlest interpretation. It may well be believed that many on both sides received all that Scripture clearly teaches, though with diverging emphasis on different elements. This may be conceded in favour of some even of the sects which took formal monophysite ground; there were others which proceeded to feats of fanciful inference not only erroneous but grotesque and mischievous. The Church pointed out hazards on both sides, and tried to settle limits of phrase by means of which those who agreed in owning both aspects might understand one another, and might avoid inferences leading into contradiction. Nor does it seem possible to do more, since the very words which we must use—as Person and Nature—prove to be at best approximate, and refuse to be restrained by invariable definitions when we carry them from man to God, and from God to man.

It is difficult to read the story without being struck with the way in which, under the influence of Scripture and Providence, compensations take place in connection with such debates as these. For though on either side unwise assertions or negations were put forward, the fears of neither side were justified by the event. The one school never lost hold of the faith that He who was found in fashion as a man was the same who was in the form of God. The other school never clearly denied that Jesus was, and continued to be, true man. Individuals, and considerable parties, may have committed themselves to phrases that conflicted with these faiths; but when sections of Christianity became separated under one or other of the contending influences, and so had the opportunity to reveal their meaning fully, the fundamental principles from which they both proceeded, along with the compensating influences of the gospel history, kept them from going further off from one another. After all, and on the whole, the thoughts concerning Jesus Christ were not very different among monophysite Armenians on the one hand, and among Nestorian Syrians on the other.

# CHAPTER XXIV

## DONATISM

Optatus Milevitanus, *De schismate Donatistarum.* Ribbeck, *Donatus u. Augustinus,* Elberf. 1858.

IT was convenient to follow out to the decision of Chalcedon the discussions regarding the Person of the Lord. Donatism takes us a good way back, for the sect originated about A.D. 311. It takes us also to the West. The forces which gave animation and character to the Trinitarian and the Christological controversies had their home mainly in the East. The importance of those issues was recognised in the West; but there questions about the method of salvation, and about the Church in relation to it, came home with special force to Christian minds.

In the year 311 the see of Carthage became vacant by the death of Mensurius, and a disputed election followed. A good deal of intrigue is alleged to have gone forward; but the parties in whose behalf the strings were pulled neither succeeded in carrying the election, nor played any prominent part afterwards. Rather unexpectedly, Cæcilianus the deacon was elected; and he was presently consecrated by Felix, bishop of Aptunga. But Cæcilianus was obnoxious to many in Carthage; and certain Numidian bishops, who conceived that no steps ought to have been taken in their absence, protested against the whole proceedings. Was Cæcilianus validly consecrated? His opponents denied it; and they formed a special ground of nullity in the allegation that Felix of Aptunga, who consecrated him, had been a *traditor*[1] in the recent time of

[1] Name given to those who saved themselves in Diocletian's persecution by delivering up the sacred books to be burnt.

persecution. He had therefore incurred deposition; all his acts were invalid; Cæcilianus, after consecration, was still no more than a deacon. This argument was supplemented by the assertion that Cæcilianus himself too had been a *traditor*—nay, that Mensurius, his predecessor, had been so also. These allegations may have had little or no foundation: certainly, repeated investigations are said, by the Catholics, to have ended always in total absence of proof. But the accusations were believed; and the inference derived from them was regarded as valid by many eager Carthaginian Christians. The opponents of Cæcilianus elected a certain Majorianus, and had him consecrated, as to a see still vacant.

So the schism began. Which of the two was to be treated as bishop of Carthage, was the question that divided the church throughout the province. Those who held communion with Cæcilianus were regarded by the other side as sharers in his sin, as outcast until they should repent, as disabled meanwhile from validly administering any Christian ordinance. But all the churches beyond the sea recognised Cæcilianus. The Emperor Constantine, to whom in this year, A.D. 312, Italy and Africa fell, was applied to by the Donatists themselves, and he referred the matter to two committees of bishops successively, both of which decided in favour of Cæcilianus. Also Constantine himself, on a final appeal to him to examine the cause in person, affirmed the sentence that had been given before. It remained for the Donatists to sustain their cause on the strength of their own judgment. All external countenance, civil or ecclesiastical, was denied them.

It is not necessary to recite minutely the details of the history. The Donatists were resolute and fierce, and neither argument nor persuasion availed to change them. They claimed to be the true Church, and those who held communion with the impure had simply unchurched themselves. The arm of the State was called in by the Catholics, and a long series of inconsistent and ill-judged measures were successively resorted to,—indefensible acts of persecution and repression being varied occasionally by weak connivance at Donatist turbulence and excess. At no time during the fourth century was the spirit of the sect, on the whole, broken, or their confidence subdued. As Donatism had the character of a popular faith and was frowned upon by the State, popular impulses were apt to connect themselves with it. Troops of fanatical persons known as Circumcelliones traversed the country districts, professed to protect the Donatists, and often assailed the Catholics. It was one of the questions discussed, how far the Donatist church, as such, was responsible for the existence and the operations of these disturbers of the peace.[1]

The series of events now rehearsed may be said to exhibit the origin of Donatism. So contemplated, it does not appear worthy of much respect. But very often such movements represent grave differences of opinion, or of tendency, which have gradually accumulated and become intense. Then some accident determines the explosion. No doubt it was so here. The Donatists represented strong convictions widely entertained in the African church; and their theory and practice alike were congenial to the African temperament. They found an energetic and fearless leader in Donatus,[2] who succeeded Majorianus as Donatist bishop of Carthage in A.D. 315.

The African church, throughout its history, was strongly characterised by a type of view and feeling which may be called in a general way puritanic. There was a strong demand that religion should declare itself by energetic strictnesses and self-denials. Tertullian was in some respects a representative African, and he may best be described as a puritanical high churchman; the puritanism—approaching even to the fifth monarchy type—being quite as vigorous as the high churchism. This type of character, we may believe, was powerfully represented among the devout people

[1] The Circumcelliones represented a vehement Africanism, with religious and socialistic inspirations, and organised with a view to terrorise opponents. The Donatists, in their own way, were the popular African church, and the Circumcelliones were in sympathy with them as such.

[2] This was Donatus the Great. There was another Donatus, of Casæ Nigræ.

of the province; and among those who were not particularly devout there were probably many who, at least, judged the devoutness of other people by a standard which embodied the same point of view. With this was probably connected, further, the disposition which existed among African Christians to cling to powerful religious individualities. They were readily swayed by men who had gained their confidence, as embodying in an impressive manner the type of character they were disposed to venerate. There is reason to think, also, that lively interest in ecclesiastical affairs,—readiness to take part in them, and to take sides about them,—was exceptionally prevalent among the Christian plebs in Africa.[1]

In particular, the great thought of the holiness of Christ's Church had laid strong hold on the African mind. This holiness must be not merely ceremonial or conventional, but real and vital. The Church of Christ is the habitation of the Spirit of grace,—the Spirit of God and of Christ. Thence comes its own blessedness, thence also its fitness or ability to perform the function by which it is to confer blessings on the world, and is to edify its own members. Therefore the sense of the Church's peculiar and characteristic holiness, and its privilege, thence arising, of communicating sanctifying influence, was to be solicitously cherished. Therefore, also, the actual holiness of the Church was to be carefully watched over and maintained. The institute, glorious as it was, had been reared in a perilous world, and there was need for constant vigilance that the canker of sin might not corrupt and ruin it. Many African Christians, accordingly, had embraced with earnestness, at an earlier period, the disciplinary severities of Montanism. Donatism reveals the same tendencies in another form. And obviously, if the pressure of the time (*ante*, p. 289) was threatening to flood the Church with questionable members, it might well seem that the vigilance ought now to be redoubled.

[1] Illustrations of these tendencies abound in the events which marked Cyprian's episcopate. Whatever the Seniores Plebis of the African churches exactly were, their existence points in the direction indicated above.

To discuss the proper place and worth of this great thought would lead us too far. But it may be remarked that it proves arduous to maintain positive and worthy conceptions of what holiness in the Church and in its members is, and to be loyal to the claims it really makes. Here, as elsewhere, it is easier to live in negative than in positive conceptions,—to fix upon certain things which are, and are to be reckoned, *unholy*, and to make holiness consist in opposing these. This is the easier working method for any mass of men; and too plainly it became the regulative method of the African Donatists.

The energy of the feeling that a holy vitality, maintained by the Spirit in the Church, and pervading it, is essential to the discharge of its functions, appears very clearly in the position sustained so resolutely in Africa, and championed, as we have seen, by Cyprian, that those who have been baptized in heresy must be baptized again, because the former baptism was null, through the defect of the minister. The sacrament in the hands of the living Church confers the blessing;—otherwise nothing is done. When the Church administers the sacrament, the living Spirit that is in the Church, and in the Church's minister, passes by that channel and communicates Himself to the receiver. But what can a society do by any manipulations if it be a society in which the Spirit of Christ is not?[1]

The Donatists said, The Church of Christ is a living and pure society in which the Holy Spirit dwells; and thus it is fitted for its function of bringing forth children to God. This continues to be so although the members and ministers of the Church are not free from failings. But there are certain sins which are recognised as rightfully separating the sinner from the communion of the Church. When a member of the Church falls into such scandalous sin, he

---

[1] Successus said, "Heretics can either do everything or they can do nothing. If they can baptize, they can also give the Holy Spirit. But if they cannot give the Holy Spirit, because they do not possess the Holy Spirit, then they cannot spiritually baptize. We give our judgment, therefore, that heretics should be rebaptized." Cypr. Opp. *Sentt. Episc.* 16.

dies. He ceases to be capable of acting as a channel for conveying what the Church has to give. He falls from the living Church; and the living Church withdraws from him. A church that cleaves to such a sinner simply reveals its own fall. Any ordinances administered by such a man are to be rejected. As a Christian, the man is null, and his ministration is null. A bishop who is a *traditor*, impenitent and unreconciled, is no bishop. He is no longer a Christian. When the Church of Christ lays hold of men, and draws them into the fellowship of His life, she puts forth a living hand, not a dead one. That is the decisive principle applicable to Cæcilianus and men like him.

It was not maintained by the Donatists that all the Catholic clergy were sinners of this type, nor that all Catholics had been baptized by men thus tainted. But the whole society fell, in adhering to the fallen. It upheld the cause of the corrupt and dead, and cherished their fellowship, as against the society which renounced such persons and disclaimed them. Of two societies that claim to be Christ's Church, which is genuine,—the one that cherishes the followers of Judas? or that which rejects them?

Following out these principles, the Donatists rebaptized those who came over to them from the Catholic Church, holding their Catholic baptism to have been null. The Catholics acted differently. Following the view of the Church of Rome as to heretical baptism (*ante*, p. 259), they received a Donatist who wished to join them, recognising the Donatist baptism as valid. On this the Donatists built an argument. They said, You own by your practice that we have the true baptism, that we have the remission of sins, that we have the Holy Spirit. But there are not *two* conflicting societies in which remission is found, in which the Holy Spirit dwells. If these privileges, as you virtually own, are ours, they cannot also be yours. " Come, therefore, to the Church, ye people, and flee the company of the *traditors*."[1]

[1] It was natural for the Donatists to clinch their indictments against their opponents by maintaining that in the Catholic Church discipline had practically failed. The Catholics had been led to their position by a defective sense

Finally, the Donatists found proof of the spurious nature of Catholic Christianity in the pressure and persecution on the part of the State, directed against Donatists, which Catholics approved and stimulated. So they fulfilled the Lord's prophecy of a generation of vipers who should slay and crucify His messengers. The Donatists got rid of a counter argument against themselves, based on the wild treatment of Catholics by the Circumcelliones, by disclaiming responsibility for anything wrong which these disturbers might have done.

It should be recognised that a genuine concern about the purity of the Church, and a desire to do right to that interest, was an element in the state of mind out of which this movement originated. The appeal to this sentiment was the strength of Donatism. But it is plain that the way of conceiving the matter—the standard of judgment about it which they set up—was of a very external kind. And the exigencies of controversy, in defending a party position inconsiderately taken up, drove them more and more into disreputable sophistries. For they themselves could not live out their own theories. They could not make out the nullity of Catholic Christianity, except by arguments which could be retorted with fatal effect on their own.[1]

of the evil of sin, and the same proclivity was manifest in their whole administration of church affairs. This, of course, was a matter of impression, or of allegation, and the Donatists were not likely to be impartial judges in regard to it. But from Augustine's way of meeting the allegation one acquires the impression that in the Catholic Church comparative laxity did prevail, and had to be justified or apologised for.

[1] The Donatist movement required for its defence this postulate, that the forgiveness of sins and the sanctifying power of the Holy Spirit are present and prevalent throughout the Church, throughout its ministry, and throughout its membership, wherever they are *not* banished by those positive and gross transgressions for which the Church inflicts discipline; on the other hand, when those transgressions occur, this spiritual vitality departs from the transgressors and, as the Donatists added, from all who symbolise with them. Some such external way of conceiving the boundary-line between the living and the dead was probably very common throughout the Church, among Catholics as among Donatists. The Donatists made this conception the basis of their church fellowship. But could they be sure that hidden sin was not vitiating it also? If they were to defend their own fellowship, then they could not help weakening their own principle by silently assuming that, some-

During the revolt of Gildo, who maintained himself as ruler of the African province (A.D. 392–398), the Donatists were sheltered from the pressure of the imperial laws.[1] But after the restoration of Roman authority the situation grew worse: the Circumcelliones on the one side, and the measures against Donatism on the other, became more active, and eventually, from about A.D. 412, the sect may be regarded as legally suppressed,—that is, they could no longer sustain a public existence,—but Donatism survived in a disorganised condition to a much later date.[2]

Far the most important feature of the Donatist dispute is the part which Augustine took in it. In his earlier days, so far as appears, it did not at all interest him, although Tagaste, his birthplace, had been a Donatist town, and became Catholic only a few years before Augustine's birth. But when he became an African ecclesiastic, he found Donatism a force to be carefully encountered. When he came to Hippo, the clear majority of the Christians there were Donatists; and at that time, he tells us, no Donatist would have baked a loaf of bread for a Catholic. He began to take a prominent part in the debate three or four years after his ordination as presbyter (which was in A.D. 392), and he prosecuted the discussion in various forms until the predominance of the Catholic Church in Africa rendered further effort unnecessary.

Augustine's was a mind perfectly disposed to engage

how or other, the fatal transgressions may be committed by ministers of the Church and yet do not hinder the communication of her life, unless they become in some measure manifest. But this modification of their theory would have weakened the attack on the Catholic fellowship. Therefore it had to be withdrawn or veiled.

[1] During this time there may have been some oppression of individual Catholics, and insufficient protection against the Circumcelliones, but from the answer of Augustine to the first book of Petilianus it does not appear that the Catholics had to complain of much persecution. Near the end of Gildo's usurpation one sees, from Augustine's conference with Fortunus of Tubursica (397), that apprehension of persecution from the Catholic side existed among the Donatists. And a few years after, about 403, symptoms of intense strain as between the parties are visible.

[2] Tillemont, *Mém.*, vol. vi., last chapter.

with predilection in such a controversy, and the position he was to take up had long been clear to him. His theory of the Church, and his advocacy of Catholic practice in connection with it, are of course the main points. In addition, he made large and successful use of the *reductio ad absurdum*. For the Donatists had laid hold of good strong principles, sufficient, if admitted, to make havoc of the Catholic positions; but these Augustine retorted upon themselves with fatal effect.[1]

Of more permanent interest are the principles which formed his theory of the Church.

The necessity of baptism to salvation was generally held, and Augustine held it. That necessity was qualified by some exceptions, but was imperative in general. That men, not yet baptized, who suffered death as martyrs, were in effect christened in their own blood was everywhere believed, and Augustine believed it. He went further, and admitted that lack of baptism would not be imputed to those who seriously designed to be baptized, but who, through no fault

[1] See the books *contr. Litt. Petiliani*, or almost any of the Donatist writings:—*e.g.* "There have been *traditors* among yourselves,—how is the world to be sure that you have expelled all of them, any more than that we have expelled all ours?" "There are some among you, as among us, who have received baptism, being secretly impenitent and living in sin,—why do you not rebaptize them when the case is discovered?" "There are some of you who, after being baptized, have gone from your communion into other sects which you reckon impure. You say that by that step those persons lost all that their baptism bestowed upon them,—why do you not baptize them over again when they come back to you?" "Some time ago a party of your people separated from you under Maximinianus; you said they were schismatics; you said they were separated from Christ and from the Spirit; in that state they baptized many catechumens; by and by they came back to you in a body,—why did you not rebaptize those converts of theirs, whom, when they baptized them, to use your own language, 'their own impure consciences disabled them from really purifying'?" "There are among you, as among us, for neither party can help it, bishops and presbyters whose lives are fair enough to man's view, but who in God's sight are ungodly men. What becomes of those who in your communion are baptized by such men? Are they after all unbaptized?" Points like these are pressed with unwearied pertinacity, and in every shape rhetorical skill could suggest. On the whole, Augustine treats his Donatist opponents with a fair measure of courtesy; but now and then his contempt for their dialectical weakness breaks through in a sentence or two of satirical banter, *e.g. c. Litt. Petiliani*, i. c. v.

of their own, died before the administration.[1] But he would not have admitted an exception, *e.g.* in the case of a member of the Society of Friends, persuaded that baptism with water ought not now to be administered.

Baptism, then, is necessary; yet, on the other hand, it is not inseparably joined to the blessings which it holds forth, *i.e.* to remission and regeneration. "Baptism is one thing, conversion of the heart is another: man's salvation is made complete through the two together."[2] A man may be baptized, and yet may be destitute of the spiritual blessing. Since this is so, Augustine finally owns it to be difficult to say *what* the intrinsic effect of the outward administration is.[3] It must be something **very** important, but what? Out of this "what" was developed the doctrine of sacramental *character*.

However, whatever it does, and whatever the manner of its working, the efficacy of baptism in no degree depends on the administrator. If in substance it is administered according to Christ's institution, then it is Christ's ordinance, and whatever is done by it, He does it. The administrator may be a secretly bad man, or a man known to be bad, he may be a schismatic or a heretic. The validity of the sacrament is not affected. It is wrong to seek Christian ordinances from heretics, but even in their hands baptism is Christ's baptism. Much more, the believer within the Catholic Church is not called upon to burden his conscience with questions about the spiritual condition of the baptizer. "Let the man's whole hope be in Christ; for it is written, Cursed is he that putteth his trust in man. It is always Christ that justifies the ungodly; it is always from Christ that faith is given; Christ always is the origin of the regenerate man, and the head of the Church."[4]

---

[1] This position is avowed in the writings against Donatism. It is not obviously consistent with the position about unbaptized infants maintained in the Pelagian controversy, but it is possible to hold both.

[2] *De Bapt.* iv. c. xxv.     [3] *Ibid.* iv. c. xxiii.

[4] *C. Pet.* i. c. vi. As baptism thus administered, even if in heresy, is still Christ's, so Augustine boldly asserts it is still the Church's. This meets Cyprian's argument that only the Church can be the true mother of Christians. See *de Bapt.* i. c. **xv.**

Baptism administered in the heretical sects is effectually and really baptism. But as outward baptism, administered in the best of circumstances, is not always accompanied by the spiritual blessings, so in these circumstances it never is. Baptism, for instance, is for remission of sins; but in the case of a man baptized in a heretical sect, either that remission never reaches him, or if it comes, it immediately departs again. For Augustine held the unity of the external Church: there is one authentic society, to be in communion with which is necessary to salvation. Outside of it spiritual life either does not exist or, if it comes, it presently dies again.

The Donatists held the same doctrine, but they grounded it and they applied it differently. They argued on the necessity of being in external organic union with that which they held to be the living society. Hence the interposition, in ministration of baptism, of a scandalous ecclesiastic breaks the conductor by which the electric influence should pass, and the man remains unbaptized and dead. Augustine's thinking was on other lines: the outward condition, baptism, may be fulfilled whenever and however administered. Also the inward conditions may be brought to pass under the influence of the Spirit, whatever agency brings the gospel to bear upon the soul, *e.g.* in a heretical meeting. Yet there is one external society, to be in communion with which is essential to life and salvation. And Augustine sought to find a reason for this necessity, which should be moral and not mechanical. It had already been advanced by Cyprian;[1] and the later writer worked it skilfully into his own system. He who forsakes the Church, or who fails to reunite himself with the Church, breaks charity. He denies the very central grace. He takes up a position of pride, censoriousness, ill-will. He refuses to bear the burden, and to be patient with the offences which, in the Church, Christ and His people endure together. A man may be truly converted outside of the Church; but the effect of that conversion will be to bring him penitently back to the Church. If he withstand that tendency, he

[1] *De Unitate*, c. 9. 15.

withstands the grace that saves, and chooses to abide in death. " When it is said that the Holy Spirit is given only in the Catholic Church, I suppose our ancestors (*i.e.* Cyprian and his fellow bishops) meant that we should understand thereby what the Apostle says,—' because the love of God is shed abroad in our hearts by the Holy Ghost, which is given to us.' This very love is that which is wanting in all who are cut off from the communion of the Catholic Church ; and for want of it, though they ' speak with the tongues of men and angels . . . it profiteth them nothing.' This is the charity which covereth the multitude of sins. And it is the especial gift of the Catholic unity and peace."[1] Obviously the assumption here made is both presumptuous and precarious. It is that outward separation necessarily and always implies an inward revolt from the love of God, and an uncharitable renunciation of what is due to the brethren. That is a fatally wide assumption, and in trying to make it good Cyprian and Augustine, and all who follow them, have been obliged themselves to sin against charity and justice.

But the principle which Augustine wields with the greatest energy of all in this department, is that of the distinction between the living and the dead, between the godly and the ungodly, in the Catholic Church itself. No Christian, perhaps, had ever denied that distinction ; and no party claiming the position and privileges of the Church could pretend that there were no ungodly persons among themselves, however much they might be disposed to denounce the impurity of other communions. But Augustine far more intensely apprehended the significance of that great unseen perpetual cleft in the Church of Christ as she is embodied in the earth. And he connected his recognition of it with a far more vivid conception of the essential contrast—of what, to the Lord's eye, makes the difference—between the godly man and the ungodly. We have seen him contending that whatever is conferred by mere authentic administration of sacraments, may be conferred and may be received by those who are strangers to

[1] *De Bapt.* iii. c. **xvi.**

the spiritual blessings for the sake of which sacraments were instituted.[1] But he carries out this argument by maintaining that persons so situated are all of them foreign to Christ's Church, aliens and strangers, as truly as are the heretics and the schismatics themselves. They may be in unchallenged communion with the Catholic Church, they may be presbyters or bishops, they may be in high repute for piety with men; but in truth they are not of the Church of Christ, and that shall be made plain in due time. No part of Augustine's argument is enforced with such energy as this. Cyprian, maintaining the nullity of heretical baptism, had argued that heretics are enemies and antichrists. Therefore their pretended ordinances are null, and their disciples, when they return to the Catholic unity, should be baptized with the one baptism, that they may be made friends and Christians. "The very same," rejoins Augustine, "may be said of all unrighteous men who are in the communion of the Catholic Church. They only *really* come to the Church who pass to Christ from the party of the devil, who build on the rock, who are incorporated with the dove, who are placed in safety in the garden enclosed and fountain sealed; but none are found there who live contrary to the precepts of Christ, whatever they may seem to be."[2] "Heretics and schismatics are only more openly, not more really, outside of the Church which is glorious, not having spot or wrinkle or any such thing."[3] Cyprian had said that heretics might baptize, if they could be shown to be "devoted to the Church, and appointed in the Church." "But neither," says Augustine, "are they devoted to the Church who *seem* to be within, yet live contrary to Christ, acting against His commandments: they do not in any way belong to that Church which He so purifies by the washing of water as to present it to Himself a glorious Church without spot or wrinkle. Now, if so, they are not in the Church of which it is said, My dove is but one, she is the only one of her mother."[4]

---

[1] See also *c. Pet.* ii. cap. 104 fin.  
[2] *De Bapt.* vii. c. xli.  
[3] *Ibid.* iii. c. xviii.  
[4] *Ibid.* iv. c. iii.

It is one thing to admit this, every sect meanwhile trying to minimise its own concern in it; it is another thing to give effect to it in the vigorous manner of Augustine. It tended to dispel the fatal confusion between the inward and the outward in Christianity; all the more because Augustine pointed out so vigorously the vital peculiarities of Christian life as distinguished from all mere methodism of Christian living. A tendency was widely prevalent to cherish large and vague assumptions as to the Christian benefit that might be conceived to arise in virtue of being in the authentic Church, even to careless people, if they were not chargeable with gross offences. And Augustine, of course, held that to be even outwardly in the fellowship of the Catholic Church was a privilege as well as a duty. "The tares that are within may be converted into wheat more easily than the tares that are without." Nay, there are sentences [1] in which he seems to admit the idea of salvation, in the Church, for a class of persons who are not quite in inward fellowship with the Lord, but who have their faces turned that way. In general, however, the vigorous wielding of the great distinction now in view unquestionably was fitted to press home the conviction that nothing will avail us, unless there be present that regeneration which he describes as "being renovated from the corruption of the old man." [2]

One way in which Augustine identified that one Catholic communion which in his view contains, embodies, and represents the true Church, though it is not identical with it, is to point to the extent of the Catholic Church as spreading over the whole world. This is a great point against the Donatists. He pleads, in connection with it, all the promises which declare that the world shall be Christ's, that the kingdom shall be visible, as a city set on a hill, and the like. Petilian, speaking of Catholic persecution, says, "You cry Peace, Peace, but where is your peace?" Augustine replies, "If you ask where peace is to be found, open your eyes to see the city which cannot be hidden, because it is built on a

---

[1] *De Bapt.* i. 15, iii. 18.  [2] *Ibid.* i. c. xi.

hill, and the mountain which grows out of a small stone and fills the whole earth. But when the same question is asked of you, what will you say? Will you show the party of Donatus, unknown to the countless nations to whom Christ is known? That, surely, is not the city which cannot be hid; and whence is this but because it is not founded on the mountain?"[1]

The treatment of the Donatists varied with the impulses and the difficulties of the Government. On the other side, the Donatists, while they complained bitterly of persecution, seem to have been ready enough to welcome the aid of State force when the possibility of such a thing seemed to open; and if the Catholics may be believed, they showed no disposition to restrain the violence of the Circumcelliones, although the more quiet and settled Donatists disclaimed responsibility for those proceedings. Augustine, indeed, declares that the Catholics would not have found it possible to live in the country districts if the Donatists in the towns had not been treated as hostages for their security.

At length, about A.D. 410, edicts were issued by Honorius, authorising the suppression of the sect by force, and from that time measures for the purpose were systematically followed out. Augustine had originally been against this course. He had maintained that pains and penalties ought not to be applied in order to bring dissidents to the Church. He had claimed only that insult and outrage, inflicted on Catholics by Donatists, should be put down; and this he supposed could be effected by fining prominent Donatists whenever injury was done to Catholics. But the Government, as we have seen, under other advice, adopted the more stringent course. And Augustine, observing that these

---

[1] *C. Pet.* ii. xiii. This was cogent reasoning when, by the conditions of argument, accepted on both sides, one or other, Donatists *or* Catholics, must be, and be exclusively, Christ's only Church on earth,—not to speak of the precarious grounds on which the Donatists unchurched the Christians of the whole world. But one does not feel sure that Augustine himself would have used the argument so confidently had the case been that of a part of Christendom, which, without unchurching the rest, saw fit to take a diverging view of some point of doctrine or practice, even if the effect were that communion was suspended on both sides.

measures seemed to be successful,—for he tells us that great numbers of Donatists came over, and that they often confessed they were glad to be rid of their old connection, though they would hardly have quitted it of their own accord,—became the advocate of persecution.[1] In support of it he quoted the Scriptures bearing on the ministry due from kings to the cause of God, and he elevated into a mournful historical significance the text, "Compel them to come in." He thus became, by precept and example, the supporter of a principle that is really diabolical; and he gave it an authority for the after age which the Reformation itself did not bring into question. It was the more easy for him to be misled, because in certain circumstances persecution works with great success of a certain kind; and the case of the Donatists is an illustration. When men have driven their own principle to extravagance,—when they have wearied themselves with the monotony of their unreasonableness, and when they have begun to feel the pressure of counter principles more profoundly conceived and more skilfully applied,—then sharp and resolute persecution sometimes precipitates a crisis, and people prove not unwilling to be driven into the new fold, though they would be slow to move spontaneously. It appeared to be so here, and yet it is questionable how far it really was so. Enough of pathetic indignation and despair appeared among the Donatists to have suggested a doubt concerning the measures which led to these results. They did not suggest such doubt to Augustine, who was capable of a certain hardness when his religious logic had sanctioned a line for him to walk in. But the storm which burst on Africa as his life was closing was not improbably a result in some degree, and so a punishment, of that mistaken policy. There is reason to believe that the progress of the Vandals was facilitated by a spirit of sedition against Roman rule which was abroad in Africa. And into this there entered doubtless, as an element, the hatred and revenge of the trampled and humiliated Donatists.[2]

[1] *De Correctione Donatistarum.*
[2] **Far** too much has been made of the conduct of the Circumcelliones as

It must be remembered, however, that at all events Augustine was not slack in employing more legitimate means of persuasion. Preaching, writing, private conference, public debate—he was eager for them all, and into all he threw his heart and his genius as well as his debating power. He had long been using these means ere he came to the conclusion that the co-operation of persecution was a desirable agency in addition.

This legitimate zeal, besides exhausting itself in various forms of prose, overflowed into verse. Augustine as a rhetorician had practised classic versification and set many a theme for such verse to pupils; but that style would not have suited the Africans. Something more fitted to the genius of the people and of the Latin language seemed to be required, and the cadence and swing of the verses written by Augustine on this subject were no doubt suggested by what he believed to be the demands of the popular ear. They may be regarded, therefore, as illustrating the conditions under which, as the lower empire was merged in barbarian kingdoms, the classic metres gave way, for religious purposes, to styles of verse governed by quite different laws.[1]

affording an explanation of, and so an apology for, the course taken by Augustine. This will not do. Certainly the conduct of the Circumcelliones called for counter measures; and, no doubt, Augustine, in arguing with the Donatists and dealing with their complaints of persecution, casts up to them the violence of the Circumcelliones as a *quid pro quo*. But Augustine distinguished perfectly between merely suppressing the Circumcelliones and oppressing the Donatists generally. He knew very well, also, that multitudes of Donatists were in no sense Circumcelliones. He advisedly argues the case on grounds which would equally apply if no Catholic had ever been assailed. He arrived at this view, approved of it in practice, and defended it in debate. Undoubtedly the complex case did present, on the Donatist side, so much of violence and unreasonableness as to afford a palliation. But supposing the case to have been otherwise, I doubt whether Augustine, arriving at his conclusion by the line of argument he describes, would have flinched merely because the heretics were inoffensive.

[1] Opp. vol. ix., *Psalmus contra partem Donati*. None of the later Christian hymns were modelled on these rough verses of Augustine; but the latter resemble the former in so far as feet dependent on quantity are superseded by accented measures. In fact the swing of Augustine's verse reminds one of some of our own Saxon rhymes.

# CHAPTER XXV

### Ecclesiastical Personages of Fourth Century

1. Eusebius was bishop of Cæsarea from A.D. 313 to 340. He may have been a native of that city, and was born probably about A.D. 260. He became celebrated as the most learned Christian of his time, and as the most productive writer. He is the father of Church history, and has preserved notices of facts, books, and personages which, but for his labours, must have remained in darkness. But he laboured in many fields. Bishop Lightfoot (in the *Dict. Christ. Biog.* ii. p. 319) has furnished a minute discussion of his work under the heads, Historical, Apologetic, Critical and Exegetical, Doctrinal, Orations, Letters: numbering forty-one distinct articles. Cæsarea had become the seat of a notable library; so had Jerusalem, which was not far off; and both furnished Eusebius with copious opportunity for study. Cæsarea had also been the home of Origen in his later years; and Eusebius was associated with Pamphilus, the scholar and champion of Origen, in defending the reputation of that great master.

Eusebius signed the Nicene Creed as finally adjusted, but not without some difficulty. He certainly was in friendly relations with leading Arians, and would have spared them the pressure of the Nicene clauses. As to his own belief, he stood nearest to those semi-Arians who deprecated the Nicene phraseology, but could not be convicted of Arianism. He inherited the subordinationism of Origen, and regarded a leaning in this direction as the necessary safeguard against Sabellianism. The phrases in the creed which created difficulty for him were $\delta\mu oo\acute{u}\sigma\iota o\varsigma$ and $\dot{\epsilon}\kappa\ \tau\hat{\eta}\varsigma\ o\dot{u}\sigma\acute{\iota}a\varsigma\ \tau o\hat{u}\ \pi a\tau\rho\acute{o}\varsigma$.

Lightfoot properly points to the personal respect with which he seems to have been regarded by his contemporaries. His most important works were, perhaps, his Ecclesiastical History in ten books; his life of Constantine in five; his *Chronica* (Chronology of General History); his Martyrs of Palestine (in two recensions, both from his own hand); his *Præparatio* and *Demonstratio Evangelica*; his works against Marcellus of Ancyra; and his *Topica*, or names of Places in Scripture. Probably half of what he is known to have written has perished.

Eusebius was one of the most cultivated men of his time, and we have reason to believe that he was personally attractive and benignant. He was greatly valued by the Emperor Constantine, whom he in turn all but worshipped. But while he occupies a place among the foremost in ecclesiastical literature, he does not rank so high in mental power or force. It has been remarked that while his conception of what his greater works ought to be is sometimes grand and striking, the execution falls short. Moreover, his Greek style has something harsh and artificial about it. His fidelity as an ecclesiastical historian has been successfully defended. As to the conception of the Church on which he proceeded, see the *History of Ecclesiastical History*, by F. C. Baur.[1] He was writing with unfailing vigour down to the end of his life.

Among bishops of the same name (and they were many) Eusebius of Cæsarea is chiefly to be distinguished from Eusebius of Nicodemia, the ecclesiastical leader of the Arians during the first half of the controversy (died bishop of Constantinople, A.D. 342). Bishops of the same name at the Cappadocian Cæsarea, at Samosata, and at Sebaste occur a little later.

2. Athanasius was born probably in the closing years of the third century. He was already a deacon at the time of the council of Nicæa (A.D. 325), the trusted attendant and the adviser of his bishop (Alexander). In three years after (A.D. 328), in spite of the antipathy of the Arians, which

[1] *Epochen*, Tüb. 1852.

he had already earned, he was elevated to the episcopal chair of Alexandria. This, in the extent of its immediate or direct jurisdiction, was then perhaps the most arduous see in Christendom. For the whole period during which he occupied it, Athanasius had to bear the strain of the Arian controversy. He died in A.D. 373; and of the forty-five years of his episcopate, twenty were spent in exile; five times he was driven from his flock, always returning again amid enthusiastic welcomes.

A legend of his boyhood (it represented him as having been baptized in play by his companions, and that the bishop held it valid); two or three stories of his attitude in the various trying conjunctures of his long life,—all significant of courage and resource; a note of his appearance—he was small of stature, but his countenance was dignified and impressive;—these are nearly all the minor personal details that have been preserved. The rest must be gathered from the survey of his work. It is obvious that he came early under the influences connected with church life, and that he developed promptly the aptitudes which it requires. His capacity for theological thought found its earliest exercise on the place and function to be ascribed to Christ the Saviour in relation to God and man;[1] that was the source of his teaching on the question which occupied his life. In defending his position he gave abundant evidence of intellectual resource and skill. But the grasp with which he held it through all turns of debate, and the mastery with which resistance and concession alike were brought into play in sustaining it, reveal character and will even more than intellect. Athanasius possessed the eye for men and for affairs, and the purpose to make all his resources tell for the cause he served, which are the main elements of statesmanship;—in his case statesmanship sustained by faith, and therefore never owning or accepting defeat.

He was not understood to possess, like Origen, the learning due to enormous reading; the circumstances of his

---

[1] *De Incarnatione* (written before the Arian controversy).

life forbade it. Nor was he a religious genius like Augustine. His knowledge and his range of religious insight and sympathy were, no doubt, adequate to the representation of a great cause, and have commanded the respect of theologians down to our time. But Athanasius was most of all a commanding personality: one who impressed, controlled, and mastered men; one whom his followers enthusiastically trusted, and whom his enemies feared and hated.

Something may be learned from the accusations with which his opponents assailed him. What they chiefly imputed to him was ambition, self-assertion amounting to treason, violent treatment of his enemies or of those whom he chose to regard as offenders. The impression we receive is of a character decisive, severe, resolute,—which would not trifle with church power or church responsibilities. In that age of many inconsistencies he very likely stretched his power in order to suppress current abuses; and he was not gentle to schismatics like the Meletians, who perplexed the situation and added to its difficulties.[1]

He did not quite live to see the result which was to reward his efforts and sacrifices; but he saw the beginning of that memorable close. And he left behind him an impression of consistent greatness hardly paralleled in the annals of the Church.

The supernaturalness of Christianity, as it was represented in Christian faith, so also claimed to be embodied in forms of Christian devotion and attainment. Athanasius was in the fullest sympathy with this feeling, and with the practices which it dictated. He was himself an ascetic; he enthusiastically sustained the claims of the monastic life, and his influence did much to recommend it in the West. The monks of Egypt were his friends and allies. Among them he found refuge when cities were no longer safe for him, and he could count securely on their support. His writings commemorate this alliance.[2] But the most re-

---

[1] Compare his outburst against the Emperor Constantius in the *Historia Arian. ad Monachos*.

[2] *Hist. Arianorum ad Monachos.*

markable monument of Athanasius' sympathy for asceticism is his life of St. Anthony. The authorship has been questioned, naturally enough; for the world of diablerie and wonder to which it introduces the reader seems incompatible with the greatness and the wisdom of the Father of Orthodoxy. But the evidence is not to be got over. And this must be said further: if the reader can assume for the moment that the strange stories were realities for Athanasius and for Anthony, then he will be touched by the gleams of good sense, of right feeling, of Christian humanity and kindness which come out, sometimes in the strangest associations.

The most important works of Athanasius are his tracts *de Incarnatione, Epistola de Nicœnis Decretis, Historia Arianorum ad Monachos, Orationes adversus Arianos*, and *Epistola de Synodis*. The life of Anthony has been mentioned already.

3. Three notable persons group themselves for the purposes of Church history as the three Cappadocians. Basil (A.D. 329–379) and Gregory of Nyssa (A.D. 336–395) were brothers; Gregory of Nazianzus (A.D. 326 ?–390) was the comrade of Basil during a prolonged student-life, and was his faithful friend in after years. All were distinguished defenders of the Church's faith by tongue and pen; while Basil attained additional eminence as an ecclesiastic, and Gregory Nazianzen as an orator and poet.

The grandmother of Basil was Macrina, a devout lady of Neo-Cæsarea. With her husband she suffered during the later persecutions, living for years in poverty and concealment. But the family possessed extensive landed property, which they resumed when the persecution passed away. Their son Basil, who studied law, married Emmelia (whose father had suffered in the persecution), and had ten children, of whom Macrina, Basil of Cæsarea, Naucratius, Gregory of Nyssa, and Peter (who became bishop of Sebaste) are known to us by name. The elder sister, Macrina, seems to have been the good genius of the family. She was led eventually to gather around her, at the family residence of Annesi, a company of devout women who lived a regulated religious life; and here she died in A.D. 380. Her brother Gregory of Nyssa was present, and has recorded the experience of her dying hours.

Basil, who stood next to Macrina in the family, aimed at intellectual and literary eminence, probably proposing to follow his father, who had combined high Christian character with eminence as an advocate and rhetorician. Leaving Cæsarea about the same time as his older friend, Gregory Nazianzen, Basil set out for Constantinople, while Gregory proceeded by Palestine to Alexandria. They met again at Athens, where Julian (afterwards the Apostate) was also pursuing his education. After long studies under various masters, Basil returned to Cappadocia at the end of A.D. 355. He came back elated with his own superiority as a man of exceptional cultivation; his reputation in foreign schools reached his native land before him, and he was provided with abundant opportunities, which he willingly embraced, for exhibiting his oratorical and other attainments. It was Macrina who confronted him with the question as to what was to be, what deserved to be, his aim in life; and the whole atmosphere of the family to which he had returned drove the question home. The result was a strong recoil from the worldly wisdom he had rated so high, and a resolution to live a life devoted to God. Probably about this time Basil was baptized. He spent about a year in visiting societies of recluses in Palestine, Egypt, etc., and finally chose a retreat near his sister at Annesi, but on the opposite bank of the river Iris. Gregory of Nazianzus was induced to join him there, but he soon returned to his own parents. Basil continued in retirement for five years, lived a strenuously ascetic life, devoted his property to ascetic purposes, promoted the formation of cœnobitic societies (as distinguished from the hermit life) throughout Pontus and Cappadocia, and planned the rule for such life, with its industries, its devotions, and its self-denial, which has continued to be fundamental in the East.[1]

See *ante*, p. 295.

Dianius, bishop of Cæsarea, having died in 362, Eusebius, a man of position and of piety, but as yet an unbaptized layman, was constrained to accept consecration, and filled the see for eight years. Basil was ordained priest. At the death of Eusebius he was chosen bishop, after a hard contest. Valens was by this time on the throne, and the later collisions of the Arian controversy were in progress. Basil had been early associated with some of those who were classed under the vague name of Semi-Arians. His own reflections led him to apprehend the truth and worth of Nicene doctrine, and his influence tended to detach from their party the more orthodox Semi-Arians, and to defeat the policy of those who were less so. This implied for him an active and troubled life. He became bishop in 370, and died in 379. He manifested extraordinary gifts as a man of affairs. In this connection he expected his friends to make every sacrifice for the cause to which he gave his own life, and some of them, Gregory of Nazianzus, for example, judged that he carried that principle too masterfully through. It must be admitted, also, that a certain hardness and impatience of temper appears, which may have served a useful purpose in connection with his commanding qualities, but which must also have added to his difficulties. The works of Basil which are most esteemed are the books against Eunomius and the treatise on the Holy Spirit; fortunately, also, three hundred and sixty-five of his letters have been preserved. Among others, he is to be distinguished from Basil of Ancyra, an older contemporary, the leader of the more orthodox Semi-Arians.

Gregory of Nyssa (335–395) was considerably younger. He shared in the gifts and also in the culture of the family, though he had not, like Basil, sought education in foreign seats of learning. Though he early became a "reader," he was for a time disposed to abandon the ecclesiastical career for that of a rhetorician, and earnest remonstrances, among others from Gregory of Nazianzus, were needed to recall him to the ecclesiastical life. Perhaps it was at this time he married; his wife's name was Theosebeia. His elevation to the episcopate was due to the energetic will of Basil, who, as metropolitan, felt the need of support from orthodox bishops, and induced Gregory to accept the obscure charge of Nyssa, ten miles from Cæsarea (A.D. 372), as unattractive apparently as it was obscure. Gregory was a loyal soldier in the war against Arianism, but he proved himself far from being a good tactician. Yet his fine personal character, and his ability in theological discussions, secured him a large share of consideration. He witnessed the death of Macrina in 380, was present at the council of Constantinople in 381, and seems to have lived until 395. His most important works are that against Eunomius, the Arian, and the *Sermo Catecheticus Magnus,* which reveals to us how he prepared catechumens for baptism. He has also left on record his impression of the dangers and disorders which attended the pilgrimages to the holy sites in Palestine.

The father of Gregory of Nazianzus (also named Gregory) was bishop of Nazianzus in South-West Cappadocia. He had been a Hypsistarian, but was brought back to the Church chiefly through the influence of his wife Nonna. A daughter, Gregoria, and a son, Cæsarius, completed the family. Gregory may have been born 325 or 326. He was educated at Cæsarea (where his friendship with Basil probably originated), afterwards at Cæsarea in Palestine, at Alexandria, and at Athens, where he again met Basil, and the friendship between them became more warm than ever. Gregory remained at Athens after Basil had departed homewards: he himself returned to Nazianzus, perhaps in 356. Then he came to the decision to consecrate his life to God's service, but without committing himself to withdraw wholly from the world. He spent some time, however, with Basil at Pontus; but returned to Nazianzus in or after 360.

Here occurred an illustration (one of several) of Gregory's shrinking from permanent official responsibility. His father was anxious to secure his help, and availed himself, in the spirit of those days, of some opportunity of practically constraining him to submit to ordination as a priest. Presently he fled, but soon felt it his duty to return.

From the time when Basil left Pontus and undertook responsible ecclesiastical activities in Cæsarea, Gregory appears as the friend whose counsel and practical aid are ever at Basil's service. Sometimes he felt that Basil's energetic will required of his friend sacrifices which were inconsiderate and excessive,—as in his committing Gregory to the squalid episcopate of Sasima, which he soon repudiated. But their friendship, though clouded a little, continued. His father died in 374, and Gregory inherited his father's estate at Arianzus (which he devoted mainly to pious purposes), and for a couple of years took charge of the vacant see. For three years more he lived in retirement in Isauria; then (after the death of Basil, 379) he felt constrained to respond to an appeal to take charge of the little flock of Nicene Christians at Constantinople. He nobly fulfilled this office, in the discharge of which he encountered various undeserved troubles. His five orations on Arianism (*Orat.* xxvii.–xxxi.) are a permanent monument of his power and eloquence in debate.

4. In the West we notice specially Hilary of Poictiers, Martin of Tours, and Ambrose of Milan.

Hilary of Poictiers (not to be confounded with Hilary of Arles, who belongs to the next century) is remarkable as the first in the West who wrote on the Arian question with freedom and power, and with a personal and independent grasp of it. At the same time, the events of his life placed him in circumstances to know at first hand the state of parties in the East, and the influences which moulded opinion there. Besides, while he firmly believed that the maintenance of faith in Christ was bound up with the prevalence of the Nicene Creed, he saw (like Athanasius) that men substantially orthodox might have difficulty about the terms of it; and therefore he was qualified to exercise a benignant and conciliatory influence. It is an interesting thing that we have from himself this statement: "I was a baptized man, and for some time a bishop, yet I never had heard the Nicene Creed till a little before I was exiled. It was the evangelists and the apostles who enabled me to understand *homo-ousia* and *homœousia*" (*De Syn.* 88).

He was born probably at Poictiers, early in the fourth century, was well educated, and perhaps well descended. He had married and was approaching middle life when he passed from a refined and thoughtful paganism to Christianity. The process was gradual, and was accompanied and completed by the study of the Scriptures, latterly more especially of the Gospel according to John. He was baptized, perhaps about 350, and set himself to live as an earnest Christian layman.

A vacancy occurred in the see of Poictiers in 353; Hilary was chosen to succeed by the popular voice, and so became bishop *per saltum*. He soon became involved in the Arian controversy as urged on in Gaul by Ursacius and Valens, and by Saturninus of Arles. Eventually he was banished by Constantius to Phrygia. He found much to displease him in the state of matters in the Eastern Church; but he was able to be of use in removing prejudices which embittered Eastern and Western men against one another. He became convinced that with many who were ranked with Semi-Arians an understanding was possible, and this conviction regulated his attitude thenceforward: that is, his object was, trusting such men as friends, to lead them to accept the Nicene Creed. Constantius allowed him to return to the West, and he reached Poictiers again in 362. While still in the East he composed his chief works, *de Synodis* and *de Trinitate*.

In the work of rallying and consolidating the Nicene party he made a long visit to Italy and Illyricum. In the former country he came into sharp collision with Auxentius of Milan, whom he disliked and distrusted. He finally died in Poictiers in 368

Hilary's statements on some points connected with the Incarnation have not been regarded as in harmony with the decisions of the third and fourth councils; but the ability and the effectiveness with which he discussed the questions that were under debate in his own day won for him great respect in the Western Church. Afterwards, the splendour of Augustine threw Hilary comparatively into the shade.

Besides the works mentioned above, and various smaller tracts, Hilary was the first in the West who regularly commented on a gospel (Matthew) from beginning to end. A certain number of hymns, in classic metre, are also ascribed to him. He touches also the history of monachism, as Martin of Tours, after he retired from military life, placed himself under Hilary's eye. Hilary's banishment, and Martin's expedition to Pannonia, to press Christianity on his father and mother, separated them. But both returned to Poictiers, and Martin founded a monastic society a few miles from that city. It was after the death of Hilary that Martin was elected to the bishopric of Tours.

Martin of Tours, born 316, was a native of Pannonia, of heathen parentage, his father being a soldier who attained the rank of military tribune. From his boyhood Christianity attracted him, and he became a catechumen; but he was obliged to enter the army, in which he served five years. During this time the incident of his giving half his cloak to a beggar occurred, and his baptism immediately followed. For some time he placed himself under the influence of Hilary of Poictiers; but with Hilary's approbation he set out for Pannonia to endeavour to convert his parents, while Hilary himself had to depart to the East, banished by the Arian emperor. Martin succeeded in winning his mother, but not his father; he suffered some persecution from Arians; and eventually came back to Poictiers, where he found Hilary, now returned to his see. Martin now set up a house for religious life in the neighbourhood of Poictiers, which is reckoned the beginning of such houses in Gaul. In 371 Martin's reputation led to his being elected, not without some opposition, to the vacant see of Tours, which he continued to occupy until A.D. 397; and he did important work in depressing and suppressing paganism in the district around Tours. In doing so he had the imperial laws to support him. But he operated mainly as a great religious character who impressed and overawed the general mind.

He came much into contact with Maximus, the usurping emperor of Gaul and Britain, who seems to have cherished a certain respect for religion, or at least appreciated the importance of winning support from religious persons. But Martin failed to obtain, as he desired, the preservation of the life of Priscillian, whose heresy he disapproved, but whose condemnation to death on that account he reckoned thoroughly unchristian. Probably the emperor judged it politic to gratify the assailants of Priscillian. Martin's conduct in the various stages of this situation leaves on the mind a strong impression of his right feeling and his courage. The date of his death has been disputed (397 or 400).

To Martin of Tours this interest attaches, that we see in him the embodiment of a lifelong religious enthusiasm, inspired and directed by the supernatural world of Christian realities as that was understood in his time. To realise it fully, to assert its incomparable claims, to anticipate in his own person, as much as might be, the eventual triumph over the secular and the transitory—this was his passion. The consequence, natural at that time, was that he selected the ascetic life as his pathway, and that he moves before us in a halo of fanciful supernaturalism, which he certainly largely believed in himself, and which the enthusiasm of his friends multiplied and enhanced. And yet, amid the deceptions which this implies, and along with some of the weaknesses which it fostered,[1] Martin must be credited with a Christian good feeling which breaks through all the rest and lends a charm of its own to his visions, his conflicts, and his other marvels.[2]

[1] *E.g.* a touch of arrogance, incidental to a man so favoured and admired.

[2] Martin's life is from the hand of a friend, Sulpicius Severus. The life was published in Martin's lifetime, and the *Dialogi*, which furnish a supplement, soon after his death. The humorous element which seldom wholly fails in legend, does not fail here. For example, Martin seeks an audience, at Treves, with Valentinian I., who is prejudiced and refuses to receive him. Martin makes his way, unauthorised, into the audience-chamber. Valentinian, offended, will not rise from his chair (as Christian emperors usually did in receiving bishops), "donec regiam sellam ignis operiret, ipsumque regem, ea parte corporis qua sedebat, adflaret incendium. Ita solio suo superbus excutitur, et Martino invitus adsurgit."

Ambrose of Milan inherited social distinction; he also had become a great officer of the empire; his capacity for affairs is approved by the whole history of his life. He is suddenly called to become the guide of the church at Milan. Once induced to accept the post, he instantly becomes a great churchman. The distinction of the Roman gentleman, the experience and the aptitudes of a governor, the dexterity and the courage of a man who has been throughout true to himself, lend themselves at once to the claims of the new position; and he is invested with a new greatness corresponding to the higher kingdom.

He was born about A.D. 340. His father had been Præfectus Prætorio of the Gauls, one of the highest administrative offices in the empire. He himself had become Prætor of Liguria and Æmilia, *i.e.* practically of Upper Italy. He belonged to a devout family; for though we do not know much of his father and mother, the character of his brother Satyrus, and of his sister Marcellina, who devoted herself to a religious life when Ambrose was still a youth, indicate the influences that had access to the household. Yet Ambrose had not been baptized when the time came for the church of Milan to call him to her service. He was known, however, to the people as a just and good governor, and as a man whose way of life made him trusted and respected.

Auxentius, the bishop of Milan, was an Arian.[1] In 374 he died. The election of a successor occasioned great excitement, for orthodox and Arian strove for victory. The story is well known how a cry got up "Ambrose for bishop," how all parties responded to it, and how Ambrose, after efforts to resist or evade the call, gave way. His baptism and his consecration were speedily arranged for and carried through.

The mark which Ambrose left on the Church was not due chiefly to his learning or to his speculative power. As

---

[1] Of what precise type we do not very accurately know. During some part of his episcopate, according to Hilary, he proposed to accept the Nicene Creed, but not sincerely. Auxentius was a friend of Ulfilas. One would like to know more of him.

to learning, he had the advantage of the education usual among the upper classes, which included facility in Greek. That enabled him to draw freely from the works of the Greek writers who were then recent (Basil of Cæsarea, perhaps, as much as any; also Athanasius). From this source his preaching and writing drew freshness, and it added a useful element to the theology of the West. As to the speculative side, he possessed a vigorous understanding, well trained in affairs. That might not qualify him to shine in the dialectics of the Arian controversy, but it gave him confidence in choosing his ground and deciding on the means by which it could best be maintained. His chief power was that of a great churchman, whose personal sincerity was never doubted, whose sagacity in affairs, secular and ecclesiastical, was conspicuous, whose courage never failed, and whose previous eminence, both of birth and of service, gave him a personal distinction which he knew very well how to make available. All this he brought to the service of Nicene Christianity. To name one department more, his ideas of ethics appear chiefly in his *De officiis ministrorum*. It leans much on Cicero, *de Officiis*, and so presents a Stoic scheme, harmonised with Christian ascetic. Here the characteristic dependence of the Christians on the philosophers for the scheme of their ethical thinking is plain enough.[1]

Ambrose occupied the chair of the church of Milan for three and twenty years. The power he exercised comes out in various striking incidents. During part of his episcopate he had to deal with Justina, widow of Valentinian I., and regent for his sons, who were still minors. Justina was an Arian, and, supported by the Arian convictions of her Gothic soldiers, she strove to advance the Arian cause. The view of duty which Ambrose took led him to concede to the Arians nothing that was the Church's. He had no physical force at his disposal; but he never flinched, and he thoroughly realised how a great community, pervaded by an intense enthusiasm, can daunt and paralyse an ad-

[1] Compare the dependence of Nilus (a younger contemporary) on Epictetus.

ministrative authority destitute of the elements of moral force. From Augustine we have a lively picture of the sensations, of the churches garrisoned by congregations at a high pitch of feeling, of the influence of hymns sung by responsive choirs, and, finally, of the enthusiasm connected with the discovery of the relics of Protasius and Gervasius, and by the miracles they wrought. This last, it must be owned, was the most questionable part of the whole business.[1] Ambrose could not be overborne; he maintained his ground. To the young Emperor Gratian he was a wise and disinterested guide, and in the unsettled and miserable period which followed Gratian's death he continued to do his utmost for the empire. When Theodosius the Great asserted himself in the West, a new prospect opened, for the emperor and the bishop had the highest regard for one another. Yet this was the time at which the bishop, on the news of the terrible massacre at Thessalonica, refused to admit the emperor to the communion, except as a penitent who made his penitence evident to all.

Ambrose introduced into the church at Milan musical methods (Antiphonal chanting is especially mentioned) which were previously unknown in the worship of Italy (Aug. *Conf.* ix. 7). Ambrose also signalised himself by Latin hymns, which could be sung, and which are still prized in the Church. They were composed in one form of the classic metres.

Personages whose lives extended into the fifth century will be referred to in another chapter.

[1] *Confessions,* ix.; *De Civ. Dei,* xxii.; Ambrose, *Epp.* xx.-xxii. The analysis of this business in Isaac Taylor's *Ancient Christianity* is still worth reading.

# CHAPTER XXVI

## Festivals, Church Services, and Sacraments

Bingham, *Chr. Antiq.* Smith and Cheetham, *Dict. of Chr. Antiq.*

### A. FESTIVALS

At the opening of this period three annual festivals were generally observed in the Church—Easter, Pentecost, and Epiphany. By the end of it Christmas also had come into general observance.

In the West, Easter was observed on the date fixed as proper by the bishop of Rome, and notified by him to the Western churches. In the East, Alexandria was recognised as the church best qualified to solve aright the difficulties of the reckoning, and accordingly the synod of Nicæa authorised the practice of that church to be followed.[1] Easter Sunday was generally the day from which everything else was reckoned, and it was itself fixed to be after the first full moon following the spring equinox. But which day of March should be reckoned the vernal equinox? In the West the 18th of March held this place, in the East the 21st. Moreover, the true day of the full moon—and in that connection the true day of the new moon (which had of course to be reckoned beforehand)—were calculated accord-

[1] Rome itself recognised the special resources of Alexandria in reckonings of this kind. Nevertheless, diverging customs and different cycles continued to create frequent misunderstandings, and in one famous case (A.D. 387) Rome celebrated five weeks before Alexandria. The custom at Alexandria was for the bishop to send out "Festal Letters" to announce the proper day for Easter. In the case of Athanasius some of these are preserved and possess historical importance.

ing to "cycles" of years, during which the varying relation of the moon to the sun's arrival at the equinox was supposed to fulfil its stages, returning at the end to what it was at the beginning. But none of these cycles was perfectly accurate, and different cycles (approximating to the facts with different degrees of accuracy) were in use.

The previous fast was now generally fixed at forty days. Six weeks corresponded with sufficient nearness, though as Sundays were not days of fasting, only thirty-six days of actual fasting were thus imposed.[1]

In the church of Jerusalem the custom had been introduced of allotting eight weeks to the fast. As both Sunday and Saturday (except Saturday before Easter) were non-fasting days in the East, eight weeks gave forty days of fasting. The period of the fast was recognised by the State, by suspension of criminal prosecutions. Also the Church held no feasts of martyrs during this time, and marriages and birthday feasts were not celebrated (Can. Laod. 52). The peculiar gaieties of Carnival are thought to have originated in Italy, and to have been connected with the Lupercalia.

In Passion week, "the great week," business was suspended, courts of justice and theatres were closed. Morning and evening service was held daily, works of mercy were specially appropriate, slaves were manumitted, and Government granted pardon to prisoners; also penitents received the Church's reconciliation. The week began with Palm Sunday, in remembrance of the entry of our Lord into Jerusalem. The Thursday (also known later as *Cœna Domini*) was the day on which our Lord instituted the Supper. The communion was celebrated morning and evening of this day, and it was the usual day for catechumens about to be baptized to repeat the creed publicly. Good Friday (*dies crucis, dominicæ passionis*) was a strict fast, and the communion was not celebrated.[2] The Saturday

---

[1] Long afterwards the beginning of Lent was carried back from Sunday to the previous Wednesday, which acquired the name of *Dies Cinerum*.

[2] Except in Syria, and in the evening; mostly in cemeteries, etc., in remembrance of the *descensus ad inferos*.

("great Sabbath") was signalised by the baptism of those whose catechumenate had been completed. Sometimes at this point, sometimes earlier in the week, a ceremony of feet-washing was introduced in connection with baptism, in which the bishop and clergy officiated (Ambr. *de Incar. sacr.* 3. 1; forbidden *Conc. Illib.* can. 48; and disapproved by Augustine).

During the night the Lenten fast closed and the joyful vigil of Easter set in, till cockcrow, when the Easter Communion was celebrated,—the newly baptized partaking. This time of religious excitement was not always free from scandals (Hieron. *adv. Vigil.* 9).

The week after Easter was marked by a succession of festal observances. The suspension of business, public and private, continued, and Jews and Heathens were obliged to submit to restrictions. The newly baptized wore their white garments for the last time on the Sunday following Easter (*Dominica in Albis*).

The fifty days after Easter were reckoned days of religious gladness and closed with Pentecost, commemorating the outpouring of the Spirit. The fortieth day commemorated the Ascension of our Lord, and in some places, for a time, this fortieth day was reckoned the closing day of the festival (*Conc. Illib.* can. 43). Both Pentecost and Ascension were reckoned great festivals.

Epiphany (on 6th January), which by degrees gathered around it various associations, had, as we have already seen, been associated with the baptism of our Lord. But as the manifestation through the Incarnation (associated with the star of the Magi) was the earlier and more fundamental manifestation of our Lord, this was now included in the significance of the festival, and became prominent. There is reason for thinking that the celebration of our Lord's birth at Epiphany continued in the West till A.D. 352. But in A.D. 354 the festival of our Lord's birth is carried back to 25th December,[1] which was already known, apart from Christianity, as *dies invicti Solis*. This date was received

[1] See ref. in W. Möller's *Lehrbuch*, i. 544.

at Constantinople A.D. 379. In A.D. 388 we find Chrysostom saying, " ten years have not yet passed since this day became plainly known to us." [1] The Armenian Church continued to celebrate the birth of Christ on Epiphany.

### B. ORDER OF SERVICE

The type of the worship of the Church is furnished by the chief service of the Lord's day. On great festivals, as at Easter, features were added to give greater fulness and emphasis; on minor occasions the service was simplified.

The term Liturgy denotes the performance of divine worship, alike as to matter and manner. It might therefore be written or unwritten, carried on with fixed forms of speech or with spontaneous prayers, or partly with both. In usage the word came to denote the form of service as written down, and different types of liturgy arose from the varying custom of different great churches.

The practice of free prayer certainly had place in the earliest churches, along with a conception of some order of service. But as always happens, the influence of revered teachers, and the recollection of sentences that seemed specially apt and edifying, would set a type. The more that forms multiplied and stages of the worship were distinguished, the more need would be felt of helps to assist the mind in conducting the service. And the more that divine service assumed the character of a rite of mystic power, the more important it would seem to secure that approved and authentic formulæ were uttered in connection with it. Perhaps the earliest collection of written prayers to which we can ascribe a date is that of Serapion of Thmuis.[2] This is not a prayer-book arranged in order of service, but a collection of prayers adapted to different situations in public worship, which could be referred to as need might require.

When our period begins, *i.e.* before the time of Constantine, many characteristic features had become fixed:—the impression of secrecy as proper in regard to Christian

[1] *Hom.* i.   [2] *Journal of Theol. Studies*, vol. i., Camb. 1899.

mysteries, the separation of the catechumen's service from the rest, the idea of offering in the Lord's Supper. The tendency to make the service more full and imposing was steadily at work, hence the local varieties of practice were discouraged, and the methods elaborated in the great churches imposed themselves as authoritative. These ways of ordering the worship passed into writing at dates which are uncertain, and great names were attached to them; liturgies of St Mark, St. James, St. Chrysostom, preserve, with later modifications, the usage of Alexandria, of Palestine, and of Constantinople. In the Latin world various types of services existed,—North African, Gallic, Gothic, Mozarabic, Milanese, etc. But the practice of the Roman church eventually prevailed; only later, and less completely in some places than in others. What concerns us at present is the practice of the fourth and part of the fifth century.

Worship began with the catechumen's service,[1] which included readings from the Scriptures,[2] with the sermon or exhortation. Singing was introduced at fitting points, and also prayer,—the most important and characteristic supplications coming at the close of this part of the service. Prayers, first in silence, then at the bidding of the deacon, and finally led by the bishop, were said for catechumens, for those possessed, and for penitents,—each class being separately dismissed after the prayer appropriate to it had been offered.

The second part of the service, from which all but baptized believers were excluded, began with a general supplication of considerable length. At a later period

[1] The division of the service into two parts was destined to pass away, chiefly because catechumens ceased to exist after infant baptism became universal, and when an adult population reared in heathenism no longer existed. Yet the ancient custom left its mark permanently on the Church's order of service.

[2] During the fourth century the practice prevailed of reading straight on through one book after another (*lectio continua*), but this was gradually interfered with and practically superseded by the reading of selected passages. But in this, and also in the number of lections read at each service, considerable variety existed.

some of the materials of this prayer were transferred to other parts of the service. Then followed the προσφορά, *oblatio*, offering, *i.e.* the gifts brought by the people (gradually confined to bread, wine, grapes, and wheat). These were collected by the deacons, and prayer was made that they might be accepted, and that blessing in return might be vouchsafed. Here followed in the East the kiss of peace: it was postponed to a later stage in the West. A portion of bread and wine being selected out of the gifts for use in the sacrament,[1] there was offered the prayer of thanksgiving, in which, with all creatures, the congregation thanked God for all His benefits, especially for the Incarnation and Redemption; and after recitation of the words of institution, the Holy Ghost was invoked to make the elements to be the body and blood of Christ.[2] The prayers went on to make supplication for the Church, the world, and also for all departed believers, including Patriarchs, Prophets,[3] etc. The Lord's Prayer followed.

All this prepared for the actual dispensation which began with the celebrant's announcement, *Sancta Sanctis* (Holy things for the Holy), with a response from the people, the Doxology, and the Hosanna. Then the congregation received in due order,—clergy, ascetics, deaconesses, virgins, and afterwards the general body of the believing people. Each received the bread from the bishop or presbyter with the words, "the body of Christ," and the cup from the officiating deacon with the words, "the blood of Christ, the cup of life." Singing (of Ps. 34) was used during the Communion. The deacon afterwards exhorted to thanks, and to prayer for a blessing on the participation; the bishop gave his benediction, and the deacon added "go in peace."

Leavened bread, *i.e.* common bread, was still everywhere

---

[1] This custom continued as late as Gregory I.

[2] This invocation was conceived to be the decisive act of consecration. The Western view, that the recitation of the words of institution occupies that place, seems to be later.

[3] The creed was read here, or in close connection with the dispensation of the elements; but not till late in fifth century: first at Antioch, A.D. 471.

in use except in Syria. There was no elevation of the elements in order to adoration, nor any idea of communion in one kind, which indeed would have incurred the charge of Manicheism. The communion of children, even of infants, *i.e.*, of course, of such as had been baptized, was recognised and practised: and they, like others, were expected to communicate fasting.

No uniform practice existed as to celebration of the Eucharist on other days besides Sunday. Daily celebration is mentioned;—also in each week Sunday, Wednesday, Friday, Saturday. Daily service, including the Eucharist with sermon, was customary in Lent, and also in the period from Easter to Pentecost. But some churches were content with Sunday alone, or Sunday and Saturday. It need hardly be said that no general attendance of the people (except in unusual circumstances) could be expected on any day but Sunday. Even on Sunday a great tendency on the part of baptized members to go away before the communion is complained of by Chrysostom and others. But there is no trace of celebration of the Eucharist by the celebrant alone, without the presence of other communicants.

Matins and Vespers afforded a daily opportunity of worship, Matins being held commonly before daybreak, so as to become a vigil. The 68th Psalm was considered appropriate to the morning, and the 141st to the evening service; there were prayers for the different classes of persons under the care of the Church, and often the Lord's Prayer. With a view to great feasts and martyrs' days, the vigils became very attractive and attended with much devotional feeling. There was much singing at these services. The ancient Greek hymn $\phi\hat{\omega}\varsigma$ $\dot{\iota}\lambda\alpha\rho\grave{o}\nu$ $\dot{\alpha}\gamma\dot{\iota}\alpha\varsigma$ $\delta\acute{o}\xi\eta\varsigma$ was a vesper hymn. The congregation joined in singing, sometimes by chanting at the end of the psalm, as sung by the psaltist or the choir, an *acrostichion* (or *akrotelcution*)—a verse which served as a sacred chorus; or they were trained to sing in unison, or by two divisions responding to one another. Development of hymns for use in public worship became notable at this time both in the East and in the West.[1]

### C. DOCTRINE OF THE EUCHARIST

F. C. Baur, *Vorlesungen über die Christliche Dogmengeschichte*, Leipzig, 1846, vol. i. 2ter Abschnitt, p. 410.

The views and the modes of speech already prevalent[2] continue in the present period; but all are emphasised and more largely developed. It is difficult to give a perfectly fair view of the doctrine really held. For the Sacrament expresses donation by the Lord and acceptance by us; it also connects in some way the sign with the thing signified, which last is eternal life in Christ, in some aspect of it. Now, as yet, the aim of writers for the most part is not to define, but to combine, these great ideas in every way that seemed fitted to awaken wonder and gratitude. In the ardour of worship one view runs easily into another.

In general, the view held is that in the Sacrament we have bread and wine and something more; and that something more, being the main thing, is often spoken of as if its presence elevated and transformed the bread and wine,—as if these lost their nature and ceased to be what they had been, merged, as it were, in that which is higher. Hence terms like μεταβολή, μεταποιεῖσθαι, μετατίθεσθαι, *convertere, transfigurare*, are used of the elements,[3] and they are used with increasing frequency; and very strong expressions regarding the real participation of the body of Christ, and its descent into our bodies, occur, for instance, in Chrysostom (*in Jo. Hom.* 45; *in Matth. Hom.* 83), Ambrose (*de init. Myst.* c. 8. 9), and Cyril of Alexandria. Yet when all the statements of these and other writers are compared, transubstantiation cannot be taken as their meaning. For the symbolical interpretation always occurs

---

[1] See well-known passage of Aug. *Conf.* ix. 6. See introduction to Trench's *Sacred Latin Poetry*, and that to Neale's *Hymns of the Eastern Church*.
[2] *Ante*, pp. 231, 232.     [3] Cyrill. Jer. *Cat.* xxii. 6.

again; also reasoning which implies that bread and wine retain their own nature, and that explanations must be based on that assumption.

Three phases may be distinguished. 1. That the body of Christ, which He took from the Virgin, is to be believed to be present and to be received. Not unfrequently this is referred to a special agency of the Holy Spirit. 2. The elements by consecration receive the same relation to the Logos which the body of our Lord holds (Greg. Nyss. *Orat. Catechet.* c. 37). 3. The symbolic view: the bread and wine are authentic signs of the body and blood of Christ. In the believing reception of them we are afresh incorporated or implanted in Christ's true body, the fellowship of the head and members (Aug. *c. Adim.* c. 12 ; *Tr. in Ev. Jo.* 26).

But the conception not only of a sacrament but of a sacrifice was now well established, not merely in reference to the gifts of the congregation, but in reference to the elements as consecrated. This offering was, in the first place, a pious commemoration of the one offering on the cross (Aug. *De Civ.* x. 5 ; Chrys. *in Hebr. Hom.* 17). But it was regarded also as having, by way of offering, value and efficiency of its own (Chrys. often). In this form the congregation was conceived to make its most effectual approach to God on behalf of the dead. As the Eucharist gave lively expression to the fellowship of believers, so in the offering they remembered the blessed dead; and having in an earlier age prayed for their repose, now the worshippers rather sought in this way benefit for themselves by the prayers of those saintly persons. But prayers for the dead in general, as well as for the various interests of human society, were offered specially in connection with this sacrifice. Also we find it administered when death was near as a *viaticum* (Aug. *Serm.* 172).

### D. BAPTISM

The ritual of baptism as it existed towards the close of the preceding period has already been sketched (p. 233).

From the time of Constantine more neophytes presented themselves, and baptisteries were enlarged. Yet the tendency to delay baptism also continued to operate; this was partly due to indifference, partly to a dread of undertaking the purity and strictness of Christian life, partly to the risk of falling into serious sin after the one forgiveness of baptism had been, as it were, expended. Constantine himself was not baptized until his last illness. In not a few cases of persons who must have looked forward for years to being baptized some time, the resolution to delay the administration no longer concurred with inward awakening: it betokened a decision to surrender themselves at once to the divine call.

Before actual baptism a period of preparation in the catechumenate was ordinarily required. To seek enrolment among the catechumens was an expression of the purpose to be baptized, and the acceptance of a neophyte in this character by the Church was equivalent to recognising him as a quasi Christian (*Christianum facere*). It was accompanied by ceremonies of signing with the cross, imposition of hands, a preliminary exorcism, and, in the West, imparting salt. The candidate was expected to be certified as to character, etc., by Christians of good repute,—clergymen often undertook this responsibility,—and candidates who had followed callings which the Church held to be questionable had to give them up. Slaves were expected to bring testimonials from their masters. The period to be spent in the catechumenate was not very definitely fixed. Some canons require it to be not less than two or three years (*Nic.* can. 2; *Illiber.* 42). But the practice varied very much according to circumstances. Persons who had been happily situated as to family connection and opportunities of instruction required less preparation. On the other hand, a long time might be spent in the catechumenate by those who shrank from the responsibilities, or, as they might view it, the risks of actual baptism. Catechumens who were taken in hand for special and final preparation, in order to be baptized at a definite and near day, were known as "*competentes.*" For example, those who were to be baptized at Easter might pass into this class at the beginning of the forty days' fast. They had now to be fully furnished with all the knowledge, theoretical and practical, that a Christian ought to have, and special exercises were enjoined with a view to chasten and discipline the soul, so that this stage of the catechumenate required patience.[1] The instructions were crowned by the communication of the actual words of the creed,[2] withheld hitherto because the tendency to treat Christian mysteries with careful secrecy was at this time in full force, and influenced the treatment of catechumens. In many churches the creed was recited by the catechumens in presence of the congregation at some stage shortly before baptism, but the precise stage varied. In large towns special clergymen might be set apart for this work of instruction or preparation.

Baptism in case of need could be administered at any time, but the regular administration of it took place at Easter and at Pentecost. Exceptions were naturally made for sick persons and for children, but as late as Leo I., and even as late as Gregory the Great, a disposition is evinced to confine the ordinary administration to the two seasons named. But in both East and West Epiphany became an additional baptismal season. And, in the West, Christmas, the festival of John the Baptist, and those of Apostles and Martyrs were also signalised in this way. It appears that for a time, baptisms of children were made to conform to those appointed periods of administration. After the catechumenate had passed away, and infant baptism had become universal, special seasons for baptism ceased to be observed.

Children even of Christian parents were not always or necessarily brought to baptism at this time. The cases of Basil (probably), Gregory Naz., Chrysostom, Jerome, and Augustine are only specimens. But the severe Augus-

[1] Greg. Naz. *Orat.* xl.
[2] With the formal *traditio symboli* it was usual to connect special sermons suitable to the occasion (specimens in Aug. and elsewhere). The final recitation by the candidates was the *redditio symboli*. Delivery and recitation of the Lord's Prayer also had a place.

tinian view of the state of unbaptized infants disposed parents to seek baptism for them, and the tendency to look on ordinances as beneficent charms worked in the same direction. Probably also the place conceded to Christianity as the public religion of the whole community operated in the same way. Infant baptism seems to have become already more general in the West than in the East. The presence of sponsors was connected with infant baptism, but they appear also in connection with adult baptism. Augustine reports it as usual for the parents, or, in the case of orphans, the grandparents, to present the children. But the substitution of sponsors prevailed. And as the relation between sponsors and those who in baptism entered on the new life took hold of men's minds, there gradually arose the imagination of the *cognatio spiritualis*. This entered eventually as an important element into the determination of forbidden degrees in marriage.

Considerable variations took place in the wording of the baptismal confession. The earliest, perhaps (see p. 73), was that short form which preceded the later and fuller Apostolic Creed; it is best known to us as the old Roman, but probably existed widely with little variation. Additional clauses were introduced in the practice of various churches (Aquileia, Spain, and Gaul) which did not materially alter its character. But in the East dogmatic discussions led to dogmatic amplifications, as in the creed of Cæsarea, and that of Jerusalem. These local Eastern creeds were gradually supplanted by the Nicene, though this in its genuine form could hardly have been quite appropriate for baptismal uses. Later than our present period the Nicene was supplanted by what was believed to be the Constantinopolitan form (that which is received as Nicene in Anglican and other prayer-books); and this form was for a time received for baptismal purposes in Rome and in Spain.

In connection with the act of baptism, the old renunciation of Satan, and the affirmation, in reply to questions, of faith and obedience, continued. In the baptistery the candidate undressed, was anointed with oil, again asked as to his faith, and baptized with threefold immersion, except in Spain, where one only was used. The account given of this Spanish peculiarity was that the one immersion expressed the essential unity of the Trinity, as against Arianism. The form of words which has persisted in the Greek Church is to this effect: "The servant of God (so and so) is baptized in the name of the Father, Amen, and of the Son, Amen, and of the Holy Ghost, Amen, now and ever more and to all eternity, Amen." In the Latin Church the threefold question of faith was mixed up with the threefold immersion. Afterwards milk and honey were given, as to a new-born child, salt also in the West; and anointing with chrism followed, betokening anointing with the Holy Spirit. In the East the imposition of hands continued to be part of the ceremonial of baptism; but in the West it was reserved to the bishop, and eventually developed into the rite of confirmation.

As regards the rites which should be reckoned to be sacraments, baptism and the Lord's Supper are mentioned by Chrysostom (*in Joh. Hom.* 84) and Augustine (*Serm.* 218) as the sacraments essential to the Church. But the term was used vaguely and with various applications. For instance, anointing the forehead of the baptized, ordination, marriage, are occasionally so termed. Augustine already suggests the later doctrine of "character" in connection with orders and with baptism. "Character" means something distinct from grace, imparted even when no grace is imparted, not lost when grace is lost. The communication of this "something" is ascribed to the two rites named, and in Romish theology to confirmation also.

### E. PREACHING

Preaching afforded a distinct line of influence by which the people could be moved; and the period before us is distinguished for its powerful and impressive preachers. From an early date, probably from the very beginning, exhortation by the presbyters in turn had followed the reading of the appointed passages of Scripture. This might to some extent continue. But addresses by individual presbyters, or by the bishops, now generally had their place at the catechumen portion of the service, *i.e.* before those who were not yet baptized were dismissed. Preachers could be heard, therefore, by those who had as yet no connection with the Church. Sometimes another discourse, adapted to believers, followed after others had withdrawn. In this period no layman could preach, however learned he might be. Presbyters were qualified for the function, but in some places they did not preach if the bishop were present. In other places the bishop, if present, followed up the presbyter's address with some words of his own. Bishops, in particular, were expected to instruct their flocks by preaching, and some of the more distinguished might preach twice on a Sunday, or, as in Lent, might preach daily. Matins and Vespers, as well as the chief Sunday service, afforded opportunities.

Instead of the homily in which the speaker commented on a passage of Scripture, suggesting the deeper sense and making edifying applications, discourses in regular form, composed according to rules of Greek rhetoric, came into use, and great reputation was acquired in this line by eminent preachers.

All manner of topics might be treated in this way, from praise of Christian celebrities to doctrinal and ethical instruction or polemical discussion. As the service otherwise proceeded chiefly in set forms, the sermon gave the opportunity to the minister to throw himself on the people, with direct appeal suited to their circumstances or to those of the Church. Great preachers were zealously attended, and produced deep impression. In Constantinople and elsewhere the habit of applauding striking passages had established itself.

It is pretty plain that while presbyters *might* preach, many of them did not feel able to discharge the duty; in many country places preaching might be rare, occurring only when the bishop or some qualified clergyman visited the place. Even in towns where the bishop's church was supplied with preaching, it would not follow that the same held of the other churches. Sozomen (vii. 19) makes the remarkable statement that in Rome neither the bishop nor anyone else taught in the church. Probably we must assume some exaggeration or misunderstanding.

In the East the brilliant age of preaching hardly survived the fourth century. Basil and the two Gregories were all of them remarkable in this department, the most distinguished being, perhaps, Gregory of Nazianzus. Chrysostom was greatest of all. His fine Greek culture and his natural gift of oratory were inspired by Christian devotedness and sincerity; and some of his sermons were unsurpassed as regards the immediate effect on the hearers. In the West Augustine introduced into preaching an experimental depth and a practical earnestness which gave a new character to preaching in that part of the Church. Leo I. of Rome and Cæsarius of Arles may be named as following him, though not with equal steps.

### F. OBJECTS OF WORSHIP

Middleton (Conyers), *Letter from Rome*, 1755; J. Dallæus, *adversus Latinorum . . . traditionem*, Genev. 1664.

The worship of saints originated chiefly from the regard paid to martyrs. As Christians commemorated the death of friends by family meetings at their tombs, it was natural that the graves of martyrs should be visited on the annual day by the Christians who had sympathised with their trial and victory.[1] The prevailing sentiment of the religious celebration on such occasions was the continued Christian fellowship between the departed and the survivors; hence oblations on their behalf were offered; in the prayer before communion the departed were remembered along with the living. For them repose was asked, and indeed participation in all Christian blessedness. By and by chapels and churches were erected over their graves. The impression

[1] Polyc. Mart., about A.D. 156; in any edition of *Apostolic Fathers*.

that such worthies did not stand in need of these supplications does not seem to have prevailed down to the end of the third century or later. Feeling on this subject became intensified when it began to be recognised that the martyr age had passed away. Christians were conscious that the heroes venerated by pagan countries and cities were for them replaced by the martyrs[1] who had overcome in the name of Christ. Their relics, therefore, were more than ever valued; for the saint's relics brought the saint himself near. And prayer for their repose began to seem less appropriate; rather prayer that, by their intercession, we might become like them, was the fitting attitude to take.[2] Direct appeals to the dead saints to intercede for us are sanctioned by the Cappadocians and by Ambrose. The tendency could not but be strengthened by the miraculous powers claimed for relics of such holy persons.[3] The appropriate place for relics in any church was under the altar. This whole development became very popular, and drew the people in large numbers to the festivals connected with it.

It was natural to ascribe like spiritual rank to others besides martyrs,—to eminent servants of God recorded in the New Testament and in the Old, and also to venerated names from the roll of worthies commemorated in the diptychs of each church. In this way a large choice of patrons was opened to worshippers; and a class of dead persons was set up about whom, as individuals, it was held that the Church on earth was entitled to assert their salvation to be certain. But no oblations, least of all the eucharist, were offered to saints. Augustine insists on this distinction in vindicating the growing veneration of the saints from the taunts of heathen controversialists.[4]

For a considerable time the Virgin Mary was not

---

[1] Eus., *Præp. Evang.* xiii.
[2] Aug., *de cura gerenda*, c. 13.
[3] Origen had made important suggestions in the direction of imputing to martyrdom a special virtue to save others. *Exhort. ad. mart.* 50.
[4] *Coll. c. Maximo.*

specially prominent in this connection. Her perpetual virginity was asserted with emphasis against those—such as Helvidius and Bonosus—who interpreted New Testament statements as implying that she was the mother of our Lord's "brethren."[1] Also, a foolish and distasteful speculation as to the birth of our Lord Himself was supposed to add something to her eminence, and received general approbation. Already in the second century her place in the order of grace was contrasted with that of Eve in the order of nature and in the history of the fall. Still, down to the fourth century church teachers continued to speak of her as not free from faults (Basil, *Ep.* 260; Chrys., *Hom.* 45). But in the fifth century Augustine declines to discuss that topic; and when the Nestorian controversy had fastened attention on her unique relation to our Lord, and suggested that above all other saints she had contributed to human salvation, the veneration of the Virgin began to receive an immense expansion. It is not certain that any church was dedicated to her name before that at Ephesus, where the council met in 431, and which was then newly built.

It was not unnatural that worship of angels as well as saints should be suggested, but as yet authorities are divided. Ambrose sanctions supplications to the guardian Angel, while Augustine rather perceives danger in it.[2] But the practice was destined to gain ground.

### G. PICTURES AND ANGELS

The early Church was jealous of associating with worship any representations of sacred persons or things. There were no such representations in churches till the fourth century; and when they began to appear, they met with discouragement.[3] Hence in the catacombs, where

---

[1] Jerome, *Contra Helv.* A.D. 303. Siricius (on Bonosus), A.D. 392, *Ep.* 9.
[2] Ambrose, *De Viduis*, 9; Aug., *Conf.* x. 43. See also Greg. the Great, *in canticum*, 8; Syn. Laod., can. 35.
[3] *Conc. Illib.*, c. 36; Eus., *Hist.* vii. 18; Epiph., *Opp.* ii. 317.

Christian art makes its earliest appearance, the embodiments of Christ are at first symbolical and allusive; and the same applies to the reliefs of Biblical scenes on early Christian sarcophagi.[1] Late in the fourth century and in the beginning of the fifth, pictures in churches begin to be described, which present the trial and death of martyrs with whom the church is associated; also Biblical scenes. These were not intended to be worshipped, but to instruct and impress. And just because our Lord is the object of worship, there is hesitation in representing Him. The cross occupies the principal place; or Christ is represented as the Lamb. The first presentation of Christ pictorially in a church as claiming the veneration of His people, is near the end of our period in the church of St. Paul beyond the walls, at Rome. Kneeling to sacred pictures falls later. But already we begin to hear of pictures which claim to be authentic portraits (by Luke, for instance), or to which miraculous powers are ascribed. The nimbus begins to encircle the head, first of Christ, then of saints. The usage was taken from representations of heathen gods, and also of the emperors.

The Nestorians were led by their theology to withstand the veneration of such pictures. They imputed to their adversary Cyril of Alexandria the blame of the new enthusiasm for having and venerating sacred pictures, and perhaps the date of Cyril may be regarded as an epoch in this matter. The great debate about it fell much later.

The subjects of this and of the preceding section reveal the tendency to popularise Christianity, by adopting objects and modes of worship hitherto regarded as characteristic of paganism. Tendencies this way had appeared much earlier but had, on the whole, been resisted. They were now becoming irresistible: and they were soon to be regarded as original and apostolic.

[1] Best seen in the Vatican Museum at Rome.

## CHAPTER XXVII

### DISCIPLINE

Greg. Nyss., *Ep. ad Letoium*, Opp. ii. 214. Basil Cæsar., **Epp. 53, 54,** 55, 160, Opp. iii. Chrys., *de Pœn. Hom.* ix. Augustin., *Serm.* 351, 352. Leo I., *Ep. ad episc. Camp.* 168. Socr., *Hist. eccl.* v. 19. Sozom., vii. 16. Bingham, *Chr. Antiq.*, Book xvi., Works, vol. vi., 1855, Oxf. Morinus, *de discipl. in adm. s. pœnitentiæ*, Par. 1651. G. F. Steitz, *d. Röm. Buss-sacr.*, Frankf. 1854. Loening, *Geschichte des deutschen Kirchenrechts*, i. 1878.

THE discipline of the Church has already been adverted to (p. 249). Known transgressions of a flagrant character incurred separation from Christian fellowship. The penitent was restored after open confession and a period of public humiliation, which tested the sincerity of the repentance, but which carried with it also, more or less, a sense of penalty inflicted for the sin. This restoration expressed the Church's charitable confidence that the penitence was real, and that the sin was forgiven by God and ought to be forgiven by her. Hence it came to be the symbol, or the outward seal, of Divine forgiveness as regards those sins; and as a tendency to lean on the outward and the sensible operated strongly in this age, the one was apt to be identified with the other. All the more therefore those Christians who were betrayed into flagrant transgressions which happened to remain concealed, if they afterwards came to serious thought, might infer that if the way of public confession and humiliation was God's way of forgiving great sins, they also must adopt it, in order to be sure of their own sincerity and of Divine pardon. It is true that public penitence in such cases must bring scandals to light that might have continued buried; and the matter is not prominent in the earlier period, although exhortations to confess are not wanting. On the other hand, it was not doubted that cases of great sin on the part of Christians did remain concealed, unsuspected, and unconfessed.[1]

As the Church extended after Constantine's accession, and the fourth century verged towards the fifth, difficulties in regard to discipline increased. The principles remained the same, but the churches had become more mixed. They included a much larger number of persons not amenable to principles which appealed only to conscience. Many sinners did not confess their sins, even when these were not absolutely secret; there was less scrutiny of Christian behaviour; serious Christians who became aware of flagrant sins of others did not inform the Church or the church authorities, partly, perhaps, because of the difficulty of producing conclusive proof, still more, probably, because the duty was felt to be invidious.

At the same time discipline came to be regarded less as a process for satisfying the Church—doing right to her sensitiveness as to her own character and calling—and more as a means of chastising, and so improving, the sinner. Both of these views had been combined before, now the second took the lead. The duty of confessing, with a view to forgiveness, cases of greater sins which had remained concealed, and of accepting in that connection the Church's penitential discipline, was still pressed. And besides, a larger range of sins came to be contemplated, especially from this point of view of benefit to the individual. For guilt might be incurred, and some special penitence might be called for in cases which did not amount to murder, or idolatry, or flagrant acts of impurity; and, on the one hand, church authorities might think it edifying to use discipline to restrain such lesser sins; on the other hand, penitent offenders might seek it for the peace of their conscience. This led to casuistical determinations: a given sin might perhaps be treated unreasonably if the full weight of the

---

[1] Tertullian's tract, *De Pœnitentia*, deserves to be read.

older discipline were imposed; but how much, then, should be reckoned appropriate? This gave new prominence to the distinction between simple ἀφορισμός, which did not contemplate so serious a separation, and might only entail the later stages of the old discipline,—not the earlier and more trying ones,—and the more serious separation, ἀποκοπή or παντελὴς ἀφορισμός, which might either be appropriate to a penitent who had very scandalous sins to confess, or might be denounced on impenitent men whose sins were public, to terrify and restrain them. The bishop decided these questions, sometimes deputing a cleric to examine and report.

The effect of this tendency of affairs was mixed. Some people complied with these admonitions, others disregarded them, others still accepted separation from communion without much concern.[1] For example, second marriages (which, of course, were public) were legitimate by the civil law; but, though their validity was not disputed, they were liable to a certain degree of disciplinary visitation by the Church's laws: people, then, who had contracted such marriages might accept exclusion from the communion and take none of the steps proper to bring it to an end. The same tendency appeared in other cases.

In this connection the old doctrine of "one repentance only after baptism" gave way. Ambrose and Augustine still cling to it, but in the East it probably passed into desuetude in the fourth century, and Sozomen frankly recognises the fact in the fifth.[2] In the West also the same change took place. The reason is plain; the sinner should be encouraged to repent more than once, of course with such precautions as may impress him with a due sense of his position.

According to the old discipline the Church knew what the sin was which had created scandal, and in connection with which the penitent was seen supplicating for restoration. Now the fear of scandal, through multiplying cases of con-

---

[1] Greg. Nyss., *Ep. ad Letoium*, Opp. ii. 114.
[2] Sozom., vii. 16.

fession, under the conditions just noticed, began to press more heavily on men's minds. Public penitence for sins, which otherwise would have remained unknown, tended to create scandal rather than to remove it. By degrees therefore steps were taken to secure that in cases of hidden sins, spontaneously confessed, the penitent in passing through the stages of penitence should be known indeed to have something on his conscience, but without disclosure (except to the bishop and his advisers) of what it was. The next step, better fitted to meet the difficulty, was to appoint the penitence itself to be transacted privately. It had still to be transacted to the satisfaction of the bishop, who closed the case finally by solemn prayer for forgiveness, and imposition of hands. But this naturally suggested the expediency of going a step further, and withdrawing the performance of penitence from observation in all cases.

In the West the sanction of private discipline and reconciliation appears first in the African Church from A.D. 360.[1] Augustine teaches that there are cases, of the graver kind, in which no man should be content with private reconciliation—those, namely, which separate from the body of Christ. Yet he owns that these sins were so numerous that the Church did not venture to excommunicate the laity for them, nor to degrade the clergy. He accepts the principle *Corripiantur secretius quæ peccantur secretius* (*Sermo* 82. 11, see also 351. 352).

In Constantinople, at the close of the fourth century, a presbyter was set apart to look after this department (πρεσβύτερος ἐπὶ μετανοίας). His business was to confer with those who had committed sins for which church canons prescribed discipline, and who desired to make satisfaction. A scandal happened to become public in connection with the administration of this office, and Nectarius (who succeeded Chrysostom in the see) was advised to abolish it.[2] The effect appears to have been,

[1] *Council of Hippo*, Can. 30; *Carthag.*, iv. (397); but see Hefele on those councils, vol. ii.
[2] Sozom., v. 19.

that while discipline still proceeded in the case of known transgressions, people were left to their own discretion as to confessing or not confessing sins which had not become otherwise known to the Church. The sufficiency of personal and private repentance in such cases was tacitly recognised.

Close to the end of our period certain bishops in Southern Italy, in the view, probably, of maintaining the old discipline, and of infusing into it some salutary pain, required penitents in their churches to read publicly a list of their sins. Leo I. reprehends this practice, and ordains a more prudent proceeding in such cases. The penitents, apparently, were still to appear publicly, but their sins were not to be published.[1]

In all these instances the range of offence contemplated is by no means that which is comprehended under the head of "mortal sins" according to the later theology of Rome. But in regard to such sins as were dealt with, the tendency to dispose of them more privately is gaining ground.

[1] *Ep.* 168 : *Ad Episcopos Campaniæ.*

# CHAPTER XXVIII

## AUGUSTINE

*Opera*, Benedictine ed., Paris, 1679, reprinted by Gaume, Paris, in 11 vols., 1838. The first vol. contains Augustine's *Confessions* and the two books of *Retractationes*, and the eleventh contains the old life by Possidius, bishop of Calama (d. after 437), and the very thorough biography by the Benedictine editors. (The new text of Aug. Opp. in the Vienna *Corpus Scriptorum*, with various readings and indices but without other apparatus, is not yet complete. Migne's reprint of the Benedictine edition is contained in tom. 32–47 of the Latin series.)

Tillemont, *Mémoires*, vol. xiii., 2nd ed., Paris, 1710; and all the Church Histories and works on Patristic. Böhringer, *Kirchengeschichte in Biographien*, 2nd ed., 11ter Theil, Zürich, 1878. Poujoulat, *Histoire de S. Augustin*, 2 vols. 8vo, Paris, 1843–1852. Bindemann, *Der heil. Augustinus*, 2 vols., Berlin, 1844–1855. K. Braune, *Monnica u. Aug.*, 12mo, Grimma, 1846. P. Schaff, *Life and Labours of S. Aug.*, London, 1851. J. Baillie, *S. Augne.*, London, 1859. Gangauf, *Metaph. Psychologie des Aug.*, Augsb. 1852. Flottes, *Études*, Paris, 1861. Nourrisson, *Philosophie de S. Augustin*, 2 vols., 2nd ed., Paris, 1866. A. Dorner, *Augustinus*, Berlin, 1873.

A very important study of Augustine is contained in Harnack's *Dogmengeschichte*, dritter Bd., pp. 1–244. See also specially Reuter, *Augustinische Studien*, Gotha, 1887.

AUGUSTINE requires a chapter to himself. From the time of his appearance on the scene, he dominates the history of the Western Church,—not that everyone agrees with his teaching or submits to his influence, but the whole situation takes colour and character from him. For that very reason it is impossible adequately to represent the man or his relation to his age; but something may be indicated.

He was born at Tagaste in Numidia on the Ides of November, 354. The father, Patricius, coarse, secular, impulsive, and no longer young, became a catechumen shortly before his death.[1] The mother, Monica, a young matron of twenty-two when Augustine was born, was an earnest Christian woman; her sincere devoutness was associated with limited knowledge, and she shared the popular superstitions; but one can gather that, along with her piety, a certain native right-mindedness and good sense sustained her influence over her son.[2] The family was not well off, but friends supplied the means necessary to enable Augustine to prosecute literary and philosophical studies at Carthage. He hoped in this line to open his way to what might be called, in modern language, University or Civil Service appointments. Carthage was a very wicked place, and Augustine tells us how it affected him. Religious impressions from his mother's influence had repeatedly touched him in his boyhood; but now as a young man a long course of wandering from the right way was before him.[3] Manicheism, with its doctrine of two principles, was vigorously pushed in Africa at that time, and Augustine became an "auditor" among the Manicheans. Their teaching included a sharp criticism of the Christian Scriptures, especially the Old Testament; it appealed to reason and experience, in the old Gnostic manner, for its conception of a radical strife between two principles in the world and in men individually. Its detail of doctrine and duty was certainly fantastic; but it was possible to regard this as only the form of a secret wisdom, which the disciple was

---

[1] He must have died before Augustine left Africa.

[2] Aug., *de Beata Vita*, vi. 10. 16; *De Ordine*, i. 31, ii. 45, etc., both in vol. i.

[3] Augustine does not spare himself. It is right to say, however, that he himself speaks of his recoil from the coarse revelry of his fellow-students (*Conf*. iii. 3). The main fact is that Augustine eventually formed a connection with a young woman (by whom he had a son, Adeodatus)—a connection which lasted for a number of years during which each was faithful to the other, so far as we know. Augustine had not accepted Christian obligations; and such a connection on the part of a non-Christian was not reckoned indecent or profligate. But Augustine had felt the claims of the Christian standard of life, which his mother exemplified; he had felt also the appeal of the philosophers to rise above sense; he was conscious of deliberately living below his ideals and transgressing his duty, in this instance especially.

eventually to reach, and in which the mind could rest. Under the influence of this hope it was that Augustine joined the sect. The step implied (1) his acceptance of their criticism of the Scriptures as unanswerable; (2) his sense of the need of a positive religion—if it was not to be Christian in the Catholic sense, it must still be a positive religion; (3) his apprehension of a conflict between evil and good which required to be strongly affirmed; and (4) he found a solace for his conscience and his self-esteem in the doctrine, that when he sinned it was not he who did so, but a certain alien nature in him, for which he was not responsible. He continued for a number of years to have some kind of connection with Manicheism; but as his mind ripened and as his expectations of successful insight continued to be disappointed, the connection became loose. Before the time of his departure for Rome (A.D. 383) it had become mainly nominal. He continued still to be a Manichean only until he should find something better.

But other influences operated. A perusal of a treatise of Cicero (the *Hortensius*—now lost—fragments in Orelli's edition) stirred his mind with the conception of a career not only of successful speculation, but of life according to wisdom, aiming at the highest and achieving it. This thought took possession of him with memorable force. It did not reform his life, but he cherished it as a glorious inspiration. The goal it propounded to him was not repudiated—only postponed.

After his arrival at Rome, where he occupied a post as teacher for a short time, and after his transference to Milan (A.D. 384), he read more largely in the philosophers, found no help in Aristotle, but was greatly impressed and attracted by the New Platonists. Their conception of the world seemed to bring him into a purer air, and some of their principles became a permanent element in Augustine's thinking. But ere long the claims of Christianity as embodied in the life and influence of the great Church began to press on him with fresh power. The magnitude and the fruitfulness of this unique phenomenon became more and more apparent to him: his mother had followed him to Milan; the preaching of Ambrose attracted him, and gradually dissipated the difficulties about the Scriptures which the Manicheans had taught him to cherish. He began to read systematically the Epistles of the Apostle Paul; he listened to what Christians told him of Christian conflict and decision. Meanwhile the personal question about his own will, and the goal to which his life should be directed, came home to him irresistibly; he felt that he had been all his life miserably and inexcusably wrong, and that he was still enslaved in the same snare. All this led to the memorable day (described in the *Conf.* viii. 8. 12) on which the struggle ended, and he passed into a new life. He was baptized by Ambrose at Easter 387: his mother died at Ostia near the end of the same year. In 388 Augustine finally left Rome and returned to Africa. He planned for himself a retired and meditative existence on his little inheritance at Tagaste. Ere long he was constrained to become presbyter and afterwards bishop at Hippo Regius (395). He died there in August 430.

Augustine's nature compelled him to think through his beliefs and his experiences; and no one in the early Church was more intent than he[1] on reducing to the unity of a coherent and consistent system the various elements of the worlds of nature and of revelation as these presented themselves to the believing and repentant man. He believed in the function of reason and in the unity of truth. But Christianity as it now possessed him was great and deep. Also in connection with it there came to him, on various lines, a wealth of suggestion and impression that placed him in relation to many forms of thought. He accepted with pious docility whatever seemed to be the teaching of the Church, not only as expressed in formal creed, but as embodied in the prevailing attitude of Christian minds, and in the prevailing sentiment of Christian life and worship. He appropriated from Scripture great thoughts to which he strove to do justice. He took something from all the

[1] A remark of Harnack's.

Christian schools of the West, from Irenæus, from Tertullian, from Cyprian, from Hilary, from Victorinus, re-shaping all he took. He had drunk deep of the Neoplatonic teaching; and while he guarded against its mystic pantheism, he had thoughts of God and of goodness, of the metaphysic of evil, and of the possible attainment of believing souls, for which he availed himself of Neoplatonic forms. Not even Augustine could really reconcile and unify these various elements; and he was fain to resort to dialectical plausibilities when true and inward harmony failed. This is one of the features which connect him with the schoolmen. But the strong grasp of the thinker compressed all at least into types that could live together in his mind; all was moulded into Augustinian forms which challenged the attention, which caught the ear and the heart of many generations. The central force of the whole lies in his consciousness of the difference between life without God in pride, self-sufficiency, and worship of the creature, and life with God in faith and love and hope. Of this last the decisive principle is Love—for Augustinian grace is the Love of God (*i.e.* towards God) shed abroad in the heart and making all new. Augustine's greatness has many elements; but chiefly it stands in the vividness, profoundness, and decisiveness of his conception of religion, or of the life of God in the soul of man.

Augustine's circumstances led him (after some essays meant to bring him to an understanding with himself as to valid method of thought) to write on the Reason of Christian Faith. At the same time he developed the argument against the Manicheans, and he found it expedient to resume this theme from time to time. His experience at Milan before and after his conversion had interested him in Arianism, and in the doctrine of the Trinity. His work on the Trinity is the chief monument in this department. Its characteristic is the strong assertion of the fundamental equality of the Divine Three, in virtue of their common possession of the unique Divine Nature and of all its attributes. On this subject, bating some refinements, the tendency at least of his thinking has been generally followed in the West.

His maturer thoughts on his own life and his conversion came out in the *Confessions*, in which he utters before God what he remembered and felt in regard to it—passing on in the later chapters to less personal meditations. His doctrine of the Church was elaborated in his controversy with the Donatists.[1] His conception of the world's history as a scene of divine permission and purpose—suggested by the difficulties of those who were losing faith in God amid the calamities of the time—is embodied in the great work *de Civitate Dei*, which occupied him occasionally during many years in the later period of his life. The questions suggested by countless phases of Christian discussion, and a great series of Biblical topics, are taken up in his letters, and in many tracts as well as in his sermons. The Pelagian and Semi-Pelagian controversies elicited during the last twenty years of his life the mass of writing which fills the famous tenth volume of the Benedictine edition and many letters and sermons besides.

All the practical questions connected with conduct, those which arose in connection with asceticism, with Christian morals, with discipline, must be added to these. For in one shape or other all the Christian interests appealed to Augustine, or were pressed upon him. We have seen how the Christian ethic had suffered in depth and thoroughness from the all but universal acceptance by Christian teachers of the form, and much of the substance, of the philosophic thinking upon virtue. It cannot be said that Augustine emancipated himself from all the effects of this state of things. And yet he left his stamp on every item of the discussion; for with him it was instinctive to seek the religious roots of ethical questions. In doctrine and in duty alike men were conscious that Augustine's way of thinking wrought a new depth and strength into Christian argument. Hence also his phrases fastened themselves on his readers; and many sayings that bear the mark of his mint have passed current among men ever since.

[1] See *ante*, Chap. XXIV.

What might be said of his attitude on the Pelagian question will come more appropriately in next chapter. Here we may notice the impression that a Manichean taint continued to keep possession of him after he had renounced Manicheism and had become a Catholic Christian. This has been often said, but it is ungrounded. The deliberate doctrine of Augustine, from the time he renounced Manicheism, laid a strong emphasis on the goodness of every created existence as it proceeds from the hand of God; and his theory of evil (the negative theory) was meant to harmonise with that position and to guard it.

The only plausible way of supporting the assertion is to say that Augustine's view of the solidarity of the race, and of the effects of the fall, introduces into human existence a fate operating adversely, as much as does the Manichean doctrine of an originally evil nature, the qualities of which can never alter, forming part of the constitution of man. But if reasoning of this kind is admitted, Manicheism may be charged on John Cassian himself. For he too admitted that without Christian revelation and ordinances men could not recover themselves from the effects of the fall, nor from the penal consequences of sin. Man in these circumstances can be described as subject to an adverse fate. But the fact of sin as it attaches to the race and the individual, and the effects of it, is a great subject of discussion which cannot be avoided in Christian theology; and the imputation of Manicheism gives no help towards a real understanding of the problem.

How far Augustine transcended the teaching of his predecessors—how far and in what respects he gave a new significance to Christian dogmas and struck a deeper and truer note of Christian experience—how far again he limited or perplexed his thinking, either by following too unreservedly single lines of thought, or (much more obviously) by the effort to harmonise the incompatible, and by the resolute purpose to make no breach with the authority of the Church,—these are topics involving a bewildering array of questions, and they cannot be entered into here. It is certain that Augustine is epoch-making, and that the theology and the religion of the Western Churches have never ceased to embody great results of his life and work. The central force lies in his realisation of Sin and Grace,—Sin as rebellion against God and separation from Him; Grace as love to God, a disposition in which the heart opens to all that is truly good—a disposition the beginning and continuation of which is itself the manifestation of the Love of God drawing near to heal and to hold communion with the undeserving and the undone. How from this centre Augustine surveys the elements of the worlds, natural and spiritual, in which he found himself, and with what success or failure he did so, is one of the historical studies which must not be entered on in a paragraph.[1]

The two books of *Retractationes* are a survey by Augustine of his own works, correcting or completing statements which, on reconsideration, he judged to be inaccurate or defective. They were written near the end of his life (A.D. 427). One or two more treatises, however, were issued later, and therefore do not appear in this review.

Augustine died of a fever while the Vandals were besieging Hippo. During the closing days he preferred to be much alone. The penitential psalms, written in large letters, were hung where he could see them. He died 28th August 430. (See note in Appendix.)

[1] The questions which may be raised regarding this central element in Augustine are very frankly suggested by Harnack (*Dogmengeschichte*, ii. Theil, 2 Buch, cap. iii., Weltgeschichtliche Stellung Augustin's als Reformator der Christlichen Frömmigkeit), and are well deserving of attention, apart from the success, more or less, to be ascribed to Harnack in dealing with those questions. The whole study of which this chapter forms a part is interesting, especially from the writer's recognition of the difficulty of mastering the complex problem presented by the thought and the influence of Augustine.

# CHAPTER XXIX

### Pelagian Controversy

The materials bearing on this subject are collected in the tenth volume of the Benedictine edition of Augustine's works (reprint by Gaume, Paris, 8vo, 1838). To these must be added the Letter of Pelagius to Demetrias, which is to be found in the Appendix to vol. ii. (p. 1380 of Gaume). The mind of Pelagius himself is best gathered from this letter. His *Libellus fidei* (in App. to vol. x.; p. 2343 of Gaume) is cautious and defensive. A commentary on the Epp. of Paul, no doubt by Pelagius,[1] is reprinted among the works of Jerome, vol. v. Ben. ed. It has been purged of passages too conspicuously Pelagian, but is still worth consulting. To the works of Augustine contained in vol. x. are to be added various letters, sermons, etc., of which a list with references is given vol. x. p. 2173. The *Commonitorium* of Marius Mercator is substantially reproduced in App. to vol. x., also the documents connected with the various ecclesiastical proceedings. The series extends over the Semi-Pelagian controversy to the Synod of Orange, A.D. 529. The works of Prosper are added in a third Appendix. G. F. Wiggers, *Pragmatische Darstellung des Augustinismus u. Pelagianismus*, Hamb. 1833. Julius Müller, *Pelagianismus*, Berlin, 1854. Fr. Wörter, *Der Pelagianismus, u.s.w.*, Freiburg, 1886. W. Cunningham, *Hist. Theol.*, Edinburgh, 1863, vol. i.

THE Pelagian controversy begins about A.D. 410, and its echoes were still audible more than twenty years after. Morals as against religion, free will as against grace, one may add, in a certain sense, reason as against revelation,

[1] Considerable retrenchments of the text must have taken place, but the commentary represents the mind of Pelagius, and is interesting in various ways. It shows, for example, how much of apostolic Christianity Pelagius could appropriate, under his own interpretation, and could adjust to his leading principles. It shows also curious results of the Pelagian position. Texts which Augustine interpreted as describing the inward grace which reforms the inward man, Pelagius habitually refers to the forgiveness of sins—because he

may be taken as a short account of the interests in collision. Yet not only were both sides in earnest, but on the Pelagian side there was, at the outset, no consciousness of disloyalty to the Church or to Christianity. The Pelagians accepted the creed and the ritual; and they believed they could strengthen a weak side of the Christianity of their time. Pelagius (who is reported as a native of Britain) was a monk, unattached apparently to any convent. The *stabilitas loci* was not yet enforced upon monks. He took up his abode at Rome before the fourth century ended, or at latest very early in the fifth, and he continued to live there till he fled, with others, from Alaric's invasion in A.D. 410. He was a devout and blameless man, chiefly anxious to see a more consistent standard of practical conduct among Christians. The virtues of the monastic life were the true Christianity; and these, or some distinct approach to them, should be visible in all Christians. Instead of this he found great laxity and worldliness, and for him the question was how to get the better of these tendencies. The reputation of Pelagius as a religious man, who had powerfully impressed people in Rome, reached Africa a considerable time before he appeared in that province himself.[1]

Pelagius, as we have said, accepted current Christianity: now, in his view, Christianity itself was intended to teach, to stimulate, and to reward morality, that, namely, which was recognised in the more earnest circles of church life. In order to this, one must enforce the maxim, "You ought, therefore you can." "When I treat of morals," he said, "and the principles of holy life, I make it my first business to establish the capacities of human nature, and to show what it can achieve: for the mind is apt to be remiss and

had a place in his system for that, while he looked with jealous eyes on Augustine's "grace." Hence in some places the commentary assumes the character of a superficial Lutheranism—though scarcely any two systems could be more opposed.

[1] It was known also that his thinking on some points differed from Augustine's. A bishop had quoted to him, from Augustine's *Confessions*, the well-known saying, "Da quod jubes, et jube quod vis." Pelagius repudiated the sentiment almost passionately.

slow to virtue, in proportion as it reckons itself unable, if it is left ignorant of its inherent power, or believes itself to have none."[1] The assertion of ability was to him the obvious way to sweep aside the pretexts on which men excuse themselves, and to force them to face their obligations. Nothing in Christianity must be taken in a sense that interferes with this fundamental view. Man is intrinsically able to do all that is required of him, if he pleases. But Christianity gives him additional encouragement and advantage, because it supplies an initial forgiveness in baptism, to those who require it, and because it promises, as the reward of virtue, not merely a happy immortality, but something more eminent which Pelagius distinguished as "the kingdom of heaven." We are not therefore "fallen in Adam": Adam's fall concerned himself. Undoubtedly men can throw away their possibilities, and they often do. But Christianity has come to illuminate and exhort us so that we may no more have any excuse for doing so. It agreed with these positions to hold, as Pelagius did, that without Christianity men may avoid sin and earn immortal blessedness, and that they often have done so. Christ therefore came not to quicken the dead, nor even to heal the (morally) sick, but to enhance the good of nature by clearer light and fairer prospects. These tenets indicate some influence from Eastern modes of thought deriving from the Apologists. And more than one circumstance in the history of Pelagius suggests that a connection with the East may have existed before his residence in Rome.

Various church historians have remarked that the confident assumption by Pelagius of complete power on the part of men to be what God would have them to be, indicates a mode of view which could obtain only in a mind free from the conflict of strong passions, in sympathy with moral order, and which had found that steady self-control could establish habits of conduct not easily overthrown. By such minds the effort to win their own respect and that of others by superior morality is often undertaken with sincerity, and

[1] *Ep. to Demetrias*, Aug. Opp. x. App.

the aim is felt to have a strong and growing attraction. But the consciousness of success, on Pelagian terms, requires for its existence a narrow and external view of duty. The breadth and depth of the commandment must be concealed, if satisfaction as to the fulfilment of it is to be maintained.

Among the adherents whom Pelagius attached to himself at Rome was Cœlestius, also a layman, apparently a man who led a studious life. He was more impulsive and disputatious than his leader. Somewhat later (about A.D. 418) Julianus, the young bishop of Eclanum, embarked in the same cause, and eventually parted with his See that he might maintain his principles. He, too, demanded well-regulated life, but conceived it less from the monastic and more from the philosophic point of view. He matched himself against Augustine in detailed discussion of the questions raised, and proved to be an able and resolute disputant.[1]

Pelagius and Cœlestius came into Africa about A.D. 410. Pelagius, after exchanging letters with Augustine, soon passed on to the East, but Cœlestius remained. He propagated his opinions with zeal, and also asked to be made a presbyter. Paulinus of Milan interposed with a challenge of the doctrinal opinions of Cœlestius: a council was called at Carthage, the explanations of Cœlestius were not reckoned satisfactory, and he was separated from the Church.[2] He departed to the East, and succeeded in procuring presbyter's orders at Ephesus. The discussion awakened interest in Africa, and Augustine began to preach and write on the subject—at first refraining from mentioning any names.

[1] The family of Julianus were among the private friends of Augustine,—and there were ties also with Paulinus of Nola. Paulinus was a poet, and we have an *Epithalamium* from his pen in connection with the marriage of Julianus, then only a lector, to a lady named Ia. The father of Julianus was also a bishop, named Memor.

[2] Errors charged—1. Adam was created mortal, and would have died apart from sin. 2. His fall injured himself alone. 3. Children are born in the same state in which Adam was before he fell. 4. The law as well as the gospel leads to the Kingdom of Heaven. 5. Even before Christ there were sinless men. These are the chief points, Mansi, iv. 289. Augustine was not present at this council.

Pelagius had found his way to Palestine. In 415 he was accused before a synod presided over by John of Jerusalem, and also before a synod at Diospolis presided over by Eugenius of Cæsarea. The real accuser was Orosius, a young Spaniard, who had letters from Augustine. The explanations of Pelagius were accepted by the council; the accusation therefore failed. At this point Jerome comes upon the scene. He did not hold, and probably did not understand, the scheme of Augustine, but he recoiled from the Pelagian extremes; he had a strong desire to cultivate the friendship of Augustine, and he seems also to have had some ground of personal irritation against Pelagius. He now came out with an attack on Pelagianism, which has not been reckoned of much importance.[1]

The African Church was not disposed to allow its sentence to be virtually reversed by these proceedings, which, besides, seemed to them to be due to misapprehension. In 416 two synods, at Carthage and Mileve, renewed the former judgment, and also communicated their proceedings to Innocent I. of Rome—who confirmed the sentence of the African synods. Innocent died in 417. A *libellus fidei* which Pelagius had sent him did not reach Rome in time. It came into the hands of Zosimus his successor, and Cœlestius also appeared in Rome, putting forth explanations which satisfied Zosimus. The latter thereupon issued a letter to the African bishops vindicating the accused, whose condemnation he ascribed to misunderstanding and overhaste.

On this, two African synods met in 417 and 418 and afresh defined their doctrine against Pelagius. A rescript from the emperor was also procured in the same sense, and subjecting the offenders to civil censure. Zosimus on this changed his attitude and issued an encyclical to all bishops, anathematising Pelagius and Cœlestius, and sanctioning the African teaching. This encyclical was to be subscribed by bishops, and those who refused were to be deposed and banished. Eighteen Italian bishops incurred these penalties, but not all of them persisted in their opposition. The most

---

[1] In a letter to Ctesiphon (*Ep.* 133) and in a *Dialogus c. Pelagium.*

distinguished was Julian, already mentioned; the most elaborate controversial efforts of Augustine's remaining years [1] were called forth by works of Julian, who maintained his ground with great acuteness.

The Pelagian leaders sought refuge again in the East, where they could find a large measure of indifference on the questions in dispute, and some positive sympathy. They are found in Constantinople in 429 when Nestorius was Patriarch. He endeavoured to befriend them—but the Emperor Theodosius II. saw no cause to interfere with a definitive sentence of the Roman see, and ordered the accused to leave the city. At the œcumenical council of Ephesus in A.D. 431, Pelagianism was condemned along with other heresies.[2]

Assuming that human salvation either involves a state of conformity to the Divine will, or that it is conditioned on this as a previous attainment, the question in hand throughout this debate has regard to the power of man to attain to this state, or the kind and degree of aid he needs with a view to it. If Christian religion is designed to promote the attainment, the question comes to be, What kind and degree of aid does that religion propose to impart?

The writings of previous church teachers presented a good deal of variety in the statement of these topics; for, in general, men had been content to oscillate between two poles, as the immediate practical object might suggest, without committing themselves to anything very conclusive.

---

[1] *Contra Julianum* and the *Opus imperfectum*, which was still in hand when he died.

[2] There is no reason to suppose that the council examined the subject; and it is generally said that the disposition to show the Pelagians some favour, evinced by Nestorius in 429, led to their being condemned along with him. The school of Antioch, however, really leant, at least, to the Pelagian side, and the leaders of the council may have perceived this. See Ἀπόκρισις πρὸς τοὺς ὀρθοδόξους in works of Justin Martyr, with Harnack's argument to affiliate it to the school of Antioch, and in particular to Diodorus of Tarsus. *Texte u. Untersuchungen*, N. F., vi. 4, Leipz. 1901. It is known that in A.D. 419 Theodorus of Mopsuestia wrote against Jerome's anti-Pelagian tracts, Πρὸς τοὺς λέγοντας φύσει καὶ οὐ γνώμῃ πταίειν τοὺς ἀνθρώπους. Fragments in Marius Mercator.

Both in the East and in the West the assertion of free will as a great Christian postulate, and as the correlative of duty, tended to sustain the thought of human competency. And in the East the Apologists and those who followed them had gone very far in this direction. And yet in the East as well as in the West, not only did the universal prevalence of sin come home to the Christian mind, especially to some minds, but Christianity as a redemption implied a fallen state, a relation to sin and death, which was dated from Adam's transgression. That, therefore, had influenced all that followed. But some made as little as possible of this bias in human nature, others dwelt on it more freely. In general a certain feebleness, darkness, and liability to the insidious attacks of evil spirits were the categories dwelt upon. It may be said that, as a rule, in making their statements men were chiefly on their guard against saying anything that might involve the assumption of an evil nature. Corruption or depravity of the race was therefore not willingly contemplated. Yet a taint of this kind is recognised by some writers; and a consciousness of it tinges the language even of those by whom a formal doctrine of depravity would not have been willingly recognised.[1]

In the West, however, as we have seen, a more pronounced doctrine of the *peccatum originis* had shaped itself. A bias to evil in human nature operating since the fall was recognised, and against this the grace of Christ was set as a counteracting force. This is prominent in the teaching of Tertullian, and it is distinctly recognised by others. This carried with it a deeper sense of the tragedy of human sin, and of the conflict of opposing forces in human hearts. Yet those who taught so did not conceive themselves to have parted with the great commonplace of free will. That continued through all earthly conditions, carrying with it always its possibilities of good and of evil. But in the West these

---

[1] In connection with this, note how Augustine himself sums up the obstacles to goodness in *ignorantia* and *difficultas*. *De Lib. Arb.*, quoted *De Natura et Gratia*, 81, and often elsewhere. Sometimes for the second member we have *infirmitas*.

wrought a deeper sense of the potency of evil in men, as needing succour, and more definite impressions of Divine grace as a positive restoring and upholding force at work within the soul. A little before the period of Augustine's activity, Ambrose had given fresh and emphatic expression to this conviction.

Pelagius considered this whole department of thought to be perfectly open,[1] as far as church authority was concerned; and he judged himself to be serving the interests of religion in striving to sway the Christian mind to one side—that which magnified human power and minimised the need of grace. Augustine regarded this as a denial of the very genius of Christian religion. Man's sin was separation from God into idolatry of self and of the creature: degrees of more consistent morality availed nothing to alter that: from God alone could come the reconciliation—the consent to God and the love to God which are decisive, which set a new goal and make a new life; and nothing less than this is the benefit which Christ brought to light. In the early stages of the debate much of Augustine's pleading is to this effect. Surely Christianity is a religion of men that pray: surely as Christians we find ourselves asking for that which we cannot achieve for ourselves, which we cannot earn and do not deserve.

Augustine had written in defence of free will against the Manicheans,[2] and he continued to maintain it as essential to moral responsibility. The whole scheme of Augustine presupposes and requires a real free will as the point of departure. But it appeared to him that the great fact of the fall must and does create new conditions for the sinning will: and free will so conditioned can never do the work of grace. Asserting the dependence of man and the supremacy of grace, Augustine accepted the full responsibilities of his

[1] *Libellus fidei* (in App. to vol. x. of Aug.).
[2] *De Libero Arbitrio*, Opp. i. One of the three books was written in 388, the second and third not till 395. The distinction between the unfallen will and the fallen is most obviously present to his mind in the last. See *Retract.* i. 9. The same subject was touched in an interesting way in *de Ordine*, written before his baptism.

assertion. The whole history of nature and grace required to be accounted for; and Augustine reckoned himself bound to present a concatenated explanation ranging over the immense array of questions. Each side, in fact, undertook to present a connected theory. That hitherto untried experiment, it seemed, could not be declined.

Not many Christians have followed **Pelagius**. But at three points in the remarkable system of Augustine vehement contest has arisen among men, on both sides earnestly Christian: 1st, as to the explanation and the effects of original sin; 2nd, as to the certain operation of grace; 3rd, as to the Divine election: and many experiments of theory have been tried to solve, or to assuage, or to veil, the difficulties. There seems no likelihood that this division will pass away; for though minor eccentricities, both of Augustinians and of anti-Augustinians, have ceased to be interesting, yet the tendency either way remains. This perhaps may be said, that those who feel bound to divide the work of grace between the two agents, God and man, must lean to the anti-Augustinian side, while those who recognise it as wholly God's, and at the same time wholly man's, sympathise with Augustinianism. As for Augustine, without undertaking to comment on his great system, it may be added here that in arguing it out he came at last to a point—the grounds of God's election—at which he recognised sheer mystery;[1] he continued, notwithstanding, to believe in perfect wisdom and goodness, but he could do nothing to expound them. Perhaps mystery should have been recognised and allowed to replace assertion and argument at earlier points of his scheme. For, indeed, the very first step—free will in a creature—is a certain fact, no doubt, but an inexplicable mystery. Yet a wise student will be thankful to the great masters who have overreached themselves in the effort to theorise the relations of the moral and spiritual world. At this point and at that, principles and analogies may have been strained in the effort to present a scheme. But thus only could they make evident to us what the reason of man

[1] There was another—the origin of human souls.

can do, and what it cannot do, in its efforts to serve the truth.

Pelagius and his followers developed their scheme as follows:—

I. As regards the religious history of the race—(*a*) No blame connected with the sin of the first man affects his children. His sin is imputed to himself alone. (*b*) No tendency to sin or moral taint is propagated from Adam to his descendants, as corruption. (*c*) Men, therefore, are now born in the same moral condition in which Adam was created: only temptations are stronger, influences tending to self-indulgence that appeal to the will have multiplied and become prevalent in the history of the race.

In connection with this part of the debate, an argument was derived from the practice of Infant Baptism, recognised throughout the churches and not contested by Pelagius. "Baptism is 'for forgiveness of sins'—why then are children baptized if they have no sins?" On this Pelagius maintained—(*a*) No sin, inherent or inherited, is remitted to infants in baptism, for infants have none. (*b*) Baptism does not confer on them "*salus*" or blessed immortality; for that is their destiny as sinless beings, apart from Christian benefit. (*c*) Baptism qualifies them for a superior and peculiarly Christian blessedness, distinguished as "the Kingdom of Heaven." (*d*) Also, it adds to the good of nature—*bonum naturale*—a special goodness, the *bonum sanctificationis*. (*e*) Pelagius eventually deferred to prevailing modes of speech by owning that baptism, even in the case of infants, is for remission of sins; but in this sense, that it introduces them into the order of things in which they shall find remission of sins to be a blessing made ready for them when they come to need it.

II. Holding all this, Pelagius laid it down as his central thesis, that as duty implies power, and men continue to be subjects of duty, free will, or the power of acting either way, in particular the power of doing right, exists after the fall just as it did before. Augustine's doctrine, he maintained, subverted free will, and so swept away the capacity of man for moral action. Pelagius distinguished—(1) the power of choice; (2) the actual choice, *e.g.*, of good; (3) the carrying out of that decision into practical concrete action. The first he said was God's gift; the other two depend on the first, but they are to be ascribed to ourselves. It is of ourselves that we use our power so. In opposition to Augustine he held that man can be without sin in this world. He can, though Pelagius did not deny that it might be difficult.

III. It had been not unusual to contrast our present state with that of man unfallen, and to paint the latter in glowing colours. Pelagius saw that the consistency of his system required him to resist this tendency. He maintained that our present state is not so very different from that in which Adam was created. It was to be believed that disease and death, natural incidents of corporeal existence, were incidental to that state as they are to ours; though possibly, if man had been faithful to his calling, immortality might have been conferred on him as a reward. Also as to his spiritual condition, though Adam was originally sinless Pelagius declined to regard him as other than equipoised between good and evil, so that free will might have play. Pelagius therefore taught practically no doctrine of original righteousness; man's great endowment was free will—which Adam possessed and which we possess, after the entrance of sin as before it. One point which came into the argument related to concupiscence, or the instinctive tendency to fleshly gratifications of various kinds. Pelagius maintained that this is simply natural, and that it existed in Paradise very much as it does now among men.

IV. Pelagius acknowledged grace, because the Scriptures speak of it; but the question was what he meant by it. And he seems to have filled up that category by setting down to it all benefits proceeding from Divine goodness, which he was still willing to recognise. In particular—
(*a*) The capacity for moral action, or the freedom of the will itself, is the primary instance of grace. This appears sometimes to be the fundamental thought of Pelagius. (*b*) The

law, or, in general, Divine revelation, including the teaching and example of Christ. (*c*) Forgiveness of sins: this meets a plain necessity, and, as it leads up to renewed hope of blessedness, it tends to establish men in goodness.

As to any such thing as an operation of the Spirit of God upon the souls of men, Pelagius did not say much, but he appears to have admitted the possibility of it, chiefly in connection with the understanding, guiding to correct knowledge. Such influence was not necessary in order to choose and do true good; and it was bestowed usually as a reward of previous effort in the use of natural power. These aids were not given, therefore, as indispensable to every good act, —*ad singulos actus*,—as Augustine maintained.

In connection with his doctrine of human nature Pelagius urged the virtuous attainments of various heathens, who were destitute of grace and yet manifested power to do what is truly good, or even to live without sin. Heathens upright in this life according to their light might have entrance into eternal life, like unbaptized infants, though not into the kingdom of heaven. He also maintained that many persons had attained to a life wholly free from sin.

In regard to the positions of Augustine:—

I. On the relation of Adam's sin to his descendants, Augustine taught—(*a*) The sin of Adam or his corrupted condition as a sinner is propagated to all his natural descendants. (*b*) This condition, and the subjection to the evil one which accompanies it, was to Adam and his descendants the punishment of the first sin: it is both *peccatum* and *pœna peccati*. (*c*) This state of things is accompanied by many other penal evils—disease, death, etc. (*d*) Man, therefore, as he now comes into the world is unfit and unable to do what is truly good. (*e*) This original sin is not anything substantial, or belonging to the substance of human nature: it is not to be conceived as a positive element in man, but rather as a negative one, a want.

II. In his early days Augustine had written largely in defence of the freedom of the will against the Manicheans, and he still maintained it. But he also taught that man, in abusing his freedom, lost his true or highest freedom, and his state now involves what may be called a certainty of sinning. Sin rules, and grace only sets men free. This is a consequence of responsible human action, in the person of our progenitor.

At the same time, a certain freedom remains; without a certain freedom we could not be the servants of sin. And a real freedom is exercised in the common actions of life. But freedom in the highest form, as power to keep God's Law in its true sense, we have not, until grace restores it.[1]

III. As regards the original state of man unfallen, Augustine had thought out a doctrine remarkable in various ways. (*a*) Man unfallen had a reasonable nature made in God's image. Hence Augustine ascribed to him a glorious eminence of knowledge and wisdom. (*b*) Man was free, so that he could sin indeed, but could also forbear to sin. This free will was a positive "*bona voluntas*," directed to what was good: and what man had to do was to persevere in the station in which he was set. (*c*) In order to man's maintaining his station an *adjutorium gratiæ* was required, and it was granted. For by reason of the frailty of the creature, man, even if purposing to persevere, is not able to persevere permanently by mere creature power. If this *adjutorium* had not been granted to him he would not have been responsible for falling. But he had it as long as he willed: it did not fail the willing mind.[2]

(*d*) In the original state the reasonable soul had full

---

[1] In the course of these discussions Augustine elaborated the thought, often reproduced since, that the freedom of moral action, the freedom which makes it moral, does not necessarily imply a capacity of actually turning from good to evil or from evil to good : nay, that the highest and truest freedom excludes for ever such a contingency. For God is most free, yet cannot sin :— and the saints confirmed in glory have secure and consummate freedom, in which they are for ever safe from falling.

[2] The aid of grace by which sinners are saved (the *salutaris gratia Christi*) is not suspended on the sinner's will: it is to be distinguished as the *adjutorium quo*; it actually produces the effect. The aid of the original state was only an *adjutorium sine quo non*: man lost this when he fell.—Students should attend to the full significance of the point indicated in the second last sentence of the text, *supra*.

dominion over the body and its desires: there was no conflict between appetite and reason. There was not therefore concupiscence in the evil sense of hankering after that which the deliberate judgment did not approve. Now, when man has rebelled against God, the appetites rebel against the reason. (*e*) Man, able not to sin, was placed under a constitution in virtue of which, by obedience, he could attain to the reward of a better state in which he should be confirmed against all possibility of sinning. The *posse non peccare* would have become a *non posse peccare*. (*f*) Although the constitution of men's bodies did not exclude the possibility of disease or death, yet so long as he continued obedient, in the right use of his freedom, man was secure against these evils: this was the *immortalitas minor*. It was a *posse non mori* corresponding to the *posse non peccare*: and if he had attained to the higher state of *non posse peccare*, that would have carried with it a final *non posse mori*, or *immortalitas major*. (*g*) Paradise was a place corresponding to this moral and corporeal well-being in its beauty and its order.

IV. As to grace: (*a*) Faith, which is the spring of all good works, is, in its beginning, middle, and end, the fruit of prevenient grace.[1] (*b*) Grace operates both on the understanding and on the will, enlightening the one, rectifying the other. The immediate influence of this grace enables us to choose aright, to desire and purpose the truly good action. So far, grace is *gratia præveniens*. Grace prevents us that we may have a good will. (*c*) Grace also is necessary to enable us to carry out and perform any good action; so it may be called *gratia cooperans*—grace working with the good will when we have it. (*d*) This grace is not given according to our deservings. (*e*) Whatever influence of a less decisive kind, tending to good, may exist, this grace certainly effects what it is given to effect: it overcomes

---

[1] Augustine had held for a time a different doctrine on this subject (a form of Semi-Pelagianism)—"quod credimus nostrum est, sed quod bonum operamur illius qui credentibus in se dat Spiritum Sanctum," but he had renounced it a number of years before the Pelagian controversy began.

the obstacles. (*f*) Even those who have this grace are not without sin in this life.[1]

These discussions naturally led on to the subject of election: it was only, however, in Augustine's latter days that active discussion on this point was forced on; though Augustine had long before reached his main position in regard to it. His developed doctrine was as follows:—(*a*) Human nature fallen must be considered as a *massa perditionis*;—it has no claim on Divine goodness, and might justly have been left to perish. Any mercy shown must by the nature of the case be absolutely sovereign and free. (*b*) God, whose purposes are everlasting, chose, without respect to human merits, whom He would deliver from condemnation and guide to blessedness: and this election is certain and unchangeable. (*c*) God uses the means of grace to effect His purpose. (*d*) Perseverance is a peculiar privilege of the elect, and of them only. (*e*) Men who are not of the elect may become pious, but not receiving the gift of perseverance they fall away. *Why*, of two men who seem pious, one should persevere and one should be allowed to fall, is a mystery known to God only. No reason can be assigned by us; but we are sure that His reasons are wise, just, and good.

Hence Augustine held that the death of Christ, as regards its full and designed efficacy, was for the elect, though some benefit by it accrues to others in various degrees.

At first it did not appear how much the controversy was to involve: at first the main point was that a penitent Christian man must surely live by the strength of another, not by his own. As time went on, however, the whole line of positions on either side came under debate.

While Pelagius on the one side and Augustine on the

---

[1] For a time Augustine had not cared to dispute the Pelagian assertion that some had lived without sin, if only Pelagians had been willing to own that in any such case grace was the cause to which this must be ascribed. But on further consideration he came to the belief that according to the criptures no mere man is wholly without sin in this life. At the same time he explained that in speaking of sin he would be understood to say nothing of the Blessed Virgin.

other, with their respective followers, contended for the positions which systematic consistency seemed to require, it is important to note the landmarks laid down by the representatives of the Church as those which Christians were called upon to recognise. Without at present anticipating later decisions we may refer for this purpose to the judgment of the African Church which was embodied in acts of a council in 411, substantially repeated in the greater council of 418.[1] They lay down:—

1. That Adam was not subject to mortality by necessity of nature, but death came to him as the penalty of sin.

2. Newborn infants are baptized for remission of sins, because the sin of Adam has passed on all his descendants, and this needs to be purged in the laver of regeneration.

3. The grace of God which justifies us, not only confers forgiveness of past sins, but gives strength against sin in time to come.

4. It does so not only by furnishing to us clearer light, but it gives power to accomplish what we see to be right.

5. It is erroneous to say that grace only renders it easier to do what could be done, though with more difficulty, by natural power.

6. The acknowledgments by holy men in Scripture of the consciousness of sin and need of forgiveness are to be taken as they sound, and are not to be explained away.

After No. 2 a canon is found in some copies which does not appear in others, condemning the assertion that there is a place of blessedness for infants who die unbaptized, although they are not admitted to the Kingdom of Heaven.

These, therefore, are the points on which it was reckoned important to make a stand.

Augustine's system of nature and grace made a profound impression on many minds. At the same time difficulties soon arose. About the year 427 his counsel was asked, in consequence of trouble which had arisen in a monastery at Adrumetum as the result of the perusal of one of Augustine's treatises. Some, asserting free will, were inclined to

[1] Hefele, ii. 102.

hold that God's grace is given according to our deserving. Others were disposed to reject free will altogether, and also to maintain that if salvation is by grace, then, in the case of those who are thus saved, no place remains for judgment according to works. Some also construed the doctrine of grace as leaving no room for remonstrance or rebuke being addressed to those who live in sin, or those who are falling back from a good life; for if they had grace they would not be as they are, and without grace they cannot be otherwise. With a view to all this Augustine wrote two tracts, *De Gratia et libero arbitrio*, and *De correptione et Gratia*.[1] In the latter he brought out very distinctly his views on Predestination and the Perseverance of the saints. These had long pertained to the consistency of his system, as it lay in his own mind, but had not as yet been so plainly argued out. This had the effect of bringing into the field a new set of opponents, who repudiated Pelagianism, and yet questioned keenly the connected system of Augustine. They were already restive under his teaching on the nature and effect of original sin; but the other doctrines, just referred to, seemed to them to require and justify a more emphatic protest. Those from whom it proceeded came to be known as the Semi-Pelagians.

[1] These are the latest of his works referred to in the *Retractationes* (Opp. vol. i.), which was itself written in 427.

# CHAPTER XXX

### SEMI-PELAGIANISM

Prosper Aquitanus, *Epistola ad Aug.* (Aug. *Ep.* 225). Hilarius, *ad Aug.* (Aug. *Ep.* 226, Opp. vol. ii.). Joannes Cassianus, *Collationes Patrum* (espec. xiii.), Opp., Vindob., 1886–88. Vincentius Lerinensis, *Commonitorium*, Migne, 50–53. Faustus, *De Gratia Dei et humanæ mentis libero arbitrio*, 2 libb., and *Professio Fidei* (in Migne, 58). Augustine, *De correptione et Gratia, De Prædestinatione sanctorum, De dono Perseverantiæ*. Prosper, *De Gratia et libero arbitrio (contra Collatorem)*. Acts of Synodus Arausicana, Mansi, vol. viii.; Hefele, ii., and Aug. Opp. vol. x. App. Jac. Sirmond, *Historia Prædestinationis*, Paris, 1648. Wiggers, *Versuch einer pragm. Darstellung d. Semipelagianismus*, Hamb. 1833. C. E. Luthardt, *Die Lehre vom freien Willen*, Leipz. 1863.

AUGUSTINE, against Julian, had copiously appealed to earlier writers to evince a Catholic consent in support of his teaching. Those quotations, however, applied mainly to the topics of the fallen condition of man, and the evil of concupiscence. If Augustine and his followers admitted a consciousness that sin and grace were handled in his works with an emphasis not reached by his predecessors, they held, at least, that the previous thought of the Church had furnished the outlines into which the deeper shading was thrown. Thus Augustinianism may be said to have offered itself as a revelation of the momentous significance of sin and grace, implied in what the Church had believed and taught, though hitherto hardly realised. But a number of persons in the churches of Southern Gaul felt it needful to protest against this. In that country, the seat of an ancient Roman civilisation, with lively aspirations after culture, there existed also a vigorous Christianity which laid a strong hand on the educated upper class as well as upon the people, was in sympathy with the church movements of the time, and felt able to take its own ground in theology. An ancient intercourse with the East had been continued or revived, which gave them access to Eastern ways of thinking.

Here an anti-Augustinian movement arose. Prosper in his letter on the subject to Augustine introduces the opponents as "servants of Christ at Marseilles." Near Marseilles there existed on the island of Lerins (Lerinum) a convent which had become influential. It was able to draw to itself a number of thinking men, serious in their Christian life, and devoted to sacred studies. This seems to have become the centre of the thinking and teaching which at a later time was called Semi-Pelagian. Besides, in Marseilles itself John Cassian had founded a monastery over which he presided.

These persons must have been dissatisfied with the strength of Augustine's teaching as to the incompetency of fallen man to the good which accompanies salvation; and we find them maintaining that the Epistle to the Romans had not been understood by church teachers, in relation to the constant and necessary precedency of grace, as it was understood by Augustine. But they no doubt shared in the sentiments of respect for Augustine's character and services, and in particular they had no wish to support the cause of Pelagius. Accordingly they seem to have refrained from audible criticism until the publication of the tracts issued by Augustine with reference to the difficulties at Adrumetum. Augustine's tenets on Predestination and Perseverance they were prepared to oppose as novelties, inconsistent with Catholic teaching. "They confirm their positions by the allegation of antiquity," Prosper reports; also, "they allege the doctrine to be unedifying and dangerous, unfit to be promulgated even if it were true" (Prosp., *Ep. ad Aug.* 3). In writing, however, they usually avoided referring to Augustine by name.

Prosper speaks also of the influence which these men

derived from their character and position. "They far excel us (the adherents of Augustine at Marseilles) in the piety of their lives, and some of them have great authority, having lately attained to the episcopate. Hardly any, except a few courageous champions of the perfect grace, venture to appear against them."

While these devout men at Marseilles were confident that Augustine's developed doctrine varied from the tradition of the Church, they were, at the same time, really opposed to Pelagius. They would not let human sinfulness be explained away as Pelagius and Cœlestius proposed. They affirmed that as the result of Adam's sin all men sin, and that no one is saved by his own works; all need the grace of God in regeneration (Prosper, *Ep. ad Aug.* 3). They recognised therefore in Christianity a real remedial force. They did not trouble themselves, like Pelagius, about the virtues of the heathen, nor, it must be added, about the condition of unbaptized infants. They explained the case of the latter by assuming that God foresaw they would not embrace the benefits of Christ's salvation if they lived: at all events both classes, being outside of Christianity, must remain unsaved. But Christian grace, which is needed by all and is offered to all, can also be welcomed and accepted by men by an act of their own will. God, it is true, can begin the work by powerfully and directly influencing an individual who is rebelling against Him. The instance of the Apostle Paul seems to have chiefly constrained them to make this concession. But ordinarily we must first individually and spontaneously respond to the general call, if we are to benefit by Christianity.

Throughout the scheme of these Semi-Pelagians one is struck by their adherence to the impressions suggested empirically by the practice of the Church and by the surface movements of Christian minds. A man unbaptized is as yet without grace. But such a man may seriously wish to be baptized, and may welcome the prospect of it. Such a man, therefore, is not whole as Pelagius said, nor yet dead as Augustine seemed to say: he is a man who is sick with an illness which he cannot himself cure, who can, however, welcome and appropriate the remedy. So, after baptism, grace is identified with the helpful influences a man *feels*, and it is conceived to come and go as the conscious moods vary. One cannot read Cassian without seeing that this superficial impression determines the method of his thinking on the whole subject.

The two most conspicuous and vigorous advocates of this theology were Joannes Cassianus, and at a later period Faustus, bishop of Reii.[1]

Schemes which avoid Pelagianism on the one hand, and Augustinianism on the other, may arrange their compromises in different ways; but Cassian and Faustus do not differ much. Faustus owns a doctrine of original sin more articulately and frankly than Cassian; but both defend the competency of " free will "; for though free will has been weakened by the fall, it can initiate the return to God, and can perform what is good. On the other hand, while Cassian teaches a real grace which enables the returning and labouring will to carry out its purpose, Faustus, while using expressions which seem to imply that grace must both precede and follow the decision of the will, has left it doubtful whether he holds real internal grace at all. Under the name of "grace," he seems to be thinking only of the moral influence of Christian truth and Christian institutions.

Cassian died two years after Augustine, A.D. 432. Faustus died not earlier than A.D. 492.

For a time, in spite of the efforts of Prosper, Semi-Pelagianism seems to have had very considerable vogue in Gaul. Under the influence of Faustus, in 472 and 475

---

[1] Besides these two and Vincentius of Lerins, are named Gennadius of Marseilles, Arnobius the younger, and the author of the tract *Prædestinatus* (which attacks as Augustinian the doctrine that sin is due to God's predestination). But it is probable that the whole cluster of devout men connected with Lerins, Hilarius, Eucherius, Honoratus, Salonius, Salvian, etc., sympathised with Cassian. The writings of some of them at least strike the reader by the absence of any echoes of Augustine's style. That was difficult to avoid on the part of men who read Augustine sympathetically.

provincial synods (at Arles and Lyons) rejected the doctrine of predestination, though they did not mention Augustine's name. The authority of Augustine, however, remained supreme among the Catholics of Africa, and it received the support of Rome also, in so far as the writings of Augustine (and Prosper) were mentioned with approbation, and by and by those of Cassian and Faustus were disapproved. On the other hand, a certain caution marked the Roman procedure. Augustine and his writings are highly commended, and opposition to them is censured, but without specifying the particular doctrines in which his teaching is to be followed; and *specific* censure of contrary teaching is avoided. In the beginning of the sixth century Cæsarius of Arles and Avitus of Vienne exerted a powerful influence in favour of Augustinianism, and were supported by Fulgentius of Ruspe in Africa, who represented a large number of African bishops banished from their sees by the Arian Vandals. At length, in the year 529, a provincial synod held at Orange (Synodus Arausicana II.) under Cæsarius, pronounced against Semi-Pelagianism. Cæsarius had been in communication with Rome, and had received papal approbation of a series of propositions drawn from the works of Augustine, or expressing his mind. These, twenty-five in number, were sanctioned by the synod. The propositions were opposed to Semi-Pelagianism, mainly as they asserted strongly the previous necessity of grace in order to the very beginning of the good will, that all good thoughts and works are God's gift, and that even the regenerate and the saints continually need Divine aid. The synod also summed up its teaching in a creed, the chief points in which are:—

1. That through the fall free will has been so weakened (*inclinatum et attenuatum*), that without prevenient grace no one can love God, believe in Him, or do good for God's sake as he ought.

2. Receiving grace through baptism, all baptized persons, with the aid and co-operation of Christ, can and ought to fulfil those things which belong to the salvation of the soul, if they are willing faithfully to exert themselves.

3. In every good work it is not we who begin, and afterwards experience Divine aid; but God Himself, no merits of ours preceding, inspires in us faith and love, so that we seek baptism, and after baptism are able with His aid to do those things which please Him.

They declared also their detestation of the doctrine that some by Divine power are predestined to sin.

In connection with these positions, they repudiated the Semi-Pelagian construction of Biblical instances which had been alleged as cases of faith and repentance beginning by natural power previous to grace.

It will be seen that the synod did not commit itself to the Augustinian doctrines of Predestination and Perseverance, nor did they say anything clearly about the certain efficacy of grace, or whether it could be frustrated by free will.[1]

Their teaching is thus inconsistent with Pelagianism and Semi-Pelagianism, for example with low Arminianism (that of Limborch), but not with evangelical Arminianism or that of Arminius himself.

As far as church authority is concerned, the Semi-Pelagian controversy may be said to have rested here.

### Note

It may be convenient to state in more detail the system of the Semi-Pelagians, as we have already stated that of Pelagius and that of Augustine.

1. In regard to the state of man unfallen, neither Cassian nor Faustus differed seriously from Augustine, though they did not set that state quite so high. But according to Cassian it was not subject to death, nor to toil and weariness, nor the other tokens of decay which mar our condition now. It comprehended a great fulness of knowledge, especially insight into God's nature and works. Also man was free, able to determine his own course; and he was in a state of moral perfection, which knew no rebellion of the flesh or strife between flesh and spirit. Thus he was in the image of God. Faustus did not differ as to this. He distinguished (with

[1] The same remark applies to the Augustinian theory of the propagation and imputation of Adam's sin.

various previous teachers) the *Imago Dei* from the *Similitudo*. The image, certainly in some of its features, is essential to man, the *similitudo* only the good possess. Faustus agreed verbally with Augustine in holding that, besides freedom of the will, man unfallen needed grace in order to be sufficiently prepared to persevere in goodness. But see below as to what Faustus meant by grace.

2. The fall. Both Cassian and Faustus agreed with Augustine that Adam's sin was essentially a sin of pride. And we, his children, are concerned in it in so far as it has entailed evil consequences upon us all. Faustus speaks of it as *peccatum originale, originale delictum, generale peccatum*. As to consequences:—

(*a*) This sin has brought to us death, toil, the various sorrows of life. Faustus speaks of these as not merely the consequence but the punishment of the fall.

(*b*) Cassian taught that mankind has suffered intellectually. The knowledge of God and of the Divine law was weakened, so that it became necessary for man's guidance that he should have a written law. Faustus does not go much into this.

(*c*) Most important are the moral consequences. Cassian traces to the fall a sickness or weakness of our moral powers, and a want of harmony, a contest, between the flesh (the appetites which seek created good) and the spirit. The will of man is now prone to be betrayed into vice rather than to adhere to virtue. This state of things is not in itself sin; it is only an inherited evil, or ill condition which involves danger. Man therefore is seriously weakened, but not so that he should be described as capable only of evil. Yet he cannot be without sin in this world.

Faustus seems to go further. He acknowledges original sin as a contagion that is positively evil, descending to us from Adam. Therefore also the remission of the guilt of it is an element in the blessing held forth in baptism. He agrees with Cassian in asserting that, notwithstanding this, a knowledge of God and a power to do what is truly good remained.

They agreed, therefore, in their teaching as to the power and freedom of the will. Fallen man has a power to will what is good, though not to carry it through without grace. He can deal with the *thoughts* that offer themselves, so as to entertain or reject them. He can make use of the opportunities which God offers. God must so far begin as to afford us an opportunity; free will has power to accept or reject it. So also it can withstand the evil one.

3. As to grace. Cassian holds that the external call affords us the opportunity of seeking salvation. Receiving that call, we can, and ordinarily we must, in the use of our own strength and freedom embrace it, will what is good, desire grace and labour for it. Then there comes an inward grace, without which we could not finally succeed. This grace influences both understanding and will, and enables us to carry out our purpose. Cassian spoke of it under four heads —Protection, Inspiration, Castigation, Exhortation. Though we do not, strictly speaking, deserve this grace, it never fails the consenting will.

Cassian was prepared also to admit the Augustinian doctrine, that with a view to being good we need this grace *singulis momentis* (= *ad singulos actus*). Only, he said, when God for any wise reason . . . for our discipline, withdraws grace, the will can *hold on for some time*, waiting and praying for its return.

This is the ordinary rule. But Cassian says that it is still open to God, if He pleases, to bestow influences of grace (unexpectedly as it were) on men who are not yet desiring grace nor purposing what is good. The conversion of the Apostle Paul is his example.

Faustus sometimes seems to express a higher doctrine than Cassian; for he says that grace must *both* precede and follow the action of the will. But then this grace appears to mean only the outwardly given truth and ordinance—what Cassian speaks of as the divinely-furnished opportunity. It has been doubted whether Faustus contemplates grace at all as a real internal influence of the Holy Spirit—as anything more than the moral influence of Christian teaching and institutions. If that be so, Faustus on this point stands nearer to Pelagius than Cassian does.

4. Predestination. In so far as this word designates the Divine purpose regarding the ultimate destiny of individuals, Cassian and Faustus alike held it to be conditioned on the moral decisions of men themselves. God's purpose is to save all, if all will consent to be saved. The views of Cassian on these points are to be made out chiefly by inferences and occasional allusions: in Faustus they are prominently inculcated and presented with the utmost decision.

Cassian does not meddle with the case of unbaptized Christian children, which was so prominent in Augustine's argument. As to the heathen and their virtues, he does not take a favourable view of them. What the school is concerned about is merely freedom of will to choose and to attain salvation under the light of Christian revelation and with the helps it offers. Beyond that, they do not seem interested in the question as to what man unaided can attain either of virtue or reward. The image in which Faustus rests as the key to the whole case is that of the sick man who cannot rise, but who on invitation stretches out his hand to lay hold of the helping hand which can raise him up.

Against the Semi-Pelagians the most pronounced controversialists were Prosper in the fifth century and Fulgentius in the sixth. Both may be said to have maintained the full doctrine of Augustine, though neither perhaps reveals a full mastery of Augustinian thought. The great point urged by them against the Semi-Pelagians was that all true good comes from grace, and therefore grace causes the very beginning of the good will. On this point the general sentiment of the Church could be more securely counted upon in support of their argument. At the same time the whole range of Augustinian positions, including those relating to Predestination and Perseverance, were maintained by Prosper and Fulgentius.[1]

---

[1] The works of Fulgentius, *De Incarnatione et Gratia* and *de Veritate Prædestinationis et Gratiæ*, in Migne, 65. The work of Cæsarius, *De gratia*, etc., is lost.

# CHAPTER XXXI

## ECCLESIASTICAL PERSONAGES

### [WHO SURVIVED A.D. 400]

JOANNES, commonly called Chrysostomus, was born at Antioch perhaps in A.D. 347. His father died early, and he grew up under the care of his mother, Anthusa, one of the notable Christian women of Church History. He was educated for the profession of an advocate, which he practised for a short time, and Libanius was one of the teachers under whom he studied. An early friend, of the name of Basil, to whom he was enthusiastically attached, was led to devote himself to monastic life, and this induced Chrysostom to adopt the same resolution. Under these influences he applied for baptism, and was ordained to the office of reader (A.D. 370). His mother's distress at the prospect of losing him led him to abandon for a time his purpose of leaving his home. But otherwise he practised the ascetic life. He now came under the instruction of Diodorus of Tarsus (*ante*, p. 375). Theodorus, afterwards of Mopsuestia, was a fellow-student. About A.D. 374 he went into seclusion among the mountains near Antioch, and continued to live a life of great privation until 380. His health was seriously affected; and he returned to Antioch, when he was ordained deacon in A.D. 381, and presbyter in 386. He immediately signalised himself as a preacher, and continued to sustain his great reputation in that respect during ten years. In the spring of 387 occurred the riot during which the statues of the Emperor Theodosius were destroyed. The outbreak was immediately followed by panic as to the consequences, and the bishop **Flavian** departed to the Court to implore for the people the emperor's forgiveness. In the interval of anxiety (three weeks) the celebrated Homilies on the Statues were delivered.

In 398 Chrysostom was consecrated to the see of Constantinople. There had been previously a large amount of splendour in the surroundings of the bishop, and much laxity among the clergy. Chrysostom revolutionised the appointments of the residence, and lived with great privacy and simplicity; a course which perhaps deprived him of friendships that it might have been useful to cultivate. He applied himself also to reform the manners of his clergy, and in doing so he raised up bitter enemies. Along with his great qualities a certain irritability attached to Chrysostom, and a disposition to break out with angry utterance on things and persons he disapproved, not only in private but in the pulpit. On the other hand, his devotedness to the duties of his office was conspicuous.

Eutropius was the man at the head of affairs who had brought Chrysostom to Constantinople: he turned against him when he found the bishop resolute to take his own course. Eutropius fell, however. Gainas, an Arian Goth, who succeeded him, quarrelled with Chrysostom over the question whether churches might not be ceded to the Arians. He also fell from power. But Chrysostom's enemies were multiplying. And Chrysostom was sometimes rash and vehement in his dealings with them. Eudoxia the empress, after some efforts to commend herself to Chrysostom, had joined their ranks: and the bishop was certainly less than prudent in the attitude he took with respect to her.

Reference has already been made to the dispute concerning Origen, and the manner in which Chrysostom was drawn into some connection with it (pp. 368, 369). When Theophilus of Alexandria appeared to lead a party against Chrysostom, his enemies felt that their opportunity was come. A string of charges, preposterous and frivolous, was got up against him, and a "council" of thirty-six bishops, chiefly Egyptian, deposed him. The emperor condemned him to banishment; but an earthquake during the night succeeding his departure impressed the general mind, so that he was recalled, and another council reversed the ecclesiastical decision. But the enmity of the empress revived, and Chrysostom was ousted and exiled in 404. Innocent of Rome denounced these proceedings, but was not listened to.

Chrysostom's first place of exile was Cucusus, in one of the ranges of Mount Taurus. It had an inclement climate, and was exposed to the raids of Isaurian marauders. He suffered severely on the journey from Constantinople, and partly also during his stay in Cucusus, from the effect of hardships on an elderly man whose health was broken; but his residence there was cheered by much friendship, as well as by his correspondence with devoted adherents in Constantinople. This did not please his enemies at Court; and after three years orders were issued to remove him to Pityus, on the north-eastern shores of the Euxine. This immense journey over a most rugged and inclement country was well fitted to kill Chrysostom, and everything was planned to increase the hardships. Three months of journeying found him and his guards near Comana. There the end came. One morning after starting they were obliged to carry him back and lay him in a chapel in which he had slept the night before. There he died, A.D. 407.

Chrysostom's correspondence during his banishment (especially with Olympias, a lady at Constantinople) throws an interesting light on his character, from the Christian humility and submission which pervade it. His last words were χάρις τῷ Θεῷ πάντων ἕνεκα. His most noted works are Homilies, Commentaries, and Letters; also his treatise, *De Sacerdotio*, and various tracts on the monastic life. Best edition is the Benedictine by Montfaucon, 13 vols., Paris, 1718. Venetian reprints, 1734, 1755, and, at Paris, 1734, and by Migne, 1863. Biographies by Neander, 2 vols., Berlin, 1844; Stephens, Lond. 1872; also Böhringer, vol. ix.

CYRIL of **Alexandria** has already been sufficiently

characterised (Chap. XXIII.). It is only necessary to add a few details.

After some years spent among the monks of Nitria, Cyril was ordained presbyter at Alexandria by his uncle, the bishop Theophilus. The latter died A.D. 412, and after a bitter contest Cyril became his successor. The early years of his episcopate were marked by extraordinary manifestations of his vehement and determined character in his conflict with Orestes, the representative of the emperor, and in the assault he made at the head of the Christian population upon the Jews. Shortly after, the lamentable event of the murder of Hypatia by a Christian mob and in a Christian church took place—an event which shed a sad light on the character of the passions which Cyril had awakened, or had failed to repress. In spite of this, however, Cyril possessed great qualities, and won for himself as a theological thinker and debater, and also as an ecclesiastical leader, genuine confidence and admiration. The Nestorian controversy occupied the latter part of his episcopate (see Chap. XXIII.). His management of the council of Ephesus was successful but not creditable; on the other hand, his writings in this cause have maintained their place as important theological documents. A few incidents of his latter days are hardly worth recording here. He died A.D. 444. Besides his Anti-Nestorian writings and his Commentaries, his answer to the attack of the Emperor Julian upon Christianity obtained celebrity. The Paris edition of his works, by Aubert, 1658, is considered the best. There is a life by Kopallik, Mainz, 1881.

THEODORETUS was a native of Antioch, born perhaps in 390, of a pious mother. He was educated at the convent of St. Euprepius, and was a friend, probably a fellow-student, of Nestorius. He became bishop of Cyrus (Cyros or Cyrrhos), in Syria, after 420. The main facts as to his relation to the debates of his time have been referred to in Chap. XXIII. Here it is only necessary to add that his personal character was attractive for kindliness, benevolence, and diligence in

the work of a rather obscure and poor bishopric. He was a
man of very considerable ability, was well-read, and knew his
ground as a defender of Antiochian theology, and he leaves
on the mind the impression of much sincerity and worth.
Besides polemical writings in the Nestorian Controversy and
his History in five books (covering A.D. 325-429), he wrote
Commentaries on books of the Old and New Testaments (that
on the Pauline Epistles is perhaps the most successful), a work
against heretics, one against the paganism of the day (*De
curandis Græcorum affectibus*), and a *Historia religiosa*, which
commemorates the virtues and the marvels of contemporary
and recent ascetics. His works by Schulze (including the
most important dissertations of Garnier), Halle, 5 vols.
1768-74, are reprinted by Migne, Gr. 80-84. Specht,
*Theodor v. Mopseustia u. Theodoret*, München, 1871.

ISIDORE of Pelusium (in Egypt), who died about A.D. 435,
is remarkable partly for the extraordinary number of his Epp.
which have been preserved (about two thousand—edited
by Schott), but also for the Christian purity of his character.
He wrote five books on interpretation of Scripture, Migne,
Gr. series, 78. Article by Niemeyer in Herzog u. Plitt,
*Real-Encycl.* vii.

JEROME[1] (Eusebius Hieronymus) was, after Eusebius,
the literary authority and celebrity of the early Church,
especially of the Latin branch of it. He was born at
Stridon, near Aquileia, perhaps about A.D. 346. His education was liberally cared for, and was completed at Rome.
He studied under Donatus, and became conversant with the
best Latin literature and a considerable range of Greek
authors also. After a period of careless life a more serious
temper gained ascendency, and he was baptized before 366.

---

[1] Earliest edition of collected works by Erasmus, 1516 fol. That by
Vallarsi, Verona, 1734-42, is reckoned the best, reprinted by Migne, 23-33.
Amédée Thierry, *Saint Jerome, etc.*, Paris, 1867. O. Zöckler, *Hieronymus,
u.s.w.*, Gotha, 1865. All Dictionaries of Biography, Ecclesiastical Encyclo-
pædias, works on Patristic and Church Histories are full on Jerome.

With his friend Bonosus he departed into Gaul, carrying with him a considerable number of books. On the way (at Aquileia ?) he made the acquaintance of Rufinus, and probably at this time the bent towards the study of ecclesiastical literature declared itself. He spent some years in Gaul, chiefly at Treves, but returned to Italy in 370. Here for some time he was associated with an interesting company of studious and devout men at Aquileia, much under the influence of Evagrius, afterwards bishop of Antioch. In 373 this company was scattered, and Jerome with Evagrius and some others departed for the East, journeying through Asia Minor to Antioch. Here (A.D. 374) he fell into a serious illness, during which he felt himself placed before the judgment-seat and condemned, as being a Ciceronian rather than a Christian. Under the impression of this dream or vision he vowed that he would study classical literature no more. The vow was not literally carried out; but he seems to have regarded this as a decisive crisis in his religious life; and in the autumn of the same year he went into the desert of Chalcis as a recluse. The life he lived here for five years is vividly described by himself (*Ep.* 22) as squalid, mournful, and agitated by mental conflicts; but it is certain that he was also busily engaged in study (including the acquisition of Hebrew). Towards the end of the period he found himself involved in theological disputes with other hermits, and he returned to Antioch in A.D. 379, spent 380 and 381 in Constantinople, and from 382 to 385 was at Rome. There, under the auspices of Pope Damasus, he began his important labours on the Latin texts of the Scriptures—revising the translation of the Psalms and of the New Testament, and commencing his systematic study of the Old Testament. To this period belong also various exegetical tracts, original and translated.

Jerome also became known at this time as an influential and vehement advocate of asceticism. He made the acquaintance of Paula, and became the centre of a circle of devout and studious ladies. In 385 strong feelings of antagonism to Jerome became manifest in Rome, especially after Blesilla, the widowed daughter of Paula, died, as it was said, from the effect of extravagant privations. Damasus too, who had been his patron, died, and was succeeded by Siricius, who showed Jerome no favour. In all such passages of Jerome's history the extraordinary violence and scurrility of his language, when he was opposed, occasioned a great part of the difficulties which he met with. He left for Palestine, accompanied by Paula and her daughter Eustochium. They arrived at Jerusalem in 386; and after a short visit to Egypt they settled at Bethlehem, where monastic institutions, hospices, and a church were built by Paula. Here Jerome continued for the remaining thirty-four years of his life.

He was occupied incessantly. The text of the LXX, Hebrew studies, the revised Latin translation (Vulgate), numerous commentaries, ascetic writings, guidance of his monastic associates, and an enormous correspondence filled up his time. There were also his controversies with Jovinian (*ante*, p. 298), with Rufinus (*ante*, p. 367) connected with the greater question of Origen, with Vigilantius. He acquired the friendship of Augustine, and took part in the Pelagian controversy. During this time invasions and troubles in the empire caused repeated and serious disturbance to the community at Bethlehem. Paula died in 403, Eustochium in 418; but a younger generation of his Roman friends supplied helpers to take their place (the younger Paula and a younger Melania). His literary activity continued almost to the end. He died in A.D. 420 on the 20th September. His Christianity, though devout, leant to the shallow, the legal, and the external type.

Jerome was an effective translator, a diligent but not an original or sagacious commentator. He had a most extensive acquaintance with books, and so with history; but his critical faculty was feeble, and modern scholars often complain bitterly of his untrustworthiness in detail, and his willingness to be thought to know when he is ignorant. Yet he possessed the genuine enthusiasms of a scholar, sustained by a most lively intelligence; and a certain real insight into the conditions on which the understanding of written documents depends, and a creditable fidelity in following out his own instincts in that respect, must be ascribed to Jerome, who is thus distinguished from all his contemporaries, unless we except Theodore of Mopsuestia. Jerome's sense of the importance of Hebrew had no support from the prejudices of his age. His admirable Latin style, his immense reading, his diligence, his real interest in ecclesiastical story, and the extensive service he rendered to literature and learning will always attract scholars, however his other qualities may repel them. He has no claim to theological power. His proneness to reckless violence in speech is an odious feature; and his self-consciousness was pronounced. In spite of this he had warm friends who never failed him. His letters and the prefaces to his commentaries are full of interesting matter. Erasmus delighted in him, and Luther strongly disliked him.

RUFINUS (Tyrannius Rufinus), b. 345, d. 410. In addition to what has been already said (*ante*, p. 366), it is only necessary to add that he was a native of Northern Italy, was baptized A.D. 371, and after some years spent in Egypt came to Palestine, where he was ordained about 390. After 397 he returned to Aquileia, but finally died in Sicily. His importance in ecclesiastical literature is chiefly due to his translations of Greek writers (from Origen downwards) into Latin, which served the useful purpose of familiarising Western men with the literature of the Eastern Church. He continued the history of Eusebius, and has left also an exposition of the creed, lives of ascetics, and several controversial works. His Christian friendship with the Roman widow lady, Melania, both in Palestine and in Italy, was a characteristic feature in his life, and was analogous to that between Jerome and Paula.

SYNESIUS, a native of Cyrene, and afterwards bishop of Ptolemais in the Libyan Pentapolis, was born sometime near 365–370. Possessed of an ample fortune, he pursued his studies at Alexandria (where he came under the influence of Hypatia) and Athens. He was a man of real ability, courageous and sympathetic, cheerful, active and romantic, happy in his married life, and devotedly attached to his children. He loved country occupations and field sports; and as a country gentleman of good estate he had every prospect of being able to gratify his desires. The main difficulty arose from his best qualities—patriotism, and sympathy with his poorer neighbours. Three years he had to waste at Constantinople pleading the cause of his native city. After his return to the Pentapolis he was kept in hot water, on the one hand, in opposing the stupidities and cruelties of local governors, on the other hand in striving to protect his neighbours from the devastating raids of desert tribes. A small organised force, well handled, would have sufficed to keep down these marauders; but the central government was too inefficient to provide for the defence of the province, and too jealous of local initiative to allow the provincials to defend themselves.

Synesius had left the schools a Neoplatonist, glowing with the devout enthusiasms of a system which could unfold itself, as the votary chose, on the religious or on the speculative side. Gradually, as the development of Christian influences and institutions went on around him, he seems to have drawn nearer to Christianity; and he had learned to respect and trust Theophilus, the bishop of Alexandria. But he still was undecided on some of the articles of Christian belief, when the bishopric of Pentapolis became vacant, and the people in the most urgent way sought Synesius for their shepherd,—a man whose character stood so high, and whose position and influence, reinforcing episcopal prestige, might do so much for them. Synesius was very unwilling:—besides his theological difficulties, he refused to separate from his wife; he foresaw the sacrifice of many innocent tastes and recreations, and the incessant pressure of many cares. Finally he left it to Theophilus to decide, who at once conjured him to undertake the task. Synesius accordingly became bishop, A.D. 409, and did his best for his people. He had already rather frankly declared for the method of an exoteric doctrine for the people and esoteric for himself; but he made this known to Theophilus and left him to judge. He was baptized and consecrated at Alexandria. Probably he did not survive the year 414. He left behind him a tract on dreams (written before his baptism), poems and hymns, a couple of homilies, speeches and letters. Synesius is a singularly interesting, because a singularly frank, sincere, and vivacious embodiment of the diverging influences of the time. It should be mentioned that his last letter is to Hypatia, full of affectionate and confiding regard; and his last poem is a prayer to Christ. (Clausen, *De Synesio Philosoph.*, Hafn. 1831. Aug. Neander, *Denkwürdigkeiten*, vol. i. 2nd ed. Kolle, *d. Bischoff Synesius*, Berlin, 1850. Dryon, *Études sur la vie, etc., de Synesius*, Paris, 1859. R. Volkmann, *Synesius von Cyrene*, Berlin, 1869. A full article in Smith's *Biographical Dictionary*.)

CASSIANUS, JOHANNES, has been referred to in Chaps. XVIII. and XXX. He belonged originally to the West, perhaps to Gaul, but early in his life resorted to Bethlehem, and participated in the monastic life there. Afterwards with a friend, Germanus, he spent ten years in Egypt, associating with monks and ascetics in the places he visited. Returning to Constantinople he was ordained deacon by Chrysostom, and afterwards passed to Rome. After 410 we find him in Southern Gaul. He founded a monastery at Marseilles, and also a convent of nuns; and there he spent the rest of his life. His two works, *De Cœnobiorum Institutis* and *Collationes Patrum*, have been described (pp. 297, 298). He wrote *De Incarnatione Domini contra Nestorium* in seven books, attacking also Pelagianism as akin to Nestorianism. He died A.D. 432. His works deserve the attention of students who wish to be acquainted with the religious atmosphere of that time. Latest edition, 2 vols., M. Petschenig, 1886–1888, in the Vienna series.

SULPICIUS SEVERUS, a native of Aquitaine, belonged to a

family of rank and fortune, and married a lady who was an heiress. After his wife's death, and while still only approaching middle age, he resolved to withdraw from the world, incurring in doing so his father's displeasure. He does not seem to have joined any monastic society, though he may have taken the monastic vow. His chief friends were Paulinus of Nola and Martin of Tours. Severus evinces a low opinion of contemporary bishops and clergy in Gaul, and sets against them the virtues and achievements of Martin. His *Vita Martini* was his earliest work (*ante*, p. 297). Next, about 403, he wrote his *Historia Sacra* or *Chronica*, which gives a rapid sketch of history from the Creation to the consulship of Stilicho, A.D. 400. There is reason to think that an interesting passage from a lost book of Tacitus can be recovered from ii. 30. The only contemporary, and so far reliable, account of Priscillianism is found in ii. 46–51, see also *Dial.* iii. 11–13. The *Dialogues* (about A.D. 405) are intended to supplement the account of St. Martin, who had now died; but one of the collocutors (i. 1–20) gives interesting reminiscences of his experiences in the East, including various monastic stories. Severus is quite worth consulting, and his Latin style, which is excellent, makes pleasant reading. Latest edition, Halm, *Sulp. Sev. Libri qui supersunt*, Vindob., 1866.

SALVIANUS, distinguished as a presbyter of Marseilles, probably belonged to Treves, and had relatives at Cologne. His family appear to have been people of condition. He married Palladia, by whom he had a daughter; afterwards they agreed to adopt the ascetic life, to the great irritation of Palladia's father, who had recently passed from paganism to Christianity, but could not sympathise with asceticism; he broke off relations with Salvian and his family. After seven years Salvian wrote to him an elaborate supplication for a renewal of friendship (*Ep.* iv.), with what effect we do not know. Salvian seems to have been in high repute as a religious and learned man; he acted as tutor to the son of Eucherius, bishop of Lyons (Eucherius having been a married man before he withdrew to monastic life at Lerins), and apparently could write with great freedom to him and to other men of ecclesiastical rank. His writings convey the impression of a sincere and intense mind, deficient in judgment. His views of the effect on human salvation of almsgiving, and in general of foregoing the use of property, are thoroughly one-sided and extravagant, and he shows no receptivity for the gracious aspects of Christianity. But his works are important as illustrating the social condition of Gaul, and partly also of other parts of the Western empire, *e.g.* the African province. His style is excessively cramped and artificial, and there are passages in his letters in which the sense seems to lose itself altogether in the effort after fine language. It is surprising how completely, alike in thought and phrase, he has escaped the influence of Augustine. Two treatises constitute his remaining works. One is *de Gubernatione Dei*, in which he undertakes to deal with the question as to the providence of God in allowing calamities to fall on the empire after it had accepted Christianity. It is suggestive not only with respect to the condition of the common people, the morals of the Gaulish gentry, and the action of the barbarians, but also as regards the imperial administration. The treatise called *Timotheus*, also *ad Ecclesiam*, also *Adversus Avaritiam*, begins oddly with an argument about pseudonymous writing—for he calls himself Timotheus, and gives his reasons. The substance of the book is an exaggerated estimate of voluntary poverty. There are also nine letters. Latest edition of works, F. Pauly, Vindob., 1883.

LEO I. was bishop of Rome from 440 to 461, and must have been born not far from 390. He is believed to have been a Roman by birth. His writings indicate no familiarity with the classics, and he was unacquainted with the Greek language. The teaching and the spirit of the Western Church possessed him. Various indications attest the importance of the influence he was already exerting as deacon and archdeacon. When Sixtus died Leo was in Gaul with a mission to reconcile Aetius and Albinus, Roman generals who were on the brink of civil war. The Roman church elected Leo to the episcopal chair in his absence, and quietly awaited his return. Before this time Cassian had dedicated to him his work against Nestorius (written at Leo's request) in terms of high respect and admiration. As pope, Leo brought into play principles which were matter of passionate conviction in his own mind. The place of Christian Rome as the centre of authority and unity, which, through the bishop, must be asserted and made effective throughout Christendom, was the thought that inspired him. A precedency granted by the Church to that see in honour of Peter came far short of his conception: the voice of the Lord Himself had granted the authority to Peter and to his successors. The firmness and consistency with which Leo upheld this principle entitle him to be regarded as the creator of the mediæval Papacy.

Leo bore himself in a manner not unworthy of these high pretensions. His interposition on behalf of his flock with Attila in 452, and with Genseric in 455, furnished two of the memorable passages of Church History; and it is not wonderful that legend stepped in to magnify what was in any view so imposing and so memorable. His firmness as a church ruler was illustrated in the case of Eastern Illyricum, which he claimed as subject to the ordinary jurisdiction of his see; and in the case of Hilary of Arles, whose alleged variations from canonical rule he claimed the right to correct in a manner which must be called not only dictatorial but extremely harsh. In this case an edict of the Emperor Valentinian III. came to his aid, which enforced in the most ample terms, throughout the West at least, all the authority which Leo claimed. In like manner he asserted his authority in Africa. It must not be thought, however, that Leo was willing in the interest of his own see to dislocate or to neglect the existing constitution of the Church. Rather, he claimed to be entitled to guard as well as to control it.

In the department of theology Leo became especially

notable by his attitude on the Eutychian controversy, described in Chap. XXIII. His letter to Flavian (*Ep.* 28) became especially famous, having acquired a kind of symbolical authority. As regards Western questions his influence was exerted against Priscillianism and Manicheism, and also against Pelagianism. As to Semi-Pelagianism, it is pretty plain that its characteristic features had no attraction for Leo: Augustine had exercised a very considerable influence upon his thinking. At the same time his is a cautious and qualified Augustinianism, so far as the question of grace is concerned.

Much more might be said of Leo; but it is a subject which rather belongs to the volume on *Latin Christianity*.

It may be added that Leo evinced a devout and, no doubt, a sincere faith in the Divine sanction of the claims he made, as well as the Divine aid on which he ought to reckon in the difficulties which he encountered. Some works have been ascribed to him on grounds which are quite uncertain. Those which are unquestionably authentic consist of ninety-six sermons and one hundred and seventy-three letters. They contain much which is illustrative of the age. Leo's style is forcible and dignified, but rather elaborate. The edition of Ballerini is still the best, reproduced by Migne (54–56). See also, among much other literature, Böhringer, *Die Kirche Christi u. ihre Zeugen*, i. 4; Milman's *Latin Christianity*, i. c. 4; Herzog's *Real-Encyclopædie*, vol. viii. (article by K. Müller); and a careful article by Canon Gore in Smith's *Biographical Dictionary*.

# CHAPTER XXXII

### Processes of Change

During the period which we have surveyed, the Church experienced rapid growth and various fortunes; and from these and from deeper causes change was always going on. We propose to enumerate some of the points to which this remark applies.

The Church's own consciousness as regards this matter of change cannot be understood, unless we have regard to an influence constantly operating. At each stage, whatever existed as approved or authoritative was apt to be regarded as having been so from the beginning; and even when men were aware that things at first had not been exactly so, they readily assumed substantial identity between past and present, and rated differences as inconsiderable. This is common in human history; for, indeed, every development comes out of *something* that existed before; there is therefore always *some* continuity; and that continuity can be represented to oneself as identity, virtual if not literal. But besides, in this case Christian piety contemplated the Church as something supernatural and divine; now that which has been all along divine must have been all along constant and steadfast; so that what men found it to be to-day, they presumed it to have been from the first. The Church undoubtedly showed a vital capacity for change; but each development, as it was accepted and approved, was consecrated; and each, as it became sacred, became also to the mind's eye a feature of an apostolic whole. Each, therefore, had a plausible claim to have been apostolic itself.[1]

---

[1] Compare the "Apostolic" Constitutions and Canons and the various early collections of laws; the traditions regarding the Apostles' Creed; the lists of

An inevitable change on the Church itself must be borne in mind. It begins with men and women who have been personally impressed by the Christian message and the Christian life: though at no time unmixed, it had at the outset the freshness and vitality to be expected in a society so constituted. In the following generations it continued to be recruited under the same influences. But its membership included also, in a growing proportion, those who had been born within the fold, children of Christian families. These had the benefit of Christian home influences, and many of them received the spirit of Christianity into their hearts; but of course it was not so with all: many of them were held to the Church in a traditionary way, and their Christianity was worn mainly as a habit of outward life. Besides this it is plain that, in spite of the unpopularity of Christianity and the persecutions that befell it, inducements existed which could persuade "false brethren" to seek and to retain a connection with the congregations.[1]

The writings of the New Testament grew into a settled form, and acquired more definite authority. From the beginning[2] the authority of the apostles was owned as of men commissioned and qualified to announce Christ's gospel and to build up His Church. Accordingly their writings were read publicly in the churches; and that seems to have been so from the earliest possible period. At first, however, the impression of the place and use of the Gospels and Epistles

---

bishops. So, after the ascetic and monastic life had made good its place, it began to be maintained that such had been the life of the earliest Church. Hieron., *Catal.* c. 11; Cassian, *Collat.* xviii. 5; *Cœnob.* ii. 5; Epiph., *Hær.* lxi. 4. This mode of view never prevailed absolutely, but it was predominant. Tertullian, and afterwards Jerome, were aware of particular changes; but that did not disturb their habitual mood, which carried back all but everything to the first days.

[1] These mixtures were inevitable. Speaking generally, however, it is reasonable to think that the lead lay with the more devoted and earnest men.

[2] The Old Testament writings had been taken over from the first, and their authority as the oracles of God was never questioned in the orthodox Church. Their divine character was all the more impressive on this account, that while primarily adapted to the Old Testament economy, they were held to be pregnant with New Testament meanings.

might be vague, and the need was not yet acutely felt of separating them conclusively from the wealth of traditions and of prophesyings still current on the one hand, and from the writings on the other, which issued occasionally from Christian pens, presumably not without some influence from the Spirit. But experience soon showed the importance of distinguishing the reliable monuments of apostolic testimony and of guarding them as the authentic monument of the Christian revelation.

The boundaries of the New Testament Canon were not finally settled; but a rapid agreement took place as to the greater and more important part of it. This amount of agreement had been reached at all events in the second century.[1] As regards the Old Testament, the allegorical principle of interpretation received a great development during our whole period. The whole Scripture was the record of Divine revelation; but the growing reliance on church authority, both as tradition and as legislation, divided the regard of the Christians and assumed a practical supremacy. As to New Testament teaching, the modes of thought of Paul, of 1 Peter, and of Hebrews are for the most part scantily apprehended and faintly felt. In the teaching of John the Logos doctrine was appreciated from the first, apparently, the other elements not till later.

The Apostle Paul sums up his gospel in such passages as 1 Cor. xv. 3–5, and the baptismal formula in Matt. xxviii.

---

[1] At what date in it is disputed. Cf. Zahn, *Geschichte des N. T. Kanons*, 8vo, 1888–1889, with A. Harnack's *Prüfung*, 1890. Zahn is apt perhaps to overargue his case; but surely a prevailing practical understanding as to *N. T. Canon* is seen operating at the middle of the century, at any rate. Six or seven books of our present Canon continued to be questioned or rejected in some churches, and some writings not now received continued for a time to be cited as "Scripture," especially at Alexandria. All along, however, the leading idea on the subject is that expressed by Clem. Al., *Strom.* vii. 16: Ἔχομεν γὰρ τὴν ἀρχὴν τῆς διδασκαλίας τοῦ Κυρίου, διά τε τῶν προφητῶν, διά τε τοῦ εὐαγγελίου, καὶ διὰ τῶν μακαρίων ἀποστόλων πολυτρόπως καὶ πολυμερῶς ἐξ ἀρχῆς εἰς τέλος ἡγουμένων τῆς γνώσεως. And again, of the heretics: Αἱροῦνται δὲ τὸ δόξαν αὐτοῖς ὑπάρχειν ἐναργέστερον ἢ τὸ πρὸς τοῦ Κυρίου διὰ τῶν προφητῶν εἰρημένον, καὶ ὑπὸ τοῦ εὐαγγελίου, πρὸς ἔτι δὲ καὶ τῶν ἀποστόλων συμμαρτυρούμενόν τε καὶ βεβαιούμενον.

expresses heads of faith. Yet the existence of a formed creed in the first century cannot be established; it would be easier to show ground for asserting the existence of short codes of Christian morality. Yet some well-considered way of expressing the mutual understanding of the Church and the neophyte at Baptism [1] was plainly desirable, and there is good ground for believing that a form of creed, suggested by the baptismal formula, but amplified, was in existence in the second century in many churches, and it may have existed earlier. This form varied in its terms a little more in the East than in the West, but not very much anywhere. It was a shorter form of what is now called the Apostles' Creed. What ancient writers call the Regula ($\kappa\alpha\nu\grave{\omega}\nu$ $\tau\hat{\eta}s$ $\dot{\alpha}\lambda\eta\theta\epsilon\acute{\iota}\alpha s$, *ecclesiastica prædicatio*) may be described as a somewhat more free conception of the way in which the Church regarded its faith, and of the way in which she was prepared to expound and apply it. The importance of definite and well-weighed utterance of faith was strongly impressed upon the Church's mind by the Gnostic controversy.

Gnosticism awakened many minds to the dangers which might assail the life of Christianity in connection with false doctrine. A watchful scrutiny of doctrine set in; and at the same time the maintenance of true doctrine became associated with the conception of the Church, as qualified and commissioned to give forth the proper watchword and to guarantee it. This seemed the shortest way to settle questions and to end disputes. Still further, in proportion as this gained ground, faith became a legal obligation; the creed was prescribed by authority, and it demanded obedience. It would be far from true to say that Christian doctrine ceased to be considered as the exhibition of objects which appeal to the heart, or as an intellectual whole which possesses the intellectual congruity of truth. But the legal and ecclesiastical view took precedence; and the attitude of mind expressed in the quotation from Clem. Al. (see last page), though never repudiated, became modified by

[1] Cf. Acts viii. 37, where the eunuch's confession is an interpolation.

reliance on the authority of the existing Church, as guaranteeing the fundamentals.

Meanwhile the Church, whose prerogatives were thus conceived, was itself changing its character. For a long time, indeed, the right of the membership to have their mind expressed and regarded in important matters was not denied. But the relative weight of the clergy steadily grew.

The distinction which came to be fixed in the terms presbyter and bishop, as names of distinct offices, was not at first of great importance, but its importance grew. The bishop, as the one person always prominent, became the centre of church life, attracted more regard, and was presently fixed on as the type or expression of the unity of his own church, as well as the natural guardian of the wider unity. He was the chosen leader; to rally round him was a point of loyalty. Important functions became fixed as proper to him only; and as perpetual chairman he could make his consent essential in nominations to office, and in many points of congregational or clerical action. When councils began to be held, the bishop, as the most representative as well as the most authoritative man of his church, was present in its behalf. In this way the rules which were adopted for the churches of a province came to be settled by the will of its bishops.

It may be believed that in many cases the bishop, as the chosen pastor of the church, was really its best representative—the man best able to express with insight and judgment the wants and the convictions of the flock. All that is suggested is that on various lines power accrued to bishops. That power assumed more and more the character of an official attribute; and as the power grew, a Divine origin for it was claimed and was conceded.

In connection with the importance attached to the witness of the churches, in ascertaining the original Christian teaching, the succession (real or supposed) of the bishops in great churches was cited, as we have seen. Hence it was suggested to be eminently their office to guard the true tradition; and, in fact, we need not doubt that Gnostic assaults had in various cases been repelled by the churches rallying round their bishops. This function was supposed to be accompanied with some grace tending to guarantee the right discharge of it; if not in the case of each single bishop, yet in the case of the episcopate.

The bishops, having such functions, appeared to the Christian mind to be carrying on the function of the Apostolate, and they themselves claimed that character; for the Apostles had been, after Christ, the authorities and teachers of the Church. Here the growth is very clear. Ignatius associates the Apostles rather with the presbyters; and he does not speak of succession, but of a kind of representation: the bishops suggest Christ, the presbyters the Apostles (*ad Magn.* vi., *ad Trall.* ii., iii., *ad Smyrn.* viii.). Irenæus, for the most part at least, includes the presbyters among the official witnesses of the faith. But soon the style of thought and speech which regards the bishops as the successors of the Apostles becomes fixed. Tertullian takes it in his larger and freer way; Hippolytus assumes it once; but Cyprian is technical, literal, and peremptory.

Again, the change took place by which the bishop, from being chief pastor of a congregation, came to have as his παροικία a city with a district around it, including various groups of Christians; various centres of worship came to be required and were provided; and the clergy were organised with a view to all this. The change raised the bishop still more decidedly above the level of the flock, and accentuated the difference of rank between him and the presbyters.

Once more, the bishop of the chief city of a province became official chairman of the provincial episcopate, and the depositary of some special powers, as metropolitan. Also, the bishops of some ancient and great churches, especially Rome, Alexandria, and Antioch, had a dignity and authority which, though vague, was more than metropolitan. Men in those great positions were really princes of the Church. So far the development had gone when our period ended.

But the inferior clergy also shared, in their degree, in the enlarging ideas of official power. It cannot be doubted that from the earliest period the office-bearers were an extremely influential class in the churches. They were so, because, as a rule, they were the most earnest, able, and energetic Christians. But things moved towards the final arrangement by which congregations were to be formed within most bishoprics, each with its presiding presbyter and clerical staff. The time of the clergy was fully occupied with clerical duties, and they became, as a rule, dependent on church funds for their support. Moreover, in connection with the functions usually fulfilled by each class, an idea was formed of the official power imparted at ordination. The presbyter, for example, in connection with the sacrificial view of the eucharist, shared so far with the bishop in what was fixed as the sacerdotal character. But what this as yet meant is vague: the time, too, when the indelible character of orders became the accepted view (so that even a deposed and excommunicated priest should not become a layman), it seems impossible to fix.

The Church, clothed with these features and associations, continued to be the object of the old faith. The Church is the assembly of Christians joined in the name and under the authority of Christ, reproducing itself everywhere. As often as they came together in this character the Christians (not then only, but then eminently) met their Lord, and expected His edifying grace. No conviction was stronger in the early Christian mind than that of the presence of the Lord to fulfil His promises. But with the perils and antagonisms of the Gnostic crisis it became a more anxious question How and Where shall we be sure of His saving presence? No doubt, in the fellowship of His Church. But were there not false churches, so false that in them men could not be sure—much the reverse? The discrimination of the true Church from the false ones became vital, because so many minds demanded to be at rest as to authentic contact with the saving forces of Christianity. In the circumstances created by Gnosticism it was a good practical answer to the question to say that the true Church was the company of churches throughout the world in fellowship through their pastors with the great historical churches. And the effective way to hold that ground was to affirm with growing vehemence that as the grace of Christ was certainly on the one side of the line, so it was wholly absent on the other. This view was rapidly extended even to churches which agreed with the great Church in doctrine, and had become separated merely on points of practice.[1]

Here especially, however, it is to be observed that various meanings combined under the one term Church. Augustine, for whom the subject had a special attraction, speaks of the Church, as others did, as the organised Society which lives in the administration and fellowship of the authentic sacraments; but yet again, and very emphatically, the true Church is the *corpus Christi*, the society of those who are vitally united to Him in faith and love, while the mass of unspiritual Christians (laymen and clergy) are not the Church, though in a sense they are in it; again, the Church is the *numerus electorum*—which does not quite agree with either of the former conceptions, for there are elect persons who are not yet in the outward fellowship— and there are persons at present holy who may fall away; again, the Church is celestial (an old thought which found in earlier days an almost Gnostic expression), only in the heavens does she reveal her true character, here she cannot. All these various lines of thought had held Christian minds. But whatever faith and whatever veneration attended any of these lines of thought, the concrete organisation which men saw—represented chiefly by the clergy—fell heir to all. That alone more and more stood for the Church in most men's minds. As the Church's state discredited the thought of an inwardly holy society, men clung the more to the belief in a society whose peculiarity and whose efficiency were outwardly guaranteed. So the Church—concrete and visible, acting and speaking through the clergy—fell heir to much of trust, veneration, and submission, which were indiscriminate and blind.

[1] Cypr., *de Unitate*, passim.

The eventual rejection of all Christianity which could not bow to the "Great" Church was no doubt due, in a large measure, to the sectarianism which has so often inspired those who claim to be Catholic Christians. But it was due also to the desire to grasp as strongly as possible the elements of security and rest that seemed to be afforded by the historical position of the "Catholic" society. "This is the Church that is right; it is so right that everything else is completely wrong." To take ground in this way, to emphasise the latter clause as well as the former, was felt to be both a comfort and a strength.

The consent, then, of the older and greater churches was a practical standard by which the true teaching should be ascertained. This was, in point of fact, a real guarantee at the end of the second century. But if so, it embodied (so men inferred) the permanent divine method, it was the proper authority in such cases.[1] As yet this principle was applied only to fundamentals, to the broad outline of the Christian faith; but by degrees it lent itself to much more detailed application. All these principles became more vigorous and insistent when it began to be possible to assemble general councils to speak for the whole Church.

In regard to the sacraments, it is not easy to make a reliable report; for definition implies discrimination, and sacramental language was always suggestive rather than discriminative.

The tendency here, as in other church relations, was to realise the spiritual through the outward and material, so as to find in the latter a definite and secure guarantee for the former. Therefore sacramental modes of speech were used with a growing tendency to assume that the outward rite carried inevitably the spiritual benefit.[2] Yet no thought-

---

[1] One great church, though entitled to influence and to respectful treatment, could not claim *authority* outside its own territory. Note the attitude of Cyprian and Firmilian towards Rome.

[2] With an interesting difference in the two cases of baptism and the eucharist. In baptism regeneration was the point of view—a change in the recipient; in the eucharist, the presence in some supernatural way of the Lord's body—a change in the elements.

ful Christian could forget that grace is a Divine presence and working, it is spirit dealing with spirit. For example, in adult baptism the spiritual blessing must relate itself to faith and repentance, which are inward and spiritual; hence the common language, which assumed or seemed to assume actual regeneration in all such cases, had to be taken, if men reflected, in a provisional sense. It was a judgment of charity. But as the proportion of infant to adult baptism increased, and that form of administration became the prevailing type, the tendency to literalism had less to control it. There could be no resistance or unbelief in an infant.

In the eucharist, also, the literal thought of a mysterious local presence of our Lord's body, and the more spiritual thought that the sacrament is an ordained sign and pledge of the gift to us of Christ, in the grace of His Incarnation and His death, to be ours,—could, either of them, be embodied in the sacramental language; and the second is the unambiguous sense of great teachers (Origen, Augustine); but the first gained ground, especially with those who welcomed every suggestion of sacred wonders embodied in the outward ministrations of the Church.

In regard to this sacrament, however, the development of the sacrificial view is the change which is more important.

As regards both ordinances, the tendency to enrich and multiply the ritual with a view to impressiveness, operated powerfully. It is to be kept in view that the application of a distinctive name (*sacramentum*, μυστήριον) to certain ordinances exclusively, had not yet become definite. The terms were used loosely, and could be applied to anything that was held sacred, especially if also it could be regarded as symbolic.

In rejecting Gnosticism and Montanism it was not necessary to *formulate* orthodoxy. Gnosticism was rejected, with all its fruits, as a perverse intellectual method, and Montanism as a claim to originate a new dispensation. Orthodox thinking was stimulated by these discussions as well as by the collision with paganism, and the Church felt so much the richer; but these treasures could remain in men's minds and writings, without being weighed and stamped. It was the third-century discussions concerning the higher nature of Christ that led to dogmatic precision in regard to propositions renounced on the one hand or affirmed on the other. Teaching definite enough, and in general harmony with the decisions of the third century, had no doubt been put forth earlier, *e.g.* by Justin and Irenæus; but we may admit that, previous to the discussions and decisions of the third century, the general mind of the churches had not reached so definite an understanding on the points involved. Yet students who follow the course of the Monarchian discussions will probably be convinced that the churches already *had* a mind which found utterance in rejecting the teaching of Sabellius and of Paul of Antioch. That is to say, that if, before these decisions, a definite doctrinal position capable of precise expression, had not yet been attained by the Church as a whole, yet an attitude of mind and heart existed, a way of thinking and feeling about Christ, which predisposed most Christians to reject alike the higher and the lower Monarchianism. Still it is to be observed that these decisions, as acquiesced in and supported by the churches, took two things for granted: first, that the Church possessed materials adequate to enable her conclusively to decide the questions raised; and second, that the points decided could be and should be treated as essential, so that conscientious dissidents on those points should no longer obtain a hearing in the Catholic Church. These positions were assumed as involved in the main question; but they were assumed silently, without being made matter of separate consideration. The writer is not disposed to question either of them; but the student may do well to attend to them in connection with the topics of the nature of church power, and the limits within which it should be exercised. The positions in question constituted, on the part of the Church, steps in the formation of a habit of action which was subsequently to receive great developments. At what point did that habit carry the Church beyond the bounds of legitimate and wholesome authority?

Down to the Council of Nicæa no creed but the baptismal one existed either for layman or clergyman: only, some Eastern churches seem to have introduced into that creed clauses or phrases which had a certain relation to current theological controversies. The best known case is the creed of Cæsarea, recited at Nicæa by Eusebius.

From the earliest period there must have been consultation with a view to mutual aid and mutual understanding between churches and between districts, and the organisation of councils to regulate this department was an obvious expedient. The religious revolution associated with the name of Constantine rendered it possible to assemble at Nicæa a council which could claim to represent the Christian Church at large. In the chapter occupied with that subject attention has been directed to the tendency of such a council to concentrate and crystallise a mass of sentiment about the Church, and to give a decisive direction to men's thoughts about the Church's competency in the field of Christian truth. What has been said need not be repeated here.

It might be thought likely that the craft and passion, the intrigue and the violence which ere long were conspicuous in the management of councils, would undermine their authority. But the set which men's minds had taken, and the craving for such an authority in order to complete the structure in which men's souls desired to live,—these forces were too strong to be affected by scandals. So the notorious personal influences, and the personal manœuvres which characterise the Vatican, seem to produce no appreciable failure of faith in Papal infallibility on the part of those who are disposed that way.

It is remarkable, however, that the Pelagian and Semi-Pelagian controversies (while they set in motion theological tendencies, Augustinian and anti-Augustinian, of a very strong and durable kind, and while at least great features of Augustinian thought and feeling became dominant in the West) produced no such clear-cut and detailed dogmatic formulæ, accepted and enforced by church authority, as were called forth by the questions about the Trinity and the Person of Christ.

It is to be noticed, finally, that the fourth century saw the tendencies in action which were destined to render multitudinism triumphant in the Church, *i.e.* to bring it to pass that the whole population of the empire, and of the kingdoms which succeeded it, became members of the Church and partakers of Christian ordinances at her hands. That was a great change from the earlier day, not so much because the number of Christians was so greatly increased, but because Christianity for the masses existed as something passively accepted, and not as the expression of individual decision. If it lay in the line of the Church's calling to resist this tendency, or effectually to control it, the ideas which prevailed as to the relation of the inward to the outward in religion rendered the task very difficult. The Church was involved in the thousand compromises arising out of this situation. Her protest against these, or rather her protest that something more individual and more decisive could be contemplated, was embodied mainly in Monasticism. Efforts to raise the standard of the common Christianity were made from time to time; very often it was an effort to carry over lessons and influences from the monasteries to the general Christian society.

One particular but important phase of the process just alluded to was the change which took place in the method of the Church's discipline and in the very conception of it. On the one hand, discipline was discouraged by the refractory and irreformable material with which it had to deal. On the other hand, the impression that the process constituted the one method of obtaining assured forgiveness, suggested the extension of discipline to sins which had not become scandals—and to sins not contemplated by the earlier discipline. In accommodating the procedure of the Church and of penitents to these impressions a step was made towards the eventual creation of the Roman Sacrament of Penance.

But a more serious result was this: with the flood of new proselytes the Church acquired a constituency which could only be dealt with on legal principles: and such principles could be applied only in the way of enjoining certain observances. That alone could be practically intelligible to the mass. The assumption followed, that when these observances were passively accepted, at least without disbelief or contradiction, they would do their work, would confer and accomplish the Christian salvation. On any other view, what must become of the mass of recognised Christians? The theory which this implied settled on men's minds like a fate. Christ has furnished us with a system of church ordinances which, if reverently complied with, do mysteriously effect salvation.

Once more, the character of the Church's new constituency accelerated the tendencies to a paganised worship. Worship of saints and martyrs, of sacred pictures and relics, of the eucharist, of the crucifix, worship which multiplied alike the objects of reverence and the splendour of ritual, became most popular, because it was far more congenial to the really pagan people who flowed into the Christian Church in the fourth and following centuries. On the other hand, this population accepted the Church's authority.

How many of these changes—and we have enumerated only some—deserve to be regarded as legitimate developments, or admissible adaptations—how many as mistakes and corruptions, and what effect should be ascribed to them on either view—also how far the essential genius of the Christian religion with its healing and renewing virtue operated through all,—these are questions not here to be further discussed. In contemplating them the student will carry with him the remembrance that our Lord's promise is for ever taking fulfilment—" Lo, I am with you alway, even to the end of the world."

# APPENDIX

## *A.* LITERATURE OF CHURCH HISTORY

IN the immense literature of Church History, some outstanding works ought to be known to students at least by name and character, though they may not be in circumstances to make much use of them. Others should be referred to by those who wish to study the subject fully. Here we name only such works as include or bear upon the period covered by this volume.

ANCIENT CHURCH WRITERS or FATHERS,—generally taken as applying to writers, especially Catholic writers, of first six centuries. See literature to Chap. III. p. 50; and for earliest, or so-called Apostolic Fathers, n. 1, 2, p. 51.

CHURCH COUNCILS.—Various collections, especially Mansi, 31 vols. folio (1 and 2 cover period of this vol.), Flor., and Ven., 1759; also Hefele, *Conciliengeschichte,* Freiburg in Breisgau, 1855 ff.

GEOGRAPHY. — The chief requisite is a good historical atlas. Spruner's, 3rd ed., by A. von Menke, 1871 ff., may be named.

CHRONOLOGY.—The great works are J. Scaliger, *De emendatione temporum,* Jena, 1629. D. Petavius, *De doctrina temporum,* Antv., 1703. *L'art de vérifier les dates* (by a Benedictine), 4th ed., by St. Alais, Paris, 1818. L. Ideler, *Lehrbuch der Chronologie,* Berlin, 1831. A handy companion on this subject will be found in *Book of Almanacs,* by A. de Morgan, Lond., 1851.

LITURGIC AND WORSHIP have a large special literature, but they are included in the general subject of *Antiquities,* which comprehends also the constitution, offices, administration, laws, and usages of the Ancient Christian Church, and the distinctive features of its social life. The classical English work is

J. Bingham, *Antiquities of the Christian Church*, 8 vols., Oxon., various editions. Originally published nearly two hundred years ago, this work retains its value in a remarkable degree. Smith and Cheetham, *Dictionary of Ecclesiastical Antiquities*, Lond., 1875. In Germany, J. W. Augusti, *Denkwürdigkeiten*, 12 vols., Leipz., 1816 ff.; Guericke, 1859 (both Lutheran), and Binterim, 17 vols. (Catholic), are usually named.

CHURCH HISTORIES: *Ancient.*—Eusebius, ten books (among many edd., Heinichen, Lips., 1868–70; Burton, Oxon., 1838), comes down to A.D. 314, Socrates (A.D. 306–439), Sozomen (A.D. 323–423), Theodoret (A.D. 325–429), Evagrius (A.D. 431–594).

*Modern* (*i.e.* since Reformation). *Protestant.*—*Ecclesiastica Historia, etc.*, Magdeburg, 1559 ff., 13 vols. folio, often called " Centuriæ Magdeburgenses," a review of the history down to A.D. 1300, in the interest of Protestantism, and against Rome. Passing over many large works, J. L. Mosheim, *Institutiones Hist. Eccl.*, Helmst., 1755, inaugurates less controversial and more philosophical treatment: J. S. Semler, *Hist. Eccl. Selecta Capita*, Halæ, 1773 ff., begins treatment on basis of rationalism. J. M. Schröck, *Christlich. Kirchengeschichte*, continued by H. G. Tzschirner, 45 vols., Leipz., 1768 ff., storehouse of results up to end of eighteenth century. Later Prot. writers named below.

*Roman Catholic.*—Cæs. Baronii, *Annales*, Rom., 1588 ff., 12 vols. folio, devoted to twelve centuries. Continuation by Raynaldus, Laderchius, and others; best ed. by G. & J. Mansi, 1738 ff. This work was the reply to the Magdeburg centuries. The author and continuators were priests of the oratory of S. Philip Neri. Natalis Alexander (French name Noel), *Hist. Eccl. Veteris et Novi Testamenti*, Paris, 1699: author a Dominican, not ultramontane: able statement of R.C. view in controverted questions. S. le Nain de Tillemont, *Mémoires pour servir à l'H. E. des six premiers siècles*, Paris, 1693 ff., 16 vols. 4to, still worth consulting: takes up the history in connection with successive biographies, diligent and candid: author a Jansenist. J. J. I. von Döllinger, *Geschichte d. Christl. K.*, Landshut, 1835: modern R.C. position as defended by a very learned man: author repudiated by the Church after the Vatican Council.

Among modern Church Histories the following deserve the attention of students. J. C. L. Gieseler, *Eccl. History*, translated (T. & T. Clark), Edin., 1846. J. A. W. Neander, *General Hist. of Chr. Ch.*, translated (T. & T. Clark), Edin., 1847. F. C. Baur, *Lectures* (partly posth.), Tüb., 1861–63. Milman,

*Latin Christianity*, 7 vols., Lond., 1854. Sohm, *Kirchengeschichte im Grundriss*, 1885. W. Möller, *Lehrbuch der K. G.*, Freiburg, 1889 ff. J. C. Robertson, *Hist. of Ch. to Reformation*, 1874.

HISTORY OF DOCTRINE.—D. Petavius, *Dogmata Theologica*, Paris, 1644 ff.; various later edd.: author a Jesuit: French name Denis Petau. Hagenbach's *Handbook of History of Doctrine* (transl., T. & T. Clark, Edin.) is still a convenient index to this subject. F.C. Baur, *Vorlesungen ü. D. G.* (posth.), 3 Bde. 1865: Hegelian, and pervaded by thought of development. Harnack, *Lehrbuch der D. G.*, 3 vols., 3rd ed. 1896 ff. Loofs, *Leitfaden z. Studium d. D. G.*, Halle, 1893.

BIOGRAPHY, besides Tillemont, Smith and Wace's *Dictionary of Ecclesiastical Biography*, Lond., 4 vols. See also articles in Herzog and Plitt, *Real-Encycl.*, which is useful also for Antiquities, Liturgie, etc. Corresponding R.C. work is Wetzer and Welte, *Kirchen-Lexicon*, 1847 ff. These works contain information also on writings and editions of Fathers. Special works on Patristic are E. Dupin, *Nouv. Bibliothèque*, Paris, 1686; and R. Ceillier, *Histoire générale des Auteurs, etc.*, last ed. Par. 1860. For Latin writers the supplementary volumes (Christian Section, 1–3) of J. C. F. Bähr, *Gesch. d. Römisch. Lit.*, Karlsruhe, 1836 ff., will be found convenient.

## B. SUPPLEMENTARY NOTES TO CHAPTERS

CHAPTER I. Add Gibbon, *Decline and Fall of Roman Empire*, notes by J. B. Bury, 7 vols., Lond., 1897. Aubé, *Histoire des persécutions d'Église, etc.*, Paris, 1875. Keim, *Rom u. Christenthum*, 1881. Uhlhorn, *Der Kampf d. Christenthums mit d. Heidenthum*, 1886. See also A. Harnack in *Real-Encycl.* viii. 772. Hardy, *Christianity and the Roman Government*, Lond., 1894. Neumann, *Der Römische Staat u. d. allgemeine Kirche*, Leipz., 1890. Merivale, *History of Rom. Emperors*, 8 vols., Lond., 1865. E. Renan, *Hist. des Origines du Christianisme*, Paris, 1867 ff.

ON THE JEWS.—Milman, *History of the Jews*, 3 vols., Lond., 1829. Gfrörer, *Jahrhundert des Heils*, 2 Bde. 1838. E. Schürer, *Geschichte des Jüdischen Volks*, 2nd ed., Leipz., 1886 ff. (very full reff. to literature).

CHAPTER II. The Early Churches.—Works on the constitution of the early churches are cited p. 32, n. 1. Among older **works which** deserve still to be kept in view are R. Hooker, *Ecclesiastical Polity*, ed. by Keble, Oxf., 1836. D. Petavius, *De Ecclesiastica Hierarchia*, lib. v. H. Hammond, *Dissertationes*, iv., Lond., 1651. D. Blondel, *Apologia pro sententia Hieronym.*, Amst., 1646. Add to later works R. Rothe, *Anfänge d. Christl. Kirche*, Witt., 1837. Bishop Kaye, *External Disc. and Govt. of Church of Christ*, Lond., 1856. Hatch, *Organisation of early Christ. Churches*, Lond., 1881; and *Growth of Christ. Institutions*, Lond., 1887.

As to the methods of early church life, besides details gathered from incidental notices in the Fathers, we have the various early collections of Church Laws—the history of which is a complicated subject. (See A. Harnack in *T. u. U.* ii., parts 1, 2, 5, 1886.) The collection best known is the *Apostolical Constitutions* (in Cotelerius, *Patres Apostolici*, see n. 1, p. 51: handy modern editions by Ueltzen, Rost.,1853, and Lagarde, Lips., 1862). Of the eight books, the composition of the first six is referred to the end of the third century or beginning of fourth; but the text as it stands contains later interpolations as well as material from earlier collections: books 7 and 8 are ascribed to different periods in the fourth century. The *Apostolic Canons* (85) belong to the fifth and sixth centuries: they are usually printed at the end of the *Ap. Const.* On Apostles' Creed, see H. B. Swete, 2nd ed., Camb., 1894.

DISCIPLINE.—Details on this subject are best studied with the aid of works on Christian Antiquities, *supra*.

MARTYRDOM.—See works cited above in connection with Chap. I.

CHAPTER III. The Church's Life. Good specimens of literature in H. M. Gwatkin, *Selections from early Writers*, Lond., 1893.

CHAPTER IV. Beliefs and Sacraments.

P. 68. On earliest asceticism, see A. Harnack in notes to his edition of *Teaching of Apostles*, Berlin, 1886. Older, S. Deyling, *Observationes Sacræ*, iii., *De ascetis Veterum*.

Pp. 70, 71. References on the doctrine concerning Christ will be found under Chap. XI.

CHAPTER V. Apologists.—Students are specially referred to A. Harnack, *Dogmengeschichte* (trans. Lond., 1875), 2nd book, 4th chapter. Loofs, *Leitfaden z. D. G.* § 18, and especially to de Pressensé, *Histoire des trois premiers siècles, etc.,* Par., 1858-64.

CHAPTER VI. Gnosticism.
P. 104, note 2. See Swete, *Gospel of S. Peter,* Lond., 1893.

CHAPTER VIII. Action of Government.—See also literature cited under Chap. I. *supra.*

CHAPTER XI. Christ and God.—On this great subject of discussion, see G. Bull, *Defensio Fidei Nicænæ,* Oxon., 1685: works by Nelson, vol. v. ff. F. C. Baur, *Die Christliche Lehre v. d. Dreieinigkeit, etc.,* Tüb., 1841–43. G. A. Meier, *Die Lehre v. d. Trinität,* Hamb., 1844. Dorner, *Entwickelungsgeschichte der Lehre v. d. Person Christi,* Stuttgart, 1845 (transl., T. & T. Clark, Edin.), and all the general histories of doctrine.

CHAPTER XII. Christian Life.—See reff. on earlier asceticism under Chap. IV. Also J. A. W. Neander, *Denkwürdigkeiten, u.s.w.,* vol. i. 3rd ed., Berlin, 1845. N. Mosler, *Zur Geschichte des Cœlibats,* Heid., 1878. A. Harnack, *Das Mönchthum, u.s.w.,* 3rd ed. 1886. How the ascetic idea commended itself to Christians is best seen in Clem. Alex. *Pædagogus,* and some tracts of Tertullian; also, later, in canons of councils.

CHAPTER XIII. Worship.—See Bingham, *Antiquities,* and Smith and Cheetham, *Dictionary of Christian Antiquities.* See also second book of *Apostolic Constitutions.*
P. 232. The recourse to O.T. to supply precedents and authorities for ecclesiastical arrangement and ritual embellishment is illustrated in first six books of *Apostolical Constitutions,* and frequently in the works of Origen.

CHAPTER XIV. Clergy.—See reff. under Chap. II. *supra.*
P. 245. Clergy in Rome, Eus. *H. E.* vi. 43. Optat. Milev. *De Schismate, etc.,* ii. 4.

CHAPTER XVI. Manicheism.—Add F. C. Baur, *Das Manichäische Religionssystem,* Tüb., 1831. Art. sub tit. in *Real-Encycl.* vol. ix. The sources are *Acta disputationis Archelai et Manetis* (referred to 4th cent.) in Routh, *Reliquiæ Sacræ,* and in Migne, *Patr. Gr.* x. Tit. Bostren, πρὸς Μανιχαίους, Lagarde, 1859. Alexander of Nicopolis, Λόγος πρὸς τὰς Μανιχαίων δόξας, in Gallandi, iv. Fresh light has been derived from Arabic sources (see in Flügel and art. in *R. E.*). Notices in Syriac works of Ephraem S. (4th cent.) and in Armenian of Esnik (5th cent.).

CHAPTER XVII. Church in Christian Empire.—Tzschirner, *Fall des Heidenthums*, Leipz., 1829. A. Beugnot, *Histoire de la destruction du Paganisme en Occident*, Paris, 1835. S. T. Rüdiger, *De statu paganorum sub. imp. Christ.*, Vratisl., 1825. J. V. A. de Broglie, *L'Eglise et l'Empire Romain au $IV^{me}$ Siècle*, 3rd ed., Paris, 1869. V. Schulze, *Geschichte des Untergangs des griech. röm. Heidenthums*, Jena, 1887. For course of legislation, see *Codex Theodos.*, by Haeneck, 6 vols., Bonn, 1842. *Codex Justinian*, by Krüger, Berol., 1877.

P. 274. On unworthy motives of many converts, Euseb. *Vita Constantin.* iv. 54.

P. 279 ff. On Julian, add to the reff. given, G. H. Rendall, *The Emperor Julian*, Lond., 1879, and H. A. Naville, *Julien l'Apostat*, Neuch., 1877.

Literary representatives of the non-Christian thinkers and scholars were Jamblichus (d. 333), Libanius (d. 395), Himerius (d. 390), Themistius (d. 390), Hypatia (d. 416), Proclus (d. 485). The historian Ammianus Marcellinus ranks on the same side, and the poet Claudius Claudianus.

CHAPTER XVIII. Monasticism.—The earliest work commonly cited is R. Hospinian, *De monachis h. e. de origine et progressu monachatus*, 2nd ed., Tiguri, 1609. Add also, Holstenius, *Cod. Regularum*, ed. Martene, 1690. J. Mabillon, *De monachis in occidente ante Benedictum* (in *Acta Sanct.*, Ord. Bened. vol. i.). H. Weingarten, *Ursprung des Mönchthums*, Gotha, 1877.

Among early sources add Rufinus, *Historia Monachorum*, Antv., 1615. Palladius, *Historia Lausiaca* (Migne, Gr. 34). Hilarii Arelat., *Vita Honorati.* Cæsarii Arelat., *Ad Monachos*, Migne, 67.

CHAPTER XIX. Clergy.
P. 311. Metropolitans and Patriarchs. See R. Loening, *Geschichte des deutschen Kirchenrechts*, i. 424 ff.

CHAPTER XX. Council of Nicæa. See J. A. Möhler *Athanasius*, Mainz, 1827-28. Harnack, *Dogmengesch.*, part ii. chap. 7.

Sources: Eus. *Vita Const. Magni.* Socrates, *Hist. Eccl*

Sozomen, *H. E.* Theodoret, *H. Eccl.* Philostorgius, fragments in Photius, cod. 40.

CHAPTER XXI. Arian Controversy, post-Nicene. Sources: Socrates, Sozomen, Theodoret, Philostorgius, Epiphanius, *Hær.* 69; and controvl. works of Athanasius, Hilary, Basil and the two Gregories, with their Epistles. *Councils* in Mansi, ii., iii.; Fuchs, *Bibliothek der Kirchenversammlungen*, Leipz., 1780, vols. i., iii.; Hahn, *Biblioth. d. Symbolik*; C. J. Hefele, *Conciliengeschichte*, Freiburg, 1855 ff., vol. i.

CHAPTER XXII. Minor Controversies.

P. 363. Apollinarian pseudonymous writings:—the confession ascribed to Athanasius was part of a letter by Apollinarius to the Emperor Jovian. A number of the followers of Apollinarius returned to the great Church and strengthened the Monophysite section.

P. 370. Origen's errors. Modern discussion of these points may be found in *Origeniana* by Huet (b. of Avranches) in vol. iv. of De la Rue's edition of Origen's works; in Redepenning's *Life of Origen*; in *Life,* by Thomasius; and in Wetzer and Welte, *Kirchenlexicon* (R. C.), vol. vii. The works of Rufinus and Jerome on the subject are Rufinus, *Præf. ad Origen.* περὶ ἀρχῶν and *Apologia in Hieron.*; Hieronymus, *Apologia adv. Rufinum*, libri iii., with *Epp.* 51–84, 87–100; also Epiphan. *Hær.* 64.

P. 371. Priscillian. P. ascribed some kind of inspiration to non-canonical writings, now lost, apparently Gnostic or semi-Gnostic. This in itself would create distrust in the minds of men like Ambrose and Damasus.

CHAPTER XXIII. Person of Christ.

On this subject it may be well to read the relative sections in Cunningham's *Historical Theology* and in Dorner's *History of the Doctrine of the Person of Christ.* The latter shares in a common Lutheran tendency to criticise and depreciate the decision of Chalcedon; also Petavius, *Dogmata Theologica.* Important as early sources are the histories of Socrates, Sozomen, and Theodoret, the latter especially, see n. 1, p. 382, —along with Cyril's Tracts and the dogmatic Epistle of Leo. The latter should not be accepted by the student at its traditional value without reconsideration.

CHAPTER XXIV. Donatism.

The importance of Donatism lies in the development of the doctrine of the Church of which it became the occasion. This topic comes up in all studies of Augustine, *e.g.* Harnack, *D. G.* iii. pp. 70 and 127. Reuter, *Augustinische Studien*, pp. 4 ff. and 231 ff. A. Dorner, *Augustinus*, p. 232.

In addition to the works cited at the head of the chapter may be named Augustin. Opp. vol. ix. M. Leydecker, *Historia Ecclesiæ Africanæ*, Ultraj., 1690. H. Noris, *Historia Donatistarum*, edited by the Ballerini, Verona, 1729-32. Bindemann, *Der heil. Augustinus*, ii., Leipz., 1829.

CHAPTER XXV.

P. 422. Eusebius. Stein, *Eusebius*, Würzb., 1859. See also in Lightfoot's reply to *Supernatural Religion*, and art. in *Dict. of Eccl. Biography*. A German translation of the Syriac version has appeared in the Berlin edition of Greek Fathers.

P. 423. Athanasius. See Böhringer, *Kirche Christi*, 2nd ed., vol. vi. 1874. Möhler, *Athanas. d. Grosse*, 1827. J. Fialon, *S. Athanase*, 1877. Opera, Montfaucon, 1693. Migne, Gr. 25-28. *Festal Letters*, preserved in Syriac, Cureton, Lond., 1848.

P. 426. Basil, born in or near A.D. 330. Opera, Garnier, Paris, 1721; Migne, 29-32; see *Vita* prefixed, and article in *Real-Encycl.* ii.

P. 428. Gregory of Nyssa. Of the three Cappadocians he adhered most to Origen; but yet, like the others, fully adopted the Athanasian position. Besides the works mentioned in the text, his *De hominis opificio* and *Apolog. de hexaēm.* may be specially noted. Opera, Fronto le Duc, Paris, 1615, and Migne, 44-48. A new edition is very desirable. Article by W. Möller in *Real-Encycl.* vol. v.

P. 430. Hilary of Poictiers. He wrote also three books against the Emperor Constantius, and a work against Auxentius of Milan. He is regarded as the father of Latin Hymnody, —stirred up, it is said, by previous efforts of the Arians,—and he communicated the impulse to Ambrose. Opp. (Bened. ed.), 1693; Migne, L. 9, 10. *Life*, Reinkens, Schaffh., 1864. On his *Theology*, see Dorner, *Entwickelungsgesch. d. Lehre v. d. P. Christi*, i. 1037.

P. 434. Ambrose, Opp. (Bened.), Paris, 1686, and Venet., 1781; new edition, Mediol., 1875; Migne, L. 14-17; *Life* by Benedictine Edd.; also Böhringer, vol. x.

CHAPTER XXVI. Festivals, etc. See Bingham, books xiii.

and xiv., and *Dict. of Christian Antiquities*; C. E. Hammond, *Ancient Liturgy of Antioch*, Oxf., 1879; L. A. Muratori, *Liturgia Romana Vetus*, Neap., 1776. Also S. Silviæ Aquitanæ, *Peregrinatio ad loca sancta*, Gamurrine, 2nd ed., Rom., 1888.

P. 444. Eucharistic doctrine; see in *Jahrb. d. deutschen Theologie*, 1864–68, articles by Steitz, *Die Abendmahlslehre d. griechischen Kirche, u.s.w.*

CHAPTER XXVIII. Augustine.

P. 467. Augustine's relations to Manicheism (cf. Chap. XVI.), to Donatism (Chap. XXIV.), to Pelagianism (Chap. XXIX.), and to Semi-Pelagianism (Chap. XXX.), are referred to in those chapters. His theory of the Catholic Church receives important exposition in works besides those against Donatism; see especially the *De Civitate Dei*. Other theological topics, which claim attention in connection with Augustine, are his theory of sacramental grace, his conception of the significance of Christ in redemption (alleged, *e.g.*, by Harnack and Loofs to be one-sided, and so defective), his free revision of earlier argument in connection with the Trinity, and his non-appreciation of the Pauline teaching on justification, while he lays so much stress on the same apostle's doctrine of grace. Hints and conjectures of this Father, which prepared the way for later developments, will be referred to when these are taken up.

# INDEX

ACACIUS of Cæsarea, 348.
Acacius of Constantinople, 347.
*Acta facientes*, 143.
Aedesius, 288.
Aerius, 370.
Aetius, 346, 348.
Africa, school of, 184 f.; Tertullian, 184-9; Cyprian, 189-97.
*Agape*, 30, 75-6, 229.
Agrippinus, 257.
Alaric, 270, 271.
Alexander of Alexandria, 326, 330, 341.
Alexander of Jerusalem, 143.
Alexandria, school of, 2nd P., 161 f.; Pantænus and Clement, 161-8; Origen, 168-79; 3rd P., 374-5, 379-80.
Allegorical Interpretation of O.T., 107, 109, 158, 510; extended to N.T. by Origen, 158, n. 2, 170.
Alogi, 211-2.
Ambrose, and Monasticism, 296; and Priscillian, 372; and prayer to the saints, 452; and inability, 475; life and works, 434-6, 530.
Ammonius Saccas, 147.
Anastasius, presb. of Antioch, 377, 378.
Anatolius of Constantinople, 396, 399, n.
Andreas of Samosata, 382, n. 1.
Anicetus, 83, 236.
Anomœans, 340, 346, 350, 352.
Antioch, s. of (Paul of S.), 214-5.
Antioch, c. at (341 A.D.), 343-4; (343 A.D.), 344-5.
Antioch, school of, 374-6, 473, n. 2.
Antoninus Pius, 17.
Antony, 293.
Apelles, 119, n. 2.
Apollinarius, 157, 358 f.
Apollinarius of Hierapolis, 180, n. 1.
Apollonius of Hierapolis, 62, 180, n. 1.

Apollonius of Tyana, 146, 155, 283.
"Apostles'" Creed, 59, 74.
Apostles in the early Church, 32-4.
Apostolici, 304.
Apuleius, 7.
Arcadius, 270.
Arianism, 205, n. 2, 324, 327, n. 3.
Arianism, Gothic, 352-3.
Ariminum, c. at (359 A.D.), 348.
Aristides, 17, 60-1, 84.
Arius, his opinions, 324-5, 326-8, 360; at Nicæa, 330-1; banished, 333; returns, 341; dies, 342; life and character, 325, 326.
Arles, s. of, and heretical baptism, 260.
Arnobius, 84, 89, 157.
Arnobius the younger, 488, n.
Art, Christian, 2nd P., 222-3; 3rd P., 454.
Artemon, 212.
Asceticism, 1st P., 68; 2nd P., 223-5; 3rd P., 291 f.
Asia Minor, school of, 180 f.; Irenæus, 180-4; Hippolytus, 180, 184.
Athanasius, archdeacon at Alexandria, 307; at Nicæa, 330; bishop, 341; in the post-Nicene debate, 341-2, 343, 344, 345, 346, 349, 350, 354-5; nature of the charges against him, 321; attitude to Origen, 364; life and works, 423-6, 530.
Athenagoras, 61, 84, 205.
Attila, 270, 271, 506.
Audiarii, 304.
Audius, 304.
Augustine, and heretical baptism, 257, n. 3; and Manicheism, 264, 267, 461-2, 466; and Monasticism, 295-6, 298, 301; and relics, 302-3, 436; and training of the clergy, 316, 319; and the Donatists, 412 f.; and veneration of the saints, 452; and

## 534  INDEX

discipline, 458 ; and Neo-Platonism, 462, 464 ; and Pelagianism, 471, 475-6, 479-82 ; and Semi-Pelagianism, 483-4. His church theory, 415-9. As preacher, 451. Character of his thinking, 463-4, 466-7. Life, 280, n. 2, 316, 460-3. Works, 271, n. 2, 464-5, 467, 473, n. 1, 475, n. 2, 484, 531.
Aurelian, 143, 144.
Aurelius, Marcus, 7, n. 2, 17, 48.
Auxentius of Milan, 434.
Avitus of Vienne, 489.
Axum, kingdom of, 288.

BABYLAS of Antioch, 142, 143.
Baptism, 1st P., 31, 75 ; 2nd P., 233-5, 237, n. 2 ; 3rd P., 290, 300, 446-9. Review, 516-7.
Baptism, heretical, 255 f. ; Augustine on, 415.
Baptismal confession, 73, 159, 448, 511.
Bar Cochba, 19.
Bardesanes of Edessa, 116, n., 119, n. 2.
*Barnabas, Epistle of,* 22, n., 55.
Basil of Ancyra, 339, 348.
Basil of Cæsarea, Neo-Platonic influence in, 156 ; post-Nicene debate, 350, 354 ; as preacher, 451 ; life and works, 295, 301, 426-8, 530.
Basilides, 113-6.
Beron, 170, n. 1, 217.
Beryllus of Bostra, 170, n. 1, 217.
Bishops, 1st P., 35-40 ; Hatch and Harnack on, 40-2 ; and discipline, 43. 2nd P., 241-5 ; election of, 245-7. 3rd P., 314, 319 ; election of, 308-9 ; celibacy of, 320. Growth of their power, 512-3.
Bishops, country, 245, 307.
Bonosus, 453.

CÆCILIANUS, 405-6.
Cæsarius of Arles, 451, 489.
Callistus of Rome, 215, 216, 217, n. 1, 251, 257.
Canon of N.T., 109-10, 158, 509-10.
Caracalla, 141.
Carpocrates, 111.
Cassian, 296, 298, 486, 488 ; his Semi-Pelagian views, 488, 490-3, 503.
Celibacy of the clergy, 2nd P., 223-4 ; 3rd P., 319-20.
Celsus, 8, n. 1, 157.
Cerinthus, 111.

Chalcedon, c. at, 396-401.
Character, doct. of, 414, 449.
*Chorepiscopoi,* 245, 307.
Chrysaphius, 393, 395.
Chrysostom, on State aid, 278 ; on Lord's Supper, 444-5 ; as preacher, 451 ; life, 295, 301, 321, 368-9, 375, 494-6 ; writings, 496.
Church, form of, in 2nd P., 239-40.
Church, idea of the, 1st P., 27-9, 71-2 ; 2nd P., 242-3, 255-6 ; Cyprian, 193-4, 256-8. 3rd P., 409 ; Augustine, 415-9. Review, 514-5.
*Circumcelliones,* 407, 411, 412, 420, n. 2.
Clemens, T. Flavius, 15.
Clement of Alexandria, and N.T. canon, 158, n. 2 ; Logos doct., 164, 166, 167, 205 ; on the Christian life, 221-2 ; life and teaching, 100, n., 161-8.
Clement of Rome, 52.
*Clement, 1st Ep. of,* 16, 52-3, 202.
*Clement, 2nd Ep. of,* 40, 53.
Clementine writings, 21-2.
Clergy, celibacy of, 2nd P., 223-4 ; 3rd P., 319-20.
Clergy, priesthood of, growth of idea, 232.
Clergy, and secular callings, 314, 319.
Clergy, training of, 3rd P., 316-8.
Cœlestinus of Rome, 379, 381.
Cœlestius, 471, 472.
*Collegia tenuiorum,* 144.
Commodian, 157.
Commodus, 4, 18, 141.
*Communicatio idiomatum,* 383, n. 2.
Communion. *See* Lord's Supper.
Constans, emp., 268 ; and post-Nicene debate, 342-3, 344-5.
Constantine, emp., 268 ; edict of Milan, 5, 145 ; religious policy, 276, 277-8 ; and the Donatists, 406 ; and Nicæa, 329, 337 ; and post-Nicene debate, 340-2.
Constantine II., 268, 342-3.
Constantinople, c. at (381 A.D.), 352, 355-7, 359.
Constantius, emp., 268, 269 ; religious policy, 276, 287 ; and Julian, 282 ; and post-Nicene debate, 343-8 ; and Hilary, 431.
Constantius Chlorus, 145.
Cornelius of Rome, 253-4, 259.
Creed, early forms of, 73-4, 511 ; "Apostles'," 59, 74 ; Nicene, 322, later form, 356 ; Chalcedon, 398-9.
Cyprian, and the "lapsed," 191-2,

251-2 ; and heretical baptism, 256-61, 417 ; on the unity of the Church, 192-4, 258 ; and Novatian, 254 ; life, 189-91 ; martyrdom, 195-7.
Cyril of Alexandria, his *contra Julianum*, 284 ; and Nestorian controversy, 379, 380-91, 400, 403 ; life and writings, 496-7.
Cyril of Ephesus, 387.
Cyril of Jerusalem, 356-7, 366.
Cyrillus of Antioch, 325.

DAMASUS of Rome, 372, 499, 500.
Deaconesses, 248.
Deacons, 1st P., 31, 35, 38 ; Hatch and Harnack on, 40-2 ; 2nd P., 241, 247 ; 3rd P., 306-7, 311, 314, 319.
Dead, Christian (2nd P.), 238.
Dead, prayers for, 239, 445.
Death, Christian view of (2nd P.), 238-9.
Decius, 142.
Dianius of Cæsarea in Cappadocia, 344, 428.
*Didache*, 58-9. On worship in the early Church, 30, 76 ; on apostles, prophets, and teachers, 33 ; on bishops and deacons, 41.
Didymus of Alexandria, 364.
Dio Chrysostom, 7.
Diocletian, 4-5, 143, 145, 267.
Diodorus, 375.
*Diognetus, Epistle to*, 55, 84, 90, 93.
Dionysius of Alexandria, 179, 217, 260.
Dionysius of Corinth, 62, 250.
Dionysius of Rome, 217, 220, n.
Dioscurus of Alexandria, 395, 397.
*Disciplina arcani*, 230.
Discipline, 42-4, 249 f., 455 f., 520.
Docetism, 95, 200.
Domitian, 15.
Domitilla, Flavia, 15-6.
Domnus of Antioch, 393, 396.
Donatism, 405 f., 530.
Donatus, 407.

EASTER, celebration of, 2nd P., 237 ; 3rd P., 437-9.
Easter, controversy as to date, 81-3, 236.
Ebionites, 21, 199, n.
Edessa, school of, 392.
Elkesaites, 21.
Ephesus, c. at (431 A.D.), 386-7, 473 ; (449 A.D.) 395-6.
Epictetus, 5, n., 6, 146.

Epiphanes, 111.
Epiphanius, 295, 356-7, 365-7.
Epiphany, 2nd P., 237 ; 3rd P., 439-40.
Episcopate. *See* Bishops.
Eucharist. *See* Lord's Supper.
Eucharistic prayers. *See* Lord's Supper.
Euchites, 304.
Eudoxia, 495, 496.
Eudoxius, 346, 348.
Eugenius, 270.
Eugenius of Cæsarea, 472.
Eunomius, 346, 348.
Eusebius of Cæsarea, on apostles in the early Church, 34 ; and Nicæa, 330, 331, 333 ; post-Nicene debate, 341, life and works, 157, 179, 422-3, 530.
Eusebius of Dorylæum, 394, 395.
Eusebius of Nicomedia, and Nicæa, 326, 330, 333 ; post-Nicene debate, 340, 341, 342 ; death, 345, 423.
Eusebius of Rome, 254.
Eusebius of Vercelli, 319.
Eustachians, 304.
Eustathius of Antioch, 321, 330, 331, 341, 342.
Eustathius of Sebaste, 304, 370.
Eutyches, 393-5.
Evagrius of Antioch, 499.
Exarchs, 312.
Exoukontians, 346.

FABIAN of Rome, 143, 253.
Fabius of Antioch, 254.
Faustus of Reii, 488, 490-3.
Felicissimus, schism of, 253, n. 2.
*Felicitas (and Perpetua), Acts of*, 130.
Felix of Aptunga, 405.
Firmilian of Cæsarea, 260.
Firmus, 270.
Flavia Domitilla, 15-6.
Flavian of Antioch, 494.
Flavian of Constantinople, 393-6.
Flavius Clemens, T., 15.
Florentius, 394.
Fortunatus, 253, n. 2.
Frumentius, 288.
Fulgentius of Ruspe, 489.

GAIUS, 157.
Galerius, 5, 145.
Gallienus, 4, 143, 144.
Gallus, 282.
Gennadius of Marseilles, 488, n.
Genseric, 271, n. 1, 286, 506.
Gildo, 270, 412.
Gnosticism, 95 f. Elements of the scheme, 96-8 ; view of the world,

99–102; the Demiurge, 103–4; the Person of Christ, 104–5; Redemption, 105–6; the three classes of men and their destiny, 106–7; Judaism and the O.T., 107–9; the N.T. canon, 109–10; Ethics, 110–1. How the scheme came to be, 117–9.
Gnostic schools, Cerinthus, Carpocrates, and Epiphanes, 111; Ophites, 111–2; Saturninus, 112–3; Basilides, 113–6; Valentinus, 116.
Gordians, the two, 141.
Goths, 285–6, 352–3.
Gratian, 269, 277, 372, 436.
Gregory of Nazianzus, and post-Nicene debate, 350, 354–5; as preacher, 451; life and works, 295, 301, 346, n., 429–30.
Gregory of Nyssa, and post-Nicene debate, 350, 354–5; as preacher, 451; life and works, 301, 428–9, 530.
Gregory Thaumaturgus, 179, 271, n. 3.

HADRIAN, 16, 19.
Hegesippus, 60.
Heliogabalus, 141.
Helvidius, 453.
Heracleon, 119, n. 2.
Heraclius, schism of, 254.
Heretical Baptism. *See* Baptism.
*Hermas, Shepherd of*, 53–4. On prophets, 33; on forgiveness of sin, 80–1; Logos doct., 202, 213, n.; on second repentance, 250.
Hermias, 60, 62, n., 84, 157.
Heterousiastians, 346.
Hierakas, 224, n. 1.
Hierocles, 157.
Hilary of Arles, 506.
Hilary of Poictiers, and post-Nicene debate, 346, 348; life and works, 430–2, 530.
Hippolytus, Logos doct., 205, 215, 219; and penitents, 251; and heretical baptism, 257; life and works, 141, 180, 184.
Homoiians, 339–40, 350, 351.
Homoiousians, 339, 348–50.
Homoousians, 348.
Honorius, 270, 419.
Hosius, 329, 330, 342, 347.
Hunerich, 286.
Hypatia, 497, 502, 503.

IBAS, 392, 393, 400.
Ignatius, on the Person of Christ, 202; on the eucharist, 76, 77, 78, n., 79, n. 1; martyrdom, 16.

*Ignatius, Epistles of*, 56–7.
Innocent I., 313, 472, 496.
Irenæus, and N.T. canon, 158, n. 2; on the eucharist, 183; on the O.T., 183–4; Logos doct., 206–7; and Easter controversy, 236; life and teaching, 129, 180–4.
Irenæus, m. of Tyre, 393.
Isidore of Pelusium, 498.
Ithacius of Emerita, 372.

JAMBLICHUS, 147, 281, n.
Jerome, 296, 298, 366–7, 472; life and writings, 498–501.
John of Antioch, 381, 382, 386–90, 400.
John of Jerusalem, 366, 472.
Jovian, 269, 349.
Jovinian, 298–9.
Julia Domna, 141.
Julian, emperor, 269; religious policy, 276–7, 278, 284, 348–9, 359; life and aims, 282–4, 285, n.
Julian of Eclanum, 471, 473.
Julius Africanus, 179.
Julius of Rome, 343, 345.
Justin Martyr, on worship in the early Church, 30–1, 75–6, 229; on the eucharist, 78–9; on Marcion, 120; Logos doct., 202, n. 1, 203–5; as apologist, 84, 88, 90, 93; life, 7, n. 3, 61; martyrdom, 17, 44–5.
Justina, 435.
Justus, followers of, 112.

LACTANTIUS, 84, 157, 442–3, 444–5.
"Lapsed," 191–2, 251–2.
Leo I., 313, 395, 396, 451, 459; life and writings, 505–7.
Lerins, convent of, and Semi-Pelagianism, 486–8. *See* Contents.
Libanius, 281.
*Libellatici*, 15, 143, n. 2.
Liberius of Rome, 347.
Licinius, 5, 145, 268.
Liturgy, 233, 440.
Logos doctrine, the Apologists, 86–8; Justin Martyr, 202, n. 1, 203–5; Irenæus, 206–7; Tertullian, 207–8; Clement, 164, 166, 167, 205; Origen, 172–3, 176, 208–9; the two Theodoti and Artemon, 212–3; Paul of Samosata, 214; Noetus and Praxeas, 215; Sabellius, 216–7; Arius, 324–5; Apollinarius, 361–2.
Lord's Supper, 1st P., 30, 75–9; 2nd P., 229–32; 3rd P., 442–5. Review 516–7.

# INDEX 537

Lord's Supper, forms of prayer in connection with, 1st P., 30, 76; 2nd P., 230-1, 233, 239; 3rd P., 441-2.
Lucian, 5, 8, n. 2, 32, 34.
Lucian of Antioch, 325-6, 327, n. 3.
Lyons (and Vienne), churches of, 17, 25, 47-8, 129.

MACARIUS of Jerusalem, 331, 342.
Macarius Magnes, 157.
Macedonians, 351.
Macedonius of Constantinople, 351.
Majorianus, 406, 407.
Mani, 262, 266.
Manicheism, 262 f.
Marcellus of Ancyra, at Nicæa, 332; his views, 337, 341, n.; and post-Nicene debate, 341, 342, 343, 344, 345, 346.
Marcellus of Rome, 254.
Marcia, 18, 141.
Marcian, 396.
Marcion, and the Canon, 109-10; life and system, 119 f.
Marcion of Arles, 254.
Marcionites, 120, 122, 127.
Marcus Aurelius, 7, n. 2, 17, 48.
Marriage, Christian view of (2nd P.), 223-5.
Marriage of the clergy, 2nd P., 223-4; 3rd P., 319-20.
Martin of Tours, 296, 297, 372; life and works, 432-3.
Martyrs, how regarded, 2nd P., 239; 3rd P., 451-2.
Maximinus, 141.
Maximus, 269, 270, 372, 433.
Maximus of Antioch, 396.
Maximus Tyrius, 7.
Meletius of Lycopolis, schism of, 254, n. 3.
Melito, 62, 180, n. 1.
Memnon of Ephesus, 387.
Mensurius, 405, 406.
Merit, doct. of, 227-8.
Mesrob, 287.
Methodius, 157, 179.
Metropolitans, rise of, 310.
Milan, edict of, 5, 145.
Miltiades, 62, 180, n. 1.
Minor Orders, 2nd P., 247-8; 3rd P., 306, 314, 315.
Minucius Felix, 62, 84, 157.
*Missa catechumenorum*, 230.
*Missa fidelium*, 231.
Monarchianism, Dynamical, 205, n. 2, 210-5, 218-9.

Monarchianism, Modalistic, 210, 215-9
Monasticism, 291 f.
Monica, 461, 463.
Monophysite teaching, 401-3.
Montanism, 128 f., 243.
Montanus, 128.

NAASSENES, 112.
Nazarenes, 21, 199, n.
Neo-Platonism, 146 f., 285, n.
Nero, 15, 16.
Nerva, 4.
Nestorianism, 287, 390, 392, 454.
Nestorius, 377-8, 381-7, 473.
New Testament, Canon of, 109-10, 158.
Nicene Council, 323 f. *See* Contents.
Nicene Creed, 332, 354; later form, 355-7.
Nitrian monks, 367-9.
Noetus, 215.
Novatian, 157, 192, 253-4.
Novatianists, 192, 254.
Novatus, 253.
Numenius, 7, 146.

OLD TESTAMENT, Christian attitude to, 1st P., 79, 107, 108-9; 2nd P., 158, Irenæus, 183-4; 3rd P., 510.
Ophites, 111-2.
Orange, s. at (529 A.D.), 489-90.
Orders, Minor, 2nd P., 247-8; 3rd P., 306, 314, 315.
Origen, Logos doct., 172-3, 176, 208-9; Neo-Platonic influence in, 156; and allegorical interpretation, 109, 158 and n. 2, 170; life and system, 168-79; as judged by a later age, 364-5, 369-70.
Origenistic controversies, 364 f., 529.
Orosius, 271, n. 2, 472.

PACHOMIUS, 294.
Pamphilus, 179.
Pantænus, 24, 34, 161-2.
Papias, 59-60.
Patriarchates, rise of, 311-2.
Patrick, apostle of Ireland, 287-8.
Patripassianism, 205, n. 2, 215.
Paul of Samosata, 213-5, 325, 327, n. 3.
Paulinus of Milan, 471.
Paulinus of Nola, 318, 471, n. 1.
Pelagian controversy, 468 f.
Pelagius, 469 f. His positions, 477-9.
Penitence, public, 1st P., 30, 43, 81; 2nd P., 250-1; 3rd P., 441, 455 f.
Peratics, 112.

*Perpetua and Felicitas, Acts of,* 47, 130.
Persecution, 141; under Decius and Valerian, 142–3, 191, 195–6; under Diocletian, 145.
Peter of Alexandria, 254.
Philip the Arabian, 141.
Philo, 146, 201.
Philostorgius, 157.
Philostratus, 155, n. 2, 283.
Photinus of Sirmium, 345, 346.
Pliny, letter to Trajan, 16, 24–5, 29–30.
Plotinus, 147, 148, 152, 154, n., 155 and n. 1.
Plutarch, 6, 146.
Polycarp, and Easter controversy, 83, 236; and Marcion, 120; martyrdom, 17, 45–6.
*Polycarp, Epistle of,* 57–8.
Polycrates, 236.
Pontianus of Rome, 141, 180, n. 2.
Pontitianus, 295–6.
Porphyry, 147, 152, 153, n., 154, n., 157.
Post-Baptismal Sin, 1st P., 79–80; 2nd P., 227–8; 3rd P., 446.
Pothinus of Lyons, 180, n. 2.
Praxeas, 129–30, 215.
Prayer, Public, 1st P., 30, 76; 2nd P., 230–1, 232–3, 239; 3rd P., 440, 441–2; posture at, 235.
Presbyters, 1st P., 35–8; Hatch and Harnack on, 40–2; 2nd P., 241, 244, 245, 247; 3rd P., 307–8, 311, 314, 319, 514.
Priesthood of the clergy, 232.
Priscillian, 371–2, 529.
Priscillianists, 371–3.
Proclus, 147, 285, n.
Proclus of Constantinople, 391.
Prophets in the early Church, 32–3.
Prosper, 486–7.
Ptolemæus, 108, n., 116, 119, n. 2.
Pulcheria, 270, 396.

QUADRATUS, 60.
Quartodecimans, 236.

RABULAS of Edessa, 391, 392.
Radagaisus, 270.
Reader, office of, 40, 247.
Regula, 74–5, 110, 159–60, 511; Origen's use of, 171.
Remoboth, 304.
Repentance, second, 250, 457.
Robber Synod, 396.
Rufinus of Aquileia, 366–7, 501.

SABELLIANISM, 205, n. 2, 216–7.
Sabellius, 216–7.
Sacrament, use of the term (3rd P.), 449.
*Sacrificati,* 143, n. 2.
Saints, growing veneration of, 451–2.
Salvian, 271, n. 2, 504–5.
Sarabaites, 304.
Sardica, c. at (343 A.D.), 344–5.
Satan, dominion of, and the death of Christ, view of Origen, 177; of Irenæus, 182–3.
Saturninus, 112–3.
Scillitan Martyrs, 18, 46–7.
Seleucia, c. at (359 A.D.), 348.
Semi-Arians, 336, 339, 347–52.
Semi-Pelagians, 485 f.; their scheme, 487–8, 490–3.
Seneca, 5, n., 7, n. 2, 146.
Sethians, 112.
Severus, Alexander, 141, 142, 144.
Severus, Septimius, 141.
Severus, Sulpicius, 297, 302, 503–4.
*Shepherd, the.* See *Hermas.*
Sin, post-baptismal, 79–80, 228, 250 f., 290. In *Hermas,* 54, 80–1, 250.
Siricius of Rome, 372, 500.
Sirmium, creeds of, 347.
Sixtus of Rome, 143.
Stephen of Rome, 257, 259–60.
Stylites, 305.
*Subintroductæ,* 224.
Sylvester of Rome, 330.
Symeon the Stylite, 305.
Symmachus, Q. Aurelius, 280.
Synesius, 156, 319, 320, 501–3.
Synods, provincial, rise of, 309–11.

TATIAN, 24, 61, 84, 116, n., 161, n. 2.
Teachers in the early Church, 32–3.
*Teaching of the Twelve Apostles.* See *Didache.*
Telemachus, 279, n.
Tertullian, and the Montanists, 130; Logos doct., 207–8; on the Christian life, 221–2; on baptism, 235, 237, n. 2; and reception of penitents, 251, n. 1; and original sin, 474; life and teaching, 84, 89, 184–9.
Theodoret of Cyrus, school of Antioch, 375; case of Nestorius, 382, 383, 384, 385, 388, 390; case of Eutyches, 393, 395, 396; at Chalcedon, 400–1; life and writings, 497–8.
Theodorus of Mopsuestia, 375–6, 391, 473, n. 2.
Theodosius I., emperor, 269–70; re-

ligious policy, 277; post-Nicene debate, 351-2; and Ambrose, 436.
Theodosius II., emperor, 270; case of Nestorius, 385-92; case of Eutyches, 394-5; and the Pelagian leaders, 473; death, 396.
Theodoti, the two, 212.
Theodotus, 161, n. 3.
Theognis of Nicæa, 333.
Theophilus of Alexandria, 279, 367-9.
Theophilus of Antioch, 61-2, 84, 205.
*Thurificati*, 143, n. 2.
Tiberius, 4.
Timæus of Antioch, 325.
Trajan, 4, 16.

ULFILAS, 286, 353.
Ulpian, 141, n.
Ursacius, 347.

VALENS, 269, 350, 351.

Valens of Mursa, 347.
Valentinian I., 267, 269, 349-50, 385.
Valentinian II., 269, 270.
Valentinian III., 270.
Valentinus, 116.
Valerian, 142-3.
Vespasian, 15.
Victor of Rome, 83, 215, 236, 313.
Victorinus, 157.
Vienne (and Lyons), churches of, 17, 25, 47-8, 129.
Vigilantius, 298-9.
Vincentius of Lerins, 488, n.

WIDOWS, 248.
Worship, public, 1st P., 29-30; 2nd P., 229-31; 3rd P., 440-3.

ZENO (Emperor), 392.
Zenobia, 213.
Zephyrinus, 215.
Zosimus, 472.

# The International Theological Library

## ARRANGEMENT OF VOLUMES AND AUTHORS

**THEOLOGICAL ENCYCLOPÆDIA.** By CHARLES A. BRIGGS, D.D., D.Litt., sometime Professor of Theological Encyclopædia and Symbolics, Union Theological Seminary, New York.

**AN INTRODUCTION TO THE LITERATURE OF THE OLD TESTAMENT.** By S. R. DRIVER, D.D., D.Litt., sometime Regius Professor of Hebrew and Canon of Christ Church, Oxford.
*[Revised and Enlarged Edition.*

**CANON AND TEXT OF THE OLD TESTAMENT.** By the Rev. JOHN SKINNER, D.D., Principal and Professor of Old Testament Language and Literature, College of the Presbyterian Church of England, Cambridge, England, and the Rev. OWEN WHITEHOUSE, B.A., Principal and Professor of Hebrew, Chestnut College, Cambridge, England.

**OLD TESTAMENT HISTORY.** By HENRY PRESERVED SMITH, D.D., Librarian, Union Theological Seminary, New York. *[Now Ready.*

**THEOLOGY OF THE OLD TESTAMENT.** By A. B. DAVIDSON, D.D., LL.D., sometime Professor of Hebrew, New College, Edinburgh.
*[Now Ready.*

**AN INTRODUCTION TO THE LITERATURE OF THE NEW TESTAMENT.** By Rev. JAMES MOFFATT, D.D., D.LITT., Hon. M.A. (Oxon.), Minister United Free Church, Broughty Ferry, Scotland. *[Revised Edition.*

**CANON AND TEXT OF THE NEW TESTAMENT.** By CASPAR RENÉ GREGORY, D.D., LL.D., sometime Professor of New Testament Exegesis in the University of Leipzig. *[Now Ready.*

# The International Theological Library

**A HISTORY OF CHRISTIANITY IN THE APOSTOLIC AGE.** By ARTHUR C. McGIFFERT, D.D., President Union Theological Seminary, New York. [*Now Ready*.

**CONTEMPORARY HISTORY OF THE NEW TESTAMENT.** By FRANK C. PORTER, D.D., Professor of Biblical Theology, Yale University, New Haven, Conn.

**THEOLOGY OF THE NEW TESTAMENT.** By GEORGE B. STEVENS, D.D., sometime Professor of Systematic Theology, Yale University, New Haven, Conn. [*Now Ready*.

**BIBLICAL ARCHÆOLOGY.** By G. BUCHANAN GRAY, D.D., Professor of Hebrew, Mansfield College, Oxford.

**THE ANCIENT CATHOLIC CHURCH.** By ROBERT RAINEY, D.D., LL.D., sometime Principal of New College, Edinburgh. [*Now Ready*.

**THE LATIN CHURCH IN THE MIDDLE AGES.** By ANDRE LAGARDE. [*Now Ready*.

**THE GREEK AND EASTERN CHURCHES.** By W. F. ADENEY, D.D., Principal of Independent College, Manchester. [*Now Ready*.

**THE REFORMATION IN GERMANY.** By T. M. LINDSAY, D.D., Principal of the United Free College, Glasgow. [*Now Ready*.

**THE REFORMATION IN LANDS BEYOND GERMANY.** By T. M. LINDSAY, D.D. [*Now Ready*.

**THEOLOGICAL SYMBOLICS.** By CHARLES A. BRIGGS, D.D., D.Litt., sometime Professor of Theological Encyclopædia and Symbolics, Union Theological Seminary, New York. [*Now Ready*.

**HISTORY OF CHRISTIAN DOCTRINE.** By G. P. FISHER, D.D., LL.D., sometime Professor of Ecclesiastical History, Yale University, New Haven, Conn. [*Revised and Enlarged Edition*.

**CHRISTIAN INSTITUTIONS.** By A. V. G. ALLEN, D.D., sometime Professor of Ecclesiastical History, Protestant Episcopal Divinity School, Cambridge, Mass. [*Now Ready*.

**PHILOSOPHY OF RELIGION.** By GEORGE GALLOWAY, D.D., Minister of United Free Church, Castle Douglas, Scotland. [*Now Ready*.

**HISTORY OF RELIGIONS.** I. China, Japan, Egypt, Babylonia, Assyria, India, Persia, Greece, Rome. By GEORGE F. MOORE, D.D., LL.D., Professor in Harvard University. [*Now Ready*.

**HISTORY OF RELIGIONS.** II. Judaism, Christianity, Mohammedanism. By GEORGE F. MOORE, D.D., LL.D., Professor in Harvard University. [*Now Ready*.

**APOLOGETICS.** By A. B. BRUCE, D.D., sometime Professor of New Testament Exegesis, Free Church College, Glasgow. [*Revised and Enlarged Edition*.

# The International Theological Library

**THE CHRISTIAN DOCTRINE OF GOD.** By WILLIAM N. CLARKE, D.D., sometime Professor of Systematic Theology, Hamilton Theological Seminary. *[Now Ready.*

**THE DOCTRINE OF MAN.** By WILLIAM P. PATERSON, D.D., Professor of Divinity, University of Edinburgh.

**THE DOCTRINE OF THE PERSON OF JESUS CHRIST.** By H. R. MACKINTOSH, Ph.D., D.D., Professor of Theology, New College, Edinburgh. *[Now Ready.*

**THE CHRISTIAN DOCTRINE OF SALVATION.** By GEORGE B. STEVENS, D.D., sometime Professor of Systematic Theology, Yale University. *[Now Ready.*

**THE DOCTRINE OF THE CHRISTIAN LIFE.** By WILLIAM ADAMS BROWN, D.D., Professor of Systematic Theology, Union Theological Seminary, New York.

**CHRISTIAN ETHICS.** By NEWMAN SMYTH, D.D., Pastor of Congregational Church, New Haven. *[Revised and Enlarged Edition.*

**THE CHRISTIAN PASTOR AND THE WORKING CHURCH.** By WASHINGTON GLADDEN, D.D., sometime Pastor of Congregational Church, Columbus, Ohio. *[Now Ready.*

**THE CHRISTIAN PREACHER.** By A. E. GARVIE, D.D., Principal of New College, London, England. *[Now Ready.*

**HISTORY OF CHRISTIAN MISSIONS.** By CHARLES HENRY ROBINSON, D.D., Hon. Canon of Ripon Cathedral and Editorial Secretary of the Society for the Propagation of the Gospel in Foreign Parts.
*[Now Ready.*

# The International Critical Commentary

## ARRANGEMENT OF VOLUMES AND AUTHORS

### THE OLD TESTAMENT

**GENESIS.** The Rev. JOHN SKINNER, D.D., Principal and Professor of Old Testament Language and Literature, College of Presbyterian Church of England, Cambridge, England. [*Now Ready*.

**EXODUS.** The Rev. A. R. S. KENNEDY, D.D., Professor of Hebrew. University of Edinburgh.

**LEVITICUS.** J. F. STENNING, M.A., Fellow of Wadham College, Oxford.

**NUMBERS.** The Rev. G. BUCHANAN GRAY, D.D., Professor of Hebrew, Mansfield College, Oxford. [*Now Ready*.

**DEUTERONOMY.** The Rev. S. R. DRIVER, D.D., D.Litt., sometime Regius Professor of Hebrew, Oxford. [*Now Ready*.

**JOSHUA.** The Rev. GEORGE ADAM SMITH, D.D., LL.D., Principal of the University of Aberdeen.

**JUDGES.** The Rev. GEORGE F. MOORE, D.D., LL.D., Professor of Theology, Harvard University, Cambridge, Mass. [*Now Ready*.

**SAMUEL.** The Rev. H. P. SMITH, D.D., Librarian, Union Theological Seminary, New York. [*Now Ready*.

**KINGS.** [*Author to be announced*.]

**CHRONICLES.** The Rev. EDWARD L. CURTIS, D.D., Professor of Hebrew, Yale University, New Haven, Conn. [*Now Ready*.

**EZRA AND NEHEMIAH.** The Rev. L. W. BATTEN, Ph.D., D.D., Professor of Old Testament Literature, General Theological Seminary, New York City. [*Now Ready*.

**PSALMS.** The Rev. CHAS. A. BRIGGS, D.D., D.Litt., sometime Graduate Professor of Theological Encyclopædia and Symbolics, Union Theological Seminary, New York. [*2 vols. Now Ready*.

**PROVERBS.** The Rev. C. H. TOY, D.D., LL.D., Professor of Hebrew, Harvard University, Cambridge, Mass. [*Now Ready*.

**JOB.** The Rev. G. BUCHANAN GRAY, D.D., Professor of Hebrew, Mansfield College, Oxford, and the Rev. S. R. DRIVER, D.D., D.Litt., sometime Regius Professor of Hebrew, Oxford. [2 *vols. Now Ready*.

# The International Critical Commentary

**ISAIAH.** Chaps. I–XXVII. The Rev. G. BUCHANAN GRAY, D.D., Professor of Hebrew, Mansfield College, Oxford. [*Now Ready.*

**ISAIAH.** Chaps. XXVIII–XXXIX. The Rev. G. BUCHANAN GRAY, D.D. Chaps. LX–LXVI. The Rev. A. S. PEAKE, M.A., D.D., Dean of the Theological Faculty of the Victoria University and Professor of Biblical Exegesis in the University of Manchester, England.

**JEREMIAH.** The Rev. A. F. KIRKPATRICK, D.D., Dean of Ely, sometime Regius Professor of Hebrew, Cambridge, England.

**EZEKIEL.** The Rev. G. A. COOKE, M.A., Oriel Professor of the Interpretation of Holy Scripture, University of Oxford, and the Rev. CHARLES F. BURNEY, D.Litt., Fellow and Lecturer in Hebrew, St. John's College, Oxford.

**DANIEL.** JAMES A. MONTGOMERY, Ph.D., S.T.D., Professor in the University of Pennsylvania and in the Philadelphia Divinity School.

**AMOS AND HOSEA.** W. R. HARPER, Ph.D., LL.D., sometime President of the University of Chicago, Illinois. [*Now ready.*

**MICAH, ZEPHANIAH, NAHUM, HABAKKUK, OBADIAH AND JOEL.** Prof. JOHN M. P. SMITH, University of Chicago; W. HAYES WARD, D.D., LL.D., New York; Prof. JULIUS A. BEWER, Union Theological Seminary, New York. [*Now ready.*

**HAGGAI, ZECHARIAH, MALACHI AND JONAH.** Prof. H. G. MITCHELL, D.D.; Prof. JOHN M. P. SMITH, Ph.D., and Prof. J. A. BEWER, Ph.D. [*Now Ready.*

**ESTHER.** The Rev. L. B. PATON, Ph.D., Professor of Hebrew, Hartford Theological Seminary. [*Now Ready.*

**ECCLESIASTES.** Prof. GEORGE A. BARTON, Ph.D., Professor of Biblical Literature, Bryn Mawr College, Pa. [*Now Ready.*

**RUTH, SONG OF SONGS AND LAMENTATIONS.** Rev. CHARLES A. BRIGGS, D.D., D.Litt., sometime Graduate Professor of Theological Encyclopædia and Symbolics, Union Theological Seminary, New York.

## THE NEW TESTAMENT

**ST. MATTHEW.** The Rev. WILLOUGHBY C. ALLEN, M.A., Fellow and Lecturer in Theology and Hebrew, Exeter College, Oxford. [*Now Ready.*

**ST. MARK.** Rev. E. P. GOULD, D.D., sometime Professor of New Testament Literature, P. E. Divinity School, Philadelphia. [*Now Ready.*

**ST. LUKE.** The Rev. ALFRED PLUMMER, D.D., late Master of University College, Durham. [*Now Ready.*

# The International Critical Commentary

**ST. JOHN.** The Right Rev. JOHN HENRY BERNARD, D.D., Bishop of Ossory, Ireland.

**ACTS.** The Rev. C. H. TURNER, D.D., Fellow of Magdalen College, Oxford, and the Rev. H. N. BATE, M.A., Examining Chaplain to the Bishop of London.

**ROMANS.** The Rev. WILLIAM SANDAY, D.D., LL.D., sometime Lady Margaret Professor of Divinity and Canon of Christ Church, Oxford, and the Rev. A. C. HEADLAM, M.A., D.D., Principal of King's College, London.
[*Now Ready*.

**I. CORINTHIANS.** The Right Rev. ARCH. ROBERTSON, D.D., LL.D., Lord Bishop of Exeter, and Rev. ALFRED PLUMMER, D.D., late Master of University College, Durham. [*Now Ready*.

**II. CORINTHIANS.** The Rev. ALFRED PLUMMER, M.A., D.D., late Master of University College, Durham. [*Now Ready*.

**GALATIANS.** The Rev. ERNEST D. BURTON, D.D., President of the University of Chicago. [*Now Ready*.

**EPHESIANS AND COLOSSIANS.** The Rev. T. K. ABBOTT, B.D., D.Litt., sometime Professor of Biblical Greek, Trinity College, Dublin, now Librarian of the same. [*Now Ready*.

**PHILIPPIANS AND PHILEMON.** The Rev. MARVIN R. VINCENT, D.D., sometime Professor of Biblical Literature, Union Theological Seminary, New York City. [*Now Ready*.

**THESSALONIANS.** The Rev. JAMES E. FRAME, M.A., Professor of Biblical Theology, Union Theological Seminary, New York City.
[*Now Ready*.

**THE PASTORAL EPISTLES.** The Rev. WALTER LOCK, D.D., Professor of Divinity in the University of Oxford and Canon of Christ Church.
[*Now Ready*.

**HEBREWS.** The Rev. JAMES MOFFATT, D.D., D.Litt., Hon. M.A. (Oxon.), Minister United Free Church, Broughty Ferry, Scotland. [*Now Ready*.

**ST. JAMES.** The Rev. JAMES H. ROPES, D.D., Bussey Professor of New Testament Criticism in Harvard University. [*Now Ready*.

**PETER AND JUDE.** The Rev. CHARLES BIGG, D.D., sometime Regius Professor of Ecclesiastical History and Canon of Christ Church, Oxford.
[*Now Ready*.

**THE JOHANNINE EPISTLES.** The Rev. E. A. BROOKE, B.D., Fellow and Divinity Lecturer in King's College, Cambridge. [*Now Ready*.

**REVELATION.** The Rev. ROBERT H. CHARLES, M.A., D.D., sometime Professor of Biblical Greek in the University of Dublin. [2 vols. *Now Ready*.